THESAURUS

DK PUBLISHING, INC.

A DK PUBLISHING BOOK

Produced for Dorling Kindersley by
PAGE*One*, Cairn House, Elgiva Lane, Chesham,
Buckinghamshire HP5 2JD

PAGE*One* team	Chris Clark, Helen Parker
DK Managing editor	Jane Yorke
Dictionary editor	Sheila Dignen
Dictionary compilers	Roz Combley
	Jessica Feinstein
	Fred McDonald
	Elaine Pollard
	Laura Wedgeworth
	John Williams

First American Edition, 1998
6 8 10 9 7

Published in the United States by DK Publishing, Inc.
95 Madison Avenue, New York, New York 10016
Visit us on the World Wide Web at http://www.dk.com

Copyright © 1998 Dorling Kindersley Limited, London

Published in Great Britain by
Dorling Kindersley Limited.

ISBN 0-7894-2809-1

Printed and bound in Italy by Legoprint

THE AIM OF THIS BOOK

The aim of a thesaurus wordfinder is to provide lists of useful synonyms or near synonyms. If you have a particular word in mind, but feel that it is not quite the word that you want to use – for example, because you have already used it once in a piece of writing, or it does not convey the exact meaning that you wish to impart – you can look the word up in this thesaurus and find a list of other words that mean the same thing, or nearly the same. You can then select the one word most appropriate for your needs. The thesaurus includes phrases as well as single words where it is felt that these may be useful. For example, the entry at dance (verb) includes not only verbs such as "jive," "twirl," and "waltz," but also phrases such as "do a jig," "leap about," and "shake a leg."

ARRANGEMENT OF ENTRIES

1 This thesaurus is arranged in strict alphabetical order. The main entries are listed in alphabetical order, and individual synonyms within the entries are also arranged in alphabetical order.

2 Different parts of speech are included as separate headwords. For example, **fence** (noun) is listed as a separate entry from **fence** (verb). They are listed next to each other in the thesaurus:

fence *n* barricade, barrier, defense, fencing, hedge, hurdle, paling, palisade, railings, rampart, stockade, wall, wire

fence *v* bound, circumscribe, confine, coop, encircle, enclose, hedge, pen, surround

3 Plural and singular nouns are listed separately. For example, **arms** (weapons) is listed as a separate entry from **arm**.

4 Parts of speech are given immediately after the headword. The following abbreviations are used throughout the wordfinder:

n	noun
v	verb
adj	adjective
adv	adverb
prep	preposition
conj	conjunction

5 Where a word has more than one meaning, each meaning is numbered and, where there is a possibility of confusion, a brief definition or example is given to make it clear which meaning is being dealt with. The following abbreviations are used throughout the book:

sb	somebody
sth	something

6 Where a particular synonym is an informal or technical word, this is indicated immediately after the synonym in question. The following labels are used throughout the book:

inf	informal
sl	slang
tech	technical

For example, at the entry for **abnormal**, the synonym "kinky" is labeled as informal and "wacko" is labeled as slang.

abnormal *adj* aberrant, anomalous, atypical, bizarre, deviant, eccentric, erratic, exceptional, extraordinary, idiosyncratic, irregular, kinky *inf*, odd, peculiar, perverse, perverted, queer, singular, strange, unexpected, unnatural, unorthodox, unusual, wacko *sl*, weird; *opp* normal

7 Where a word has a clear or useful opposite, this is given at the end of the list of synonyms. Sometimes more than one opposite may be given if it is useful. For example:

noisy *adj* blaring, blasting, boisterous, deafening, ear-splitting, loud, piercing, raucous, riotous, rowdy; *opp* quiet, silent

THESAURUS

abandon v 1 (leave sb) desert, ditch *inf*, dump *inf*, forsake, jilt, leave, leave behind, maroon, run out on *inf*, strand, throw over *inf*. 2 (leave a place) depart from, evacuate, go away from, quit, vacate, withdraw. 3 (give sth away) cede, deliver, forfeit, give up, renounce, relinquish, resign, surrender, waive, yield. 4 **abandon yourself to** give yourself up to, give way to, indulge in, lose yourself in, lose yourself to

abashed *adj* ashamed, discomfited, disconcerted, embarrassed, humiliated, mortified, shamefaced; *opp* unabashed

abate v die down, diminish, ease, fade, lessen, let up, subside

abbreviate v abridge, clip, compress, condense, crop, curtail, cut, cut down, précis, prune, reduce, shorten, summarize, trim, truncate; *opp* lengthen

abbreviation *n* contraction, shortened form

abdicate v 1 (give up throne) cede, give up, quit, renounce, resign, retire, stand down, step down *inf*, vacate, waive, yield. 2 (give up responsibility) cast aside, disown, give up, refuse, relinquish, renounce, repudiate, surrender, turn your back on, wash your hands of

abduct v carry off, hold for ransom, kidnap, make off with, run away with, run off with, seize, snatch *inf*

abhor v abominate, detest, dislike, hate, loathe, recoil from, shrink from, shudder at

abhorrent *adj* abominable, detestable, disgusting, distasteful, execrable, hated, hateful, horrible, horrid, loathsome, nauseating, obnoxious, odious, offensive, repellent, repugnant, repulsive, revolting

abide v 1 accept, bear, endure, put up with, stand, stomach, suffer, tolerate. 2 **abide by** adhere to, agree to, comply with, conform to, follow, keep to, obey, observe, stand by, stick to, submit to

ability *n* adeptness, adroitness, aptitude, bent, capability, capacity, cleverness, competence, competency, expertise, expertness, facility, faculty, flair, gift, knack, know-how *inf*, power, proficiency, prowess, skill, talent

abject *adj* 1 (of conditions) deplorable, hopeless, miserable, pathetic, pitiable, piteous, wretched. 2 (of people) base, contemptible, cringing, despicable, groveling, ignominious, ingratiating, low, mean, obsequious, servile, slavish, sniveling, submissive, sycophantic, toadying, vile, worthless, wretched

ablaze *adj* 1 (on fire) afire, alight, blazing, burning, fiery, flaming, ignited, lighted, on fire, raging. **2** (full of light) aglow, bright, brilliant, flashing, gleaming, glowing, illuminated, incandescent, lit up, luminous, radiant, shimmering, sparkling

able *adj* accomplished, adept, capable, clever, competent, experienced, expert, gifted, masterly, proficient, qualified, skilled, strong, talented

abnormal *adj* aberrant, anomalous, atypical, bizarre, deviant, eccentric, erratic, exceptional, extraordinary, idiosyncratic, irregular, kinky *inf*, odd, peculiar, perverse, perverted, queer, singular, strange, unexpected, unnatural, unorthodox, unusual, wacko *sl*, weird; *opp* normal

abolish *v* annul, ax, cancel, destroy, do away with, eliminate, end, eradicate, extinguish, get rid of, nullify, put an end to, quash, rescind, revoke, stamp out, stop, terminate, wipe out

abominable *adj* abhorrent, contemptible, despicable, detestable, disgusting, foul, hateful, horrible, horrid, loathsome, nasty, obnoxious, odious, offensive, repellent, revolting, terrible, vile, wretched

abort *v* **1** (end pregnancy) have a miscarriage, miscarry, terminate. **2** (end mission) call off, come to a halt, end, fail, halt, stop, terminate

abortion *n* miscarriage, termination

abortive *adj* failed, fruitless, futile, ineffective, ineffectual, pointless, unproductive, unsuccessful, useless, vain, worthless; *opp* successful

abound *v* **1** (be full of) be alive with, be crawling with *inf*, be full of, overflow

with, swarm with, teem with. **2** (be plentiful) be plentiful, flourish, thrive

abrasive *adj* **1** (rubbing a surface) caustic, chafing, coarse, corrosive, eroding, harsh, rough, sharp. **2** (of people) aggressive, biting, cutting, grating, harsh, hurtful, nasty, rough, sharp, unpleasant

abridge *v* abbreviate, compress, condense, cut, cut down, précis, prune, reduce, shorten, summarize, trim, truncate

abrupt *adj* **1** (rude) blunt, brisk, brusque, curt, direct, gruff, impolite, rough, rude, short, snappish, terse, uncivil, ungracious. **2** (sudden) hasty, hurried, instantaneous, quick, rapid, sharp, sudden, swift, unexpected, unforeseen

abscond *v* bolt, decamp, disappear, escape, flee, make a quick getaway, make off, run away, run for it, slip away, sneak away, steal away, take flight, take to your heels

absence *n* **1** (person missing) absenteeism, non-attendance, non-appearance, truancy; *opp* presence. **2** (thing missing) deficiency, lack, need, omission, privation, want

absent *adj* **1** (not present) away, elsewhere, gone, lacking, missing, not present, off, out, unavailable, wanting; *opp* present. **2** (not paying attention) absentminded, blank, day-dreaming, distracted, dreaming, dreamy, empty, far-away, inattentive, oblivious, preoccupied, unaware, unconscious, vacant, vague

absentminded *adj* absorbed, abstracted, bemused, distracted, dreaming, engrossed, forgetful, preoccupied, unaware, vague

absolute *adj* 1 (complete) complete, downright, entire, out-and-out, outright, perfect, pure, sheer, thorough, total, unmitigated, unqualified, utter. 2 (definite) categorical, certain, conclusive, decided, definite, positive, sure, undoubted, unequivocal, unquestionable. 3 (absolute power) authoritarian, autocratic, despotic, dictatorial, full, sovereign, supreme, unbounded, unconditional, unlimited, unqualified, unrestrained

absolutely *adv* 1 (completely) completely, entirely, fully, perfectly, totally, utterly, wholly. 2 (definitely) certainly, definitely, positively, surely, truly, undoubtedly, unequivocally, unquestionably, unreservedly, without a doubt

absolve *v* acquit, clear, discharge, exempt, excuse, exonerate, forgive, free, liberate, let off, pardon, release, reprieve, set free, vindicate

absorb *v* 1 (take in substance) assimilate, digest, draw in, draw up, mop up, soak up, sop up, suck up, take in. 2 (engross) captivate, engage, engross, enthrall, fascinate, immerse, occupy, preoccupy, rivet. 3 (take over) appropriate, incorporate, swallow, take over

absorbed *adj* captivated, engrossed, fascinated, fixed, held, immersed, involved, lost, occupied, preoccupied, rapt, riveted, spellbound

absorbing *adj* captivating, fascinating, gripping, intriguing, riveting, spellbinding

abstain *v* 1 avoid, decline, deny yourself, desist, forbear, forgo, give up, go without, hold back, refrain, refuse, renounce, shun. 2 (not drink) be on the wagon *inf*, be teetotal, take the pledge

abstemious *adj* abstinent, austere, frugal, moderate, puritanical, self-denying, sober, sparing, temperate

abstract *adj* 1 abstruse, complex, conceptual, deep, general, intellectual, metaphysical, obscure, philosophical, theoretical. 2 (art) non-representational, nonrealistic, symbolic, unrealistic

abstract *n* digest, outline, précis, resume, summary, synopsis

abstract *v* detach, extract, isolate, remove, separate, take away, take out, withdraw

absurd *adj* crazy, daft *inf*, farcical, foolish, idiotic, illogical, inane, hare-brained, laughable, ludicrous, nonsensical, paradoxical, preposterous, ridiculous, risible, silly, stupid, surreal, zany

abundance *n* affluence, bountifulness, copiousness, heaps *inf*, loads *inf*, plentifulness, plenty, profusion, stacks *inf*, tons *inf*

abundant *adj* ample, bounteous, bountiful, copious, flourishing, full, generous, great, huge, large, lavish, liberal, luxuriant, overflowing, plentiful, profuse, rampant, rich, teeming

abuse *n* 1 (wrong use) corruption, misapplication, mishandling, misuse. 2 (cruel behavior) beating, cruelty, exploitation, harm, ill-treatment, maltreatment, mistreatment, oppression, torture, wrongdoing.

3 (insults) blame, censure, curses, cursing, defamation, expletives, insults, invective, obscenity, rebuke, reproach, revilement, slander, swearing, swear-words, upbraiding, vilification, vituperation

abuse *v* **1** (use sth wrongly) misapply, mishandle, misuse. **2** (behave cruelly to sb) batter, beat, harm, hurt, ill-treat, ill-use, injure, maltreat, manhandle, mistreat, molest, oppress, torture. **3** (insult) blame, call sb names *inf*, castigate, censure, criticize, curse, denigrate, disparage, insult, malign, rebuke, revile, scold, smear, swear, upbraid, vilify

abusive *adj* acrimonious, angry, censorious, critical, cruel, disparaging, hurtful, insulting, libelous, obscene, offensive, rude, scornful, slanderous

abysmal *adj* appalling, awful *inf*, bad, deplorable, dreadful, dire, lousy, poor, terrible

abyss *n* bottomless pit, chasm, depths, gulf, hole, pit, void

academic *adj* **1** (to do with education) educational, instructional, pedagogical, scholastic. **2** (of a person) bookish, brainy *inf*, cerebral, cultured, erudite, high-brow, intellectual, learned, literary, scholarly, studious, well-read. **3** (theoretical) abstract, conjectural, hypothetical, impractical, speculative, theoretical

academic *n* don, fellow, lecturer, pedagogue, professor, pupil, scholar, student, teacher, thinker, tutor

accelerate *v* **1** go faster, hurry, pick up speed, speed up; *opp* slow down. **2** (make

sth go faster) advance, expedite, hasten, precipitate, speed up, spur on, stimulate

accent *n* **1** (way of talking) articulation, brogue, cadence, dialect, enunciation, inflection, intonation, modulation, pronunciation, tone. **2** (stress) accentuation, emphasis, force, stress. **3** (written mark) acute accent, cedilla, circumflex, diacritic, grave accent, mark, sign, tilde, umlaut

accept *v* **1** accede, acknowledge, acquiesce, admit, agree, approve, assume, buy *sl*, comply, concur, consent, cooperate, go along with, take on, undertake. **2** (receive) acquire, come by, gain, get, obtain, receive, secure, take. **3** (tolerate) put up with, stand, submit to, suffer, take, tolerate. **4** (believe) be convinced, believe, credit, have faith, trust

acceptable *adj* **1** (welcome) agreeable, delightful, desirable, gratifying, pleasing, welcome. **2** (satisfactory) adequate, admissible, all right, fair, moderate, OK, okay, passable, satisfactory, so-so *inf*, tolerable. **3** (of risks) admissible, allowable, bearable, supportable, tolerable

accepted *adj* acknowledged, admitted, agreed, approved, authorized, conventional, customary, normal, recognized, standard, time-honored, traditional, usual

access *n* accessibility, admission, admittance, entrance, entrée, entry, right of entry, way in

accessible *adj* **1** (able to be reached) available, exposed, get-at-able *inf*, handy, near, nearby, obtainable, on

hand, open, reachable, within reach. 2
(able to be understood) comprehensible,
fathomable, intelligible, understandable.
3 (of a person) affable, agreeable,
approachable, available, cordial, easygoing, friendly, informal, obliging

accessory n 1 addition, add-on, adjunct,
appendage, attachment, component,
extra, supplement. 2 (crime)
accomplice, assistant, associate,
confederate, helper, partner

accident n 1 blunder, calamity,
catastrophe, disaster, mishap,
misfortune, tragedy. 2 (road accident)
collision, crash, pile-up, smash.
3 (chance) chance, coincidence, fate,
fluke inf, fortune, hazard, luck,
serendipity, twist of fate

accidental adj arbitrary, chance,
coincidental, fortuitous, fortunate,
inadvertent, lucky, random, unexpected,
unforeseen, unintentional, unplanned,
unpremeditated, unwitting

accidentally adv by accident, by chance,
by mistake, inadvertently,
unintentionally, unwittingly

acclaim v announce, applaud, approve,
celebrate, cheer, clap, commend,
declare, exalt, extol, hail, honor, praise,
proclaim, salute

acclimatize v accommodate, accustom,
adapt, adjust, become seasoned,
familiarize yourself, get used to,
habituate yourself

accommodate v 1 (give a room to)
board, cater for, entertain, house, lodge,
put up, shelter, take in. 2 (help) aid,
assist, help, lend a hand, meet sb's needs,
oblige, do sb a favor. 3 (give sth to sb)

equip, furnish, grant, oblige, provide,
serve, supply. 4 (adapt) accustom, adapt,
adjust, conform

accommodating adj agreeable,
complaisant, compliant, considerate,
cooperative, helpful, hospitable, kind,
obliging, polite, unselfish, willing

accommodation n board, digs inf, home,
housing, lodging, pied-à-terre, premises,
quarters, shelter

accompany v 1 attend, chaperon,
conduct, escort, go with, guide, tag
along with inf, travel with. 2 (musically)
provide backing for, play for, support

accomplice n accessory, ally, assistant,
collaborator, colleague, confederate,
conspirator, friend, helper, henchman,
mate, right-hand man, sidekick inf

accomplish v achieve, attain, bring
about, bring off, carry off, do, effect,
execute, finish, fulfill, perform, produce,
realize, succeed

accomplished adj able, adept, capable,
competent, consummate, deft, expert,
gifted, masterly, polished, practiced,
proficient, skillful, skilled, talented

accomplishment n 1 (talent) ability,
achievement, attainment, capability,
proficiency, skill, talent. 2 (thing done)
achievement, act, attainment, coup,
deed, exploit, feat, success, triumph

accost v address, buttonhole inf, confront,
grab, greet, hail, nab inf, salute, speak to

account n 1 (report) chronicle,
description, explanation, history,
portrayal, record, report, statement,
story, tale. 2 accounts balance, balance
sheet, books, reckoning, tally

account for v explain, give reasons

for, justify

accountable adj answerable, liable, responsible

accrue v accumulate, amass, build up, collect, gather, grow, increase, mount up

accumulate v accrue, amass, assemble, build up, collect, gather, grow, hoard, increase, pile up, stash away inf, stockpile

accumulation n buildup, collection, heap, hoard, mass, pile, stack, stock, stockpile, store, supply

accuracy n authenticity, carefulness, correctness, exactness, faithfulness, meticulousness, precision, rightness, truth, truthfulness, validity, veracity; *opp* inaccuracy

accurate adj careful, correct, exact, faithful, literal, meticulous, precise, reliable, right, scrupulous, sound, spot on inf, strict, sure, true, truthful, valid; *opp* inaccurate

accusation n allegation, blame, charge, complaint, denouncement, indictment, recrimination, summons

accuse v arraign, blame, censure, charge, condemn, denounce, hold sb responsible, point the finger at inf

accustomed adj 1 (usual) common, customary, established, fixed, general, habitual, normal, ordinary, regular, routine, set, typical, usual.
2 **accustomed to** given to, in the habit of, seasoned, trained, used to

ache n discomfort, hurt, pain, pang, smarting, soreness, throb, twinge

ache v be painful, be sore, hurt, pound, smart, sting, throb

achieve v accomplish, acquire, arrive at,

attain, bring about, carry out, do, earn, effect, engineer, execute, finish, fulfill, gain, get, manage, obtain, perform, procure, reach, realize, win

achievement n accomplishment, act, action, attainment, deed, exploit, feat

acid adj 1 (taste) acrid, biting, bitter, pungent, sharp, sour, tangy, tart, vinegary. 2 (remarks) acerbic, caustic, cutting, sarcastic, sharp, vitriolic

acknowledge v 1 (notice sb) address, greet, hail, notice, recognize, respond, say hello to inf. 2 (answer a letter) answer, reply, respond. 3 (admit sth) accept, admit, allow, concede, own, recognize

acknowledgment n acceptance, admission, agreement, answer, appreciation, notice, reaction, recognition, reply, response

acquaintance n 1 (person) associate, colleague, contact. 2 (knowledge) awareness, familiarity, knowledge, understanding

acquainted adj aware, conscious, familiar, informed, privy to

acquiesce v accept, agree, assent, bow, comply, concur, consent, go along with, submit, yield

acquire v amass, appropriate, buy, collect, come by, gain, gather, get, earn, obtain, pick up, procure, purchase, receive, win

acquisition n addition, buy, gain, possession, prize, property, purchase

acquit v absolve, clear, discharge, exonerate, find innocent, free, let off inf, liberate, reprieve, set free, vindicate

acrimonious adj acerbic, bad-tempered, bitter, caustic, cutting, harsh, hostile, hot-tempered, petulant, quarrelsome, rancorous, sarcastic, spiteful, unpleasant, vitriolic

act n 1 (thing done) accomplishment, achievement, action, deed, exploit, feat, move. 2 (law) bill, decree, edict, judgment, law, measure, ruling, statute. 3 (piece of entertainment) item, performance, routine, sketch, skit, show, turn. 4 (pretending) affectation, fake, feigning, front, pose, pretense, sham, show

act v 1 (do sth) be active, do sth, function, get involved, move, react, strike, take action, take steps. 2 (behave) behave, carry on. 3 (perform on stage) act out, appear as, be an actor, be an actress, dramatize, enact, mime, perform, play, play a part, portray, represent, take a part, tread the boards inf. 4 (have an effect) operate, take effect, work. 5 (pretend) affect, dissemble, fake, feign, pose, pretend, put on

acting adj deputy, fill-in inf, interim, pro tem, provisional, stopgap, substitute, surrogate, temporary, vice-

action n 1 accomplishment, achievement, act, deed, effort, endeavor, initiative, maneuver, measure, move, operation, step. 2 activity, energy, force, forcefulness, get-up-and-go inf, liveliness, spirit, vigor, vim, vitality. 3 the action activity, bustle, drama, events, excitement, goings-on inf, happenings, incidents. 4 (war) battle, combat, conflict, fighting, warfare. 5 (legal) case, lawsuit, litigation, proceedings

activate v arouse, energize, excite, fire, galvanize, initiate, kick-start, mobilize, motivate, prod, prompt, rouse, set going, set off, start, stimulate, switch on, trigger, turn on

active adj 1 animated, bustling, busy, dynamic, energetic, enthusiastic, hyperactive, industrious, lively, mobile, nimble, on the go inf, on the move inf, quick, sprightly, spry, vibrant, vigorous, vivacious. 2 effective, effectual, functioning, in force, live, moving, operating, operative, potent, powerful, running, working

activist n campaigner, lobbyist, man of action, militant, woman of action

activity n 1 (things happening) action, bustle, comings and goings inf, commotion, flurry, hurly-burly, hustle and bustle, industry, life, movement, stir, toing and froing inf, tumult. 2 (sth that you do) enterprise, hobby, job, occupation, pastime, project, pursuit, scheme, task, undertaking, venture, work

actor, actress n artist, artiste, lead, leading man, leading woman, performer, play-actor, player, star, starlet, supporting actor, Thespian, tragedian, trouper

actual adj authentic, bona fide, confirmed, definite, genuine, indisputable, legitimate, physical, real, tangible, true, undeniable, verified, veritable

actually adv as a matter of fact, indeed, in fact, in truth, literally, really, truly

acute adj 1 alert, astute, canny, clever, discerning, incisive, intuitive, keen, observant, penetrating, perceptive, perspicacious, quick, sharp, smart. 2 (of senses) discerning, keen, sensitive, sharp; *opp* dull. 3 (very great) critical, dangerous, grave, great, pressing, serious, severe, urgent, vital. 4 (of pain) excruciating, fierce, intense, piercing, racking, sharp, stabbing, shooting, sudden, violent

adamant *adj* determined, firm, inflexible, intransigent, obdurate, resolute, stubborn, unbending, uncompromising, unyielding

adapt *v* 1 adjust, alter, change, convert, modify, remodel, reorganize, reshape, tailor, transform. 2 (get used to) accommodate, adjust, become conditioned, become hardened, conform, familiarize yourself, get used to, habituate yourself

adaptable *adj* adjustable, convertible, flexible, malleable, modifiable, pliant, resilient, variable, versatile

add *v* 1 attach, affix, append, combine, include, integrate, join, tack on *inf*. 2 (figures) add up, compute, count, reckon, total, tot up *inf*

addict *n* 1 (drug addict) abuser, dope-fiend *sl*, freak *inf*, junkie *inf*, user. 2 (sb who is keen on sth) buff *inf*, devotee, enthusiast, fan, follower, freak *inf*, nut *inf*

addicted *adj* dependent, hooked *inf*, obsessed

addiction *n* compulsion, craving, dependence, dependency, fixation, habit, obsession

addition *n* adjunct, appendage, appendix, attachment, augmentation, enlargement, extension, extra, gain, increase, increment, supplement

additional *adj* added, extra, fresh, further, more, new, other, supplementary

address *n* 1 (place where sb lives) abode, domicile, dwelling, home, house, location, lodging, pad *sl*, residence. 2 (speech) lecture, oration, sermon, speech, talk

address *v* 1 (give a speech) lecture, preach, sermonize, speak, spout *inf*, talk. 2 (talk to) buttonhole *inf*, engage sb in conversation, greet, hail, salute, speak to, talk to

adept *adj* able, accomplished, adroit, clever, dexterous, expert, practiced, proficient, skillful, skilled

adequate *adj* acceptable, ample, competent, enough, fair, mediocre, middling, OK, passable, presentable, reasonable, satisfactory, sufficient, suitable

adhere *v* attach, bind, bond, cling, fix, stick

adjacent *adj* abutting, adjoining, alongside, attached, bordering, close, near, neighboring, touching

adjoining *adj* abutting, adjacent, attached, bordering, connected, connecting, joining, next door, neighboring, touching

adjourn *v* break off, delay, interrupt, postpone, put off, suspend

adjournment *n* break, delay, interruption, pause, postponement, recess

adjudicate *v* arbitrate, decide, determine, give a ruling, judge, referee, settle, umpire

adjust *v* 1 adapt, alter, change, modify,

move, position, put right, rearrange, remodel, set, tailor, tune, vary. **2** (adjust to a situation) acclimatize, assimilate, become accustomed, conform, get used to, settle

adjustment *n* alteration, change, modification, rearrangement, rectification, repair, setting, tuning

ad-lib *v* extemporize, improvise, make up, speak impromptu, speak off the cuff

administration *n* **1** (managing sth) control, management, overseeing, running, supervision. **2** (government) executive, governing body, government, ministry, regime

administrative *adj* controlling, directorial, executive, governmental, management, managerial, organizational, regulatory, supervisory

admirable *adj* commendable, creditable, estimable, exemplary, fine, good, great, honorable, laudable, marvelous, praiseworthy, wonderful, worthy

admiration *n* adoration, appreciation, approval, awe, esteem, praise, regard, respect, veneration, wonder

admire *v* applaud, approve, carry a torch for *inf*, esteem, have a high opinion of, hero-worship, idolize, like, look up to, love, praise, respect, revere, sing the praises of, think highly of, value, venerate, wonder at, worship

admirer *n* **1** beau, boyfriend, girlfriend, lover, suitor, sweetheart. **2** aficionado, devotee, disciple, enthusiast, fan, follower, freak *inf*, supporter, worshipper

admissible *adj* acceptable, allowable, allowed, permissible, permitted, tolerated

admission *n* **1** (getting in) access, admittance, entrance, entry, right of entry, ticket. **2** (admitting sth) acceptance, acknowledgement, avowal, confession, declaration, profession, revelation; *opp* denial

admit *v* **1** (let in) accept, allow in, give access, give admission to, grant access, let in, permit entry, receive, take in. **2** (admit that sth is true) accept, acknowledge, allow, concede, confess, declare, own, own up, recognize, reveal; *opp* deny

adolescent *adj* boyish, childish, girlish, immature, juvenile, pubescent, puerile, teenage, young, youthful

adolescent *n* teenager, young man, young person, young woman, youngster, youth

adopt *v* **1** accept, approve, assume, back, champion, choose, endorse, espouse, follow, ratify, sanction, select, support, take on, take up. **2** (adopt a child) foster, take care of, take in

adorable *adj* appealing, attractive, captivating, charming, cute, darling, dear, delightful, gorgeous, lovable, sweet

adore *v* cherish, dote on, idolize, love, praise, revere, worship

adorn *v* beautify, bedeck, deck, decorate, embellish, enhance, festoon, garnish, ornament, trim

adult *adj* full-grown, full-size, fully developed, fully grown, grown-up, mature, of age; *opp* immature

adulterate *v* contaminate, debase, degrade, dilute, pollute, spoil, taint, thin, water down, weaken

adultery *n* a bit on the side, extramarital affair, infidelity, unfaithfulness

advance n breakthrough, development, finding, improvement, invention, progress

advance v 1 (move) come forward, forge ahead, gain ground, go ahead, go forward, make headway, move along, move forward, press on, proceed, push forward, push on inf; opp retreat. 2 (quicken) accelerate, expedite, forward, hasten, quicken, speed up, step up. 3 (develop) develop, evolve, flourish, grow, improve, progress, thrive. 4 (lend money) give, lend, loan, provide, supply on credit. 5 (put forward a theory) offer, propose, put forward, recommend, submit, suggest. 6 (help) assist, benefit, boost, facilitate, further, promote

advantage n 1 asset, benefit, blessing, boon, convenience, gain, good point, help. 2 (have an advantage over sb) edge, head start inf, lead, power, superiority, supremacy, upper hand

advantageous adj beneficial, constructive, convenient, helpful, invaluable, positive, profitable, useful, valuable, worthwhile

adventure n 1 (sth exciting that happens) escapade, experience, exploit, incident, occurrence. 2 (go out looking for adventure) danger, excitement, peril, risk, uncertainty

adventurous adj 1 bold, brave, courageous, daredevil, daring, intrepid; opp cautious. 2 challenging, dangerous, difficult, exciting, hazardous, precarious, perilous, risky

adversary n antagonist, competitor, enemy, foe, opponent, rival

adverse adj 1 (bad conditions) bad, disadvantageous, dreadful, inauspicious, unfavorable, unlucky; opp favorable. 2 (unkind) antagonistic, critical, derogatory, hostile, hurtful, negative, unfavorable, unfriendly, unkind, unsympathetic

adversity n affliction, bad luck, calamity, disaster, hardship, ill luck, misfortune, sorrow, suffering, tribulation, woe

advertise v 1 (try to sell sth) market, plug inf, promote, publicize, push inf, tout. 2 (tell people sth) advise, announce, broadcast, make known, notify, proclaim, publish

advertisement n advert inf, announcement, blurb inf, commercial, notice, poster, promotion, publicity, sign, small ad inf

advice n counsel, counseling, guidance, help, idea, opinion, recommendation, suggestion, tip, warning

advisable adj appropriate, desirable, expedient, judicious, politic, prudent, recommended, seemly, sensible, wise

advise v advocate, argue for/against caution, counsel, encourage, exhort, give guidance, guide, help, prescribe, recommend, suggest, urge, warn

adviser n confidant, confidante, consultant, coach, counselor, guide, mentor

advocate n backer, champion, fan inf, promoter, spokesman, spokesperson, spokeswoman, supporter

advocate v advise, argue for, back, campaign for, champion, endorse, plead for, promote, recommend, speak for, uphold, urge

affair *n* **1** activity, business, case, episode, happening, issue, matter, project, question, subject, thing, topic. **2** attachment, bit on the side *inf*, intrigue, involvement, liaison, love affair, relationship, romance

affect *v* **1** (have an effect on) act on, alter, change, have an effect on, have an impact on, impinge on, influence, sway, transform. **2** (upset) concern, distress, disturb, grieve, hit *inf*, move, stir, touch, trouble, upset. **3** (put on) adopt, assume, fake, feign, pretend, put on *inf*, simulate

affectation *n* airs, airs and graces, facade, insincerity, mannerism, pose, posturing, pretense, pretension, sham, show, simulation

affected *adj* **1** (not real) artificial, contrived, fake, feigned, insincere, put on *inf*, simulated, studied, unnatural; *opp* natural. **2** (of style) high-flown, ostentatious, pompous, precious, pretentious

affection *n* devotion, fondness, friendliness, friendship, liking, love, soft spot *inf*, tenderness, warmth

affectionate *adj* caring, fond, friendly, kind, loving, tender, warm, warm-hearted

affinity *n* closeness, compatibility, connection, kinship, likeness, liking, relationship, resemblance, similarity, sympathy

affirm *v* assert, attest, avow, certify, confirm, declare, say, state, swear, testify

afflict *v* bother, cause suffering to, distress, grieve, harm, hurt, plague, rack, torment, torture, trouble, try, vex, worry

affliction *n* distress, grief, hardship, misery, misfortune, ordeal, pain, scourge, sorrow, suffering, torment, trouble, woe, wretchedness

affluent *adj* **1** (people) flush *inf*, loaded *inf*, moneyed, opulent, prosperous, rich, wealthy, well-heeled *inf*, well-off, well-to-do; *opp* poor. **2** (life style) comfortable, expensive, lavish, luxurious, opulent, pampered, sumptuous

afford *v* **1** (be able to buy sth) find money for, have the means for, meet the expense of, pay for, spare the price of. **2** (be able to stand sth happening) bear, sustain, stand. **3** (give) bestow, furnish, give, offer, provide, supply

affront *n* aspersion, indignity, insult, outrage, provocation, slight, slur, snub, slap in the face *inf*

afraid *adj* alarmed, anxious, apprehensive, chicken *inf*, fearful, frightened, horror-struck, nervous, panic-stricken, scared, terrified, terror-stricken, timid, worried; *opp* fearless

age *n* **1** (period of history) date, days, epoch, era, generation, period, time. **2** (old age) advancing years, declining years, dotage, maturity, old age, senescence, senility, seniority. **3** (a long time) aeon, eternity, hours on end, lifetime, long time

age *v* become obsolete, decline, degenerate, deteriorate, get older, grow older, look older, mature, mellow, ripen, wither

aged *adj* ancient, antique, decrepit, elderly, getting on *inf*, gray, in your dotage, long in the tooth *inf*, old, past it *inf*, senile

agency n bureau, business, company, department, office, organization

agenda n list, plan, program, schedule, scheme, timetable

agent n 1 broker, delegate, emissary, envoy, executor, go-between, intermediary, middleman, negotiator, proxy, rep inf, representative, spokesman, spokeswoman. 2 mole inf, spook inf, spy

aggravate v 1 compound, exacerbate, heighten, inflame, intensify, make worse, worsen. 2 (inf) (annoy sb) annoy, exasperate, get on sb's nerves, hassle inf, irritate, provoke, rub sb the wrong way

aggression n attack, assault, hostility, invasion, offensive, onslaught, raid

aggressive adj argumentative, assertive, attacking, belligerent, forceful, hostile, provocative, pugnacious, pushy inf, quarrelsome, warlike

aggrieved adj distressed, hurt, ill-used, injured, peeved inf, piqued, resentful, unhappy, upset, wronged

agile adj acrobatic, active, fit, graceful, lithe, mobile, nimble, quick, sprightly, spry, supple

agility n activity, fitness, sprightliness, suppleness

agitated adj alarmed, anxious, confused, disconcerted, disturbed, excited, fazed, flustered, nervous, nervy, unnerved, unsettled, upset, worked up, worried; *opp* calm

agonize v deliberate, fret, labor, struggle, suffer, worry, wrestle

agonizing adj distressing, excruciating, harrowing, painful, racking, tormenting

agony n anguish, distress, hurt, misery, pain, suffering, torment, torture, woe

agree v 1 accept, acknowledge, acquiesce, admit, allow, concede, consent, grant, promise. 2 (two people agree) accord, be of the same mind, concur, get on, see eye to eye inf. 3 (figures) add up, match, tally

agreeable adj 1 amiable, charming, congenial, delightful, friendly, lovely, nice, pleasant, satisfying, to your liking; *opp* disagreeable. 2 (willing to do sth) accommodating, amenable, compliant, consenting, well-disposed, willing; *opp* unwilling

agreement n 1 accord, affinity, compatibility, concord, concurrence, congruity, consensus, harmony, unanimity, union. 2 (a deal) arrangement, bargain, contract, deal inf, pact, pledge, treaty, truce, understanding

aid n assistance, cooperation, encouragement, guidance, help, support

aid v abet, assist, benefit, encourage, facilitate, help, lend a hand, relieve, support

aim n ambition, aspiration, desire, dream, end, focus, goal, hope, intention, objective, plan, target, wish

aim v 1 (aim at sth) beam, direct, focus, line up, point, take aim, train, zero in. 2 (try to do sth) aspire, attempt, endeavor, hope, intend, resolve, seek, set your sights on, strive

air n 1 (space above earth) atmosphere, heavens, sky, space. 2 (breeze) blast, breath of air, breeze, draft, fresh air, oxygen, puff, ventilation, waft, wind. 3 (impression) appearance, aspect, atmosphere, aura, bearing, character, characteristic, demeanor, effect, feeling, flavor, look, manner, mood, quality, tone, vibes *inf*. **4** (tune) melody, theme, tune, song

air *v* **1** (air an opinion) communicate, declare, disclose, divulge, express, give vent to, make known, reveal, say, state, tell, voice. **2** (air a room or clothes) dry, freshen, ventilate

alarm *n* **1** angst, anxiety, apprehension, consternation, dismay, fear, fright, horror, nervousness, panic, shock, terror, uneasiness, worry; *opp* calmness, composure. **2** bell, distress signal, fire alarm, flare, red alert, siren, warning

alarm *v* daunt, dismay, distress, frighten, make sb nervous, panic, perturb, scare, scare sb stiff *inf*, shake, terrify, trouble, unnerve, worry

alarmed *adj* anxious, apprehensive, concerned, dismayed, fearful, frightened, horrified, nervous, perturbed, shocked, terrified, uneasy, worried; *opp* calm, collected, composed, cool

alarming *adj*, daunting, distressing, disturbing, dreadful, frightening, scary, shocking, startling, ominous, terrifying, unnerving, worrying; *opp* reassuring

alcoholic *n* alky *slang*, dipsomaniac, drunk, drunkard, hard drinker, heavy drinker, wino *slang*

alert *adj* **1** (ready to respond) attentive, awake, eagle-eyed, on your guard, on your toes, prepared, ready, sharp-eyed, vigilant, wary, watchful, wide-awake; *opp* off guard. **2** (with a lively mind) bright, lively, on the ball *inf*, perceptive, quick, quick off the mark, sharp-witted, with your wits about you; *opp* slow.

3 alert to alive to, aware of, clued up on *inf*, conscious of, sensitive to

alert *n* alarm, danger signal, emergency, flare, mayday, red-alert, signal, siren, warning

alert *v* advise, draw sb's attention to, notify, raise the alarm, tip sb off, warn

alibi *n* defense, excuse, explanation, justification, pretext, reason

alien *adj* extraterrestrial, foreign, outlandish, strange, unfamiliar, unnatural, weird; *opp* familiar

alight *v* dismount, disembark, get down, get off, get out. **2** land, come down, settle, perch

alight *adj* **1** (burning) aflame, blazing, burning, flaming, lit, on fire; *opp* burnt out, dead, extinguished, out. **2** (lit up) bright, glowing, illuminated, lit up, radiant, shining; *opp* dark, dead, dim, dull

alike *adj* cast in the same mold, comparable, duplicate, equivalent, identical, like, like peas in a pod, much the same, parallel, resembling, similar, the same, twin, uniform; *opp* different, dissimilar, unlike

alive *adj* **1** alive and kicking, animate, breathing, in the land of the living *inf*, living; *opp* dead, deceased, lifeless. **2** (continuing) continuing, current, in action, in existence, in operation, on-going; *opp* dead, defunct. **3** (lively) active, alert, energetic, full of life, lively, sprightly, vibrant, vigorous, vivacious; *opp* dead, dull, lifeless. **4** (alive to a problem) aware of, alert to, conscious of, sensitive to. **5** (alive with people, insects) bustling, crawling, heaving, swarming, teeming

allay *v* alleviate, assuage, calm, diminish, lessen, pacify, quell, reduce, relieve, soothe; *opp* exacerbate, make worse, inflame

allegation *n* accusation, assertion, charge, claim

allege *v* accuse, assert, aver, contend, claim, declare, insist, maintain, profess, say, state, suggest

allergic *adj* hypersensitive, sensitive, susceptible

allergy *n* allergic reaction, hypersensitivity, sensitivity, susceptibility

alleviate *v* allay, assuage, deaden, ease, lessen, mitigate, moderate, reduce, relieve, soothe; *opp* exacerbate, make worse

alliance *n* affiliation, agreement, association, coalition, confederation, federation, league, marriage, pact, partnership, relationship, treaty, union; *opp* divorce, separation

allied *adj* associated, connected, linked, related, similar

allocate *v* allot, assign, dish out *inf*, distribute, dole out *inf*, earmark, give, give out, grant, set aside, share out

allot *v* allocate, assign, dish out *inf*, distribute, dole out *inf*, earmark, give, give out, grant, set aside, share out

all-out *adj* complete, determined, full, maximum, no-holds-barred, thorough, total, unmitigated, utmost, wholehearted, wholesale

allow *v* 1 (permit) approve, authorize, give sb the go-ahead *inf*, give sb the green light, let, permit, sanction.

2 (allocate) allocate, allot, assign, give, grant, set aside. 3 (take sth into account) bear sth in mind, make allowances for, make provision for, take into account, take into consideration, provide for. 4 (accept that) accept, acknowledge, admit, concede, confess, grant

allowance *n* 1 grant, maintenance, payment, pocket money, remittance, stipend. 2 allocation, quota, ration, share

allude to *v* hint at, imply, mention, refer to, suggest, touch upon

allusion *n* hint, implication, insinuation, intimation, mention, reference, remark, suggestion

ally *n* accomplice, associate, collaborator, colleague, co-worker, friend, helper, partner in crime, sidekick; *opp* enemy

alone *adj*, *adv* 1 apart, by yourself, detached, isolated, lone, separate, solitary, unaccompanied, unattended. 2 (without help) by yourself, single-handed, solo, unassisted, unaided. 3 abandoned, deserted, forsaken, lonely. 4 (you alone, this alone) exclusively, just, nothing but, purely, only, simply, solely

aloof *adj* cold, cool, distant, haughty, inaccessible, indifferent, reserved, standoffish, unapproachable, unfriendly, unsociable; *opp* friendly, sociable, warm

aloud *adv* audibly, clearly, distinctly, out loud, plainly; *opp* silently, to yourself

alter *v* adapt, adjust, amend, change, convert, do sth differently, make sth different, modify, remodel, reshape, revise, transform, vary

alteration n adaptation, adjustment, amendment, change, conversion, difference, modification, revision, transformation, variation

alternate adj alternating, every other, every second, turn and turn about

alternate v follow in turn, intersperse, rotate, take turns, vary

alternative n choice, option, other, substitute

always adv 1 (every time) consistently, every time, invariably, without exception, without fail. 2 (continually) continually, constantly, incessantly, interminably, perpetually, repeatedly. 3 (forever) eternally, endlessly, forever, forever more

amalgamate v combine, fuse, incorporate, integrate, join, link, merge, mix, unify, unite; **opp** separate, split

amalgamation n combination, fusion, incorporation, integration, linking, joining, merger, unification; **opp** separation

amass v accumulate, assemble, collect, gather together, hoard, save, stash away inf, stockpile, store away

amaze v astonish, astound, bowl sb over inf, dumbfound, floor inf, leave sb speechless, shock, stagger, stun, surprise, take sb's breath away

amazed adj astonished, astounded, bowled over inf, dumbfounded, floored inf, left speechless, shocked, staggered, stunned, surprised, thunderstruck

amazement n astonishment, awe, surprise, shock, wonder

amazing adj 1 (very good) brilliant, excellent, fabulous, fantastic, great,

incredible, marvelous, superb, terrific, tremendous, wonderful. 2 (surprising) astonishing, astounding, shocking, staggering, stunning, surprising

ambassador n attaché, consul, diplomat, emissary, envoy, representative

ambiguous adj cryptic, double-edged, enigmatic, equivocal, obscure, puzzling, unclear, vague, with a double meaning; **opp** clear, plain, obvious, unequivocal

ambition n 1 determination, drive, enterprise, get up-and-go inf, motivation; **opp** apathy, indifference. 2 aim, aspiration, desire, dream, goal, objective

ambitious adj 1 determined, eager, enterprising, go-ahead, keen, motivated. 2 challenging, demanding, difficult

ambush n surprise attack, trap

ambush v attack, lie in wait for, trap, waylay

amenable adj accommodating, agreeable, flexible, open to persuasion, open to suggestion, responsive

amend v adjust, alter, change, correct, improve, modify, revise

amendment n addendum, adjustment, alteration, change, correction, improvement, modification, revision

amenity n facility, feature, resource, service

amiable adj affable, agreeable, approachable, endearing, engaging, friendly, genial, good-natured, kindly, likeable, pleasant, sociable

amicable adj amiable, civil, cordial, courteous, friendly, good-humored, good-natured, harmonious, peaceable

ammunition n ammo inf, armaments,

bombs, bullets, cartridges, explosives, grenades, missiles, munitions, pellets, rounds, shot

amnesty *n* dispensation, forgiveness, immunity, pardon, remission, reprieve

amorous *adj* adoring, ardent, doting, enamored, erotic, in love, lecherous, lovesick, loving, lustful, passionate, randy, sexual, sexy

amount *n* 1 degree, extent, magnitude, quantity, number, size, value, volume. 2 lot, measure, sum, sum total, total

amount to *v* 1 add up to, come to, equal, make, run to, total. 2 add up to, be equivalent to, be tantamount to, be the same as, mean

ample *adj* 1 adequate, enough, more than enough, plenty, sufficient. 2 abundant, generous, lavish, plentiful. 3 big, expansive, full, large, roomy, spacious, substantial, voluminous

amplify *v* 1 boost, intensify, increase, magnify, make louder, strengthen. 2 develop, elaborate on, enlarge on, expound, flesh out, go into details, say more about

amputate *v* chop off, cut off, lop off, remove, sever

amuse *v* 1 entertain, make sb laugh, make sb smile, regale sb with. 2 (find sth to do) entertain, keep sb happy, occupy

amused *adj* 1 entertained, tickled, tickled pink. 2 absorbed, engrossed, entertained, occupied

amusement *n* 1 delight, enjoyment, hilarity, laughter, pleasure. 2 diversion, entertainment, occupation, recreation

amusing *adj* comical, droll, funny, hilarious, humorous, ludicrous, ridiculous, witty

analogy *n* correlation, correspondence, parallel, resemblance, similarity

analysis *n* 1 examination, study, investigation, evaluation. 2 (of blood sample) test, breakdown

analytical *adj* detailed, diagnostic, methodical, investigative, systematic

analyze *v* 1 evaluate, examine, investigate, study, work out. 2 (analyze a blood sample) break down, do an analysis of, separate out, test

anarchic *adj* chaotic, disorderly, lawless, rebellious, uncontrolled, undisciplined, unpredictable; *opp* orderly

anarchy *n* anarchism, chaos, disorder, lawlessness, rebellion

ancestor *n* family, forbear, forefather, previous generation

ancient *adj* 1 (very old) aged, aging, antiquated, elderly, old. 2 (old-fashioned) antiquated, archaic, behind the times, dated, obsolete, old-fashioned, old hat, outmoded, out-of-date, passé; *opp* latest, modern, up-to-date. 3 (in early history) early, prehistoric, primeval, primitive, primordial

anecdote *n* account, cautionary tale, reminiscence, story, tale

angel *n* 1 cherub, seraph, archangel. 2 dear, gem, marvel, saint, star, treasure

anger *n* annoyance, exasperation, displeasure, fury, irritation, outrage, rage, temper

angle *n* 1 bend, corner, crook, fork, point. 2 approach, aspect, direction, point of view, position, perspective, side, slant, standpoint, viewpoint

angry *adj* annoyed, cross, mad, fuming, furious, heated, hopping mad, hot under the collar, incensed, infuriated, irate, irritated, mad, outraged, uptight *inf*; *opp* calm, laid-back

anguish *n* agony, distress, grief, heartbreak, misery, pain, sorrow, suffering, torment, trauma

animal *n* beast, creature, mammal

animated *adj* 1 enthusiastic, excited, lively, impassioned, passionate, vehement, vigorous. 2 cartoon, lifelike, moving

animosity *n* acrimony, antagonism, bad feeling, bitterness, conflict, disapproval, distaste, hatred, hostility, loathing, rancor, resentment

annihilate *v* decimate, defeat, destroy, eradicate, exterminate, extinguish, liquidate, take out, wipe out

announce *v* declare, give out, go public on, make known, publicize, publish, release, reveal, say

announcement *n* bulletin, communiqué, declaration, disclosure, notice, statement, press release, pronouncement, report, revelation

annoy *v* aggravate, anger, bother, exasperate, get on sb's nerves, get to sb *inf*, infuriate, hassle *inf*, irritate, madden, make sb mad, pester, vex

annoyance *n* 1 anger, displeasure, infuriation, irritation. 2 (nuisance) bind *inf*, bother, hassle *inf*, nuisance, pain *inf*, pain in the neck *inf*, pest, pig *inf*

annoyed *adj* angry, cross, exasperated, fuming, furious, hopping mad, hot under the collar, incensed, infuriated, irate, irritated, mad, outraged, uptight *inf*

annoying *adj* aggravating, exasperating, galling, infuriating, irritating, maddening, tiresome, troublesome

annual *adj* once a year, yearly

anomaly *n* abnormality, fluke *inf*, freak, inconsistency, irregularity, oddity, peculiarity, quirk, rarity, unusual occurrence

anonymous *adj* nameless, unassigned, unidentified, unknown, unsigned

answer *n* 1 reply, response, retort. 2 explanation, solution

answer *v* 1 acknowledge, react to, reply, respond to, retort. 2 find a solution to, resolve, solve. 3 (satisfy a need) fit the bill, fulfill, meet, satisfy, suit

answerable *adj* accountable, responsible

antagonistic *adj* against, aggressive, anti, disapproving, hostile, in opposition to, on the other side, opposed

antagonize *v* alienate, annoy, bother, estrange, infuriate, irritate, offend, pester, rub sb the wrong way *inf*

anthology *n* collected works, collection, compendium, compilation, selection

anticipate *v* assume, count on, expect, forecast, foresee, look forward to, predict, think of in advance

anticlimax *n* bathos, comedown, failure, fiasco, flop, disappointment, letdown, wash-out *inf*

antics *n* messing about, mischief, shenanigans, silliness, tomfoolery, tricks

antidote *n* antitoxin, antivenin, cure, remedy

antiquated *adj* 1 aged, ancient, elderly, old. 2 (old-fashioned) ancient, archaic, behind the times, dated, obsolete, old-fashioned, old hat, out-of-date, outmoded, passé; *opp* latest, modern, up-to-date

antique *adj* antiquarian, classic, old, veteran, vintage

antisocial *n* 1 (of people) cold, standoffish, unapproachable, unfriendly, unsociable, withdrawn; *opp* friendly, gregarious. 2 (of behavior) offensive, unacceptable

anxiety *n* angst, apprehension, bother, concern, hang-up *inf*, misgiving, nervousness, stress, tension, trauma, uneasiness, worry

anxious *adj* apprehensive, bothered, concerned, nervous, on tenterhooks, stressed-out, tense, uneasy, worried; *opp* calm, cool, laid-back, relaxed

apartment *n* living quarters, penthouse, pied-à-terre, room, rooms, studio flat

apathetic *adj* indifferent, lazy, lethargic, listless, uninterested

apathy *n* indifference, laziness, lethargy, listlessness

apologetic *adj* contrite, repentant, remorseful, sorry

apologize *v* eat crow *inf*, eat humble pie *inf*, eat your words, grovel *inf*, make an apology, say sorry, take back what you said

apology *n* confession, excuse, expression of regret

appall *v* disgust, dismay, horrify, outrage, shock

appalled *adj* disgusted, dismayed, horrified, outraged, shocked

appalling *adj* atrocious, awful, disgusting, dreadful, foul, ghastly, grim, hideous, horrendous, horrible, horrific, horrifying, outrageous, really bad, shocking, terrible

apparatus *n* contraption, device, equipment, gear, tackle

apparent *adj* 1 clear, evident, noticeable, obvious, plain, visible, unmistakable. 2 ostensible, outward, seeming, superficial

apparently *adv* evidently, rumor has it that, seemingly

appeal *n* 1 application, call, entreaty, petition, plea, request, suit. 2 attraction, charm, fascination, interest

appeal *v* 1 ask for, beg for, call for, implore, petition for, put in a request for, request. 2 (seem attractive or interesting) attract, draw, fascinate, interest, please, tempt

appealing *adj* attractive, fascinating, interesting, pleasing, tempting

appear *v* 1 arrive, come into view, come out, come to light, crop up, emerge, materialize, pop up, show up, turn up. 2 look like, seem. 3 (in a show) perform, play, star, take part

appearance *n* 1 arrival, emergence, materialization. 2 air, aspect, demeanor, dress, expression, impression, look. 3 (illusion) front, guise, illusion, outward appearance, pretense, show

appease *v* calm down, mollify, pacify, placate, soften up, soothe

appendix *n* addendum, addition, adjunct, codicil, supplement

appetite *n* craving, desire, hunger, keenness, relish, stomach, will

appetizing *adj* delicious, inviting, mouth-watering, tasty

applaud *v* 1 clap, bring the house down, give a standing ovation to, give sb a big hand, give sb a round of applause, put your hands together for, raise the roof.

2 approve, commend, have great admiration for, praise, support, welcome

applause n clapping, curtain call, encore, ovation

applicable adj apposite, appropriate, pertinent, relevant, suitable, to the point, valid

applicant n candidate, claimant, interviewee

application n claim, form, petition, request

apply v 1 (be relevant) appertain, be applicable, be appropriate, be relevant, be valid, concern, involve, pertain, relate. 2 (use) carry out, employ, implement, make use of, put into operation, put into practice, use, utilize. 3 (apply medication, glue) cover with, put on, rub in, spread on

appoint v choose, elect, employ, name, nominate, put into office, select, sign, take on

appointment n 1 date, engagement, meeting, rendezvous. 2 job, office, position, post, role, situation, situation vacant

apportion v allocate, dish out inf, dispense, distribute, divide up, dole out inf, hand out, share out

appraise v assess, cast your eye over, evaluate, give sth the once-over inf, judge, review, size up inf

appreciable adj apparent, considerable, discernible, noticeable, significant, substantial

appreciate v 1 (be grateful) be appreciative of, be grateful for, be thankful for, value. 2 (appreciate art, good food) like, prize, rate, rate highly,

respect, think a lot of, value. 3 (realize) accept, be aware of, be conscious of, realize, recognize, understand

appreciation n 1 gratitude, thanks. 2 (understanding) acceptance, awareness, realization, recognition, understanding

appreciative adj 1 grateful, pleased, thankful. 2 admiring, enthusiastic, supportive

apprehend v arrest, capture, detain, nail inf, nick inf, pick up inf, run in inf, take in, take in for questioning, take into custody

apprehension n 1 alarm, anxiety, butterflies in the stomach, concern, disquiet, doubt, fear, foreboding, misgiving, mistrust, nervousness, presentiment, the heebie-jeebies, the shakes, trepidation, unease, uneasiness, worry. 2 arrest, capture, detention, seizure. 3 appreciation, awareness, comprehension, conception, discernment, grasp, perception, realization, recognition, understanding

apprehensive adj afraid, alarmed, anxious, concerned, fearful, frightened, mistrustful, nervous, scared, uneasy, worried

approach n 1 (coming nearer) advance, advancing, advent, arrival, nearing. 2 (to a place) access road, avenue, drive, driveway, entrance, entry, passage, path, road, way. 3 (to a person) advances, appeal, application, invitation, overtures, proposal, proposition. 4 (to doing something) attitude, course, manner, means, method, mode, procedure, style, technique, way

approach v 1 advance, arrive, catch up,

come close, come near, come to, draw near, gain on, go towards, meet, move towards, near, reach. **2** (talk to sb) address, greet, hail, speak to, start talking to. **3** (ask sb for sth) appeal, apply, ask, broach the matter with, chat up *inf*, make advances, make a proposal, make overtures, proposition, solicit, sound out, suggest to. **4** (do sth) begin, commence, embark on, make a start on, set about, tackle, undertake. **5** approximate, be close to, be like, be near to, be comparable with, be similar to, come close to, come near to, compare with, resemble, suggest

approachable *adj* accessible, affable, amicable, easygoing, friendly, informal, kind, open, relaxed, sympathetic, understanding, well-disposed; *opp* aloof, severe, stuffy

appropriate *adj* apposite, apt, becoming, befitting, belonging, correct, fit, fitting, going well with, pertinent, proper, relevant, right, suitable, to the point, to the purpose, well-suited, well-timed

approval *n* **1** (liking) acceptance, acclaim, acclamation, admiration, applause, appreciation, approbation, commendation, esteem, favor, good opinion, high regard, liking, praise, regard, respect. **2** (agreement) acceptance, acquiescence, agreement, assent, authorization, blessing, confirmation, consent, endorsement, leave, mandate, permission, ratification, sanction, the go-ahead *inf*, the green light *inf*, the okay *inf*

approve *v* **1** acclaim, admire, applaud, appreciate, be pleased with, commend, esteem, favor, have a good/high opinion of, have a high regard for, like, praise, regard highly, respect, think highly of, think well of. **2** accept, agree to, authorize, consent to, endorse, give the go-ahead *inf*, give the green light to *inf*, give the nod to *inf*, give the OK to *inf*, give your backing to, give your blessing to, go along with, pass, permit, ratify, recommend, sanction, validate

approximate *adj* estimated, imprecise, inexact, loose, rough

approximately *adv* **1** about, around, close to, give or take *inf*, in the region of, just about, loosely, more or less, not far off, or so, roughly. **2** (with dates) circa

approximation *n* conjecture, ballpark figure *inf*, estimate, guess, guesstimate *inf*, guesswork, rough calculation, rough figure, rough idea

apt *adj* **1** applicable, appropriate, apposite, correct, felicitous, fitting, pertinent, proper, relevant, suitable, to the point. **2** able, adept, astute, bright, clever, competent, gifted, intelligent, quick, quick to learn, sharp, smart, talented. **3** apt to given, inclined, liable, likely, of a mind, prone

aptitude *n* ability, faculty, flair, gift, knack, quickness, talent

arbitrary *adj* erratic, irrational, personal, random, subjective

arbitrate *v* adjudicate, decide, determine, judge, mediate, settle

arbitration *n* adjudication, decision, judgment, settlement

archaic *adj* ancient, behind the times, old, old-fashioned, outdated, outmoded

ardent *adj* eager, emotional, enthusiastic, fervent, intense, keen, passionate, zealous

arduous *adj* back-breaking, demanding, exhausting, grueling, hard, strenuous, taxing, tiring, uphill, wearying; *opp* easy

area *n* **1** district, environment, neighborhood, patch *inf*, quarter, region, sector, space, surroundings, territory, turf *sl*. **2** acreage, expanse, extent, measurements, size. **3** (of knowledge) branch, discipline, field, province, realm, sphere, world

arena *n* **1** amphitheater, field, ground, ring, stadium. **2** battleground, domain, realm, scene, sphere

argue *v* **1** be at each other's throats, bicker, clash, disagree, fall out *inf*, feud, fight, have a bone to pick with sb, have a row, pick a fight, quarrel, squabble, wrangle. **2** debate, discuss, dispute, reason, remonstrate. **3** assert, claim, insist, put forward, say, state, suggest

argument *n* **1** clash, controversy, difference of opinion, disagreement, discussion, dispute, feud, fight, quarrel, row, showdown, squabble, tiff. **2** assertion, case, claim, contention, hypothesis, idea, plea, proposition, reasoning, reasons, statement, view

argumentative *adj* awkward, belligerent, combative, contrary, difficult, opinionated, quarrelsome

arid *adj* desert, dried up, dry, parched, waterless

arise *v* **1** appear, begin, come up, come to light, crop up *inf*, emerge, happen, occur, originate. **2** be caused by, be the result of, come of, come out of, follow,

proceed, result, spring from, stem from. **3** get out of bed, get to your feet, get up, stand up

aristocrat *n* grandee, lady, lord, nob *sl*, noble, nobleman, noblewoman, patrician, peer, peeress

aristocratic *adj* blue-blooded, elite, noble, posh *inf*, privileged, upper-class, titled, well-born

arm *n* **1** appendage, limb, upper limb. **2** branch, department, division, extension, offshoot, section, sector

arm *v* **1** equip, fit with, issue with, provide, supply. **2** (prepare yourself) brace, fortify, gird your loins, prepare, steel

armed *adj* **1** (carrying weapons) in arms, tooled up *slang*, under arms. **2** equipped, fortified, prepared, primed, provided, ready, strengthened,

armored *adj* armor-plated, bombproof, bulletproof, fortified, protected, strengthened

arms *n* **1** armaments, firearms, guns, ordnance, weaponry, weapons. **2** coat of arms, crest, emblem, escutcheon, insignia, shield

army *n* **1** armed forces, forces, land force, soldiers, the military, troops. **2** crowd, horde, host, mob, multitude, pack, swarm, throng

aroma *n* bouquet, fragrance, odor, perfume, scent, smell

aromatic *adj* fragrant, perfumed, piquant, pungent, scented, sweet-smelling

arouse *v* **1** awake, rouse, waken, wake up. **2** agitate, animate, egg on, enliven, excite, goad, incense, inflame, provoke, spur on, wind up *inf*. **3** cause, foster, induce, kindle, provoke, set off, sow the seeds of, stimulate, stir up, trigger, whip up. **4** excite, stimulate, turn on *inf*

arrange *v* **1** align, classify, grade, group, lay out, line up, order, organize, put in order, rank, set out, sort, sort out, tidy. **2** agree, decide, fix up, make a date, make an appointment, make arrangements, organize, pencil in, plan, schedule, settle on , set up. **3** (music) adapt, orchestrate, score, set to music

arrangement *n* **1** alignment, array, classification, design, display, formation, grouping, layout, line-up, order, organization, pattern, ranking, set-up, structure, system. **2** agreement, appointment, date, plan, preparations. **3** adaptation, interpretation, orchestration, score, version

array *n* arrangement, collection, display, formation, group, line-up, presentation

array *v* arrange, assemble, draw up, group, line up, order, organize, place, position, range, rank

arrival *n* **1** appearance, approach, beginning, coming, dawn, entrance, entry. **2** (a person) immigrant, newcomer, visitor

arrive *v* appear, come, come along, come on the scene, enter, get here/there, make an entrance, put in an appearance, reach, roll up *inf*, show up *inf*, turn up

arrogant *adj* big-headed, boastful, brash, cavalier, cocky *inf*, conceited, contemptuous, disdainful, egotistical, haughty, high-and-mighty, high-handed, lordly, overbearing, patronizing, pompous, proud, scornful, self-important, smug, superior, supercilious, vain

arrow *n* **1** bolt, dart, shaft. **2** indicator, marker, pointer

art *n* **1** knack, knowledge, method, skill, technique, trick. **2** aptitude, artistry, craft, craftsmanship, dexterity, expertise, ingenuity, proficiency, skillfulness, skill. **3** craft, culture, fine art, the arts

article *n* **1** artifact, item, object, piece, thing, unit. **2** (in a newspaper) account, essay, feature, item, piece, report, story, write up

articulate *v* enunciate, express, pronounce, say, speak, state, talk, utter, voice

articulate *adj* **1** (of a person) eloquent, expressive, fluent, having the gift of the gab *inf*, lucid, silver-tongued; *opp* inarticulate. **2** (of language) clear, coherent, comprehensible, eloquent, fluent, intelligible, lucid, understandable

artificial *adj* **1** man-made, manufactured, synthetic; *opp* real, natural. **2** bogus, counterfeit, ersatz, fake, false, imitation, mock, phony, pseudo-, sham, simulated; *opp* real, genuine. **3** affected, assumed, fake, false, feigned, forced, insincere, put on, unnatural, unreal; *opp* real, genuine

artistic *adj* **1** (of people) accomplished, creative, cultured, gifted, talented. **2** attractive, beautiful, decorative, elegant, esthetic, exquisite, graceful, ornamental, stylish, tasteful

artistry *n* **1** ability, brilliance, creativity, expertise, flair, gift, proficiency, skill, talent, virtuosity. **2** art, craftsmanship, style, workmanship

ascend *v* climb, climb up, float up, fly up,

gain height, go up, lift off, mount, move up, rise, scale, soar, take off; **opp** descend

ascent *n* climb, gradient, hill, incline, ramp, rise, slope; **opp** descent

ascertain *v* 1 determine, discover, establish, ferret out *inf*, find out, get to know, learn. 2 confirm, establish, identify, make certain, make sure, settle, verify

ascetic *adj* abstemious, abstinent, austere, celibate, chaste, frugal, harsh, hermit-like, plain, puritanical, restrained, rigorous, self-denying, self-disciplined, severe, simple, Spartan, strict, temperate

ascribe *v* assign, attribute, blame, charge, credit sb with, give credit to, impute, put down, refer, set down

ashamed *adj* apologetic, chastened, conscience-stricken, contrite, embarrassed, guilty, humiliated, mortified, red-faced, remorseful, repentant, shamefaced, sheepish, sorry, unable to look sb in the face

ask *v* 1 (ask questions) ask around, canvass, enquire, inquire, make inquiries, query, question. 2 (question sb) fire questions at, give sb the third degree *inf*, grill *inf*, interrogate, interview, pick sb's brains, put sb on the spot *inf*, question, quiz. 3 (ask for sth) appeal, apply, beg, beseech, call upon, claim, demand, implore, petition, plead, pray, request, seek, solicit. 4 invite, summon

asleep *adj* catnapping, comatose, dead to the world *inf*, dormant, dozing, having a nap, having a snooze, hibernating, out like a light, resting, sleeping, slumbering, snoozing; **opp** awake

aspect *n* 1 angle, face, feature, part, side, slant, standpoint, viewpoint. 2 air, appearance, attitude, bearing, demeanor, expression, look, manner, mien

aspiration *n* aim, ambition, desire, dream, goal, hankering, hope, intention, longing, objective, purpose, wish, yearning

aspire *v* aim, be ambitious, desire, dream of, hanker after *inf*, hope, long, pursue, seek, set your sights on, wish, yearn

aspiring *adj* ambitious, budding, eager, hopeful, potential, striving, wannabe *inf*, would-be

assail *v* 1 (attack) assault, attack, bombard, fall on, lay into, pelt, set about, set on. 2 (criticize) abuse, berate, blast, criticize, harangue, lambast, malign, pillory, put down, revile, vilify

assassin *n* contract killer, executioner, hit man *inf*, killer, murderer, slayer

assassinate *v* eliminate, execute, hit *slang*, kill, liquidate, murder, slay

assault *n* 1 act of aggression, attack, invasion, offensive, raid, strike. 2 assault and battery, mugging, rape

assault *v* 1 (a place) assail, attack, invade, storm. 2 (a person) attack, fly at *inf*, hit, lay into *inf*, set about *inf*, set upon, work over *inf*. 3 (sexually) grope, interfere with, molest, rape, sexually assault

assemble *v* 1 (of people) call together, come together, congregate, convene, flock, gather, get together, herd together, marshal, meet, muster, rally, round up. 2 (of things) amass, bring together, collect, gather, get together, pile up. 3 (put parts together) build, cobble together *inf*, connect, construct, erect, fabricate, fit together, join, make, piece together, put together, set up

assembly *n* 1 body, company, congregation, convention, council, crowd, flock, gathering, group, mass, meeting, throng. 2 accumulation, collection

assert *v* 1 affirm, allege, announce, argue, claim, contend, declare, insist, maintain, profess, say, state, stress. 2 **assert yourself** act confidently, be assertive, exert your influence, insist, make your presence felt, put your foot down, stand firm, stand up for yourself, stick up for yourself, stick to your guns

assertion *n* affirmation, allegation, argument, claim, contention, declaration, insistence, pronouncement, statement

assertive *adj* 1 confident, decided, definite, emphatic, firm, forceful, insistent, positive, self-assured, strong-willed. 2 bossy, dogmatic, domineering, not backward in coming forward *inf*, opinionated, peremptory, pushy *inf*, stubborn, uncompromising

assess *v* appraise, calculate, determine, estimate, evaluate, gauge, judge, price, rate, reckon, size up *inf*, value, weigh up

assessment *n* appraisal, estimate, estimation, gauging, judgment, rating, valuation

asset *n* advantage, benefit, blessing, boon, godsend, help, resource, support

assets *n* capital, estate, funds, goods, means, money, possessions, property, reserves, wealth

assign *v* 1 (to a job) appoint, choose, commission, designate, name, nominate, select. 2 (give) allocate, allot, consign, give, share out

assimilate *v* 1 (absorb) absorb, digest, incorporate, take in. 2 (fit in) adapt, become adjusted, become like, blend in, conform with, fit in

assist *v* 1 (help) aid, collaborate, cooperate with, help, help out, lend a hand, play a part, rally round *inf*, succor, support, work; *opp* hinder. 2 (make easier) expedite, facilitate, further, help, make easier; *opp* hinder

assistance *n* 1 a hand, a helping hand, aid, benefit, collaboration, cooperation, help, support; *opp* hindrance. 2 (financial) aid, backing, back-up, help, patronage, reinforcement, sponsorship, subsidy, support

assistant *n* 1 (colleague) accessory, accomplice, ally, associate, collaborator, colleague, comrade, helper, partner. 2 (subordinate) aide, auxiliary, deputy, helper, henchman, mate, personal assistant, right-hand man, right-hand woman, second in command, secretary, subordinate

associate *n* ally, colleague, companion, comrade, co-worker, follower, friend, mate, partner, workmate

associate *v* 1 (in the mind) connect, couple, link, relate, think of together, tie in, tie up *inf*. 2 (of people) ally yourself, band together, be friends, fraternize, gang up *inf*, get pally with *inf*, go round with, hang out *inf*, hobnob, join up, keep company, make friends, mingle, mix, pal up, socialize. 3 (of organizations) affiliate, ally, amalgamate, attach, combine, connect, join, link up, unite, yoke

association n 1 (group) alliance, band, body, brotherhood, cartel, clique, club, coalition, company, confederacy, confederation, cooperative, corporation, federation, firm, fraternity, gang, group, league, order, organization, partnership, society, syndicate, union. 2 (joining) amalgamation, blend, combination, connection, mixture, pairing, relation, tie in, union

assorted adj different, diverse, heterogeneous, miscellaneous, mixed, motley, multifarious, sundry, varied, various

assortment n choice, collection, hotchpotch, jumble, medley, miscellany, mishmash, mixed bag inf, mixture, range, selection, variety

assume v 1 believe, deduce, expect, fancy, guess, have a hunch inf, have an idea, imagine, infer, presume, presuppose, reckon, surmise, suspect, take for granted, think, understand. 2 (assume responsibility) accept, shoulder, take on, take up, take on yourself, undertake. 3 affect, feign, pretend, put on, simulate

assumption n belief, conjecture, expectation, guess, hunch inf, hypothesis, inference, premise, presumption, surmise, suspicion, theory

assurance n 1 certainty, confidence, coolness, self-assurance, self-confidence, nerve, poise. 2 guarantee, oath, pledge, promise, vow, word, word of honor. 3 insurance

assure v convince, give your word, guarantee, persuade, promise, reassure, soothe, swear, vow

astonish v amaze, astound, bewilder, daze, dazzle, shock, stagger, stun, stupefy, surprise, take your breath away

astonished adj amazed, astounded, dumbfounded, shocked, speechless, staggered, surprised, taken aback

astonishing adj amazing, astounding, bewildering, breathtaking, hard to believe, mind-boggling inf, shocking, striking, stunning, surprising

astonishment n amazement, bewilderment, confusion, disbelief, shock, surprise, wonder

astounding adj amazing, astonishing, awe-inspiring, bewildering, impressive, staggering, striking, surprising

astute adj artful, calculating, canny, clever, crafty, cunning, discerning, knowing, nobody's fool, perceptive, sharp, shrewd, sly

asylum n a haven, protection, refuge, safety, sanctuary, shelter

atheist n free-thinker, non-believer, unbeliever

athlete n 1 competitor, contender, fitness fanatic, fitness freak inf, gymnast, player, runner, sportsman, sportsperson, sportswoman. 2 (in particular events) decathlete, distance runner, heptathlete, high jumper, long jumper, sprinter, triple jumper

athletic adj active, brawny, energetic, fit, muscular, powerful, robust, sporty, strapping, strong, sturdy, well-built

atmosphere n 1 (around the earth) air, ionosphere, sky, stratosphere. 2 (general mood) air, ambience, aura, character, climate, feel, feeling, flavor, mood, quality, spirit, tone, vibes *inf*

atrocious *adj* abominable, appalling, awful, bad, dreadful, ghastly, grim, horrendous *inf*, horrible, horrific, terrible, unspeakable

atrocity *n* abomination, barbarity, bloodbath, brutality, crime against humanity, killing, massacre, outrage, slaughter, war crime

attach *v* add, add on, affix, append, connect, couple, fasten, fit, fix, hitch, hitch up, hook up, join, link, pin, secure, stick, tie; *opp* detach

attachment *n* 1 (thing attached) accessory, accoutrement, addition, add-on, adjunct, affix, extension. 2 (feeling) affection, affinity, bond, devotion, emotional tie, fondness, friendship, liking, love, loyalty, tenderness

attack *n* 1 act of aggression, assault, incursion, invasion, onslaught, raid, storming. 2 (against person) assault, beating, mugging, rape

attack *v* 1 invade, raid, storm. 2 (attack a person) assail, assault, beat, beat up, lay into, mug, rape

attacker *n* 1 aggressor, invader, raider. 2 assailant, mugger, rapist. 3 (in sport) forward, goalscorer, striker

attain *v* achieve, accomplish, acquire, arrive at, earn, fulfill, gain, get, obtain, reach, realize, secure, win

attempt *n* crack *inf*, effort, endeavor, go, shot, stab *inf*, try

attempt *v* aim, do your best, endeavor, give it a whirl *inf*, have a bash at *inf*, have a crack at *inf*, have a go at, have a shot at, have a stab at *inf*, make an

effort, seek, set out, strive, take it upon yourself, try, undertake, venture

attend *v* 1 (be at a place) be present at, go to, visit. 2 (serve sb) accompany, escort, help, serve, wait on, wait on sb hand and foot. 3 attend to deal with, do, handle, see to, set your mind to

attendant *n* aide, assistant, butler, companion, equerry, escort, guard, helper, lackey, lady-in-waiting, minder *inf*, servant, squire, steward, usher, valet

attention *n* 1 attentiveness, awareness, concentration, consideration, heed, notice, observation, regard, scrutiny, thought. 2 (medical) care, therapy, treatment. 3 attentions attendance, civilities, compliments, concern, courtesies, gallantry, ministrations, respects

attentive *adj* 1 alert, all ears *inf*, awake, aware, heedful, listening, looking, mindful, observant, on guard, on the lookout, on your guard, vigilant, watchful, watching, wide awake; *opp* inattentive. 2 (considerate) chivalrous, concerned, conscientious, considerate, courteous, dancing attendance, gallant, gracious, kind, obliging, polite, respectful, thoughtful

attitude *n* 1 (mental) approach, disposition, feeling, opinion, outlook. 2 (physical) pose, position, posture

attract *v* allure, bewitch, captivate, charm, draw, enchant, entice, fascinate, interest, intrigue, pull, seduce, tempt; *opp* repel

attractive *adj* 1 (of person) alluring, beautiful, captivating, comely, enchanting, good-looking, gorgeous, handsome, lovely, pretty, seductive, sexy, striking, stunning; **opp** repulsive. **2** (of things, qualities) agreeable, appealing, charming, engaging, fascinating, fetching, interesting, inviting, nice, pleasant, pleasing, tempting

attribute n aspect, characteristic, facet, feature, hallmark, mark, property, quality, virtue

attribute v ascribe, assign, charge, credit, impute, lay at the door of, put down to

audacious adj adventurous, bold, brave, cheeky, intrepid, reckless, risky

audible adj clear, discernible, distinct, perceptible, within earshot, within hearing

audience n **1** assembly, congregation, crowd, fans, gallery, house, listeners, public, spectators, turnout, viewers. **2** (for particular views or publications) aficionados, devotees, fans, following, market, public. **3** (meeting with important person) consultation, reception, hearing, interview, meeting

audit n bookkeeping, check, examination, inspection, monitoring, review, scrutiny

audit v check, examine, go through, inspect, monitor, oversee, review, scrutinize

auspicious adj bright, encouraging, favorable, felicitous, rosy, good, hopeful, opportune, promising, propitious, timely; **opp** inauspicious

austere adj **1** (of place, conditions) hard, harsh, plain, spare, spartan. **2** (of person) abstemious, ascetic, forbidding, frugal, puritan, sober, solemn, stern, strict

austerity n belt-tightening, frugality,

hardship, poverty, recession, straitened circumstances

authentic adj authenticated, bona fide, genuine, kosher inf, real, true

author n authoress, biographer, composer, creator, dramatist, essayist, journalist, librettist, lyricist, novelist, originator, playwright, poet, poetess, songwriter, writer

authoritarian adj autocratic, despotic, dictatorial, disciplinarian, dominant, dominating, domineering, imperious, strict, totalitarian, tyrannical, undemocratic

authority n **1** (power to command or decide) command, competence, control, charge, dominion, influence, jurisdiction, power, prerogative, remit, rule, sovereignty, supremacy. **2** (the right to do sth) authorization, clearance, license, permission, right, sanction, warrant. **3** (controlling body) board, body, executive, institution, local authority, regulator, regulatory body. **4** (person with special knowledge) expert, fount of knowledge, pundit, scholar, source, specialist, witness

authorize v agree to, allow, approve, assent to, clear, countenance, empower, enable, entitle, give the go-ahead to, give the green light to, let, license, permit, sanction

autocratic adj absolutist, authoritarian, despotic, dictatorial, dominant, dominating, domineering, imperious, tyrannical, undemocratic

automatic adj **1** (of machines) mechanical, electronic, remote-control; **opp** manual. **2** (happening by itself) instinctive, involuntary, unconscious

autonomous adj free, independent, self-contained, self-governing, sovereign

available adj accessible, free, handy, in plentiful supply, obtainable, on hand, on tap inf, ready, to be had, to hand, vacant

avarice n acquisitiveness, greed, meanness, miserliness, parsimony, selfishness, stinginess inf

avenge v get back at, retaliate against, take vengeance on, take revenge on

avenue n 1 boulevard, path, road, street, thoroughfare. 2 choice, opening; opportunity, possibility

average adj everyday, medium, middle-sized, middling, moderate, normal, ordinary, run-of-the-mill, standard, typical, unexceptional, usual

average n median, mean, midpoint, norm, standard

averse adj antipathetic, disinclined, hostile, ill-disposed, loath; opposed, reluctant, unfavorable, unwilling

aversion n abhorrence, animosity, antipathy, detestation, disinclination, dislike, disgust, distaste, hate, hatred, horror, hostility, loathing, opposition, reluctance, repugnance, repulsion, revulsion, unwillingness

avert v avoid, prevent, stop, turn aside, turn away

avid adj eager, enthusiastic, greedy, hungry, keen, thirsty

avoid v 1 elude, escape, evade, keep away from, shirk, shun, stay away from. 2 (not do sth) abstain from, get out of, refrain from

avoidable adj escapable, preventable, unnecessary

await v anticipate, expect, wait for

awake adj alert, aware, compos mentis inf, conscious, vigilant, wide awake; **opp** asleep

awaken v rouse, wake, wake up

award n 1 (for achievement) decoration, presentation, prize, reward, trophy. 2 (legally or officially granted) adjudication, compensation, damages, grant, order

award v accord, allot, assign, bestow, confer, endow, give, grant, hand out, present

aware adj 1 attentive, alert, awake, conscious. 2 aware of able to recognize, alive to, conscious of, conversant with, familiar with, mindful of, wise to

awareness n cognition, cognizance, consciousness, perception, recognition

awe n admiration, adoration, amazement, fear, wonder

awesome adj amazing, astonishing, awe-inspiring, incredible, magnificent, marvelous, stupendous, unbelievable, wonderful

awful adj abominable, appalling, atrocious, bad, deplorable, devastating, disgusting, dire, dreadful, frightful, ghastly, grim, hideous, horrendous inf, horrible, horrific, shocking, sickening, terrible, unspeakable; **opp** great, terrific, wonderful

awfully adj dreadfully, extremely, frightfully, horrendously inf, incredibly, really, terribly, unspeakably, very

awkward adj 1 (of a person) clumsy, embarrassed, ill-at-ease, maladroit, nervous, uncoordinated, ungainly. 2 (of a problem, situation) difficult,

embarrassing, thorny, tricky
awkwardness *n* clumsiness,
  embarrassment, nervousness
ax *v* abolish, dismiss, do away with, fire,
  get rid of, give sb the boot *inf*, kick out
  inf, make redundant, remove, repeal,
  sack

B

baby *n* babe, babe in arms, child, infant, neonate *tech*, newborn, tiny tot, toddler, tot, young child

back *n* **1** end, hind quarters, rear, rear end, reverse, stern, tail; *opp* front. **2** backbone, spine

back *v* **1** (give or express support for) advocate, agree with, approve, approve of, back up, bet on, champion, encourage, endorse, favor, finance, invest in, sanction, second, side with, sponsor, subsidize, support, underwrite. **2** (move backwards) back away, back up, backtrack, retreat, reverse. **3 back down** back off, backpedal, backtrack, climb down, concede, give in, give way, retreat, submit, surrender, withdraw, yield. **4 back out of** abandon, back away from, cancel, chicken out of *inf*, get cold feet about, go back on, have second thoughts about, renege on, welsh on, withdraw from. **5 back up** (back up a statement) confirm, corroborate, prove, substantiate, support

backer *n* advocate, benefactor, champion, investor, patron, promoter, punter, sponsor, supporter, underwriter

backfire *v* blow up in sb's face, boomerang, fail, go wrong, miscarry, misfire, rebound

background *n* **1** (of a picture) backdrop, decor, distance, hinterland, middle distance, scenery. **2** (of a person) breeding, credentials, culture, education, experience, life history, origins, past, qualifications, upbringing. **3** (of events, situation) circumstances, context, events leading up to, history

backing *n* agreement, aid, approval, assistance, cooperation, endorsement, finance, help, helping hand, encouragement, sponsorship, support

backward *adj* **1** primitive, uncivilized, underdeveloped, undeveloped, unsophisticated. **2** (of a person) educationally subnormal, mentally retarded, retarded, slow, subnormal, with special needs

bad *adj* **1** (of low quality) appalling, atrocious, awful, defective, deficient, dreadful, faulty, imperfect, inferior, lousy *inf*, low-quality, mediocre, poor, rotten, substandard, terrible, useless, worthless; *opp* good. **2** (not what is wanted or needed) adverse, difficult, disagreeable, distressing, grim, inadequate, inappropriate, incorrect, nasty, unacceptable, uncomfortable, undesirable, unfavorable, unfortunate, unlucky, unnecessary, unpleasant, unsuitable, unwanted, unsatisfactory, unwelcome, wrong; *opp* good. **3** (bad accident or illness) acute, chronic, critical, disastrous, dreadful, grave, serious, severe, terrible. **4** (causing damage or harm) damaging, dangerous, deleterious, destructive, detrimental, harmful, injurious, noxious, poisonous, ruinous, unhealthy; *opp* good. **5** (of a person) badly behaved, base, corrupt, criminal, crooked, delinquent, depraved, dishonest, dishonorable, evil, immoral, nasty *inf*, naughty, sinful, unruly, unscrupulous, vile, villainous, wicked; *opp* good. **6** (of food) contaminated, decaying, festering, moldy, off, putrescent, putrid, rancid, rotten, sour, spoiled, tainted. **7 not bad** acceptable, adequate, all right, average, fair, moderate, OK *inf*, passable, satisfactory, so-so *inf*, tolerable

baffle *v* bamboozle, bewilder, confound, confuse, flummox, have sb scratching his head, mystify, nonplus, perplex, puzzle, stump

bag *n* basket, case, container, handbag, holdall, rucksack, sack, satchel, shopping bag, shoulder bag

baggage *n* bags, belongings, cases, gear, kit, luggage, suitcases, things

balance *n* **1** (personal quality) composure, equanimity, even-handedness, fairness, level-headedness, objectivity, poise, stability, steadiness. **2** (between different factors or interests) balance of power, correspondence, due proportion, equality, equilibrium, equity, parity, symmetry. **3** (machine) scales, weighing machine. **4** (sum of money) difference, outstanding amount, remainder, residue, rest; *opp* deposit.

5 in the balance at a crisis, at a crossroads, at a turning point, critical, finely balanced, uncertain, undecided. **6 on balance** all in all, all things considered, on the whole, taking everything into account, taking everything into consideration, when all's said and done

balance *v* **1** (place carefully) adjust, perch, place/put carefully, stabilize, steady. **2** (balance different factors or interests) counterbalance, equalize, give equal weight to, offset, weigh, weigh up. **3** (of figures, amounts) add up, balance out, balance up, correspond, match

balanced *adj* evenhanded, fair, objective, unbiased

bald *adj* bald as a coot, bald-headed, bare, hairless, receding, thin on top, with thinning hair

ballot *n* election, franchise, plebiscite, poll, polling, referendum, vote, voting

ban *n* boycott, censorship, embargo, moratorium, prohibition, suppression, taboo, veto

ban *v* abolish, banish, bar, criminalize, debar, end, exclude, forbid, make illegal, outlaw, prohibit, proscribe, put an end to, put a stop to, stop, suppress, veto

banal *adj* bland, clichéd, common, commonplace, everyday, hackneyed, humdrum, meaningless, ordinary, pedestrian, stale, tired, trite, trivial, vapid

band *n* **1** (of people) bevy, brigade, bunch, clique, company, crew *inf*, gang, group, mob, pack, set, troop. **2** (of musicians) brass band, combo *inf*, ensemble, group, orchestra. **3** (narrow piece) bar, line, ribbon, sash, streak, strip, stripe

bandit n brigand, highwayman, outlaw, robber, thief

bang n boom, detonation, explosion, gunshot, thud, thump

banish v 1 (banish a person) ban, bar, boot out *inf*, cast out, deport, drive away, eject, evict, exclude, exile, expel, kick out *inf*, throw out. 2 (banish a feeling) dismiss, dispel, get rid of, shake off

bank n 1 (where money is kept) building society, depository, financial institution, investment bank, merchant bank, reserve, savings and loan association, savings bank. 2 (of a river) embankment, riverside, shore, verge, waterside, waterfront, water's edge

bank v 1 (put money in an account) deposit, pay in

bank on count on, depend on, expect, rely on

bankrupt adj broke *inf*, bust, cleaned out *inf*, failed, in liquidation *tech*, insolvent *tech*, penniless, poor, ruined, without a penny to your name

banner n colors, flag, pennant, placard, standard, streamer

banquet n blow-out *inf*, dinner, dinner party, feast, formal dinner, repast

banter n chaff, gossip, idle chat, joking, joshing, patter, small talk, talk, teasing

baptize v christen, name

bar n 1 (piece of metal) barrier, bolt, ingot, rail, rod. 2 (for drinking) club, lounge, lounge bar, pub, public bar, saloon. 3 (sth that prevents progress) barrier, glass ceiling, hindrance, obstacle

bar v ban, exclude, forbid, keep out, prevent, prohibit, rule out

barbarian n boor, brute, hooligan, lout, monster, ruffian, savage

barbaric adj barbarous, brutal, cruel, primitive, savage, uncivilized, uncouth, wild

bare adj 1 (without clothes) exposed, in the buff *inf*, in the nude, in your birthday suit *inf*, naked, nude, stark naked, stripped, unclothed, undressed, with nothing on; *opp* clothed, dressed. 2 (of a room) austere, empty, plain, spare, unfurnished, vacant. 3 (of landscape) austere, barren, bleak, desolate, empty, exposed, exposed to the elements, featureless, open, scanty, stark, treeless

barefaced adj audacious, blatant, bold, brash, brazen, glaring, impudent, open, patent, shameless, undisguised

barely adv by the skin of your teeth, hardly, just, only just, scarcely

bargain n 1 agreement, arrangement, contract, deal, negotiation, pact, pledge, transaction, treaty, understanding. 2 (sth cheap) discount, good buy, good deal, good value, give-away, reduction. 3 into the bargain also, as well, besides, in addition, moreover

bargain v agree, negotiate, transact

bark v bay, growl, howl, snarl, woof, yap, yelp

barrage n 1 (of gunfire) battery, bombardment, salvo, shelling, volley, wall of fire. 2 (of abuse, criticism) burst, hail, onslaught, storm, stream, torrent

barren adj 1 childless, infertile, sterile; *opp* fertile. 2 arid, desert, desolate, infertile, unfruitful, unproductive, waste; *opp* fertile

barricade n bar, barrier, blockade, bulwark, obstacle, obstruction, palisade, rampart, roadblock, stockade

barrier n 1 bar, barricade, blockade, fence, obstacle, obstruction, railing, roadblock, wall. 2 (to achieving sth) check, handicap, hurdle, impediment, limitation, obstacle, restraint, restriction, stumbling block

base adj contemptible, corrupt, debased, depraved, despicable, dishonorable, disreputable, dissolute, evil, foul, ignoble, immoral, low, reprobate, scandalous, shameful, sinful, sordid, unprincipled, vile, villainous, vulgar, wicked

base n 1 bed, bottom, foot, foundation, pedestal, rest, stand, support; opp top. 2 basis, core, essence, essentials, heart, key, origin, principal, root, source. 3 camp, headquarters, post, settlement, starting point, station

base v build, construct, derive, establish, fasten, form, found, ground, hinge, rest, root

bash n attempt, crack inf, go inf, shot inf, stab inf, try

bash v bang, belt inf, biff inf, crash, deck inf, hit, punch, smash, sock inf, strike, wallop inf, whack

basic adj central, elementary, essential, fundamental, indispensable, intrinsic, key, necessary, primary, rudimentary, underlying, vital; opp peripheral

basically adv at bottom, at heart, essentially, firstly, for the most part, fundamentally, inherently, in the main, intrinsically, mainly, mostly, primarily

basics n brass tacks inf, core, essentials, facts, fundamentals, hard facts, nitty-gritty inf, nuts and bolts, practicalities, principles, realities, rudiments

basis n base, footing, foundation, grounds, reasoning, support

bask v 1 laze, lie, loll, lounge, relax, sunbathe. 2 delight, rejoice, revel, savor, take pleasure

batch n accumulation, amount, collection, crowd, group, lot, mass, pack, quantity, set

bath n dip, douche, shower, soak, soaping, wash

bathe v clean, cleanse, immerse, moisten, rinse, soak, steep, wash, wet

batter v 1 (of a person) abuse, assault, bash inf, beat, clobber inf, hit, smack, whack. 2 (of the weather) buffet, lash, pelt, pound, pummel, smash, thrash, wallop inf, whack inf

battle n action, affray, attack, campaign, clash, combat, conflict, confrontation, contest, encounter, engagement, fight, fray, hostilities, scuffle, skirmish, struggle, tussle, war, warfare

battle v 1 contend, fight, strive, struggle. 2 (argue) argue, bicker, disagree, dispute, feud, fight, have a row, quarrel, row inf, squabble, wrangle

bawdy adj blue, coarse, crude, dirty, disgusting, filthy, gross, indecent, indelicate, lascivious, lecherous, lewd, licentious, naughty, obscene, pornographic, prurient, racy, risqué, rude, smutty, salacious, steamy inf, suggestive, ribald, vulgar

bawl v 1 bellow, call, cry, howl, roar, scream, screech, shout, yell. 2 blubber, cry, snivel, sob, squall, wail, weep

bay n 1 cove, gulf, harbor, inlet, sound. 2 alcove, niche, nook, opening, recess

beach n coast, coastline, sand, seashore, seaside, water's edge

beacon n beam, bonfire, flare, lighthouse, sign, signal, warning light, watchtower

beam n 1 board, girder, joist, plank, rafter, support, timber. 2 flash, gleam, glimmer, glint, glow, ray, shaft, streak, stream

beam v 1 emit, glare, gleam, glitter, glow, radiate, shine. 2 grin, smile

bear v 1 bring, carry, convey, fetch, move, take, tote, transport. 2 endure, put up with, stand, stomach, suffer, tolerate, undergo. 3 (bear a child, bear fruit) beget, breed, bring forth, engender, give birth to, produce, yield

bearable adj acceptable, endurable, manageable, passable, sufferable, sustainable, tolerable; *opp* unbearable

bearing n 1 (sb's bearing) air, aspect, attitude, behavior, demeanor, manner, mien, posture. 2 (a ship's bearing) course, direction. 3 (have a bearing on) connection, pertinence, relation, relevance

bearings n course, direction, location, orientation, position, situation, track, way, whereabouts

beast n 1 (animal) animal, brute, creature, monster. 2 (person) animal, barbarian, brute, fiend, monster, ogre, sadist, savage

beat v 1 bang, batter, buffet, hammer, hit, knock, pound, pummel, strike, thrash. 2 (beat up a person) abuse, assault, bash *inf*, beat up, clobber *inf*, hit, knock about *inf*, lay into, punch, rough up *inf*, slap, smack, strike, thrash, thump, wallop *inf*,

work over *inf*. 3 conquer, defeat, lick *inf*, master, outdo, overcome, quash, rout, subdue, surpass, thrash *inf*, vanquish, walk all over *inf*

beautiful adj alluring, appealing, attractive, becoming, charming, comely, delightful, elegant, exquisite, fair, fine, glamorous, good-looking, gorgeous, graceful, handsome, lovely, pleasant, pleasing, pretty, radiant, ravishing, seemly, stunning; *opp* ugly

beauty n 1 allure, appeal, attractiveness, bloom, charm, elegance, fairness, glamour, good looks, grace, handsomeness, loveliness, prettiness, seemliness; *opp* ugliness. 2 belle, charmer, femme fatale, goddess, knockout *inf*, seductress, stunner *inf*

beckon v bid, call, gesticulate, gesture, motion, nod, signal, summon, wave

becoming adj attractive, comely, chic, elegant, flattering, graceful, handsome, lovely, neat, pretty, stylish, tasteful; *opp* ugly

bedlam n chaos, clamor, commotion, disarray, disorder, furor, hubbub, hullabaloo, pandemonium, tumult, turmoil, uproar; *opp* calm

bedraggled adj dirty, disheveled, disordered, drenched, messy, muddied, muddy, soaking, sodden, soiled, stained, sullied, tatty, unkempt, untidy; *opp* tidy

befall v arise, chance, come about, crop up, ensue, follow, happen, materialize, occur, result, take place, transpire

beg v 1 ask for, beseech, entreat, implore, importune, plead, request. 2 (for money) cadge *inf*, scrounge, sponge *inf*

beggar n down-and-out, mendicant,

scrounger *inf*, sponger *inf*, tramp, vagrant

begin *v* commence, get going, get the ball rolling, get the show on the road, inaugurate, initiate, instigate, institute, kick off, set about, set in motion, set on foot, start; *opp* end, finish

beginner *n* amateur, apprentice, fledgling, fresher, freshman, learner, new recruit, novice, probationer, rookie, trainee; *opp* expert

beginning *n* 1 (earliest time) birth, commencement, dawn, emergence, inauguration, inception, initiation, onset, outset, start, starting point; *opp* end, finish. 2 (of a book) foreword, introduction, opening, preface, prelude, start, starting point; *opp* end

begrudge *v* be jealous, envy, grudge, not be happy about, resent

behave *v* 1 act, function, operate, perform, work. 2 acquit yourself well, be good, behave yourself, be on your best behavior, mind your manners; *opp* misbehave

behavior *n* 1 actions, conduct, demeanor, deportment, manner, manners, ways. 2 (of a machine) action, functioning, operation, performance, reaction, response

being *n* animal, beast, body, creature, entity, human, human being, individual, living thing, man, mortal, person

belief *n* 1 conviction, feeling, impression, judgment, notion, opinion, persuasion, way of thinking, theory, thinking, view, viewpoint. 2 credo, creed, doctrine, dogma, faith, ideology, teaching

believable *adj* acceptable, conceivable, credible, imaginable, likely, not beyond the realms of possibility, plausible, possible, probable, reliable, trustworthy; *opp* implausible

believe *v* 1 accept, be certain of, be convinced of, buy *inf*, fall for *inf*, have faith in, swallow *inf*, swear by, trust. 2 assume, be of the opinion that, consider, gather, guess, have an opinion, imagine, judge, postulate, presume, reckon, speculate, suppose, think, understand

believer *n* adherent, devotee, disciple, follower, supporter

bellow *v* bawl, call, clamor, cry, holler, howl, roar, scream, screech, shout, shriek, yell

belong *v* 1 belong to be at the disposal of, be held by, be owned by, be the property of. 2 belong to be affiliated with, be allied with, be a member of, be associated with, be included in. 3 attach to, be connected with, be part of, fit, go with, relate to, relevant to

belongings *n* effects, gear, goods, property, possessions, stuff, things

beloved *adj* adored, cherished, darling, dear, dearest, idolized, loved, precious, prized, sweet, treasured, worshipped

belt *n* band, cummerbund, girdle, girth, sash, strap, waistband

bench *n* 1 form, pew, seat. 2 counter, table, workbench, worktable. 3 (in a court) bar, court, courtroom, judge, judiciary, magistrate, tribunal

bend *n* angle, arc, corner, crook, curve, hook, loop, spiral, turn, twist

bend *v* 1 arch, bow, buckle, contort, crook, curl, curve, flex, turn, twist, warp. 2 (a road bends) curve, deviate, diverge, go round, swerve, turn, twist, veer.

3 (a person bends) crouch, hunch, lean, stoop

beneficial *adj* advantageous, favorable, good, helpful, profitable, useful, valuable; *opp* harmful

benefit *n* advantage, aid, asset, assistance, blessing, boon, favor, fringe benefit, gain, good, help, perk, profit; *opp* disadvantage

benefit *v* advance, advantage, aid, assist, avail, be an advantage to, better, contribute to, enhance, further, help, improve, profit, promote, serve; *opp* harm

benevolent *adj* altruistic, amiable, caring, compassionate, considerate, friendly, generous, helpful, humane, kind, kind-hearted, magnanimous, obliging, sympathetic, thoughtful, warm-hearted; *opp* unkind

benign *adj* 1 amiable, benevolent, cordial, friendly, genial, gentle, kind, sympathetic; *opp* unkind. 2 (of a tumor) curable, harmless, innocent, nondangerous, nonmalignant, treatable; *opp* malignant

bent *adj* 1 angled, arched, bowed, contorted, crooked, curved, hunched, stooped, twisted, warped; *opp* straight. 2 bent on determined, insistent, resolved, set. 3 ability, aptitude, capacity, flair, forte, gift, inclination, knack, leaning, penchant, predisposition, proclivity, talent

bequeath *v* bestow, cede, commit, consign, endow, entrust, give, grant, hand down, leave to, pass on, will

bequest *n* estate, gift, heritage, inheritance, legacy, settlement, trust

bereavement *n* death, deprivation, loss, passing

berserk *adj* crazed, crazy, frenzied, hysterical, insane, mad, manic, rabid, raging, raving, uncontrollable, violent, wild; *opp* calm

berth *n* 1 bed, bunk, sleeping accommodation. 2 anchorage, dock, harbor, mooring, pier, port, quay, wharf

besiege *v* beleaguer, beset, blockade, encircle, encompass, lay siege to, surround

besotted *adj* doting, infatuated, in love, smitten, spellbound; *opp* indifferent

best *adj* chief, cream, elite, finest, first, first-class, first-rate, foremost, greatest, highest, leading, most fitting, most suitable, outstanding, pick, pre-eminent, prime, right, supreme, top, unsurpassed; *opp* worst

bet *n* gamble, pledge, risk, speculation, stake, venture, wager

bet *v* gamble, pledge, risk, speculate, stake, venture, wager

betray *v* blow the whistle on, break your promise, double-cross *inf*, inform on, sell out *inf*, stab sb in the back, swindle, tell on *inf*

betrayal *n* back-stabbing *inf*, breach of faith, disloyalty, double-dealing, duplicity, falseness, treachery, treason, subversion, trickery; *opp* loyalty

beware *v* avoid, be careful, be on the alert, be on the lookout, be on your guard, heed, look out, mind, steer clear of, take heed, watch out

bewildered *adj* baffled, bemused, confused, dazed, disconcerted, flummoxed, muddled, mystified, nonplussed, perplexed, puzzled, startled, surprised, taken aback, thrown off balance

bewildering adj baffling, confusing, disconcerting, mystifying, perplexing, puzzling, startling, surprising

bewitched adj beguiled, captivated, charmed, enchanted, enraptured, entranced, fascinated, mesmerized, spellbound; **opp** indifferent

bias n 1 bigotry, favoritism, narrow-mindedness, one-sidedness, partiality, prejudice, unfairness. 2 bent, inclination, leaning, penchant, predisposition, propensity, tendency

biased adj distorted, one-sided, partial, prejudiced, slanted, weighted; **opp** impartial

bicker v argue, disagree, dispute, fall out, feud, fight, have a row, quarrel, squabble

bid n 1 offer, price, proposal, proposition, submission, sum, tender. 2 attempt, effort, try, venture

bid v 1 (bid money) offer, proffer, propose, put forward, submit, tender. 2 (bid sb farewell, good-day) call, greet, say, tell, wish. 3 (bid sb do sth) ask, charge, command, demand, direct, enjoin, instruct, invite, order, require, solicit, summon, tell

big adj 1 (in size) beefy, bulky, burly, colossal, enormous, extensive, gigantic, great, huge, hulking, immense, large, mammoth, massive, muscular, prodigious, sizable, spacious, strapping, thickset, substantial, tall, vast, voluminous; **opp** small. 2 (in importance) eminent, important,

leading, main, momentous, powerful, principal, prominent, serious, significant, valuable, weighty; **opp** small. 3 (in generosity) altruistic, benevolent, generous, gracious, kind, heroic, magnanimous, unselfish; **opp** petty, selfish

bigot n chauvinist, dogmatist, fanatic, homophobic, racist, sexist

bigoted adj dogmatic, fanatical, homophobic, intolerant, narrow-minded, opinionated, prejudiced, racist, sexist

bill n 1 account, charges, check, invoice, statement, tally. 2 act, measure, piece of legislation, proposal

bill v charge, debit, invoice

bind v 1 attach, chain, fasten, fetter, glue, hitch, lash, paste, secure, stick, strap, tether, tie. 2 (make sb do sth) compel, constrain, force, impel, obligate, oblige, prescribe. 3 (make doing sth difficult) confine, detain, hamper, hinder, inhibit, restrain, restrict; **opp** help. 4 (bind a wound) bandage, cover, dress, strap

binding adj compulsory, irrevocable, mandatory, obligatory, unalterable

biography n account, life, life story, memoir, memoirs, profile

birth n 1 childbirth, confinement, delivery, nativity, parturition. 2 beginning, beginnings, commencement, emergence, genesis, origin, rise, start, source. 3 ancestry, background, blood, breeding, descent, extraction, family, genealogy, heritage, line, lineage, origin, parentage, pedigree, race, stock

bit n chip, chunk, crumb, flake, fragment,

grain, iota, jot, lump, mite, morsel, part, particle, piece, scrap, shred, sliver, speck, trace, whit

bitchy adj backbiting, catty, cruel, malicious, mean, nasty, rancorous, snide, spiteful, venomous, vicious, vindictive, waspish

bite n 1 nibble, nip, puncture. 2 morsel, mouthful, snack. 3 edge, piquancy, punch, pungency, spice, spiciness

bite v chew, champ, crunch, gnaw, masticate, munch, nibble, nip, pierce, pinch, snap, tear

biting adj 1 (of wind) bitter, cold, cutting, freezing, harsh, nipping, penetrating, piercing, stinging. 2 (of remarks) acid, caustic, cutting, sarcastic, scathing, sharp, stinging, trenchant, vitriolic

bitter adj 1 (of taste) acid, acrid, astringent, pungent, sharp, sour, tart, unsweetened, vinegary. 2 acrimonious, angry, begrudging, embittered, hostile, hurt, morose, piqued, rancorous, resentful, sore, sour, sullen

bizarre adj abnormal, curious, eccentric, extraordinary, fantastic, freakish, grotesque, ludicrous, odd, oddball inf, offbeat, outlandish, outré, peculiar, queer, strange, unconventional, unusual, way-out inf, wacky inf, weird; **opp** normal

black adj 1 coal-black, dark, dusky, ebony, inky, jet, murky, pitch-black, raven, sable, starless, swarthy. 2 dark, depressing, dismal, distressing, doleful, foreboding, funereal, gloomy, hopeless, lugubrious, melancholy, mournful, pessimistic, ominous, sad, somber. 3 bad, devilish, diabolic, evil, foul, heinous, iniquitous, nefarious, villainous, wicked

blacklist v ban, bar, boycott, debar, exclude, expel, ostracize, proscribe, reject

blackmail v extort, exact, extract, force, hold to ransom, intimidate, threaten

blame n 1 accountability, culpability, fault, guilt, liability, onus, responsibility. 2 accusation, castigation, censure, charge, condemnation, incrimination, indictment, recrimination, reprimand, reproof

blame v accuse, censure, charge, condemn, hold accountable, hold to account, indict, find fault with, find guilty, reprehend, reprimand, reproach, reprove, take to task; **opp** absolve

blameless adj above suspicion, beyond reproach, faultless, guiltless, innocent, in the clear, irreproachable, not to blame, perfect, stainless, unblemished, unimpeachable, upright, virtuous

bland adj 1 (of flavor) boring, dull, flavorless, insipid, mild, plain, tasteless, weak. 2 (of a person, remarks) boring, dull, insipid, middle-of-the-road, mediocre, nondescript, neutral, safe, uncontroversial, uninspiring, uninteresting, vapid

blank adj 1 bare, clean, clear, empty, plain, spotless, unfilled, unmarked, vacant, void, white. 2 at a loss, baffled, bewildered, confounded, confused, expressionless, nonplussed, perplexed, puzzled, uncomprehending

blare v bellow, blast, boom, honk, hoot, peal, resound, roar, trumpet

blasé adj apathetic, bored, casual, indifferent, jaded, laid-back, lukewarm, nonchalant, phlegmatic, offhand, relaxed, unconcerned, unenthusiastic, unimpressed, uninterested, unmoved, unperturbed, weary, world-weary

blaspheme *v* curse, damn, desecrate, profane, swear

blasphemous *adj* godless, impious, irreverent, profane, sacrilegious, ungodly, unholy

blast *n* 1 bang, blowing-up, boom, crash, detonation, explosion, salvo, volley. 2 blare, boom, honk, hoot, peal, trumpeting, wail

blast *v* 1 bomb, blow up, demolish, destroy, detonate, explode, fire, fire-bomb, raze, ruin, shatter. 2 blare, boom, honk, hoot, peal, sound, trumpet, wail

blatant *adj* brazen, conspicuous, flagrant, glaring, naked, obvious, open, ostentatious, outright, overt, prominent, shameless, sheer, unashamed, unconcealed

blaze *n* 1 bonfire, conflagration, fire, flame, flames, inferno. 2 beam, brilliance, flare, flash, glare

blaze *v* 1 (of a fire) be ablaze, burn, burst into flames, catch fire, flame, glow. 2 (of light) be ablaze, burn, beam, flare, flash, glare, gleam, glow, shine

bleach *v* blanch, fade, pale, peroxide, lighten, take the color out of, whiten

bleak *adj* 1 bare, barren, desolate, exposed, open, raw, unsheltered, waste, windswept. 2 cheerless, dark, depressing, dismal, drab, dreary, gloomy, grim, hopeless, joyless, miserable, somber, unpromising, wretched

bleary *adj* blurred, blurry, clouded, dim, fogged, foggy, fuzzy, hazy, indistinct, misty, unclear; *opp* clear

blemish *n* 1 (on skin) blotch, defect, disfigurement, fault, flaw, imperfection, mark, mole, patch, scab, scar, smudge, speck, spot, stain, taint. 2 (on character) blot, defect, disgrace, dishonor, fault, flaw, imperfection, stain, taint

blemished *adj* blotted, blotchy, defective, disfigured, faulty, flawed, imperfect, marked, patchy, smudged, speckled, spotted, spotty, stained, tainted; *opp* clear

blend *n* alloy, amalgam, amalgamation, combination, composite, compound, cross, fusion, mix, mixture, synthesis, union

blend *v* amalgamate, coalesce, combine, cross, fuse, merge, mingle, mix, synthesize, unite

bless *v* 1 consecrate, dedicate, exalt, extol, glorify, praise, sanctify, thank. 2 (bless sb with sth) bestow, endow, favor, grace, grant, provide. 3 approve, be in favor, condone, consent, endorse, sanction, support

blessed *adj* 1 adored, beatified, consecrated, divine, exalted, hallowed, holy, sanctified, sacred. 2 (blessed with sth) endowed, favored, fortunate, gifted, lucky

blessing *n* 1 benediction, benison, consecration, dedication, grace, invocation, praise, thanksgiving. 2 approval, assent, backing, consent, endorsement, permission, sanction, support. 3 advantage, benefit, boon, endowment, gift, godsend, good fortune, favor, windfall

blight *n* 1 affliction, bane, cancer, curse, pestilence, plague, scourge, woe.

2 (in plants) canker, disease, fungus, infestation, mildew, pest, pestilence, rot

blight v 1 afflict, blast, crush, curse, dash, destroy, kill, ruin, wreck. 2 (blight a plant) blast, destroy, infest, kill, rot, shrivel, wither

blind adj 1 sightless, unseeing, visually impaired. 2 dense, heedless, ignorant, inattentive, insensitive, neglectful, oblivious, unaware, unconscious, unmindful, unobservant

bliss n delight, ecstasy, elation, euphoria, gladness, happiness, heaven, joy, paradise, pleasure, rapture

blissful adj delightful, ecstatic, euphoric, happy, heavenly, joyful, rapturous, wonderful

blitz n assault, attack, blitzkrieg, bombardment, bombing, offensive, onslaught, raid, strike

bloated adj dilated, distended, enlarged, full, inflated, puffed up, swollen

blob n ball, bead, dab, dollop, drop, droplet, glob, globule, lump, mass

block n bar, brick, cake, chunk, cube, hunk, lump, ingot, piece, rectangle, square, wedge

block v 1 choke, clog, close, obstruct, plug, stop up. 2 bar, check, hinder, impede, obstruct, prevent, stop, thwart

blockage n bar, barrier, clog, impediment, jam, obstacle, obstruction, occlusion, plug, stoppage

blond(e) adj fair, fair-haired, flaxen, golden, golden-haired

blood n 1 gore, lifeblood, vital fluids. 2 ancestry, birth, descent, extraction, family, genealogy, heritage, kindred,

kinship, line, lineage, origin, parentage, pedigree, race, relation, relative, stock, strain

bloodshed n blood bath, bloodletting, butchery, carnage, gore, killing, massacre, murder, slaughter, slaying, violence, war

bloodthirsty adj barbaric, barbarous, brutal, cruel, ferocious, murderous, ruthless, sadistic, savage, vicious, violent, warlike

bloody adj 1 bleeding, bloodstained, blood-soaked, blood-spattered, gory. 2 barbaric, barbarous, bloodthirsty, brutal, gory, murderous, sadistic, savage, vicious, violent

bloom n 1 blossom, blossoming, bud, flower. 2 blush, flush, freshness, glow, health, luster, radiance, rosiness

bloom v 1 be in bloom, be in blossom, be in flower, blossom, bud, burgeon, flower, open. 2 (of a person) blossom, flourish, glow, thrive

blossom n bloom, blossoming, bud, flower

blossom v 1 be in bloom, be in blossom, be in flower, bud, burgeon, flower, open. 2 (of a person) bloom, flourish, glow, thrive

blot n 1 blemish, blotch, blur, dot, mark, patch, smudge, speck, spatter, speckle, spot, stain. 2 (on reputation) blemish, blur, defect, disgrace, dishonor, fault, flaw, imperfection, stain, taint

blow n 1 bang, bash, buffet, clout, hit, knock, punch, rap, slap, smack, stroke, thump, thwack, wallop inf, whack. 2 bombshell, calamity, catastrophe, disappointment, disaster, jolt, letdown,

misfortune, reverse, setback, shock,
upset

blow v 1 blast, breathe, exhale, fan, huff,
pant, puff. 2 (move by air, wind) buffet,
flap, flutter, sweep, toss, waft, wave,
whirl, whisk. 3 pipe, play, sound, toot.
4 **blow up** blast, bomb, burst, detonate,
fire, explode, go off, pop, rupture, shatter

blue adj 1 azure, cobalt, indigo, navy,
sapphire, sky-blue, turquoise,
ultramarine. 2 dejected, depressed,
despondent, down inf, downcast,
downhearted, fed up inf, gloomy, glum,
low, melancholy, miserable, sad,
unhappy; **opp** happy

blues n dejection, depression,
despondency, doldrums, dumps inf,
gloom, gloominess, glumness, low spirits,
melancholy, misery, sadness,
unhappiness

bluff v con, deceive, delude, fake, feign,
hoax, lie, mislead, pretend, put it on,
sham, take in, trick

blunder n boob inf, error, faux pas, gaffe,
mistake, oversight, slip

blunt adj 1 dull, rounded, unsharpened;
opp sharp. 2 abrupt, bluff, brusque,
candid, direct, forthright, frank, honest,
outspoken, plainspoken, straight,
straightforward, tactless, to the point

blur n dimness, fog, haze, indistinctness,
mist, obscurity, smear, smudge

blur v blotch, cloud, darken, dim, fog,
mask, mist up, obscure, smear, smudge,
steam up, veil

blurred adj bleary, blurry, clouded, dim,
faint, fogged, foggy, fuzzy, hazy,
indistinct, misty, nebulous, obscure, out
of focus, smeared, smudged, unclear,

vague; **opp** clear

blurt out v babble, blab, cry, disclose,
exclaim, let out, let slip, reveal, say, spill
the beans inf, tattle, tell

blush v color, flush, go pink, go red,
redden, turn pink, turn red

board n 1 beam, panel, plank, slat,
timber. 2 body, committee, council,
directorate, directors, panel, trustees

board v 1 embark, enter, go aboard, go on
board, mount. 2 accommodate, feed,
house, lodge, put up, quarter, take in

boast n 1 bluster, bragging, crowing,
exaggeration, self-congratulation,
showing off, swagger, swank. 2 gem,
jewel, pride, pride and joy, treasure

boast v 1 blow your own trumpet inf,
bluster, brag, crow, exaggerate, show off,
strut, swagger, swank, talk big inf, vaunt.
2 enjoy, have, own, possess, pride
yourself on

bodily adj carnal, corporal, corporeal,
fleshly, material, physical

body n 1 build, figure, form, flesh, frame,
physique, shape, torso, trunk. 2 cadaver,
carcass, corpse, dead body, remains.
3 bulk, essence, main part, majority,
mass, material, matter, substance.
4 association, authority, band,
committee, company, corporation,
group, organization, society

bog n fen, marsh, mire, morass, quagmire,
swamp, wetland

boggy adj marshy, muddy, soft, swampy,
wet

bogus adj artificial, counterfeit, dummy,
ersatz, fake, false, forged, fraudulent,
imitation, mock, phony inf, pseudo,
sham, spurious; **opp** genuine

boil *n* blister, carbuncle, pustule, spot, swelling

boil *v* bubble, come to the boil, cook, churn, foam, froth, seethe, simmer, steam, stew

boiling *adj* baking, blistering, hot, roasting, scorching, searing, sweltering; *opp* freezing

boisterous *adj* bouncy, exuberant, lively, loud, noisy, riotous, rollicking, rough, rowdy, spirited, unruly, uproarious, wild

bold *adj* 1 adventurous, audacious, brash, brave, cheeky, courageous, daring, dauntless, enterprising, fearless, intrepid, presumptuous, valiant; *opp* timid. 2 bright, colorful, conspicuous, eye-catching, flashy, loud, lurid, prominent, showy, striking, strong, vivid; *opp* muted

bolster *v* aid, assist, boost, brace, buoy up, buttress, help, hold up, maintain, prop up, reinforce, shore up, strengthen, support

bolt *n* 1 bar, catch, fastener, latch, lock. 2 peg, pin, rivet, rod

bolt *v* 1 abscond, bound, dart, dash, escape, flee, fly, hurtle, leap, run, rush, sprint. 2 bar, fasten, lock, secure. 3 (bolt food) cram, devour, down, gobble, gulp, guzzle, stuff, wolf

bomb *n* blast, booby-trap, charge, device, explosive, grenade, incendiary, mine, shell, torpedo

bomb *v* attack, blast, blitz, blow up, bombard, booby-trap, destroy, detonate, explode, fire, firebomb, shell, torpedo

bombard *v* 1 assault, attack, blast, blitz, bomb, fire on, open fire, pound, shell, strafe, torpedo. 2 (with questions) assail, attack, barrage, besiege, beset, bother,

harass, hassle *inf*, hound, pester

bond *n* 1 affinity, attachment, connection, link, relation, relationship, tie, union. 2 binding, chain, cord, fastening, fetters, manacles, shackles, rope. 3 agreement, bargain, compact, commitment, contract, covenant, deal, guarantee, obligation, pledge, promise, treaty, word

bond *v* bind, cement, fasten, fix, fuse, glue, join, stick

bonus *n* benefit, boon, bounty, commission, dividend, extra, gift, gratuity, hand-out, perk *inf*, perquisite, plus, prize, reward, tip

book *n* leaflet, magazine, manual, publication, text, title, tome, tract, treatise, volume, work

book *v* arrange, charter, engage, line up, make a reservation, organize, reserve, schedule

boom *n* 1 bang, bellow, blast, clap, crash, explosion, reverberation, roar, roll, rumble, shout, thunder. 2 advance, burgeoning, development, expansion, gain, growth, increase, progress, success, spurt, upsurge, upturn

boom *v* 1 bang, bellow, blare, blast, crash, echo, explode, resound, reverberate, roar, roll, rumble, shout, thunder. 2 advance, burgeon, develop, expand, flourish, grow, increase, progress, prosper, succeed, thrive

boost *n* advance, assistance, augmentation, encouragement, help, improvement, increase, inspiration, plug *inf*, praise, promotion, stimulus, rise, support

boost *v* advance, amplify, assist, augment,

enlarge, encourage, facilitate, foster, further, heighten, help, improve, increase, inflate, inspire, plug *inf*, praise, promote, raise, stimulate, support, uplift

border *n* **1** boundary, brim, brink, edge, edging, fringe, hem, limit, margin, outskirts, perimeter, rim, skirt, verge. **2** (between countries) borderline, boundary, frontier

bore *v* be tedious, bother, exhaust, fatigue, pall, put sb to sleep, tire, vex, wear out, weary; *opp* inspire

bored *adj* apathetic, blasé, fatigued, fed up *inf*, indifferent, jaded, languorous, lukewarm, tired, unenthusiastic, unimpressed, uninspired, uninterested, unmoved, weary

boredom *n* apathy, dullness, monotony, sameness, tediousness, tedium, weariness; *opp* excitement

boring *adj* dead, dull, humdrum, insipid, monotonous, repetitious, routine, stale, tedious, tiresome, uneventful, unexciting, uninteresting

borrow *v* acquire, adopt, appropriate, cadge *inf*, commandeer, filch, help yourself to, pinch, pirate, plagiarize, scrounge *inf*, sponge *inf*, take, use; *opp* lend

boss *n* chief, employer, foreman, head, master, overseer, owner, supervisor

boss *v* bully, domineer, order about, order around, push around, ride roughshod over, throw your weight about

bossy *adj* assertive, bullying, dominating, domineering, high-handed, imperious, lordly, officious, overbearing, pushy *inf*, self-assertive

botch *v* bungle, fumble, make a hash *inf*,

make a mess, mess up *inf*, mismanage, ruin, spoil

bother *n* annoyance, difficulty, effort, exertion, fuss, hassle *inf*, inconvenience, irritation, nuisance, strain, trouble, worry

bother *v* **1** (bother sb) annoy, disturb, exasperate, give sb a hard time *inf*, harass, hassle *inf*, irritate, molest, nag, pester, provoke, torment, vex, worry. **2** (needn't bother) be concerned, care, concern yourself, go to any trouble, inconvenience yourself, make the effort, mind, put yourself out, take the time, trouble yourself. **3** (sth bothers you) alarm, concern, dismay, distress, perturb, upset, trouble, worry

bottom *n* **1** base, bed, depth, floor, foot, foundation, underneath, underside. **2** backside, behind, bum *inf*, butt *inf*, buttocks, hindquarters, rear, rear end, seat, tail. **3** basis, cause, center, core, essence, heart, nitty-gritty, origin, root, source, substance

bounce *n* **1** elasticity, give, resilience, spring, springiness. **2** animation, dynamism, energy, go *inf*, life, liveliness, oomph *inf*, pep, spirit, vigor, vitality, vivacity, zip *inf*. **3** bound, leap, jump, skip, spring

bounce *v* bob, bound, jump, leap, rebound, recoil, ricochet, spring

bound *adj* **1** (bound to happen) certain, destined, doomed, fated, predestined, sure, very likely. **2** (bound with rope) fettered, lashed, roped, secured, strapped, tethered, tied, tied up, trussed. **3** (obliged to do sth) committed, compelled, constrained, duty-bound, forced, obligated, obliged, required

bound v bob, bounce, caper, frisk, frolic, gambol, hop, jump, leap, pounce, prance, skip, spring, vault

boundary n barrier, border, bounds, brink, demarcation, edge, end, extremity, fringe, frontier, limits, margin, perimeter, threshold

boundless adj endless, immeasurable, incalculable, infinite, never-ending, unbounded, unending, untold, vast

bounds n boundary, border, confines, edges, limitations, limits, periphery, perimeter

bouquet n 1 (flowers) arrangement, bunch, buttonhole, corsage, garland, posy, spray, wreath. 2 (wine) aroma, fragrance, odor, perfume, savor, scent, smell

bout n 1 (fighting) competition, contest, encounter, engagement, fight, match, set-to inf. 2 (of illness) attack, fit, spell. 3 (of activity) period, run, spell, stint, stretch, time, turn

bow n bob, curtsy, genuflexion, nod, obeisance

bow v 1 bend, bob, curtsy, genuflect, incline your head, kowtow, make obeisance, nod, prostrate yourself, salaam, stoop. 2 **bow to** capitulate, give in, give way, submit, surrender, yield

bowels n 1 entrails, guts, innards inf, insides inf, intestines. 2 belly, core, depths, heart, inside, interior

bowl n basin, container, dish, tureen, vessel

box n carton, case, chest, container, crate, pack, package, trunk

boy n fellow, kid inf, lad, schoolboy, son, youngster, youth

boycott n ban, embargo, prohibition

boycott v ban, bar, blacklist, ostracize, place an embargo on, reject, spurn

boyfriend n date, lover, man, sweetheart, young man

brace n 1 buttress, clamp, prop, reinforcement, stanchion, stay, strut, support, truss. 2 couple, duo, pair, two

brace v bolster, buttress, fortify, hold up, prop up, reinforce, secure, shore up, steady, strengthen

braced adj prepared, ready, rigid, set, steady, tense

brain n 1 brainpower, gray matter inf, intellect, intelligence, mind, reason, sense, understanding, wit. 2 (clever person) genius, intellectual, mastermind, thinker

brainwash v condition, indoctrinate, influence, reeducate

brake v check, decelerate, reduce speed, slow, slow down, stop

branch n 1 (of a tree) arm, bough, limb, offshoot, prong, stem, twig. 2 (of an organization) department, division, office, part, section, subdivision, subsection, tributary, wing

brand n 1 class, grade, kind, line, make, quality, sort, species, trademark, trade name, type, variety. 2 hallmark, label, marker, sign, stamp, symbol, tag

brand v 1 (cattle) burn, mark, scar, sear, stamp. 2 (give sb a bad name) characterize, denounce, discredit, stigmatize, vilify. 3 (impress on sb's mind) engrave, fix, impress, imprint, print, stamp

brandish v flaunt, flourish, shake,

swing, wave, wield

brash *adj* arrogant, bold, brazen, cocky *inf*, forward, impertinent, insolent, pushy *inf*, rude

bravado *n* arrogance, audacity, bluster, boastfulness, boldness, bombast, bragging, machismo, swagger

brave *adj* bold, courageous, daring, dauntless, fearless, gutsy *inf*, heroic, intrepid, tough, unafraid, undaunted, unshrinking; *opp* cowardly

bravery *n* boldness, courage, daring, fearlessness, gallantry, guts *inf*, heroism, nerve *inf*, pluck, spirit, valor; *opp* cowardice

brazen *adj* barefaced, blatant, brash, flagrant, immodest, insolent, rude, saucy, shameless, unashamed

breach *n* 1 aperture, break, chasm, cleft, crack, fissure, fracture, gap, hole, opening, split. 2 breaking, contravention, infringement, transgression, violation

breach *v* 1 break through, burst through, open up, rupture. 2 break, contravene, defy, disobey, infringe, violate

breadth *n* 1 (distance across) broadness, latitude, span, spread, thickness, wideness, width. 2 (wide range) comprehensiveness, extensiveness, extent, range, scale, scope, sweep

break *n* 1 breach, breakage, cleft, crack, division, hole, fissure, fracture, gap, gash, hole, opening, rent, rift, rupture, split, tear. 2 (pause) breather *inf*, breathing-space, halt, hiatus, interlude, interval, lull, pause, respite, rest, stop, time out *inf*. 3 breach, disruption, estrangement, lapse, rift, schism, separation,

split, suspension

break *v* 1 (break into parts) bust *inf*, chip, crack, crumple, damage, demolish, destroy, fracture, fragment, part, separate, sever, shatter, shiver, smash, smash to smithereens, snap, splinter, split, tear, wreck. 2 (break a rule) contravene, defy, disobey, disregard, flout, infringe, transgress, violate. 3 (break a person) bankrupt, bring sb to his knees, cow, cripple, crush, defeat, dispirit, make bankrupt, overwhelm, ruin, subdue, tame, weaken. 4 (stop) discontinue, interrupt, knock off *inf*, pause, rest, stop, take a break, take five *inf*. 5 (break a record) beat, cap *inf*, exceed, go beyond, outdo, outstrip, pass, shatter, smash, surpass. 6 (of news) announce, appear, become public, be revealed, disclose, divulge, emerge, make public, reveal, tell. 7 (of waves) crash, dash, hit. 8 (break a code) decipher, decode, unravel, solve. 9 **break down** collapse, come to grief, conk out *inf*, crack up *inf*, fail, fall through, go to pieces, seize up, stop, stop working. 10 **break in** barge in, break and enter, burgle, burst in, butt in, interfere, interrupt, intervene, intrude, invade, push your way in, rob, thrust your way in. 11 **break off** detach, divide, pull off, separate, sever, splinter. 12 **break off** bring to an end, call a halt, cease, discontinue, end, finish, stop, suspend, terminate. 13 **break out** abscond, bolt, break loose, escape, flee, free yourself. 14 **break out** (spots) appear, emerge, occur. 15 **break up** adjourn, come to an end, dismantle, disrupt, dissolve, divorce, end, part, scatter, separate, split up, stop, terminate

breakdown *n* 1 collapse, destruction, disintegration, failure, malfunction, nervous breakdown, ruin, stoppage. 2 analysis, categorization, classification, diagnosis, dissection, rundown *inf*

breakthrough *n* advance, development, discovery, innovation, invention, leap forward, progress, revolution

breast *n* bosom, bust, chest, front

breath *n* 1 air, breathing, exhalation, gasp, gulp, pant, respiration, wheeze. 2 (suggestion) hint, murmur, suggestion, suspicion, touch, trace, undertone, whisper

breathe *v* 1 exhale, gasp, inhale, pant, puff, respire, wheeze. 2 murmur, say, sigh, tell, whisper

breathless *adj* 1 exhausted, choking, gasping, gulping, out of breath, panting, puffed *inf*, puffing, spent, tired out, wheezing, winded. 2 (with excitement) agog, all agog, avid, eager, excited, on tenterhooks, openmouthed, with bated breath

breed *n* class, family, kind, line, lineage, pedigree, race, stock, strain, type, variety

breed *v* bear, bring up, hatch, increase, multiply, nurture, procreate, produce, propagate, raise, rear, reproduce

breeze *n* draft, gentle wind, gust, light wind, puff of air, waft

brew *n* beer, beverage, blend, concoction, drink, infusion, liquor, mixture, potion, preparation, tea

brew *v* 1 boil, concoct, ferment, infuse, prepare, simmer, steep, stew. 2 (of trouble) contrive, cook up *inf*, devise,

foment, hatch, plan, plot, scheme, stir up

bribe *n* backhander *sl*, bribery, carrot *inf*, enticement, hush money *sl*, inducement, kickback *inf*, pay-off *inf*, sweetener *inf*

bribe *v* buy off, corrupt, get at *inf*, give an inducement to, grease sb's palm *inf*, pay sb off, tempt

bridge *n* 1 aqueduct, arch, causeway, crossing, footbridge, overpass, span, viaduct. 2 bond, connection, link, stepping stone, tie

bridge *v* bind, connect, cross, join, link, span, straddle, traverse, unite

brief *adj* 1 compact, concise, condensed, crisp, incisive, pithy, short, succinct, terse, thumbnail, to the point; *opp* lengthy, long. 2 ephemeral, fleeting, impermanent, passing, quick, short, short-lived, swift, temporary, transient, transitory; *opp* lengthy, long

brief *n* advice, briefing, description, guidance, information, instructions, orders, outline, summary

brief *v* advise, fill sb in *inf*, give the facts to, instruct, prepare, prime, put sb in the picture *inf*

bright *adj* 1 (of light) beaming, blazing, brilliant, dazzling, flashing, gleaming, glittering, glowing, illuminated, incandescent, intense, luminous, radiant, scintillating, shining, shiny, sparkling, twinkling, vivid; *opp* dark, dull. 2 (clever) acute, astute, clever, intelligent, inventive, quick, sharp, smart; *opp* dull. 3 (of weather) clear, cloudless, fair, sunny; *opp* dull. 4 (of prospects) encouraging, favorable, good, hopeful, optimistic, promising, propitious, rosy; *opp* gloomy. **5** (of a person) cheerful, gay, happy, jolly, joyful, light-hearted, lively, merry; *opp* miserable. **6** (of color) bold, brilliant, colorful, fresh, gaudy, intense, rich, vivid; *opp* pale

brighten *v* **1** cheer up, enliven, gladden, illuminate, lighten, light up, liven up, make brighter, perk up, revitalize. **2** (of weather) clear, clear up; *opp* cloud over

brilliance *n* **1** (of light) brightness, dazzle, glare, intensity, luminosity, radiance, sheen, sparkle, vividness. **2** (of an occasion) glamour, glitter, grandeur, luster, magnificence, splendor. **3** (genius) braininess, cleverness, eminence, fame, genius, giftedness, talent

brilliant *adj* **1** (shining) bright, dazzling, glittering, intense, radiant, scintillating, shining, sparkling, vivid. **2** (good) excellent, fabulous, great, good, marvelous, superb, wonderful. **3** (clever) bright, celebrated, clever, exceptional, famous, gifted, intelligent, remarkable, smart, talented

bring *v* **1** (take somewhere) accompany, bear, carry, convey, deliver, escort, fetch, gather, guide, import, lead, take, transport. **2** (lead to sth happening) attract, cause, contribute to, create, draw, earn, effect, generate, give rise to, inflict, lead to, occasion, produce, prompt, provoke, result in, wreak. **3 bring about** accomplish, achieve, cause, create, effect, give rise to, lead to, make happen, occasion, produce, result in. **4 bring up** care for, educate, nurture, raise, rear, support. **5 bring up** (bring up

a subject) allude to, broach, introduce, mention, refer to, touch on/upon

brink *n* border, brim, edge, fringe, limit, rim, threshold, verge

brisk *adj* **1** (a brisk walk) energetic, lively, quick, smart, spanking *inf*, speedy, vigorous; *opp* leisurely. **2** (of weather) bracing, crisp, exhilarating, fresh, invigorating, keen, nippy *inf*, refreshing. **3** (of business) active, bustling, busy, hectic; *opp* slow

brittle *adj* breakable, crisp, crumbling, delicate, easily broken, fragile, frail, hard, splintery, weak

broach *v* bring up, introduce, mention, propose, raise, speak about, suggest, talk about, touch on

broad *adj* **1** (wide) ample, boundless, capacious, extensive, large, open, spacious, sweeping, vast, wide, widespread; *opp* narrow. **2** (of knowledge) comprehensive, encyclopedic, far-reaching, general, wide, wide-ranging. **3** (of sb's mind) liberal, open, permissive, progressive, tolerant, unbiased, unprejudiced; *opp* narrow. **4** (of a description) general, imprecise, inexact, loose, sweeping, vague; *opp* detailed. **5** (of taste) all-embracing, catholic, eclectic, varied; *opp* narrow

broadcast *n* program, show, transmission

broadcast *v* advertise, air, announce, beam, circulate, disseminate, make known, make public, proclaim, publish, report, spread, televise, transmit

broaden *v* develop, enlarge, expand, make broader, make wider, open up, spread, stretch, swell, widen

broad-minded adj enlightened, flexible, liberal, open-minded, permissive, tolerant, unbiased, unprejudiced, unshockable; *opp* narrow-minded

brochure n booklet, catalog, circular, folder, hand-out, leaflet, pamphlet, prospectus

broken adj 1 burst, bust *inf*, cracked, demolished, destroyed, fractured, fragmented, punctured, severed, shattered, smashed, split, torn; *opp* whole. 2 (not working) broken down, bust *inf*, damaged, defective, faulty, kaput, out of order. 3 (not continuous) discontinuous, disrupted, disturbed, erratic, fragmentary, intermittent, interrupted, spasmodic. 4 (having lost the will to fight) beaten, crippled, crushed, defeated, demoralized, discouraged, dispirited, subdued, tamed, vanquished

brood n chicks, children, clutch, family, litter, offspring, progeny, young

brood v 1 agonize, dwell upon, fret, mope, mull over, muse, ponder, sulk, think, worry. 2 hatch, incubate, sit on

brown adj 1 beige, buff, chocolate, cocoa, copper, coppery, dun, ecru, fawn, hazel, khaki, mahogany, maroon, ochre, russet, rust, sepia, tan, tawny, terracotta, umber. 2 (of hair) auburn, chestnut, dark, ginger. 3 (of skin) bronze, bronzed, coffee-colored, dark, sunburnt, sun-tanned, tanned

browse v 1 dip into, flip through, leaf through, look through, scan, skim. 2 look round, window-shop. 3 crop, eat, feed, graze, nibble

bruise n black eye, blemish, bump, contusion, discoloration, mark, shiner *inf*, swelling, welt

bruise v blacken, blemish, crush, damage, discolor, knock, make black and blue, mark

brush v 1 buff, clean, comb, groom, polish, sweep, tidy, wash. 2 caress, contact, flick, glance, graze, kiss, scrape, stroke, sweep, touch. 3 brush up go over, polish up, read up, refresh your memory, relearn, revise, study

brutal adj barbaric, barbarous, bloodthirsty, bloody, callous, cold-blooded, cruel, heartless, inhuman, merciless, murderous, pitiless, remorseless, ruthless, sadistic, savage, vicious, violent; *opp* gentle

brutality n atrocity, barbarism, barbarity, bloodiness, bloodthirstiness, cruelty, ferocity, savageness, savagery

brutalize v abuse, corrupt, dehumanize, harden, inure, make brutal, toughen

brute n 1 animal, beast, creature, dumb animal, wild animal. 2 barbarian, beast, bully, devil, fiend, monster, ruffian, sadist, savage, swine

bubble v 1 effervesce, fizz, fizzle, foam, froth, gurgle, sparkle. 2 boil, percolate, simmer

buckle n catch, clasp, clip, fastener, fastening, hasp

buckle v 1 bend, bulge, cave in, crumple, curve, dent, fold, kink, twist, warp. 2 clip, do up, fasten, hitch, hook up, secure

budding adj aspiring, burgeoning, fledgling, flowering, growing, potential, promising, would-be *inf*

budge v 1 dislodge, give way, go, move,

push, remove, roll, shift, slide.
2 acquiesce, change, change your mind, convince, give in, give way, persuade, sway, yield

budget n accounts, allowance, cost, finances, financial plan, funds, means, resources

budget v allocate, allow, apportion, cost, estimate, plan, provide, ration, save, set aside

buffer n bulwark, bumper, cushion, fender, guard, safeguard, screen, shield

bug n 1 creepy-crawly inf, flea, insect, mite. 2 bacterium, germ, infection, microorganism, virus. 3 (in a computer program) breakdown, defect, error, fault, flaw, gremlin inf, malfunction, mistake, virus

bug v 1 eavesdrop, listen to, phone-tap, spy on, tap, wiretap. 2 anger, annoy, get on sb's nerves inf, hassle inf, infuriate, irk, irritate, provoke

build v 1 assemble, construct, erect, form, make, manufacture, put together, put up, raise. 2 base, begin, establish, found, originate, set up, start

building n construction, edifice, premises, structure

build-up n accumulation, collection, gathering, heap, hoard, mass, stockpile, store

bulge n bump, hump, lump, projection, protuberance, rise, swelling

bulging adj ballooning, bloated, distended, full, lumpy, popping, protruding, sticking out, swelling, swollen

bulk n 1 bulkiness, extent, immensity, largeness, magnitude, mass, massiveness,

quantity, size, weight. 2 best part inf, greater part, lion's share, main part, majority, mass, most, nearly all

bullet n missile, pellet, shot, slug

bulletin n announcement, communication, communiqué, message, news-flash, notification, report, statement

bully n abuser, oppressor, persecutor, ruffian, thug, tormentor, tyrant

bully v browbeat, coerce, domineer, frighten, intimidate, oppress, persecute, pick on inf, push around inf, ride roughshod over, terrorize, threaten, tyrannize

bump n 1 bang, blow, collision, crash, jolt, knock, smash, thud, thump.
2 (a bump on sth) bulge, hump, knob, lump, nodule, protrusion, protuberance, swelling, welt

bump v 1 (hit sth) bang, collide, crash, hit, hurt, injure, jar, knock, ram, slam inf, smash into, strike, thump. 2 (bump up and down) bounce, jerk, jolt, rattle, shake. 3 **bump into** chance upon, come across, encounter, happen on, meet, run into, see

bunch n 1 (of things) batch, bundle, cluster, collection, group, heap, load, mass, pack, quantity, set. 2 (of flowers) bouquet, clump, posy, sheaf, spray.
3 (of people) band, crowd, gang, group, knot, party

bunch v 1 assemble, bundle, cluster, collect, crowd, flock, gather, group, herd, huddle, mass, pack; **opp** separate. 2 bunch up, fold, gather, pleat; **opp** lie flat

bundle n 1 assortment, batch, bunch, collection, heap, pile. 2 bag, pack, package, parcel, roll, sheaf

bundle v bind, fasten, muffle, pack, package, roll, swathe, tie, truss, wrap

bungle n blunder, botch, error, fiasco, mess, mistake, mix-up, muddle, pig's ear *sl*, slip-up *inf*

bungle v blunder, botch, fudge, make a hash *inf*, make a mess *inf*, mess up *inf*, mismanage, muck up *inf*, ruin, spoil

buoyant *adj* 1 able to float, floating, light. 2 blithe, bouncy, bright, cheerful, jaunty, light-hearted, upbeat *inf*; *opp* depressed, low

burden n 1 anxiety, care, difficulty, duty, obligation, problem, responsibility, sorrow, stress, trial, trouble, worry. 2 cargo, encumbrance, load, weight

burden v afflict, bother, encumber, hamper, impose, load, lumber *inf*, overload, saddle *inf*, strain, tax, trouble, weigh down, worry

bureaucracy n administration, civil service, government, ministry, officialdom, red tape *inf*, rules and regulations

burglar n cat burglar, housebreaker, intruder, robber, thief

burglary n break-in, breaking and entering, housebreaking, larceny, robbery, stealing, theft, thieving

burly *adj* beefy, brawny, bulky, hefty, hulking, muscular, powerful, stocky, strong, sturdy, well-built; *opp* thin, weedy

burn v 1 be ablaze, be on fire, blaze, consume, flame, flare, flicker, glow, go up in flames, ignite, incinerate, kindle, light, reduce to ashes, set alight, set on fire, smoke, smolder, spark. 2 (damage)

blister, char, parch, scald, sear, shrivel, singe, toast, wither

burning *adj* 1 alight, blazing, fiery, flaming, flickering, glowing, hot, incandescent, lit up, raging, scorching, smoking, smoldering. 2 ardent, eager, fervent, impassioned, intense, passionate, vehement. 3 biting, irritating, painful, prickling, searing, smarting, stinging. 4 acrid, caustic, corrosive, harsh, pungent, reeking, scorching, smoky

burrow n den, earth, hole, lair, shelter, tunnel, warren

burst n bang, blast, crack, discharge, explosion, rupture

burst v blow up, break, crack, disintegrate, erupt, explode, fly open, force open, fragment, give way, pierce, pop, puncture, rupture, shatter, split, tear

bury v 1 conceal, cover, cover up, embed, enclose, engulf, enshroud, hide, immerse, plant, sink, submerge. 2 (a dead person) entomb, inter, lay to rest

business n 1 (a firm) company, concern, enterprise, establishment, firm, industry, organization, outfit *inf*, partnership, practice, set-up *inf*, venture. 2 (to be in business) buying and selling, commerce, dealings, marketing, merchandising, selling, trade, transactions. 3 (business to be dealt with) affair, case, issue, matter, problem, question, subject, topic. 4 (line of business) career, job, line of work, occupation, profession, trade, work

businesslike *adj* efficient, methodical, neat, organized, professional, systematic, thorough, well-ordered

bustle n activity, ado, agitation, commotion, excitement, flurry, fuss, haste, hurry, movement, toing and froing *inf*, tumult

bustle v dash, fuss, hurry, scamper, scramble, scurry, scuttle, tear, whirl

busy adj 1 (to be busy) active, employed, engaged, engrossed, hard at it *inf*, hard at work, industrious, occupied, on the go *inf*, rushed off your feet, slaving, up to your eyes *inf*, working; *opp* unoccupied. 2 (a busy life) chaotic, energetic, frantic, full, hectic, strenuous, tiring; *opp* quiet

butcher n killer, murderer, slaughterer, slayer

butcher v 1 (meat) carve, cut, kill, prepare, slice. 2 (people) kill, murder, massacre, put to death, slaughter, slay

butt n 1 (cigarette butt) end, stub. 2 (butt of a joke) dupe, laughing-stock, object, subject, target, victim

buy v acquire, come by, get, invest in *inf*, obtain, pay for, procure, purchase, shop for

bypass v avoid, circumvent, detour around, evade, go around, sidestep, skirt

bystander n eyewitness, observer, onlooker, passerby, spectator, witness

cabin *n* **1** chalet, hut, lodge, log cabin, shack, shed, shelter. **2** (on a ship) berth, compartment, quarters, room

café *n* cafeteria, coffee bar, coffee shop, diner, restaurant, snack bar, tearoom

cage *n* aviary, birdcage, corral, enclosure, hutch, pen, pound

cage *v* confine, coop up, corral, fence in, imprison, incarcerate, lock up, pen, restrain, shut up

calculate *v* **1** assess, consider, determine, evaluate, figure out, gauge, judge, rate, reckon, weigh up, work out.
2 (numbers) add, compute, count, estimate, find out, measure, reckon, total, weigh

calculated *adj* considered, deliberate, intended, intentional, on purpose, planned, premeditated

calculating *adj* canny, crafty, cunning, devious, manipulative, scheming, shrewd, sly; *opp* ingenuous

calculation *n* answer, computation,

estimate, forecast, judgment, reckoning, result

call *n* **1** bellow, cry, exclamation, roar, shout, shriek, signal, song, whoop, yell. **2** appeal, command, demand, invitation, plea, request

call *v* **1** (call to sb) cry, cry out, exclaim, hail, shout, yell. **2** (using a telephone) call up, contact, give sb a buzz *inf*, give sb a ring, phone, ring, ring up *inf*, telephone. **3** (call somewhere) drop in *inf*, pay a call, pop in *inf*, stop by, visit. **4** (name sb or sth) christen, designate, dub, entitle, label, name, style, term, title. **5** (call a meeting) announce, convene, convoke, gather, order. **6** (call an ambulance) ask for, fetch, order, send for, summon. **7 call for** demand, entail, justify, necessitate, need, require

calling *n* business, career, job, occupation, profession, trade, vocation, work

callous *adj* cold, cool, dispassionate, hardened, hard-hearted, heartless, indifferent, insensitive, ruthless, soulless, stony-hearted, thick-skinned, uncaring, unemotional, unfeeling; *opp* sensitive

calm *adj* **1** airless, balmy, flat, mild, motionless, peaceful, placid, quiet, restful, serene, slow-moving, smooth, still, tranquil, windless. **2** (relaxed) collected, composed, controlled, cool, laid-back *inf*, level-headed, patient, relaxed, sensible, together *inf*, unexcited, unfazed *inf*, unflappable *inf*, unmoved, unruffled, untroubled; *opp* frantic

calm *n* **1** peace, peacefulness, quietness, restfulness, serenity, stillness, tranquillity. **2** composure, equanimity, impassivity, poise, sang-froid, self-control

calm v **1** (calm a situation) appease, compose, control, cool, mollify, smooth; *opp* inflame. **2** (calm a baby) hush, lull, pacify, placate, quieten, relax, settle, soothe, tranquilize; *opp* disturb

camouflage n blind, concealment, cover, disguise, facade, guise, markings, mask, mimicry, protective covering, veil

camouflage v cloak, conceal, cover, disguise, hide, mask, obscure, screen, veil

campaign n **1** action, crusade, drive, effort, fight, movement, promotion, struggle. **2** (military) attack, battle, expedition, offensive, push, war

campaign v agitate, battle, canvass, crusade, fight, push, struggle, work

cancel v **1** abandon, abolish, abort, annul, call off, declare void, invalidate, nullify, postpone, quash, repeal, rescind, revoke, scrap, scrub *inf*, wipe out, write off. **2** cross out, delete, erase, strike out

cancer n canker, carcinoma, growth, malignancy, melanoma, tumor

candid adj blunt, forthright, frank, honest, open, outspoken, plain, straightforward, truthful, upfront *inf*; *opp* cagey, deceitful

candidate n applicant, competitor, contender, contestant, entrant, nominee, possibility, runner *inf*

canvass v **1** (seek votes) campaign, drum up support *inf*, electioneer. **2** (investigate) analyze, examine, find out, inspect, investigate, scan, sift, study. **3** (seek opinions) ask for, discuss, poll, solicit

cap v **1** beat, better, eclipse, exceed, excel, outdo, outstrip, surpass, top, transcend. **2** coat, cover, crown, top

capability n ability, aptitude, capacity, competence, faculty, means, potential, power, skill, wherewithal

capable adj able, adept, clever, competent, efficient, experienced, gifted, handy *inf*, intelligent, masterly, practiced, proficient, qualified, skillful, skilled, talented, trained

capacity n **1** amplitude, dimensions, extent, magnitude, range, room, scope, size, space, volume. **2** ability, aptitude, cleverness, competence, intelligence, potential, power, skill, talent. **3** duty, function, job, office, position, post, responsibility, role

capital adj **1** (letters) big, block, initial, large, upper-case. **2** cardinal, central, chief, foremost, important, key, leading, main, major, paramount, primary, prime, principal

capital n **1** assets, cash, finance, funds, investments, liquid assets, money, principal, property, resources, savings, stock, wealth, wherewithal. **2** center of government, chief city, first city, seat of government

capitulate v acquiesce, admit defeat, back down, be defeated, concede, give in, give up, relent, submit, succumb, surrender, throw in the towel *inf*, yield

capsize v flip over, invert, keel over, knock over, overturn, tip over, turn over, turn upside down, upset

captain n boss, chief, commander, head, leader, master, officer, pilot, skipper

captive *adj* caged, captured, chained, confined, enslaved, fettered, imprisoned, in captivity, incarcerated, interned, jailed, locked up, taken prisoner, under lock and key *inf*; *opp* free

captive *n* convict, detainee, hostage, internee, prisoner, prisoner of war, slave

captivity *n* bondage, confinement, custody, detention, imprisonment, incarceration, internment, slavery; *opp* freedom

capture *n* apprehension, arrest, imprisonment, seizure

capture *v* apprehend, arrest, catch, collar *inf*, corner, ensnare, nab *inf*, nick *inf*, seize, take captive, take into custody, take prisoner, trap

car *n* automobile, vehicle, wheels *sl*

carcass *n* body, cadaver, corpse, dead body, meat, remains

care *n* 1 anxiety, burden, concern, difficulty, hardship, problem, sorrow, stress, trouble, woe, worry. 2 (do sth with care) attention, carefulness, caution, circumspection, concentration, consideration, diligence, forethought, heed, meticulousness, prudence, thought, vigilance, watchfulness. 3 (in sb's care) charge, control, custody, guardianship, keeping, management, protection, safekeeping, supervision

care *v* 1 be concerned, be interested, be troubled, bother, concern yourself with, give a hoot *inf*, mind, worry. 2 **care for** (look after sb or sth) cherish, foster, look after, mind, minister to, mother, nurse, protect, provide for, take care of, tend, watch over. 3 **care for** (like sb) be fond of, be in love with, cherish, hold dear,

like, love. 4 **care for** (want sth) desire, enjoy, fancy, want

career *n* business, calling, employment, livelihood, living, métier, occupation, profession, trade, vocation, work

carefree *adj* 1 blasé, casual, cheerful, contented, easygoing, happy, happy-go-lucky, insouciant, laid-back *inf*, light-hearted, nonchalant, relaxed, unworried; *opp* anxious. 2 (a carefree time) peaceful, quiet, relaxing, restful, trouble-free; *opp* stressful

careful *adj* 1 (careful in your work) accurate, conscientious, methodical, meticulous, neat, painstaking, particular, precise, rigorous, systematic, thorough, well-organized; *opp* careless. 2 (be careful) alert, attentive, cautious, circumspect, discreet, heedful, mindful, observant, on guard, solicitous, thoughtful, vigilant, wary, watchful; *opp* careless. 3 (careful with money) canny, cautious, economical, thrifty; *opp* wasteful

careless *adj* 1 absentminded, forgetful, hasty, inattentive, inconsiderate, indiscreet, irresponsible, negligent, rash, reckless, remiss, scatterbrained, thoughtless, unguarded, unthinking, unwary; *opp* careful. 2 (careless with your work) casual, disorganized, hasty, imprecise, inaccurate, messy, shoddy, slapdash, slipshod, sloppy *inf*, untidy; *opp* careful

caress *n* cuddle, embrace, hug, kiss, pat, touch

caress *v* cuddle, embrace, fondle, hug, kiss, nuzzle, pat, pet, stroke, touch

caretaker *n* curator, custodian, janitor,

keeper, porter, superintendent, warden, watchman

cargo n baggage, consignment, contents, freight, goods, haul, load, merchandise, shipment

caricature n cartoon, lampoon, parody, satire, send-up inf, spoof, take-off inf, travesty

caring adj altruistic, charitable, compassionate, concerned, considerate, helpful, humane, interested, kind, kind-hearted, kindly, loving, solicitous, sympathetic, thoughtful, understanding, unselfish, well-meaning; **opp** uncaring

carnage n bloodbath, bloodshed, butchery, gala, massacre, murder, slaughter

carnival n celebration, fair, festival, fête, fiesta, gala, jamboree, holiday, merrymaking, parade, procession, revelry

carriage n 1 cab, car, coach, compartment. 2 bearing, comportment, demeanor, gait, manner, mien, posture, stance

carry v 1 (take sth somewhere) bear, bring, cart inf, conduct, convey, ferry, fetch, haul, lug inf, manhandle, move, remove, ship, shoulder, take, transfer, transmit, transport. 2 (support sth) bear, hold, support, sustain, underpin. 3 (carry a punishment) demand, entail, involve, lead to, occasion, require, result in. **4 carry on** continue, endure, go on, keep, keep going, last, maintain, persevere, persist. **5 carry out** accomplish, achieve, carry through, do, effect, fulfill, perform, realize

cartoon n animated film, animation, comic strip, drawing, sketch

carve v cut, cut in, chisel, engrave,

etch, form, hack, scratch, sculpture, shape. 2 (carve meat) cut up, do the honors, serve, slice, slice up

case n 1 box, carton, chest, container, crate, holder, pack. 2 bag, briefcase, hand luggage, luggage, suitcase, trunk. 3 casing, cover, covering, jacket, sheath, outer shell, wrapper. 4 (display case) cabinet, display cabinet, display case, glass case, showcase. 5 circumstances, example, illustration, instance, occasion, occurrence, position, situation. 6 (legal action) action, dispute, hearing, inquiry, investigation, lawsuit, legal action, proceedings, trial, tribunal

cash n change, coins, currency, dough sl, funds, money, notes, pennies inf, resources, small change

cast n 1 actors, cast list, characters, company, dramatis personae tech, performers, players, troupe. 2 casting, impression, mold, shape

cast v 1 chuck inf, fling, heave, hurl, lob, scatter, sling, throw, toss. 2 discard, get rid of, shed, slough off, throw off. 3 (cast a glow) direct, emit, give off, send out, shed

castle n citadel, chateau, fort, fortress, mansion, pile, stately home, stronghold

casual adj 1 blasé, carefree, careless, couldn't-care-less, cursory, easygoing, free and easy, happy-go-lucky, indifferent, informal, laid-back, nonchalant, offhand, relaxed, slap-happy, sloppy, unconcerned. 2 accidental, chance, impromptu, occasional, random, unexpected, unintentional, unplanned

casualty n fatality, injured, injured

person, hospital case, stretcher case, victim, wounded

catalog n 1 classification, directory, inventory, record, register. 2 booklet, brochure, guide, leaflet

catastrophe n blow, disaster, calamity, crisis, devastation, fiasco, mishap, tragedy

catch n 1 clasp, clip, fastener, fastening, hook, latch, lock. 2 (disadvantage) bad news, difficulty, disadvantage, downside, drawback, fly in the ointment, problem, snag. 3 bag, haul, prize, take

catch v 1 apprehend, arrest, capture, collar inf, grab, grab hold of, grasp, nab inf, seize, snatch; *opp* drop, let go. 2 catch sb red-handed, discover, expose, surprise, take sb by surprise. 3 (catch flu) be affected by, contract, get, develop, be down with. 4 (catch a train) get, get on, go by, take, travel by; *opp* miss. 5 catch on be all the rage, be in demand, be popular. 6 catch on get it, get the picture, realize, sth dawns on you, the penny drops, understand

catching adj contagious, communicable, infectious, transmissible, transmittable

categorical adj absolute, clear, complete, definite, explicit, express, out-and-out, total, unambiguous, unequivocal

category n class, classification, division, department, group, grouping, heading, kind, nature, section, sector, sort, type, variety

cater v look after, provide, satisfy, supply

catty adj bitchy, malicious, nasty, spiteful, vicious, vindictive

cause n 1 basis, grounds, incentive, motive, origin, reason, source; *opp* effect, result. 2 aim, campaign, end, movement, objective, purpose, struggle, undertaking

cause v be the cause of, bring about, bring on, create, end in, generate, give rise to, instigate, lead to, make, produce, provoke, result in, set off, spark off, trigger

caution n 1 care, carefulness, circumspection, discretion, prudence, vigilance, wariness; *opp* recklessness. 2 admonition, reprimand, talking-to, telling-off, warning

caution v 1 admonish, give sb a caution, reprimand, reprove, tell off, warn. 2 admonish, advise, counsel, urge

cautious adj alert, careful, chary, guarded, tentative, vigilant, wary; *opp* reckless

cave n cavern, chamber, grotto

cavernous adj deep, huge, massive, vast, yawning

cavity n aperture, gap, hole, hollow, opening, pit

cease v break off, bring sth to a halt, come to an end, die away, end, fizzle out, grind to a halt, finish, pack in inf, pack up inf, quit, stop; *opp* begin, start

celebrate v 1 commemorate, drink to, eulogize, honor, observe, toast. 2 enjoy yourself, have fun, let your hair down, live it up, paint the town red, party

celebrated adj acclaimed, distinguished, eminent, famed, famous, illustrious, legendary, renowned, revered, well-known

celebration n 1 commemoration, remembrance. 2 bash inf, do inf, event, festivity, party, shindig inf

celebrity n big name, bigwig inf,

dignitary, luminary, personality, star, VIP, worthy

celibate adj chaste, innocent, pure, virgin, virginal

cell n cubicle, dungeon, lock-up, prison, room

censor v ban, bowdlerize, blue-pencil, clean up, cut, edit, expurgate, prohibit, remove

censure n blame, castigation, criticism, condemnation, disapproval, rebuke, reproach

censure v berate, blame, castigate, condemn, criticize, denounce, lambast, rebuke, reprimand, reproach, take to task, upbraid

center n central point, core, crux, focal point, heart, hub, middle, mid-point, nucleus

central adj 1 mid, middle, inner, interior; *opp* outer, peripheral. 2 basic, chief, core, fundamental, important, key, main, pivotal, principal

centralize v amalgamate, center, concentrate, consolidate, converge, focus, rationalize; *opp* decentralize, devolve

ceremonial adj formal, official, ritual, ritualistic

ceremony n celebration, commemoration, formal occasion, function, rite, service

certain adj 1 (sure in your mind) confident, convinced, definite, positive, satisfied, sure. 2 beyond question, bound to happen, clear, definite, evident, inescapable, inevitable, irrevocable, in the bag inf, obvious, plain

certainty n 1 assurance, confidence,

conviction, sureness. 2 dead cert inf, foregone conclusion, inevitability, open-and-shut case, safe bet

certificate n authorization, accreditation, award, degree, diploma, document, guarantee, license, pass, qualification, voucher, warrant

certify v accredit, authenticate, authorize, confirm, declare, guarantee, license, validate, verify

chain n progression, sequence, series, string, succession, train

chain v bind, fasten, fetter, fix, shackle, secure, tether, tie

chairman, chairwoman n chair, chairperson, convenor, moderator

challenge n 1 dare, invitation, taunt. 2 hard task, hurdle, job-and-a-half inf, obstacle, test, uphill struggle, venture

challenge v 1 (challenge sb to do sth) dare, defy, test, throw down the gauntlet. 2 (question sth) campaign against, contest, dispute, object to, query, question, raise an objection to, stand up to

champion n 1 gold-medalist, prize-winner, title-holder, victor, winner. 2 advocate, backer, campaigner, defender, promoter, supporter

chance n 1 (fate) accident, coincidence, destiny, fate, fluke, fortune, luck, providence. 2 risk, gamble. 3 likelihood, odds, probability, prospect. 4 (opportunity) opening, opportunity, possibility, prospect

change n about-turn, alteration, difference, innovation, metamorphosis, modification, mutation, reorganization, sea change, transformation, variation, volte-face

change v 1 alter, do an about-face *inf*, modify, rearrange, reform, reorganize, restyle, shift, transform, vary. 2 exchange, replace, substitute, swap

changeable adj changing, erratic, fickle, fluctuating, fluid, irregular, mercurial, shifting, uncertain, unpredictable, unstable, vacillating, variable, volatile

channel n canal, conduit, culvert, ditch, duct, groove, gutter, strait, waterway

channel v direct, force, guide, lead, move, send, steer

chant v intone, sing

chaos n bedlam, confusion, disorder, disarray, pandemonium, mayhem, shambles, tumult, turmoil

chaotic adj confused, disordered, disorganized, haywire, in a mess, in chaos, messy, muddled, topsy-turvy, untidy

character n 1 (nature) disposition, flavor, individuality, make-up, manner, nature, personality, quality, temperament. 2 (a person) case *inf*, eccentric, individual, oddball *inf*, oddity, person, sort

characteristic adj distinctive, distinguishing, individual, peculiar, typical

characteristic n attribute, feature, idiosyncrasy, mannerism, peculiarity, quality, quirk, trait

charade n absurdity, farce, fiasco, game, humbug, nonsense, pantomime, parody, pretense, put-up job *inf*, sham, show, travesty, whitewash

charge n 1 cost, fare, fee, levy, price, rate,

rent, toll. 2 accusation, allegation, indictment. 3 care, custody, safe hands, safekeeping

charge v 1 ask, bill, debit, demand, invoice, set a price, want. 2 dash, hurtle, run, rush, stampede, storm, tear, zoom. 3 accuse, arraign, bring charges against, indict, put on trial

charitable adj 1 big-hearted, compassionate, forgiving, generous, indulgent, kind, magnanimous, sympathetic, tolerant, understanding; *opp* mean, uncharitable. 2 benevolent, humanitarian, philanthropic

charity n aid, alms, assistance, handouts, relief, welfare

charm n allure, appeal, attraction, charisma, fascination, lure, magic, magnetism, pull, seduction

charm v attract, beguile, bewitch, captivate, delight, enchant, fascinate, mesmerize

charming adj attractive, beautiful, captivating, delightful, enchanting, lovely, picturesque, pleasant, pretty, sweet; *opp* unattractive, horrid

chart n diagram, map, plan, table

chart v log, map out, mark, note, plot, record, show, sketch

charter n agreement, bill of rights, canon, code, constitution, contract, mission statement

chase v 1 follow, hound, pursue, run after, set off after, shadow, sit on sb's tail, tail, track. 2 drive away, see off, send packing

chaste adj celibate, innocent, pure, undefiled, unsullied, virgin, virginal; *opp* immoral, licentious

chastity n celibacy, innocence, purity,

virginity, virtue

chat *n* chit-chat, confab *inf*, discussion, gossip, heart-to-heart, one-to-one, small talk, talk

chat *v* chatter, chew the fat *inf*, cozy up to *inf*, discuss, gossip, have a chat, have a heart-to-heart *inf*, talk

chatter *v* chat, discuss, gossip, have a chat, talk

cheap *adj* 1 bargain-rate, budget, cut-price, dirt-cheap *inf*, discounted, economical, economy, marked-down, inexpensive, knock-down, low-cost, low-priced, reasonable, reduced, rock-bottom *inf*, sale; *opp* expensive, extortionate, over-priced, top-rate. 2 cheapo *inf*, second-rate, shoddy, tacky, tawdry, trashy

cheat *n* con man *inf*, fraud, racketeer, shark *inf*, swindler

cheat *v* con *inf*, deceive, defraud, do *inf*, double-cross, fleece *inf*, hoodwink, overcharge, pull a fast one *inf*, rip off *inf*, rob *inf*, sting *inf*, swindle, take sb for a ride *inf*, take sb to the cleaners *inf*, trick

check *n* 1 examination, inspection, test, once-over *inf*, spot-check. 2 brake, curb, delay, halt, slow-down, stoppage

check *v* 1 confirm, make sure, see, verify. 2 check out, check over, examine, give sth the once-over *inf*, inspect, look at, test. 3 curb, halt, inhibit, limit, obstruct, put the brakes on, restrain, slowdown, stem, stop

cheek *n* audacity, effrontery, gall, impudence, nerve, temerity

cheeky *adj* discourteous, impertinent, impudent, insolent, rude, sassy; *opp* polite

cheer *n* cheering, hooray, hurrah, shout, whoop

cheerful *adj* bright and breezy, bright-eyed and bushy-tailed, chipper, contented, full of beans, full of the joys of spring, enthusiastic, happy, in a good mood, in high spirits, optimistic, perky, sanguine, smiling, upbeat

cheer up *v* bring a smile to sb's face, buck up *inf*, buoy up, console, liven up, make sb happier, raise sb's spirits, perk up *inf*, uplift

cherish *v* 1 adore, care for, hold dear, love, revere, treasure, value. 2 (cherish a hope) foster, harbor, have, maintain, nurse, nurture

chest *n* 1 box, case, casket, coffer, crate, trunk. 2 chest of drawers, tallboy. 3 bosom, breast

chew *v* champ, chomp, crunch, gnaw, masticate, munch

chief *adj* central, first, foremost, key, leading, main, most important, paramount, premier, primary, principal, top, uppermost, vital

chief *n* bigwig *inf*, boss, controller, director, head, leader, manager, number one, person in charge, person at the top, principal, ringleader, ruler, superior, supremo, top dog *inf*

child *n* baby, boy, daughter, girl, infant, juvenile, kid, kiddie, little one, minor, mite, offspring, son, teenager, toddler, tot, youngster

childhood *n* adolescence, babyhood, boyhood, early days, formative years, girlhood, infancy, school days, teens, young days, youth

childish *adj* adolescent, babyish, boyish,

girlish, immature, infantile, juvenile, naive, puerile, silly

childlike *adj* artless, innocent, naive, simple, youthful

chill *adj* chilly, cold, cool, fresh, icy, raw

chill *v* cool, cool down, make cold, put on ice, refrigerate; *opp* warm

chip *n* 1 break, nick, notch. 2 fragment, bit, shaving, shard, flake, sliver, splinter

chivalrous *adj* courteous, courtly, gallant, gentlemanly, gracious, honorable, knightly, noble, polite, protective

choice *adj* best, desirable, exclusive, fine, first-class, first-rate, prime, quality, select, special, superior, top-quality; *opp* low-quality, poor, second-rate

choice *n* 1 alternative, decision, option, pick, possibility, preference, selection, vote. 2 array, assortment, range, selection, supply, variety

choke *v* 1 asphyxiate, smother, strangle, suffocate, throttle. 2 cough, gag, gasp for air, retch. 3 block, block up, clog, congest, jam, obstruct

choose *v* decide on, desire, fix on, name, opt for, pick, pick out, prefer, select, single out, vote for

chore *n* 1 job, daily grind, duty, hack work, housework, task, toil. 2 bore, burden, drag *inf*, drudgery

chorus *n* call, refrain, response, shout

chronic *adj* 1 appalling, awful, bad, boring, dire, dreadful, tedious, terrible. 2 confirmed, constant, habitual, incessant, incurable, lifelong, long-term, nonstop, persistent

chunk *n* bit, hunk, lump, part, piece, section, wedge

circle *n* ball, band, disk, hoop, ring, round, sphere. 2 (of people) band, clique, crowd, gang, group, set

circle *v* 1 circumnavigate, draw a ring round, encircle, ring. 2 gyrate, revolve, rotate, spin, turn, wheel, whirl

circuit *n* course, journey, lap, loop, ring, round, tour, track

circuitous *adj* indirect, meandering, labyrinthine, roundabout, tortuous; *opp* direct

circular *adj* 1 ring-shaped, disk-shaped, round, spherical. 2 (circular argument) going nowhere, illogical, repetitive, tautologous

circulate *v* broadcast, disseminate, distribute, pass round, promulgate, send around, spread, transmit

circumstance *n* accident, event, factor, happenstance, occasion, position, situation

circumstances *n* how things stand, position, situation, state of affairs

citizen *n* civilian, man/woman in the street, member of society, person, resident, subject, taxpayer, voter

city *n* concrete jungle, conurbation, downtown, town, metropolis, metropolitan area, urban area

civil *adj* 1 cordial, courteous, pleasant, polite, well-mannered; *opp* rude. 2 civic, domestic, home, internal, municipal, public, state

civilization *n* country, culture, life, people, society, way of life

civilize *v* advance, cultivate, develop, educate, improve, refine

civilized *adj* 1 advanced, cultivated, developed, educated, refined, social. 2 comfortable, enjoyable, luxurious, pleasant

claim n 1 allegation, assertion, protestation, statement. 2 application, call, demand, request, right

claim v 1 allege, assert, declare, maintain, profess, say, state. 2 ask for, collect, demand, get, pick up, request, send off for

clamber v climb, scrabble, scramble, shin

clan n clique, faction, family, gang, group, set, tribe

clap v applaud, give sb a round of applause, put your hands together, show your appreciation in the usual way

clarify v disambiguate, elucidate, explain, make clear, put your cards on the table, simplify, spell out what you mean, resolve

clash n brush, confrontation, disagreement, dispute, fight, quarrel, row, showdown

clash v come into conflict, come to blows, confront, cross swords, fall out, fight, quarrel, squabble, wrangle

clasp v clutch, embrace, grasp, hold, hug

class n 1 category, classification, division, grade, group, league, rank, set, sort, status, type, variety. 2 lesson, period, seminar, study group, tutorial

class v arrange, categorize, classify, grade, group, order, rank, rate

classic adj 1 brilliant, definitive, excellent, fine, first-rate, great, superlative. 2 archetypal, copybook, model, prototypical, typical. 3 (a classic style) elegant, simple, timeless, traditional

classical adj 1 Greek, Latin, Roman. 2 elegant, harmonious, simple,

traditional, well-proportioned

classification n 1 arrangement, cataloging, codification, grading, grouping, ordering, organization, taxonomy. 2 category, class, division, grade, group, rank

classify v arrange, categorize, catalog, class, grade, group, order, rank, rate

clause n condition, item, part, passage, point, proviso, section, statement, stipulation, subsection

clean adj 1 clean as a whistle, hygienic, immaculate, laundered, polished, pristine, scrubbed, shining, spick and span, spotless, sterile, sterilized, washed; **opp** dirty. 2 (clean water) clear, fresh, pure, uncontaminated, unpolluted; **opp** contaminated, polluted

clean v dust, polish, sanitize, scrub, spring-clean, sterilize, sweep, vacuum, wash, wipe

clear adj 1 apparent, beyond doubt, beyond question, coherent, distinct, evident, lucid, obvious, plain, unambiguous, understandable, unmistakable; **opp** unclear. 2 (clear glass, water) clean, colorless, see-through, transparent, unclouded. 3 (clear sky) bright, cloudless, fine, moonlit, sunny, starlit; **opp** cloudy, dull, overcast. 4 empty, free, open, unblocked, unobstructed; **opp** blocked

clear v 1 clean, clean out, empty, free, get rid of, remove, unblock, unclog, tidy, tidy up. 2 (clear sb) absolve, acquit, excuse, exonerate, vindicate. 3 (the sky clears) brighten, brighten up, lighten. 4 **clear up** (solve a mystery) crack inf, explain, find an answer to, resolve,

solve, unravel. **5 clear up** (tidy things away) pack up, put sth in order, put things away, sort out, tidy up. **6 clear up** get better, improve

clearly adv distinctly, evidently, obviously, patently, plainly, visibly

clever adj astute, brainy inf, bright, brilliant, canny inf, competent, educated, intelligent, ingenious, knowledgable, quick, sharp, shrewd, smart, streetwise, talented

cliché n adage, hackneyed phrase, maxim, platitude, saying, stereotype, truism, well-worn expression

client n consumer, customer, patron, regular, user

climate n **1** (weather) atmospheric conditions, microclimate, temperature, weather. **2** atmosphere, conditions, feeling, mood, spirit, setting, situation

climax n apogee, crowning point, culmination, finale, height, peak, pinnacle, zenith

climax v **1** culminate, peak, come to a head, result, end. **2** have an orgasm

climb v **1** ascend, clamber, climb up, go up, move up, mount, rise, shin up, shoot up, soar. **2** (climb a mountain) ascend, conquer, reach the summit of, reach the top of, scale

cling v adhere, attach yourself, cling on, grip, hold, hold fast, hold on, stick

clip n **1** clasp, fastener, paper clip, pin. **2** clipping, cutting, excerpt, extract, passage, scene, snippet

clip v **1** attach, fasten, fix, pin, staple. **2** crop, cut, cut off, lop, prune, shear, shorten, snip, trim

cloak n cape, coat, overcoat, shawl, wrap

clog v block, block up, choke, clog up, congest, jam, jam up, obstruct, stop up

close adj **1** (in space) adjacent, adjoining, close by, convenient, handy, hard by, near, nearby, neighboring, at hand; *opp* distant. **2** (in time) approaching, at hand, imminent, impending, near, nigh; *opp* distant. **3** (of friends) dear, devoted, inseparable, intimate, loving. **4** (of weather) humid, muggy, oppressive, sultry, sweaty, sweltering

close n cessation, completion, conclusion, dénouement, end, ending, finish, termination

close v **1** bolt, fasten, lock, seal, shut, slam; *opp* open. **2** (close an investigation) bring to a close, bring to an end, cease, complete, conclude, end, finish, terminate, wind up; *opp* open. **3** (get nearer) approach, catch up, chase, near, pursue

closed adj **1** bolted, fastened, locked, sealed, shut, unopened; *opp* open. **2** completed, concluded, ended, finished, over, over and done with, resolved, settled

cloth n **1** fabric, material, textile. **2** (piece of cloth) cover, dishcloth, dishtowel, napkin, serviette, tablecloth, wipe

clothes n apparel, attire, clothing, costume, dress, garb, garments, gear inf, get-up inf, outfit, raiment, togs inf, wardrobe, wear

cloud n **1** cloud cover, fog, haze, mist, vapor, water vapor. **2** cirrus, cumulus, nimbus, stratus

cloudy adj **1** (of sky, weather) dull, foggy, hazy, misty, overcast. **2** (of liquid, glass) frosted, milky, misty, muddy, murky, opaque, smoky, steamed up

clown n 1 (performer) comedian, comic, fool, jester, pierrot. 2 buffoon, fool, idiot, joker

club n 1 association, brotherhood, circle, federation, fraternity, group, guild, league, organization, society, sorority, team, union. 2 bar, cabaret, disco inf, discothèque, nightclub, night spot. 3 baton, blackjack, bludgeon, cudgel, shillelagh, stave, stick, truncheon

clue n hint, idea, indication, inkling, key, lead, pointer, sign

clumsy adj awkward, blundering, bumbling, bungling, gawky, graceless, ham-fisted, lumbering, maladroit, unco-ordinated, ungainly

cluster n accumulation, bunch, clump, collection, gathering, group, knot, mass

cluster v accumulate, bunch, coalesce, gather, group, mass, press

clutch v clasp, cling to, grasp, grip, hang on to, hold, hold on to

clutter n chaos, disorder, jumble, litter, mess, garbage, untidiness

clutter v encumber, fill, fill up, litter, pack, pile high, strew, stuff

coach v direct, drill, exercise, guide, instruct, manage, prepare, teach, train, tutor

coalition n alliance, allies, amalgamation, association, bloc, compact, confederacy, confederation, league, merger, pact, union

coarse adj 1 crude, rough, tough, uneven, unrefined. 2 (in manners) boorish, common, crude, gross, ill-mannered, uncouth, vulgar

coast n coastline, littoral, shore, seaboard, seaside, shoreline

coast v cruise, drift, freewheel, glide, relax, slide

coat n 1 anorak, cloak, duffel coat, fleece, jacket, mac inf, mackintosh, overcoat, parka, raincoat, topcoat. 2 (of an animal) fleece, fur, hair, pelt. 3 (of paint) coating, covering, film, finish, glaze, layer, patina

coat v cover, plaster, spread, smear

coax v cajole, encourage, entice, induce, inveigle, persuade, talk sb into/out of sth, sweet-talk inf, wheedle

code n 1 (system of rules, beliefs) canon, code of conduct, convention, custom, ethics, etiquette, manners, oath, rules. 2 (for writing and understanding messages) coding system, cipher, key, notation. 3 (sequence of letters or numbers) combination, password, PIN, user ID. 4 (types of code) Morse code, semaphore, sign language

coerce v compel, constrain, force, intimidate, make, persuade, twist sb's arm

coherent adj articulate, clear, cogent, cohesive, consistent, intelligible, logical, lucid, organized, reasoned, sound, systematic, well-ordered, well-structured; **opp** incoherent

coil v curl, entwine, loop, snake, spiral, twine, twist, wind

coincide v accord, agree, be the same, clash, combine, come together, concur, correspond, happen at the same time, line up, match, tally

coincidence n accident, chance, fluke, stroke of luck

cold *adj* **1** arctic, biting, bitter, chill, chilled, chilly, cool, drafty, freezing, fresh, frigid, frosty, frozen, glacial, ice-cold, icy, nippy *inf*, refrigerated, wintry; *opp* hot, warm. **2** (of a person, atmosphere) aloof, callous, chilly, cold-blooded, cold-hearted, cool, distant, forbidding, frigid, frosty, hard-hearted, heartless, indifferent, inhospitable, inhuman, insensitive, passionless, reserved, standoffish, stony, uncaring, unemotional, unfeeling, unfriendly, unsympathetic, unwelcoming; *opp* warm

cold *n* bug *inf*, chill, common cold, flu, influenza, sniffle *inf*, viral infection, virus

collaborate *v* assist, band together, collude, connive, conspire, cooperate, help, join forces, pool resources, pull together, team up, work together

collaborator *n* **1** accomplice, assistant, associate, co-author, confederate, colleague, fellow worker, helper, helpmate, partner. **2** (with an enemy) Judas, quisling, traitor, turncoat

collapse *n* breakdown, disintegration, failure, implosion

collapse *v* **1** (of an object) cave in, come apart, fall apart, fall down, fall in, fall over, fall to pieces, give way, implode, subside. **2** (of a person) be taken ill, crumple, faint, fall over, keel over, pass out. **3** (of an idea) break down, disintegrate, fail, fall apart, fall through, fall to pieces, fold, founder; *opp* succeed, thrive

colleague *n* associate, collaborator, comrade, fellow worker, partner, peer, workmate

collect *v* accumulate, assemble, bring together, gather, hoard, marshal, pile up, stock, stockpile, store

collected *adj* **1** accumulated, assembled, assorted, complete. **2** (of a person) calm, composed, cool, focused

collection *n* accumulation, anthology, array, assemblage, assembly, assortment, cluster, compilation, gathering, group, heap, hoard, pile, set, stack, stock, stockpile, store

collide *v* bang, bump into, crash into, come into collision with, meet head-on, smash into, strike, strike against

collision *n* bang, bump, crash, impact, smash

colloquial *adj* common, conversational, everyday, idiomatic, informal, popular, slang, spoken, vernacular

color *n* **1** coloration, coloring, hue, pigment, pigmentation, shade, tinge, tint, tone. **2** (attractive quality) excitement, interest, spice, variety, vividness

color *v* color in, dye, paint, stain, tinge, tint

colorful *adj* **1** bright, brilliant, gaudy, iridescent, multicolored, psychedelic, vibrant, vivid; *opp* drab, dull. **2** (of a story, event) exciting, exotic, graphic, interesting, lively, stimulating, striking, vivid; *opp* dull. **3** (of a person) dashing, eccentric, distinctive, extrovert, flamboyant, glamorous, larger-than-life, unusual; *opp* dull

column *n* **1** monument, pilaster, pile, pillar, pole, post, shaft, support, strut, upright. **2** (in a newspaper) article, diary, editorial, feature, leader, leading article, section. **3** (of people) file, line, procession, queue, trail, train

comb v examine, look in, rummage through, scour, search, turn inside out

combat n battle, battlefield, conflict, fighting, hand-to-hand combat, hostilities, struggle, war

combat v battle against, defeat, fight, oppose, resist, struggle against, wage war against

combination n alliance, amalgam, amalgamation, blend, conjunction, fusion, integration, merger, mix, mixing, union

combine v **1** (combine things, people) add together, ally, amalgamate, bind, blend, bring together, fuse, integrate, intertwine, interweave, join, join together, lump together, marry, merge, mingle, mix, pool, put together, synthesize, unite. **2** (people, things combine) ally, amalgamate, blend, club together, coalesce, coincide, come together, conspire, co-occur, cooperate, form an alliance, fuse, gang up, integrate, intertwine, interweave, join, join forces, join together, merge, mingle, mix, team up, unite

come v **1** (move toward) advance, appear, approach, come up, draw nearer, enter, move toward, reach. **2** (come to an event or place) arrive, attend, be present, get (to), show up, turn up, visit. **3 come about** come to pass, fall out, happen, occur, take place. **4 come across** encounter, find, meet, see. **5 come back** get back, retrace your steps, return. **6 come from** be derived from, be made from, have its origin(s)

in, have its source in, originate from, originate in. **7 come from** (of a person) be a native of, be born in, be from, be originally from, hail from. **8 come around** (after being unconscious) recover, recover consciousness, regain consciousness, wake up. **9 come around** (to sb's home) come over, drop in inf, pay a visit, pop in inf, pop over inf, visit. **10 come around to** (= agree with) accede to, acquiesce in, agree, be convinced of, be converted to, be persuaded of. **11 come up with** deliver, devise, discover, find, invent, offer, produce, propose, provide, put forward, submit, suggest, turn up

comeback n recovery, resurrection, return, revival

comedian n clown, comedienne, comic, entertainer, humorist

comedy n **1** clowning, humor, situation comedy, slapstick, stand-up comedy; *opp* tragedy. **2** (individual play or performance) sitcom, situation comedy, sketch, turn. **3** (of a situation) absurdity, amusement, funny side, humor, ridiculousness, silliness

comfort n ease, luxuriousness, luxury, opulence, warmth, well-being; *opp* discomfort

comfortable adj **1** (of furniture, surroundings) comfy inf, cozy, de luxe, easy, homey, luxurious, opulent, padded, plush, relaxing, snug, soft, upholstered, warm. **2** (of a person) at ease, comfy inf, cozy, relaxed, snug

comforting adj compassionate, considerate, consoling, fatherly, gentle, kind, paternal, reassuring, supportive, sympathetic

comic *adj* absurd, amusing, comical, droll, facetious, funny, hilarious, humorous, joking, light, rib-tickling, side-splitting, silly, waggish, whimsical, witty; *opp* tragic

comical *adj* absurd, amusing, comic, farcical, funny, laughable, ludicrous, rich, silly, ridiculous

coming *adj* approaching, at hand, future, imminent, impending, in store, next, upcoming

command *n* 1 (words to be obeyed) commandment, decree, directive, edict, injunction, instruction, order. 2 (power to command) ascendancy, authority, charge, control, direction, domination, dominion, government, leadership, mastery, power, superiority, supremacy

command *v* 1 (tell sb to do sth) ask, charge, decree, direct, instruct, order, tell. 2 (command an army) be in charge of, be in control of, control, dominate, have authority over, have dominion over, have power over, have superiority over, have supremacy over, have the ascendancy over, direct, govern, head, head up, lead, outrank

commander *n* 1 boss, chief, commandant, commanding officer, head, leader, superior, superior officer, supremo. 2 (military and police ranks) admiral, captain, commander-in-chief, field marshal, general

commemorate *v* celebrate, honor, pay homage to, pay your respects to, remember, salute

commendable *adj* admirable, creditable, estimable, exemplary, laudable,
meritorious, praiseworthy, valiant, worthy

comment *n* 1 allusion, mention, observation, opinion, reaction, reference, remark, response. 2 (in writing) annotation, footnote, note

comment *v* 1 express an opinion, interpose, note, observe, opine, react, remark, respond, say, venture. 2 **comment on** allude to, annotate, discuss, mention, refer to, talk about

commentary 1 (spoken) comments, narration, narrative, remarks, running commentary, voice-over. 2 criticism, discussion, exegesis, interpretation, review

commentator 1 announcer, broadcaster, DJ, narrator, presenter, pundit, reporter, speaker. 2 critic, expert, reviewer, specialist, writer

commerce *n* business, buying and selling, commercial activity, dealing, money-making, trade, trading

commercial *adj* business, capitalist, entrepreneurial, financial, mercenary, money-making, profit-making

commiserate *v* comfort, console, empathize, sympathize; *opp* congratulate

commission *n* 1 (sth to be done) brief, instruction, mandate, remit, task. 2 (official body) authority, board, committee, tribunal

commission *v* appoint, contract, employ, engage, hire, order, request

commit *v* 1 carry out, do, effect, execute, perform, perpetrate. 2 (commit sth to sb's care) assign, certify, consign, deliver, entrust, give, hand over, send. 3 **commit yourself** bind yourself, engage, give an assurance, give an undertaking, make a decision, make up your mind, pledge, promise, swear, take the plunge

committed *adj* active, ardent, card-carrying, confirmed, dedicated, determined, devoted, diehard, earnest, engaged, fervent, firm, loyal, militant, passionate, persevering, resolute, resolved, single-minded, stalwart, staunch, sworn, unswerving, unwavering, wholehearted, zealous

commitment *n* 1 (dedication) ardor, dedication, determination, devotion, fervor, loyalty, passion, perseverance, resolution, single-mindedness, support, zeal. 2 (sth you have committed yourself to) engagement, oath, promise, undertaking

committee *n* board, executive, panel, steering group

common *adj* 1 (ordinary) common-or-garden, commonplace, customary, everyday, familiar, habitual, normal, ordinary, plain, regular, routine, run-of-the-mill, standard, stock, traditional, typical, unexceptional, usual. 2 (not rare) frequent, numerous, plentiful, popular, widespread; *opp* rare. 3 collective, communal, general, in common, joint, jointly owned, mutual, reciprocal, same, shared. 4 (of a person, manners) coarse, crude, earthy, ill-bred, lower-class, plebeian, uneducated, vulgar

common sense *n* intelligence, level-headedness, practicality, prudence, reason, sense

commotion *n* agitation, bedlam *inf*, chaos, confusion, din, disorder,

disturbance, excitement, ferment, fray, furor, fuss, hubbub, hullabaloo *inf*, pandemonium, racket *inf*, rumpus, sensation, stir, to-do *inf*, trouble, tumult, turmoil, unrest, uproar

communal *adj* collective, common, community, general, in common, joint, jointly owned, public, same, shared

communicate *v* 1 (with sb) be in communication, be in contact, be in touch, commune, contact, get through to, interact, speak to, talk to. 2 (communicate an idea) convey, express, get across, get over, impart, transmit

communication *n* 1 broadcasting, contact, correspondence, exchange, interaction, intercourse, speech, telecommunications. 2 (letter, message) announcement, bulletin, cable, card, communiqué, conversation, dialogue, directive, dispatch, E-mail, fax, letter, memo, memorandum, message, note, notice, piece of news, report, signal, statement, telegram, telephone call, transmission, wire

communicative *adj* chatty, expressive, forthcoming, informative, open, outgoing, talkative

community *n* colony, commune, group, neighborhood, settlement, society

compact *adj* compressed, concise, condensed, dense, miniature, neat, small, tightly packed

companion *n* assistant, associate, chaperone, comrade, colleague, confidant, confidante, consort, escort, fellow traveler, friend, mate, partner, servant, sidekick

companionship n company, comradeship, friendship, partnership

company n 1 business, concern, corporation, enterprise, establishment, firm, organization. 2 (group of people) assembly, audience, band, crew, crowd, ensemble, gang, gathering, group, troop, troupe. 3 companionship, friends, friendship, guests, society, visitors

comparable adj alike, analogous, equal, equivalent, like, matching, parallel, related, similar

compare v 1 balance, contrast, differentiate, juxtapose, set against. 2 draw a parallel, draw/make a comparison, equate, liken, look like, match, resemble

comparison n 1 (make a comparison) analogy, contrast, difference, distinction, juxtaposition, parallel. 2 (there's no comparison) comparability, correlation, likeness, resemblance, similarity

compartment n area, berth, booth, carriage, cell, chamber, cubby-hole inf, cubicle, locker, pigeonhole, section, slot, space

compassion n benevolence, concern, consideration, heart, humanitarianism, humanity, kind-heartedness, kindness, leniency, mercy, pity, soft-heartedness, sorrow, sympathy, tenderness, understanding

compassionate adj benevolent, considerate, gentle, humane, humanitarian, kind, kind-hearted, lenient, merciful, soft-hearted, sympathetic, tender, understanding

compatible adj 1 (of people) in-tune, like-minded, similar, suitable, suited,

well-matched; opp incompatible. 2 (of claims, ideas) consistent, in keeping, reconcilable; opp incompatible

compensate v 1 atone, expiate, indemnify, make amends, make good, pay back, pay compensation, recompense, refund, reimburse, repay. 2 (one thing compensates for another) balance, cancel, counteract, counterbalance, even up, make up for, neutralize, nullify, offset, redress

compensation adj atonement, damages, indemnity, recompense, refund, reimbursement, reparation, repayment, redress, restitution

compete v be a contestant, be in competition, challenge, contend, contest, fight, oppose, participate, pit yourself against, rival, take part, vie

competent adj able, accomplished, adept, capable, clever, effective, experienced, expert, fit, good, handy inf, proficient, qualified, skillful, skilled, trained; opp inept

competition n 1 championship, contest, game, heat, match, race, rally, tournament. 2 conflict, contention, opposition, rivalry, strife, struggle

competitive adj aggressive, ambitious, antagonistic, combative, cutthroat, dog-eat-dog

competitor n adversary, antagonist, candidate, challenger, contender, contestant, entrant, opponent, opposition, participant, rival

compile v accumulate, amass, arrange, assemble, collate, collect, compose, draw up, gather, organize, put together

complacent adj at ease, pleased, satisfied,

self-assured, self-satisfied, smug, unconcerned

complain v bellyache *inf*, bemoan, carp, criticize, find fault, fuss, go on about *inf*, gripe *inf*, grouch *inf*, grouse, grumble, moan, nag, object, protest, remonstrate, whine

complaint n 1 accusation, charge, condemnation, criticism, grievance, gripe *inf*, grouch *inf*, grumble, moan, objection, protest, remonstrance. 2 (medical) affliction, ailment, condition, disease, disorder, illness, infection, sickness, upset

complementary adj corresponding, interdependent, interrelating, matching, paired, reciprocal, twin

complete adj 1 comprehensive, entire, exhaustive, full, in its entirety, intact, total, unabbreviated, unabridged, unbroken, uncut, unedited, whole; *opp* partial. 2 (finished) accomplished, achieved, completed, concluded, done, ended, finished, over; *opp* incomplete. 3 (total) absolute, arrant, consummate, downright, out-and-out, outright, thorough, total, unmitigated, unqualified, utter

complete v accomplish, achieve, clinch, close, conclude, discharge, do, effect, end, execute, finalize, finish, fulfill, realize, round off, settle, terminate, wind up *inf*, wrap up; *opp* begin

completely adv absolutely, altogether, entirely, from beginning to end, fully, perfectly, thoroughly, totally, utterly, wholly

complex adj complicated, convoluted, difficult, elaborate, intricate, involved, knotty, problematic, sophisticated, tangled, tortuous; *opp* simple

complex n fixation, hang-up, mania, neurosis, obsession, phobia, preoccupation

complexion n cast, color, coloring, hue, skin, skin tone, tinge

complicate v compound, confound, confuse, entangle, jumble, mix up, muddle; *opp* simplify

complicated adj complex, convoluted, difficult, elaborate, intricate, involved, knotty, problematic, sophisticated, tangled, tortuous; *opp* simple

complication n 1 difficulty, drawback, obstacle, problem, setback, snag. 2 complexity, confusion, convolution, difficulty, dilemma, intricacy, mix-up, muddle

compliment n accolade, commendation, endorsement, eulogy, flattery, honor, plaudits, praise, tribute; *opp* insult

complimentary adj 1 admiring, appreciative, approving, commendatory, favorable, flattering, generous, laudatory; *opp* critical. 2 free, free of charge, gratis, on the house

comply v abide by, accede, acquiesce, adhere to, agree, assent, conform, consent, fall in, fit in, follow, fulfill, heed, keep, meet, obey, observe, respect, satisfy, submit, yield; *opp* disobey

component n bit, constituent, element, ingredient, part, piece, section, segment

compose v 1 (music, poetry) arrange, concoct, create, devise, invent, make up, produce, think up, write. 2 (compose yourself) calm down, calm yourself, collect your thoughts, relax

composed adj at ease, calm, confident, cool, laidback, level-headed, poised, relaxed, sedate, self-controlled, self-possessed, serene, undisturbed, unfazed, unflappable, unperturbed, unruffled, together inf; opp disturbed, upset

composition n 1 arrangement, configuration, constitution, design, form, formation, layout, make-up, organization, structure. 2 creation, essay, literary work, opus, piece, study, work, work of art

compound n blend, combination, composite, fusion, mixture, synthesis

compound v 1 amalgamate, blend, combine, fuse, mix, put together, synthesize. 2 add to, aggravate, augment, complicate, exacerbate, heighten, intensify, magnify, make worse, worsen; opp alleviate

comprehend v appreciate, apprehend, catch on inf, conceive, discern, fathom, follow, get inf, grasp, know, make out, realize, see, take in, understand

comprehension n appreciation, grasp, knowledge, perception, realization, sense, understanding

comprehensive adj all-embracing, all-inclusive, blanket, broad, complete, exhaustive, extensive, far-reaching, full, inclusive, thorough, total, umbrella, universal, wide, wide-ranging; opp selective, partial

comprise v be composed of, consist of, contain, cover, embody, embrace, encompass, include, incorporate, involve

compromise n agreement, bargain, concession, deal, give-and-take, happy medium, middle course, settlement, trade-off, understanding

compromise v 1 (compromise on sth) come to an understanding, concede, make concessions, meet halfway, negotiate a settlement, settle, strike a balance. 2 (compromise sb's reputation) bring into disrepute, damage, discredit, endanger, imperil, jeopardize, prejudice, risk, undermine, weaken

compulsion n 1 desire, drive, fixation, necessity, need, obsession, preoccupation, urge. 2 coercion, constraint, duress, enforcement, force, oppression, pressure, requirement

compulsive adj 1 (compulsive drinker, gambler) addicted, habitual, incurable, obsessive, persistent. 2 (compulsive viewing) compelling, fascinating, gripping, irresistible

compulsory adj mandatory, necessary, obligatory, required, requisite, statutory; opp optional

computer n machine, mainframe, PC, personal computer, system, word-processor

comrade n ally, associate, colleague, confederate, co-worker, crony inf, fellow-worker, friend, mate inf, pal inf

conceal v 1 (from view) blot out, camouflage, cloak, cover, disguise, hide, keep out of sight, mask, obscure, screen, secrete, shelter. 2 (conceal a fact) cover up, gloss over, hush up, keep quiet, keep secret, keep the lid on, veil; opp reveal

concede v 1 accede, accept, acknowledge, admit, make a concession. 2 capitulate, cave in inf, cede, give in, give up, hand over, relinquish, resign, submit, surrender, yield

conceited *adj* arrogant, big-headed, boastful, cocky, egotistical, full of yourself, immodest, puffed up, self-important, smug, vain; *opp* modest

conceivable *adj* believable, not beyond the realms of possibility, credible, feasible, imaginable, likely, possible, thinkable; *opp* inconceivable

conceive *v* 1 (a plan, idea) conjure up, contrive, create, design, develop, devise, draw up, dream up *inf*, evolve, form, formulate, hatch, initiate, invent, make up, plan, think up. 2 (understand) apprehend, believe, comprehend, envisage, grasp, imagine, suppose, think, understand, visualize

concentrate *v* 1 apply yourself, be absorbed, be attentive, consider closely, engross yourself, give your attention to, pay attention, put your mind to, rack your brains, think, work hard. 2 (in a place) accumulate, center, cluster, collect, congregate, converge, gather, mass; *opp* scatter

concentrated *adj* 1 (concentrated effort) all-out *inf*, concerted, consolidated, intense, intensive, rigorous, vigorous; *opp* half-hearted . 2 rich, strong, thick, undiluted; *opp* diluted

concentration *n* 1 absorption, application, close attention, heed, single-mindedness. 2 (in a place) accumulation, cluster, collection, congregation, convergence, gathering, group, mass

concept *n* conception, hypothesis, idea, notion, theory, view

conception *n* 1 (biological) conceiving, fertilization, impregnation, insemination, pregnancy. 2 beginning, birth, creation, design, formation, inception, invention, origin, outset; *opp* completion. 3 plan, project, proposal. 4 (have no conception of) appreciation, clue, comprehension, concept, idea, inkling, notion, perception, understanding

concern *n* 1 anxiety, apprehension, disquiet, distress, disturbance, fear, malaise, solicitude, worry. 2 (that's my concern) affair, business, department, duty, field, interest, job, matter, problem, regard, responsibility, subject, task. 3 business, company, corporation, enterprise, establishment, firm, house, organization

concern *v* 1 affect, apply, be relevant to, have a bearing on, interest, involve, pertain, refer, regard, relate, touch. 2 bother, distress, disturb, perturb, preoccupy, trouble, worry

concerned *adj* 1 anxious, bothered, distressed, disturbed, fearful, perturbed, troubled, uneasy, unhappy, upset, worried; *opp* unconcerned. 2 (the people concerned) affected, connected, implicated, interested, involved, mixed up, privy to, relevant

concerted *adj* collaborative, collective, combined, cooperative, coordinated, joint, mutual, shared, unified, united

concession *n* 1 acknowledgment, acceptance, admission, allowance, ceding, giving in, recognition, relinquishment, settlement, surrender, yielding. 2 (make a concession) adjustment, allowance, compromise, exception, indulgence, modification, privilege

conciliatory *adj* accommodating, appeasing, mollifying, obliging, pacifying, peaceable, placatory; *opp* aggressive

concise *adj* brief, compact, compressed, condensed, pithy, pointed, short, small, succinct, summary, terse, to the point

conclude *v* 1 bring to an end, cease, close, come to an end, complete, end, finish, halt, round off, stop, terminate, wind up *inf*. 2 assume, come to the conclusion, conjecture, decide, deduce, gather, infer, judge, presume, reckon, suppose, surmise

conclusion *n* 1 close, completion, end, ending, finale, finish, rounding-off, termination; *opp* beginning. 2 consequence, culmination, issue, outcome, result, solution, upshot. 3 (belief) answer, belief, conviction, decision, deduction, inference, judgment, opinion, resolution, settlement, verdict

conclusive *adj* categorical, certain, clinching, convincing, decisive, definite, definitive, final, incontestable, irrefutable, persuasive, unambiguous, unanswerable, unequivocal, unquestionable; *opp* inconclusive

concoct *v* contrive, cook up *inf*, design, devise, formulate, hatch, invent, make up, manufacture, plan, plot, prepare, project, put together, think up

concrete *adj* actual, definite, existing, explicit, factual, firm, material, objective, palpable, physical, real, solid, specific, substantial, tangible,

visible; *opp* abstract

condemn *v* 1 berate, blame, castigate, censure, chide, criticize, damn, decry, denounce, deprecate, disapprove, disparage, rebuke, reproach, reprove, upbraid; *opp* commend, praise. 2 convict, find guilty, judge, pass judgment, pass sentence, punish, sentence; *opp* acquit

condemnation *n* blame, censure, criticism, denunciation, deprecation, disapproval, disparagement, rebuke, reproach, reprobation, reproof, stricture; *opp* praise

condense *v* 1 (make shorter) compress, contract, curtail, cut, reduce, shorten, summarize; *opp* expand, lengthen. 2 (of liquid) concentrate, distill, reduce, thicken; *opp* dilute

condescend *v* 1 deign, descend, humble yourself, lower yourself, stoop, submit. 2 look down your nose at, patronize, talk down to

condescending *adj* disdainful, haughty, high-and-mighty, imperious, patronizing, pompous, snobbish, snooty *inf*, stuck-up *inf*, supercilious, superior

condition *n* 1 case, circumstances, plight, position, predicament, situation, state, state of affairs. 2 demand, essential, necessity, precondition, prerequisite, provision, proviso, qualification, requirement, requisite, restriction, stipulation, terms. 3 fettle, fitness, form, health, kilter, order, shape. 4 (medical) affliction, ailment, disease, disorder, illness, infection, sickness

condition *v* acclimatize, accustom, adapt, educate, equip, habituate, inure, make ready, prepare, train

conditional adj contingent, dependent, provisional, restricted, subject to, with conditions, with reservations, with restrictions, with strings attached inf; **opp** unconditional

condone v accept, allow, approve, endorse, excuse, forgive, ignore, let pass, look the other way, make allowances, overlook, pardon, put up with, tolerate, turn a blind eye

conduct n 1 actions, behavior, manners, mien, ways. 2 administration, control, command, direction, government, handling, leadership, management, organization, regulation, running, supervision

conduct v 1 administer, be in charge, be in control, chair, command, control, direct, govern, handle, head, lead, look after, manage, organize, oversee, preside, regulate, rule, run, steer, supervise. 2 accompany, escort, guide, lead, pilot, take, usher

confer v 1 compare notes, consult, converse, debate, discuss, exchange ideas, exchange views, have discussions, put your heads together inf, seek advice. 2 award, bestow, give, grant, invest, present

conference n colloquium, congress, convention, forum, meeting, seminar, symposium

confess v accept blame, acknowledge, admit, come clean, concede, confide, disclose, divulge, own up, plead guilty, reveal, tell all, unburden yourself

confession n admission, disclosure, divulgence, owning-up, revelation

confide v admit, confess, disclose, divulge, open your heart, reveal, spill the beans, unburden yourself

confidence n 1 assertiveness, assurance, boldness, composure, courage, nerve, poise, self-assurance, self-confidence, self-possession; **opp** shyness. 2 belief, certainty, credence, dependence, faith, reliance, trust; **opp** doubt

confident adj 1 assertive, bold, brave, cocksure, composed, courageous, fearless, outgoing, poised, self-assured, self-confident, self-possessed; **opp** shy. 2 certain, convinced, positive, satisfied, sure; **opp** doubtful

confidential adj classified, hush-hush inf, intimate, off the record, personal, private, secret

confine v bind, cage, coop up inf, detain, enclose, hem in, imprison, incarcerate, intern, jail, limit, lock up, repress, restrain, restrict, shut up; **opp** liberate

confirm v 1 authenticate, back up, bear out, corroborate, endorse, establish, give credence to, prove, show, substantiate, verify; **opp** disprove. 2 (confirm a deal) authorize, clinch, establish, formalize, fix, settle, ratify, sanction. 3 (confirm sb's doubts) add to, increase, strengthen, make firmer, reinforce, fortify; **opp** assuage

confirmation n 1 corroboration, endorsement, evidence, proof, substantiation, testimony, verification. 2 acceptance, agreement, approval, assent, authorization, endorsement, ratification

confirmed adj chronic, compulsive, established, habitual, hardened, ingrained, inveterate, long-established, seasoned, through-and-through

confiscate v commandeer, expropriate, impound, remove, seize, take, take possession of

conflict n 1 (violent) altercation, battle, brush inf, clash, combat, confrontation, encounter, engagement, fight, strife, war, warfare. 2 antagonism, antipathy, bad blood, difference of opinion, disagreement, discord, dissension, feud, friction, hostility, opposition

conflict v 1 clash, contradict, contrast, differ, disagree. 2 clash, contend, contest, cross swords, fight, struggle

conflicting adj at odds, at variance, clashing, contradictory, contrary, contrasting, differing, discordant, incompatible, inconsistent, mutually exclusive, opposed, opposing, paradoxical; opp similar

conform v be good, behave conventionally, blend in, do what you are told inf, comply, fall in with, fit in, follow the crowd, keep in step, obey, run with the pack, toe the line; opp rebel

confront v accost, brave, challenge, defy, encounter, face, face up to, meet head on, oppose, resist, stand up to, tackle, take on; opp avoid

confrontation n battle, clash, conflict, contest, crisis, encounter, head-to-head, set-to inf, showdown

confuse v 1 (confuse sb) baffle, befuddle, bemuse, bewilder, disconcert, disorient, flummox, fluster, mystify, perplex, puzzle. 2 jumble, mess up, mingle, mix up, muddle, snarl up, tangle, throw into disarray, upset

confused adj 1 at a loss, at sea, baffled, bamboozled, befuddled, bemused, bewildered, dazed, disorganized, flummoxed, muddled, mystified, nonplussed, perplexed, puzzled, taken aback, thrown inf; opp clear. 2 chaotic, disordered, disorderly, disorganized, in disarray, in disorder, jumbled, messy, misunderstood, mixed up, muddled, out of order, tangled, untidy; opp tidy

confusing adj ambiguous, baffling, bewildering, complex, complicated, contradictory, difficult, disorganized, disorientating, disorienting, incomprehensible, jumbled, misleading, mixed up, muddled, mystifying, perplexing, puzzling, unclear; opp clear

confusion n 1 bafflement, befuddlement, bemusement, bewilderment, mystification, perplexity, puzzlement. 2 chaos, commotion, disarray, disorder, hodge-podge, jumble, mess, mix-up, muddle, shambles inf, tangle, turmoil; opp order

congenital adj constitutional, hereditary, inborn, inbred, inherent, inherited, innate, natural; opp acquired

congested adj blocked, clogged, crammed, crowded, jammed, obstructed, overcrowded, overfilled, overflowing, packed, plugged, stuffed, teeming; opp clear

congratulate v applaud, compliment, offer your congratulations

congratulations n best wishes, compliments, felicitations, good wishes

congregate v assemble, collect, come together, convene, converge, convoke, crowd around, flock, gather, group together, mass, meet, muster, rally, rendezvous, swarm, throng; *opp* disperse

congregation *n* assembly, audience, brethren, convocation, crowd, fellowship, flock, gathering, group, host, laity, listeners, mass, meeting, multitude, parish, parishioners, rally, throng

congress *n* assembly, chamber, conclave, conference, convention, convocation, council, delegates, gathering, house, legislature, meeting, parliament, representatives, synod

conjugal *adj* bridal, connubial, marital, married, matrimonial, nuptial, wedded

conjure *v* 1 do magic, do tricks, juggle. 2 **conjure up** bring forth, call up, create, evoke, produce, recall, recreate

connect *v* 1 affix, attach, combine, couple, fasten, fix, join, link, relate, tie, unite; *opp* disconnect. 2 associate, bracket, equate, identify, link, relate

connection *n* 1 attachment, coupling, fastening, joint, junction, link, tie. 2 affinity, alliance, association, bond, correspondence, equivalence, link, relatedness, relation, relationship, relevance, tie. 3 acquaintance, ally, associate, contact, friend

connive *v* 1 collaborate, collude, conspire, intrigue, plot, scheme. 2 **connive at** abet, aid, allow, be an accessory to, be party to, condone, let sth pass, overlook, pass over, shut your eyes to, tolerate, turn a blind eye to

connoisseur *n* aficionado, authority, buff *inf*, cognoscenti, devotee, epicure, expert, fan, gourmet, savant, specialist

conquer *v* annex, beat, capture, crush, defeat, get the better of, invade, lick *inf*, master, occupy, overcome, overpower, overrun, overthrow, prevail, quell, rout, seize, subdue, subjugate, surmount, take, thrash *inf*, triumph, trounce, vanquish, win

conqueror *n* champion, hero, lord, master, vanquisher, victor, winner

conquest *n* annexation, appropriation, capture, coup, crushing, defeat, invasion, licking *inf*, mastery, occupation, overpowering, overrunning, overthrow, quelling, rout, seizing, subjugation, taking, thrashing *inf*, triumph, trouncing, vanquishing, victory

conscience *n* better nature, better self, compunction, ethics, morals, moral sense, principles, qualms, scruples

conscientious *adj* careful, dedicated, diligent, dutiful, faithful, hard-working, meticulous, painstaking, particular, perfectionist, punctilious, responsible, rigorous, scrupulous, thorough

conscious *adj* 1 alert, alive to, awake, aware, cognizant, knowing, responsive, sensible, sensitive to, sentient, wise to; *opp* unconscious. 2 calculated, deliberate, intended, intentional, knowing, on purpose, premeditated, studied, voluntary, willful, willed; *opp* unconscious

consciousness *n* alertness, awareness, cognizance, knowledge, perception, realization, recognition, responsiveness, sense, sensibility, sentience; *opp* unconsciousness

consecrate *v* bless, dedicate, devote, make holy, make sacred, ordain, sanctify, set apart

consecutive *adj* continuous, following, in a row, in sequence, in turn, one after another, running, sequential, serial, succeeding, successive, unbroken, uninterrupted

consensus *n* agreement, common consent, common ground, concord, concurrence, general opinion, harmony, unanimity

consent *n* acceptance, acquiescence, agreement, approval, assent, compliance, concurrence, go-ahead *inf*, permission, say-so *inf*, sanction, seal of approval, support; *opp* refusal

consent *v* accept, acquiesce, agree, allow, approve, assent, comply, concede, concur, condone, go along with, permit, sanction, support, yield; *opp* refuse

consequence *n* 1 aftermath, by-product, effect, end, follow-up, issue, outcome, repercussion, result, reverberation, sequel, side-effect, upshot.
2 importance, moment, note, relevance, significance, value, weight

consequent *adj* ensuing, following, resultant, resulting, subsequent

conservation *n* care, charge, custody, husbandry, keeping, maintenance, preservation, preserving, protection, safeguarding, safekeeping, saving, upkeep

conservative *adj* careful, cautious, conventional, die-hard, guarded, hidebound, narrow-minded, old-fashioned, old-school, orthodox, reactionary, right-wing, stick-in-the-mud, straitlaced, traditional, traditionalist; *opp* progressive

conserve *v* be economical with, hoard, keep, maintain, preserve, protect, safeguard, save, store, take care of; *opp* waste

consider *v* 1 cogitate, contemplate, deliberate, examine, meditate, mull over, ponder, reflect, ruminate, study, think, weigh. 2 allow for, bear in mind, have regard for, make allowances for, reckon with, remember, respect, take into account, take into consideration. 3 believe, be of the opinion, deem, hold, judge, reckon, regard, think

considerable *adj* abundant, ample, appreciable, decent, enormous, goodly, great, huge, large, lavish, notable, not inconsiderable, respectable, significant, sizeable, substantial, tolerable; *opp* negligible

considerably *adv* a great deal, a lot, appreciably, enormously, greatly, hugely, markedly, notably, significantly, substantially, very much

considerate *adj* accommodating, attentive, aware, caring, compassionate, concerned, discreet, helpful, kind, mindful, obliging, sensitive, solicitous, tactful, thoughtful, unselfish; *opp* inconsiderate

consideration *n* 1 awareness, compassion, concern, discretion, kindness, sensitivity, solicitude, tact, thought, thoughtfulness, unselfishness. 2 attention, cogitation, contemplation, deliberation, discussion, examination, inspection, perusal, reflection, regard, review, scrutiny, study, thought

consignment *n* batch, cargo, delivery, goods, load, shipment

consist of *v* be composed of, be made up

of, comprise, contain, include, incorporate, involve

consistent adj constant, dependable, predictable, reliable, regular, stable, steady, true, unchanging, undeviating, uniform, unvarying; **opp** inconsistent

consolation n cheer, comfort, ease, encouragement, help, relief, solace, soothing, succor, support, sympathy

console v assuage, calm, cheer, comfort, ease, encourage, hearten, placate, relieve, solace, soothe, succor, support, sympathize

consolidate v cement, fortify, reinforce, secure, stabilize, strengthen; **opp** weaken

conspicuous adj apparent, blatant, clear, evident, flagrant, glaring, intrusive, loud, manifest, marked, noticeable, obtrusive, obvious, ostentatious, patent, prominent, striking, unconcealed, visible; **opp** inconspicuous

conspiracy n cabal, collusion, connivance, frame-up inf, intrigue, machination, plot, scheme, stratagem, treason

conspirator n collaborator, plotter, schemer, traitor

conspire v be in cahoots inf, be in league, collaborate, collude, connive, contrive, devise, hatch a plot, intrigue, maneuver, plot, scheme

constant adj 1 ceaseless, continual, continuous, endless, eternal, everlasting, incessant, interminable, never-ending, nonstop, perpetual, persistent, relentless, sustained, unbroken, unceasing, unending, unrelenting, unremitting. 2 dependable, even, faithful, firm, fixed, immutable, invariable, loyal, permanent,

regular, reliable, steadfast, steady, staunch, true, trusty, unchanging, uniform, unvarying; **opp** changeable

constantly adv all the time, always, ceaselessly, continually, continuously, endlessly, eternally, incessantly, interminably, nonstop, perpetually, persistently, relentlessly, unceasingly, unrelentingly, unremittingly

constituent n component, element, factor, ingredient, member, part, principle, unit

constitute v 1 compose, comprise, form, make, make up. 2 create, establish, form, found, inaugurate, institute, make, set up

constitution n 1 charter, code, law, rules, principles, system. 2 condition, disposition, health, make-up, nature, temperament. 3 creation, establishment, formation, forming, foundation, founding, inauguration, organization, setting up

constitutional adj 1 chartered, constituted, legal, legitimate, statutory, vested. 2 congenital, inborn, inbred, inherent, innate, intrinsic, natural, organic

constrain v 1 compel, coerce, drive, force, impel, oblige, pressure, pressurize, push. 2 bind, check, curb, hinder, hold back, impede, limit, restrain, restrict, tie

constraint n 1 compulsion, coercion, force, impulsion, necessity, obligation, pressure. 2 check, curb, hindrance, limit, limitation, obstacle, restraint, restriction, tie

construct v assemble, build, compose, create, design, devise, erect, establish, fabricate, fashion, forge, form, formulate, found, frame, make, manufacture, organize, produce, put together, put up, raise, set up, shape

construction n assembly, building, composition, creation, design, edifice, erection, fabric, figure, form, formation, framework, shape, structure

constructive v cooperative, creative, helpful, positive, practical, productive, useful, valuable; **opp** destructive

consult v ask, call in, compare notes, confer, debate, deliberate, discuss, interrogate, question, refer to, seek advice, turn to

consultant n adviser, authority, expert, specialist

consultation n appointment, audience, conference, council, deliberation, dialogue, discussion, examination, hearing, interview, meeting, session, talk

consume v absorb, burn, deplete, devour, drain, eat up, exhaust, expend, finish off, guzzle inf, polish off inf, ingest, spend, use, use up, utilize, wear out

contact n 1 communication, connection, contiguity, correspondence, join, juxtaposition, proximity, touch, union. 2 (sb you know) acquaintance, ally, associate, connection, friend

contact v approach, call, communicate, correspond, get in touch, get hold of, notify, reach, ring, speak, talk, telephone, write

contagious adj catching, communicable, epidemic, infectious, passed on, pestilential, spreading, transmissible, transmittable

contain v 1 accommodate, carry, enclose,

have capacity for, have room for, hold, seat. 2 be composed of, be made up of, comprise, consist of, include, incorporate, involve

container n holder, receptacle, vessel

contaminate v adulterate, corrupt, debase, dirty, foul, infect, poison, pollute, soil, stain, sully, taint, tarnish; **opp** purify

contemplate v 1 brood, cogitate, consider, deliberate, examine, gaze, look, meditate, mull over, muse, ponder, reflect, ruminate, study, view. 2 (contemplate doing sth) consider, envisage, expect, foresee, have in mind, imagine, intend, plan, propose, think

contemporary adj 1 coeval, coexistent, coexisting, concurrent, contemporaneous, simultaneous, synchronous. 2 à la mode, current, fashionable, in fashion, latest, modern, newfangled inf, present-day, recent, trendy inf, up-to-date, with it inf; **opp** old, outdated

contempt n abhorrence, derision, disdain, disregard, disrespect, distaste, loathing, mockery, ridicule, scorn, sneering; **opp** respect

contemptible adj abhorrent, abject, base, cheap, despicable, detestable, distasteful, hateful, ignominious, loathsome, low, mean, pathetic, ridiculous, shabby, shameful, vile, worthless

contemptuous adj cutting, derisive, disdainful, disrespectful, haughty, insulting, jeering, mocking, scathing, scornful, sneering, snide, snobbish, snotty inf, supercilious, superior, withering; **opp** respectful

contend v 1 affirm, allege, argue, assert, avow, claim, hold, maintain, put forward, say, state, testify. 2 battle, challenge, clash, compete, contest, fight, oppose, strive, struggle, vie, wrestle

content adj at ease, at peace, cheerful, comfortable, contented, fulfilled, gratified, happy, pleased, relaxed, replete, satisfied, tranquil, untroubled, unworried; **opp** dissatisfied, unhappy

content n cheer, comfort, contentment, ease, equanimity, fulfillment, gratification, happiness, peace of mind, pleasure, satisfaction, tranquillity; **opp** unhappiness

content v appease, cheer, comfort, fulfill, gladden, gratify, mollify, pacify, placate, please, put at ease, relax, satisfy, soothe; **opp** anger, annoy

contented adj at ease, at peace, cheerful, comfortable, content, fulfilled, gratified, happy, pleased, relaxed, replete, satisfied, tranquil, untroubled, unworried; **opp** dissatisfied, unhappy

contentious adj 1 arguable, controversial, debatable, disputable, dubious, tendentious; **opp** uncontroversial. 2 aggressive, argumentative, bickering, combative, competitive, cross, disputatious, factious, fractious, peevish, perverse, pugnacious, quarrelsome, querulous, wrangling; **opp** conciliatory

contentment n cheer, cheerfulness, comfort, content, ease, equanimity, fulfillment, gladness, gratification, happiness, peace, pleasure, repletion, satisfaction, serenity, tranquillity; **opp** dissatisfaction, unhappiness

contents n components, constituents, ingredients, material, matter, subject matter, substance, theme

contest n battle, competition, fight, game, head-to-head, match, rivalry, tournament, trial

contest v 1 battle, compete, contend, fight, fight over, strive, struggle, tussle, vie. 2 argue, call into question, challenge, debate, disagree with, dispute, doubt, object, oppose, question

contestant n adversary, candidate, competitor, contender, entrant, opponent, participant, player, rival

context n background, circumstances, conditions, environment, frame of reference, framework, milieu, setting, situation, surroundings

continual adj ceaseless, constant, continuous, endless, eternal, everlasting, incessant, interminable, never-ending, nonstop, ongoing, perpetual, persistent, recurrent, regular, relentless, repeated, sustained, unbroken, unceasing, unending, unrelenting, unremitting

continually adv all the time, always, ceaselessly, constantly, continuously, endlessly, eternally, incessantly, interminably, nonstop, perpetually, persistently, recurrently, regularly, relentlessly, repeatedly, unceasingly, unrelentingly, unremittingly

continue v abide, carry on, endure, go on, keep on, last, live on, maintain, persevere, persist, proceed, remain, rest, resume, stay, subsist, survive

continuous adj connected, consecutive, constant, continuing, endless, extended, never-ending, nonstop, prolonged, sustained, unbroken, unceasing, unending, uninterrupted

contract *n* agreement, arrangement, bargain, bond, commitment, compact, convention, covenant, deal, lease, pact, settlement, transaction, treaty, understanding

contract *v* 1 abridge, compress, condense, constrict, curtail, dwindle, lesson, narrow, reduce, shorten, shrink, shrivel, tighten, wither, wrinkle; *opp* expand. 2 (contract to do sth) agree, arrange, bargain, pledge, stipulate, undertake. 3 (contract an illness) be/become infected with, catch, develop, get, go down with

contradict *v* argue, be at odds, be at variance, belie, challenge, clash, conflict, counter, deny, disagree, dispute, dissent from, negate, oppose, rebut, refute; *opp* agree

contradiction *n* clash, conflict, counter, denial, disagreement, dissension, incompatibility, incongruity, inconsistency, negation, opposite, paradox, rebuttal, variance; *opp* agreement

contradictory *adj* antagonistic, at odds, at variance, clashing, conflicting, contrary, dissenting, incompatible, incongruous, inconsistent, irreconcilable, opposite, paradoxical

contrary *adj* 1 clashing, conflicting, contradictory, different, discordant, hostile, incompatible, incongruous, inconsistent, inimical, irreconcilable, opposed, opposite. 2 (of a person) awkward, headstrong, intractable, intransigent, obstinate, perverse,

stubborn, uncooperative, wayward, willful; *opp* amenable, obliging

contrast *n* clash, comparison, difference, disparity, dissimilarity, distinction, divergence, foil, opposition

contrast *v* 1 compare, differentiate, discriminate, distinguish, juxtapose, oppose, put side by side. 2 be at variance, clash, differ, diverge, oppose, set off

contribute *v* add, bestow, chip in *inf*, donate, endow, furnish, give, grant, pitch in *inf*, provide, subscribe, supply

contribution *n* donation, gift, grant, hand-out *inf*, offering, payment, present, subscription

contrive *v* concoct, construct, design, devise, engineer, improvise, invent

contrived *adj* artificial, forced, labored, unnatural

control *n* 1 authority, charge, command, discipline, dominance, influence, leadership, management, mastery, power, rule, supervision, supremacy. 2 (lose control) direction, grip, hold, restraint, self-control

control *v* 1 administer, be at the helm *inf*, be in charge, direct, dominate, govern, handle, have control, lead, look after, manage, manipulate, oversee, preside, rule, run, supervise. 2 (control a vehicle) command, pilot, steer. 3 (control your temper) bridle, check, constrain, curb, hold back, master, restrain, subdue

controversial *adj* arguable, at issue, contentious, controvertible, debatable, disputable, disputed, doubtful, open to question, questionable

controversy n altercation, argument, debate, disagreement, discussion, dispute, dissension, quarrel, row, squabble, wrangle

convene v assemble, bring together, call, come together, congregate, convoke, gather, meet, summon

convenience n accessibility, appropriateness, availability, expedience, fitness, handiness, suitability, timeliness, usefulness

convenient adj 1 (easy to use) accessible, at hand, available, close at hand, handy, labor-saving, nearby, neat, useful; **opp** inconvenient. 2 (suitable) appropriate, favorable, helpful, opportune, suitable, timely; **opp** inconvenient

convention n 1 code, custom, etiquette, matter of form, practice, propriety, protocol, tradition. 2 conclave, conference, congress, convocation, meeting

conventional adj 1 accepted, commonplace, correct, customary, expected, formal, mainstream, normal, ordinary, orthodox, proper, received, standard, straight, traditional, usual; **opp** unconventional. 2 (of people) conformist, conservative, pedestrian, reactionary, stuffy inf, unadventurous; **opp** unconventional

conversation n chat, dialogue, discussion, exchange, gossip, heart-to-heart inf, talk, tête-à-tête

converse v chat, communicate, discuss, have a conversation, speak, talk

conversion n adaptation, alteration, change, exchange, metamorphosis, modification, rebuilding, reorganization, substitution, transfiguration, transformation

convert v 1 alter, change, modify, reconstruct, reshape, transform, transmute, transpose, turn, switch. 2 (convert sb) change sb's mind, convince, persuade, reeducate, reform, rehabilitate, save, win

convey v 1 (take sth) bear, bring, carry, cart, ferry, fetch, move, send, shift, ship, take, transfer, transport. 2 (convey meaning) communicate, disclose, impart, imply, mean, reveal, signify, transmit

convict v condemn, find guilty, sentence; **opp** acquit

conviction n 1 assurance, certainty, confidence, earnestness, firmness. 2 belief, creed, faith, persuasion, principle

convince v assure, persuade, prove to, reassure, satisfy, sway, talk round, win over

convinced adj assured, certain, confident, persuaded, positive, satisfied, sure; **opp** uncertain

convincing adj 1 (of a theory) believable, cogent, compelling, credible, likely, logical, plausible, probable, valid; **opp** unconvincing. 2 (of a result) conclusive, decisive, impressive, unambiguous

convoy n caravan, company, escort, group, line

cool adj 1 chilled, chilly, cold, fresh, iced, lukewarm, nippy; **opp** warm. 2 calm, collected, composed, dignified, laid-back inf, self-possessed, sensible, together inf, unflustered, unruffled; **opp** flustered. 3 aloof, distant, indifferent, offhand, reserved, standoffish *inf*, unfriendly, unwelcoming; *opp* friendly, warm. **4** bold, brazen, cheeky, impudent, shameless. **5** streetwise *inf*, urbane; *opp* uncool. **6** brilliant, excellent, good, great, marvelous, splendid, terrific, wonderful; *opp* bad

cool *n* **1** coolness, freshness, coldness. **2** calmness, composure, control, poise, self-control

cool *v* become cold, chill, cool off, freeze, refrigerate; *opp* heat. **2** assuage, calm, dampen, diminish, lessen, reduce; *opp* inflame

cooperate *v* assist, collaborate, combine, help, join forces, pitch in *inf*, unite, work together

cooperation *n* assistance, collaboration, contribution, give-and-take, help, helpfulness, participation, support, teamwork, unity

cooperative *adj* **1** accommodating, constructive, helpful, keen, obliging, supportive, willing; *opp* unhelpful. **2** collaborative, collective, combined, communal, joint, mutual, shared; *opp* individual

coordinate *v* arrange, integrate, match, organize, synchronize

cope *v* carry on, get by, get through, make do, make out *inf*, manage, muddle through, survive

copious *adj* abundant, ample, bountiful, extensive, extravagant, full, generous, lavish, luxuriant, overflowing, plentiful, profuse, rich, unstinting

copy *n* carbon copy, clone, counterfeit, double, duplicate, facsimile, fake, forgery, image, imitation, likeness, model, pattern, photocopy, print, replica, representation, reproduction, transcript, twin

copy *v* **1** (make a copy of) counterfeit, duplicate, forge, photocopy, reproduce, replicate, transcribe. **2** (copy sb's work) crib, plagiarize, steal. **3** ape, echo, imitate, mimic, mirror, parrot, repeat

cordon *n* barrier, chain, fence, line, ring

core *n* center, crux, essence, gist, heart, inside, kernel, middle, nitty-gritty *inf*, nub, nucleus

corner *n* **1** angle, bend, intersection, joint, junction, turn, turning. **2** cranny, hideaway, hole, niche, nook, recess

corporation *n* business, company, conglomerate, firm, organization, partnership, trust

corpse *n* body, cadaver, carcass, dead body, remains, skeleton, stiff *inf*

correct *adj* **1** (of behavior) appropriate, conventional, proper, seemly, suitable; *opp* improper. **2** (of work) accurate, exact, faultless, flawless, perfect, right; *opp* wrong

correct *v* **1** (correct sth) adjust, alter, amend, cure, fix, improve, mark, put right, rectify, redress, remedy, repair, right. **2** (correct sb) admonish, chastise, criticize, discipline, punish, rebuke, reprimand, scold, tell off *inf*

correction *n* adjustment, alteration, amendment, improvement, rectification, revision

correspond *v* **1** communicate, exchange letters, keep in touch, write. **2** agree, be analogous, be consistent, be equivalent, be similar, coincide, compare, correlate, fit, match, tally

correspondence n 1 communication, letters, e-mail, mail, memoranda, notes, post, writing. 2 analogy, accord, conformity, correlation, resemblance, similarity

corresponding adj analogous, comparable, equivalent, matching, parallel, reciprocal, similar

corroborate v attest, authenticate, back up, bear out, confirm, endorse, establish, support, verify

corrode v abrade, consume, eat away, erode, gnaw, oxidize, rot, rust, tarnish, wear away

corrosive adj abrasive, caustic, corroding, destructive, eroding, virulent, wearing

corrupt adj bent inf, crooked, degenerate, depraved, dirty inf, dishonest, evil, fraudulent, immoral, perverted, rotten, sinful, unethical, unprincipled, untrustworthy, wicked; opp honest

corrupt v 1 bribe, buy off, deprave, fix inf, influence, lead astray, pervert, seduce, subvert, tempt, warp.
2 contaminate, debase, infect, taint

corruption n 1 bribery, dishonesty, extortion, fraud, profiteering, villainy.
2 (corruption in society) decadence, degeneration, depravity, evil, immorality, iniquity, perversion, sinfulness, vice, wickedness

cosmopolitan adj 1 (of people) cultured, sophisticated, urbane, well-traveled, worldly, worldly-wise. 2 (of a place) international, multiracial

cost n 1 amount, charge, damage inf, expenditure, expense, fare, figure, outlay, payment, price, quotation, rate, tariff, value, worth. 2 damage, detriment,

harm, hurt, loss, penalty, sacrifice, suffering

cost v be priced at, be valued at, be worth, come to, fetch, go for, realize, sell at, sell for, set you back

council n assembly, board, cabinet, chamber, committee, convocation, governing body, house, local authority, panel, parliament, synod

counsel n advice, direction, guidance, information, opinion, recommendation, suggestion, warning

counsel v advise, advocate, caution, discuss, exhort, give help, recommend, urge, warn

count v 1 add, add up, calculate, compute, enumerate, estimate, figure out, number, reckon, score, tally, tot up, work out. 2 be important, be of account, carry weight, have significance, matter, mean sth, signify. 3 count on bank on, believe in, depend on, put your faith in, rely on, swear by, trust

counter v answer, combat, come back at inf, contradict, dispute, oppose, rebut, refute, reply, resist, respond, retaliate

counteract v be an antidote to, cancel out, check, counterbalance, cross, defeat, foil, frustrate, hinder, invalidate, negate, neutralize, offset, resist, thwart, work against

counterfeit adj artificial, bogus, copied, ersatz, faked, false, feigned, forged, fraudulent, imitation, phony inf, pretend inf, pseudo- inf, sham, simulated, spurious, synthetic; opp genuine

counterfeit v copy, fabricate, fake, falsify, forge, sham, simulate

countless adj endless, immeasurable,

incalculable, infinite, innumerable, myriad, numerous, untold, without end, without limit

country n 1 empire, kingdom, nation, principality, realm, state. 2 fatherland, homeland, land of your birth, motherland, native land. 3 (people) citizens, inhabitants, nation, people, populace, public, society, voters. 4 countryside, farmland, green belt, provinces, rural area, sticks, wilds. 5 (landscape) area, land, landscape, scenery, terrain, territory

coup n 1 accomplishment, achievement, deed, exploit, feat, maneuver, stratagem, stroke, stunt, tour de force. 2 coup d'etat, overthrow, revolt, revolution

couple n brace, duo, pair, twosome

courage n boldness, bravery, daring, determination, fearlessness, fortitude, gallantry, guts inf, heroism, intrepidity, nerve, pluck, resolution, spirit, valor; opp cowardice

courageous adj bold, brave, daring, fearless, gutsy sl, heroic, indomitable, intrepid, plucky, stout-hearted, tough, unafraid, undaunted, valiant; opp cowardly

course n 1 advance, continuity, development, flow, march, movement, progress, progression, sequence, succession, unfolding. 2 channel, circuit, direction, line, orbit, passage, path, road, route, tack, track, trail, trajectory, way. 3 circuit, lap, race, racecourse, round. 4 classes, curriculum, lectures, program, studies, syllabus

court n 1 cloister, courtyard, piazza, plaza, quad inf, quadrangle, square, yard.

2 assizes, bar, bench, court of justice, court of law, law court, tribunal. 3 castle, palace, royal residence. 4 attendants, entourage, followers, retinue, royal household

court v 1 (court sb) date, go out with, make advances to, run after, woo. 2 (court sth) ask for inf, attract, bring on yourself, crave, invite, provoke, risk, seek

courteous adj attentive, chivalrous, civil, considerate, gallant, gracious, polite, refined, respectful, well-mannered; opp rude

courtesy n 1 chivalry, civility, courteousness, good breeding, good manners, politeness, respect. 2 (as a courtesy) benefit, consideration, favor, indulgence, kindness, service

courtyard n area, court, enclosure, forecourt, patio, quad inf, quadrangle, square, yard

cover n 1 blanket, canopy, cap, case, coating, covering, lid, roof, top, wrapper. 2 (blow sb's cover) disguise, facade, front, pretense, smokescreen. 3 (seek cover) concealment, hiding place, protection, refuge, sanctuary. 4 (insurance) compensation, indemnity, insurance, protection

cover v 1 (cover sth) blanket, carpet, bury, cloak, clothe, coat, conceal, disguise, drape, encase, enclose, envelop, hide, house, mask, obscure, plaster, screen, shade, sheathe, shelter, shroud, veil, wrap. 2 (stand in for sb) fill in, relieve, replace, stand in, take over. 3 (cover a story) describe, investigate, recount, report, write up. 4 (cover a topic) contain, deal with, encompass, include, incorporate, involve, take in, treat. **5 cover up** conceal, hide, hush up, keep secret, repress, suppress

covering n blanket, canopy, casing, cladding, coat, coating, cover, film, layer, rind, sheet, skin, surface, veneer, wrapping

covet v crave, desire, hanker after, long for, lust after, set your heart on, thirst for, want, wish for, yearn for

coward n chicken sl, scaredy-cat inf, wimp inf

cowardly adj fainthearted, fearful, gutless inf, lily-livered, scared, soft, spineless, timorous, weak, wimpish inf, yellow inf; **opp** brave

cower v cringe, crouch, draw back, flinch, grovel, hide, quail, recoil, shrink, skulk, tremble

coy adj bashful, demure, diffident, evasive, flirtatious, modest, reticent, shy, self-conscious

cozy adj **1** (of a house) comfortable, comfy inf, homely, safe, secure, sheltered, snug, warm; **opp** drafty. **2** (a cozy chat) easy, friendly, intimate, reassuring; **opp** awkward

crack n (break in sth) break, chink, chip, cleft, crevice, fissure, flaw, fracture, gap, opening, rift, slit, split. **2** (sound) burst, clap, crash, explosion, pop. **3** (have a crack at sth) (inf) go inf, stab inf, try. **4** (funny remark) (inf) dig inf, gag inf, insult, jibe, joke, quip, wisecrack, witticism

crack v **1** (be broken) break, chip, craze, fracture, fragment, snap, splinter, split. **2** (of thunder) boom, crackle, go bang,

resound, ring out. **3** (hit a part of your body) bang, bash, bump, clout, hit, knock, smack, strike, whack. **4** (of people) break down, collapse, give way, go to pieces, lose control, succumb, yield

cracked adj broken, chipped, crazed, damaged, faulty, flawed, imperfect, split

craft n **1** ability, art, artistry, craftsmanship, expertise, handiwork, knack, skill, technique, workmanship. **2** aircraft, boat, ship, spacecraft, vessel

crafty adj artful, calculating, canny, clever, conniving, cunning, deceitful, devious, dodgy inf, furtive, guileful, scheming, sharp, shifty, shrewd, sly, sneaky inf, wily

cram v compact, compress, crowd, crush, fill, force, jam, overcrowd, overfill, pack, press, squeeze, stuff

cramped adj awkward, close, closed in, confined, congested, crowded, hemmed in, narrow, overcrowded, packed, restricted, small, tight, uncomfortable; **opp** spacious

crash n **1** bang, boom, clang, clash, din, explosion, racket, thunder. **2** accident, bump, collision, disaster, pile-up inf, smash. **3** (financial) bankruptcy, collapse, depression, failure, fold, ruin

crash v **1** bang, batter, boom, clash, clatter, dash, shatter, smash, splinter. **2** dive, fall, give way, hurtle, lurch, overbalance, pitch, plummet, plunge, topple, tumble. **3** (of a vehicle) crash into, collide, hit, plough into, smash into. **4** (of a driver) bump, crash-land, drive into, wreck, write off. **5** (of a business) collapse, fail, fold, go bust inf, go to the wall inf, go under

crate n box, case, container, packing case, tea chest

crater n chasm, depression, dip, hole, hollow, pit

crave v be dying for, cry out for *inf*, desire, fancy *inf*, hanker after, hope for, hunger after, long for, lust after, need, pine for, require, thirst for, want, yearn for

craving n addiction, appetite, desire, hankering, hope, hunger, longing, lust, need, thirst, urge, yearning

crawl v 1 clamber, creep, drag yourself, edge, go on all fours, inch, move on hands and knees, pull yourself along, slither, worm your way, wriggle, writhe. 2 be obsequious, flatter, grovel, humble yourself, suck up *sl*

craze n enthusiasm, fad, fashion, infatuation, mania, novelty, obsession, passion, pastime, rage, thing *inf*, trend, vogue

crazy adj 1 berserk, cracked *sl*, crazed, delirious, demented, deranged, hysterical, idiotic, insane, loopy *inf*, lunatic, mad, maniacal, nuts *sl*, touched, unbalanced, unhinged; *opp* sane. 2 (of ideas) bizarre, confused, eccentric, fantastic, impractical, odd, outrageous, peculiar, ridiculous, silly, strange, wacko *sl*, weird, wild, zany; *opp* sensible. 3 **crazy about sth** enthusiastic, fanatical, fervent, keen, mad, nuts *inf*, passionate

creak v grate, grind, jar, rasp, scrape, scratch, screech, squeak, squeal

cream n liniment, lotion, ointment, paste, salve

crease n corrugation, crinkle, fold, furrow, groove, line, pleat, pucker, ridge, tuck, wrinkle

crease v crimp, crinkle, crumple, crush, fold, furrow, groove, pleat, pucker, ridge, rumple, wrinkle

create v bring into being, build, coin, compose, conceive, concoct, construct, design, develop, devise, dream up *inf*, establish, forge, formulate, found, generate, give life to, hatch, initiate, invent, make, originate, produce, shape, think up

creation n 1 beginning, birth, building, establishment, formation, foundation, generation, genesis, inception, making, origin, procreation, setting up. 2 (sth a person has made) achievement, brainchild, concoction, handiwork, invention, masterpiece, opus, pièce de résistance, work, work of art

creative adj artistic, fertile, imaginative, inspired, inventive, original, productive, visionary

creativity n imagination, ingenuity, inspiration, inventiveness, originality, productivity, talent

creator n architect, author, designer, inventor, maker, producer, writer

creature n animal, beast, being, brute, living thing, organism

credentials n authorization, certificate, diploma, documentation, documents, identity card, license, passport, permit, proof of identity, recommendation, reference, testimonial, warrant

credible adj believable, conceivable, convincing, imaginable, likely, persuasive, plausible, possible, reasonable; *opp* unbelievable

credit n acknowledgment, approval, commendation, distinction, esteem, fame, glory, honor, kudos, merit, praise, prestige, recognition, thanks, tribute

credit v 1 (accept that sth is true) accept, believe, buy inf, fall for inf, have faith in, swallow inf, trust; opp doubt. 2 (give sb credit for sth) accredit, ascribe to, assign to, attribute, chalk up to, impute to

credulity n blind faith, credulousness, greenness, gullibility, naiveté; opp skepticism

creed n articles of faith, belief, canon, catechism, credo, doctrine, dogma, principles, statement of beliefs, teaching, tenet

creep v 1 (of creatures) crawl, glide, slither, squirm, worm, wriggle, writhe. 2 (of people) crawl, dawdle, drag yourself, edge, go on all fours, inch, move on hands and knees, move quietly, move slowly, move stealthily, pussyfoot, skulk, slink, sneak, steal, tiptoe. 3 bow and scrape, butter up inf, curry favor, flatter, grovel, suck up sl

crest n 1 (of a hill) apex, brow, crown, peak, pinnacle, ridge, summit, top. 2 (feathers) comb, plume, tassel, mane, tuft. 3 (family crest) badge, bearing, coat of arms, device, emblem, heraldic device, insignia, regalia, seal, shield, symbol

crestfallen adj dejected, depressed, despondent, disappointed, disconsolate, disheartened, dispirited, downcast, downhearted; opp cheerful

crevice n chink, cleft, crack, cranny, fissure, rift, slit, split

crew n 1 band, company, corps, force, gang, party, posse, squad, team. 2 (on a ship) hands, sailors, ship's company

crime n 1 (a crime) felony, misdeed, misdemeanor, offense, outrage, transgression, unlawful act, violation, wrong. 2 (crime in general) delinquency, dishonesty, lawbreaking, lawlessness, wrongdoing

criminal adj 1 bent inf, corrupt, crooked inf, culpable, dishonest, evil, illegal, illicit, immoral, unlawful, villainous, wicked, wrong. 2 deplorable, immoral, reprehensible, scandalous, shameful, shocking, wrong

criminal n con inf, convict, crook inf, culprit, delinquent, desperado, felon, jailbird, lawbreaker, miscreant, offender, outlaw, sinner, villain, wrongdoer

cringe v cower, draw back, duck, flinch, quail, recoil, shrink, shy away, tremble, wince

cripple v 1 (cripple sb) disable, enfeeble, handicap, incapacitate, make sb lame, maim, paralyze, weaken. 2 (cripple sth) damage, mutilate, paralyze, put out of action, ruin, sabotage, spoil

crisis n 1 calamity, catastrophe, dilemma, dire straits, disaster, emergency, predicament, quandary, trouble. 2 climax, critical point, crunch inf, crux, height, moment of truth, turning point

crisp adj 1 (of food) breakable, crispy, crumbly, crunchy, dry, firm, fresh; opp soggy. 2 (of the wind) bracing, brisk, cool, fresh, invigorating, refreshing

criterion n benchmark, gauge, measure, norm, principle, rule, scale, standard, test, touchstone, yardstick

critic n 1 commentator, connoisseur, expert, judge, pundit, reviewer. 2 attacker, backbiter, detractor, faultfinder, nit-picker *inf*; *opp* supporter

critical *adj* 1 carping, censorious, criticizing, derogatory, disapproving, disparaging, fault-finding, hypercritical, judgmental, nagging, niggling, nit-picking *inf*, quibbling, uncomplimentary, unfavorable; *opp* complimentary.
2 (a critical moment) deciding, decisive, important, key, momentous, pivotal.
3 (a critical situation) crucial, dangerous, grave, perilous, risky, serious, touch-and-go, urgent

criticism *n* 1 (criticism in general) bad press, censure, character assassination, condemnation, disapproval, disparagement, fault-finding, outcry, stick *sl*; *opp* approval. 2 complaint, diatribe, rebuke, reprimand, reproach, tirade. 3 (a criticism) analysis, appraisal, appreciation, assessment, comment, critique, evaluation, judgment, review

criticize *v* blame, castigate, censure, complain, condemn, disapprove, disparage, find fault, give flak *inf*, knock *inf*, nag, nit-pick *inf*, pick holes, slam *inf*; *opp* praise

croak *v* caw, gasp, grunt, speak hoarsely, speak huskily, squawk, wheeze

crook *n* cheat, criminal, robber, rogue, swindler, thief, villain

crooked *adj* 1 (not straight) bent, bowed, contorted, curved, curving, deformed, distorted, gnarled, irregular, misshapen, twisted, twisting, warped, winding, zigzag; *opp* straight. 2 (not even) askew, aslant, asymmetric, at an angle, awry, lopsided, off-center, slanted, slanting, sloping, tilted, uneven, unsymmetrical.
3 (not honest) bent *sl*, corrupt, criminal,

deceitful, dishonest, dubious, fraudulent, illegal, questionable, shady *inf*, shifty, underhand; *opp* honest

crop *n* fruits, gathering, harvest, produce, season's growth, sowing, vintage, yield

crop *v* 1 clip, cut, lop, mow, pare, prune, shear, shorten, snip, trim. 2 **crop up** arise, come up, emerge, happen, occur, turn up

cross *adj* angry, annoyed, bad-tempered, disagreeable, fractious, fretful, grouchy, grumpy *inf*, ill-humored, in a bad mood, irritable, irritated, short, short-tempered, sullen, surly, testy, upset, vexed; *opp* cheerful

cross *n* 1 crucifix, rood. 2 amalgam, blend, combination, cross-breed, hybrid, hybridization, mix, mixture, mongrel

cross *v* 1 (cross a river) bridge, cut across, ford, pass over, span, traverse.
2 (of lines) crisscross, intersect, intertwine, meet, zigzag. 3 (of breeds) blend, cross-breed, cross-fertilize, cross-pollinate, interbreed, mix. 4 **cross out** cancel, delete, obliterate, strike out

crossing *n* 1 crossroads, intersection, junction, pedestrian crossing. 2 (a rough crossing) journey, passage, ride, trip, voyage

crouch *v* bend down, bow, duck, kneel, squat, stoop

crowd *n* 1 (group of people) army, bevy, bunch, circle, clique, company, flock, gang, group, herd, horde, host, lot, mass, mob, multitude, pack, rabble, set, swarm, throng. 2 (people watching sth) audience, gate, house, spectators, turnout

crowd *v* assemble, cluster, concentrate,

congregate, cram, flock, gather, huddle, jam, pile *inf*, press, push, squeeze, stuff, surge, swarm, throng

crowded adj busy, congested, cramped, crushed, full, jam-packed *inf*, packed, swarming, teeming

crown n 1 circlet, coronet, diadem, tiara. 2 apex, brow, head, peak, ridge, summit, top

crown v 1 anoint, appoint, enthrone, inaugurate, invest, install. 2 be the climax of, be the culmination of, cap, complete, consummate, finish, fulfill, put the finishing touch to, round off, top

crucial adj central, critical, decisive, determining, essential, high-priority, important, major, momentous, pivotal, significant

crude adj 1 coarse, crass, dirty, gross, indecent, indelicate, lewd, obscene, raunchy *inf*, smutty, tasteless, uncouth, vulgar. 2 natural, unprocessed, unrefined. 3 awkward, clumsy, inelegant, makeshift, primitive, rough, rough-and-ready, rudimentary, sketchy, undeveloped, unfinished, unskillful; *opp* sophisticated

cruel adj 1 (of people) barbaric, barbarous, brutal, callous, cold-blooded, fiendish, hard-hearted, heartless, inhuman, malevolent, merciless, murderous, pitiless, ruthless, sadistic, savage, spiteful, stony-hearted, unfeeling, unkind, vengeful, vicious; *opp* kind. 2 (of conditions) atrocious, bitter, fierce, grim, hard, harsh, hellish, painful, raw, severe, unrelenting

cruise v coast, drift, move, sail, travel, voyage

crumb n bit, bite, grain, morsel, particle, scrap, shred, speck

crumble v 1 (of food) break into pieces, break up, crush, granulate, grind, pound, powder, pulverize. 2 (of materials) come to dust, decay, decompose, disintegrate, fall apart, fall to pieces, molder, perish, rot

crumple v crease, crinkle, crush, fold, pucker, rumple, wrinkle

crunch v bite, chew, chomp, crush, munch, scrunch *inf*, smash, squash

crusade n campaign, cause, drive, holy war, jihad, military campaign, movement, struggle

crush v 1 break, bruise, compress, crumble, crunch, grind, mangle, mash, pound, press, pulp, pulverize, shatter, smash, squeeze. 2 (of fabric) crease, crinkle, crumple, rumple, wrinkle. 3 conquer, defeat, overcome, overpower, put down, quash, quell, stamp out, subdue, thrash, vanquish. 4 (crush sb's spirit) chagrin, humiliate, mortify, shame

crust n coating, covering, outer layer, outside, rind, scab, shell, skin, surface, topping

crux n core, essence, gist, heart, nub, point

cry n 1 bellow, howl, scream, shriek, shout, whoop, yell, yelp. 2 blub *inf*, howl, keening, lamentation, sob, sobbing, wail, weep, weeping

cry v 1 bawl, blubber, grizzle, howl, lament, shed tears, snivel, sob, wail, weep, whimper, whine. 2 bawl, bellow, call, call out, exclaim, roar, scream, screech, shout, shriek, sing out, yell

cryptic *adj* coded, enigmatic, hidden, mysterious, mystical, obscure, puzzling, secret, unclear, veiled; *opp* clear, obvious

cuddle *v* 1 clasp, embrace, fondle, hold closely, hug, kiss, neck *inf*, pet, smooch *inf*. 2 curl up, nestle, snuggle

cue *n* hint, nod, prompt, reminder, sign, signal, suggestion

culminate *v* build up to, climax, close, come to a crescendo, come to a head, conclude, end, finish, peak, terminate

culprit *n* bad guy *inf*, delinquent, guilty party, miscreant, offender, person responsible, wrongdoer

cult *n* 1 church, denomination, faction, group, order, party, religion, sect

cultivate *v* 1 dig, farm, fertilize, grow, harvest, hoe, plant, plough, prepare, produce, raise, sow, take cuttings, tend, till, turn, work. 2 court, develop, devote yourself to, encourage, foster, improve, promote, pursue, support. 3 civilize, educate, enlighten, polish, refine, train

cultivation *n* 1 agriculture, farming, gardening, growing, horticulture. 2 advancement, development, encouragement, fostering, furtherance, promotion, support

cultural *adj* 1 (cultural experiences) artistic, broadening, civilizing, edifying, educational, elevating, enriching, highbrow, improving. 2 (cultural diversity) ethnic, racial

culture *n* 1 civilization, customs, lifestyle, mores, society, way of life. 2 (person of culture) education, enlightenment, erudition, good taste, refinement, sophistication

cultured *adj* accomplished, civilized, cultivated, educated, enlightened, erudite, genteel, intellectual, knowledgeable, learned, refined, scholarly, versed, well-educated, well-read; *opp* ignorant

cunning *adj* artful, astute, canny, clever, crafty, devious, guileful, imaginative, ingenious, resourceful, sharp, shrewd, subtle, wily

cup *n* 1 beaker, chalice, glass, goblet, mug, tankard, tumbler. 2 prize, trophy

curb *v* bite back, bridle, check, constrain, contain, control, hinder, hold back, impede, inhibit, keep in check, limit, moderate, muzzle, put a brake on, repress, restrain, restrict, suppress

cure *n* 1 antidote, cure-all, medication, medicine, palliative, panacea, prescription, remedy, solution, therapy, treatment. 2 convalescence, healing, improvement, progress, recovery

cure *v* 1 (make sb better) heal, make better, make well, rehabilitate, restore to health, treat. 2 (put sth right) correct, fix, put right, rectify, remedy, repair, solve. 3 (preserve food) dry, preserve, salt, smoke

curiosity *n* 1 inquisitiveness, interest, interference, meddling, nosiness *inf*, prying, snooping. 2 (sth unusual) freak, novelty, oddity, phenomenon, rarity, spectacle

curious *adj* 1 (a curious mind) inquiring, inquisitive, interested, probing, puzzled, questioning. 2 (nosy) inquisitive, interfering, intrusive, meddlesome, meddling, nosy *inf*, prying, snooping. 3 (a curious object) bizarre, exotic, mysterious, novel, odd, puzzling, strange, unusual, wonderful

curl v 1 bend, coil, corkscrew, curve, entwine, loop, meander, ripple, snake, spiral, turn, twine, twirl, twist, wind, wreathe, writhe. 2 (of hair) corkscrew, crimp, crinkle, frizz, kink, perm, wave

curly adj curling, crimped, crinkly, frizzy, fuzzy, permed, wavy; *opp* straight

current adj 1 alive, contemporary, continuing, existing, fashionable, happening inf, in inf, in fashion, in vogue, living, modern, now inf, popular, present, present-day, prevailing, trendy inf, up-to-date; *opp* old, outdated

current n 1 (of water) course, drift, flow, river, stream, tide, undercurrent, undertow. 2 (of air) draft, movement, thermal, wind

curriculum n course, program, syllabus

curse n 1 bad language, blasphemy, expletive, oath, obscenity, profanity, swear word. 2 (put a curse on sb) evil eye, imprecation, jinx. 3 affliction, bane, evil, hardship, misfortune, plague, scourge, tribulation

curse v 1 be foul-mouthed, blaspheme, cuss inf, swear, take God's name in vain, use bad language. 2 damn, jinx, put a curse on, put a jinx on, put the evil eye on

cursory adj brief, careless, casual, desultory, fleeting, hasty, hurried, perfunctory, quick, superficial

curtail v abbreviate, break off, cut short, dock, pare down, reduce, restrict, shorten, stop, terminate, trim; *opp* extend

curve n arc, arch, bend, bow, bulge, camber, circle, crescent, curvature, half-moon, loop, spiral, twist, undulation

curve v arc, arch, bend, bow, coil, curl, loop, meander, snake, swerve, swirl, turn, twist, wind

curved adj arched, bent, bowed, concave, convex, crooked, curvilinear, curvy, humped, rounded, sinuous, twisted, undulating

custody n 1 (in custody) arrest, detention, imprisonment, incarceration. 2 (in sb's custody) care, charge, control, guardianship, keeping, possession, protection, safe-keeping, supervision, trusteeship

custom n convention, etiquette, form, formality, habit, manner, observance, practice, ritual, routine, tradition, usage, way, wont

customary adj accepted, common, conventional, established, everyday, familiar, general, habitual, normal, ordinary, regular, routine, traditional, typical, usual

customer n buyer, client, consumer, patron, purchaser, regular inf, shopper

cut n 1 gash, graze, groove, incision, laceration, nick, opening, rent, rip, slash, slit, snip, split, tear, wound. 2 cutback, economy, fall, lowering, reduction, saving

cut v 1 (injure sb) gash, gouge, graze, knife, lacerate, lance, nick, open, sever, slash, snick, stab, wound. 2 (cut sth) carve, chip, chisel, chop, cleave, clip, crop, dice, dissect, divide, engrave, grate, guillotine, hack, hew, lop, mow, notch, pare, pierce, prune, saw, score, sculpt, shave, shear, shred, slice, slit, whittle. 3 (reduce) abbreviate, abridge, condense, curtail, cut back, decrease, delete, economize, edit, excise, lessen, rationalize, reduce, retrench, shorten, slash, slim down, trim, truncate; *opp* increase. **4 cut down** bring down, chop down, fell, flatten, hew, level, lop, raze. **5 cut off** break off, disconnect, interrupt, isolate, remove, separate, sever, suspend. **6 cut out** delete, excise, extract, remove. **7 cut up** carve, chop, dice, divide, mince, slice

cutback *n* cut, decrease, economy, reduction

cutthroat *adj* **1** bloodthirsty, bloody, cruel, ferocious, fierce, homicidal, murderous, savage, violent. **2** competitive, dog-eat-dog, fierce, merciless, relentless, ruthless, unprincipled

cutting *adj* acerbic, acid, barbed, biting, hurtful, incisive, malicious, sarcastic, scathing, sharp, stinging, spiteful, trenchant, wounding

cycle *n* circle, revolution, rotation, round, sequence, series, succession

cynic *n* doubting Thomas, killjoy, pessimist, skeptic

cynical *adj* doubting, full of doom and gloom, negative, pessimistic, skeptical, scornful, sneering; *opp* optimistic

cynicism *n* doubt, pessimism, skepticism, scorn, suspicion

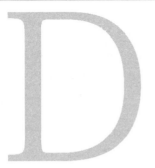

dagger *n* blade, knife, sheath knife

daily *adj, adv* common, day-to-day, everyday, regular, routine, usual

dainty *adj* delicate, elegant, fine, graceful, neat, petite, pretty

dam *n* 1 barrage, barricade, barrier, wall, weir. 2 artificial lake, lake, reservoir

dam *v* barricade, block, check, dam up, hold back, stop

damage *n* abuse, detriment, devastation, harm, havoc, hurt, injury, loss, sabotage, vandalism

damage *v* bend, break, bruise, bump, bust *inf*, chip, crack, crash, deface, dent, harm, hurt, impair, injure, rip, ruin, sabotage, scrape, scratch, spoil, tear, vandalize, warp, wreck

damaging *adj* critical, detrimental, discreditable, disparaging, harmful, hurtful, injurious, prejudicial

damp *adj* clammy, dank, humid, misty, moist, muggy, soggy, steamy, sticky, wet; *opp* dry

damp *n* clamminess, dampness, humidity, moisture, mist, mugginess, steaminess, wetness

dance *n* ball, ballet, bop *inf*, dancing, disco, hop, jig, square dance

dance *v* cavort, do a jig, jive, leap about, shake a leg *inf*, smooch, sway, take the floor, twirl, waltz

danger *n* hazard, jeopardy, menace, peril, pitfall, risk, threat

dangerous *adj* chancy, daredevil, foolhardy, hairy *inf*, hazardous, life-threatening, nasty, perilous, risky, ugly, unsafe; *opp* safe

dare *n* challenge, provocation, taunt

dare *v* 1 challenge, defy, goad, provoke, taunt, throw down the gauntlet. 2 brave, have the courage, have the guts *inf*, have the nerve, pluck up the courage, risk, take the plunge, take the risk, venture

daring *adj* adventurous, audacious, bold, brave, fearless, rash, wild; *opp* timid

dark *adj* 1 black, cloudy, dim, dingy, gloomy, inky, overcast, poorly lit, shadowy, unlit; *opp* bright, light. 2 (of complexion) black, brown, dark-skinned, olive, swarthy, tanned; *opp* pale. 3 (of colors) deep, dense, rich; *opp* light

dark *n* blackness, darkness, dusk, gloom, murkiness, night, nightfall, nighttime, shade, shadows, twilight

darken *v* blacken, cloud over, dim, get dark, grow dim, make dark, shade

darkness *n* blackness, dark, dusk, gloom, murkiness, night, nightfall, nighttime, shade, shadows, twilight

darling *n* dear, dearest, love, pet,

sweetheart, sweetie

dart v bolt, dash, fly, hop, hurtle, nip, race, run, rush, scuttle, shoot, sprint, tear

dash v 1 bolt, charge, chase, fly, hurry, hurtle, race, run, rush, speed, sprint, tear, zoom inf. 2 crash, fling, hurl, pitch, slam, smash, throw

data n details, facts, figures, information, statistics

date n 1 age, day, day and age, epoch, era, period, time, vintage, year. 2 appointment, assignation, engagement, meeting, rendezvous

dated adj ancient, antiquated, fuddy-duddy inf, fusty, obsolete, old, old-fashioned, old-hat, outmoded, passé, stale, unfashionable; **opp** latest, modern, up-to-date

daunting adj disconcerting, discouraging, frightening, intimidating, overwhelming, scary, terrifying, unnerving

dawdle v amble, dilly-dally, drag your feet, go slowly, hang about, lag behind, linger, loiter, saunter, shilly-shally, take your time, waste time; **opp** rush

dawn n 1 crack of dawn, daybreak, daylight, first light, start of the day, sunrise, sun-up; **opp** dusk, sunset. 2 advent, beginning, birth, genesis, onset, start; **opp** end

dawn v 1 begin, break, come into being, emerge, start. 2 (sth dawns on you) come to you, enter your mind, flash across your mind, hit, occur to you, register, strike

day n 1 daytime, daylight; **opp** night. 2 age, date, day and age, epoch, era,

generation, period, point in time, time

daybreak n crack of dawn, dawn, daylight, first light, start of the day, sunrise, sun-up; **opp** dusk, sunset

daydream n castle in the air, dream, fantasy, pipe-dream, reverie

daydream v be in your own little world, be lost in thought, dream, fantasize, imagine, let your thoughts wander, stare into space

daze v bemuse, bewilder, confuse, floor inf, numb, shock, stagger, stun, stupefy

dazed adj bemused, bewildered, confused, dizzy, floored inf, fuddled, muddled, numbed, shocked, staggered, stunned, stupefied

dazzle v 1 blind, confuse, disorientate. 2 bedazzle, bowl over inf, impress, overwhelm, stagger, stun, take your breath away

dazzling adj amazing, brilliant, glittering, magnificent, sensational, sparkling, splendid, terrific, stunning

dead adj 1 deceased, departed, late, lifeless, no more, out of your misery, passed away, pushing up the daisies inf, six feet under inf, stillborn; **opp** alive. 2 (obsolete) extinct, obsolete; **opp** living. 3 (unresponsive) cold, emotionless, indifferent, inert, lifeless, numb, paralyzed, unresponsive, without feeling, wooden. 4 (not working) broken, defunct, had it, kaput, out of order, worn out; **opp** working. 5 boring, dreary, dull, flat, lifeless, uninteresting; **opp** lively

deaden v blunt, dull, muffle, numb, soothe, smother, stifle, suppress

deadlock n checkmate, dead end,

impasse, logjam, stalemate, standoff, standstill

deadly *adj* **1** fatal, lethal, malignant, noxious, poisonous, virulent. **2** (boring) awful, boring, dire, dull, tedious, terrible

deaf *adj* hard of hearing, stone deaf, with a hearing problem, with impaired hearing

deafen *v* make deaf, damage sb's hearing, hurt your ears

deafening *adj* at full blast, at full volume, blaring, ear-splitting, loud, roaring, thudding, thunderous

deal *n* agreement, arrangement, bargain, business deal, contract, pact, transaction, understanding, venture

deal *v* **1** (share out) allocate, allot, dish out, distribute, dole out, give, hand out, share out. **2 deal in** buy and sell, do business, handle, trade, traffic. **3 deal with** attend to, do, fix, handle, see to, sort *inf*, sort out, tackle, take care of, take on, take responsibility for

dealer *n* agent, broker, buyer, handler, retailer, seller, trader, vendor, wholesaler

dear *adj* **1** cost-a-fortune *inf*, costly, exorbitant, expensive, extortionate, high-priced, luxury, overpriced, pricey, steep *inf*, stiff *inf*, top-rate, up-market, upscale; *opp* cheap, inexpensive. **2** (much-loved) close, close to your heart, darling, intimate, loved, much-loved

dear *n* darling, dearest, love, pet, sweetheart, sweetie

death *n* **1** bloodshed, curtains *inf*, decease, demise, dying, end, fatality, killing, loss of life, massacre, slaughter. **2** (end) annihilation, destruction, downfall, end, eradication,

extermination, finish, obliteration, ruin

debase *v* cheapen, degrade, demean, devalue, discredit, disgrace, lower, shame, spoil, sully

debatable *adj* arguable, borderline, controversial, doubtful, dubious, iffy *inf*, open to question, questionable

debate *n* argument, deliberation, disagreement, discussion, dispute

debate *v* argue, deliberate, disagree, discuss, talk about

debris *n* detritus, dross, garbage, litter, remains, rubbish, rubble, trash, waste

debt *n* arrears, credit, dues, liability, loan, money owing, mortgage, overdraft

debut *n* appearance, entrance, first appearance, inauguration, introduction, launch, première

decadent *adj* corrupt, debauched, decaying, declining, degenerate, depraved, dissipated, dissolute, immoral, licentious, permissive

decay *n* collapse, corrosion, crumbling, death, decline, decomposition, disintegration, going bad, rot, rotting, putrefaction, withering away

decay *v* corrode, crumble, decompose, die, disintegrate, go bad, mold, rot, perish, putrefy, shrivel, waste away, wither

deceased *adj* dead, departed, late, no more, passed away, passed on

deceit *n* cheating, deception, dishonesty, disloyalty, double-dealing, duplicity, false pretenses, fraud, lying, misrepresentation, pretense, subterfuge, treachery, trickery, untruthfulness

deceitful *adj* bogus, crooked, dishonest, disloyal, double-dealing, false,

fraudulent, lying, sham, two-faced,
underhand, untrustworthy, untruthful;
opp honest

deceive *v* cheat, cheat on, con *inf*,
double-cross, dupe, fool, lead sb on,
mislead, hoodwink, pull a fast one, pull
the wool over sb's eyes, swindle, take for
a ride, take in, trick

decency *n* civility, courtesy, correctness,
dignity, good manners, honesty,
propriety, respectability

decent *adj* **1** courteous, dependable,
dignified, good, honest, honorable, nice,
proper, respectable, suitable, trustworthy,
upright, worthy. **2** (adequate)
acceptable, adequate, fair, good,
reasonable, sufficient

deception *n* **1** cheating, deceit,
dishonesty, double-dealing, duplicity,
false pretenses, fraud, lying,
misrepresentation, pretense, subterfuge,
treachery, trickery, untruthfulness. **2** con
inf, cover-up, dodge, fiddle *inf*, hoax, lie,
pretense, ruse, sham, swindle, trick

deceptive *adj* deceiving, false, illusory,
misleading, unreliable

decide *v* choose, come to a conclusion,
conclude, determine, give your verdict,
go for, make a decision, make up your
mind, opt for, resolve, settle, settle for,
settle on, take the plunge

decision *n* choice, conclusion, finding,
judgment, outcome, pronouncement,
resolution, result, ruling, verdict

decisive *adj* **1** definite, firm, forceful,
positive, resolute, self-confident, strong-
minded, sure of yourself, unfaltering,
unwavering; *opp* hesitant, indecisive,
tentative. **2** critical, crucial, deciding,

definitive, determining, key, pivotal,
significant

declaration *n* announcement, assertion,
decree, disclosure, edict, notice, press
release, proclamation, revelation,
statement

declare *v* affirm, announce, assert, claim,
contend, disclose, maintain, make
known, proclaim, profess, reveal, say,
state

decline *n* degeneration, deterioration,
downturn, downward trend, drop, fall,
reversal, slump

decline *v* **1** refuse, reject, say no, send
your apologies, turn down; *opp* accept.
2 decrease, degenerate, deteriorate,
diminish, dwindle, fade, fall, fall off, get
worse, go down, go downhill, go to the
dogs *inf*, peter out, sink, tail off, wane,
weaken; *opp* get better, improve,
increase

decorate *v* **1** do up *inf*, paint, paper,
refurbish, smarten up, wallpaper. **2** deck,
embellish, garnish, festoon, trim

decoration *n* **1** decor, color scheme.
2 bauble, embellishment, fancywork,
flounce, frill, garnish, ornamentation,
spangle, tinsel, trimmings

decorative *adj* nonfunctional,
ornamental, ornate; *opp* functional

decoy *n* bait, distraction, inducement,
lure, trap

decoy *v* attract, bait, entice, induce,
inveigle, lure, tempt

decrease *n* cutback, decline, downsizing,
downturn, drop, fall, let-up, reduction,
shrinkage; *opp* increase

decrease *v* abate, cut, cut back on,
decline, diminish, downsize, dwindle,

drop, fall off, go down, lessen, lower, peter out, reduce, subside, taper off; *opp* increase

decree *n* announcement, command, dictum, directive, edict, injunction, judgment, law, order, policy statement, regulation, rule, ruling

decree *v* announce, dictate, direct, lay down, prescribe, ordain, order, proclaim, pronounce, rule, say, state

decrepit *adj* broken-down, derelict, dilapidated, doddering, incapacitated, on its last legs, ramshackle, rickety, run-down, tottering, worn-out, wrecked

dedicate *v* 1 assign, commit, devote, give over to, pledge. 2 bless, consecrate, sanctify

dedicated *adj* committed, devoted, enthusiastic, keen, loyal, single-minded, wholehearted, zealous

dedication *n* 1 commitment, determination, devotion, keenness, loyalty, single-mindedness, zeal. 2 address, inscription, message

deduce *v* come to a conclusion, conclude, infer, gather, realize, surmise, understand, work out

deduct *v* allow, cut, discount, knock off *inf*, subtract, take away, take off; *opp* add

deduction *n* 1 allowance, cut, discount, markdown, rebate, reduction, stoppage, subtraction. 2 assumption, conclusion, inference, presumption, reasoning

deed *n* 1 achievement, act, action, effort, enterprise, exercise, exploit, feat, job, operation, undertaking. 2 agreement, contract, deed of covenant, document, indenture, paper, policy, proof of ownership, record, title deed

deep *adj* 1 abyssal, bottomless, cavernous, yawning; *opp* shallow. 2 broad, large, wide. 3 (of a voice) bass, booming, low, low-pitched, rich; *opp* high. 4 (of a color) dark, intense, rich, strong, vivid; *opp* light, pale. 5 (of an emotion) deep-rooted, deep-seated, heartfelt, intense, passionate, profound, strong; *opp* superficial

deface *v* damage, disfigure, mutilate, spoil, vandalize

default *v* backslide, be negligent, dodge, evade, fail to fulfill, fail to pay, fall into arrears, get behind, let sb down, shirk, stop payment, withhold payment

defeat *n* 1 conquest, drubbing *inf*, overthrow, rout, thrashing, trouncing, victory, win. 2 collapse, disappointment, downfall, failure, frustration, reverse, ruin; *opp* victory

defeat *v* annihilate, beat, conquer, foil, get the better of, hammer *inf*, get the upper hand, knock the socks off *inf*, knock the stuffing out of *inf*, outclass, overthrow, rout, thrash, thwart, topple, trounce, vanquish, wipe the floor with *inf*

defect *n* blemish, bug *inf*, deficiency, error, failing, fault, flaw, mistake, shortcoming, weakness, weak spot

defect *v* change sides, desert, desert the cause, go over to the other side, join the opposition, turn traitor

defective *adj* broken, damaged, faulty, flawed, malfunctioning, not working, out of order

defend *v* 1 fortify, guard, protect, safeguard, secure; *opp* attack. 2 champion, espouse, justify, speak up for, stand by, stand up for, support, uphold; **opp** attack

defendant n accused, appellant, culprit, litigant, offender, prisoner, respondent, suspect

defense n 1 (protection) barricade, bastion, cover, deterrent, fortification, fortress, protection, shelter, shield. 2 (military matters) armaments, armed forces, the military, weapons. 3 (justification) case, excuse, explanation, justification, vindication

defenseless adj exposed, helpless, impotent, powerless, unarmed, vulnerable, weak; **opp** strong

defensive adj 1 feeling accused inf, sensitive, uptight inf, wary. 2 protective

defer v adjourn, delay, hold over, postpone, put off, put on ice, put on the back burner, shelve, table

defiant adj belligerent, challenging, disobedient, noncompliant, intransigent, rebellious, recalcitrant, scornful, stubborn, uncooperative; **opp** compliant, submissive

deficiency n dearth, deficit, inadequacy, lack, scarcity, shortage

deficient adj inadequate, lacking, meager, scant, scarce, short, skimpy

deficit n arrears, deficiency, loss, shortage, shortfall

define v clarify, describe, elucidate, explain, give the meaning of, outline, set out, specify, spell out

definite adj 1 certain, confident, confirmed, guaranteed, positive, sure. 2 clear, clear-cut, explicit, marked, obvious, precise, unmistakable

definition n description, explanation, meaning

definitive adj 1 conclusive, decisive, final, unconditional. 2 authoritative, complete, exhaustive, reliable

deflect v bounce off, change course, divert, glance off, ricochet, shy, swerve, turn aside, veer

deformed adj contorted, damaged, disfigured, distorted, injured, maimed, malformed, misshapen, mutilated, twisted

defraud v cheat, con inf, embezzle, fleece, pull a fast one inf, rip off inf, rob, rook, sting inf, swindle, take sb for a ride

defunct adj deceased, dead, expired, extinct, gone, invalid, obsolete

defy v challenge, confront, disobey, disregard, flout, foil, frustrate, rebel against, resist, thumb your nose at inf, thwart, withstand

degenerate adj corrupt, decadent, degraded, depraved, dissolute, fallen, immoral, low, unacceptable

degenerate v decline, deteriorate, fall off, get worse, go downhill, go from bad to worse, go to rack and ruin, go to seed inf, go to the dogs inf, sink, slide

degrade v cheapen, debase, demean, devalue, discredit, disgrace, dishonor, downgrade, lower, shame

degrading adj demeaning, embarrassing, humiliating, mortifying, shameful, undignified

degree n amount, extent, intensity, level, limit, point, stage, standard

deign v bother, condescend, consent, lower yourself, stoop

deity n divinity, god, goddess, holy being, object of worship, spirit

dejected adj cut up inf, depressed, despairing, despondent, disappointed, discouraged, disgruntled, dispirited, down, downhearted, down in the dumps inf, gloomy, miserable, out of sorts, sad, with a long face

delay n break, hiatus, hitch, holdup, interruption, lull, postponement, setback, suspension, time-lag, wait

delay v 1 adjourn, defer, hold, hold over, postpone, put off, put on ice, put on the back burner, shelve, table. 2 detain, hold up, make late, slow down

delegate n agent, emissary, envoy, go-between, messenger, representative, spokesman, spokesperson, spokeswoman

delegate v 1 (a task) assign, devolve, hand over, pass on, transfer. 2 (a person) appoint, authorize, choose, empower, mandate

delegation n contingent, delegates, deputation, group, mission, representatives

delete v cancel, cut out, cross out, erase, get rid of, remove, rub out, strike out, take out, wipe out

deliberate adj 1 calculated, cold-blooded, conscious, intentional, knowing, preconceived, premeditated, willful; opp accidental, unintentional. 2 careful, determined, measured, methodical, painstaking, patient, ponderous, resolute, slow; opp hasty

deliberate v 1 (think about) consider, evaluate, mull over, ponder, reflect, review, ruminate, think over, think, weigh. 2 (discuss) consider, debate, discuss

deliberately adj 1 consciously, in cold-blood, intentionally, knowingly, on purpose, willfully, wittingly; opp accidentally, unintentionally. 2 carefully, determinedly, methodically, painstakingly, patiently, resolutely, slowly; opp hastily

delicacy n 1 daintiness, elegance, fineness, flimsiness, fragility, intricacy. 2 (sensitivity) care, diplomacy, discretion, sensitivity, tact. 3 (a luxury food) luxury, titbit, treat

delicate adj 1 dainty, elegant, fine, flimsy, fragile, graceful, intricate. 2 (pastel) muted, pale, pastel, soft, subtle, understated. 3 (sensitive) awkward, difficult, diplomatic, discreet, sensitive, tactful, tricky

delicious adj appetizing, gorgeous, mouth-watering, scrumptious, tasty, tempting, yummy inf

delight n amusement, ecstasy, elation, enjoyment, enthusiasm, excitement, happiness, joy, jubilation, pleasure, thrill

delight v amuse, captivate, cheer, enchant, entertain, excite, please, thrill, tickle

delighted adj captivated, ecstatic, enchanted, glad, happy, in raptures, jubilant, on cloud nine inf, on top of the world, overjoyed, pleased, thrilled, tickled pink inf

delightful adj agreeable, amusing, appealing, attractive, captivating, charming, cute, enchanting, engaging, enjoyable, entertaining, fascinating, lovely, nice, pleasant, pleasurable, thrilling, wonderful; opp unpleasant

delinquent n hoodlum, hooligan, rowdy, ruffian, thug, tough, troublemaker, vandal, young offender

delirious adj **1** demented, deranged, distracted, feverish, hallucinating, incoherent, lightheaded, rambling, raving. **2** carried away, ecstatic, euphoric, on a high inf

deliver v **1** (deliver goods) bring, dispatch, hand over, produce, send, supply, take, transfer, transport. **2** (deliver a speech or verdict) announce, declare, give, make, pronounce, read. **3** (deliver a ball or punch) administer, aim, deal, direct, hit, hurl, inflict, send, throw

delivery n **1** carriage, conveyance, dispatch, distribution, shipment, transfer, transport, transportation. **2** batch, consignment, load, shipment

deluge n **1** downpour, flash flood, flood, inundation, overflowing, rainstorm, torrent. **2** barrage, flood, rush, spate; *opp* trickle

delusion n dream, error, false impression, fancy, fantasy, hallucination, illusion, mirage, misapprehension, misbelief, misconception, mistake, misunderstanding; *opp* reality

demand n **1** appeal, claim, clamor, entreaty, insistence, pressure, request, requisition. **2** challenge, inquiry, interrogation, question. **3** (the demands of sth) exigency, necessity, need, requirement. **4 in demand** all the rage inf, fashionable, in vogue, popular, sought after, trendy inf

demand v **1** (ask for sth) appeal, ask, call for, claim, clamor for, cry out for, insist on, lay claim to, make a claim for, press for, request, urge. **2** (ask a

question) ask, challenge, inquire, interrogate, question. **3** call for, entail, involve, necessitate, need, require, take, want

demanding adj arduous, challenging, daunting, difficult, exacting, exhausting, grueling, hard, taxing, tiring, tough, trying, wearing; *opp* undemanding

demeanor n air, appearance, bearing, behavior, carriage, conduct, deportment, manner, mien

democratic adj autonomous, classless, egalitarian, free, of the people, popular, populist, representative, republican, self-governing; *opp* totalitarian

demolish v bulldoze, destroy, dismantle, flatten, knock down, level, pull down, raze, ruin, tear down, trash sl, wreck; *opp* build

demon n devil, evil spirit, fiend, goblin, imp, monster

demonstrate v **1** (demonstrate that sth is true) confirm, establish, indicate, prove, show, testify, validate, verify; *opp* disprove. **2** (demonstrate how to do sth) describe, explain, give a demonstration, give an idea of, illustrate, make clear, show how, teach. **3** lobby, march, parade, picket, protest, rally, sit in

demonstration n **1** (of the truth of sth) confirmation, evidence, illustration, proof, testimony, validation, verification. **2** (how to do sth) description, explanation, exposition, illustration, lesson, presentation. **3** lobby, march, parade, picket, protest, rally, sit-in

demonstrative adj affectionate, effusive, emotional, expressive, gushing, lovey-dovey *inf*, loving, open, uninhibited, unreserved, unrestrained; **opp** reticent

demoralize *adj* break, crush, daunt, depress, discourage, dishearten, dispirit, unnerve, weaken; **opp** encourage

demure *adj* bashful, coy, diffident, modest, quiet, reserved, reticent, retiring, sedate, shy, sober, staid, unassuming; **opp** wild

den *n* 1 cave, cavern, haunt, hideaway, hideout, hiding place, hole, lair, shelter. 2 retreat, sanctum, sanctuary

denial *n* backpedaling, disavowal, disclaimer, retraction, taking back; **opp** admission, confession. 2 (not allowing sb to do sth) prohibition, rebuff, refusal, rejection, thumbs-down *inf*, veto; **opp** permission

denote *v* be the sign for, express, indicate, mark, mean, represent, show, signal, signify, stand for, symbolize

denounce *v* 1 attack, castigate, condemn, criticize, damn, decry, revile, stigmatize, vilify; **opp** praise. 2 accuse, betray, blame, incriminate, report

dense *adj* 1 close, compact, compressed, concentrated, condensed, heavy, impenetrable, lush, opaque, solid, substantial, thick; **opp** thin. 2 bird-brained, brainless, clueless, dim *inf*, dopey, dumb, ignorant, simple, slow, stupid, thick *inf*, unintelligent; **opp** clever

dent *n* chip, crater, depression, dimple, dip, hollow, indentation

dent *v* buckle, crumple, depress, knock in, press in, push in

deny *v* 1 refute, retract, take back; **opp** admit, confess. 2 (deny sb sth) give

the thumbs down, prohibit, rebuff, refuse, reject, revoke, turn down, veto, withhold; **opp** allow

depart *v* abscond, be off *inf*, be on your way *inf*, clear off *inf*, disappear, emigrate, exit, go, go away, hit the road *inf*, leave, make tracks *inf*, migrate, move away, move off, quit, retire, retreat, split *inf*, take your leave, take yourself off, vanish, withdraw; **opp** arrive

department *n* 1 agency, branch, bureau, division, office, section, sector, subdivision, unit. 2 (sb's department) area, concern, domain, field, function, job, line, realm, responsibility, specialty, sphere. 3 canton, county, district, province, region, state, territory

departure *n* 1 disappearance, emigration, exit, exodus, going, leaving, migration, retreat, withdrawal; **opp** arrival. 2 (from the norm) deviation, difference, digression, divergence, shift, variation. 3 (a new departure) branching out, change, change of direction, innovation, novelty

depend *v* 1 bank on, be dependent on, cling to, count on, lean on, need, put your faith in, rely on, trust in, turn to. 2 be based on, be dependent on, be determined by, be subject to, hinge on, pivot on, rest on, revolve around

dependable *adj* consistent, faithful, reliable, reputable, responsible, sensible, stable, staunch, steadfast, trustworthy, trusty, unfailing; **opp** unreliable

dependent *adj* 1 conditional, contingent, controlled by, determined by, liable to, relative to, subject to. 2 (dependent children) defenseless, helpless, reliant, vulnerable, weak; **opp** independent

depict v describe, draw, illustrate, narrate, outline, paint, picture, portray, represent, reproduce, show, sketch

deplete v consume, cut, decrease, diminish, drain, empty, evacuate, exhaust, expend, impoverish, lessen, lower, reduce, use up

deplorable adj abominable, atrocious, awful, despicable, disgraceful, disreputable, dreadful, reprehensible, scandalous, shameful, shocking

deplore v abhor, censure, condemn, decry, denounce, deprecate, disapprove of, object to, regret; **opp** approve

deport v banish, exile, expatriate, expel, extradite, oust, remove, send abroad/overseas

depose v dethrone, dismiss, displace, get rid of, oust, overthrow, remove, topple, unseat

deposit n 1 advance payment, down-payment, initial payment, installment, part-payment, retainer, security, stake. 2 accumulation, layer, sediment, silt, sludge

depot n 1 arsenal, base, depository, repository, store, storehouse, warehouse. 2 bus station, terminal, terminus, train station

depraved adj base, corrupt, debased, debauched, degenerate, dissolute, evil, immoral, indecent, lewd, licentious, obscene, perverted, profligate, sinful, unprincipled, vicious, vile, wicked

depress v dampen your spirits, discourage, dishearten, dismay, dispirit, sadden, upset, weigh down; **opp** encourage

depressed adj blue, dejected, despondent, discouraged, disheartened, dismayed, dispirited, down, down in the dumps, downcast, fed up, gloomy, glum, low, melancholy, miserable, moody, morose, sad, saddened, unhappy, upset; **opp** cheerful

depressing adj black, bleak, discouraging, disheartening, dismal, dispiriting, distressing, dreary, gloomy, hopeless, melancholy, miserable, sad, somber; **opp** encouraging

depression n 1 dejection, desolation, despair, despondency, dolefulness, downheartedness, gloominess, hopelessness, low spirits, melancholy, misery, sadness, the blues, weariness; **opp** cheerfulness. 2 (economic) bad times, decline, hard times, recession, slump, stagnation; **opp** boom

deprive v deny, dispossess, rob, starve, strip, take away, withdraw

deprived adj bereft, destitute, disadvantaged, forlorn, in need, lacking, needy, poor; **opp** advantaged

depth n 1 deepness, drop, extent, measure, profundity. 2 (of forest) bowels, middle, midst; **opp** edge. 3 (of sea) bottom, deepest part; **opp** surface

deputy adj assistant, proxy, representative, second in command, sidekick, understudy, vice-chairman, vice-president

derelict adj abandoned, crumbling, decrepit, deserted, dilapidated, falling-down, neglected, ramshackle, ruined, rundown, tumbledown

derisory adj 1 (a derisory amount) contemptible, inadequate, insulting, laughable, ludicrous, outrageous, preposterous, ridiculous, tiny; **opp** fair. 2 (derisory remarks) contemptuous, derisive, jeering, mocking, scornful

derive v acquire, collect, draw, elicit, extract, gain, gather, get, glean, infer, lift, obtain, pick up, procure, receive

derogatory adj damaging, defamatory, disapproving, disparaging, injurious, insulting, offensive, uncomplimentary, unfavorable, unflattering; **opp** complimentary

descend v 1 come down, drop, fall, go down, move down, plummet, plunge, sink, tumble; **opp** rise. 2 (the path descends) go down, dip, incline, slant, slope; **opp** rise

descent n 1 dip, drop, fall, plunge, slump, swoop; **opp** rise. 2 (family background) ancestry, background, blood, extraction, genealogy, heredity, lineage, origin, parentage, stock

describe v define, depict, detail, explain, express, give a description, give an account, give details, illustrate, narrate, outline, portray, put into words, recount, relate, report, sketch, specify, tell

description n account, chronicle, depiction, explanation, illustration, narrative, outline, portrayal, report, representation, sketch

descriptive adj colorful, detailed, explanatory, expressive, graphic, illustrative, striking, vivid; **opp** bland

desecrate v abuse, contaminate, corrupt, debase, defile, degrade, dishonor, infect, pervert, pollute, profane, vandalize, violate; **opp** revere

desert n sand, waste, wasteland, wilderness, wilds

desert v abandon, forsake, give up, jilt, leave, leave high and dry, leave in the lurch, maroon, strand, turn your back on, walk out on

deserted adj abandoned, derelict, desolate, empty, forlorn, godforsaken, isolated, lonely, neglected, solitary, uninhabited, unoccupied, vacant; **opp** bustling

deserter n defector, escapee, fugitive, outlaw, renegade, runaway, traitor, truant

deserve v be entitled to, be worthy of, earn, gain, have a claim to, have a right to, justify, merit, rate, warrant, win

design n 1 (a design of a building) blueprint, draft, drawing, model, outline, plan, sketch. 2 (pattern) arrangement, motif, pattern, shape

design v 1 conceive, create, devise, draft, draw, draw up, hatch, invent, originate, outline, plan, sketch, think up. 2 **designed for** aimed at, intended for, tailor-made for

designer n architect, creator, inventor, originator, stylist

desirable adj 1 advantageous, advisable, beneficial, in sb's interest, profitable, worthwhile; **opp** undesirable. 2 (of a person) alluring, attractive, beguiling, erotic, fetching, seductive, sexually attractive; **opp** undesirable

desire n ambition, appetite, ardor, aspiration, craving, hunger, inclination, longing, lust, need, passion, preference, urge, wish, yearning

desire v aspire to, covet, crave, dream of, fancy, hanker after, have a yen for, hope for, hunger for, itch for *inf*, long for, lust after, set your heart on, set your sights on, strive for, thirst for, want, wish for, yearn for

desolate *adj* 1 (of a place) bare, barren, bleak, cheerless, deserted, dreary, godforsaken, inhospitable, isolated, remote, solitary, uninhabited, waste, wild. 2 (of a person) abandoned, alone, dejected, depressed, despairing, despondent, downcast, forlorn, gloomy, grieving, inconsolable, lonely, melancholy, miserable, neglected, sad, unhappy, wretched; *opp* cheerful

despair *n* defeatism, dejection, depression, desperation, despondency, distress, gloom, hopelessness, misery, pessimism, wretchedness; *opp* enthusiasm, happiness, optimism

despair *v* give in, give up, lose heart, lose hope, quit, resign yourself, surrender, throw in the towel; *opp* hope

desperate *adj* 1 at your wits end, despairing, frantic, inconsolable, wretched. 2 (a desperate situation) acute, critical, dangerous, drastic, grave, hopeless, irretrievable, pressing, risky, serious, severe, urgent

despicable *adj* abominable, base, cheap, contemptible, detestable, disgraceful, disgusting, disreputable, hateful, ignominious, loathsome, low, mean, odious, reprehensible, shameful, sordid, vile, worthless, wretched

despise *v* abhor, be contemptuous of, can't bear, can't stand, detest, disdain, hate, loathe, revile

despondent *adj* blue, dejected, discouraged, disheartened, dismayed,

dispirited, down, down in the dumps, downcast, fed up, gloomy, glum, low, melancholy, miserable, unhappy, upset; *opp* cheerful

despot *n* authoritarian, autocrat, dictator, tyrant; *opp* democrat

destination *n* end of the line, journey's end, landing-place, port of call, resting-place, stop, terminus; *opp* starting point

destined *adj* 1 bound for, en route to, heading for. 2 bound to, certain, doomed, fated, intended, meant, pre-ordained, unavoidable

destiny *n* chance, doom, fate, fortune, lot, providence

destitute *adj* badly off *inf*, bankrupt, bereft, broke *inf*, disadvantaged, hard up *inf*, impoverished, in need, lacking, needy, on the breadline, penniless, poor, poverty-stricken, without two pennies to rub together; *opp* rich

destroy *v* annihilate, break, break down, crush, decimate, demolish, devastate, dismantle, knock down, level, obliterate, ravage, raze, ruin, shatter, smash, spoil, trash *sl*, wipe out, wreck

destruction *n* annihilation, decimation, demolition, devastation, dismantling, downfall, end, extermination, havoc, obliteration, ruin, ruination, wrecking

destructive *adj* damaging, deadly, detrimental, devastating, fatal, harmful, hurtful, injurious, lethal, malignant, pernicious; *opp* beneficial

detach *v* cut loose, cut off, disconnect, disengage, disentangle, free, isolate, loosen, part, pull off, release, remove, sever, take off, tear off, uncouple, undo, unfasten; *opp* attach

detached *adj* 1 disconnected, disengaged, disentangled, free, isolated, loose, released, removed, separate, severed, uncoupled, undone, unfastened; *opp* connected. 2 aloof, cool, disinterested, dispassionate, distant, formal, remote, removed, reserved, standoffish, unapproachable; *opp* friendly. 3 fair, impartial, neutral, objective, unbiased, uncommitted, uninvolved, unprejudiced; *opp* biased

detail *n* aspect, component, element, fact, factor, feature, intricacy, item, part, particular, point, respect, technicality

detail *v* 1 (detail sb to a place/job) allocate, appoint, assign, charge, commission, delegate, detach, send. 2 (detail in a list) catalog, cite, enumerate, indicate, itemize, list, point out, set out, specify, spell out, relate

detailed *adj* all-inclusive, blow-by-blow, complete, comprehensive, elaborate, exact, exhaustive, full, intricate, in (minute) detail, specific, thorough; *opp* vague

detain *v* 1 (make sb late) delay, hinder, hold up, keep, slow down. 2 (in custody) arrest, confine, hold, impound, imprison, incarcerate, intern, lock up, restrain; *opp* release

detect *v* ascertain, catch, discern, discover, distinguish, find, find out, identify, note, notice, observe, recognize, scent, spot, uncover

detective *n* investigator, police officer, private eye, sleuth *inf*

detention *n* arrest, confinement, custody, imprisonment, incarceration, internment, quarantine, restraint

deter *v* daunt, discourage, dissuade, frighten, inhibit, intimidate, prevent, put off, scare, stop, talk sb out of, warn off; *opp* encourage

deteriorate *v* crumble, decay, decline, decompose, degenerate, depreciate, disintegrate, fade, fall apart, get worse, go downhill *inf*, go to pot *inf*, go to the dogs *inf*, spoil, weaken, worsen; *opp* improve

determination *n* backbone, commitment, conviction, dedication, doggedness, drive, fortitude, grit *inf*, guts *inf*, perseverance, persistence, resolution, resolve, single-mindedness, staying power, tenacity, willpower

determine *v* 1 (determine what will happen) agree on, arbitrate, decide, decree, judge, ordain, regulate, settle. 2 (learn) ascertain, calculate, detect, discover, establish, find out, learn, work out. 3 (determine to do sth) choose, decide, elect, make up your mind, resolve

determined *adj* 1 (determined to do sth) bent on, fixed on, intent on, resolved, set on. 2 (a determined person) dedicated, dogged, firm, focused, insistent, persistent, purposeful, resolute, resolved, singleminded, steadfast, strong-willed, tenacious, tough, unwavering; *opp* irresolute

deterrent *n* check, curb, discouragement, disincentive, restraint, turn-off *inf*; *opp* encouragement

detest *v* abhor, abominate, despise, disdain, dislike, hate, loathe, scorn; *opp* love

detract from *v* devalue, diminish, lessen,

lower, reduce, take away from;
opp enhance

detrimental *adj* adverse, damaging,
destructive, harmful, inimical, injurious,
pernicious, prejudicial, unfavorable;
opp advantageous, helpful

devastate *v* 1 demolish, destroy, flatten,
lay waste, level, obliterate, ravage, raze,
ruin, spoil, trash *sl*, wreck. 2 disappoint,
horrify, overwhelm, shock, take aback,
traumatize

devastating *adj* 1 deadly, destructive,
ruinous, savage. 2 (devastating news)
disappointing, horrifying, overwhelming,
shocking, traumatic, upsetting

develop *v* 1 advance, enlarge, evolve,
expand, flourish, grow, mature, progress,
ripen, spread. 2 (develop an idea)
amplify, augment, broaden, dilate on,
elaborate, enlarge on, expand.
3 (develop a habit, illness) acquire,
catch, contract, get, pick up

development *n* 1 advance,
advancement, enlargement, evolution,
expansion, flourishing, growth, increase,
maturing, maturity, progress,
progression, ripening, spreading.
2 change, circumstance, event,
happening, incident, occurrence,
outcome, result, situation, turn of
events, upshot

deviate *v* branch off, deflect, depart,
differ, digress, diverge, drift, err, part,
stray, swerve, turn aside, vary, veer,
wander

device *n* 1 apparatus, appliance,
contraption, gadget, gizmo *inf*,
implement, instrument, machine, tool,
utensil, widget *inf*. 2 (a trick) artifice,

con, expedient, fraud, gambit,
machination, maneuver, plan, ploy, ruse,
scheme, sleight, strategy, stunt,
subterfuge, tactic, trick, wile

devil *n* 1 Beelzebub, demon, Evil One,
evil spirit, fiend, Lucifer, Prince of
Darkness, Satan. 2 beast, brute, fiend,
monster, ogre, savage, terror, thug,
villain

devious *adj* artful, calculating, crafty,
crooked, cunning, deceitful, dishonest,
evasive, guileful, indirect, insidious,
insincere, misleading, scheming, sly,
sneaky, surreptitious, treacherous, tricky,
underhand, wily; *opp* direct, ingenuous

devise *v* arrange, come up with, conceive,
concoct, construct, contrive, cook up
inf, create, design, dream up, engineer,
form, formulate, frame, imagine, invent,
plan, plot, prepare, scheme, think up,
work out

devoid *adj* barren, bereft, deficient,
denuded, destitute, empty, free from,
lacking, missing, vacant, void, wanting,
without

devote *v* allocate, allot, apply, assign,
commit, consign, dedicate, give, pledge,
reserve, set aside

devoted *adj* adoring, ardent, attentive,
besotted, caring, committed, concerned,
conscientious, constant, dedicated,
devout, dutiful, enthusiastic, faithful,
fond, loving, loyal, passionate, staunch,
steadfast, true, unswerving, zealous

devotion *n* adherence, adoration,
allegiance, ardor, attentiveness, caring,
commitment, concern, constancy,
dedication, devotedness, enthusiasm,
faithfulness, fervor, fidelity, fondness,

love, loyalty, passion, staunchness, steadfastness, zeal

devout adj dutiful, God-fearing, godly, holy, orthodox, pious, prayerful, religious, reverent, righteous, zealous

dexterous adj adept, adroit, agile, clever, deft, expert, handy, neat, nimble, proficient, sharp, skilled, skillful; **opp** clumsy

diagnose v detect, determine, distinguish, identify, interpret, isolate, pinpoint, recognize

diagnosis n analysis, conclusion, explanation, interpretation, judgment, opinion, pronouncement, recommendation, verdict

diagram n chart, drawing, figure, illustration, outline, picture, representation, sketch, symbol, table

dialect n accent, argot, idiom, jargon, language, patois, regionalism, slang, speech, tongue, variety, vernacular

dialogue n 1 chat, communication, conference, conversation, discourse, discussion, exchange, interchange, talk. 2 (of a film) conversation, lines, script

diary n annals, appointment book, calendar, chronicle, engagement book, journal, log, memoir, personal organizer, record

dictate v 1 command, declare, decree, direct, enjoin, give orders, impose, lay down, ordain, order, prescribe. 2 read out, say, speak, recite, transmit, utter

dictator n absolute ruler, autocrat, despot, oppressor, tyrant

die v 1 be no more, bite the dust inf, cease to exist, croak sl, decease, depart, expire, kick the bucket inf, lose your life, meet

your end, pass away, pass on, perish, snuff out inf. 2 come to an end, decay, decline, decrease, disappear, dwindle, ebb, end, fade, lapse, pass, sink, vanish, wane, wilt, wither. 3 (of a machine) break down, come to a halt, fail, fizzle out, halt, lose power, peter out, run down, stop

diet n alimentation, consumption, fare, food, intake, nourishment, nutrition, provisions, rations, regime, regimen, subsistence, viands, victuals

diet v abstain, cut down, fast, go on a diet, lose weight, reduce, slim

differ v 1 be different, be dissimilar, be distinct, be unlike, contrast, deviate, diverge, vary. 2 argue, be at odds, clash, conflict, contradict, debate, disagree, dispute, dissent, diverge, object, oppose, quarrel, quibble, take issue; **opp** agree

difference n 1 contrast, discrepancy, disparity, dissimilarity, distinction, divergence, incongruity, nonconformity, peculiarity, singularity, variation, variety; **opp** similarity. 2 altercation, argument, clash, conflict, controversy, debate, difference of opinion, disagreement, dispute, objection, quarrel, quibble, tiff, wrangle; **opp** agreement

different adj 1 assorted, clashing, contradictory, contrasting, contrastive, disparate, dissimilar, distinct, diverging, diverse, incongruous, inconsistent, miscellaneous, mixed, other, peculiar, separate, singular, various, varying, unlike; **opp** similar. 2 abnormal, bizarre, distinctive, eccentric, interesting, novel, odd, original, peculiar, singular, special, strange, striking, uncommon, unconventional, unique, unorthodox, unusual, weird; *opp* ordinary

differentiate *v* contrast, discern, discriminate, distinguish, identify, make a distinction, mark off, separate, sort, tell apart, tell the difference

difficult *adj* 1 arduous, burdensome, challenging, complex, complicated, demanding, daunting, exacting, formidable, grueling, hard, laborious, onerous, painful, problematic, strenuous, taxing, thorny, tough, tricky, wearisome; *opp* easy. 2 (of a person) argumentative, awkward, contrary, demanding, fastidious, fractious, fussy, intractable, obstreperous, perverse, quarrelsome, tiresome, troublesome, trying, uncooperative, unmanageable; *opp* cooperative

difficulty *n* 1 adversity, arduousness, awkwardness, challenge, hardship, laboriousness, labor, ordeal, pain, problem, strain, struggle, toughness, tribulation. 2 dilemma, distress, fix *inf*, jam *inf*, mess, pickle *inf*, plight, predicament, quandary, scrape *inf*, spot *inf*, straits

diffident *adj* apprehensive, backward, bashful, constrained, coy, doubtful, fearful, hesitant, humble, inhibited, insecure, introverted, meek, modest, nervous, shy, reluctant, reserved, retiring, self-conscious, self-effacing, sheepish, shrinking, tentative, timid, timorous, unassertive, unassuming, unconfident, unsure, withdrawn; *opp* brash

dig *v* 1 burrow, delve, excavate, fork,

gouge, grub, harrow, hoe, hollow, mine, penetrate, pierce, plow, quarry, scoop, till, tunnel, turn over. 2 (dig for information) delve, go into, investigate, probe, research, search. 3 (dig sb in the ribs) jab, nudge, poke, prod, punch, push, shove

digest *v* 1 absorb, assimilate, break down, consume, dissolve, eat, incorporate, take in. 2 (digest information) absorb, assimilate, comprehend, consider, contemplate, grasp, master, mull over, ruminate, ponder, study, take in, understand

dignified *adj* ceremonious, decorous, distinguished, elegant, formal, graceful, gracious, grave, honorable, imposing, impressive, lofty, noble, proper, proud, regal, solemn, stately, tasteful; *opp* undignified

dignitary *n* celebrity, luminary, notability, notable, official, personage, public figure, VIP, worthy

dignity *n* ceremony, class, decorum, distinction, elegance, formality, grace, grandeur, gravitas, gravity, hauteur, honor, loftiness, majesty, nobility, pride, propriety, solemnity, stateliness, taste

digress *v* depart, deviate, diverge, drift, get off the subject, get sidetracked, go off at a tangent, lose your thread, meander, ramble, stray, veer, wander

digression *n* aside, departure, detour, deviation, divergence, diversion, drifting, footnote, meander, rambling, straying, wandering

dilapidated *adj* battered, broken-down, crumbling, decaying, decrepit, derelict, falling apart, falling down, in disrepair, in ruins, neglected, peeling, ramshackle, rickety, ruined, rundown, shabby, tumbledown, uncared-for, worn out

dilemma n catch-22, difficulty, fix inf, impasse, jam inf, perplexity, pickle inf, plight, predicament, problem, puzzle, quandary, scrape inf, spot inf, straits, vicious circle

diligent adj assiduous, attentive, busy, careful, conscientious, dutiful, earnest, hard-working, indefatigable, industrious, meticulous, painstaking, patient, persevering, persistent, punctilious, scrupulous, sedulous, studious, thorough, tireless; **opp** careless, slapdash

dilute v adulterate, cut inf, mix, thin, water down, weaken; **opp** concentrate

dim adj 1 bleary, blurred, blurry, cloudy, dark, dingy, dull, dusky, faint, foggy, fuzzy, gloomy, hazy, indistinct, misty, murky, muted, obscure, obscured, shadowy, unclear, vague; **opp** bright. 2 dense, dozy inf, dull, dull-witted, dumb inf, obtuse, slow, stupid, thick inf; **opp** bright

dim v blur, cloud, darken, dull, fade, fog, lower, mask, obscure, shade, shadow, shroud, turn down

dimensions n amplitude, area, bulk, capacity, extent, greatness, largeness, magnitude, measurements, proportions, range, scale, scope, size, volume

diminish v abate, contract, curtail, cut, decline, decrease, dwindle, ebb, lessen, lower, peter out, recede, reduce, shrink, subside, wane, weaken

dine v banquet, eat, feast, feed, have dinner, sup

dingy adj cheerless, dark, depressing, dim, dirty, dismal, drab, dreary, dull, faded, gloomy, grimy, murky, rundown, seedy, shabby, soiled, somber, threadbare, worn; **opp** bright

dinner n banquet, feast, meal, repast, spread inf, supper

dip n 1 bathe, ducking, dunking, immersion, plunge, rinse, soak, soaking, sousing, submersion, swim. 2 concavity, declivity, dent, depression, hole, hollow, incline, slope, valley. 3 (a dip in amount) decline, dive, drop, fall, lowering, plunge, slip, slump

dip v 1 bathe, douse, drench, duck, dunk, immerse, lower, plunge, rinse, soak, souse, steep, submerge. 2 decline, descend, dive, drop, fall, go down, lower, plunge, sag, slip, slump

diplomacy n adroitness, delicacy, discretion, finesse, sensitivity, skill, subtlety, tact

diplomat n ambassador, conciliator, emissary, envoy, go-between, intermediary, mediator, moderator, negotiator, peacemaker, politician, representative, statesman

diplomatic adj adept, adroit, careful, considerate, delicate, discreet, judicious, politic, prudent, sensitive, subtle, tactful

dire adj alarming, appalling, atrocious, awful, calamitous, catastrophic, chronic, disastrous, dreadful, frightful, ghastly, grievous, horrendous, horrible, horrifying, shocking, terrible, unspeakable, woeful

direct adj 1 immediate, non-stop, shortest, straight, through, unbroken, uninterrupted; **opp** indirect. 2 blunt, candid, categorical, clear, explicit, forthright, frank, honest, open, outspoken, plain, plainspoken, straight, straightforward, to the point, unambiguous, unequivocal, upfront; *opp* indirect. 3 (direct opposite) absolute, complete, diametrical, downright, exact, thorough, total, utter

direct *v* 1 administer, be in charge of, conduct, control, govern, guide, handle, head, manage, orchestrate, oversee, preside, regulate, run, superintend, supervise. 2 bid, command, dictate, enjoin, instruct, order, require, tell. 3 (direct sb to a place) conduct, escort, give directions, guide, indicate, lead, navigate, pilot, point, show the way, steer, usher

direction *n* 1 bearing, course, line, orientation, path, road, route, tack, track, way. 2 administration, command, control, government, guidance, handling, leadership, management, orchestration, order, overseeing, regulation, running, supervision. 3 bidding, command, decree, edict, injunction, instruction, order, ruling

directions *n* briefing, guidance, guide, guidelines, indications, instructions, map, plan, recommendations

director *n* administrator, boss, chair, chairman, chairwoman, chief, conductor, controller, executive, governor, head, manager, managing director, organizer, overseer, president, principal, regulator, supervisor

dirt *n* dust, earth, filth, gunge, gunk, impurity, mire, muck, mud, ordure, pollution, slime, smudge, spot, stain, soil, tarnish

dirty *adj* 1 contaminated, dusty, filthy, foul, grimy, grubby, grungy *inf*, impure, marked, messy, mucky *inf*, muddy, nasty, polluted, smudged, soiled, spotted, stained, sticky, sullied, tainted, tarnished, unclean; *opp* clean. 2 corrupt, crooked, deceitful, dishonest, dishonorable, fraudulent, illegal, treacherous, unfair, unscrupulous, unsporting; *opp* honest. 3 bawdy, blue, coarse, improper, indecent, lascivious, lewd, obscene, offensive, pornographic, ribald, risqué, rude, salacious, sleazy *inf*, smutty, suggestive, vulgar; *opp* clean

disability *n* affliction, ailment, defect, disadvantage, disorder, handicap, impairment, incapacity, infirmity, malady

disabled *adj* afflicted, crippled, debilitated, disadvantaged, handicapped, immobilized, impaired, incapacitated, infirm, lame, maimed, mutilated, paralyzed, weak, weakened; *opp* able-bodied

disadvantage *n* defect, disability, downside, drawback, fault, flaw, handicap, hindrance, hitch, impediment, inconvenience, minus, obstacle, problem, snag, weakness; *opp* advantage

disagree *v* argue, bicker, clash, conflict, contend, contest, contradict, counter, debate, differ, discuss, dispute, dissent, diverge, fall out, fight, object, oppose, quarrel, question, quibble, squabble, take issue, wrangle; *opp* agree

disagreeable *adj* bad-tempered, churlish, cross, crotchety, difficult, horrible, ill-natured, irritable, nasty, objectionable, obnoxious, peevish, rude, surly, unfriendly, ungracious, unpleasant; **opp** agreeable

disagreement n altercation, argument, clash, conflict, contention, contradiction, controversy, debate, difference, discord, discussion, dispute, dissent, divergence, division, falling out, fight, objection, opposition, quarrel, row, squabble, strife, tiff, wrangle; **opp** agreement

disallow v ban, bar, boycott, cancel, deny, dismiss, embargo, forbid, prohibit, proscribe, refuse, reject, repudiate, veto; **opp** allow

disappear v 1 become invisible, be lost to view, dematerialize, dissolve, evaporate, fade, flee, melt away, recede, vanish, vaporize, wane; **opp** appear. 2 become extinct, cease, come to an end, die, die out, end, evaporate, expire, go, pass away, perish, stop, vanish; **opp** appear

disappearance n dissolving, ebbing, ending, evaporation, fading, fleeing, going, invisibility, melting, passing, receding, vanishing; **opp** appearance

disappoint v depress, disenchant, dishearten, disillusion, dismay, dispirit, dissatisfy, fail, frustrate, let down, sadden, thwart, upset; **opp** satisfy

disappointed adj cast down, depressed, despondent, discouraged, disenchanted, disheartened, disillusioned, dismayed, dispirited, dissatisfied, downcast, frustrated, let down, sad, saddened, thwarted; **opp** satisfied

disappointing adj depressing, discouraging, disenchanting, disheartening, disillusioning, dismaying,

dispiriting, dissatisfying, frustrating, inadequate, insufficient, paltry, pathetic, unsatisfactory, upsetting; **opp** encouraging, satisfying

disappointment n 1 depression, discouragement, disenchantment, disillusionment, dismay, dissatisfaction, frustration, regret, sadness; **opp** satisfaction. 2 blow, disaster, failure, fiasco, letdown, setback; **opp** success

disapprove v be against, censure, condemn, criticize, deplore, deprecate, dislike, frown on, look askance at, not take kindly to, object to, reject, take a dim view, take exception; **opp** approve

disaster n accident, act of God, adversity, blow, calamity, cataclysm, catastrophe, misadventure, mischance, misfortune, mishap, reverse, ruin, tragedy, trouble

disastrous adj adverse, appalling, awful, calamitous, cataclysmic, catastrophic, destructive, devastating, dire, dreadful, fatal, fateful, ill-fated, ill-starred, ruinous, terrible, tragic, unfortunate, unlucky

discard v abandon, cast aside, chuck out inf, dispense with, dispose of, ditch inf, drop, dump inf, get rid of, jettison, junk inf, reject, repudiate, scrap, shed, throw away, throw out

discharge n 1 emission, excretion, matter, pus, secretion. 2 dismissal, expulsion, firing, redundancy, removal, sacking. 3 acquittal, clearance, exoneration, freeing, liberation, pardon, release

discharge v 1 belch, eject, emit, excrete, exude, give off, produce, release, secrete, send out, spew. 2 dismiss, expel, fire, let go, make redundant, relieve, remove, sack. **3** absolve, acquit, clear, exonerate, free, let go, liberate, pardon, release, set free. **4** detonate, fire, let off, shoot

disciple n acolyte, adherent, apostle, believer, convert, devotee, follower, partisan, proselyte, pupil, supporter

discipline n **1** chastisement, control, correction, drilling, exercise, punishment, regime, regulation, rules, strictness, training. **2** control, organization, restraint, self-control, self-discipline, self-restraint, strength, will-power

discipline v chastise, control, correct, penalize, punish, rebuke, regulate, reprimand, train

disclose v admit, bring to light, confess, divulge, expose, impart, let slip, make known, make public, reveal, tell, unveil

discomfort n ache, disquiet, distress, hardship, hurt, inconvenience, irritation, nuisance, pain, pang, soreness, trouble, twinge, uneasiness, vexation; **opp** comfort

disconcerting adj alarming, baffling, bewildering, dismaying, distracting, disturbing, off-putting, perplexing, perturbing, puzzling, troubling, unnerving, unsettling, upsetting, worrying; **opp** reassuring

disconnect v break off, cut off, detach, disengage, divide, part, separate, sever, uncouple, undo, unplug

discontented adj annoyed, disaffected, disgruntled, displeased, dissatisfied, fed up, fretful, impatient, restless, troubled, unfulfilled, unhappy, unsatisfied, unsettled; **opp** contented

discontinue v abandon, ax inf, break off, cancel, cease, cut, drop, end, give up, halt, interrupt, put an end to, quit, stop, suspend, terminate; **opp** continue

discord n **1** arguing, argument, clashing, conflict, contention, controversy, difference, disagreement, disharmony, dispute, dissent, disunity, division, falling-out, friction, hostility, opposition, quarreling, rupture, strife, variance, wrangling; **opp** agreement. **2** cacophony, din, dissonance, harshness, jangle, jarring, racket; **opp** harmony

discount v **1** disbelieve, disregard, gloss over, ignore, overlook, pass over, pay no attention to, reject, take no notice of. **2** cut, lower, mark down, reduce, take off, slash

discourage v **1** abash, cast down, dampen, daunt, demoralize, depress, deter, dishearten, dismay, dissuade, intimidate, put off, unnerve; **opp** encourage. **2** advise against, caution against, disapprove, dissuade, deter, frown on, oppose, put off, repress, take a dim view, urge against; **opp** encourage

discouraged adj abashed, cast down, cowed, crestfallen, dashed, daunted, dejected, demoralized, depressed, despondent, deterred, disheartened, dismayed, dispirited, downhearted, intimidated, put off, unnerved; **opp** encouraged

discouragement n **1** dejection, demoralization, depression, despondency, dismay, downheartedness; **opp** encouragement. **2** barrier, check, constraint, curb, damper, deterrent,

discincentive, hindrance, impediment, obstacle, restriction; *opp* encouragement

discouraging *adj* daunting, demoralizing, depressing, disheartening, dismaying, dispiriting, inauspicious, intimidating, off-putting, unnerving, worrying; *opp* encouraging

discourse *n* **1** chat, communication, conversation, dialogue, discussion, exchange, interchange, speech, talk. **2** address, dissertation, essay, lecture, oration, paper, speech, study, treatise

discourse *v* **1** chat, communicate, confer, converse, debate, discuss, have a conversation, speak, talk. **2** declaim, deliver a paper, expatiate, give a talk, hold forth, lecture, make a speech, orate, speak

discover *v* **1** come across, come upon, dig up, find, light on, locate, track down, turn up, uncover, unearth. **2** ascertain, come to know, detect, determine, disclose, expose, find out, identify, learn, perceive, realize, recognize, see, spot, uncover

discovery *n* **1** detection, digging up, disclosure, exposing, finding, identification, locating, location, recognition, spotting, tracking down, uncovering, unearthing. **2** breakthrough, coup, find, innovation, invention

discredit *v* blacken sb's name, cast doubt on, decry, denigrate, disparage, show up

discreet *adj* careful, circumspect, diplomatic, judicious, polite, politic, prudent, tactful, tasteful; *opp* indiscreet

discrepancy *n* anomaly, contradiction, difference, disparity, error, inconsistency, inequality, miscalculation, mismatch, mistake, shortfall

discretion *n* care, circumspection, diplomacy, politeness, prudence, tact, tactfulness

discriminate *v* **1 discriminate against** be biased against, be intolerant of, be prejudiced against, pick on, segregate, single out, treat unfairly, victimize. **2** choose, differentiate, distinguish, draw a distinction, judge, make a distinction, select

discriminating *adj* choosy, cultivated, discerning, fastidious, refined, selective, tasteful

discrimination *n* **1** ageism, apartheid, bias, bigotry, intolerance, male chauvinism, prejudice, racism, segregation, sexism, victimization. **2** culture, discernment, fastidiousness, judgment, refinement, sensitivity, taste

discuss *v* argue, confer, consider, converse, debate, deliberate, put your heads together, talk, talk about, talk over

discussion *n* argument, conference, conversation, debate, deliberation, dialogue, pow-wow *inf*, talk

disdainful *adj* aloof, contemptuous, disparaging, disrespectful, proud, scornful, sneering, superior

disease *n* ailment, bug *inf*, complaint, disorder, illness, infection, malady, sickness, syndrome, virus

diseased *adj* **1** ailing, festering, infected, ill, septic, sick, swollen, unhealthy; *opp* healthy. **2** (with a particular disease) arthritic, asthmatic, cancerous, gangrenous, leprous, rabid

disembark *v* alight, arrive, get off, get

out, go ashore, land; **opp** embark

disentangle v 1 disengage, extricate, loose, undo, unravel, untangle, untie, unwind; **opp** entangle. 2 ascertain, decipher, disembroil, resolve, solve, sort out, straighten out, understand

disgrace n abasement, abjection, discredit, dishonor, disrepute, embarrassment, humiliation, rejection, shame, stigma

disgrace v 1 discredit, drag through the mud, dishonor, embarrass, humiliate, shame, stigmatize. 2 **disgrace yourself** abase yourself, degrade yourself, demean yourself, dishonorable, prostitute yourself, stoop to

disgraceful v 1 (morally) abject, contemptible, corrupt, degrading, disgusting, dishonorable, ignominious, outrageous, shameful. 2 (very bad) appalling, awful, dreadful, pathetic, shocking, terrible

disguise n 1 camouflage, concealment, costume, cover, false identity, fancy dress, mask. 2 **in disguise** disguised, incognito, undercover

disguise v 1 camouflage, cloak, cover, cover up, conceal, dissemble, fake, falsify, hide, mask. 2 **disguise yourself as** dress up as, impersonate, masquerade as

disgust n contempt, dislike, distaste, loathing, nausea, offense, outrage, repugnance, repulsion, revulsion

disgust v appal, make sick, nauseate, offend, outrage, put off, repel, revolt, sicken

disgusting adj appalling, awful, disgraceful, distasteful, gross, horrible, nauseating, obscene, offensive,

off-putting, outrageous, repugnant, repellent, repulsive, revolting, sickening, ugly, unpleasant, unsavory

dish n 1 (container) bowl, plate, platter, serving dish, vessel. 2 (food) course, creation, delicacy, meal, recipe, specialty

dishearten v dampen sb's spirits, deflate, deject, depress, demoralize, deter, discourage, dismay, put off, sadden; **opp** hearten

disheveled adj bedraggled, messy, ruffled, slovenly, tousled, unkempt, untidy

dishonest adj cheating, criminal, crooked, deceitful, dishonorable, duplicitous, lying, unscrupulous, untrustworthy; **opp** honest

dishonesty n cheating, criminality, deceit, deception, duplicity, lies, unscrupulousness

disillusioned adj alienated, cynical, disabused, disaffected, disappointed, disenchanted, fed up

disinfect v bathe, clean, clean out, cleanse, sterilize

disintegrate v break down, collapse, decay, fall apart, fall to pieces, implode

disinterested adj above the fray, aloof, detached, dispassionate, impartial, objective, unbiased, unselfish, with no ax to grind

dislike n antipathy, aversion, detestation, distaste, hate, hatred, hostility; **opp** liking

dislike v be disgusted by, be hostile to, be put off by, detest, hate, have an aversion to; **opp** like

disloyal adj disobedient, false, mutinous, perfidious, traitorous, treacherous, seditious, unfaithful; **opp** faithful, loyal

dismal *adj* **1** bleak, cheerless, demoralizing, depressing, disheartening, dispiriting, gloomy, miserable, sad. **2** (of weather) appalling, awful, dark, dreadful, gloomy, murky, rainy, miserable, shocking, terrible, unpleasant, wet, wretched; *opp* lovely, wonderful

dismantle *v* disassemble, strip down, take apart, take down, take to pieces

dismay *n* annoyance, disappointment, consternation, displeasure, frustration, shock

dismay *v* annoy, disconcert, dishearten, disappoint, displease, frustrate, shatter, sadden, shock, upset

dismiss *v* **1** (from sb's presence) banish, cast out, chuck out *inf*, exclude, excuse, send away, send out, throw out. **2** (from a job) downsize, fire, get rid of, kick out *inf*, remove, sack. **3** (dismiss an idea) brush aside, brush off, discount, disregard, forget about, ignore, reject, ridicule

disobedient *adj* cheeky, defiant, disrespectful, dissenting, dissident, disloyal, insubordinate, mutinous, naughty, unruly; *opp* obedient

disobey *v* **1** (disobey a rule) break, contravene, defy, disregard, flout, infringe, transgress; *opp* obey. **2** (act disobediently) answer back, mutiny, rebel, refuse, resist, revolt, stand firm, stand up to; *opp* obey

disorder *n* **1** chaos, clutter, disarray, jumble, muddle, untidiness; *opp* order. **2** (violent) anarchy, chaos, civil disobedience, discontent, insurrection, rioting, trouble, turbulence, turmoil, unrest, unruliness, violence; *opp* order.

3 (medical) ailment, complaint, disease, dysfunction *tech*, illness, malady, sickness, syndrome

disorganized *adj* **1** anarchic, chaotic, disorderly, in disarray, jumbled, random, uncontrolled, unplanned, unstructured, unsystematic, untidy; *opp* organized. **2** (of a person) aimless, in disarray, illogical, muddled, undisciplined, unsystematic; *opp* organized

disown *v* deny, disclaim, dissociate yourself from, distance yourself from, reject, repudiate

disparaging *adj* belittling, contemptuous, critical, disapproving, disdainful, insulting, scornful

dispassionate *adj* calm, cool, detached, disinterested, distant, unbiased, unsentimental

dispatch *n* consignment, message, missive, package, parcel, report

dispatch *v* **1** distribute, forward, mail, post, send, send off, send out. **2** (dispatch a task) conclude, deal with, dispose of, expedite, finish off, make short work of, polish off *inf*

dispel *v* clear up, deny, put an end to, put a stop to, scotch

dispense *v* **1** distribute, disseminate, give, give out, hand out, impart, prescribe, provide, vend. **2 dispense with** cancel, do without, eliminate, forget, forget about, get rid of, go without, not bother with, remove, scrap

disperse *v* **1** (of a crowd) break up, separate, scatter, leave, melt away, spread out. **2** banish, drive away, scatter

displace *v* **1** (move out of position) disturb, misplace, move, remove, shift, transpose. 2 (cause sb to lose position) dislodge, drive out, force out, oust, replace, supplant, take the place of

display n array, demonstration, exhibition, exposure, presentation, show

display v 1 (display goods) arrange, exhibit, present, put on view, show, show off. 2 (display an emotion) betray, reveal, show

displease v anger, annoy, disappoint, frustrate, irk, irritate, offend, upset; *opp* please

displeasure n anger, annoyance, disappointment, dissatisfaction, frustration, indignation, irritation, offense; *opp* pleasure

disposable adj 1 biodegradable, expendable, nonreturnable, paper, plastic, temporary, throwaway. 2 (disposable income) after tax, available, net, take-home, to spend

disposal n 1 clearance, destruction, dumping, elimination, removal, scrapping. 2 **at your disposal** accessible, at your discretion, available, free, handy, obtainable, to hand

dispose of v chuck away inf, dispense with, dump, eliminate, finish off, get rid of, polish off inf, remove, scrap, throw away

disprove v demolish, explode, invalidate, prove wrong, refute; *opp* prove

dispute n 1 altercation, argument, battle, conflict, controversy, difference of opinion, differences, disagreement, feud, fight, friction, quarrel, row. 2 (between workers and management) go slow, grievance, industrial action, lock-out, strike. 3 **beyond dispute** crystal clear,

definite, incontrovertible, unarguable, undisputed

dispute v 1 contest, deny, reject, oppose, question, wrangle over. 2 (dispute the leadership) battle for, challenge for, compete for, contend for, contest, fight over, vie for

disqualify v ban, bar, debar, disallow, exclude, make ineligible, rule out

disregard v brush aside, discount, dismiss, ignore, take no notice of

disreputable adj crooked, dishonest, dishonorable, dubious, of ill repute, shady, unscrupulous

disrespect n cheek, contempt, disdain, disobedience, impertinence, impudence, insolence, insults, irreverence, insubordination, scorn; *opp* respect

disrespectful adj cheeky, contemptuous, disdainful, disobedient, impertinent, impolite, impudent, insolent, insubordination, insulting, irreverent, scornful; *opp* respectful

disrupt v disturb, impede, interfere with, interrupt, sabotage, throw into disarray, upset

disruptive adj badly behaved, distracting, ill-behaved, interfering, naughty, troublesome, unruly

dissatisfied adj angry, annoyed, displeased, frustrated, irked, irritated, unfulfilled, unsatisfied; *opp* satisfied

dissent n argument, defiance, disagreement, discontent, disobedience, dissension, dissidence, nonconformism, opposition; *opp* agreement

dissent v break ranks, contest, defy, disagree with, disobey, dissociate yourself from, distance yourself from, oppose, reject, speak out against

dissident n critic, dissenter, non-conformist, opponent, political prisoner, prisoner of conscience

dissipate v 1 blow away, break up, disappear, disperse, evaporate, melt away, scatter, vanish. 2 (use wastefully) consume, expend, fritter, misspend, spend, squander, use up, waste

dissociate v dissociate yourself from break away from, break ranks with, deny, disclaim, dissent from, disown, distance yourself from, repudiate, reject, say no to, sever your connections with

dissolve v 1 (add to liquid) dilute, melt, mix, mix in, stir in. 2 (of feelings) crumble, disappear, dissipate, evaporate, fade, fade away, melt away, vanish. 3 (dissolve a partnership, an organization) annul, break up, disband, end, terminate, wind up

dissuade v deter, discourage, persuade against, prevent, put off, stop, talk sb out of

distance n 1 interval, length, long way, remoteness, space, way. 2 **in the distance** a long way away, distantly, far away, far off, just in sight, just in view, on the horizon, yonder

distant adj 1 faint, far, faraway, far-off, remote, yonder. 2 (of a person) aloof, cold, day-dreaming, detached, haughty, other-worldly, preoccupied, private, superior, unfriendly

distaste n antipathy, aversion, disgust, disapproval, dislike, displeasure, repugnance

distasteful adj disgusting, gross, in bad taste, in poor taste, obscene, repugnant,

repellent, unpleasant, unsavory

distinct adj 1 (that can be noticed) audible, clear, clear as a bell, definite, discernible, noticeable, perceptible, tangible, unmistakable, visible; **opp** indistinct. 2 (distinct from each other) contrasting, different, discrete, independent, individual, separate, unconnected

distinction n 1 contrast, difference, differentiation, dissimilarity, dividing line, division, separation. 2 (personal quality) eminence, excellence, prestige, refinement, standing. 3 award, commendation, credit, decoration, honor

distinctive adj characteristic, distinguishing, own, peculiar, specific, tell-tale

distinguish v 1 discern, hear, make out, notice, perceive, see. 2 (distinguish between two things) differentiate, discriminate, draw a distinction, make a distinction, tell apart, tell the difference

distinguished adj award-winning, celebrated, eminent, experienced, favored, honored, respected

distort v bend out of shape, change, deform, falsify, misrepresent, pervert, twist, warp

distract v beguile, confuse, disturb, disturb sb's concentration, divert sb's attention, put off, sidetrack

distracted adj confused, day-dreaming, inattentive, other-worldly, preoccupied, wandering

distraction n 1 confusion, day-dreaming, inattention, lack of concentration, other-worldliness. 2 (sth which distracts) amusement, digression, disturbance, diversion, interruption, irruption, sideshow. **3 to distraction** bonkers *inf*, crazy, frantic, insane, mad, nuts *inf*, off the wall *inf*

distress *n* agony, anguish, anxiety, grief, misery, pain, sadness, suffering, torment, trauma, trouble, worry

distress *v* afflict, aggrieve, grieve, perturb, traumatize, trouble, upset, worry

distressed *adj* anguished, anxious, distraught, grieving, in distress, in pain, jumpy, nervous, panicky, suffering, traumatized, troubled, upset, worried

distressing *adj* difficult, disturbing, painful, sad, stressful, traumatic, troubling, trying, upsetting, worrisome, worrying

distribute *v* allocate, allot, deal, deal out, deliver, dispense, dispatch, disseminate, divide up, give out, hand out, issue, send out, share out

distribution *n* allocation, delivery, dispatch, dissemination, division, transport

district *n* area, borough, constituency, division, locality, neighborhood, part of town, postal district, quarter, ward

distrust *v* be skeptical of, be suspicious of, be wary of, disbelieve, doubt, have doubts about, have no confidence in, have no faith in, mistrust, suspect; *opp* trust

disturb *v* **1** bother, butt in, distract, hassle *inf*, harass, hinder, interrupt, intrude, pester; *opp* leave alone. **2** (upset) agitate, alarm, concern, distress, fluster, perturb, shake, trouble, unnerve, unsettle, upset, worry;

opp reassure. **3** (disturb sth) interfere with, mess about *inf*, mix up, move, muddle, rearrange, throw into confusion, touch; *opp* leave alone

disturbance *n* agitation, confusion, disorder, fracas, interruption, intrusion, riot, upheaval, uproar

disturbed *adj* **1** (a disturbed child) neurotic, psychotic, troubled, unbalanced, upset. **2** (feeling disturbed) alarmed, concerned, distracted, distraught, troubled, uneasy, worried

disturbing *adj* alarming, distressing, frightening, harrowing, troubling, unsettling, upsetting, worrying; *opp* reassuring

disused *adj* abandoned, dead, discarded, idle, neglected, unused

ditch *n* channel, drain, dike, gully, gutter, moat, trench

ditch *v* abandon, chuck *inf*, discard, dispose of, drop, dump *inf*, get rid of, junk *inf*, scrap, throw out

dive *v* **1** (dive into water) go under, jump, leap, plunge. **2** (dive behind a hedge) dart, disappear, dodge, drop, duck. **3** (dive through the air) fall, nosedive, plummet, swoop

diverse *adj* assorted, different, differing, dissimilar, distinct, miscellaneous, mixed, separate, several, sundry, varied, various

diversify *v* branch out, broaden, change, develop, expand, mix, spread out, vary

diversion *n* amusement, entertainment, fun, game, hobby, interest, play, recreation, relaxation, sport

diversity *n* difference, diverseness, mixture, range, variety

divert v 1 alter, change the course of, deflect, redirect, reroute, switch, turn aside. 2 deflect, distract, sidetrack. 3 amuse, delight, enchant, entertain, keep happy, occupy

diverting adj amusing, enjoyable, entertaining, fun, interesting

divide v 1 cut, detach, disconnect, halve, part, partition, quarter, segregate, separate, sever, shear, split, subdivide. 2 (share) allocate, deal out, dole out, measure out, parcel out, share. 3 (of a road) branch, diverge, fork, split. 4 (divide into categories) arrange, classify, group, organize, separate, sort

divine adj 1 angelic, celestial, godlike, heavenly, holy, saintly. 2 (to do with God) religious, sacred. 3 beautiful inf, glorious, lovely, marvelous, perfect, splendid, super inf, wonderful

divinity n 1 deity, god, goddess, spirit. 2 divine nature, holiness, sanctity

division n 1 category, class, compartment, department, group, part, piece, portion, section, sector, segment, share, slice. 2 border, boundary, frontier, line, partition, wall. 3 arm, branch, department, unit

divorce n annulment, break-up inf, separation, split inf

divorce v (get divorced) annul the marriage, dissolve the marriage, part, separate, split up

divulge v betray, disclose, impart, leak, let slip, make known, reveal, tell

dizzy adj dazed, faint, giddy, light-headed, muddled, reeling, shaky, staggering, swimming, unsteady, weak at the knees, wobbly, woozy inf

do v 1 accomplish, achieve, carry out, cause, complete, finish, perform, undertake. 2 (make sth) arrange, create, design, get ready, look after, make, manufacture, organize, prepare, produce, provide, see to. 3 (do a crossword) complete, figure out, solve, understand, work out. 4 (do a play) act, perform, present, put on. 5 (this will do) be adequate, be enough, be sufficient, satisfy, serve, suffice

docile adj compliant, cooperative, obedient, passive, submissive

dock n boatyard, harbor, jetty, landing stage, marina, pier, waterfront, wharf

doctor n consultant, general practitioner, GP, medic inf, physician, quack inf, surgeon

doctrine n belief, canon, conviction, creed, dogma, principle, teaching, theory

document n certificate, diploma, documentation, manuscript, paper, record, report

document v authenticate, back up, certify, chart, corroborate, prove, record, report, support, validate, verify

dodge v 1 (dodge sb) elude, escape, evade, give sb the slip. 2 (move) dart, dive, sidestep, swerve, veer, weave. 3 (dodge doing sth) avoid, get out of, shirk, steer clear of, wriggle out of

dog n bitch, canine, cur, hound, mongrel, mutt inf, pooch inf, puppy

dogma n article, belief, creed, doctrine, orthodoxy, principle, tenet, truth

dogmatic adj arrogant, assertive, authoritarian, dictatorial, hard-line inf, imperious, insistent, overbearing

dole *n* benefit, income support, welfare

dole out *v* administer, allocate, deal out, dispense, distribute, divide, give out, hand out, share

domestic *adj* 1 (domestic problems) family, home, personal, private. 2 (domestic animal) domesticated, house-trained, pet, tame; *opp* wild. 3 (domestic affairs) home, internal, national; *opp* foreign

domesticated *adj* 1 (of an animal) broken-in, house-trained, tame, tamed, trained; *opp* wild. 2 (of a person) domestic, home-loving, house-trained *inf*

dominant *adj* 1 assertive, controlling, domineering, leading, most influential, ruling, superior; *opp* self-effacing, passive. 2 (of a feature) biggest, conspicuous, eye-catching, highest, imposing, largest, main, major, tallest

dominate *v* 1 (of a person) be in the driver's seat, boss *inf*, command, control, direct, govern, have the upper hand, influence, lead, monopolize, outnumber, prevail, rule, take control, tyrannize, wear the pants. 2 (of a feature) dwarf, loom over, overlook, overshadow, stand over, tower above

domineering *adj* bossy *inf*, bullying, forceful, high-handed, menacing, overbearing, strict, threatening, tyrannical; *opp* passive

donate *v* chip in *inf*, contribute, give, kick in *inf*, make a gift of, present, supply

donation *n* contribution, gift, grant, offering, present

donor *n* backer, benefactor, contributor, giver, sponsor, supporter

doom *n* 1 destiny, end, fate, kismet. 2 annihilation, catastrophe, death, destruction, downfall, extinction, ruin. 3 doomsday, end of the world, Judgment Day, Last Judgment

doomed *adj* condemned, fated, hopeless, ill-fated, ruined, star-crossed, unlucky

door *n* barrier, doorway, entrance, entry, exit, gate, opening

dormant *adj* asleep, hibernating, inactive, motionless, quiet, resting, sleeping, sluggish, slumbering; *opp* active

dose *n* amount, measure, portion, prescribed amount, quantity

dot *n* 1 circle, dab, fleck, jot, mark, point, speck, speckle, spot. 2 decimal point, full stop

dote on *v* admire, adore, idolize, love, prize, treasure, worship

doting *adj* adoring, devoted, fond, indulgent, loving

double *adj* coupled, doubled, dual, duplicate, in pairs, paired, twice, twin, twofold, two-ply

double *v* enlarge, grow, increase, magnify, multiply by two, rise; *opp* halve

doubt *n* apprehension, cynicism, disbelief, fear, hesitation, incredulity, lack of confidence, lack of conviction, lack of faith, misgivings, mistrust, qualms, reservations, skepticism, suspicion, uncertainty, uneasiness, worries

doubt *v* be dubious, be undecided, be skeptical, be suspicious, distrust, fear, have doubts, have misgivings, have reservations, have scruples, hesitate, question, suspect

doubtful adj 1 (not likely to happen) iffy *inf*, improbable, in doubt, uncertain, unconfirmed, unlikely, unsettled, vague; *opp* certain. 2 (feeling doubt) distrustful, hesitating, incredulous, mistrustful, skeptical, suspicious, tentative, unconvinced, unsure, wavering; *opp* certain. 3 (open to doubt) ambiguous, debatable, dodgy *inf*, dubious, equivocal, inconclusive, obscure, open to question, problematic, questionable

downfall n collapse, defeat, disgrace, fall, overthrow, ruin, undoing

downpour n cloudburst, deluge, flood, rainstorm, torrents of rain

downward adj descending, downhill, earthbound, earthward, going down

drab adj colorless, dingy, dismal, dowdy, dreary, dull, flat, gray, lackluster, mousy, somber; *opp* bright

draft n 1 first version, outline, plan, rough version, sketch. 2 breeze, current, flow, movement, wind

draft v compose, design, draw, draw up, formulate, outline, plan, put together, sketch, work out

drag v 1 haul, lug, pull, tow, trail, tug, yank. 2 (the afternoon dragged) be tedious, crawl, creep, go on too long, go slowly, move slowly, stretch out

drain n channel, conduit, culvert, ditch, drainpipe, gutter, outlet, pipe, sewer, sink, trench

drain v 1 (get liquid out) bleed, draw off, dry, empty, filter, milk, pump, remove, tap, withdraw. 2 (of liquid) drip, ebb, flow, leak, ooze, seep, trickle. 3 (use up resources) consume, deplete, expend,

exhaust, spend, strain, use up. 4 (make sb tired) enervate, exhaust, sap, tax, weary

drama n 1 (a play) comedy, dramatization, melodrama, play, production, show, tragedy. 2 (studying drama) acting, dramatic art, improvisation, stagecraft, theater. 3 crisis, excitement, histrionics, scene, spectacle

dramatic adj 1 breathtaking, electrifying, exciting, impressive, melodramatic, powerful, sensational, startling, tense, thrilling, unexpected, vivid. 2 (a dramatic gesture) artificial, exaggerated, flamboyant, large, overdone, showy, stagy. 3 stage, theatrical

drastic adj desperate, dire, extreme, radical, severe, strong

draw n 1 allure, attraction, enticement, lure, pull *inf*. 2 (in a game) dead heat, stalemate, tie. 3 lottery, raffle, sweepstake

draw v 1 color, depict, design, make a drawing, make a picture, paint, pencil, sketch, trace. 2 (draw the crowds) attract, coax, entice, lure, persuade, pull. 3 (draw a caravan) haul, pull, tow. 4 (draw a weapon) bring out, produce, pull out, remove, take out, unsheathe. 5 (draw in a game) be equal, be neck and neck, tie. 6 **draw up** compose, draft, frame, put in writing, put together, write out

drawback n catch, disadvantage, downside, flaw, fly in the ointment *inf*, hitch, hurdle, obstacle, problem, snag, stumbling-block; *opp* advantage

drawing n cartoon, depiction, diagram,

illustration, outline, picture, portrait, portrayal, representation, sketch, study

dread n alarm, apprehension, cold feet inf, dismay, fear, foreboding, fright, horror, terror, trepidation, uneasiness, worry

dread v be afraid of, be terrified of, fear, shrink from, worry about

dreadful adj appalling, awful, dire, disgusting, distressing, fearful, frightful, ghastly, grim, gruesome, harrowing, hideous, horrible, horrifying, monstrous, nasty, repugnant, revolting, shocking, terrible, very bad

dream n 1 daydream, delusion, fantasy, hallucination, illusion, imagination, mirage, nightmare, reverie, stupor, trance, vision. 2 aim, ambition, aspiration, desire, fantasy, goal, hope, pipedream, wish

dream v daydream, fantasize, hallucinate, have dreams, have nightmares, have visions, imagine, muse, think

dreary adj 1 boring, colorless, comfortless, depressing, drab, dull, flat, funereal, gloomy, joyless, melancholy, miserable, monotonous, mournful, sad, somber, sorrowful, uninteresting, wretched. 2 (dreary weather) bleak, dark, dismal, downcast, gloomy, overcast; *opp* bright

dregs n deposit, dross, grounds, remains, residue, scum, sediment

drench v douse, drown, flood, saturate, soak, wet

dress n 1 frock, gown, robe, shift. 2 (in strange dress) attire, clothes, clothing, costume, garb, gear inf, get-up inf

dress v 1 (put clothes on) don, get changed, get dressed, put on, slip on.

2 (decorate) adorn, decorate, trim. 3 (dress a wound) attend to, bandage, bind, cover, put a plaster on, tend, treat. **4 dress up** dress smartly, get dolled up inf. **5 dress up** (dress up as sb) disguise yourself, put fancy dress on, wear a disguise. **6 dress up** (make sth look better) beautify, decorate, embellish, improve, ornament, trim

dribble v 1 drip, drop, leak, ooze, run, seep, trickle. 2 drool, slaver, slobber

drift v be carried, coast, float, ramble, roam, stray, waft, wander

drill n discipline, exercise, instruction, practice, training

drill v 1 bore, make a hole, pierce, puncture. 2 coach, discipline, exercise, instruct, practice, put sb through his paces, rehearse, teach, train

drink n 1 alcohol, beverage, booze inf, grog, hard stuff inf, liquid refreshment, liquor, spirits. 2 cup, dram inf, glass, gulp, nip inf, sip, slug inf, swig inf, tot

drink v 1 gulp, guzzle, knock back inf, lap, sip, suck, swallow, swig inf. 2 (drink alcohol) booze inf, carouse, get drunk, have a few, hit the bottle inf, indulge, take a drop inf

drip n 1 bead, dribble, drop, leak, plop, splash, spot, tear, trickle. 2 coward, weakling, weak person, wimp inf

drip v dribble, drizzle, drop, filter, plop, splash, sprinkle, trickle

drive n 1 excursion, jaunt, journey, outing, ride, run, spin inf, trip. 2 (determination) ambition, determination, energy, enterprise, enthusiasm, get-up-and-go inf, initiative, motivation, vigor. 3 (sales drive) campaign, effort, push

drive v 1 (make sth or sb go) direct, guide, herd, move, propel, push, send, steer, urge. 2 (go in a car) chauffeur, give sb a lift, go by car, ride, run. 3 (drive a machine) operate, push, work. 4 (make sb do sth) coerce, compel, force, goad, impel, oblige, prod, put pressure on, spur. 5 (push sth in) bang, hammer, hit, knock, ram, thrust

droop v bend, dangle, drop, fall, flop, hang, sag, sink, slump, stoop, wilt

drop n 1 (drop of liquid) bead, blob, drip, droplet, globule, pearl, tear. 2 (amount) dab, dash, mouthful, sip, smidgen inf, splash, spot, taste, trace, trickle. 3 (a drop in unemployment) cut, decline, decrease, dip, downturn, fall-off, reduction; *opp* rise. 4 (a steep drop) cliff, descent, precipice, slope

drop v 1 (go downwards) descend, dip, dive, fall, fall away, go downhill, plummet, plunge, sink, subside, tumble; *opp* rise. 2 (of liquid) dribble, drip, fall, plop. 3 (of prices) collapse, decrease, dip, fall, lessen, plummet; *opp* rise. 4 (drop sth) let fall, let go; *opp* hold. 5 (lose interest in) abandon, chuck inf, desert, discontinue, ditch inf, finish with, give up, kick inf, stop; *opp* take up. 6 **drop off** decline, decrease, diminish, drop, dwindle, fall off, lessen; *opp* increase. 7 **drop off** doze off, fall asleep, nod off inf. 8 **drop out** abandon, back out, cop out sl, give up, leave, quit, resign, stop

drought n dry spell, lack of rain

drown v 1 deluge, drench, engulf, flood, immerse, inundate, submerge, swamp.

2 (of people) go under, sink. 3 (of noise) deaden, drown out, muffle, overpower, swallow up

drudge n hack, menial, servant, slave, worker

drudgery n chores, grind inf, hard work, labor, slavery, slog, toil

drug n 1 medication, medicine, remedy, treatment. 2 barbiturate, illegal substance, narcotic, opiate

drug v 1 anesthetize, knock out, sedate, tranquillize. 2 dope inf, dose, give drugs to, medicate, poison, treat

drum v beat, pulsate, rap, reverberate, tap, throb, thrum

drunk adj blind drunk, inebriated, intoxicated, loaded sl, out of it inf, plastered inf, sloshed inf, smashed inf, tight inf, tipsy, under the influence; *opp* sober

drunk n alcoholic, boozer inf, drunkard, heavy drinker, wino inf

dry adj 1 arid, baked, barren, dead, dehydrated, dried up, moistureless, parched, shriveled, waterless, wilted, withered, wizened. 2 (of food) desiccated, dried, hard, stale; *opp* fresh. 3 (of humor) deadpan, droll, ironic, laconic, sarcastic. 4 (of a text) boring, dreary, dull, monotonous, tedious, uninteresting; *opp* exciting

dry v dehydrate, desiccate, drain, dry off, dry out, dry up, make dry, parch, sear, shrivel, wither, wilt

dual adj binary, double, duplicate, linked, matched, paired, twin, twofold

dubious adj 1 (dubious about sth) doubtful, hesitant, skeptical, suspicious, uncertain, unconvinced, undecided, unsure, wavering; **opp** sure. 2 ambiguous, debatable, dodgy *inf*, doubtful, equivocal, fishy *inf*, iffy *inf*, indefinite, obscure, problematic, unclear, unresolved, unsettled, up in the air, vague

duck v 1 bend, bob, bow, crouch, drop, lower yourself, squat, stoop. 2 (duck sb) dunk, immerse, plunge, push under, submerge

due adj 1 (the money due) in arrears, outstanding, owed, owing, payable, unpaid. 2 (with the respect that was due) appropriate, decent, deserved, fit, fitting, merited, proper, right. 3 (train is due) awaited, expected, scheduled

duel n battle, clash, competition, contest, engagement, fight

dull adj 1 (of a person) dense, dim, dim-witted, obtuse, slow, stupid, unintelligent; **opp** bright.
2 boring, dreary, mind-numbing, tame, tedious, unexciting, unimaginative, uninteresting; **opp** exciting. 3 (of colors) dark, dingy, drab, dreary, faded, flat, lackluster, matt, muted, somber, toned down, washed-out; **opp** bright.
4 (of weather) cloudy, dark, dismal, gloomy, gray, murky, overcast; **opp** bright, sunny. 5 (a dull expression) apathetic, blank, dead, empty, expressionless, lifeless, unresponsive.
6 (feeling dull) depressed, drowsy, idle, inactive, lethargic, listless, sleepy, slow, sluggish, stagnant. 7 (a dull blade) blunt, blunted, dulled, unsharpened; **opp** sharp. 8 (a dull thud) deadened, indistinct, muffled, muted

dumb adj 1 at a loss for words,

inarticulate, mute, silent, soundless, speechless, tongue-tied, unable to speak, wordless. 2 (stupid) dense, dim, slow, stupid, unintelligent; **opp** clever

dump n garbage heap, junkyard, refuse heap, tip

dump v 1 (put) deposit, drop, fling down, park *inf*, put, throw. 2 (dump garbage) dispose of, ditch *inf*, empty out, get rid of, jettison, scrap, throw away, throw out, unload. 3 (dump sb) (*inf*) chuck *inf*, ditch *inf*, finish with, leave, stop going out with

dungeon n cage, pit, prison

duplicate adj alternative, copied, corresponding, identical, matched, matching, second, twin

duplicate n carbon copy, clone, copy, double, exact match, facsimile, imitation, photocopy, replica, spitting image *inf*, twin

duplicate v clone, copy, do again, double, echo, photocopy, print, repeat, replicate, reproduce

dusk n dark, evening, gloaming, nightfall, sundown, sunset, twilight

dust n dirt, earth, grime, grit, powder, smut, soil, soot

dusty adj 1 dirty, dust-covered, filthy, grimy, sooty, undusted, unswept.
2 chalky, crumbly, dry, fine, gritty, powdery, sandy

dutiful adj attentive, conscientious, devoted, faithful, hard-working, obedient, obliging, reliable, respectful, submissive, willing

duty n 1 (sth you have to do) assignment, chore, job, mission, obligation, responsibility, task. 2 (a sense of duty) allegiance, deference, loyalty, obligation, respect, responsibility. **3** (pay duty on sth) charge, customs, dues, levy, tariff, tax, toll

dwarf *adj* baby, miniature, pocket, small, tiny, undersized

dwarf *n* midget, pygmy

dwarf *v* dominate, overshadow, tower above, tower over

dwell *v* hang out *inf*, inhabit, live, lodge, remain, reside, rest, settle, stay, stop

dwelling *n* abode, home, house, residence

dye *n* color, coloring, pigment, stain, tint

dye *v* color, stain, tint

dynamic *adj* active, energetic, enterprising, enthusiastic, forceful, go-ahead *inf*, go-getting, high-powered, lively, motivated, powerful, spirited, vigorous

eager adj agog, anxious, ardent, bursting, committed, enthusiastic, excited, greedy, hungry, impatient, intent, itching inf, keen, longing, passionate, raring, thirsty; *opp* unenthusiastic

early adj 1 advanced, ahead of time, before time, forward, precocious, premature, untimely. 2 (early people) ancient, first, prehistoric, primitive

earn v 1 (earn money) bring in inf, clear inf, gain, get, gross, make, net, pocket, pull in, realize, receive, take home inf. 2 (earn points) accumulate, collect, gain, qualify for, receive, win. 3 (earn respect) be entitled to, be worthy of, deserve, gain, have a right to, merit, rate, secure, win

earnest adj 1 (of people) committed, conscientious, dedicated, determined, grave, hard-working, intense, purposeful, resolved, serious, solemn, studious, zealous. 2 (an earnest plea) heartfelt, impassioned, passionate, sincere, wholehearted

earnings n fee, income, pay, remuneration, return, reward, salary, wages

earth n 1 globe, planet, sphere, world. 2 clay, dirt, ground, land, loam, soil, turf

earthly adj human, material, mortal, terrestrial, worldly

ease n 1 calmness, comfort, composure, contentment, enjoyment, happiness, leisure, peace, relaxation, serenity, tranquillity. 2 (do sth with ease) casualness, dexterity, easiness, effortlessness, nonchalance

easy adj 1 (easy work) cushy inf, light, simple, soft, straightforward, undemanding; *opp* demanding, difficult. 2 (easy to do) child's play, clear, foolproof, idiot-proof inf, not difficult, simple, uncomplicated, user-friendly; *opp* complicated. 3 (an easy climb) gentle, leisurely, smooth, undemanding, unhurried; *opp* hard. 4 (an easy life) carefree, comfortable, cozy, peaceful, pleasant, quiet, troublefree, uncomplicated; *opp* hard

easygoing adj calm, carefree, casual, even-tempered, flexible, informal, laid-back inf, lenient, liberal, mellow, permissive, patient, placid, relaxed, tolerant, understanding

eat v 1 (eat food) bolt, chew, consume, devour, digest, gobble, graze inf, munch, nibble, put away inf, stuff yourself inf, swallow, wolf. 2 (time to eat) dine, feast, have a meal, lunch, snack inf

eavesdrop v bug inf, listen, listen in, monitor, overhear, snoop, spy, tap

ebb v 1 (of the tide) fall away, flow back,

go out, recede, retreat, subside, withdraw. 2 (of sb's confidence) decline, decrease, die, diminish, drop, dwindle, fade, flag, lessen, peter out, sink, wane, weaken

eccentric *adj* abnormal, bizarre, cranky, dotty *inf*, erratic, freakish, idiosyncratic, irregular, nutty *inf*, odd, outlandish, peculiar, queer, strange, uncommon, unconventional, unusual, wacky *sl*, way-out *inf*, weird, zany

echo *n* 1 answer, repetition, resounding, reverberation, ringing. 2 (echoes of another occasion) hint, memory, overtones, reminder, suggestion, trace

echo *v* 1 (of a sound) repeat, resound, reverberate, ring, sound again. 2 (echo sb) copy, imitate, mimic, mirror, parrot, reflect

eclipse *n* 1 blocking, blotting out, dimming, shading, veiling. 2 decline, deterioration, failure, fall, weakening; *opp* rise

eclipse *v* 1 block, blot out, cloud, darken, dim, obscure, overshadow, shroud, veil. 2 dwarf, exceed, excel, outdo, outshine, outstrip, put in the shade, surpass, transcend

economic *adj* 1 (for economic reasons) business, commercial, financial, industrial, trade. 2 (not economic) cost-effective, money-making, productive, profitable, profit-making, solvent, viable. 3 (economic policy) budgetary, financial, fiscal, monetary

economical *adj* 1 cheap, cost-effective, efficient, inexpensive, money-saving, time-saving; *opp* uneconomical. 2 (of a person) careful, economizing, frugal,

mean, miserly, parsimonious, prudent, scrimping, sparing, thrifty; *opp* wasteful

economics *n* budgeting, finance, money

economize *v* be economical, be frugal, be sparing, cut back, cut corners, save, scrimp, tighten your belt; *opp* splash out

economy *n* 1 carefulness, meanness, miserliness, prudence, restraint, saving, stinginess, thrift. 2 (a country's economy) budget, economic affairs, financial management, wealth

edge *n* 1 border, boundary, brim, brink, circumference, fringe, limit, line, lip, margin, outline, perimeter, periphery, rim, side, threshold, verge. 2 (have the edge) advantage, dominance, head start, lead, superiority, upper hand

edible *adj* digestible, eatable, fit to eat, good to eat, palatable, safe to eat, wholesome; *opp* inedible

edit *v* adapt, amend, annotate, arrange, assemble, censor, check, compile, correct, polish, prepare, put together, rephrase, revise, rewrite

edition *n* copy, impression, issue, number, printing, publication, version, volume

educate *v* 1 (educate sb at school) coach, discipline, drill, indoctrinate, inform, instruct, lecture, nurture, prepare, school, teach, train, tutor. 2 (travel educates you) civilize, cultivate, develop, edify, enlighten, inform

educated *adj* civilized, cultivated, cultured, enlightened, experienced, informed, knowledgable, learned, literate, well-informed, well-read; *opp* ignorant

education *n* instruction, knowledge, scholarship, schooling, teaching, training, tuition

educational *adj* edifying, enlightening, improving, informative, instructive

eerie *adj* awesome, creepy *inf*, fearful, frightening, ghostly, mysterious, scary *inf*, spine-chilling, spooky *inf*, strange, uncanny, unearthly, unnatural, weird

effect *n* 1 (the effect of sth) aftermath, conclusion, consequence, outcome, repercussion, result, upshot. 2 (create an effect) feeling, illusion, impression, sensation, sense

effect *v* (effect a change) accomplish, achieve, bring about, carry out, cause, complete, create, execute, fulfill, give rise to, implement, initiate, make, perform, produce, put into effect

effective *adj* 1 (effective argument, lighting) compelling, convincing, impressive, moving, noticeable, persuasive, powerful, striking, strong. 2 (working well) capable, competent, efficacious, efficient, powerful, productive, serviceable, strong, successful, useful. 3 (in force) active, current, in force, in operation, valid

effeminate *adj* feminine, girlish, unmanly, weak, wimpish *inf*, womanly; *opp* manly

effervescent *adj* 1 (of liquid) bubbling, bubbly, carbonated, fizzing, fizzy, foaming, foamy, frothing, gassy, sparkling. 2 (of personality) animated, bubbly, exuberant, irrepressible, lively, vivacious

efficiency *n* ability, capability, competence, economy, effectiveness, organization, power, skill

efficient *adj* 1 (an efficient worker) able,

businesslike, capable, competent, effective, organized, productive, proficient. 2 (an efficient use of time) cost-effective, economic, effective, productive, profitable, sensible; *opp* inefficient

effort *n* 1 application, challenge, diligence, elbow grease *inf*, endeavor, energy, exertion, force, labor, muscle, power, strain, stress, struggle, trouble, work. 2 (a good effort) attempt, crack *inf*, shot *inf*, stab *inf*, try. 3 accomplishment, achievement, attainment, exploit, feat, outcome, result

effortless *adj* easy, painless, simple, uncomplicated, undemanding; *opp* difficult

egotism *n* egocentricity, egoism, narcissism, pride, self-absorption, self-centeredness, self-importance, selfishness, vanity

egotist *n* bighead *inf*, egomaniac

egotistic(al) *adj* boastful, conceited, egocentric, egoistic, full of yourself, narcissistic, proud, self-centered, self-important, selfish, vain

eject *v* 1 (get rid of sb) banish, boot out *inf*, cast out, chuck out *inf*, deport, discharge, dismiss, evict, exile, expel, get rid of, kick out *inf*, oust, remove, sack, throw out, turn out. 2 (get rid of sth) disgorge, emit, excrete, expel, exude, release, send out, shoot out, spew, spout, throw out, vomit. 3 (remove) dislodge, extract, remove, take out; *opp* insert

elaborate *adj* 1 (worked out carefully) careful, detailed, exact, exhaustive, painstaking, precise, thorough;

opp vague. 2 (complicated) complex, complicated, fancy, fussy, intricate, involved, ornate, showy; *opp* simple

elaborate *v* add detail, add to, amplify, develop, embellish, embroider, enlarge, expand, fill out, flesh out, improve, polish, refine

elapse *v* go by, lapse, pass, roll, slip away, slip by

elastic *adj* bendy, bouncy, flexible, plastic, pliable, resilient, rubbery, springy, stretchy, supple, yielding

elect *v* adopt, appoint, cast your vote, choose, decide upon, nominate, opt for, pick, plump for, prefer, select, settle on, vote

election *n* ballot, hustings, poll, referendum, vote, voting

elector *n* constituent, voter

electric *adj* 1 (of a speech) charged, dynamic, electrifying, galvanizing, rousing, stimulating, stirring, tense, thrilling. 2 (of an appliance) battery-operated, electrical

elegant *adj* 1 (elegant clothes) beautiful, chic, fashionable, stylish, tasteful. 2 (of sb's body) delicate, fine, handsome. 3 (elegant manners) charming, debonair, genteel, graceful, nice, polished, refined, sophisticated, suave. 4 (an elegant apartment) beautiful, luxurious, posh *inf*, smart, stylish, sumptuous, tasteful

element *n* component, constituent, factor, feature, ingredient, part, piece, unit

elementary *adj* 1 easy, plain, rudimentary, simple, straightforward, understandable. 2 basic, early, first,

fundamental, initial, primary, introductory

elements *n* 1 basics, essentials, first principles, foundations, principles, rudiments. 2 atmosphere, climate, environment, weather

elevate *v* 1 hoist, lift, make higher, raise; *opp* lower. 2 advance, promote, upgrade

eligible *adj* acceptable, allowed, authorized, equipped, fit, qualified, suitable, suited, worthy

eliminate *v* cut out, exclude, get rid of, leave out, reject, remove, take out

elite *n* 1 best, cream *inf*, flower, pick, top. 2 aristocracy, nobility, upper class

elope *v* abscond, run away, run off, slip away, steal away

eloquent *adj* articulate, fluent, graceful, moving, persuasive, plausible, powerful, well-expressed

elude *v* avoid, dodge, escape, evade, get away, give the slip to, lose, shake off, slip away from, throw sb off the scent

elusive *adj* evasive, hard to find, hard to pin down, indefinable, intangible, shifting, shifty, slippery, subtle

emanate *v* arise, come forth, derive, emerge, flow, issue, originate, proceed, spring, stem

emancipate *v* 1 deliver, free, let go, liberate, release, set free, unchain, unshackle; *opp* enslave. 2 enfranchise, give rights to, give the vote to

embargo *n* ban, bar, boycott, prohibition, restriction, seizure, stoppage

embark *v* 1 (board a ship) board, go on board, go aboard. 2 (embark on a venture) begin, enter into, go into, have a go at, launch, set about, set out, take on, take the plunge, take up, undertake, venture into

embarrass v fluster, humiliate, make sb blush, make sb feel awkward, make sb go red, mortify, shame, show up

embarrassed adj ashamed, awkward, blushing, flustered, humiliated, mortified, red, red-faced, self-conscious, shamefaced, sheepish

embarrassing adj awkward, humiliating, mortifying, tricky, uncomfortable

embarrassment n awkwardness, bashfulness, humiliation, mortification, self-consciousness, shame

emblem n badge, crest, insignia, logo, symbol, sign

embody v 1 (include) comprise, constitute, embrace, encompass, include, incorporate, take in. 2 (represent) personify, represent, stand for, symbolize, typify

embrace v 1 (hug) clasp, cuddle, fold sb in your arms, hold, hug. 2 (include) comprise, embody, encompass, include, incorporate, take in, subsume. 3 (welcome) adopt, espouse, support, take up, take on board, welcome

emerge v 1 appear, come into view, come out, emanate, materialize, surface. 2 arise, become apparent, become known, crop up, come out, come to light, develop, get around, transpire, turn out

emergency n accident, crisis, critical situation, danger, dire straits, disaster, fix, hole, pickle inf, predicament

emigrate v go to live abroad, migrate, move, relocate

eminent adj celebrated, distinguished,

esteemed, important, notable, prominent, renowned, respected

emission n discharge, leakage, outflow, output, radiation, release

emit v belch, discharge, disgorge, exude, give off, leak, let out, pour out, radiate, release, send out, spew out, spout

emotion n excitement, feeling, fervor, passion, sensation, sentiment, sentimentality

emotional adj ardent, demonstrative, excitable, fervent, fiery, heated, hot-blooded, impassioned, moved, moving, passionate, poignant, sensitive, sentimental, warm

emotive adj 1 controversial, delicate, sensitive. 2 emotional, heart-rending, moving, touching

emphasis n accent, attention, force, importance, priority, significance, stress, weight

emphasize v accentuate, bring out, feature, focus on, give prominence to, heighten, highlight, point up, press home, spotlight, stress, underline, underscore

emphatic adj absolute, categorical, decided, definite, determined, firm, forceful, positive, powerful, pronounced, strong, unequivocal, unmistakable; *opp* hesitant, tentative

empire n colonies, commonwealth, domain, dominion, jurisdiction, kingdom, protectorate, realm, territory

employ v 1 (hire) commission, engage, hire, put on the payroll, recruit, sign up, take on. 2 (use) exercise, make use of, use

employed adj earning, in a job, in

employment, in work, working, waged;
opp unemployed

employee *n* member of staff, worker,
workforce

employer *n* boss, management, manager,
owner

employment *n* business, job, livelihood,
living, occupation, profession, trade,
vocation, work

emptiness *n* 1 bareness, barrenness,
blank, vacuum, void. 2 futility,
hollowness, meaninglessness,
senselessness, triviality, worthlessness

empty *adj* 1 bare, barren, blank, clear,
deserted, unfilled, vacant, with nothing
inside. 2 futile, hollow, meaningless,
purposeless, senseless, trivial, worthless

enable *v* allow, authorize, empower,
entitle, equip, facilitate, make sth
possible, open the way for, prepare,
qualify; *opp* prevent

enamored *adj* besotted, captivated, crazy
about *inf*, infatuated, in love, keen on,
nuts about *inf*, smitten *inf*, sweet on

enchant *v* allure, bewitch, captivate, cast
a spell on, charm, delight, entrance,
fascinate

enchanted *adj* 1 bewitched, captivated,
charmed, delighted, entranced,
fascinated, spellbound. 2 charmed,
magic, magical, under a spell

enchanting *adj* alluring, attractive,
bewitching, captivating, charming,
delightful, fascinating, spellbinding

enclose *v* 1 cocoon, encase, encircle,
fence off, ring, shut in, surround, wall in,
wrap. 2 (enclose sth with a letter)
include, insert, put in with, send with

enclosure *n* arena, compound, corral,

paddock, pen, pound, ring, run,
stockade, yard

encounter *n* confrontation, meeting

encounter *v* be faced with, bump into,
come across, come up against, confront,
meet, run into

encourage *v* be conducive to, bolster,
buoy up, cheer on, egg on *inf*, foster, give
courage to, give hope to, hearten,
inspire, reassure, root for, spur on,
stimulate, strengthen, support, urge;
opp discourage

encouragement *n* boost, incentive,
inspiration, pep talk, reassurance, shot
in the arm, support; *opp* discouragement

encouraging *adj* heartening, hopeful,
inspiring, optimistic, promising,
reassuring, supportive, uplifting;
opp discouraging

encroach *v* barge in *inf*, get in on *inf*,
impinge, interfere, intrude, invade,
make inroads, muscle in, obtrude, poke
your nose in *inf*, tread on sb's toes,
trespass

end *n* 1 cessation, climax, close,
completion, conclusion, culmination,
finale, finish. 2 boundary, edge, extent,
limit, margin, terminus, tip.
3 (remnant) butt, leftover, remnant,
stub. 4 (death) curtains *inf*, death,
demise, destruction, downfall,
extermination, extinction, ruin.
5 (objective) aim, goal, intention,
motive, object, objective, purpose

end *v* 1 abolish, conclude, finish, halt,
phase out, put an end to, put a stop to,
stop, terminate, wind up; *opp* begin,
start. 2 break off, cease, close, come to
an end, conclude, culminate, finish,

peter out, stop, terminate; **opp** begin, start. **3 end up** become, come to, come to rest, finish up, reach, turn out, wind up

endanger v expose, jeopardize, put at risk, risk, threaten

endearing adj adorable, captivating, charming, cute, engaging, lovable, sweet; **opp** repulsive

endless adj continual, continuous, everlasting, incessant, interminable, limitless, never-ending, nonstop, perpetual, unbroken, unending, uninterrupted, unremitting

endorse v **1** advocate, approve, authorize, back, champion, give approval to, give sth the go-ahead, give sth the red light, okay, sanction, second, support, vote for. **2** countersign, initial, sign

endure v bear, cope with, face, go through, put up with, stand, stick inf, stomach, tolerate, withstand. **2** carry on, continue, exist, last, live, persist, prevail, survive

enemy n adversary, foe, opponent, rival, them inf, the opposition, the other side; **opp** ally, friend, one of us

energetic adj active, animated, brisk, dynamic, forceful, hard-working, lively, spirited, tireless, vigorous; **opp** lethargic, sluggish

energy n animation, drive, dynamism, enthusiasm, get-up-and-go inf, life, liveliness, potency, stamina, strength, vigor, vitality, vivacity; **opp** lethargy, weakness

enforce v administer, carry out, implement, impose, insist on, put into force

engage v **1** (engage sb's interest) attract, allure, captivate, capture, catch, draw, engross, gain, grip, hold, occupy. **2** (engage gear) interconnect, interlock, lock on. **3** (employ) appoint, commission, employ, hire, put on the payroll, take on. **4 engage in** be/get involved in, join in, participate in, practice, tackle, take part in

engaged adj **1** busy, occupied, tied up, unavailable. **2** betrothed, spoken for

engagement n **1** appointment, commitment, date, meeting. **2** betrothal

engine n generator, locomotive, machine, motor, turbine

engineer n architect, designer, mechanic, planner, technician

engineer v bring about, create, devise, effect, manage, mastermind, orchestrate, plan

engrave v carve, chisel, cut, etch, gouge, inscribe, scratch

engraving n block, carving, etching, inscription, plate, print

engrossed adj absorbed, fascinated, immersed, intent, involved, preoccupied, rapt, riveted, wrapped up

enhance v add to, augment, boost, emphasize, enrich, improve, increase, intensify, reinforce, strengthen, upgrade

enigma n conundrum, mystery, paradox, puzzle, riddle

enigmatic adj baffling, curious, inexplicable, mysterious, obscure, puzzling, strange, weird

enjoy v **1** adore, get a buzz from inf, get a kick out of inf, get pleasure from, go in for inf, like, love, luxuriate in, relish, revel in; **opp** dislike, hate. **2 enjoy**

yourself celebrate, have a field day, have a good time, have fun, have the time of your life, let your hair down, party, treat yourself

enjoyable *adj* brilliant, entertaining, fun, good, good fun, great, lovely, nice, pleasant, super, superb, wonderful; *opp* awful, dreadful

enjoyment *n* amusement, delight, entertainment, fun, gratification, joy, pleasure, relish, satisfaction

enlarge *v* add to, blow up, broaden, deepen, expand, extend, increase, inflate, lengthen, let out, magnify, make bigger, stretch, widen; *opp* contract, reduce, shrink

enlighten *v* advise, edify, educate, fill sb in on, inform, instruct, make aware, make sb understand, put sb in the picture, put sb right, teach, tell sb about

enlightened *adj* 1 aware, educated, informed, knowledgeable, learned, well-informed, wise; *opp* ignorant. 2 broad-minded, fair-minded, liberal, open-minded, tolerant; *opp* bigoted, prejudiced

enlist *v* employ, engage, enroll, hire, join up, recruit, register, sign up, take on, volunteer for

enormous *adj* astronomic, big, colossal, excessive, giant, gigantic, huge, immense, jumbo, mammoth, massive, vast; *opp* minuscule, small, tiny

enough *adj* adequate, ample, as much as you need, plenty, sufficient

enrich *v* augment, embellish, enhance, improve, make richer, supplement; *opp* impoverish

enroll *v* admit, enlist, join, recruit, register, sign on, sign up, take on

ensue *v* come after, derive, flow, follow, happen afterwards, occur as a result, result, stem from, turn out

ensure *v* certify, confirm, guarantee, make certain, make sure, secure

entail *v* call for, give rise to, involve, lead to, necessitate, require, result in

enter *v* 1 (go inside) board, come in, come inside, get into, get onto, go in, go inside, penetrate. 2 (enter information) add, document, log, note, put down, register, take down, write down, write in. 3 (enroll) become a member, enlist, enroll, go in for, join, participate in, put your name down for, sign up for, take part in

enterprise *n* 1 business, effort, endeavor, operation, project, scheme, undertaking, venture. 2 ambition, drive, enthusiasm, get-up-and-go *inf*, gumption, imagination, initiative

enterprising *adj* adventurous, ambitious, entrepreneurial, go-ahead, imaginative, resourceful; *opp* staid, stick-in-the-mud, unimaginative

entertain *v* amuse, divert, keep sb amused, keep sb happy, keep sb's attention, occupy

entertainer *n* artist, artiste, performer

entertaining *adj* amusing, diverting, funny, hilarious, interesting, witty; *opp* boring, dull

entertainment *n* 1 amusement, distraction, diversion, enjoyment, fun, pleasure, treat. 2 performance, presentation, production, show, spectacle

enthralled *adj* captivated, engrossed,

fascinated, gripped, intrigued, hypnotized, riveted, spellbound, taken up with

enthusiasm n commitment, eagerness, excitement, exuberance, fervor, gusto, keenness, passion, relish; *opp* apathy

enthusiast n addict, buff *inf*, devotee, fan, fanatic, fiend *inf*, follower, freak *inf*, lover, supporter

enthusiastic adj avid, crazy *inf*, dead keen *inf*, eager, keen, excited, fanatical, mad about *inf*, passionate, raring to go, vehement, wholehearted; *opp* apathetic, half-hearted

entice v allure, encourage, induce, lead on, lure, seduce, tempt

entire adj complete, full, total, whole

entitle v authorize, empower, enable, give sb the right, license, make sb eligible, permit, qualify

entourage n attendants, band, escort, followers, groupies *inf*, retinue

entrails n bowels, guts *inf*, innards, insides, intestines

entrance n 1 (way in) access point, door, doorway, entry, foyer, gate, gateway, lobby, mouth, opening, portal, threshold, way in. 2 (admission) access, admission, admittance, entry, right of entry

entrant n applicant, candidate, competitor, contestant, participant, player

entrenched adj deep-rooted, deep-seated, established, firmly held, fixed, ingrained, well-established

entry n 1 (way in) access point, door, doorway, entrance, foyer, gate, gateway, lobby, opening, threshold, way in.

2 (admission) access, admission, admittance, entrance, right of entry.
3 (in a diary) account, description, item, note, record

envelop v blanket, cover, encase, enclose, enfold, engulf, shroud, surround, swathe, veil, wrap

envelope n bubble bag, case, casing, cover, covering, folder, mailing bag, sheathe, skin, wrapper

enviable adj desirable, favored, fine, fortunate, privileged, plum *inf*, sought-after, worth having

envious adj green-eyed, green with envy, jealous, resentful

environment n conditions, context, environs, habitat, locale, locality, milieu, setting, situation, surroundings

envisage v anticipate, conceive of, contemplate, expect, imagine, picture, see, suppose, visualize

envoy n agent, ambassador, consul, delegate, emissary, go-between, intermediary, messenger, representative

envy n enviousness, jealousy, resentfulness, resentment

ephemeral adj brief, evanescent, fleeting, momentary, passing, short-lived, temporary, throwaway, transient

epidemic n outbreak, plague, rash, scourge, wave

epidemic adj global, pandemic, prevalent, rampant, rife, spreading, sweeping, universal, widespread

episode n 1 affair, chapter, escapade, event, experience, incident, interlude, matter, occasion, occurrence. 2 edition, installment, part, scene, section

epitome n embodiment, essence, model,

personification, prototype

epoch *n* age, date, day, era, generation, period, time

equal *adj* **1** alike, comparable, identical, equivalent, on a par, similar, the same, uniform. **2** even, evenly matched, fifty-fifty, level, neck-and-neck. **3** egalitarian, even-handed, fair, impartial, just, unbiased

equal *n* clone, counterpart, equivalent, match, twin

equality *n* egalitarianism, equal opportunity, fairness, impartiality, justice; *opp* discrimination, inequality

equalize *v* balance, compensate, equate, even up, level, level the score, make equal, match, standardize

equate *v* associate, be equivalent, compare, correspond to, draw a parallel between, group together, liken, link, pair, regard as the same, talk of in the same breath

equation *n* calculation, sum

equilibrium *n* balance, evenness, stability, symmetry

equip *v* arm, fit out, furnish, prepare, provide, supply

equipment *n* apparatus, gear, instruments, kit *inf*, machinery, materials, rig, stuff, supplies, tackle, things, tools, trappings, utensils

equivalent *adj* alike, analogous, comparable, corresponding, equal, identical, interchangeable, matching, on a par, similar, the same, twin; *opp* dissimilar

equivocal *adj* ambiguous, ambivalent, doubtful, dubious, evasive, hesitant, qualified, questionable, uncertain, vague; *opp* categorical, definite, unequivocal

era *n* age, date, day, epoch, generation, period, stage, time

eradicate *v* abolish, annihilate, destroy, eliminate, expunge, exterminate, get rid of, obliterate, remove, root out, stamp out, take out, weed out, wipe out

erase *v* blot out, cancel, cross out, delete, remove, rub out, scratch out, scrub out, wipe out

erect *adj* perpendicular, rigid, standing, stiff, straight, straight as a ramrod, upright, vertical

erect *v* assemble, build, construct, pitch, put together, put up, set up; *opp* demolish, dismantle, take down

erode *v* abrade, corrode, eat away, rub away, wash away, wear away, weather

erotic *adj* amorous, aphrodisiac, pornographic, raunchy, sensual, sexual, sexy, steamy, suggestive

err *v* be mistaken, be wrong, blunder, do wrong, get it wrong, get the wrong end of the stick, go wrong, make a mistake, make an error, miscalculate, slip up

errand *n* assignment, chore, job, message, task

erratic *adj* changeable, chaotic, fickle, inconsistent, irregular, meandering, sporadic, unpredictable, unreliable; *opp* constant, regular

error *n* blunder, boo-boo *inf*, bug, fault, gaffe, miscalculation, misprint, mistake, oversight, slip-up *inf*

erupt *v* blow up, burst out, explode, flare up, go off, gush, spew out, spout

escalate *v* accelerate, climb, get worse, grow, heighten, increase, intensify, mount, rise, spiral, step up

escapade n adventure, affair, episode, exploit, incident, prank, stunt

escape n 1 breakout, flight, flit, getaway, jailbreak. 2 discharge, emission, leak, leakage, seepage

escape v 1 abscond, bolt, break loose, break out, get away, get free, get out, run away, run off, flit *inf*. 2 (escape doing sth) avoid, dodge, duck, evade. 3 (leak) bleed, discharge, drain, leak, ooze, seep

escort n attendant, bodyguard, chaperon, companion, date, entourage, guard, outrider, partner, retinue

escort v accompany, conduct, go with, guide, lead, partner, shepherd, take

essay n article, assignment, comment, composition, critique, paper, piece, treatise, review, writings

essence n 1 core, crux, essential part, fundamental principle, heart, innermost being, marrow, nature, spirit, substance. 2 concentrate, essential oil, extract, flavoring, tincture

essential adj critical, crucial, important, indispensable, key, necessary, vital. 2 basic, cardinal, fundamental, inherent, intrinsic, principal

establish v 1 create, form, found, install, put in place, set up, start. 2 confirm, demonstrate, prove, show, verify

established adj accepted, deep-rooted, entrenched, ingrained, long-standing, orthodox, official, settled, traditional, tried-and-tested

establishment n 1 creation, formation, foundation, inauguration, inception, setting up. 2 business, company, concern, firm, household, office,

organization, outfit *inf*, residence, shop, store. 3 **the Establishment** big brother *inf*, bureaucracy, the authorities, the government, the powers that be, the ruling classes, the system

estate n 1 domain, holding, land, park, property. 2 assets, belongings, fortune, inheritance, possessions, property

esteem n acclaim, admiration, approbation, favor, good opinion, honor, kudos, prestige, regard, respect, reverence

estimate n approximation, assessment, ballpark figure, calculation, evaluation, guess, guesstimate *inf*, judgment, reckoning, rough figure

estimate v 1 (cost) assess, calculate, evaluate, gauge, judge, reckon, value, work out. 2 (believe) appraise, assess, believe, consider, judge, rate, reckon, surmise, think, view

estimation n 1 (opinion) appraisal, assessment, belief, consideration, considered opinion, evaluation, judgment, opinion, view, way of thinking. 2 (esteem) admiration, approval, esteem, good opinion, regard, respect

estranged adj alienated, antagonized, apart, at odds, divided, going their separate ways, separated

eternal adj 1 abiding, everlasting, deathless, immortal, infinite, permanent, perpetual, timeless, unceasing, undying, without end. 2 ceaseless, constant, continual, continuous, endless, everlasting, incessant, interminable, never-ending, nonstop, perpetual, unending

eternity n 1 ages, an age, endlessness, forever, infinity, long time, timelessness. 2 afterlife, heaven, paradise, the hereafter, the next world, world without end

ethical adj correct, decent, fair, good, honest, honorable, just, moral, principled, proper, right, upright, virtuous

ethics n moral code, morality, morals, principles, standards, values

ethnic adj 1 cultural, national, native, racial, tribal. 2 folk, traditional

etiquette n 1 (politeness) civility, courtesy, decorum, good manners, politeness, propriety. 2 (convention) accepted behavior, code of behavior, code of conduct, code of practice, convention, custom, manners, propriety, protocol, the proprieties

evacuate v abandon, desert, flee, go away from, leave, move out of, pull out of inf, quit, retreat from, vacate, withdraw from

evade v 1 avoid, dodge, duck inf, elude, escape, give sb the slip, keep out of the way of, shake off, sidestep, steer clear of; **opp** confront. 2 (evade a question or issue) avoid, beat about the bush, dodge, equivocate, fudge, hedge, not give a straight answer to, quibble about, prevaricate. 3 (evade work) avoid, dodge, shirk, skive inf

evaluate v appraise, assess, estimate, gauge, judge, put a value on, rate, reckon, size up, value, weigh up

evaporate v 1 dry, dry up, vaporize. 2 disappear, disperse, dissipate, dissolve, fade away, melt away, vanish

evasive adj 1 (of a person, tactic) artful, cagey inf, cunning, devious, disingenuous, elusive, shifty. 2 (of a reply) ambiguous, disingenuous, equivocal, indirect, misleading, oblique, prevaricating; **opp** direct

even adj 1 (level) flat, flush, horizontal, level, plane, smooth, uniform. 2 (steady, constant) consistent, constant, regular, stable, steady, unbroken, unchanging, uniform, unvarying. 3 (equal) alike, all square, balanced, equal, identical, level, much the same, on an equal footing, similar, the same, tied. 4 (fair) balanced, disinterested, equitable, evenhanded, fair, impartial, just, unbiased. 5 get even be revenged, get your own back, get your revenge, give as good as you get, pay sb back, reciprocate, revenge yourself, settle the score

event n 1 episode, experience, happening, occasion, occurrence, phenomenon. 2 (sporting event) competition, contest, fixture, game, match, race, round, tournament

even-tempered adj calm, cool, easy-going, equable, laid back inf, imperturbable, peaceable, placid, relaxed, serene, unflappable, unruffled

eventful adj action-packed, active, busy, exciting, full, lively, never a dull moment

eventual adj concluding, consequent, ensuing, final, future, later, resulting, ultimate

eventually adv after all, at last, at the end of the day, finally, in the end, in the long run, in time, sooner or later, one day, one fine day inf, some day, sooner or later, when all is said and done

everlasting *adj* 1 deathless, enduring, eternal, immortal, imperishable, indestructible, infinite, lasting, never-ending, perpetual, timeless, undying, unending. 2 ceaseless, constant, continual, continuous, eternal, incessant, interminable, never-ending, nonstop, perpetual, tiresome, without let-up

everyday *adj* common, commonplace, customary, familiar, habitual, mundane, nothing special, ordinary, regular, routine, run-of-the-mill, standard, usual, workaday

evict *v* bounce *inf*, chuck out *inf*, dislodge, dispossess, drive out, eject, expel, give notice to quit, kick out *inf*, oust, put out, remove, show sb the door, throw out, throw sb out on his ear, turn out

evidence *n* 1 confirmation, corroboration, data, facts, indication, information, mark, proof, sign, substantiation, support, verification. 2 affidavit, declaration, deposition, statement, testimony. 3 **give evidence** swear on oath, testify, witness. 4 **in evidence** conspicuous, evident, having a high profile, noticeable, obvious, on display, on view

evident *adj* (easy to see or understand) apparent, clear, easy to see, incontestable, incontrovertible, indisputable, manifest, noticeable, obvious, palpable, perceptible, plain, plain as the nose on your face *inf*, self-explanatory, tangible, transparent, undeniable, undoubted, unmistakable, visible

evidently *adv* 1 apparently, as far as you can tell, from all appearances, it appears, it seems, ostensibly, outwardly, seemingly. 2 clearly, obviously, surely, undoubtedly, without question

evil *adj* atrocious, bad, base, corrupt, cruel, demonic, diabolic, depraved, fiendish, foul, heinous, immoral, iniquitous, malicious, malevolent, shameful, sinful, vicious, vile, villainous, wicked; *opp* good

evil *n* 1 atrocity, badness, corruption, cruelty, depravity, immorality, vice, villainy, wickedness, wrong, wrong-doing. 2 affliction, calamity, curse, disaster, hardship, harm, misery, misfortune, pain, suffering, wrong

evocative *adj* bringing to mind, redolent, reminiscent, suggestive

evoke *v* 1 (a response or emotion) arouse, awaken, cause, elicit, excite, give rise to, induce, inspire, kindle, provoke, stimulate, stir up. 2 (an image or memory) call to mind, call up, conjure up, invoke, inspire, recall, summon up

evolution *n* 1 advance, development, emergence, growth, maturing, progress, progression, unfolding. 2 natural selection

evolve *v* change, develop, grow, expand, improve, mature, open out, progress, unfold

exact *adj* 1 (an exact copy) accurate, careful, correct, explicit, faithful, literal, precise, strict, true, word for word. 2 (of a person) accurate, careful, conscientious, meticulous, painstaking, precise, punctilious

exact *v* call for, compel, demand, enforce, extort, extract, impose, insist on, require

exactly *adv* 1 (quite right) absolutely, certainly, definitely, indeed, precisely, quite, quite right, quite so. 2 accurately, carefully, correctly, faithfully, precisely, strictly, to the letter, word for word. 3 **not exactly** by no means, not at all, not really

exaggerate *v* amplify, embellish, embroider, magnify, make a drama out of, make a mountain out of a molehill, make too much of, overemphasize, overestimate, overrate, overstate, stretch the truth, talk up *inf*

exaggeration *n* embellishment, embroidery, hyperbole, inflation, overestimation, overstatement

examination *n* 1 (the examination of sth) appraisal, analysis, consideration, exploration, inspection, investigation, observation, perusal, probe, review, scrutiny. 2 (undergo an examination) check-up, inspection, the once-over *inf*. 3 (of a witness) cross-examination, interrogation, questioning. 4 assessment, exam, test

examine *v* 1 analyze, appraise, assess, check out, consider, explore, look into, scrutinize, study, weigh, weigh up. 2 check, give the once-over *inf*, go over, inspect, look at, look over, observe, peruse, scan, take a look at. 3 (examine a witness) cross-examine, grill *inf*, interrogate, question, test

example *n* 1 case, case in point, illustration, instance, sample, specimen. 2 ideal, model, paragon, pattern, standard. 3 **for example** as an illustration, e.g., for instance, such as

exasperate *v* anger, annoy, drive crazy *inf*,

enrage, get on your nerves, incense, infuriate, irk, irritate, madden, make your blood boil, needle *inf*, provoke, rouse, try the patience of, vex, wind up *inf*

excavate *v* burrow, dig, dig out, dig up, hollow out, mine, tunnel, uncover, unearth

exceed *v* 1 (be better than) beat, be better than, be greater than, better, do more than, excel, outdo, outshine, outstrip, surpass. 2 (be more than) be greater than, be more than, go beyond, pass, top. 3 (go beyond a limit) do more than, go beyond, go over, go over the top, overstep

excel *v* 1 (be better than) beat, be better than, be superior to, do better than, eclipse, outdo, outclass, outshine, outstrip, overshadow, surpass. 2 (be very good) be excellent, be outstanding, be very good, do well, shine, stand out

excellence *n* distinction, eminence, greatness, high quality, merit, quality, perfection, superiority, value, worth

excellent *adj* 1 (very good) ace *inf*, brilliant *inf*, exceptional, fabulous *inf*, fantastic *inf*, great, marvelous, outstanding, perfect, superb, superior, wonderful; *opp* awful, dreadful. 2 (of good quality) A1, choice, exquisite, fine, first-class, first rate, good quality, of high quality, prime, select. 3 (admirable) admirable, exemplary, superior, supreme, worthy

exception *n* 1 anomaly, departure, deviation, freak, irregularity, oddity, special case. 2 exclusion, omission. 3 **with the exception of** apart from, bar,

but for, except, except for, excepting.
4 take exception be offended, object to, resent, take offense, take umbrage

exceptional *adj* 1 (unusually good) excellent, outstanding, phenomenal, prodigious, remarkable, special.
2 (unusual) abnormal, atypical, odd, out of the ordinary, peculiar, rare, unusual; *opp* normal, usual

excerpt *n* clip, extract, part, passage, quotation, quote, selection

excess *n* 1 abundance, glut, more than enough, overdose, overkill *inf*, surfeit, surplus, too much, too many. **2** leftovers, overflow, remainder, residue.
3 debauchery, dissipation, intemperance, overindulgence

excessive *adj* exaggerated, extravagant, immoderate, inordinate, lavish, needless, overdone, over the top *inf*, superfluous, uncalled-for, undue, unnecessary, unreasonable, unwarranted

exchange *n* barter, dealing, give and take, interchange, substitution, swap *inf*, switch, trade, trade-off

exchange *v* 1 barter, do a swap *inf*, reciprocate, swap *inf*, trade. **2** change, interchange, replace, substitute, swap *inf*, switch, trade in

excitable *adj* 1 edgy, emotional, highly strung, jumpy, lively, nervous, restive, volatile. **2** hasty, hot-headed, quick-tempered, temperamental, testy, touchy; *opp* calm

excite *v* 1 (make sb excited) agitate, arouse, disturb, get sb going *inf*, inflame, provoke, rouse, set off *inf*, stimulate, stir up, thrill, titillate, turn on *inf*, upset, wind up *inf*, work up *inf*. **2** (arouse

feelings) arouse, awaken, cause, evoke, incite, inspire, kindle, stir up

excited *adj* 1 agog, animated, aroused, boisterous, enthusiastic, exhilarated, exuberant, high *inf*, in high spirits, intoxicated, thrilled, turned on *inf*.
2 agitated, at fever pitch, frantic, frenzied, hysterical, in a frenzy, overwrought, wound up

excitement *n* 1 agitation, animation, anticipation, elation, exhilaration, enthusiasm, ferment, tumult.
2 adventure, kick *inf*, thrill

exciting *adj* 1 (of an experience) dramatic, electrifying, exhilarating, heady, stimulating, stirring, thrilling; *opp* dull, boring. **2** (of a story, film) action-packed, dramatic, fast-moving, gripping, riveting, spectacular, spine-tingling; *opp* dull, boring

exclaim *v* blurt out, call, call out, come out with, cry, cry out, shout, utter, yell

exclude *v* 1 (keep out) ban, bar, blacklist, debar, forbid, ignore, keep out, leave out, ostracize, pass over, prohibit, proscribe, refuse, reject, repudiate, shut out. **2** (be exclusive of) be apart from, be exclusive of, except; *opp* include

exclusive *adj* 1 closed, limited, posh *inf*, private, restricted, select, selective, smart, snobbish. **2** only, single, sole, unique. **3 exclusive of** apart from, excluding, not including

excursion *n* day trip, expedition, jaunt, outing, pleasure trip, tour, trip

excuse *n* 1 apology, defense, explanation, justification, mitigation, mitigating circumstances, plea, pretext, reason.
2 cop-out *inf*, ostensible reason,

pretense, pretext, rationalization

excuse v 1 (a person) absolve, allow sb to get away with sth, exonerate, forgive, let off, make allowances for, pardon.
2 (excuse bad behavior) condone, defend, explain, explain away, forgive, ignore, justify, mitigate, pardon.
3 (excuse sb from doing sth) exempt, free sb from, let sb off, liberate sb from, release sb from, relieve, spare

execute v 1 carry out the death sentence, kill, lynch, put to death. 2 (execute a plan) accomplish, achieve, carry out, discharge, do, effect, enact, fulfill, implement, perform, put into practice, realize

execution n 1 capital punishment, death sentence, killing, putting to death. 2 (the execution of a plan) accomplishment, achievement, carrying out, discharge, effecting, fulfillment, implementation, performance, realization

executioner n hit-man inf, killer

executive adj administrative, controlling, decision-making, directing, governing, managerial

executive n 1 administrator, boss inf, chief inf, director, manager, officer, official. 2 administration, government, leadership, management, top brass inf

exemplify v 1 (give an example of) demonstrate, give an example, illustrate, show. 2 (be an example) be an example of, be typical of, epitomize, represent, symbolize, typify

exempt adj excepted, excused, free from, immune, let off, not liable to, released from, spare

exempt v except, exclude, excuse, free sb from, grant immunity from, let sb off, make an exception for, release sb from, spare

exercise n 1 (physical exercise) activity, effort, exertion, games, gym, gymnastics, keep fit, movement, sport, training, workout. 2 (use) application, employment, practice, use, utilization

exercise v 1 (take exercise) do exercises, drill, exert yourself, take exercise, train, work out. 2 (use) apply, employ, exert, make use of, practice, use, utilize

exert v 1 apply, bring to bear, employ, make use of, use, utilize, wield. 2 (exert yourself) apply yourself, do your best, do your utmost, drive yourself hard, give your all, go all out, make an effort, push yourself, put yourself out, strain, strive, struggle, toil, work hard

exertion n activity, action, effort, endeavor, exercise, hard work, strain, toil, work

exhaust v 1 (tire) burn out inf, debilitate, do in inf, drain, enervate, fatigue, knock out inf, overtax, sap your strength, take it out of you, tire, tire out, wear out, weary. 2 (use up) consume, deplete, dissipate, drain, empty, finish off, finish up, run out of, run through, spend, squander, use up, waste

exhausted adj 1 (tired) all in, burnt out, bushed, dead beat inf, dead on your feet inf, debilitated, dog-tired inf, drained, enervated, faint, fatigued, prostrate, ready to drop, shattered inf, spent, tired out, worn out. 2 (used up) all gone, at an end, depleted, finished, spent, used up

exhausting *adj* arduous, back-breaking, debilitating, enervating, fatiguing, grueling, laborious, punishing, taxing, wearing, wearying; *opp* easy

exhaustive *adj* all-embracing, careful, complete, comprehensive, full, in-depth, intensive, thorough

exhibit *v* 1 (exhibit things) demonstrate, display, flaunt, parade, present, put on display, put on a show, put on view, show, show off, unveil. 2 (exhibit a quality, feeling) betray, disclose, display, express, give away, flaunt, indicate, reveal, show, show off

exhibition *n* 1 (of things) demonstration, display, exposition, fair, presentation, show. 2 (of feelings) demonstration, display, expression, indication, revelation

exhilarating *adj* breathtaking, exciting, thrilling

exile *n* 1 banishment, deportation, expulsion, transportation. 2 (a person) deportee, displaced person, outcast, refugee

exile *v* banish, bar, deport, drive out, eject, evict, expel, send into exile, uproot

exist *v* 1 be, be extant, be found, be in existence, be real, happen, live, occur. 2 (survive) continue, endure, last, live, persist, remain, stay alive, stay in existence, subsist, survive

existence *n* 1 actuality, being, existing, fact, living, reality. 2 (survival) duration, endurance, persistence, subsistence, survival. 3 (way of life) life, lifestyle, way of life

exit *n* 1 escape, outlet, passage, vent, way out. 2 departure, escape, exodus, going, leaving, retreat, withdrawal

exodus *n* emigration, escape, exit, flight, leaving, migration, retreat; *opp* arrival

exorbitant *adj* excessive, extortionate, extreme, high, inordinate, outrageous, preposterous, ridiculous, steep, unreasonable; *opp* modest

exotic *adj* 1 (foreign) alien, foreign, imported, introduced, non-native. 2 (different and exciting) bizarre, colorful, curious, extraordinary, fascinating, glamorous, mysterious, novel, odd, outlandish, peculiar, sensational, striking, unusual

expand *v* 1 (make sth bigger) amplify, augment, broaden, build up, develop, dilate, distend, diversify, elaborate, enlarge, extend, fill out, increase, inflate, make bigger, make larger, open up, widen. 2 (become bigger) become bigger, become larger, get bigger, grow, increase in size, open out, stretch, swell, widen; *opp* contract

expanse *n* 1 (size) area, breadth, extent, range, spread, vastness. 2 (expanse of land, sea) area, plain, stretch, sweep, tract

expect *v* 1 assume, believe, calculate, guess, imagine, presume, reckon, suppose, surmise, suspect, think, think likely, trust. 2 anticipate, await, be prepared for, envisage, foresee, hope for, look forward to, plan for, predict, wait for. 3 call for, consider necessary, demand, insist on, look for, require, want

expectant *adj* 1 anxious, eager, expecting, hopeful, in suspense, keyed up, looking forward to, on tenterhooks, ready, ready and waiting. 2 (expecting a baby) expecting, having a baby, in the family way *inf*, pregnant

expectation *n* 1 assumption, belief, calculation, conjecture, forecast, likelihood, presumption, probability, reckoning, surmise, supposition, trust. 2 anticipation, expectancy, hope, readiness

expectations *n* hopes, outlook, prospects

expedition *n* enterprise, excursion, exploration, journey, mission, outing, pilgrimage, quest, safari, tour, trek, trip, voyage

expel *v* 1 (send sb away) ban, banish, cast out, chuck out *inf*, deport, drive out, eject, evict, exile, kick out *inf*, oust, remove, send away, send packing *inf*, throw out, turn out. 2 (send sth out) belch, discharge, eject, emit, force out, give off, push out, send out, spew out

expend *v* 1 (time, money) disburse, dish out *inf*, fork out *inf*, fritter, fritter away, lavish, lay out, pay out, shell out *inf*, spend, squander, waste. 2 (use up) consume, deplete, drain, exhaust, finish off, use, use up

expendable *adj* dispensable, disposable, inessential, nonessential, replaceable, unimportant, unnecessary

expenditure *n* costs, disbursements, expenses, outgoings, overheads, payments, spending; *opp* income, revenue

expense *n* 1 cost, expenditure, investment, money, outlay, price, spending. 2 at the expense of in place of, instead of, rather than, to the detriment of, to the disadvantage of

expensive *adj* beyond sb's means, costly, dear, exorbitant, extortionate, overpriced, pricey, prohibitive; *opp* cheap, inexpensive

experience *n* 1 (sth that happens to you) encounter, episode, event, incident, occurrence, perception, sensation. 2 competence, expertise, familiarity, grounding, knowledge, maturity, record, track record, wisdom; *opp* inexperience

experienced *adj* competent, expert, familiar, knowledgable, mature, versed, well-versed, wise; *opp* inexperienced

experiment *n* 1 attempt, pilot study, test, trial, try-out, venture. 2 (the practice of experimenting) experimentation, innovation, research, testing, trial and error

experiment *v* 1 carry out experiments, conduct experiments, explore, improvise, innovate, play around. 2 **experiment with** explore, investigate, pilot, research, test, try, try out

experimental *adj* avant-garde, exploratory, innovative, new, pilot, probationary

expert *adj* adept, advanced, brainy *inf*, capable, competent, experienced, practiced, proficient, qualified, skillful, skilled, specialist, technical

expert *n* academic, authority, brain, brains, connoisseur, egghead *inf*, maestro, mastermind, professional, pundit, sage, specialist

expertise *n* command, competence, dexterity, experience, proficiency, skillfulness, skill, mastery, professionalism, proficiency, specialism

expire v 1 breathe your last, depart this world, die, kick the bucket *inf*, pass away, pass on, perish, snuff it *inf*. 2 (of a document) become invalid, cease, come to an end, end, finish, go out of date, lapse, run out

explain v account for, answer, clarify, clear up, describe, give a reason for, interpret, make clear/plain, solve, spell out, throw light on

explanation n account, answer, clarification, defense, description, elucidation, excuse, explication, hypothesis, interpretation, justification, reason, reply

explanatory adj descriptive, illuminating, illustrative, informative, revealing, theoretical

explicit adj categorical, clear, crystal clear, definite, detailed, direct, distinct, exact, express, obvious, overt, patent, plain, precise, specific, straightforward, unambiguous, unequivocal; *opp* implicit

explode v 1 (sth explodes) blow up, burst, erupt, fly apart, go bang, go off, go up, implode. 2 (explode sth) blast, blow up, detonate, drop, let off, set off, trigger

exploit n accomplishment, achievement, adventure, deed, feat, stunt, triumph

exploit v 1 (use sth) capitalize on, develop, employ, make use of, press into service, put to good use, take advantage of, use, utilize, work. 2 (use sb unfairly) abuse, impose on, manipulate, overwork, take advantage of, use, walk all over

exploration n 1 discovery, expedition, journey, travel, visit, voyage. 2 (of an issue, problem) analysis, consideration, discussion, examination, inquiry, investigation, research, study, survey

explore v 1 discover, journey, look around, travel, visit, voyage. 2 analyze, consider, discuss, examine, go into, inquire into, investigate, look into, probe, research, survey

explosion n 1 bang, blast, boom, burst, detonation, eruption, gunshot, mushroom cloud, report. 2 (of new developments, ideas) escalation, expansion, flowering, growth, increase, outbreak, mushrooming

explosive adj 1 combustible, exploding, flammable, incendiary, inflammable, unstable, volatile. 2 (likely to cause trouble) controversial, highly charged, sensational, tense, unstable, volatile

explosive n charge, dynamite, gunpowder, plastic explosive, TNT

exponent n advocate, apologist, backer, champion, practitioner, propagandist, promoter, proponent, supporter

expose v 1 bare, denude, display, exhibit, flash, lay bare, reveal, show, uncover, unveil. 2 (expose dishonesty) bring to light, draw attention to, highlight, reveal, uncover, unmask

exposed adj bare, for all to see, in full view, naked, on display, open, public, unprotected, vulnerable

exposure n 1 (publicity) advertising, coverage, publicity. 2 (revealing of sth) baring, disclosure, display, revelation, showing, uncovering, unmasking, unveiling

express adj 1 clear, conscious, deliberate, distinct, explicit, expressed, intentional, manifest, plain, willful. 2 fast, first-class, nonstop, prompt, quick, rapid, special, speedy, swift

express v announce, articulate, communicate, convey, declare, describe, display, give vent to, indicate, make known, manifest, put into words, say, show, speak, state, utter, verbalize, voice

expression n 1 announcement, articulation, communication, declaration, demonstration, description, display, exhibition, indication, manifestation, reflection, statement, voicing. 2 (group of words) figure of speech, idiom, phrase, proverb, saying, utterance. 3 (on sb's face) air, appearance, countenance, face, look, mien

expressive adj articulate, colorful, demonstrative, descriptive, eloquent, emotional, explicit, lyrical, moving, poetic, poignant, suggestive, vivid

exquisite adj artistic, beautiful, delicate, excellent, fine, high-quality, lovely, ornate, perfect, refined, superb, sublime, tasteful

extend v 1 (make bigger) add to, augment, elongate, enlarge, expand, increase, lengthen, prolong, spread, stretch, stretch out. 2 (extend to full size) pay out, pull out, put up, stretch out, uncoil, unfold, unroll. 3 (extend over an area) cover, range, reach, span, spread, stretch. 4 (extend a deadline) postpone, protract, put back, put off, relax, reschedule. 5 (give) advance, give, grant, hold out, impart, offer, make available, proffer

extension n 1 accessory, addition, adjunct, add-on, appendage, enlargement, expansion. 2 (to a house)

annex, conservatory, lean-to, outbuilding, outhouse, wing

extensive adj comprehensive, considerable, enormous, great, large, lengthy, long, prolonged, sizeable, vast, wide, wide-ranging, widespread

extent n area, breadth, dimensions, expanse, length, magnitude, range, scope, size, spread

extenuating adj exceptional, exonerating, justifying, mitigating, qualifying

exterior adj external, outer, outermost, outside, outward, surface

exterior n facade, face, outside, outward appearance, shell, surface

exterminate v annihilate, destroy, eliminate, eradicate, extirpate, kill, massacre, slaughter, wipe out

external adj exterior, outer, outermost, outside, outward, surface

extinct adj dead, defunct, died out, exhausted, extinguished, gone, lost, vanished, wiped out

extinguish v 1 destroy, end, eradicate, kill, quench, snuff out, stifle, suppress. 2 (extinguish a fire, light) blow out, put off, put out, smother, snuff out, switch off, turn off, turn out

extortionate adj dear, excessive, exorbitant, expensive, outrageous, overpriced

extra adj added, additional, bonus, further, more, supplementary, surplus

extra n 1 accessory, addition, additive, add-on, bonus, supplement, surplus. 2 (in a film) bit part, chorus girl, non-speaking part, walk-on part

extract n 1 concentrate, derivative,

essence. 2 (piece of writing) cutting, excerpt, highlight, part, quotation, quote, selection

extract v abstract, derive, distill, draw, draw out, obtain, pull out, remove, select, take out

extraordinary adj amazing, astonishing, exceptional, incredible, marvelous, out of the ordinary, outstanding, rare, remarkable, singular, striking, unique, unusual, wonderful; **opp** ordinary

extravagant adj excessive, immoderate, overgenerous, spendthrift, squandering, wasteful

extreme adj 1 (great) absolute, acute, drastic, great, high, intense, severe, utmost. 2 furthest, furthest away, most distant, outer, remotest. 3 (extreme views, measures) drastic, exaggerated, excessive, fanatical, harsh, radical, uncompromising, unreasonable, over-the-top

extreme n absolute, boundary, edge, end, extremity, height, limit, maximum, ultimate

extremist n diehard, fanatic, militant, radical, ultra, zealot; **opp** moderate

extremity n boundary, edge, end, extreme, limit, tip

extricate v disembroil, disentangle, free, loose, rescue, unravel, untangle

extroverted adj boisterous, extrovert, friendly, fun-loving, gregarious, lively, loud, outgoing, outward-looking, sociable, talkative; **opp** introverted

exuberant adj celebrating, cheerful, effervescent, elated, enthusiastic, irrepressible, joyful, joyous, jubilant, rejoicing, sparkling, vivacious

eye v gaze at, glance at, inspect, keep an eye on, look at, peer at, regard, scrutinize, stare at, study, survey, watch

eyesight n eyes, perception, powers of observation, range of vision, sight, vision

eyesore n blemish, blight, blot on the landscape, disfigurement, monstrosity, scar

eyewitness n bystander, observer, onlooker, spectator, witness

fabric n 1 cloth, material, textile. 2 (the fabric of society) constitution, essence, framework, make-up, nature, structure

fabricate v 1 (falsely) concoct, fake, forge, invent, make up. 2 assemble, construct, make, make up, manufacture, produce, put together

fabulous adj 1 (good) ace inf, brilliant, fantastic, good, great, super, superb, wonderful. 2 (imaginary) fantastic, imaginary, invented, legendary, make-believe, mythical

face n 1 complexion, countenance, expression, head, mug inf, physiognomy, visage. 2 (outward appearance) appearance, aspect, facet, side, surface

face v 1 (of a person) gaze at, look sb in the face, look towards, stare at, turn to, turn towards. 2 (of a building) be opposite, front onto, give onto, have a view of, look out on, overlook. 3 (in a contest) be opposed to, confront, meet, play, play against. 4 (face a problem) accept, come to terms with, confront, deal with, face up to; **opp** avoid. 5 (a problem that faces sb) be before sb, be in store, confront, lie ahead, present itself

facetious adj flippant, frivolous, humorous, ironic, jocular, jokey, joking, sarcastic, silly, teasing, tongue-in-cheek

facile adj banal, glib, oversimplified, shallow, silly, trite; **opp** profound

facilitate v aid, allow, assist, enable, encourage, help, make easier, permit, simplify, speed up

facility n 1 facilities amenities, comforts, equipment, resources, service. 2 dexterity, ease, effortlessness, elegance, fluency, simplicity

fact n 1 actuality, certainty, reality, truth. 2 in fact actually, as a matter of fact, as it happens, in actual fact, indeed, in point of fact, in reality, in truth, really

faction n band, camp, caucus, clique, group, lobby, party, pressure group, ring, section, set, splinter group

factor n aspect, component, consideration, detail, element, facet, influence, ingredient, part

factory n foundry, industrial unit, mill, plant, works, workshop

factual adj accurate, authentic, exact, faithful, informative, objective, real, real-life, true, true to life, truthful, unbiased; **opp** fictional

faculty n 1 (in a university) department, division, section, school. 2 ability, aptitude, capability, capacity, sense. 3 faculties awareness, cognition, consciousness, perception, reason, understanding

fade v 1 (of colors) become pale, dim, dull, grow pale. 2 (become less) decline, die away, disappear, dwindle, grow faint, vanish, wane

fail v 1 be defeated, break down, collapse, come to grief, crash, draw a blank, fall down, fall flat, fall short, fall through, founder, go bankrupt, go under, lose, malfunction, miscarry, misfire, miss, stumble; **opp** succeed. 2 **fail to do sth** avoid, decline, neglect, omit, refuse. 3 (fail a person) abandon, desert, disappoint, forsake, let down. 4 (fail an exam) be unsuccessful, drop out, flunk; **opp** pass

failing n defect, drawback, failure, fault, imperfection, inadequacy, shortcoming, weakness

failure n 1 bankruptcy, breakdown, collapse, defeat, malfunction; **opp** success. 2 (failure to do sth) dereliction of duty, inability, omission, oversight, refusal. 3 (sb who has failed) incompetent, loser. 4 (sth that has failed) disaster, dud, flop, washout; **opp** success

faint adj 1 barely audible, barely perceptible, barely visible, blurred, dim, feeble, indistinct, quiet, soft, unclear, weak; **opp** bright, loud. 2 (feel faint) dizzy, giddy, light-headed, weak, woozy inf

faint v black out, collapse, lose consciousness, pass out, swoon; **opp** come round, come to

fair adj 1 balanced, equitable, even-handed, honest, impartial, just, legitimate, objective, reasonable, right, sporting, unbiased, unprejudiced.

2 (of hair) blond, blonde, flaxen, yellow. 3 (of skin) light, pale, white

faith n 1 commitment, confidence, conviction, expectation, hope, loyalty, sincerity, trust. 2 (religious belief) belief, communion, confession, congregation, creed, denomination, religion

faithful adj 1 committed, loyal, reliable, true, trusting, trusty. 2 **be faithful to** believe in, have confidence in, keep faith with, stand by, stick to, trust in

fake adj artificial, counterfeit, fabricated, false, forged, fraudulent, imitation, sham; **opp** genuine

fake v copy, counterfeit, fabricate, falsify, forge, pretend, simulate

fall n 1 collapse, descent, slip, stumble, trip, tumble. 2 collapse, decline, decrease, dip, drop, falling-off; **opp** rise. 3 (the fall of sb in power) defeat, demise, dismissal, downfall, end, fall from grace, impeachment, removal, resignation; **opp** rise

fall v 1 (move downwards) be dropped, collapse, come crashing down, descend, drop, plop, plummet, sink, stumble, tip over, topple over, trip, tumble. 2 (of a person) collapse, fall down, fall over, keel over, lose your balance, slip, stumble, trip, tumble. 3 (of a price, amount) be marked down, collapse, come down, decline, decrease, drop, fall off, go down, plummet, slump, tumble; **opp** rise. 4 (of sb in power) be defeated, be dismissed, be impeached, be kicked out inf, be ousted, be voted out, fall from grace, lose office, lose power, resign, stand down. 5 **fall out** argue, disagree, have a difference of opinion, quarrel, row

fallacy n error, misconception, mistake, paradox

fallible adj erring, error-prone, flawed, human, imperfect, sinful, unreliable, weak; **opp** infallible

false adj 1 erroneous, fallacious, incorrect, invalid, mistaken, spurious, unfounded, untrue, wrong; **opp** true. 2 (of a person) deceitful, dishonest, disloyal, insincere, unfaithful. 3 artificial, counterfeit, fake, forged, imitation, mock, synthetic; **opp** real

falsify v alter, counterfeit, doctor, fabricate, fake, forge, lie about, manipulate, misrepresent, retouch, tamper with, touch up

falter v bumble, go wrong, hesitate, stammer, stutter

fame n celebrity, distinction, eminence, esteem, greatness, importance, infamy, note, notoriety, pre-eminence, renown, reputation, stardom

familiar adj 1 common, commonplace, conventional, customary, everyday, frequent, habitual, household, mundane, normal, ordinary, predictable, recognizable, regular, routine, run-of-the mill, stock, usual, well-known; **opp** unusual. 2 (of people) amiable, casual, close, confidential, cordial, easy, free, friendly, informal, intimate, open, relaxed, sociable, unceremonious, unreserved; **opp** formal. 3 **familiar with** acquainted with, at home with, aware of, conscious of, conversant with, expert in, informed about, no stranger to, trained in, versed in, well up in

familiarize v accustom, acquaint, get to know, habituate, make familiar with, make conversant with

family n brood, flesh and blood, household, issue, kin, nearest and dearest inf, relations, relatives, tribe

famine n food shortage, hunger, lack of food, starvation

famished adj dying of hunger, dying of starvation, hungry, ravenous, starved, starving, undernourished; **opp** full

famous adj acclaimed, big, celebrated, eminent, famed, illustrious, legendary, much-publicized, notorious, prominent, renowned, well-known, world-famous; **opp** unknown

fan n adherent, admirer, aficionado, buff inf, devotee, enthusiast, fanatic, follower, lover, nut inf, supporter, zealot

fanatic n 1 (sports fanatic) enthusiast, fan, follower, lover, nut inf, supporter. 2 (religious fanatic) activist, extremist, maniac, militant, radical, zealot

fanatical adj enthusiastic, excessive, extreme, fervent, fervid, frenzied, mad, obsessive, overenthusiastic, passionate, rabid, wild, zealous; **opp** moderate

fanciful adj 1 (of a design) extravagant, fabulous, fairy-tale, fancy; **opp** simple. 2 (of an idea) fabulous, fantastic, ideal, imaginary, legendary, mythical, poetic, romantic, unreal, wild; **opp** realistic. 3 (of a person) capricious, imaginative, inventive, whimsical

fancy adj decorated, decorative, elaborate, elegant, embellished, embroidered, glitzy inf, intricate, jazzy inf, lavish, ornamental, ornamented, ornate, posh inf, showy, snazzy inf; **opp** plain

fancy v 1 (fancy that sth will happen) believe, conceive, conjecture, guess, imagine, infer, reckon, suppose, surmise, think. 2 (fancy a drink) crave, feel like, long for, want, would like, wish for, yearn for. 3 (fancy sb) be attracted to, be infatuated by, be mad on, desire, fall for, have a crush on, lust after, take a shine to, take to

fantastic adj 1 ace inf, brilliant, excellent, fabulous, first-class, first-rate, great, magnificent, marvelous, outstanding, phenomenal, sensational, splendid, super, superb, terrific, tremendous, wonderful; *opp* terrible. 2 (fantastic notions) absurd, amazing, eccentric, exaggerated, exotic, fanciful, far-fetched, freakish, grotesque, incredible, odd, peculiar, quaint, queer, strange, weird, whimsical, wild; *opp* ordinary

fantasy n daydream, delusion, fancy, illusion, imagination, invention, make-believe, reverie; *opp* reality

far adv 1 afar, a good way, a great distance, a long way, deep. 2 (far better) considerably, decidedly, greatly, incomparably, much; *opp* slightly. 3 so far thus far, to date, until now, up to now, up to the present, up to this point

farce n 1 (type of humor) buffoonery, comedy, parody, satire, slapstick. 2 joke, mockery, nonsense, sham, travesty

farcical adj 1 (of a type of humor) amusing, comic, droll, funny, satirical, slapstick. 2 (not good) absurd, derisory, foolish, laughable, ludicrous, nonsensical, preposterous, ridiculous, risible, silly; *opp* reasonable

far-fetched adj doubtful, dubious, improbable, ridiculous, unbelievable, unconvincing, unlikely, unnatural, unrealistic; *opp* realistic

farm n holding, homestead, land, plantation, ranch

farm v cultivate, operate, plant, plow, work

farming n agriculture, cultivation, food-production, husbandry

far-reaching adj broad, comprehensive, extensive, important, significant, sweeping, widespread

fascinate v absorb, beguile, bewitch, captivate, charm, delight, enchant, engross, enrapture, enthrall, entrance, hypnotize, intrigue, mesmerize, rivet, transfix; *opp* bore

fascinated adj absorbed, captivated, enchanted, engrossed, enraptured, enthralled, entranced, hypnotized, intrigued, mesmerized, riveted, spellbound, transfixed; *opp* uninterested

fascinating adj absorbing, captivating, compelling, enchanting, engaging, engrossing, enrapturing, enthralling, entrancing, gripping, hypnotizing, interesting, intriguing, irresistible, mesmerizing, riveting; *opp* dull

fashion n 1 (the latest fashion) convention, craze, custom, fad, the latest thing, trend, vogue. 2 (in such a fashion) manner, method, mode, style, system, way

fashionable adj à la mode, chic, current, in inf, in fashion, in vogue, latest, modern, trendy inf, up-to-date, up-to-the-minute, with it inf; *opp* unfashionable

fast *adj* breakneck, brisk, hasty, high-speed, hurried, quick, rapid, speedy, supersonic, swift; *opp* slow

fast *n* abstinence, fasting, hunger strike

fast *v* abstain, go hungry, go on hunger strike, go without food

fasten *v* affix, anchor, attach, bind, bolt, buckle, chain, clamp, connect, couple, do up, fix, hitch, join, link, seal, secure, tether, tie; *opp* unfasten

fastener *n* anchor, binding, bolt, buckle, chain, clamp, connection, coupling, link, seal

fat *adj* beefy, chubby, corpulent, flabby, heavy, large, obese, overweight, plump, portly, pudgy, rotund, solid, squat, stocky, stout, tubby, weighty; *opp* thin

fat *n* blubber, bulk, corpulence, extra weight, flab, paunch

fatal *adj* 1 (resulting in sb's death) deadly, final, incurable, killing, lethal, malignant, mortal, pernicious, terminal; *opp* harmless. 2 (resulting in sth unpleasant) calamitous, catastrophic, dire, disastrous, lethal, ruinous; *opp* harmless

fatality *n* casualty, death, loss, victim; *opp* survivor

fate *n* 1 chance, destiny, doom, fortune, lot, predestination, providence. 2 (the fate of sth) end, future, issue, outcome, result, upshot

fateful *adj* catastrophic, disastrous, lethal, fated, ruinous

father *n* 1 dad, daddy, male parent, old man *inf*, pa *inf*, papa, pop *inf*. 2 (the father of sth) architect, creator, discoverer, founder, initiator, maker, originator

fatigue *n* exhaustion, heaviness, languor, lethargy, listlessness, overtiredness, tiredness, weariness; *opp* liveliness

fault *n* 1 blemish, defect, deficiency, drawback, failing, flaw, imperfection, shortcoming, snag, weakness, weak point. 2 blunder, boob *inf*, error, faux pas, gaffe *inf*, howler *inf*, inaccuracy, miscalculation, misspelling, mistake, omission, oversight, slip, slip-up

faulty *adj* bad, broken, damaged, defective, deficient, flawed, erroneous, impaired, imperfect, malfunctioning, on the blink *inf*, out of order, unusable, weak, wrong; *opp* faultless

favor *n* 1 (win sb's favor) acceptance, approbation, approval, backing, benevolence, esteem, good opinion, good will, liking, partiality, support. 2 (do sb a favor) courtesy, good turn, kindness, service

favor *v* 1 (favor doing sth) advocate, approve, back, be in sympathy with, endorse, promote, recommend, sanction, support; *opp* disapprove. 2 (favor sb) indulge, pamper, reward, show favoritism towards, spoil. 3 (favor sth) be partial to, go for *inf*, go in for *inf*, incline towards, like best, prefer; *opp* dislike

favorable *adj* 1 advantageous, appropriate, auspicious, beneficial, conducive, convenient, fair, fit, good, helpful, hopeful, in your favor, on your side, opportune, positive, promising, suitable, timely; *opp* unfavorable. 2 (favorable comments) approving, complimentary, congratulatory, encouraging, enthusiastic, good,

laudatory, praising, well-disposed;
opp unfavorable

favorite *adj* best, best-loved, choice,
chosen, dearest, favored, ideal, most-
liked, preferred, selected

favorite *n* 1 choice, first choice, pick,
preference. 2 (a child) apple of your eye,
darling, idol, pet, teacher's pet

fear *n* 1 alarm, anxiety, apprehension,
butterflies, cowardice, dread, fearfulness,
faintheartedness, foreboding, fright,
horror, nervousness, panic, qualms,
shivers, terror, timidity, trepidation,
uneasiness; *opp* courage. 2 (a fear of sth)
aversion, hang-up, horror, neurosis,
nightmare, phobia; *opp* love

fear *v* be afraid of, be scared of, dare not,
dread, live in fear/terror of, shrink from,
shudder at, take fright, tremble at, worry
about

fearful *adj* 1 (fearful of sth) afraid,
alarmed, anxious, apprehensive,
frightened, intimidated, nervous, panic-
stricken, scared, scared stiff, terrified,
timid, uneasy. 2 (a fearful noise)
appalling, awful, dire, dreadful,
frightful, ghastly, horrible, terrible

fearless *adj* bold, brave, confident,
courageous, daring, gallant, gutsy *inf*,
hard *inf*, heroic, intrepid, plucky,
unafraid, undaunted, valiant;
opp cowardly

fearsome *adj* alarming, awesome,
daunting, formidable, frightening, hair-
raising, horrifying, intimidating,
menacing, terrifying, unnerving

feasible *adj* achievable, attainable,
doable, likely, possible, practicable,
realizable, reasonable, viable,

workable; *opp* impossible

feast *n* banquet, blow out *sl*, dinner,
spread *inf*, treat

feat *n* accomplishment, achievement,
act, action, attainment, deed, exploit,
performance

feature *n* 1 aspect, attribute,
characteristic, detail, facet, factor, mark,
peculiarity, point, property, quality, side,
trait. 2 (in a newspaper) article, column,
item, piece, report, story

feature *v* 1 accentuate, emphasize, focus
on, give prominence to, highlight, play
up, present, promote, spotlight, stress.
2 (in a film) act, appear, figure,
participate, perform, play a role, star

features *n* appearance, countenance, face,
look

fed up *adj* annoyed, bored, depressed,
discontented, dissatisfied, down, gloomy,
glum, miserable, sad, weary; *opp* happy

fee *n* bill, charge, cost, dues, fare,
payment, price, rate, remuneration,
subscription, tariff, toll

feeble *adj* 1 decrepit, debilitated, delicate,
doddering, exhausted, failing, faint,
fragile, frail, infirm, languid, listless,
poorly, puny, sickly, weak; *opp* strong.
2 (not determined) inadequate,
incompetent, indecisive, ineffectual,
irresolute, spineless, wimpy, wishy-washy
inf; *opp* tough. 3 (a feeble excuse)
flimsy, futile, inadequate, ineffective,
insubstantial, lame, paltry, poor,
unconvincing; *opp* good

feed *v* 1 cater for, give food to, nourish,
nurture, provide for, provision, suckle,
support, supply, sustain. 2 (feed on sth)
devour, dine, eat, graze, live on, subsist

feel n 1 (a leathery feel) finish, surface, texture. 2 (the feel of a place) ambience, atmosphere, aura, impression, mood

feel v 1 (with your fingers) caress, finger, fondle, handle, manipulate, maul, paw, stroke, thumb, touch. 2 (in your mind) be aware of, be conscious of, detect, discern, endure, enjoy, experience, go through, have, know, notice, observe, perceive, suffer, undergo. 3 (feel your way) explore, fumble, grope, test, try. 4 (have an opinion) be convinced, believe, be of the opinion that, consider, have a (funny) feeling, intuit, judge, sense, think. 5 **feel like** desire, fancy, want, wish for, would like, yearn for

feeling n 1 sensation, sense of touch, sensitivity. 2 (have a feeling) funny feeling, hunch, idea, impression, inkling, notion, suspicion. 3 (sb's feeling about sth) attitude, belief, inclination, instinct, opinion, thought, view

feelings n ego, emotions, self-esteem, sensitivities, sentiments, susceptibilities

fell v chop down, cut down, demolish, flatten, floor, hew, knock down, level

feminine adj delicate, elegant, gentle, girlish, girly inf, graceful, ladylike, soft, tender, womanly; **opp** masculine

fen n bog, lowland, marsh, quagmire, swamp

fence n barricade, barrier, defense, fencing, hedge, hurdle, paling, palisade, railings, rampart, stockade, wall, wire

fence v bound, circumscribe, confine, coop, encircle, enclose, hedge, pen, surround

ferment v 1 boil, brew, bubble, fizz, foam, froth, heat, leaven, rise. 2 agitate,

excite, incite, inflame, instigate, provoke, rouse, stir up; **opp** calm

ferocious adj barbaric, bloodthirsty, brutal, fierce, predatory, ruthless, savage, vicious, violent, wild; **opp** harmless

ferry v bring, carry, chauffeur, convey, fetch, shift, ship, shuttle, take, taxi, transport

fertile adj fecund, fruitful, lush, productive, prolific, rich, yielding; **opp** infertile

fertilize v 1 impregnate, inseminate, make pregnant, pollinate. 2 (fertilize soil) compost, dress, enrich, feed, make fertile, manure, mulch, nourish

fervent adj ardent, avid, devout, eager, earnest, emotional, enthusiastic, excited, fanatical, fiery, heartfelt, heated, impassioned, intense, keen, passionate, vehement, wholehearted, zealous; **opp** lukewarm

fester v 1 become infected, become inflamed, become poisoned, discharge, go septic, ooze, putrefy, ulcerate. 2 decay, decompose, disintegrate, go bad, go off, rot

festival n 1 (a public festival) anniversary, bank holiday, commemoration, day of observance, feast, holiday, holy day, saint's day. 2 carnival, celebration, festivities, gala, jubilee

festive adj celebratory, cheerful, convivial, gay, happy, holiday, jolly, jovial, joyful, joyous, merry

festivity n amusement, celebration, conviviality, entertainment, fun, fun and games, gaiety, joviality, joyfulness, merriment, merrymaking, mirth, pleasure, revelry

fetch v 1 bring, carry, conduct, convey, deliver, escort, get, go and get, import, obtain, retrieve, transport. 2 (fetch a price) bring in, earn, go for, make, raise, realize, sell for, yield

fete n bazaar, fair, festival, gala, garden party, sale of work, show

feud n 1 argument, conflict, disagreement, dispute, falling-out, quarrel, running battle. 2 (a state of feud) animosity, antagonism, argument, bad blood, conflict, disagreement, discord, dispute, dissension, estrangement, grudge, hostility, rivalry, strife, unfriendliness; *opp* harmony

fever n delirium, feverishness, high temperature, temperature

feverish adj 1 (of a person) burning up *inf*, delirious, flushed, hot. 2 (of activity) agitated, desperate, excited, distracted, excited, frantic, frenetic, frenzied, hectic, passionate; *opp* calm

fiasco n catastrophe, debacle, disaster, failure, farce, flop *inf*, mess, rout, washout; *opp* success

fiber n filament, hair, strand, thread

fickle adj capricious, changeable, changing, disloyal, erratic, fitful, flighty, inconstant, unpredictable, up and down *inf*, vacillating, volatile; *opp* constant

fiction n 1 fable, fantasy, legend, make-believe, myth, romance, story, tale; *opp* real life. 2 (sth not true) cock and bull story *inf*, deception, fabrication, falsehood, fancy, fantasy, fib, imagination, invention, lie, tall story, untruth, whopper *inf*; *opp* truth

fictional adj fictitious, imaginary,

invented, made-up, make-believe, pretend, nonexistent, unreal; *opp* real

fictitious adj assumed, bogus, counterfeit, fabricated, fake, false, feigned, imaginary, imagined, invented, made-up, mythical, sham, spurious, unreal, untrue; *opp* genuine

fiddle v 1 fidget, finger, fuss, interfere, meddle, mess about, mess around, play, tamper, tinker, toy, trifle. 2 cheat, falsify, fix, maneuver, racketeer, swindle, wangle

fidelity n 1 allegiance, commitment, constancy, dependability, devotion, faithfulness, integrity, loyalty, reliability, staunchness, trustworthiness; *opp* disloyalty. 2 accuracy, adherence, authenticity, closeness, correspondence, exactness, faithfulness, precision; *opp* inaccuracy

fidget v fiddle, fuss, have ants in your pants, mess about, mess around, play about, shuffle, squirm, twitch, wriggle

fidgety adj agitated, frisky, impatient, jerky, jittery, jumpy, nervous, on edge, restless, twitchy, uneasy; *opp* still

field n 1 clearing, enclosure, grassland, green, meadow, paddock, pasture. 2 (a sports field) arena, court, ground, pitch, playing field, recreation ground, stadium, turf. 3 (a field of activity) area, discipline, domain, line, province, specialty, sphere, subject, territory

fiend n 1 demon, devil, evil spirit, goblin, imp, Satan, spirit. 2 addict, devotee, enthusiast, fan, fanatic, follower, freak *inf*, lover, maniac, nut *inf*, supporter, zealot

fiendish adj accursed, atrocious, barbaric,

bloodthirsty, brutal, cruel, demonic, devilish, diabolical, hellish, implacable, infernal, inhuman, malevolent, malicious, malignant, merciless, monstrous, pitiless, ruthless, satanic, savage, ungodly, unspeakable, vicious, wicked; *opp* godly, good

fierce *adj* barbaric, brutal, cold-blooded, cruel, dangerous, fearsome, ferocious, menacing, murderous, passionate, ruthless, savage, threatening, uncontrollable, untamed, vicious, violent, wild; *opp* gentle

fight *n* 1 action, affray, attack, battle, bout, brawl, clash, conflict, contest, engagement, fracas, fray, joust, scrap *inf*, skirmish, struggle, tussle, war, wrestle. 2 altercation, argument, brush, disagreement, dispute, falling out, feud, quarrel, squabble, wrangle

fight *v* 1 attack, battle, box, brawl, clash, come to blows, contend, engage, grapple, have a fight, joust, scrap *inf*, skirmish, spar, struggle, tussle, war, wrestle. 2 challenge, contest, defy, dispute, oppose, resist, struggle against, take a stand against, withstand. 3 argue, be at odds, bicker, clash, dispute, fall out, feud, quarrel, squabble, wrangle. 4 **fight back** counterattack, defend yourself, hit back, put up a fight, reply, resist, retaliate, stand up for yourself. 5 **fight off** beat off, fend off, hold at bay, repel, repulse, stave off, ward off

fighter *n* boxer, combatant, contender, pugilist, soldier, warrior, wrestler

figure *n* 1 amount, cipher, digit, integer, number, numeral, sum, value. 2 body, build, form, frame, outline, physique,
shape, silhouette. 3 chart, diagram, graph, illustration, symbol, table

figure *v* 1 comprehend, decipher, fathom, make out, see, realize, understand, work out. 2 **figure out** assess, calculate, compute, reckon, solve, work out

file *n* 1 data, document, dossier, folder, portfolio, record. 2 column, line, procession, queue, row, stream, string, train

file *v* 1 categorize, classify, document, enter, organize, put on record, record, register. 2 march, parade, troop. 3 abrade, rasp, rub, scrape, shape, smooth

fill *v* block, cram, crowd, gorge, jam, load, pack, refill, replenish, satisfy, stock, stuff

filling *n* contents, insides, middle, padding, stuffing, wadding

film *n* 1 flick *inf*, motion picture, movie, picture, video. 2 coat, coating, covering, haze, layer, membrane, scum, skin, tissue, veil, veneer

filter *v* clarify, filtrate, purify, refine, screen, sieve, sift, strain

filth *n* 1 contamination, dirt, dung, effluent, excrement, feces, filthiness, foulness, grime, muck, ordure, pollution, refuse, sewage, sludge, squalor. 2 impurity, indecency, obscenity, pornography, smut, vulgarity

filthy *adj* 1 begrimed, contaminated, defiled, dirty, foul, grimy, grubby, mucky, polluted, squalid; *opp* clean. 2 bawdy, blue *inf*, coarse, impure, indecent, lewd, licentious, obscene, pornographic, raunchy, rude, smutty, sordid, vulgar

final *adj* closing, concluding, conclusive, dying, end, eventual, finishing, last, parting, terminating, ultimate; *opp* first

finale n climax, close, conclusion, culmination, denouement, end, epilogue, finish, last act

finalize v agree, arrange, clinch, complete, conclude, confirm, decide, settle, tie up, wrap up

finance n 1 (dealing with money) accounting, banking, business, commerce, economics, investment, stock market. 2 (money) accounts, assets, capital, cash, funds, money, resources, revenue, wealth, wherewithal

finance v back, fund, guarantee, invest in, pay for, subsidize, support, underwrite

financial adj budgetary, commercial, economic, fiscal, monetary, money, pecuniary

find n acquisition, asset, bargain, discovery, good buy, innovation, invention

find v 1 (find sth new) chance upon, come across, discover, encounter, espy, happen on, hit on, light on, spot, turn up, uncover, unearth. 2 (find sth lost) get back, locate, recoup, recover, rediscover, regain, retrieve, trace, track down; *opp* lose. 3 become aware, conclude, discover, note, notice, observe, perceive, realize. 4 **find out** become aware, bring sth to light, detect, discover, expose, learn, observe, realize, reveal, see

fine adj 1 admirable, beautiful, choice, classic, consummate, elegant, excellent, exceptional, exquisite, first-class, first-rate, good, great, high-class, high-quality, magnificent, outstanding, quality, rare, refined, select, splendid, superb, superior, supreme, top-notch *inf*, world-class. 2 acceptable, agreeable, all right, OK *inf*, satisfactory, suitable. 3 (a fine day) balmy, bright, clear, cloudless, dry, fair, pleasant, sunny; *opp* wet. 4 (fine porcelain) dainty, delicate, flimsy, fragile, light, minute, narrow, slender, slim, small, thin, translucent; *opp* coarse. 5 (a fine distinction) abstruse, discriminating, exact, fastidious, fine-drawn, hair-splitting, minute, nice, precise, subtle; *opp* clear, obvious

fine n charge, forfeit, penalty, punishment

finesse n adroitness, artfulness, cleverness, craft, delicacy, expertise, grace, polish, refinement, savoir-faire, skill, subtlety

finish n 1 cessation, close, closing, completion, conclusion, culmination, denouement, end, ending, finale, termination; *opp* start. 2 coating, gloss, lacquer, luster, patina, polish, sheen, shine, smoothness, surface, veneer

finish v 1 accomplish, achieve, bring to an end, clinch, close, complete, conclude, culminate, discharge, end, execute, finalize, fulfill, get done, perfect, settle, wrap up. 2 break off, cease, desist, discontinue, halt, interrupt, pack up, phase out, stop, suspend, terminate, wind up. 3 annihilate, beat, be too much for, bring down, conquer, destroy, dispose of, exterminate, get rid of, get the better of, kill, overcome, overpower, ruin. 4 consume, devour, dispatch, dispose of, drink up, eat up, get through, polish off *inf*

finished adj 1 clinched, closed, complete, completed, done, ended, final, finalized, over, perfect, settled, through, tied up, wrapped up. 2 beaten, defeated, done for inf, doomed, overcome, past it inf, ruined, through, undone, washed up inf, wrecked

finite adj calculable, certain, countable, definable, defined, determinable, fixed, limited, measurable, numbered, restricted; **opp** infinite

fire n 1 blaze, burning, combustion, conflagration, flame, inferno, pyre. 2 barrage, bombardment, gunfire, salvo, shelling, shooting, shot, sniping. 3 ardor, energy, fervor, intensity, life, passion, spark, spirit, vehemence, vigor, vivacity, zeal

fire v 1 (set fire to sth) burn, ignite, kindle, put a match to, set sth alight, set fire to, set sth on fire, torch. 2 (fire a gun) detonate, discharge, launch, let off, pull the trigger, set off, shoot. 3 (fire sb) discharge, dismiss, down-size, get rid of, give sb the boot inf, let sb go, make sb redundant, sack, throw sb out

firm adj 1 compact, compressed, condensed, dense, hard, inflexible, resilient, resistant, rigid, set, solid, solidified, strong, taut, tight, stiff, unyielding; **opp** soft. 2 anchored, braced, embedded, fast, fixed, immovable, motionless, rooted, secured, solid, stable, steady, strong, sturdy, tight, unmoving; **opp** loose. 3 adamant, certain, constant, definite, determined, fixed, immovable, inflexible, intransigent, obdurate, resolute, resolved, set, settled, staunch, stalwart, steadfast, strict, stubborn, sure,

unalterable, unbending, unmoving, unshakable, unswerving, unwavering, unyielding

firm n association, business, company, concern, corporation, enterprise, establishment, house, group, organization, partnership

first adj 1 earliest, initial, maiden, opening, original, preliminary, primeval, primitive, primordial. 2 chief, dominant, foremost, head, highest, leading, pre-eminent, premier, prime, principal, ruling, superior, supreme, uppermost. 3 axiomatic, basic, cardinal, elementary, essential, fundamental, key, primary, rudimentary

first-rate adj admirable, choice, classic, consummate, excellent, exceptional, first class, high-class, high-quality, magnificent, outstanding, quality, rare, refined, select, splendid, superb, superior, superlative, top-notch inf, world class

fit adj 1 energetic, healthy, in shape, robust, strapping, strong, toned, trim, vigorous, well; **opp** unfit. 2 able, adequate, appropriate, capable, competent, correct, decent, eligible, equipped, fitting, good enough, qualified, proper, right, suitable, up to the job inf, worthy; **opp** unfit

fit n attack, bout, convulsion, eruption, explosion, outbreak, outburst, paroxysm, seizure, spasm, spell, turn

fit v 1 accord, agree, be right, belong, concur, dovetail, interlock, match, meet, suit, tally. 2 arrange, assemble, build, construct, install, interlock, join, match, put in, put together. 3 adapt, adjust, alter, cut, modify, shape, tailor

fitting *adj* adequate, appropriate, becoming, correct, decent, decorous, good enough, proper, right, seemly, suitable, worthy

fix *n* bind *inf*, corner, difficulty, dilemma, jam *inf*, mess, pickle *inf*, plight, predicament, problem, quandary, scrape *inf*, spot *inf*

fix *v* **1** anchor, attach, connect, embed, fasten, fit, install, join, secure, stick, tie. **2** agree, appoint, arrange, arrive at, conclude, decide, define, determine, establish, finalize, limit, name, resolve, set, settle, specify. **3** mend, patch up, put right, remedy, repair, restore, sort out

fixed *adj* **1** attached, immobile, permanent, rigid, secured; *opp* movable. **2** agreed, arranged, definite, established, planned, prearranged, predetermined, set, settled

fixture *n* arrangement, date, engagement, event, game, match, meeting

fizzy *adj* bubbling, bubbly, carbonated, effervescent, gassy, sparkling; *opp* still

flag *n* banner, bunting, colors, ensign, pennant, standard, streamer

flag *v* **1** fade, fail, decline, decrease, diminish, ebb, taper off, tire, wane, weaken, weary. **2** indicate, label, mark, pick out, signal

flagrant *adj* barefaced, blatant, bold, brazen, glaring, gross, obvious, open, ostentatious, outrageous, overt, scandalous, shameless, shocking, unashamed, unconcealed, undisguised

flair *n* **1** ability, aptitude, facility, feel, genius, gift, knack, skill, talent. **2** chic, dash, elegance, panache, style, taste

flamboyant *adj* bold, colorful, dashing, dazzling, extravagant, fancy, flashy, gaudy, glamorous, ostentatious, outrageous, shocking, showy, splendid, swashbuckling, theatrical

flame *n* **1** blaze, conflagration, fire, tongue. **2** ardor, fervor, fire, intensity, passion, warmth

flame *v* be ablaze, blaze, burn, flare, flash, glare, glow, shine

flap *v* **1** agitate, beat, flail, flutter, oscillate, shake, swing, swish, thrash, wag, waggle, wave. **2** be agitated, be in a state, fuss, get flustered, panic

flare *v* blaze, burn, dazzle, flash, flicker, glare, gleam, glint, shine

flash *n* **1** beam, blaze, bolt, burst, flare, flicker, glare, gleam, glimmer, glint, ray, shaft, shimmer, shine, spark, sparkle, twinkle. **2** instant, jiffy *inf*, minute, moment, second, split second, twinkling of an eye

flash *v* beam, blaze, dazzle, flare, flicker, glare, gleam, glimmer, glint, glisten, glitter, light up, reflect, shimmer, shine, sparkle, twinkle

flashy *adj* bold, brash, bright, extravagant, fancy, flamboyant, garish, gaudy, glitzy, loud, ostentatious, showy, tacky *inf*, tasteless, tawdry, vulgar; *opp* understated

flat *adj* **1** even, horizontal, level, leveled, plane, smooth, unbroken. **2** lying down, outstretched, prone, prostrate, reclining, recumbent, sprawling, spread-eagled, stretched out, supine. **3** bland, boring, dead, dry, dull, insipid, lackluster, lifeless, monotonous, prosaic, stale, tedious, uninteresting, unvarying, vapid; *opp* interesting

flatten *v* **1** compact, compress, even out, iron out, level out, plane, press down, smooth out. **2** crush, demolish, destroy, knock down, level, raze, squash, trample

flatter *v* blandish, butter up, cajole, compliment, court, eulogize, fawn, get round *inf*, gush, humor, kiss up to *inf*, lay it on thick *inf*, lick sb's boots *inf*, pander to, pay court to, play up to *inf*, praise, soft-soap *inf*, suck up to *sl*, sweet-talk *inf*, wheedle

flattery *n* adulation, blandishments, blarney, boot-licking *inf*, buttering-up, cajoling, compliments, eulogy, fawning, gushing, kissing up *inf*, obsequiousness, pandering, praise, soft soap *inf*, sucking-up *sl*, sweet talk *inf*, wheedling

flavor *n* **1** aroma, essence, extract, odor, piquancy, relish, savor, seasoning, smack, tang, taste, tastiness, zest. **2** ambience, atmosphere, aura, character, essence, feel, feeling, nature, quality, soul, spirit, tone

flavor *v* add flavor to, add piquancy to, imbue, infuse, lace, season, spice

flaw *n* blemish, defect, failing, fault, foible, imperfection, shortcoming, weakness

flawed *adj* blemished, broken, chipped, cracked, damaged, defective, faulty, imperfect, marred, spoilt, unsound; *opp* perfect

flee *v* abscond, beat a retreat, beat it *inf*, bolt, decamp, disappear, escape, fly, make off, run away, run off, take flight, take off, vanish

fleet *n* armada, convoy, flotilla, naval force, navy, task force, warships

fleeting *adj* brief, ephemeral, momentary, passing, quick, rapid, short, short-lived, swift, transient, transitory

flesh *n* **1** brawn, carrion, fat, meat, muscle, tissue. **2** body, carnality, physicality, sensuality

flexible *adj* **1** bendable, ductile, giving, elastic, malleable, plastic, pliable, springy, stretchy, supple, yielding; *opp* rigid. **2** adaptable, amenable, biddable, compliant, fluid, malleable, open, responsive, tractable, yielding; *opp* inflexible

flicker *v* blink, flash, flutter, glimmer, glint, glitter, oscillate, quiver, tremble, twinkle, vibrate, waver, wink, wobble

flicker *n* blink, flash, flutter, glimmer, glint, glitter, twinkle, spark, wink

flight *n* **1** journey, trajectory, trip. **2** aviation, flying, soaring, winging. **3** absconding, decamping, departure, disappearance, escape, exit, exodus, fleeing, getaway, retreat, vanishing

flimsy *adj* **1** breakable, brittle, delicate, fine, fragile, frail, insubstantial, lightweight, makeshift, ramshackle, rickety, shaky, slight, thin, weak; *opp* strong. **2** (a flimsy excuse) feeble, implausible, inadequate, pathetic, poor, thin, transparent, trifling, trivial, unconvincing, unsatisfactory, weak; *opp* sound

flinch *v* balk, blench, cower, cringe, dodge, duck, flee, jump, quail, recoil, retreat, shirk, shrink, shy away, start, swerve, wince, withdraw

fling *v* cast, chuck *inf*, heave, hurl, launch, lob *inf*, pitch, propel, send, shy, sling, throw, toss

flippant *adj* casual, cheeky, disrespectful, facetious, flip, frivolous, glib, light-hearted, impertinent, impudent, irreverent, jokey, offhand, pert, shallow, superficial, thoughtless

flirt *n* coquette, heartbreaker, philanderer, tease

flirt *v* lead sb on, make advances, ogle, philander, tease, toy with, trifle with

flirtatious *adj* coquettish, coy, flirty, philandering, playful, provocative, teasing

float *v* be buoyant, bob, drift, glide, hang, hover, poise, sail, slide, slip, stay afloat; *opp* sink

floating *adj* **1** afloat, bobbing, buoyant, drifting, gliding, hanging, hovering, poised, sailing, suspended. **2** changeable, fluctuating, unattached, uncommitted, undecided, variable, wandering

flock *n* **1** (of animals) drove, flight, gaggle, herd. **2** (of people) assembly, company, congregation, crowd, gathering, group, horde, host, mass, multitude, throng

flock *v* amass, assemble, congregate, converge, crowd, gather, group, herd, huddle, mass, swarm, throng, troop

flog *v* beat, cane, chastise, flagellate, flay, lash, scourge, thrash, whip

flood *n* **1** deluge, downpour, flash flood, inundation, overflow, spate, tidal wave, tide, torrent. **2** abundance, excess, flow, glut, plethora, profusion, rush, stream, surfeit, surge

flood *v* **1** (to flood an area) cover, deluge, drown, engulf, fill, immerse, inundate, submerge, sweep. **2** (of a river) break its banks, brim over, overflow, pour,

stream, surge, swell

floor *n* deck, level, stage, story, tier

flop *n* debacle, disaster, dud *inf*, failure, fiasco, loser, no-hoper *inf*, nonstarter, washout *inf*; *opp* success

flop *v* **1** collapse, dangle, droop, drop, fall, flag, hang, sag, slump, topple, tumble, wilt. **2** bomb *inf*, close, fail, fall flat, founder

flounder *v* blunder, flail, fumble, grope, muddle, struggle, stumble, thrash, wallow

flourish *n* brandishing, display, gesture, shaking, show, swing, swish, twirl, wave

flourish *v* **1** be fruitful, be successful, bloom, blossom, burgeon, grow, prosper, succeed, thrive; *opp* fail. **2** brandish, hold up, shake, swing, swish, twirl, wave, wield

flourishing *adj* blooming, blossoming, booming, burgeoning, fruitful, growing, prosperous, successful, thriving; *opp* ailing, failing

flout *v* defy, disobey, disregard, ignore, insult, jeer at, laugh at, make a mockery of, mock, ridicule, scorn, show contempt for, sneer at, spurn, treat sth with disdain

flow *v* cascade, circulate, course, dribble, drip, ebb, glide, gush, leak, move, ooze, pour, roll, run, rush, seep, slide, slip, spill, spout, squirt, stream, surge, sweep, swirl, trickle, well, whirl

flower *n* **1** bloom, blossom, bud, floret. **2** best, choice, cream, elite, height, pick

flower *v* bloom, blossom, bud, burgeon, flourish, open, unfold

fluctuate *v* alternate, be unsteady, change, hesitate, oscillate, move, seesaw, shift, swing, vacillate, vary, veer, waver, yo-yo

fluent *adj* articulate, easy, effortless, eloquent, flowing, fluid, mellifluous, natural, ready, smooth, voluble

fluid *adj* 1 flowing, liquefied, liquid, melted, molten, running, runny, sloppy, watery; *opp* solid. 2 adaptable, adjustable, changeable, flexible, floating, indefinite, mobile, mutable, open, shifting, variable; *opp* fixed

flurry *n* bustle, commotion, excitement, flap, fluster, flutter, hubbub, stir, tumult, whirl

flush *n* bloom, blush, color, glow, radiance, redness, rosiness

flush *v* 1 (of a face) blush, burn, color, flame, glow, go red, redden. 2 clean out, cleanse, flood, hose down, rinse, wash down, wash out

fly *v* 1 flit, flutter, glide, hover, sail, soar, swoop, take flight, take to the air, take wing. 2 (of a pilot) control, maneuver, operate, pilot, take off. 3 (of a flag) display, flap, flutter, hoist, raise, show, wave. 4 (of time) elapse, pass, race, roll on, slip away, slip past. 5 dart, dash, hurry, race, rush, shoot, sprint, tear, zoom

foam *n* bubbles, froth, head, lather, scum, spray, spume, suds

foam *v* boil, bubble, effervesce, fizz, froth, lather

focus *n* center, core, focal point, heart, hub, pivot, target

focus *v* 1 aim, concentrate, direct attention, fix, home in, pinpoint, spotlight. 2 (of a lens) bring into focus, turn, zoom in

fog *n* cloud, gloom, haze, mist, mistiness, murk, murkiness, smog

foggy *adj* blurred, blurry, clouded, cloudy, dim, gray, hazy, indistinct, misty, murky, obscure, smoggy; *opp* clear

foil *v* baffle, defeat, frustrate, outwit, prevent, stop, thwart

fold *n* bend, corrugation, crease, crinkle, furrow, gather, layer, line, overlap, pleat, pucker, turn, wrinkle

fold *v* 1 bend, crease, crimp, crinkle, crumple, double, gather, jackknife, overlap, pleat, pucker, tuck, turn. 2 (fold sth in your arms) embrace, enclose, enfold, entwine, envelop, hold, wrap. 3 (of a business) close, collapse, crash, fail, go bankrupt, go bust *inf*, go under *inf*

follow *v* 1 (go behind sb or sth) chase, dog, hound, hunt, pursue, shadow, stalk, tag along *inf*, tail *inf*, track, trail. 2 (follow a rule) abide by, comply with, conform, honor, obey, observe, stick to. 3 (come after sb or sth) replace, step into sb's shoes, succeed, supersede, supplant, take sb's place

follower *n* admirer, apostle, believer, convert, devotee, disciple, enthusiast, fan, groupie *inf*, pupil, supporter, worshiper

folly *n* foolishness, idiocy, insanity, lunacy, madness, nonsense, silliness, stupidity

fond *adj* 1 adoring, affectionate, amorous, caring, devoted, loving, warm. 2 **fond of** addicted to, attached to, enamored of, hooked on, in love with, keen on, mad about, partial to

fondle *v* caress, cuddle, pat, pet,

stroke, touch

food n 1 cooking, cuisine, diet, eats inf, fare, foodstuffs, grub inf, meals, nosh sl, nourishment, provisions, refreshments, sustenance. 2 fodder, feed

fool n 1 blockhead, clot inf, dope inf, fat-head inf, half-wit, idiot, jerk sl, moron, nerd sl, nincompoop, nit, nitwit, twerp inf, twit inf. 2 buffoon, clown, comedian, comic, jester

fool v 1 bamboozle, beguile, bluff, cheat, con inf, deceive, delude, dupe, hoax, hoodwink, kid inf, make a fool of, mislead, play a trick on, string sb along inf, take sb in, trick. 2 **fool around** act the fool, clown around, joke, mess about inf, play tricks, tease

foolish adj brainless, crazy, daft, dumb inf, hare-brained, idiotic, ill-advised, inane, ludicrous, mad, ridiculous, senseless, silly, simple, stupid, thoughtless, unintelligent, unwise; **opp** sensible

foolproof adj certain, guaranteed, infallible, safe, sure

foot n 1 base, bottom, end, foundation. 2 claw, hoof, paw, trotter

forbid v ban, bar, deny, exclude, inhibit, make illegal, prevent, prohibit, refuse, rule out, say no to, stop, veto; **opp** allow

forbidden adj against the law, banned, outlawed, out of bounds, prohibited, restricted, secret, taboo, wrong

force n 1 effort, energy, exertion, impact, might, muscle, power, pressure, stamina, strength, stress. 2 (making sb do sth) aggression, arm-twisting inf, coercion, compulsion, duress, pressure, violence. 3 (force of an argument) effect,

effectiveness, influence, persuasiveness, power, strength, validity, weight. 4 (spoke with force) drive, emphasis, feeling, fierceness, intensity, passion, persistence, vehemence, vividness. 5 army, battalion, body, corps, division, group, squad, squadron, troops, unit

force v 1 (make sb do sth) bulldoze inf, coerce, compel, constrain, dragoon, impose, make, oblige, press-gang, pressurize, railroad inf, twist sb's arm. 2 (force sth open) blast, break open, thrust, use force, wrench. 3 (force sth out) drag, exact, extort, wring. 4 (force sth along) drive, press, propel, push, urge

forced adj (a forced smile) affected, artificial, false, insincere, self-conscious, stiff, strained, unnatural, wooden; **opp** natural

forceful adj assertive, compelling, convincing, dynamic, effective, powerful, strong; **opp** weak

foreboding n anxiety, apprehension, chill, dread, fear, feeling, forewarning, intuition, misgiving, omen, premonition, presentiment, suspicion, warning, worry

forecast n guess, outlook, prediction, prognosis, projection, prophecy, speculation

forecast v divine, estimate, foresee, foretell, forewarn, predict, prophesy

foreign adj 1 (foreign lands) alien, distant, exotic, faraway, outlandish, remote, strange, unfamiliar, unknown. 2 (foreign affairs) external, international, outside, overseas; **opp** domestic

foreigner n alien, immigrant, newcomer, outsider, stranger, visitor

forerunner n 1 ancestor, forebear, forefather, predecessor. 2 harbinger, herald, precursor

foresee v anticipate, divine, envisage, expect, forebode, forecast, foretell, predict, prophesy

foresight n anticipation, care, farsightedness, forethought, looking ahead, precaution, prescience, vision

forest n coppice, copse, jungle, plantation, trees, wood, woodland

foretell v forecast, foresee, foreshadow, forewarn, herald, predict, prophesy

forfeit n damages, fee, fine, loss, penalty

forfeit v be deprived of, give up, hand over, lose, relinquish, renounce, surrender

forge v 1 (forge metal) beat, cast, form, hammer, make, mold, shape, work. 2 (forge an object) coin, copy, counterfeit, fake, falsify, imitate, make illegally, reproduce

forgery n copy, counterfeit, fake, imitation, replica, reproduction

forget v disregard, fail to remember, ignore, lose sight of, neglect, omit, overlook, put out of your mind; **opp** remember

forgetful adj absentminded, careless, distracted, dreamy, inattentive, neglectful, oblivious, preoccupied, vague

forgive v absolve, acquit, condone, excuse, exonerate, ignore, let off, overlook, pardon, spare

forgiveness n absolution, amnesty, clemency, compassion, exoneration, leniency, mercy, pardon, reprieve

forgiving adj compassionate, lenient, magnanimous, merciful, mild, soft-hearted, tolerant, understanding

forgo v do without, give up, go without, relinquish, renounce, sacrifice, surrender

forgotten adj blotted out, buried, dead, gone, left behind, lost, obliterated, out of mind, past

forlorn adj 1 alone, desolate, lonely, miserable, pathetic, pitiable, pitiful, unhappy, wretched. 2 abandoned, deserted, forgotten, forsaken, neglected. 3 (a forlorn hope) desperate, hopeless

form n 1 (the shape of sth) arrangement, configuration, design, formation, pattern, shape, structure. 2 (type) kind, sort, type, variety. 3 (form to fill in) application, document, paper, sheet. 4 (a slim form) anatomy, body, build, figure, frame, outline, physique, shape, silhouette

form v 1 build, cast, concoct, construct, create, fashion, forge, make, model, mold, produce, shape, stamp. 2 appear, arise, become visible, come into existence, develop, grow, materialize, take shape. 3 devise, draw up, dream up inf, formulate, plan, think up. 4 assemble, bring about, establish, found, organize, set up. 5 comprise, constitute, make up

formal adj 1 (of an occasion) ceremonial, dignified, elaborate, official, posh inf, ritualistic, sophisticated; **opp** informal. 2 (of people) aloof, conventional, correct, prim, reserved, rigid, stuffy, unbending, unfriendly; **opp** relaxed. 3 (of an agreement) binding, contractual, legal, official, proper;

opp informal

formality *n* 1 (a formality) ceremony, convention, custom, form, gesture, rite, ritual, rule. 2 ceremoniousness, correctness, decorum, etiquette, procedure, protocol, red tape

formative *adj* developing, forming, growing, impressionable, shaping, susceptible

former *adj* 1 (his former wife) ex-, last, late, one-time, previous. 2 (former times) ancient, bygone, earlier, long gone, old, past

formidable *adj* 1 (of a person) alarming, daunting, frightening, intimidating, scary *inf*. 2 (of a sight) awe-inspiring, awesome, daunting, fearful, frightful, horrible, menacing, petrifying, terrifying. 3 (of a task) arduous, challenging, daunting, difficult, onerous, overwhelming; *opp* simple. 4 (of an enemy) mighty, invincible, powerful, strong

formula *n* blueprint, method, prescription, procedure, recipe, technique

formulate *v* 1 articulate, define, express, frame, give form to, set out, specify. 2 create, devise, draw up, evolve, map out, plan, work out

fort *n* camp, castle, citadel, fortification, fortress, garrison, stronghold, tower

forthcoming *adj* 1 (the forthcoming exam) approaching, coming, imminent, impending, prospective, upcoming. 2 (of a person) chatty, communicative, talkative, voluble

fortification *n* barricade, battlement, bulwark, castle, defense, fort, fortress, parapet, rampart, stronghold

fortify *v* 1 (make sth stronger) brace, buttress, defend, guard, protect, reinforce, secure, shore up, stiffen, strengthen. 2 (encourage yourself) boost, buoy up, cheer, embolden, encourage, hearten, invigorate, reassure, revive, sustain; *opp* discourage

fortress *n* castle, citadel, fort, stronghold

fortunate *adj* 1 blessed, favored, happy, lucky, prosperous, successful; *opp* unfortunate. 2 auspicious, favorable, felicitous, opportune, propitious, timely

fortune *n* 1 affluence, assets, inheritance, millions *inf*, money, prosperity, riches, treasure, wealth. 2 accident, chance, destiny, fate, kismet, luck, providence

fortune-teller *n* astrologer, clairvoyant, crystal-gazer, oracle, palmist, prophet, seer, soothsayer, stargazer *inf*

forward *adj* 1 advanced, early, precocious, premature, well-developed; *opp* backward. 2 bold, brash, brazen, impudent, insolent, overfamiliar, presumptuous, shameless; *opp* shy

forward *v* 1 dispatch, readdress, send, send on, transmit. 2 advance, encourage, further, hasten, help, promote, speed up

foster *v* 1 adopt, bring up, care for, look after, raise, rear, take care of. 2 (foster links) cultivate, encourage, promote, support. 3 (foster hopes) cherish, entertain, harbor, sustain

foul *adj* 1 bad, contaminated, dirty, disgusting, fetid, filthy, impure, infected, polluted, putrid, rank, repugnant, repulsive, revolting, rotten, smelly, squalid, stinking, unclean; *opp* clean.

2 atrocious, contemptible, cruel, disgraceful, evil, horrible, scandalous, sordid, vicious, violent, wicked. **3** (foul language) blasphemous, coarse, filthy, obscene, offensive, rude, vulgar. **4** (a foul day) blustery, foggy, rainy, rough, stormy, wet, wild, windy; *opp* beautiful, lovely

foul v blacken, contaminate, defile, dirty, pollute, smear, stain, taint

found v begin, bring about, create, endow, establish, organize, set up, start

foundation n **1** base, basis, bottom, cornerstone, footing, substructure. **2** basis, fundamentals, origin, principles, rudiments

founder n beginner, benefactor, builder, designer, inventor, maker, organizer, originator

founder v **1** be lost, be wrecked, capsize, go down, run aground, sink. **2** come to grief, fail, fall through, go wrong

fountain n fount, jet, spout, spray, spring, well

fraction n division, part, portion, small part, subdivision

fracture n break, crack, fissure, opening, rift, rupture, split

fracture v break, crack, rupture, split, suffer a fracture

fragile adj breakable, brittle, delicate, feeble, flimsy, frail, insubstantial, thin, weak; *opp* robust

fragment n bit, chip, crumb, fraction, morsel, particle, piece, portion, remnant, scrap, shard, shred, sliver

fragment v break, chip, crack, disintegrate, fall apart, fracture, shatter, shiver, smash, splinter

fragrance n **1** aroma, bouquet, perfume, scent, smell. **2** cologne, perfume, scent

fragrant adj aromatic, perfumed, sweet-scented, sweet-smelling

frail adj **1** (of a person) decrepit, delicate, feeble, fragile, ill, infirm, puny, sickly, slight, unwell, unsteady, vulnerable, weak; *opp* strong. **2** (of an object) breakable, dainty, easily damaged, flimsy, fragile, insubstantial, rickety, thin; *opp* strong

frame n **1** body, casing, chassis, framework, scaffolding, shell, skeleton, structure, substructure. **2** border, edge, mount, mounting, setting

frame v **1** compose, devise, draft, draw up, formulate, sketch. **2** box in, encase, enclose, mount, put in a frame, set off, surround. **3** (frame sb) accuse, implicate, incriminate, point the finger at, set up

framework n bare bones, core, fabric, foundation, groundwork, outline, plan, shell, skeleton, structure, support

frank adj blunt, candid, direct, forthright, free, honest, no-nonsense inf, open, outspoken, plain, sincere, straight, straightforward, truthful, unconcealed, undisguised, upfront inf

frantic adj agitated, berserk, beside yourself, crazy, desperate, distracted, distraught, excitable, frenetic, frenzied, furious, hectic, hysterical, mad, overwrought, panic-stricken, raving, wild

fraternize v associate, consort, go around with, hang around with inf, keep company with, mingle, mix, socialize

fraud n **1** (accused of fraud) cheating, deceit, deception, dishonesty, double-dealing, fraudulence, sharp practice, skulduggery, treachery, trickery. **2** (a trick) con inf, deception, hoax, put-up job inf, ruse, scam sl, trick. **3** (a person) cheat, confidence trickster, con man inf, fake, hoaxer, imposter, phony inf, pretender, quack, scoundrel, swindler. **4** (sth not genuine) counterfeit, fake, forgery, phony inf

fraudulent adj bent inf, bogus, corrupt, criminal, crooked inf, deceitful, deceptive, dishonest, false, forged, illegal, phony inf, spurious, unscrupulous; **opp** honest

freak adj abnormal, atypical, bizarre, exceptional, extraordinary, freakish, odd, peculiar, queer, rare, unexpected, unpredictable, unusual, weird; **opp** normal, usual

freak n **1** aberration, abnormality, anomaly, curiosity, monster, monstrosity, mutant, quirk, rarity. **2** addict, buff inf, enthusiast, fan, fanatic

free adj **1** (free tickets) at no cost, complimentary, for nothing, free of charge, on the house inf. **2** (free to move) able, allowed, at large, at liberty, clear, liberated, loose, unchained, unhindered, unblocked, unobstructed, unrestrained. **3** easygoing, footloose, independent, liberated, relaxed, unconstrained, uninhibited; **opp** tied down. **4** (a free country) autonomous, democratic, independent, self-governing. **5** (available for use) available, empty, extra, spare, unoccupied, unused, vacant. **6 free with** generous, hospitable, lavish, open-handed, unsparing

free v cut loose, discharge, emancipate, extricate, let go, let out, liberate, loose, release, rescue, save, turn loose, unchain, undo, unleash, untie

freedom n **1** (freedom to do what you want) carte blanche, flexibility, free hand, free rein, latitude, leeway, license, opportunity, range, scope. **2** (fighting for freedom) autonomy, deliverance, emancipation, home rule, independence, liberty, sovereignty

freely adv **1** (go freely) of your own accord, of your own free will, voluntarily, willingly. **2** (speak freely) bluntly, candidly, frankly, honestly, openly

freeze v **1** become frozen, chill, harden, ice over, ice up, solidify; **opp** thaw. **2** be cold, chill, cool, go numb, make cold, numb. **3** be immobilized, go rigid, stand still, stop dead, stop in your tracks; **opp** move

freezing adj arctic, biting, bitter, cutting, frosty, ice-cold, icy, raw, snowy, wintry; **opp** boiling

freight n cargo, consignment, goods, load, merchandise, shipment

frenzied adj agitated, excited, frantic, frenetic, furious, hysterical, maniacal, rabid, uncontrolled, wild; **opp** calm

frenzy n **1** agitation, delirium, excitement, fury, hysteria, insanity, lunacy, madness, mania, paroxysm, passion, rage, seizure. **2** bout, fit, outburst

frequent adj common, constant, continual, customary, everyday, familiar, habitual, incessant, innumerable, many, numerous, persistent, recurrent, repeated; *opp* rare

frequent *v* go to, hang out at *inf*, haunt, spend time at, visit

fresh *adj* 1 (fresh colors) bright, clean, crisp, unfaded, vivid. 2 (fresh food) crisp, healthy, natural, raw, unprocessed, untreated; *opp* processed. 3 (fresh water) clean, clear, drinkable, pure, refreshing, sweet, uncontaminated; *opp* stale. 4 (fresh ideas) different, innovative, modern, new, novel, original, up-to-date; *opp* old. 5 (fresh-faced) bright, clear, fair, healthy, pink, rosy, wholesome. 6 (feel fresh after a shower) alive, awake, bright, energetic, full of beans *inf*, invigorated, lively, perky *inf*, refreshed, restored, revived, tingling; *opp* tired. 7 (a fresh wind) bracing, brisk, chilly, cool, invigorating, strong; *opp* gentle. 8 (fresh supplies) additional, extra, further, more, other. 9 (fresh bedding) clean, crisp, laundered, starched, unused, washed; *opp* dirty

freshen *v* 1 liven up, refresh, restore, revitalize, revive, rouse. 2 air, purify, ventilate

fret *v* agonize, be distressed, brood, complain, feel unhappy, grumble, lose sleep, whine, worry

friction *n* 1 abrasion, chafing, erosion, grating, irritation, resistance, rubbing, scraping. 2 (friction between people) antagonism, arguing, bad feeling, conflict, disagreement, dissension, hostility, resentment

friend *n* boyfriend, buddy *inf*, chum, companion, comrade, girlfriend, mate *inf*, pal *inf*, partner, pen pal, playmate

friendliness *n* amiability, helpfulness, hospitality, kindliness, kindness, neighborliness, sociability, warmth

friendly *adj* affectionate, agreeable, amicable, approachable, civil, companionable, helpful, hospitable, intimate, kind, kindhearted, kindly, neighborly, sociable, sympathetic, warm, welcoming; *opp* unfriendly

friendship *n* affection, closeness, companionship, harmony, intimacy, rapport, relationship

fright *n* 1 (fear) alarm, apprehension, dismay, dread, fear, horror, panic, terror, trepidation. 2 (have a fright) scare, shock, surprise

frighten *v* 1 alarm, intimidate, make you afraid, make your blood run cold, make your hair stand on end, petrify, scare, spook *inf*, startle, terrify, unnerve, upset. 2 browbeat, bully, menace, persecute, terrorize, threaten, tyrannize

frightened *adj* afraid, alarmed, anxious, apprehensive, cowardly, fearful, horrified, horror-struck, panicky, panic-stricken, petrified, scared, shocked, startled, terrified, trembling, unnerved, upset

frightening *adj* alarming, blood-curdling, creepy *inf*, daunting, dreadful, eerie, fearful, fearsome, ghostly, hair-raising, horrifying, intimidating, menacing, scary, shocking, sinister, spine-chilling, terrifying, weird

frigid *adj* 1 aloof, forbidding, formal, icy, remote, rigid, stiff, unfeeling, unfriendly, unresponsive; *opp* warm. 2 arctic, bitter, cold, cool, frosty, frozen, glacial, icy, wintry

fringe *n* 1 border, boundary, edge, limits,

margin, outskirts, perimeter, periphery.
2 edging, flounce, frill, ruffle, tassel,
trimming

frisk v 1 caper, cavort, dance, frolic,
gambol, jump, play, romp, skip.
2 inspect, search

frisky adj active, bouncy, full of beans inf,
high inf, high-spirited, lively, playful,
sprightly

frivolous adj empty-headed, facetious,
flighty, flip inf, flippant, foolish, giddy,
idle, inconsequential, juvenile, pointless,
puerile, shallow, silly, superficial, trivial,
unimportant; *opp* serious

frolic v caper, cavort, dance, frisk,
gambol, have fun, play, prance, romp,
skip

front adj first, foremost, head, lead,
leading

front n 1 exterior, facade, face,
foreground, forepart, frontage.
2 beginning, front line, head, top,
vanguard. 3 (just a front) blind, cover,
disguise, facade, pretext, show

frontier n border, boundary, confines,
edge, limit

froth n bubbles, foam, head, lather, scum,
suds

froth v bubble over, bubble up, effervesce,
fizz, foam, lather

frothy adj 1 bubbly, foaming, foamy,
lathery. 2 frivolous, insignificant,
insubstantial, light, slight, trivial,
worthless

frown v glare, glower, knit your brows,
look sullen, scowl

frozen adj 1 (frozen wastes) arctic,
chilled, frosted, glacial, hard, icebound,
icy, polar, Siberian. 2 (without feeling)

anesthetized, asleep inf, deadened, frigid,
numb. 3 (not able to move) petrified,
rooted to the spot, stock-still, suspended

fruit n 1 crop, harvest, produce, yield.
2 effect, outcome, profit, result, return,
reward

fruitful adj 1 beneficial, productive,
profitable, rewarding, successful, useful,
well-spent, worthwhile; *opp* fruitless.
2 abundant, copious, fertile, flourishing,
lush, luxurious, plentiful, potent,
prolific, rich

frustrate v annoy, defeat, disappoint,
discourage, dishearten, embitter, foil,
hinder, prevent, spoil, stymie, thwart,
vex

frustrated adj annoyed, disappointed,
discontented, discouraged, disheartened,
embittered, resentful, unfulfilled,
unsatisfied

frustration n anger, annoyance,
dissatisfaction, disappointment,
exasperation, irritation, resentment,
vexation

fudge v 1 avoid, dodge, equivocate,
hedge, waffle. 2 botch, fake

fuel n 1 coal, diesel, electricity, gas,
kerosene, oil, paraffin. 2 ammunition,
encouragement, fodder, incentive,
provocation, stimulus

fugitive n deserter, escapee, refugee,
runaway

fulfill v 1 (do sth) accomplish, achieve,
bring about, carry out, complete, do,
execute, finish, implement, make sth
come true, realize. 2 (satisfy sth) answer,
comply with, conform to, fill, meet,
obey, satisfy

full adj 1 (full of sth) brimful, brimming,

bursting, filled, gorged, loaded, overflowing, replete, sated, satisfied, saturated, stuffed, well-stocked; *opp* empty. 2 (detailed) complete, comprehensive, copious, detailed, entire, exhaustive, thorough, unabridged, whole. 3 (full lips) ample, broad, curvaceous, fat, generous, large, plump, rounded; *opp* thin. 4 (a full bus) chock-full *inf*, crammed, crowded, jammed, jam-packed *inf*, packed; *opp* empty

full-grown *adj* adult, developed, fully grown, grown-up, mature, ripe

full-scale *adj* all-out, comprehensive, extensive, in-depth, major, proper, thorough, wide-ranging

fumble *v* 1 botch, bungle, drop, flounder, make a mess of *inf*, mess up, mishandle, miss, muff, spoil, stumble. 2 (fumble in your pocket) feel around, grope, scrabble

fume *v* 1 emit fumes, smoke, smolder. 2 be angry, be enraged, be incensed, be livid, blow your top *inf*, boil, flip your lid *inf*, fly off the handle *inf*, rage, rant, rave, see red *inf*, seethe, storm

fumes *n* exhaust, gases, pollution, smog, smoke, vapor

fun *n* amusement, distraction, diversion, enjoyment, entertainment, games, jokes, joking, joy, laughter, merriment, pleasure, recreation, relaxation, sport

function *n* 1 aim, purpose, raison d'être, use. 2 capacity, duty, job, responsibility, role. 3 affair, do *inf*, event, occasion, party, reception, social occasion

function *v* act, behave, go, operate, perform, run, serve, work

functional *adj* hard-wearing, practical, serviceable, useful, utilitarian, working

fund *n* hoard, kitty, mine, pool, repository, reserve, reservoir, stock, store, storehouse, supply, treasury

fund *v* finance, pay for, subsidize, support, underwrite

fundamental *adj* basic, central, crucial, elementary, essential, first, important, inherent, intrinsic, key, necessary, principal, quintessential, underlying, vital

funds *n* assets, capital, cash, endowments, finance, investments, means, money, resources, riches, savings, wealth

funeral *n* burial, cremation, entombment, interment

funny *adj* 1 amusing, comic, comical, daft *inf*, droll, entertaining, hilarious, humorous, ironic, ludicrous, mad, nonsensical, preposterous, ridiculous, riotous, satirical, side-splitting, uproarious, witty. 2 (strange) curious, mysterious, odd, peculiar, puzzling, strange, suspicious, unusual; *opp* normal. 3 (feel funny) (*inf*) dizzy, ill, off-color *inf*, queasy, sick

fur *n* bristles, coat, down, fleece, hair, wool

furious *adj* 1 angry, beside yourself, enraged, foaming at the mouth *inf*, fuming, hot under the collar *inf*, incensed, infuriated, irate, livid *inf*, mad. 2 fierce, frantic, frenetic, intense, stormy, turbulent, violent, wild

furnish *v* 1 decorate, equip, fit out. 2 give, offer, present, provide, supply

furniture *n* equipment, fittings, furnishings, household goods, possessions

furtive *adj* clandestine, conspiratorial,

covert, disguised, hidden, secret,
secretive, shifty, skulking, slinking, sly,
sneaking, sneaky, stealthy, surreptitious,
underhand

fury *n* **1** anger, frenzy, madness, passion,
rage, wrath. **2** ferocity, force, intensity,
power, savagery, tempestuousness,
violence

fuss *n* **1** bother, bustle, confusion,
excitement, flurry, tumult, uproar.
2 (make a fuss) argument, dispute, furor,
objection, protest, row, squabble,
trouble, upset

fuss *v* bustle about, complain, fidget, flap,
fret, get in a stew *inf*, get worked up *inf*,
gripe *inf*, grumble, kick up a fuss, make
a fuss, take on *inf*, worry

fussy *adj* choosy, difficult, finicky, hard
to please, nit-picking *inf*, particular,
picky *inf*

futile *adj* fruitless, ineffectual, in vain,
pointless, to no avail, unproductive,
unsuccessful, useless, wasted, worthless;
opp useful

future *n* **1** (in the future) hereafter, time
ahead, time to come, tomorrow. **2** (no
future) expectations, outlook, prospects

future *adj* **1** (a future time) approaching,
awaited, coming, forthcoming,
impending, prospective, subsequent, to
come. **2** (his future wife) destined,
eventual, expected, intended, planned,
prospective

gadget *n* appliance, contraption, contrivance, device, instrument, invention, novelty, tool, utensil

gag *n* crack *inf*, funny remark, jest, joke, one-liner *inf*, quip, wisecrack *inf*, witticism

gag *v* 1 keep sb quiet, muffle, muzzle, quiet, silence, smother, stifle, suppress. 2 choke, gasp, heave, retch

gain *n* acquisition, advantage, attainment, benefit, earnings, improvement, income, increase, profit, return, rise, winnings, yield; *opp* loss

gain *v* achieve, acquire, attain, build up, capture, collect, earn, get, make, net, obtain, pick up, reach, secure, win, yield

gale *n* blast, cyclone, hurricane, squall, storm, tempest, tornado, typhoon, wind

gallant *adj* attentive, bold, brave, chivalrous, courageous, courteous, courtly, daring, dashing, fearless, heroic, honorable, intrepid, manly, noble, polite, valiant, valorous

gallop *v* canter, go at full speed, hurry, hurtle, race, run, rush, sprint, tear

galvanize *v* arouse, awaken, electrify, excite, inspire, jolt, shock, spur, stimulate, stir, urge

gamble *v* 1 (bet money) bet, lay bets, stake money, wager. 2 (take a chance) speculate, stick your neck out *inf*, take a chance, take a risk, trust, venture

game *adj* 1 brave, courageous, daring, plucky, unafraid. 2 agreeable, eager, happy, interested, ready, willing

game *n* 1 amusement, entertainment, pastime, recreation, sport, toy. 2 (just a game) fun, joke, laugh, prank, trick. 3 (a game you play) competition, contest, match, round, tournament

gang *n* band, clique, club, crew *inf*, crowd, group, herd, horde, lot, mob, pack, posse, team

gangster *n* bandit, brigand, desperado, gunman, robber, thug, tough

gap *n* 1 (gap between two things) aperture, blank, breach, break, cavity, chink, crack, crevice, divide, gulf, hole, opening, rift, space, void. 2 (gap in time) break, breathing-space, interlude, interruption, interval, lull, pause, respite, rest, suspension, wait. 3 (gap between people) difference, distance, division, divergence, gulf, incompatibility

gape *v* 1 gawk, gaze, goggle, ogle, stare. 2 crack, open, part, split, yawn

garbled *adj* confused, distorted, jumbled, misquoted, mixed up, twisted; *opp* clear

garish *adj* brassy, bright, crude, flash *inf*, flashy, gaudy, loud, lurid, showy, tacky *inf*, tasteless, vulgar

garland n crown, loop, wreath

garment n article of clothing, attire, clothing, costume, dress, garb, item of clothing, outfit

garnish v adorn, beautify, decorate, embellish, enhance, grace, ornament, set off, trim

gash n cut, incision, laceration, slash, slit, tear, wound

gash v cut, gouge, lacerate, nick, score, slash, slit, split, tear, wound

gate n barrier, door, doorway, entrance, exit, gateway, portal, portcullis, turnstile

gather v 1 (collect) accumulate, amass, collect, heap, hoard, pile up, stockpile. 2 (of people) assemble, congregate, convene, crowd, get together, flock, group, herd, marshal, mass, mobilize, round up, summon, swarm, throng. 3 (understand) assume, believe, deduce, draw the conclusion, guess, hear, infer, learn, understand. 4 (gather flowers) harvest, pick, pluck, reap

gathering n assembly, congregation, convention, crowd, get-together inf, group, horde, meeting, mob, party, rally

gaudy adj bright, brilliant, flash inf, flashy, garish, glaring, harsh, loud, ostentatious, showy, tasteless, tawdry, vivid, vulgar

gauge n 1 (size) bore, caliber, capacity, depth, dimensions, height, measure, size, thickness, width. 2 (instrument) dial, indicator, instrument, meter. 3 (yardstick) benchmark, guide, guideline, indication, indicator, model, standard, yardstick

gauge v 1 (gauge an amount) ascertain, calculate, check, count, determine, measure, value, weigh, work out.

2 (gauge sb's response) assess, discern, estimate, evaluate, guess, judge, reckon

gaunt adj angular, bony, drawn, emaciated, haggard, hollow-cheeked, lanky, pinched, scrawny, skinny, starving, thin, wasted; opp fat, plump, well-rounded

gay adj 1 (of colors) bright, colorful, rich, showy, vivid; opp dull. 2 (happy) cheerful, happy, jolly, merry, vivacious; opp sad. 3 homosexual, lesbian; opp straight

gaze n look, stare

gaze v eye, gape, look, stare, watch

gear n 1 belongings, bits and pieces, equipment, kit, paraphernalia, possessions, stuff, things, tools, trappings. 2 cog, cogwheel, gearwheel, machinery, mechanism. 3 clothes, clothing, dress, get-up inf, outfit, rig, togs inf

gem n 1 gemstone, jewel, precious stone, stone. 2 pearl, prize, star, treasure

general adj 1 across-the-board, all-encompassing, blanket, broad, comprehensive, global, inclusive, overall, universal; opp specific. 2 accepted, common, customary, normal, regular, typical, usual. 3 approximate, ballpark, broad, loose, outline, rough, vague; opp precise

generally adv 1 (on the whole) as a rule, broadly speaking, by and large, commonly, mostly, normally, on the whole, typically, usually. 2 (widely) commonly, popularly, universally, widely

generate v arouse, bring about, cause, engender, give rise to, lead to, produce, stir up

generation n 1 age group, contemporaries, day, era, period, time. 2 arousal, creation, production, stirring up

generic adj across-the-board, broad, typical, universal

generosity n benevolence, kindness, lavishness, magnanimity, munificence, philanthropy; **opp** meanness

generous adj 1 benevolent, big-hearted, charitable, kind, magnanimous, philanthropic; **opp** mean. 2 abundant, huge, large, lavish, plentiful

genius n 1 expert, know-all inf, mastermind, prodigy, boy wonder, girl wonder, master, virtuoso, whiz-kid inf, whiz inf. 2 ability, aptitude, brains, brilliance, flair, gift, talent

genteel adj cultured, elegant, ladylike, polished, polite, posh inf, refined, well-mannered

gentle adj 1 (of a person) amiable, easy-going, kind, kindly, mild, placid, soft-hearted, soft, tender. 2 delicate, easy, light, mild, muted, peaceful, quiet, soft, soothing. 3 (of a slope) easy, gradual, moderate, slight, smooth, steady; **opp** steep

genuine adj 1 authentic, bona fide, guaranteed, kosher, legitimate, original, pukka inf, real, solid, true. 2 candid, honest, open, sincere, straight, unaffected

germ n bacteria, bug inf, infection, micro-organism, virus

germinate v develop, grow, shoot, sprout, start growing, start, take root

gesticulate v gesture, indicate, motion, sign, signal, wave

gesture n gesticulation, hand movement, indication, motion, sign, signal, wave

gesture v gesticulate, indicate, motion, sign, signal, wave

get v 1 (obtain) achieve, acquire, attain, come by, come into possession of, earn, gain, inherit, land inf, lay your hands on, make, obtain, procure, receive, secure, win. 2 (get old) become, go, grow, turn. 3 collect, fetch, pick up. 4 arrest, capture, collar, grab, nail, seize, trap. 5 (get sb to do sth) encourage, make, persuade, prevail on. 6 (get flu) be infected by, catch, come down with, contract, develop, fall ill with, go down with, pick up. 7 (get to a place) arrive, come, reach. 8 get along (be friendly) be friendly, be on good terms, get on, hit it off. 9 get at (criticize) attack, blame, carp, criticize, make fun of, nag, pick on, taunt, tease. 10 get at (imply) hint, imply, insinuate, mean, suggest. 11 get away (escape) abscond, break free, break out, depart, disappear, escape, get out, leave, run away. 12 get on (get on a bus, ship, bike) board, catch, climb on, embark, get, go on board, mount. 13 get on (manage) cope, do, get along, make out, manage, progress. 14 get on (carry on working) carry on, continue, get cracking inf, press on, proceed. 15 get around avoid, bypass, circumvent, evade, skirt

ghastly adj appalling, awful, bad, dreadful, foul, grim, gruesome, hideous, horrendous, horrible, horrid, nasty, terrible

ghost n apparition, ghoul, phantom, poltergeist, shade, specter, spirit, spook inf, wraith

ghostly adj creepy, eerie, ghostlike, phantom, spectral, spooky inf, supernatural, unearthly

giant n behemoth, colossus, Goliath, leviathan, monster, titan, whopper inf

giddy adj dizzy, faint, light-headed, reeling, spinning, unsteady

gift n 1 bequest, contribution, donation, endowment, freebie inf, gratuity, hand-out, honorarium, legacy, offering, present, tip. 2 ability, flair, genius, knack, power, talent

gifted adj accomplished, brainy inf, bright, brilliant, clever, expert, skillful, talented

gigantic adj colossal, enormous, giant, huge, immense, jumbo inf, king-size, mammoth, massive, monstrous, towering, vast

giggle v chortle, chuckle, laugh, snigger, titter

gimmick n dodge, gizmo, publicity stunt, stunt, trick

girdle n 1 band, cummerbund, sash, waistband. 2 corset, pantie-girdle

girl n daughter, female, kid, lass, schoolgirl, woman, young woman, youngster

girlfriend n date, lover, sweetheart, young lady, woman

girth n circumference, perimeter

gist n drift, essence, idea, meaning, nub, point, sense, significance, substance

give v 1 allocate, award, contribute, deliver, dish out, dole out, donate, grant, hand over, let sb have, present, provide, share out, supply. 2 (give a speech, information) announce, communicate, deliver, make, reveal, tell, utter. 3 (give sb medicine, a punishment) administer,

dish out, dispense, impose, inflict, prescribe. 4 (give a party) arrange, have, organize, put on. 5 (yield) buckle, fall, give way, sink, yield. 6 **give in** capitulate, comply, concede defeat, give up, quit, submit, succumb, surrender, throw in the towel. 7 **give out** (share out) deal, distribute, dole out inf, hand out. 8 **give out** (emit) discharge, emit, exude, give off, produce, release. 9 **give out** (announce) advertise, announce, broadcast, make known, make public, notify, publish. 10 **give up** (give up an attempt) abandon the attempt, capitulate, comply, concede defeat, give in, lose heart, quit, submit, succumb, surrender, throw in the towel. 11 **give up** (give up smoking) abandon, cut out, leave off, quit, stop

glad adj 1 (happy) cheerful, delighted, elated, happy, joyful, pleased, satisfied, thrilled, well-pleased; opp disappointed. 2 (willing) delighted, eager, happy, keen, more than willing, pleased, ready, willing; opp unwilling

glamorous adj appealing, attractive, beautiful, beguiling, dazzling, exciting, flashy, glittering, glitzy inf, glossy, prestigious, smart

glamour n appeal, attraction, beauty, glitter, magic, prestige

glance n glimpse, look, peek, peep, quick look

glance v cast an eye over, dip into, flick through, have a quick look at, leaf through, look, peek, peep, scan

glare n 1 black look, frown, look, scowl, stare. 2 blaze, brightness, brilliance, dazzle

glare v frown, give sb a black look, glower, look daggers at, scowl, stare

glaring adj 1 blatant, conspicuous, obvious. 2 blazing, bright, dazzling

glass n beaker, crystal, flute, glassware, goblet, tumbler, wineglass

glaze v coat, enamel, lacquer, varnish

gleam v flash, glimmer, glint, glisten, glow, shine, sparkle, twinkle

glee n delight, excitement, happiness, joy, pleasure, triumph; **opp** misery

glide v coast, drift, sail, skate, skim, slide, slip, soar

glimmer n flash, flicker, gleam, glow, shimmer, sparkle, twinkle

glimmer v blink, flicker, gleam, glint, glow, shimmer, shine, sparkle, twinkle

glimpse v catch sight of, notice, see, spot

glint v flash, gleam, glisten, glitter, shimmer, shine, sparkle, twinkle

glisten v gleam, glint, glitter, shimmer, shine, sparkle

glitter v flash, glint, glisten, shine, sparkle, twinkle

gloat v boast, brag, crow about, revel in, rub it in, show off, wallow in

global adj 1 international, universal, worldwide; **opp** local, parochial. 2 across-the-board, all-encompassing, all-inclusive, general, universal, wide-ranging

globe n 1 ball, orb, sphere. 2 earth, planet, planet earth, world

gloom n 1 dejection, depression, despair, despondency, low spirits, misery, pessimism, sadness, unhappiness; **opp** happiness. 2 dark, darkness, dimness, dusk, murkiness, shadow; **opp** brightness

gloomy adj 1 dejected, depressed, dismal, down in the dumps inf, down, low, miserable, pessimistic, sad; **opp** cheerful. 2 dark, dim, dull, murky, overcast; **opp** bright

glorious adj beautiful, brilliant, fine, gorgeous, lovely, magnificent, splendid, superb, terrific, wonderful; **opp** awful, dreadful, terrible

glory n 1 credit, distinction, fame, honor, kudos, prestige, triumph. 2 brilliance, grandeur, magnificence, radiance, splendor, wonder

glory v exult in, revel in, take pride in

gloss n 1 gleam, luster, polish, sheen, shine, varnish. 2 (outward appearance) appearance, outward appearance, semblance, veneer. 3 (explanation) comment, definition, explanation, note, paraphrase, translation

glossy adj gleaming, lustrous, polished, shining, shiny, sleek; **opp** dull, matt

glow n brightness, flush, gleam, light, luster, radiance, redness, rosiness, shine

glow v burn, gleam, light up, redden, shine, smolder

glower v give sb a black look, glare, look daggers at sb, scowl

glowing adj 1 bright, flushed, radiant, red, rich, rosy, vivid. 2 complimentary, enthusiastic, favorable, full of praise, warm

glue n adhesive, cement, paste

glue v bond, cement, fasten, fix, paste, stick

glut n excess, overabundance, oversupply, surplus; **opp** scarcity

glutton n gourmand, overeater, pig inf

gnarled adj arthritic, contorted,

knotted, twisted

gnaw v bite, chew, chomp, eat, eat away, munch, nibble, wear away

go v **1** (leave) beat it *inf*, buzz off *inf*, depart, disappear, get away, get going, get moving, leave, retreat, set off, set out, shove off *inf*, vanish. **2** (move) make for, move, pass, proceed, progress, travel. **3** (work) be working, function, operate, run, work. **4** (this road goes to Boston, our land goes as far as the river) continue, extend, lead to, reach, spread, stretch. **5** (time goes quickly) elapse, fly, pass, slip by. **6** (go gray) become, get, grow, turn. **7** (the interview went well, how is the project going?) develop, end up, fare, happen, pan out, proceed, turn out, work out. **8 go by** (time goes by) elapse, fly, pass. **9 go by** (use as a guide) be guided by, follow, obey, observe, use as a guide. **10 go for** (fetch) collect, fetch, go and get, go to pick up. **11 go for** (attack) assault, attack, launch yourself at, lunge at. **12 go for** (like) choose, like, prefer. **13 go off** (explode) detonate, explode, go bang. **14 go over** check, examine, inspect, look through, rehearse, review, run through, scan, study. **15 go through** (look through) check, examine, hunt through, inspect, look through, run through, scan, study. **16 go through** (endure) brave, endure, experience, have to put up with, suffer, undergo. **17 go without** abstain from, deny yourself, do without, forego, go short, manage without

goad v egg on *inf*, prod, prompt, provoke, push, spur, stimulate, urge

goal n aim, ambition, aspiration, end,

objective, target

godforsaken adj desolate, dismal, dreary, gloomy, miserable, wretched

godsend n bit of luck, blessing, boon, miracle, unexpected bonus

golden adj **1** (gold) fair, gilded, gilt, gold, yellow. **2** (golden opportunity) excellent, fortuitous, ideal, opportune, perfect, wonderful

good adj **1** brilliant, delicious, enjoyable, excellent, first-class, great, hunky-dory *inf*, interesting, lovely, nice, pleasant, satisfactory, suitable, super; *opp* awful, bad, terrible. **2** (good at a job) accomplished, capable, clever, competent, conscientious, efficient, professional, proficient, skillful, skilled, talented. **3** (a good person) caring, considerate, decent, generous, honest, honorable, kind, kindhearted, trustworthy, virtuous; *opp* bad, evil, wicked. **4** (well-behaved) obedient, well-behaved; *opp* naughty

good-bye interj adieu, au revoir, bye, bye-bye, cheerio, ciao *inf*, farewell, see you, so long

good-looking adj attractive, beautiful, gorgeous, handsome, pretty; *opp* ugly

goods n **1** freight, merchandise, products, stock. **2** belongings, effects, possessions, property, stuff, things

gorge n canyon, chasm, gully, ravine

gorge v be greedy, cram, devour, eat as much as you can, eat ravenously, fill yourself up, gobble, gulp down, make a pig of yourself *inf*, overeat, shovel, stuff, wolf

gorgeous adj beautiful, brilliant, glorious, good-looking, handsome, impressive, lovely, magnificent, stunning, superb, terrific, wonderful

gory *adj* blood-and-guts *inf*, blood-stained, bloody, brutal, grisly, gruesome, savage, violent

gospel *n* creed, doctrine, message, teaching, word

gossip *n* 1 hearsay, report, rumor, scandal. 2 (a person) busybody, scandalmonger

gossip *v* blab, chat, chatter, spread rumors, talk

gourmet *n* connoisseur, epicure

govern *v* 1 administer, be in power, control, look after, manage, oversee, reign, rule, run. 2 affect, control, decide, determine, influence

government *n* 1 administration, authorities, executive, parliament, regime, ruling party, state, the powers that be. 2 control, leadership, management, regulation, rule

governor *n* administrator, commissioner, director, executive, head, leader, manager, ruler

grab *v* catch hold of, collar *inf*, get hold of, grasp, seize, snap up, snatch, take hold of

grace *n* charm, elegance, finesse, gracefulness, poise, polish

grace *v* adorn, decorate, dignify, enhance, favor, honor

graceful *adj* attractive, charming, deft, elegant, natural, polished, tasteful

grade *n* category, class, level, position, rank, rung, stage

grade *v* categorize, classify, group, order, rank, size, sort

gradient *n* hill, incline, rise, slope

gradual *adj* 1 continuous, even, progressive, regular, steady, step-by-step; *opp* abrupt, sudden. 2 easy, gentle, moderate; *opp* steep

gradually *adv* bit by bit, evenly, gently, little by little, progressively, slowly, steadily, step by step; *opp* abruptly, suddenly

graduate *v* 1 become a graduate, get your degree, pass, qualify. 2 calibrate, classify, grade, group, mark off, order, rank, sort

grain *n* 1 cereal, corn, seed. 2 atom, bit, crumb, granule, iota, jot, piece, scrap, speck

grand *adj* elegant, imposing, impressive, luxurious, magnificent, majestic, palatial, regal, stately

grandeur *n* elegance, luxury, magnificence, opulence, pomp, splendor

grandiose *adj* ambitious, extravagant, grand, imposing, majestic, ostentatious, over-the-top *inf*, pretentious, splendid

grant *n* allowance, award, bursary, donation, endowment, scholarship

grant *v* 1 allocate, allot, assign, award, bestow, confer, donate, give. 2 (allow) accept, acknowledge, admit, allow, concede, go along with, permit

graph *n* bar chart, chart, diagram, pie chart

graphic *adj* blow-by-blow, clear, descriptive, detailed, explicit, realistic, striking, vivid

grapple *v* clash, fight, struggle, tackle, tussle, wrestle

grasp *n* 1 clutches, grip, hold. 2 (understanding) awareness, comprehension, knowledge, mastery, understanding. 3 (ability to achieve sth) capabilities, capacity, limitations, limits,

reach. 4 (power) clutches, control, domination, dominion, possession, power

grasp v **1** grab, catch, clutch, grip, hold, seize, take hold of. **2** comprehend, follow, get your mind around, get, realize, see, understand

grasping adj avaricious, grabbing, greedy, mean, mercenary, miserly, selfish, stingy, tight-fisted

grateful adj appreciative, full of gratitude, indebted, pleased, thankful; **opp** ungrateful

gratitude n appreciation, gratefulness, thankfulness, thanks; **opp** ingratitude

gratuitous adj needless, uncalled-for, undeserved, unjustifiable, unjustified, unnecessary, unprovoked, unwarranted, without reason

grave adj **1** grim, serious, sober, solemn, somber, stony-faced. **2** (a grave situation) critical, crucial, serious, severe, worrying

grave n burial chamber, crypt, mausoleum, sepulcher, tomb, vault

graveyard n burial ground, cemetery, churchyard

gravity n consequence, importance, magnitude, seriousness, solemnity, urgency, weightiness

gray adj **1** (of sb's face) ashen, pale, white. **2** (of weather) cloudy, dull, foggy, gloomy, leaden, misty, murky, overcast

graze n abrasion, cut, scrape, scratch

graze v cut, scrape, scratch

grease n fat, lubrication, oil, tallow

greasy adj fatty, oily, slimy, slippery, smeary, waxy

great adj **1** (excellent) brilliant, classic, excellent, marvelous, outstanding, superb, terrific, wonderful; **opp** awful, dreadful, terrible. **2** (large) big, enormous, huge, immense, large, massive, vast. **3** (considerable) acute, considerable, extreme, intense, severe. **4** (important) celebrated, chief, distinguished, eminent, famous, important, leading, main, prominent, renowned. **5** (very skillful) ace inf, expert, gifted, good, skillful, talented

greed n **1** gluttony, greediness, piggishness inf, voraciousness. **2** avarice, miserliness, selfishness, tight-fistedness

greedy adj **1** gluttonous, piggish inf, voracious. **2** avaricious, grasping, miserly, money-grabbing, selfish, tight-fisted

green adj **1** grassy, leafy, lush, verdant. **2** callow, gullible, inexperienced, naive, new, raw, wet behind the ears. **3** ecological, environmental, environmentally friendly, environmentally sound

greet v meet, receive, say hello to, welcome

greeting n good wishes, hello, message, nod, reception, regards, tidings, wave, welcome

grief n anguish, bereavement, despair, heartache, misery, mourning, sadness, unhappiness

grievance n allegation, charge, complaint, dispute, gripe inf, grouse inf, injustice

grieve v be distressed, be in mourning, be sad, despair, fret, lament, mourn, suffer; **opp** rejoice

grim adj **1** (gruesome) appalling, dreadful,

ghastly, grisly, gruesome, harrowing, shocking, terrible. **2** (unpleasant) awful, dire, dreadful, horrendous, horrid, unattractive, unpleasant. **3** (stern) gloomy, morose, serious, somber, sour, stern, sullen. **4** (stubbornly determined) determined, obdurate, obstinate, resolute, unrelenting

grimace n expression, face, frown, scowl, wry expression

grind v **1** crush, granulate, mill, powder, pulverize. **2** file, polish, sharpen, smooth

grip n **1** grasp, hold. **2** clutches, control, influence, power

grip v **1** clasp, grab, grasp, hold, seize, take hold of. **2** capture, enthrall, fascinate, hold spellbound, mesmerize

gripping adj absorbing, compulsive, exciting, fascinating, heady, interesting, riveting, sensational, thrilling; **opp** boring

grisly adj appalling, dreadful, ghastly, gory, grim, gruesome, horrifying, macabre, shocking, sickening

groan v cry out, moan, object, protest, sigh, wail

groom v **1** arrange, brush, clean, comb, fix, make tidy, smarten up, spruce up, tidy, titivate. **2** coach, drill, get ready, instruct, prepare, prime, school, teach, train

groove n channel, cutting, furrow, gouge, gutter, hollow, indentation, rut, slot, track

grope v **1** feel, finger, touch. **2** (seek by touch) feel about for, feel for, fish for, fumble for, search blindly, seek

gross adj **1** (fat) bloated, bulky, fat, heavy, huge, massive, obese, overweight;

opp skinny, thin. **2** coarse, crude, disgusting, offensive, rude, vulgar. **3** (a gross error) blatant, flagrant, glaring, outrageous, serious, shameful, shocking

grotesque adj **1** absurd, bizarre, curious, fantastic, outlandish, peculiar, strange, surreal, unnatural, weird. **2** deformed, distorted, gnarled, misshapen, twisted, ugly

ground n **1** (soil) dirt, earth, mud, soil. **2** (under your feet) deck inf, earth, floor, terra firma. **3** (for sports) arena, field, pitch, playing field, stadium

groundless adj baseless, false, irrational, unfounded, unjustified, unreasonable, unwarranted, without cause, without foundation; **opp** true

grounds n pl **1** (around a building) area, estate, gardens, land, park, surroundings. **2** (reason) basis, cause, excuse, foundation, justification, motive, pretext, rationale, reason, reasons

groundwork n elements, essentials, fundamentals, preparation, preparations, spadework

group n **1** (small group of people) band, bunch inf, cluster, company, congregation, crew, gaggle inf, gang, party, team. **2** (large group of people) assembly, crowd, flock, gathering, horde, host, mob, multitude, rabble, swarm, throng. **3** (exclusive group of people) association, cadre, circle, clique, club, faction, ring, school, sect, set. **4** (of animals) flock, herd, swarm. **5** (of things) assortment, batch, bunch, bundle, category, class, cluster, collection, lot, set

group v **1** (make a group) arrange,

assemble, bring together, categorize, classify, collect, gather, marshal, organize, put together, set out. 2 (become a group) associate, cluster, come together, congregate, flock, gather, get together, swarm, team up, throng

grovel v abase yourself, bow and scrape, crawl, creep, fawn, humble yourself, ingratiate yourself with, kowtow, lick sb's boots inf, prostrate yourself, suck up to

grow v 1 (get bigger) develop, enlarge, expand, extend, fill out, get bigger, get taller, heighten, increase, lengthen, multiply, spread, swell, thicken, widen. 2 (come from) arise, issue, originate, spring, stem. 3 (grow old) become, come to be, get, turn. 4 (of a business) develop, expand, flourish, make headway, make progress, progress, prosper, thrive. 5 (of plants) come up, flourish, shot up, spring up, sprout. 6 cultivate, farm, plant, produce, propagate, raise

growth n 1 development, enlargement, evolution, expansion, extension, increase, multiplication. 2 advance, expansion, improvement, progress, proliferation, rise, success. 3 (of plants) crop, harvest, produce, yield. 4 (on the body) cancer, cyst, lump, swelling, tumor

grub n 1 caterpillar, larva, maggot. 2 (food) a bite inf, a bite to eat inf, fast food inf, junk food inf, meal, nosh inf, refreshments, snacks, something to eat

grudge n bitterness, grievance, hard feelings, pique, rancor, resentment

grudge v 1 begrudge, give unwillingly. 2 begrudge, be jealous of, envy, mind, resent

grudging adj envious, guarded, half-hearted, hesitant, jealous, reluctant, resentful, unenthusiastic, ungracious; *opp* enthusiastic

grueling adj arduous, backbreaking, demanding, exhausting, laborious, punishing, strenuous, taxing, tiring, tough, wearying; *opp* easy

gruesome adj awful, disgusting, dreadful, ghastly, grim, grisly, horrendous, horrible, horrific, horrifying, macabre, repulsive, shocking, sickening

gruff adj 1 (of a voice) hoarse, husky, rasping, rough, throaty. 2 (of a person) abrupt, bad-tempered, brusque, crabby inf, crotchety, crusty, curt, grouchy inf, grumpy, impolite, rough, rude, surly, uncivil

grumble v bellyache inf, bitch inf, carp, complain, find fault with, go on about inf, groan, gripe inf, grouch inf, grouse inf, moan, object, protest, whine

guarantee n 1 (of good quality) warranty. 2 assurance, bond, oath, pledge, promise, word, word of honor. 3 (financial) bond, collateral, security, surety

guarantee v 1 assure, certify, give a guarantee, give an assurance, give your word, pledge, promise, vouch for, swear, vow, warrant. 2 (guarantee a loan) back, be a guarantor for, provide collateral for, provide security for, underwrite

guard n 1 (of a person) bodyguard, escort, guardian, protector. 2 (of a place) bouncer inf, custodian, defender, lookout, night watchman, patrol, security guard, sentry, watch, watchman.

3 (prison guard) jailer, prison officer, warden. **4 off (your) guard** unprepared, unready, with your defenses down. **5 on your guard** alert, careful, cautious, on the lookout, prepared, ready, vigilant, wary

guard v **1** (people or animals) escort, keep, keep under guard, keep watch over, mind, protect, save, secure, shelter, shield, tend, watch, watch over. **2** (a place) cover, defend, patrol, police, secure, watch over. **3 guard against** be alert, be on the lookout for, beware of, be wary of, keep an eye out for, keep your eyes open, take care

guardian n **1** caretaker, curator, custodian, keeper, steward, warden. **2** champion, defender, protector, preserver, trustee

guerrilla n freedom fighter, member of the resistance, partisan, terrorist

guess n assumption, conjecture, estimate, feeling, guesstimate, hypothesis, prediction, speculation, suspicion, surmise

guess v conjecture, estimate, have a feeling, have a hunch, have an idea, hazard a guess, make a guess, postulate, predict, speculate, surmise, suppose, think likely

guest n **1** caller, house guest, visitor. **2** (in a hotel) customer, patron, resident

guidance n advice, brief, counsel, counseling, direction, guidelines, hint, instruction, leadership, management, supervision, teaching, tip

guide n **1** attendant, courier, director, escort, leader, usher. **2** advisor, counselor, guru, mentor, teacher, tutor.

3 beacon, clue, guiding light, key, landmark, sign. **4** directory, guidebook, guidelines, handbook, instructions, manual, tourist guide

guide v **1** (to a place) accompany, conduct, direct, escort, lead, lead the way, pilot, shepherd, show, show the way, steer, usher. **2** advise, brief, counsel, give counseling to, give advice, give a hint, give a pointer, give a tip, give guidance, influence, inform, instruct, make suggestions, take sb by the hand inf. **3** command, control, govern, handle, manage, preside over, regulate, steer, supervise

guilt n **1** blame, culpability, fault, liability, responsibility; **opp** innocence. **2** bad conscience, contrition, disgrace, dishonor, penitence, regret, remorse, repentance, self-reproach, shame

guilty adj **1** at fault, blameworthy, convicted, criminal, culpable, responsible, to blame; **opp** innocent. **2** (feel guilty) ashamed, conscience-stricken, contrite, penitent, remorseful, repentant, shamefaced, sheepish

gulf n **1** bay, bight, inlet. **2** abyss, breach, canyon, chasm, cleft, gap, gorge, ravine, rent, rift, split. **3** (between people) difference, division, rift, split

gullible adj credulous, easily taken in, foolish, green, innocent, naive, silly, simple, trusting, unsuspecting; **opp** shrewd

gulp v bolt, devour, gobble, guzzle, knock off inf, swallow, swig inf, toss off, wolf, wolf down

gumption n ability, acumen, common-sense, enterprise, get-up-and-go, horse sense *inf*, initiative, judgment, resourcefulness, savvy *inf*, sense, shrewdness

gun *n* firearm, machine-gun, musket, pistol, revolver, rifle, shotgun

gunman *n* armed robber, bandit, gangster, gunfighter, gunslinger *inf*, hired gun, hit man *inf*, hold-up man, terrorist

gurgle *v* 1 (of water) babble, bubble, murmur, splash, tinkle. 2 (of a baby) babble, burble, chuckle, crow

gush *n* burst, cascade, flood, jet, spate, spurt, stream, surge, torrent

gush *v* 1 burst out, cascade, flood, flow, pour, rush, spout, spurt, stream, surge; *opp* trickle. 2 (of a person) babble, be effusive, be overenthusiastic, bubble over, get carried away *inf*, make too much of sth, prattle, speak effusively, wax lyrical

gust *n* blast, flurry, puff, rush, squall

gusto *n* appetite, delight, enjoyment, enthusiasm, excitement, pleasure, relish, verve, zest

guts *n* 1 alimentary canal, entrails, innards *inf*, intestines, viscera. 2 boldness, bravery, courage, daring, grit, mettle, nerve, pluck, spirit

gutter *n* channel, conduit, culvert, ditch, drain, open sewer, sluice, trench, trough

guzzle *v* bolt, cram yourself, devour, gobble, gulp down, knock off *inf*, swallow, swig *inf*, swill, toss off *inf*, stuff yourself *inf*, wolf down

habit *n* 1 convention, custom, practice, procedure, routine, rule, second nature, tradition, way, wont. 2 bent, inclination, leaning, predisposition, propensity, tendency. 3 addiction, compulsion, craving, dependence

habitation *n* abode, accommodation, domicile, dwelling, home, housing, lodging, pad *inf*, place *inf*, quarters, residence

habitual *adj* 1 accustomed, common, customary, established, familiar, fixed, natural, normal, ordinary, regular, routine, standard, traditional, usual. 2 (having a habit) addicted, chronic, confirmed, hardened, inveterate

hack *v* carve, chop, cut, cut down, gash, hew, lacerate, mutilate, slash

hackneyed *adj* banal, clichéd, commonplace, conventional, corny *inf*, overworked, platitudinous, predictable, stale, stereotyped, stock, trite, unoriginal, worn-out; *opp* new, original

haggard *adj* drawn, emaciated, gaunt, pinched, scraggy, thin, tired, wan, wasted, worn out

haggle *v* 1 bargain, beat sb down, drive a hard bargain. 2 argue, bicker, dispute, quarrel, squabble, wrangle

hail *v* 1 acknowledge, greet, salute, say hello to, welcome. 2 accost, call out to, flag down, signal to, shout to, wave to. 3 acclaim, applaud, extol, glorify, honor, praise, sing the praises of

hair *n* 1 head of hair, locks, mop, shock, tresses. 2 coiffure, cut, haircut, hairdo, hairstyle, style. 3 (of an animal) bristles, coat, fleece, fur, mane, pelt, wool

hairy *adj* bearded, bristly, fleecy, furry, hirsute, long-haired, shaggy, unshaven, woolly

half *n* division, equal part, equal share, fifty percent, percentage

half-hearted *adj* apathetic, cool, cursory, indifferent, lackluster, lukewarm, perfunctory, superficial, unenthusiastic; *opp* enthusiastic

hall *n* 1 assembly room, auditorium, meeting room. 2 entrance hall, entry, foyer, lobby, vestibule

hallmark *n* 1 authentication, endorsement, mark, seal, sign, stamp, symbol. 2 badge, indicator, mark, sign, stamp, sure sign, trademark

hallucination *n* apparition, delusion, dream, fantasy, figment of the imagination, illusion, mirage, vision

halt *n* 1 (temporary) break, breather *inf*, breathing space, hiatus, interruption, interval, pause, stoppage, time out *inf*. 2 (permanent) cessation, end, standstill, stop, termination; *opp* start

halt v 1 break off, cease, come to a standstill, come to a stop, draw up, pull up, stand still, stop, wait. 2 (stop sth happening) arrest, block, check, crush, end, nip in the bud, put an end to, put a stop to, stop, terminate

halve v bisect, cut in half, cut in two, divide equally, reduce by fifty percent, share equally, split in half, split in two

hamper v block, delay, encumber, foil, frustrate, hinder, hold back, hold up, impede, inhibit, interfere with, obstruct, restrain, slow down, stymie, thwart; *opp* help

hand n 1 fist, mitt inf, palm, paw inf. 2 (of a dial) indicator, needle, pointer. 3 (helping hand) aid, assistance, help, helping hand, support. 4 (worker) artisan, employee, laborer, worker. 5 calligraphy, handwriting, penmanship, script. 6 **a big hand** applause, ovation, round of applause. 7 **at hand** about to happen, approaching, imminent, impending. 8 **to hand** accessible, available, handy, ready, within reach. 9 **try your hand** attempt, have a go, have a shot inf, make an attempt, try your skill

hand v 1 convey, deliver, give, offer, pass, present. 2 **hand down** bequeath, hand on, leave, pass down, pass on, will. 3 **hand out** deal out, disburse, dish out inf, dispense, distribute, dole out inf, give out, share out. 4 **hand over** deliver, donate, give, present, surrender, turn over

handicap n 1 disability, impairment. 2 disadvantage, hindrance, impediment, limitation, obstacle, problem, stumbling block

handiwork n 1 artifacts, craft, craftsmanship, handicraft. 2 achievement, creation, design, doing, product, production, work

handle n grip, haft, hand-grip, hilt, knob, shaft, stock

handle v 1 feel, finger, grasp, hold, maul, paw inf, stroke, turn over in your hands. 2 administer, be in charge of, control, cope with, deal with, direct, manage, take care of. 3 (handle goods) deal in, market, sell, stock, trade in, traffic in

handsome adj 1 (of a man) attractive, good-looking, gorgeous. 2 (of a woman) elegant, fine, fine-looking, good-looking, striking. 3 (of a gift) big, bountiful, generous, large, lavish, liberal, magnanimous, sizable, valuable

handy adj 1 accessible, at your fingertips, available, close at hand, convenient, nearby, on tap inf, ready, to hand, within reach. 2 convenient, easy to use, functional, helpful, practical, serviceable, useful. 3 (handy with sth) adept, capable, clever, competent, deft, dexterous, good with your hands, nimble-fingered, proficient, skillful

hang v 1 be suspended, dangle, droop, flap, swing. 2 attach, drape, fix, pin up, put up, suspend. 3 (in the air) be poised, drift, float, hover. 4 (hang sb) execute, lynch, put the noose around sb's neck, send sb to the gallows. 5 **hang on** (hold on to sth) cling, cling on to, clutch, grasp, grip, hold, hold on to. 6 **hang on** (wait) hold on, hold the line, stop, wait, wait a minute. 7 **hang on sb's words** be all ears, be rapt, be very attentive,

concentrate on, give sb your undivided
attention, listen closely

haphazard adj **1** accidental, chance,
random, unplanned. **2** aimless, careless,
casual, disorganized, hit or-miss,
indiscriminate, slapdash, slipshod,
unmethodical, unplanned, unsystematic

happen v **1** arise, come about, come to
pass, crop up, occur, take place,
transpire. **2** (happen to sb) become of,
befall. **3** (happen by chance) chance,
fall out, pan out inf, turn out inf

happening n accident, adventure, affair,
event, incident, occurrence

happiness n **1** bliss, good fortune, heaven
inf, prosperity, well-being; **opp** misery.
2 (happy feeling) cheerfulness,
cheeriness, contentment, delight,
ecstasy, elation, enjoyment, euphoria,
gaiety, gladness, high spirits, joy,
merriment, pleasure; **opp** misery

happy adj **1** carefree, cheerful, cheery,
contented, glad, in a good mood, in
good spirits, jolly, jovial, light-hearted,
merry, pleased, satisfied, smiling,
untroubled; **opp** miserable, sad, unhappy.
2 (very happy) blithe, delighted,
ecstatic, euphoric, in high spirits, in
seventh heaven inf, joyful, joyous, on
cloud nine inf, on top of the world inf,
overjoyed, radiant, rapt, starry-eyed inf,
thrilled, thrilled to bits inf. **3** (fortunate)
advantageous, auspicious, beneficial,
convenient, fortunate, lucky, opportune,
welcome

harass v annoy, badger, be on sb's back
inf, bother, exasperate, give sb a hard
time inf, harry, hassle inf, hound,
persecute, pester, plague, tease,
torment, trouble, vex

harassed adj agitated, careworn,
distraught, hassled inf, strained, stressed,
under pressure, vexed

harbor n **1** anchorage, dock, haven,
marina, port. **2** asylum, haven, place of
safety, refuge, safe house, sanctuary,
shelter

harbor v **1** (a person) conceal, give
shelter to, grant asylum to, hide, protect,
shelter, shield. **2** (a feeling) brood over,
cherish, cling on to, hold on to, nurse,
maintain, retain

hard adj **1** (of a substance) close-packed,
compact, dense, firm, inflexible, rigid,
rocklike, solid, solidified, stiff, stony,
tough, unyielding; **opp** soft. **2** (of work)
arduous, backbreaking, daunting,
difficult, exhausting, grueling, heavy,
Herculean, laborious, no easy task,
onerous, strenuous, taxing, tiring;
opp easy. **3** (of a problem) baffling,
complex, complicated, daunting,
difficult, perplexing, puzzling, thorny inf,
tough; **opp** easy. **4** (of a person) callous,
cold, cruel, hard-hearted, harsh,
heartless, implacable, inflexible,
merciless, pitiless, ruthless, severe, stern,
strict, unbending, unfeeling, unkind.
5 (of conditions) austere, bad, difficult,
distressing, grim, harsh, intolerable,
unbearable, unpleasant; **opp** good.
6 (of a worker) assiduous, conscientious,
diligent, dogged, enthusiastic,
indefatigable, industrious, keen, steady,
untiring, zealous. **7** (of a blow) forceful,
heavy, powerful, strong, violent;
opp light, soft

hard and fast adj binding, immutable,

inflexible, invariable, rigorous, strict, stringent, unalterable

harden v 1 bake, cake, clot, coagulate, congeal, freeze, jell, ossify, petrify, set, solidify, stiffen; **opp** soften. 2 (a person) brutalize, deaden, make callous, make tough, numb, toughen

hardened adj 1 (a hardened criminal) experienced, habitual, incorrigible, inveterate, irredeemable, reprobate, shameless. 2 (hardened to sth) accustomed, habituated, inured, seasoned, toughened, used to

hardheaded adj astute, practical, pragmatic, rational, sensible, shrewd, tough, unsentimental

hard-hearted adj callous, cold, cruel, hard, heartless, insensitive, merciless, pitiless, stony-hearted, uncaring, unfeeling, unkind, unmoved, unsympathetic

hardly adv barely, faintly, just, only just, scarcely, with difficulty

hardship n adversity, affliction, austerity, deprivation, destitution, difficulty, misery, misfortune, need, poverty, privation, tribulation, trouble, want

hard-working adj assiduous, busy, conscientious, diligent, energetic, indefatigable, industrious, zealous; **opp** lazy

hardy adj fit, hale, healthy, hearty, robust, rugged, sound, stalwart, stout, strong, sturdy, tough, vigorous; **opp** delicate, weak

harm n abuse, damage, detriment, disservice, hurt, impairment, injury, loss, misfortune, ruin

harm v abuse, be harmful to, damage,

hurt, ill-treat, impair, injure, maltreat, spoil, wound

harmful adj damaging, destructive, detrimental, evil, hurtful, injurious, noxious, pernicious, poisonous, prejudicial, toxic, unhealthy, unwholesome

harmless adj benign, innocent, innocuous, inoffensive, nonviolent, safe, tame; **opp** dangerous

harmony n accord, agreement, concord, conformity, cooperation, peace, peacefulness, unison, unity; **opp** discord

harness n bridle, gear, lead, reins, straps, tack, tackle, yoke

harness v 1 attach, bind, couple, fasten, hitch, hitch up, join, tether, tie, yoke. 2 appropriate, channel, control, employ, exploit, put to use, use, utilize

harrowing adj distressing, excruciating, frightening, heartbreaking, heartrending, horrifying, painful, terrifying, traumatic

harsh adj 1 (of a voice) croaking, grating, gravelly, guttural, rasping, raucous, rough. 2 (harsh conditions) austere, bleak, difficult, grim, hard, spartan. 3 (of a person, a punishment) brutal, cruel, despotic, domineering, draconian, excessive, hard, heavy-handed, severe, stern, strict, unfair, unjust, unkind; **opp** lenient

harvest n 1 crops, flowers, fruit, grain, produce, vintage, yield. 2 (things won or gained) fruits, gains, haul, prize, return, reward, spoils, winnings

harvest v 1 (harvest crops) bring in, dig up, gather in, pick, pluck, pull up, reap, uproot. 2 be rewarded with, collect, gain, obtain, reap, secure, win

hassle n annoyance, aggravation, argument, bother, difficulty, grief inf, harassment, irritation, pain inf, problem, trouble, upset

hassle v annoy, argue with, bother, get on sb's back inf, harass, harry, irritate, pester, plague, trouble

haste n hurry, impetuosity, recklessness, rush, speed, urgency

hasten v bring forward, bring on, encourage, speed, speed up, urge on

hasty adj hurried, impetuous, premature, rash, rushed, urgent

hatch v 1 be born, break open, breed, emerge, incubate. 2 (hatch a plot) conceive, concoct, cook up inf, design, devise, formulate, instigate, think up

hate n abhorrence, antipathy, aversion, contempt, detestation, dislike, enmity, hatred, hostility, ill-will, loathing, odium, spite; opp love

hate v 1 abhor, be contemptuous of, be unable to bear, be unable to stand, despise, detest, dislike, loathe; opp love. 2 (hate doing sth) be averse to, be reluctant to, be unwilling to, shy away from, shrink from

hateful adj 1 abominable, abhorrent, atrocious, contemptible, despicable, detestable, foul, hated, heinous, obnoxious, odious, ugly, unpleasant. 2 (feeling hate) angry, bitter, contemptuous, hostile, jealous, resentful, spiteful

hatred n abhorrence, antipathy, aversion, contempt, detestation, dislike, enmity, hate, hostility, ill-will, loathing, odium, spite

haughty adj aloof, arrogant, condescending, disdainful, proud, snooty inf, superior

haul n bag, booty, catch, gains, harvest, loot, spoils, winnings

haul v drag, draw, heave, lug, pull, tow, tug

haunt v 1 (go to a place frequently) frequent, hang around inf, inhabit, patronize, visit. 2 (haunt a person) beset, hang over, nag at, obsess, preoccupy, worry

haunted adj 1 cursed, possessed, scary, spooky inf. 2 (haunted look) haggard, hagridden, troubled, tormented, tortured, worried

haunting adj eerie, evocative, fascinating, nagging, poignant, spine-tingling, unforgettable

have v 1 be blessed with, enjoy, hold, keep, own, possess, retain. 2 (have a walk, bath, meal) enjoy, go for, indulge in, manage, partake of, take. 3 (have an illness, accident, operation) be affected by, experience, get, meet with, suffer, sustain, undergo. 4 (have a baby) bear, beget, bring into the world, give birth to, produce. 5 (have sb do sth) ask, command, commission, compel, direct, force, instruct, make, order, request, tell. 6 **have to** be bound to, be compelled to, be forced to, be made to, be obliged to, be ordered to, be required to, be to, be told to, must, need to

haven n hideaway, hideout, love nest, oasis, refuge, retreat, safe haven, sanctuary, shelter

havoc n anarchy, chaos, destruction, mayhem, trouble, violence

hazard *n* danger, difficulty, obstacle, pitfall, problem, risk

hazardous *adj* dangerous, difficult, poisonous, risky, toxic, tricky

haze *n* fog, heat haze, mist, pollution, smog, smoke, steam, vapor

hazy *adj* 1 foggy, misty, polluted, smoky, steamy, vaporous. 2 (a hazy memory) blurred, confused, distant, faint, indistinct, obscure, unclear, vague

head *adj* chief, commanding, first, foremost, highest, leading, principal, senior, supreme, top

head *n* 1 brain, cranium, face, mind, skull. 2 boss, chairman, chief, chief executive, director, headmaster, headmistress, head teacher, leader, manager, principal. 3 (highest part) apex, beginning, start, summit, tip, top, vertex; *opp* foot

head *v* 1 be in charge of, control, direct, head up, lead, manage, run. 2 (head a list) be at the head of, be at the top of, begin, lead, lead off, start, start off, top. 3 (go in a particular direction) aim, go, make a beeline *inf*, move, set off, set out, travel. 4 **head off** block, counter, deflect, forestall, obstruct, preempt, prevent, stop

heading *n* 1 caption, headline, name, rubric, subheading, title. 2 category, class, classification, division, head, section

headlong *adj* direct, fast, nonstop, onrushing, straight, wild

headstrong *adj* determined, driven, overconfident, rash, reckless, self-willed, uncontrollable, willful

heal *v* cure, make better, mend, remedy, restore to health, soothe, treat

health *n* 1 (good health) fitness, healthiness, strength, vigor, vitality, well-being; *opp* illness, sickness. 2 (state of your body) condition, constitution, medical history, shape, state of health. 3 (public health) health care, health service, hygiene, medical science, medicine, public health, sanitation

healthy *adj* 1 fit, fit as a fiddle *inf*, hale and hearty, in fine fettle, in good health, in good shape, in tiptop condition *inf*, sound, strong, vigorous, well; *opp* ill, sick, unhealthy. 2 good for you, health-giving, hygienic, invigorating, nourishing, nutritious, restorative, wholesome; *opp* unhealthy

heap *n* 1 accumulation, collection, hoard, lot, mass, mound, mountain, pile, quantity, stack. 2 **heaps** a lot, a great deal, loads, lots, masses, plenty, stacks, tons

heap *v* amass, heap up, pile, pile up, stack, stack up

hear *v* catch, detect, hark, heed, listen, notice, overhear, perceive

hearing *n* 1 ears, earshot, hailing distance, sound. 2 audience, case, court martial, inquest, proceedings, session, trial

heart *n* 1 center, core, hub, kernel, middle, nerve center, nucleus. 2 affection, courage, emotions, feelings, love, mercy, pity, soul, sympathy, tenderness, warmth. 3 **by heart** by rote, from memory, without looking, without notes, word for word

heartbreaking *adj* agonizing, crushing, devastating, distressing, heart-rending, painful, shattering, upsetting

heartbroken adj anguished, crushed, devastated, grief-stricken, sad, shattered

heartfelt adj deep, earnest, emotional, from the heart, genuine, honest, sincere, warm

heartless adj cold, cruel, harsh, merciless, pitiless, ruthless, uncaring, unfeeling, unsympathetic

heart-to-heart adj confessional, frank, intimate, man-to-man, personal, sincere, woman-to-woman

hearty adj 1 cordial, expansive, extrovert, hail-fellow-well-met, jolly, jovial, loud, welcoming. 2 (a hearty meal) big, filling, large, nourishing, square, substantial, sumptuous

heat n 1 energy, fire, heating, sun, temperature, warmth. 2 (emotional) anger, emotion, energy, excitement, pressure, urgency, vehemence

heat v boil, heat up, microwave, raise the temperature of, reheat, warm, warm up

heated adj angry, emotional, energetic, excited, fierce, frenzied, furious, passionate, vehement, vigorous, violent, worked up

heathen n barbarian, idolater, infidel, pagan, savage

heave v cart inf, drag, lift, lug, pull, push, raise, shove, struggle with, tow, tug

heaven n 1 Elysian Fields, Elysium, heavens, Olympus, paradise, sky, Valhalla; *opp* hell. 2 (happiness) bliss, dream come true, heaven on earth, Nirvana, paradise, perfection; *opp* hell

heavy adj 1 big, cumbersome, dense, fat, heavyweight, large, overweight, weighty; *opp* light. 2 (heavy pressure, rainfall)

abundant, considerable, great, hard, high, intense, severe, strong; *opp* light. 3 (of a discussion) deep, dense, difficult, profound, serious, solemn, weighty; *opp* light

heckle v answer back, argue, catcall, interrupt, jeer, mock, shout, take issue with

hectic adj busy, chaotic, exciting, fevered, feverish, frantic, frenetic, frenzied, rushed

hedge n border, boundary, bushes, fence, hedgerow, hurdle, privet, shrubs, topiary

hedge v dither, dodge, duck, equivocate, evade, hesitate, prevaricate, play for time, sidestep

heed v acknowledge, bear in mind, consider, follow, hearken, listen to, notice, obey, pay attention to, pay heed to, pay regard to, respect, take account of, take heed of, take notice of; *opp* ignore

hefty adj big, cumbersome, enormous, great, heavy, huge, large, strong, weighty, whopping inf

height n 1 altitude, depth, elevation, size, stature. 2 (high place) apex, cliff, crest, hill, mountain, peak, pinnacle, summit. 3 (the height of bad manners) acme, apogee, culmination, embodiment, essence, pinnacle, ultimate

heighten v add to, augment, boost, enhance, improve, increase, intensify, pile on, sharpen, stimulate, wind up

heir n beneficiary, daughter, heiress, inheritor, next in line, son, successor

hell n 1 Hades, inferno, nether world, other place, purgatory, underworld; *opp* heaven. 2 (unhappiness) agony, hell on earth, misery, murder *inf*, nightmare, suffering, torture; *opp* heaven

help *n* aid, assistance, contribution, donation, hand, helping hand, hint, service, succour

help *v* 1 advise, aid, assist, come to the rescue, contribute, give sb a hand, help out, lend sb a hand, rescue, serve, succor, volunteer. 2 (can't help doing sth) avoid, prevent, resist, stop

helper *n* aide, adviser, assistant, collaborator, contributor, helpmate, partner, volunteer

helpful *adj* 1 (of a person) accommodating, amenable, benevolent, cooperative, friendly, kind, generous, obliging, supportive. 2 beneficial, constructive, convenient, handy, positive, practical, productive, profitable, serviceable, useful, valuable

helping *n* dollop *inf*, plate, plateful, portion, ration, serving, share

helpless *adj* 1 (not knowing what to do) at a loss, bewildered, floundering, forlorn, hapless, incapable, incompetent, struggling, uncomprehending, useless. 2 (unable to defend yourself) defenseless, exposed, impotent, powerless, unprotected, vulnerable, weak

herd *n* crowd, flock, group, mob, rabble, troop

herd *v* assemble, bring together, collect, drive, flock, gather, rally, muster, shepherd

hereditary *adj* 1 (in biology) congenital, family, genetic, inborn, inherited, innate. 2 (hereditary wealth) ancestral, by divine right, family, genealogical, handed down, inherited

heresy *n* blasphemy, dissent, idolatry, nonconformism, sacrilege

heretic *n* agnostic, atheist, blasphemer, dissenter, free thinker, idolater, infidel, nonconformist, pagan, renegade, skeptic, unbeliever

heretical *adj* agnostic, atheistic, blasphemous, dissenting, idolatrous, nonconformist, pagan, renegade, sacrilegious, skeptical

heritage *n* birthright, culture, endowment, inheritance, legacy, patrimony, tradition

hermit *n* anchorite, loner, recluse, solitary

hero *n* 1 (brave person) celebrity, champion, conqueror, daredevil, star, superhero, superman, superstar, victor. 2 (of a story) lead, leading man, main character, protagonist, star. 3 (person who is looked up to) example, exemplar, ideal, idol, inspiration, role model

heroic *adj* 1 bold, brave, courageous, daring, gallant, fearless, intrepid, valiant. 2 (a heroic achievement) enormous, epic, huge, monumental, painstaking, tremendous

heroine *n* 1 celebrity, champion, daredevil, star, superstar, superwoman *inf*, victor. 2 (of a story) lead, leading lady, main character, protagonist, star. 3 (woman who is looked up to) example, exemplar, ideal, idol, inspiration, role model

heroism *n* bravery, courage, daring, fearlessness, gallantry, valor; *opp* cowardice

hesitant *adj* dithering, doubting,

equivocal, evasive, hesitating,
indecisive, reluctant, reticent, uncertain,
undecided, unsure

hesitate v delay, dither, equivocate, falter,
hang back, have doubts, have second
thoughts, hedge, pause, stall, think
carefully, think twice, wait

hesitation n delay, dithering, doubt,
equivocation, evasion, hedging,
indecision, pause, reluctance, reticence,
thought, uncertainty, wait

hidden adj concealed, in disguise, in
hiding, invisible, lurking, secret,
undetectable, undercover

hide v 1 conceal, cover, cover up,
disguise, hide away, keep secret, mask,
obscure, put away, secrete; **opp** reveal.
2 go into hiding, hole up, lie low, lurk,
take cover, take refuge

hideous adj disfigured, disgusting, ghastly,
gruesome, horrible, horrific,
nightmarish, repulsive, ugly, unsightly

hiding n 1 **in hiding** hidden,
incommunicado, on the run, under
cover. 2 (a good hiding) beating,
corporal punishment, drubbing, flogging,
smack, spanking, thrashing

high adj 1 elevated, lofty, high up, raised,
tall, top, upper; **opp** low. 2 (high in an
organization) chief, commanding,
elevated, high-ranking, high up,
influential, leading, powerful, senior,
superior, supreme, top; **opp** lowly.
3 (high in amount) abundant, buoyant,
considerable, elevated, excessive,
expensive, extreme, great, heavy, hot,
intense, loud, severe; **opp** low.
4 (a high voice) alto, falsetto, fluting,
high-pitched, soprano, squeaky,

treble; **opp** deep

high-class adj aristocratic, choice, classy
inf, de luxe, elite, first-class, five-star,
high-quality, luxurious, pedigree, posh
inf, quality, select, superior, top, up-
market, upper-class

highlight n climax, excerpt, extract,
good point, strong point

highly adv abundantly, considerably,
extremely, greatly, intensely, really,
seriously, severely, very

highly strung adj delicate, edgy inf,
emotional, irritable, nervous, nervy,
neurotic, temperamental, tense,
unstable

hijack v appropriate, car-jack,
commandeer, expropriate, seize, skyjack,
take control of, take over, steal

hike n march, ramble, tramp, trek, trudge,
walk, wander

hike v backpack, march, ramble, tramp,
trek, trudge, walk, wander

hilarious adj a great laugh, amusing,
comic, comical, funny, humorous,
hysterical inf, side-splitting, uproarious,
witty, zany

hill n elevation, fell, foothill, height, high
land, hillock, hillside, hilltop, knoll,
mound, mount, mountain, peak, pike,
prominence, ridge, summit

hinder v arrest, bar, block, check, curb,
delay, deter, encumber, frustrate, get in
the way, hamper, handicap, hold back,
hold up, impede, inhibit, interrupt, keep
back, limit, obstruct, oppose, prevent,
restrain, restrict, retard, sabotage, slow
down, slow up, stand in the way, stop,
thwart; **opp** aid, help

hindrance n bar, barrier, block, check,

curb, deterrent, difficulty, disadvantage, drawback, encumbrance, handicap, hitch, hold-up, impediment, inconvenience, limitation, obstacle, obstruction, restraint, restriction, snag, stumbling block; **opp** aid, help

hinge v center, depend, hang, pivot, rest, revolve, turn

hint n 1 allusion, clue, idea, implication, indication, inkling, innuendo, insinuation, intimation, mention, reminder, sign, suggestion, tipoff. 2 (give sb a hint) advice, help, pointer, suggestion, tip. 3 (a hint of sth) breath, dash, scent, soupçon, speck, sprinkling, suggestion, suspicion, taste, tinge, touch, trace, undertone, whiff, whisper

hint v allude, imply, indicate, insinuate, intimate, mention, signal, suggest, tip off

hire n charge, cost, fee, lease, price, rent, rental

hire v appoint, book, contract, employ, engage, enlist, sign on, sign up, take on

hiss n 1 buzz, fizz, purr, rasp, rustle, shrill, sizzle, wheeze, whir, whistle, whizz. 2 boo, catcall, condemnation, damnation, derision, hoot, jeer, mocking, ridiculing, scoff, taunt; **opp** applause

hiss v 1 buzz, fizz, purr, rasp, rustle, shrill, sizzle, wheeze, whir, whistle, whizz. 2 boo, catcall, condemn, damn, decry, deride, hoot, jeer, mock, ridicule, scoff, scorn, taunt; **opp** applaud

historic adj celebrated, extraordinary, famous, important, memorable, momentous, notable, outstanding, remarkable, significant; **opp** ordinary

historical adj 1 (historical reasons)

ancient, bygone, former, old, past, prior; **opp** current. 2 (a historical figure) actual, attested, authentic, chronicled, confirmed, documented, factual, real, real-life, recorded, true, verifiable; **opp** fictional

history n 1 antiquity, before, bygone days, former times, the good old days, the old days, the past, time gone by, yesterday, yesteryear; **opp** today. 2 (a history) account, biography, chronicle, diary, memoirs, narration, narrative, recital, record, relation, report, saga, story, study, tale

hit n 1 bang, bash, blow, bump, clash, clout sl, clip, collision, crash, cuff, impact, knock, punch, slap, smack, smash, spank, strike, swat, thump, wallop, whack. 2 sellout, sensation, success, triumph, winner inf; **opp** flop

hit v 1 (deliberately) bang, bash, batter, beat, belt sl, clout sl, clobber sl, cuff, deck sl, knock, lay one on sl, punch, slap, smack, sock sl, spank, strike, swat, thump, wallop, whack. 2 (accidentally) bang into, bump, clip, collide, crash, run into, smash into

hitch n catch, check, delay, difficulty, drawback, encumbrance, hindrance, hold-up, impediment, inconvenience, mishap, obstacle, obstruction, problem, restraint, snag, stumbling block, trouble

hitch v attach, bind, connect, couple, fasten, harness, join, tether, tie, yoke; **opp** unhitch

hoard n accumulation, cache, collection, fund, heap, mass, pile, reserve, reservoir, stash inf, stock, stockpile, store, supply

hoard v accumulate, amass, assemble, buy

up, collect, deposit, gather, put by, save, stash *inf*, stockpile, stock up, store

hoarse *adj* croaky, grating, gravely, growling, gruff, guttural, harsh, husky, rasping, rough, throaty; *opp* smooth

hoax *n* cheat, con *inf*, deception, fake, fast one *inf*, fraud, jest, joke, practical joke, prank, ruse, scam, spoof, swindle, trick

hobby *n* diversion, interest, leisure activity, pastime, pursuit, recreation, relaxation, sideline

hoist *n* crane, elevator, jack, lift, pulley, tackle, winch

hoist *v* elevate, erect, heave, jack up, lift, pull up, raise, rear, winch

hold *n* **1** clasp, clutch, grasp, grip. **2** anchorage, foothold, footing, leverage, prop, purchase, stay, support, vantage

hold *v* **1** (hold sth in your hand) bear, carry, clasp, clinch, cling to, clutch, grasp, grip, hang on to, hug. **2** (hold sb in your arms) cradle, cuddle, embrace, enfold, hug . **3** (hold a passport) have, keep, maintain, own, possess, retain. **4** (hold sb in custody) arrest, bind, check, confine, detain, impound, imprison, incarcerate, keep in custody, lock up, put behind bars, restrain; *opp* release. **5** (hold a view) assume, believe, consider, deem, esteem, judge, maintain, presume, reckon, regard, think. **6** (hold a meeting) assemble, call, conduct, convene, have, organize, run. **7** (a theater holding 500 people) accommodate, comprise, contain, have a capacity of, seat, take. **8** (hold the weight of sth) bear, brace, buttress, carry, keep up, prop, shoulder, support, sustain, take. **9** (my offer still holds) be

unaltered, carry on, continue, endure, go on, persist, remain, stay. **10** hold out carry on, continue, endure, hang on *inf*, keep going, last, persevere, persist, remain, resist, stand fast, stand firm, stick at it, withstand; *opp* give in. **11** hold up delay, detain, hinder, impede, obstruct, retard, set back, slow, slow down, stop; *opp* speed up

holder *n* bearer, custodian, incumbent, keeper, owner, possessor, proprietor, purchaser

holdup *n* bottleneck, delay, difficulty, hindrance, hitch, impediment, inconvenience, obstacle, obstruction, restraint, setback, snag, stoppage, trouble, wait

hole *n* **1** aperture, breach, break, chink, crack, fissure, gap, opening, orifice, perforation, puncture, rift, rip, slit, slot, space, split, tear, vent. **2** (in the ground) abyss, cavity, chasm, crater, dent, depression, dip, excavation, hollow, indentation, pit, pocket, pothole, shaft. **3** (in sb's argument) crack, defect, discrepancy, error, fault, flaw, inconsistency

holiday *n* **1** break, day/week off, leave, recess, respite, rest, sabbatical, semester break, time off, vacation. **2** (public holiday) celebration, day of observance, feast, federal holiday, festival, gala, holy day, saint's day

hollow *adj* **1** cavernous, concave, deep-set, depressed, dimpled, indented, sunken; *opp* convex. **2** empty, hollowed-out, unfilled, vacant, void; *opp* solid. **3** (a hollow sound) deep, dull, flat, low, muffled, muted, rumbling, toneless;

opp clear. **4** (a hollow promise) artificial, empty, false, hypocritical, insincere, two-faced; ***opp*** sincere. **5** (a hollow victory) fruitless, futile, insignificant, meaningless, pointless, useless, vain, worthless; ***opp*** meaningful

hollow *n* cavity, crater, dent, depression, dimple, dint, dip, excavation, hole, indentation, pit, trough

holocaust *n* annihilation, bloodbath, butchery, carnage, destruction, devastation, ethnic cleansing, extermination, genocide, massacre, mass murder, ravaging, slaughter

holy *adj* **1** (of an object) blessed, consecrated, divine, hallowed, revered, sacred, sacrosanct. **2** (of a person) devout, faithful, God-fearing, godly, pious, pure, religious, reverent, righteous, saintly, spiritual, virtuous; ***opp*** atheistic

home *n* **1** abode, base, domicile, dwelling, dwelling-place, habitation, house, lodging, pad *inf*, quarters, residence. **2** birthplace, country of origin, fatherland, homeland, home town, motherland, native land. **3** (the home of the cheetah) environment, habitat, haunt, home ground, range, territory. **4 at home** at ease, comfortable, familiar, relaxed; ***opp*** uncomfortable

homeless *adj* abandoned, destitute, displaced, dispossessed, down-and-out, evicted, exiled, itinerant, nomadic, of no fixed abode, rootless, vagrant, wandering, without a roof over your head

homicidal *adj* dangerous, deadly, lethal, maniacal, mortal, murderous, violent

homicide *n* assassination, bloodshed, killing, manslaughter, murder, slaughter, slaying

honest *adj* **1** (of a person) aboveboard, decent, ethical, genuine, high-minded, honorable, law-abiding, reliable, reputable, scrupulous, straight *inf*, trustworthy, trusty, truthful, upright, upstanding, virtuous; ***opp*** dishonest. **2** (an honest answer) blunt, candid, direct, forthright, frank, open, outright, plain, sincere, upfront

honesty *n* ethics, honor, incorruptibility, integrity, morality, morals, reliability, reputability, scrupulousness, straightness, trustworthiness, truthfulness, uprightness, veracity, virtue; ***opp*** dishonesty

honor *n* **1** (a sense of honor) decency, fairness, goodness, honesty, integrity, loyalty, morality, principle, rectitude, righteousness, uprightness, virtue. **2** (it would be an honor) compliment, credit, pleasure, privilege. **3** (the honor of representing your country) credit, dignity, distinction, eminence, esteem, fame, glory, good name, prestige, rank, renown, reputation, repute. **4** (treat sb with honor) acclaim, accolade, commendation, deference, homage, kudos, prestige, recognition, regard, respect, reverence, tribute; ***opp*** disrespect

honor *v* acclaim, admire, applaud, appreciate, celebrate, commemorate, commend, dignify, esteem, exalt, glorify, hallow, praise, prize, respect, revere, value, venerate, worship

honorable *adj* admirable, chivalrous,

creditable, decent, dependable, ethical, fair, faithful, good, honest, irreproachable, just, law-abiding, moral, principled, proper, reliable, righteous, straight *inf*, true, truthful, trustworthy, trusty, upright, upstanding, virtuous, worthy; *opp* dishonorable

honorary *adj* complimentary, ex-officio, formal, nominal, titular, unofficial, unpaid

honors *n* awards, decorations, dignities, distinctions, prizes, rewards, titles

hook *n* 1 (on clothing) catch, clasp, clip, fastener, hasp, link, lock. 2 (coat hook) holder, nail, peg

hook *v* catch, clasp, fasten, fix, secure

hooligan *n* bully, delinquent, hoodlum, lout, ruffian, tearaway, thug *inf*, trouble-maker, vandal

hoop *n* band, circle, girdle, loop, ring, wheel

hoot *n* 1 (of an owl) call, cry, screech, toot, whoop. 2 (of people) boo, catcall, hiss, jeer, scoff, taunt. 3 (it was a hoot) laugh, scream

hoot *v* 1 (of an owl) call, cry, screech, toot, whoop. 2 (of people) boo, catcall, condemn, damn, decry, deride, hiss, jeer, mock, ridicule, scoff, scorn, taunt; *opp* applaud

hop *v* bounce, bound, caper, dance, jump, leap, prance, skip, spring, vault, trip

hope *n* 1 ambition, aspiration, craving, desire, dream, longing, wish, yearning. 2 anticipation, assumption, assurance, belief, conviction, expectation

hope *v* 1 aspire, crave, desire, dream, long, wish, yearn. 2 anticipate, assume, await, be hopeful, believe, contemplate,

expect, foresee, look forward to, trust

hopeful *adj* 1 (of a person) buoyant, confident, expectant, optimistic, positive, sanguine; *opp* pessimistic. 2 (of news) auspicious, cheerful, cheering, encouraging, favorable, heartening, promising, propitious, reassuring, rosy; *opp* gloomy

hopefully *adv* 1 (full of hope) confidently, expectantly, full of hope, optimistically, positively, with anticipation, with assurance, with hope; *opp* pessimistically. 2 all being well, if everything goes according to plan, most likely, probably, with any luck

hopeless *adj* 1 (feel hopeless) defeated, dejected, demoralized, despairing, desperate, despondent, disconsolate, downhearted, forlorn, in despair, negative, pessimistic, resigned, without hope; *opp* hopeful. 2 (a hopeless case) beyond (all) hope, helpless, incurable, irremediable, irreparable, irretrievable, irreversible, lost. 3 (a hopeless task) forlorn, futile, impossible, impracticable, no-win, pointless, unattainable, useless, vain

horde *n* army, band, crew, crowd, drove, flock, gang, group, host, mass, mob, multitude, pack, press, swarm, throng, tribe, troop

horizontal *adj* even, facedown, flat, level, lying down, prone, prostrate, supine; *opp* vertical

horrible *adj* abominable, appalling, awful, cruel, disagreeable, disgusting, dreadful, fearful, frightful, ghastly, grim, grisly, gruesome, hateful, heinous, hideous, horrendous, horrid, loathsome, macabre, mean, nasty, objectionable, obnoxious, repulsive, revolting, shameful, shocking, terrible, unkind, unpleasant, vile; *opp* pleasant

horrid adj abominable, appalling, awful, cruel, disagreeable, disgusting, dreadful, fearful, frightful, ghastly, hateful, heinous, hideous, horrendous, horrible, loathsome, mean, nasty, objectionable, obnoxious, repulsive, revolting, shameful, shocking, terrible, unkind, unpleasant, vile; *opp* pleasant

horrific adj appalling, atrocious, blood-curdling, disgusting, dreadful, frightening, grisly, gruesome, hair-raising, harrowing, horrendous, horrifying, nauseating, shocking, sickening, unthinkable

horrified adj 1 alarmed, frightened, petrified, scared, scared out of your wits, scared stiff, scared to death, terrified. 2 appalled, disgusted, dismayed, outraged, revolted, scandalized, shocked, sickened

horrify v 1 alarm, frighten, petrify, scare, scare sb out of his wits, scare sb stiff, scare sb to death, terrify. 2 appal, disgust, dismay, outrage, revolt, scandalize, shock, sicken

horrifying adj 1 alarming, frightening, petrifying, scary, terrifying. 2 appalling, disgusting, dismaying, outrageous, revolting, shocking, sickening

horror n 1 alarm, apprehension, consternation, dismay, dread, fear, fearfulness, fright, panic, terror, trepidation, uneasiness; *opp* delight. 2 (have a horror of sth) abhorrence, antipathy, aversion, disgust, dislike,

distaste, hatred, loathing, repugnance, revulsion; *opp* love

horse n colt, filly, foal, gelding, hack, mare, mount, mule, mustang, nag *inf*, packhorse, pony, racehorse, stallion, steed

hospitable adj amicable, convivial, cordial, courteous, friendly, generous, genial, gracious, kind, neighborly, sociable, warm, warmhearted, welcoming; *opp* unwelcoming

hospital n clinic, health center, hospice, infirmary, medical center, nursing home, sanatorium, sick bay

hospitality n cheer, conviviality, cordiality, courtesy, friendliness, generosity, geniality, graciousness, kindness, neighborliness, sociability, warmheartedness, warmth, welcome; *opp* unfriendliness

host n 1 anchor man, announcer, entertainer, interviewer, master of ceremonies, MC, presenter. 2 hostess, landlord, owner, proprietor. 3 army, band, crew, crowd, drove, flock, gang, group, hoard, mass, mob, multitude, pack, press, swarm, throng, tribe, troop

host v introduce, officiate, present, preside

hostage n captive, pawn, prisoner, security, surety

hostile adj 1 aggressive, antagonistic, anti *inf*, belligerent, combative, confrontational, contrary, inimical, malevolent, opposed, unfriendly, unkind, unsympathetic, unwelcoming; *opp* friendly. 2 (hostile conditions) adverse, inauspicious, unfavorable, unhelpful; *opp* favorable

hostilities n conflict, confrontation, fighting, military action, strife, war, warfare

hostility n aggression, anger, animosity, antagonism, antipathy, aversion, bad feeling, belligerence, enmity, friction, hatred, ill will, malevolence, malice, opposition, rancor, resentment, spite, unfriendliness, unkindness, wrath; **opp** friendliness

hot adj 1 baking, blistering, boiling, burning, fiery, flaming, heated, piping, red-hot, roasting, scalding, scorching, searing, steaming, sultry, sweltering, thermal, torrid, tropical, warm; **opp** cold. 2 (spicy) peppery, piquant, pungent, sharp, spicy, strong; **opp** mild

hound v 1 annoy, badger, browbeat, bully, harass, harry, nag, persecute, pester. 2 chase, drive, follow, hunt, pursue, shadow, stalk, trail

house n 1 abode, building, domicile, dwelling, edifice, habitation, home, pad inf, place inf, residence. 2 (a publishing house) business, company, concern, corporation, enterprise, establishment, firm, organization, outfit inf

house v accommodate, board, harbor, keep, lodge, place, put up, shelter, sleep, take in

hovel n cabin, den, dump inf, hole inf, hut, shack, shanty, shed

hover v 1 be suspended, drift, float, flutter, fly, hang, poise. 2 hang about, hang around, linger, loiter, wait about

howl v 1 bay, bellow, cry, holler, roar, scream, shout, shriek, yell, yelp. 2 bawl, cry, sob, wail, weep

huddle n band, bevy, bunch, cluster, crowd, gang, gathering, group, knot, mass, pack, posse, throng, troupe

huddle v 1 bunch, cluster, converge, cram, crowd, flock, gather, group, herd, jam, pile, squeeze, swarm, throng; **opp** spread out. 2 crouch, cuddle, curl up, hug, hunch, nestle, snuggle; **opp** stretch

hug n bearhug, clinch inf, cuddle, embrace, squeeze

hug v 1 (hug a person) cuddle, embrace, enfold, hold, squeeze. 2 (hug sth) clasp, cling, crush, nurse, squeeze

huge adj colossal, elephantine, enormous, extra-large, gargantuan, giant, gigantic, great, hulking, immense, jumbo inf, large, mammoth, massive, mighty, monster inf, mountainous, outsize, vast, whopping inf; **opp** tiny

hulk n body, carcass, frame, hull, shell, skeleton, wreck

hull n body, casing, covering, frame, framework, skeleton, structure

hum v 1 buzz, drone, murmur, purr, sing, throb, thrum, vibrate, whir. 2 (be humming with activity) be active, be busy, bustle, buzz, pulsate, pulse, stir, vibrate

human adj 1 anthropoid, hominid, mortal. 2 compassionate, considerate, humane, kind, rational, reasonable, sensible, sensitive, sympathetic, thoughtful, understanding; **opp** inhuman. 3 (only human) fallible, frail, mortal, natural, normal, vulnerable, weak

humane adj altruistic, benevolent, benign, charitable, compassionate, feeling, forgiving, gentle, good, humanitarian, kind, kindhearted, lenient, magnanimous, merciful, mild, sympathetic, tender, understanding, unselfish, warmhearted; **opp** inhumane

humanitarian adj altruistic, beneficent, benevolent, charitable, compassionate, gentle, good, humane, kind, lenient, merciful, philanthropic, public-spirited, sympathetic

humanity n humankind, man, mankind, men, mortals, people, the human race

humanize v civilize, cultivate, educate, polish, refine, soften, tame

humble adj 1 deferential, docile, meek, modest, submissive, unostentatious, unpretentious; **opp** brash. 2 (a humble cottage) common, commonplace, ignoble, insignificant, low, lowly, modest, ordinary, poor, simple, undistinguished, unimportant; **opp** great

humdrum adj banal, boring, dreary, dull, everyday, mind-numbing, monotonous, mundane, ordinary, repetitious, routine, run-of-the-mill, tedious, tiresome, uninteresting; **opp** exciting

humid adj clammy, close, damp, dank, moist, muggy, steamy, sticky, sultry, wet

humiliate v abase, chasten, crush, deflate, debase, degrade, demean, disgrace, embarrass, humble, make sb feel small, mortify, put down, put sb in his place, shame, show sb up inf, take sb down a peg inf

humiliating adj chastening, crushing, deflating, degrading, demeaning, embarrassing, humbling, ignominious, mortifying, shameful, shaming

humiliation n abasement, crushing, debasement, degradation, disgrace, dishonor, embarrassment, humbling,

ignominy, indignity, loss of face, mortification, shame

humility n deference, diffidence, humbleness, lack of pride, lowliness, meekness, modesty, self-effacement, servility, submissiveness, unpretentiousness; **opp** arrogance

humor n 1 banter, comedy, drollness, farce, fun, hilarity, jesting, jocularity, jokes, joking, laughter, ludicrousness, merriment, quips, repartee, ridiculousness, satire, wisecracks, wit, witticisms. 2 (mood) disposition, frame of mind, mood, state of mind, spirits, temper, temperament

humorist n caricaturist, comedian, comic, jester, joker, satirist, sketch-writer

humorous adj amusing, comic, comical, droll, entertaining, facetious, farcical, funny, hilarious, laughable, ludicrous, ridiculous, satirical, witty

hump n bulge, bump, growth, hunch, lump, mound, projection, protrusion, protuberance, swelling

hunch n 1 feeling, guess, idea, impression, inkling, intuition, premonition, presentiment, sixth sense, suspicion. 2 bulge, bump, growth, hump, lump, swelling

hunger n 1 appetite, emptiness, famine, hungriness, ravenousness, starvation. 2 (have a hunger for sth) appetite, craving, desire, eagerness, greed, hankering, itch, keenness, longing, lust, pining, yearning

hunger v crave, desire, hanker, have a hankering, have an appetite for, itch, long, lust, pine, yearn

hungry adj 1 empty, famished, hollow, malnourished, ravenous, starved, starving, underfed, undernourished, voracious. 2 (hungry for sth) aching, craving, desperate, eager, greedy, hankering, itching, keen, longing, lusting, pining, yearning

hunk n block, chunk, lump, mass, piece, slab, wedge

hunt n chase, course, pursuit, quest, search, trail

hunt v 1 chase, course, hound, pursue, stalk, track, trail. 2 ferret out, forage, look for, search, seek, scour, trace, track down

hurdle n barrier, block, handicap, hindrance, impediment, obstacle, obstruction, stumbling block

hurl v cast, chuck inf, fire, fling, heave, launch, lob inf, pitch, propel, send, shy, sling, throw, toss

hurricane n cyclone, gale, storm, tempest, tornado, typhoon, whirlwind, windstorm

hurry n acceleration, bustle, dispatch, expeditiousness, flurry, haste, rush, rushing, speed, urgency

hurry v 1 belt, dash, fly, hasten, get a move on inf, make haste, run, rush, scurry, speed, step on it inf. 2 (hurry sth) accelerate, expedite, hasten, press, push through, quicken, speed up, urge; *opp* slow down

hurt n 1 (emotional) affliction, distress, grief, offense, pain, sadness, upset. 2 (physical) burning, discomfort, pain, smarting, soreness, stinging, throbbing

hurt v 1 bruise, cut, damage, disable, harm, impair, injure, mar, spoil, wound. 2 (sth hurts) ache, be painful, be sore, burn, smart, sting, throb. 3 affect, afflict, aggrieve, be hurtful, cut, distress, grieve, insult, offend, pain, sadden, sting, upset, wound

husky adj croaking, croaky, deep, gravely, gruff, harsh, hoarse, low, rasping, rough, throaty

hut n cabin, hovel, lean-to, refuge, shack, shanty, shed, shelter

hybrid adj amalgam, blend, composite, compound, cross, crossbreed, half-blood, half breed, mix, mixture, mongrel

hygiene n cleanliness, health, purity, sanitation

hygienic adj aseptic, clean, disinfected, healthy, germ-free, pure, salubrious, sanitary, sterile, sterilized, uncontaminated, unpolluted; *opp* unhygienic

hype n advertising, build-up, exaggeration, plugging inf, PR, promotion, propaganda, publicity

hypnotic adj fascinating, magnetic, mesmeric, mesmerizing, narcotic, soporific, spellbinding, stupefying

hypnotize v entrance, fascinate, magnetize, mesmerize, put a spell on, put sb in a trance, spellbind, stupefy

hypocrisy n cant, deceit, deception, dishonesty, dissembling, double standards, duplicity, falsity, humbug, insincerity, pretense, sham, two-facedness inf

hypocrite n charlatan, deceiver, dissembler, fake, fraud, imposter, liar, phony inf, pretender

hypocritical adj deceitful, dishonest, dissembling, duplicitous, fake, false,

fraudulent, hollow, inconsistent,
insincere, phony *inf*, pretended,
sanctimonious, sham, spurious,
two-faced *inf*

hypothesis *n* assumption, axiom,
conjecture, guess, idea, postulate,
premise, proposition, speculation,
theorem, theory, thesis

hypothetical *adj* academic, assumed,
conjectured, imaginary, notional,
possible, presumed, proposed, putative,
speculative, suggested, theoretical

hysteria *n* delirium, frenzy, hysterics,
madness, mania, panic

hysterical *adj* berserk, beside yourself,
crazed, delirious, distracted, distraught,
frantic, frenzied, in hysterics, irrational,
manic, out of control, raving,
uncontrollable

icy *adj* **1** arctic, biting, bitter, chill, chilly, freezing, frosty, frozen, glacial, ice-cold, polar, raw; *opp* hot. **2** aloof, cold, cool, chilly, distant, frigid, frosty, glacial, steely, stony, unfriendly; *opp* warm

idea *n* **1** abstraction, belief, concept, conception, construct, hypothesis, image, impression, notion, opinion, perception, principle, tenet, thought, theory, understanding, view. **2** (a new idea) brainwave, creation, design, inspiration, plan, proposal, scheme, suggestion. **3** (give an idea of sth) approximation, clue, estimate, estimation, guess, guidelines, impression, inkling, intimation

ideal *adj* archetypal, classic, complete, consummate, exemplary, faultless, flawless, model, optimum, perfect, quintessential, supreme

idealist *n* dreamer, optimist, romantic, Utopian, visionary

idealistic *adj* impracticable, impractical, optimistic, quixotic, romantic, starry-eyed, unrealistic, Utopian, visionary; *opp* realistic

identical *adj* alike, duplicate, equal, indistinguishable, interchangeable, like, matching, the same, twin; *opp* different

identify *v* **1** discern, distinguish, label, name, pick out, pinpoint, recognize, single out, specify, spot. **2** (identify a problem) ascertain, detect, diagnose, discover, establish, find, find out, uncover

identity *n* **1** ID *inf*, name. **2** character, distinctiveness, ego, existence, individuality, nature, personality, self, selfhood, uniqueness

ideology *n* belief, convictions, credo, creed, doctrine, dogma, philosophy, politics, principles, teaching, tenets, theory, thesis

idiom *n* **1** colloquialism, expression, manner of speaking, phrase, turn of phrase. **2** argot, dialect, jargon, language, parlance, patois, speech, usage, vernacular

idiosyncrasy *n* characteristic, eccentricity, feature, habit, mannerism, oddity, peculiarity, quirk, trait, trick, way

idiosyncratic *adj* characteristic, distinctive, eccentric, individual, odd, particular, peculiar, personal, quirky, singular, unique, unusual

idiot *n* blockhead, bonehead *inf*, dimwit, dummy *inf*, dunce, fool, halfwit, ignoramus, imbecile, moron, nitwit, numbskull, simpleton, twit *inf*

idiotic *adj* asinine, crazy, daft *inf*, dense, dimwitted, dumb *inf*, fatuous, foolish, half-witted, inane, moronic, senseless, stupid

idle *adj* **1** apathetic, indolent, lazy, loafing, shiftless, slothful, sluggish, torpid; *opp* hard-working, industrious.
2 (not working) inactive, inoperative, jobless, not working, out of action, out of use, redundant, unemployed, unoccupied, unproductive, unused.
3 (idle gossip) fatuous, frivolous, fruitless, futile, inane, insignificant, irrelevant, pointless, superficial, trivial, useless, worthless; *opp* serious

idle *v* coast, drift, hang around *inf*, laze around, lie around, loaf, loll, lounge, mess around *inf*, shirk, sit around, slack, take it easy *inf*, vegetate, waste time

idol *n* deity, god, guru, hero, heroine

idolize *v* adore, adulate, deify, glorify, hero-worship, look up to, love, revere, venerate, worship

idyllic *adj* Arcadian, blissful, ideal, heavenly, lovely, perfect, picturesque, wonderful; *opp* awful, terrible

ignite *v* burn, catch fire, fire, inflame, kindle, light, set alight, set fire to, set on fire, spark off

ignorant *adj* benighted, blind, ill-informed, inexperienced, innocent, naive, oblivious, stupid, unaware, unconscious, uneducated, unenlightened, unknowing, unwitting; *opp* knowledgable

ignore *v* brush aside, discount, disregard, neglect, omit, overlook, pass over, pay no attention, reject, shut your eyes, take no notice, turn a blind eye

ill *adj* **1** ailing, groggy *inf*, indisposed, infected, infirm, invalid, not well, off-color, out of sorts, poorly, sick, sickly, under the weather, unhealthy, unwell; *opp* well. **2** bad, damaging, detrimental, evil, foul, harmful, injurious, ruinous, unfavorable, unfortunate, unlucky, vile, wicked; *opp* good

ill-bred *adj* badly brought up, bad-mannered, boorish, coarse, crass, discourteous, ill-mannered, impolite, indelicate, loutish, rude, uncivil, uncouth, ungentlemanly, unladylike, unmannerly, vulgar

illegal *adj* against the law, banned, barred, black-market, criminal, felonious, forbidden, illegitimate, illicit, lawless, outlawed, prohibited, proscribed, unauthorized, unlawful, unlicensed, unofficial, wrongful; *opp* legal

illegible *adj* incomprehensible, indecipherable, indistinct, obscure, scrawled, scribbled, unintelligible, unreadable; *opp* legible

illegitimate *adj* **1** illegal, illicit, improper, incorrect, invalid, irregular, unauthorized, unlawful, unwarranted, wrongful; *opp* legitimate. **2** (of a person) bastard, born out of wedlock, fatherless; *opp* legitimate

illicit *adj* banned, forbidden, furtive, illegal, illegitimate, immoral, improper, irregular, prohibited, proscribed, unauthorized, unlawful, unlicensed, wrong, wrongful

illiterate *adj* unable to read, uncultured, uneducated, unlettered, unschooled, untaught; *opp* educated, literate

illness *n* affliction, ailment, attack, bug *inf*, complaint, condition, disease, disorder, ill-health, indisposition, infection, infirmity, invalidity, malady, malaise, sickness

illogical adj absurd, fallacious, faulty, inconsistent, incorrect, invalid, irrational, meaningless, senseless, specious, spurious, unreasonable, unscientific, unsound, untenable; **opp** logical

ill-treat v abuse, be cruel, damage, harm, hurt, injure, maltreat, mistreat, misuse, oppress, treat sb badly, wrong

illusion n 1 apparition, daydream, fantasy, figment, hallucination, mirage, phantasm, phantom. 2 delusion, error, fallacy, false impression, misapprehension, misconception, mistake

illustrate v 1 bring home, clarify, demonstrate, elucidate, emphasize, exemplify, exhibit, explain, interpret, prove, show. 2 adorn, decorate, embellish, illuminate

illustrated adj decorated, embellished, graphic, illuminated, pictorial, with pictures

illustration n 1 decoration, diagram, drawing, embellishment, figure, graphic, picture, plate, sketch. 2 analogy, case, clarification, demonstration, elucidation, example, explanation, instance, sample, specimen

image n 1 depiction, figure, likeness, photograph, picture, portrayal, projection, reflection, representation, semblance. 2 conception, idea, mental picture, notion, perception. 3 (improve your image) impression, name, perception, reputation, repute, standing, status

imaginable adj conceivable, credible, feasible, likely, plausible, possible, thinkable; **opp** unimaginable

imaginary adj dreamed-up, fabulous, fanciful, fantastic, fictional, ideal, illusory, imagined, invented, legendary, made-up, mythical, mythological, non-existent, shadowy, supposed, unreal, visionary; **opp** real

imagination n creativity, fancy, ingenuity, insight, inspiration, inventiveness, originality, vision

imaginative adj clever, creative, fanciful, ingenious, innovative, inspired, inventive, novel, original, unique, visionary; **opp** unimaginative

imagine v 1 conceive, conjure up, create, devise, dream up, envisage, fantasize, invent, make believe, picture, pretend, project, think of, think up, visualize. 2 assume, believe, conjecture, deduce, gather, guess, infer, judge, presume, reckon, suppose, surmise, suspect, think

imitate v 1 ape, caricature, counterfeit, do an impression of, duplicate, echo, impersonate, mimic, mirror, mock, parody, repeat, simulate. 2 copy, emulate, follow, follow sb's example, model yourself on

imitation n 1 aping, copying, impersonation, impression, mimicry, parody. 2 clone, copy, counterfeit, dummy, duplication, fake, forgery, look-alike, mock-up, model, replica, reproduction, sham, simulation

imitative adj copied, derivative, mock, parrot-like, plagiarized, unoriginal; **opp** original

immaculate adj 1 clean, impeccable,

neat, spick and span, spotless, spruce,
squeaky-clean. **2** faultless, flawless,
guiltless, impeccable, innocent,
irreproachable, perfect, pure, sinless,
spotless, squeaky-clean, unpolluted,
unstained, unsullied, untainted,
untarnished, virtuous

immature *adj* **1** (not fully developed)
crude, green, half-formed, raw,
undeveloped, unformed, unripe, young;
opp mature. **2** (of a person) adolescent,
babyish, backward, callow, childish,
infantile, juvenile, puerile; *opp* mature

immediate *adj* instant, instantaneous,
on the spot, prompt, quick, rapid,
speedy, sudden, swift, unhesitating.
2 adjacent, close, direct, near, next

immense *adj* colossal, elephantine,
enormous, extensive, gargantuan, giant,
gigantic, great, huge, infinite,
mammoth, massive, mighty,
monumental, prodigious, stupendous,
titanic, tremendous, vast; *opp* tiny

immerse *v* **1** bathe, cover, dip, douse,
drench, duck, dunk, lower, plunge, sink,
soak, submerge. **2** absorb, engage,
engross, lose yourself, occupy, preoccupy

immigrant *n* alien, expatriate, migrant,
newcomer, settler

imminent *adj* approaching, at hand,
close, coming, forthcoming, gathering,
impending, looming, near, on the
horizon, on the way

immobilize *v* bring to a standstill,
cripple, disable, freeze, halt, paralyze,
put out of action, stop, transfix

immoral *adj* bad, base, corrupt,
debauched, degenerate, depraved,
dishonest, dissolute, evil, impure,

indecent, lewd, licentious, obscene,
sinful, unethical, unprincipled,
unscrupulous, vicious, vile, villainous,
wicked, wrong; *opp* moral

immortal *adj* abiding, ageless, constant,
deathless, endless, enduring, eternal,
evergreen, everlasting, imperishable,
indestructible, infinite, lasting, never-
ending, perennial, perpetual, timeless,
undying, unfading

immortalize *v* celebrate, commemorate,
enshrine, exalt, glorify, keep alive,
memorialize, perpetuate, preserve

immovable *adj* **1** anchored, fast, firm,
fixed, immobile, jammed, riveted,
rooted, secure, set, stable, stationary,
stuck. **2** adamant, constant, determined,
dogged, immutable, inflexible, obdurate,
resolute, staunch, steadfast, stubborn,
unbending, unchanging, unshakable,
unswerving, unwavering

immune *adj* exempt, free, immunized,
invulnerable, proof against, protected,
resistant, safe, unaffected

immunize *v* inoculate, protect, safeguard,
vaccinate

impact *n* **1** bang, blow, bump, collision,
contact, crash, force, impetus, jolt,
knock, shock, smash, stroke, thump.
2 bearing, consequence, effect, force,
impression, influence, repercussions,
result

impair *v* blunt, damage, debilitate,
deteriorate, diminish, disable, enfeeble,
harm, hinder, hurt, impede, injure,
lessen, mar, reduce, spoil, undermine,
weaken, worsen

impart *v* **1** communicate, convey,
disclose, make known, pass on, relate,

reveal, tell, transmit. 2 accord, bestow, confer, contribute, give, grant, lend

impartial *adj* balanced, detached, disinterested, dispassionate, equal, equitable, evenhanded, fair, fair-minded, just, neutral, objective, open-minded, unbiased, unprejudiced; *opp* biased

impassable *adj* blocked, closed, impenetrable, insurmountable, obstructed, unconquerable

impasse *n* dead end, deadlock, full stop, stalemate, standoff, standstill, stop

impatience *n* abruptness, agitation, eagerness, edginess, impetuosity, intolerance, irritability, restiveness, restlessness, shortness; *opp* patience

impatient *adj* 1 (waiting for sth) agitated, edgy, fidgety, intolerant, irritable, restive, testy; *opp* patient. 2 (eager to do sth) anxious, eager, keen, longing, raring *inf*. 3 (impatient with sb) abrupt, brusque, hasty, irritable, peevish, quick-tempered, short-tempered, snappish, terse; *opp* patient

impeccable *adj* 1 exact, exquisite, faultless, flawless, perfect, precise. 2 innocent, irreproachable, pure, virtuous

impediment *n* bar, block, defect, deterrent, difficulty, disadvantage, handicap, obstacle, problem, snag, stumbling block

impending *adj* approaching, at hand, brewing, close, coming, gathering, imminent, looming, menacing, near, on the horizon, threatening

imperative *adj* critical, crucial, essential, important, necessary, vital

imperceptible *adj* faint, fine, inaudible, indistinct, insignificant, invisible, microscopic, negligible, shadowy, slight, subtle, tiny, undetectable, unnoticeable, unobtrusive, vague; *opp* obvious

imperfect *adj* blemished, broken, chipped, cracked, damaged, defective, faulty, flawed, incomplete, limited, partial, spoilt, unfinished; *opp* perfect

imperfection *n* blemish, defect, deficiency, failing, fault, flaw, inadequacy, shortcoming, spot, stain, weakness, weak point

imperial *adj* 1 kingly, majestic, princely, queenly, regal, royal, sovereign. 2 grand, great, high, imposing, magnificent, majestic, noble, stately, superior

impersonal *adj* businesslike, cold, cool, detached, disinterested, dispassionate, distant, formal, mechanical, remote, stiff, unfriendly, without emotion; *opp* friendly, warm

impersonate *v* do *inf*, do an impression of, imitate, masquerade as, mimic, parody, pose as, pretend to be, take off *inf*

impertinent *adj* brazen, cheeky, cocky *inf*, disrespectful, forward, fresh *inf*, impolite, impudent, insolent, irreverent, rude, saucy; *opp* respectful

impervious *adj* 1 (not letting sth in) impenetrable, impermeable, nonporous, resistant, sealed, waterproof, watertight. 2 (impervious to her charms) immune, resistant, unaffected, unmoved, unreceptive, untouched

impetuous *adj* ardent, careless, eager, hasty, hot-headed, impromptu, impulsive, quick, rash, reckless, spontaneous, spur-of-the-moment, thoughtless, unplanned, unthinking

impetus n 1 encouragement, impulse, incentive, inducement, motivation, push, spur, stimulus. 2 force, momentum, power, propulsion, thrust

implement v achieve, bring about, carry out, enforce, execute, fulfill, perform, put into effect, put into practice

implicate v 1 connect, concern, embroil, entangle, imply, include, involve. 2 (implicate sb in the crime) accuse, blame, compromise, incriminate, involve

implication n assumption, hint, inference, innuendo, meaning, overtone, significance, suggestion

implicit adj 1 (implicit in sth) contained, hinted at, implied, inherent, tacit, understood, unspoken; *opp* explicit. 2 (implicit obedience) absolute, complete, total, unconditional, unquestioning, utter

implied adj implicit, indirect, inherent, insinuated, suggested, tacit, unspoken

imply v hint, indicate, insinuate, intimate, mean, point to, signify, suggest

impolite adj bad-mannered, discourteous, disrespectful, ill-mannered, impertinent, insolent, rough, rude, uncivil, uncouth, vulgar; *opp* polite

import v bring in, introduce, ship in; *opp* export

importance n 1 gravity, momentousness, newsworthiness, prestige, rarity, seriousness, significance, status. 2 (of no importance) consequence, interest, relevance, usefulness, value, worth

important adj 1 (of things, issues) basic, big, cardinal, central, chief, far-reaching,

grave, historic, key, main, major, momentous, principal, salient, serious, significant, urgent, weighty; *opp* unimportant. 2 (of a person) celebrated, distinguished, eminent, famous, high-ranking, influential, leading, powerful, prominent, well-known; *opp* ordinary. 3 (it's important that you do this) critical, crucial, essential, necessary, pivotal, pressing, vital

impose v 1 (impose sth on sb) apply, dictate, enforce, exact, foist, force, inflict, introduce, levy, prescribe, put, saddle *inf*, set. 2 (don't want to impose) abuse, be a burden, butt in *inf*, crash *inf*, exploit, force yourself, intrude, take advantage

imposing adj commanding, effective, grand, impressive, lofty, majestic, striking

impossible adj 1 (not possible) difficult, hopeless, impracticable, impractical, inconceivable, insoluble, insuperable, out of the question, unattainable, unimaginable, unthinkable, unworkable; *opp* possible. 2 (not true) absurd, incredible, outrageous, preposterous, unbelievable. 3 (of people) (*inf*) insufferable, unbearable, unmanageable

impostor n charlatan, cheat, con man *inf*, fake, fraud, hypocrite, phony *inf*, swindler, trickster

impotent adj feeble, helpless, inadequate, incapable, incapacitated, ineffective, ineffectual, paralyzed, powerless, unable, weak

impoverished adj 1 bankrupt, needy, penniless, poor, poverty-stricken, ruined; *opp* rich, wealthy. 2 barren, bare, depleted, desolate, empty, exhausted, spent, weakened

impracticable *adj* awkward, impossible, inconvenient, not feasible, unattainable, unsuitable, useless

impractical *adj* abstract, academic, idealistic, impossible, ineffective, romantic, theoretical, unbusinesslike, unrealistic, visionary; **opp** practical

imprecise *adj* ambiguous, approximate, estimated, hazy, inaccurate, indefinite, inexact, loose, rough, sloppy *inf*, unscientific, vague; **opp** precise

impregnable *adj* impenetrable, invincible, invulnerable, safe, secure, strong, unassailable

impress *v* 1 (impress sb) affect, be memorable, excite, influence, inspire, leave your mark, make an impression, make an impact, persuade, stick in sb's mind *inf*, stir, sway, touch. 2 (impress sth on sb) emphasize, instill, stress. 3 emboss, engrave, print, stamp

impression *n* 1 (do an impression of sb) imitation, impersonation, parody, take-off *inf*. 2 (I had the impression that she was lying) feeling, hunch, idea, inkling, sensation, sense, suspicion. 3 (made a good impression) effect, impact, mark, response. 4 (your impression of sth) idea, memory, opinion, recollection, view. 5 (an impression on the grass) dent, hollow, imprint, indentation, mark

impressionable *adj* easily influenced, gullible, inexperienced, open, receptive, sensitive, susceptible, vulnerable

impressive *adj* awe-inspiring, awesome, exciting, formidable, grand, inspiring, magnificent, memorable, moving,

powerful, stirring, striking, touching; **opp** unimpressive

imprison *v* confine, detain, incarcerate, jail, lock up, put away, put in prison, remand, send down *inf*, send to prison, shut up; **opp** free

improbable *adj* doubtful, dubious, fanciful, far-fetched, hard to believe, highly unlikely, implausible, incredible, questionable, unbelievable, unconvincing, unlikely; **opp** likely

impromptu *adj* ad-lib, improvised, off the cuff *inf*, off the top of your head *inf*, spontaneous, unplanned, unpremeditated, unrehearsed, unscripted

improve *v* 1 (make sth better) correct, enhance, enrich, help, mend, modernize, put right, rectify, refine, reform, repair, revise, touch up, update, upgrade. 2 (get better) advance, develop, gain strength, get better, get well, increase, look up *inf*, make headway, pick up *inf*, progress, rally, recover; **opp** worsen

improvement *n* advance, amendment, correction, development, enhancement, gain, growth, increase, progress, recovery, rise, upswing, upturn

improvise *v* 1 ad-lib, make it up as you go along, play it by ear. 2 concoct, devise, invent, make do, throw together

imprudent *adj* careless, foolish, ill-advised, ill-judged, indiscreet, irresponsible, rash, reckless, thoughtless, unwise; **opp** prudent, wise

impudent *adj* bad-mannered, bold, brazen, cheeky *inf*, disrespectful, forward, fresh *inf*, immodest, impertinent, insolent, presumptuous, rude, saucy

impulse n 1 force, impetus, momentum, movement, pressure, push, stimulus. 2 desire, drive, instinct, urge, whim

impulsive adj 1 (of an action) automatic, hasty, impetuous, instinctive, quick, rash, spontaneous, sudden, unplanned; **opp** planned. 2 (of a person) demonstrative, emotional, hot-headed, intuitive, passionate, spontaneous; **opp** cautious

impurity n contamination, dirt, dirtiness, filth, foreign body, infection, pollution

inability n impotence, incapability, incompetence, powerlessness, uselessness

inaccessible adj cut off, god-forsaken, impassable, inconvenient, isolated, off the beaten track inf, out of reach, remote, unattainable, unobtainable

inaccuracy n error, falsehood, fault, imprecision, inconsistency, miscalculation, misprint, mistake, slip, slip-up inf, unreliability

inaccurate adj 1 careless, erroneous, false, faulty, flawed, imprecise, incorrect, inexact, misleading, mistaken, out, unfaithful, untrue, wrong; **opp** accurate. 2 (an inaccurate shot) off-target, out, wide, wild; **opp** accurate

inactive adj asleep, dormant, hibernating, idle, immobile, inert, lazy, lethargic, out of action, passive, quiet, sedentary, sleepy, slothful, sluggish, unoccupied, unused, vegetating; **opp** active

inadequate adj 1 deficient, disappointing, incapable, incompetent, incomplete, unacceptable, unqualified,

unsatisfactory, unsuitable; **opp** adequate. 2 (inadequate rainfall) insubstantial, insufficient, limited, meager, not enough, scanty, scarce

inadvisable adj foolish, ill-advised, ill-judged, imprudent, misguided, unwise; **opp** advisable, wise

inane adj fatuous, foolish, frivolous, idiotic, mindless, senseless, silly, stupid

inanimate adj cold, dead, defunct, extinct, inert, lifeless, unconscious; **opp** living

inarticulate adj dumb, faltering, halting, hesitant, incoherent, incomprehensible, indistinct, muffled, mute, shy, silent, speechless, stammering, stuttering, tongue-tied, unclear, unintelligible, wordless; **opp** articulate

inaudible adj faint, hard to hear, indistinct, low, muted, quiet, soft, unheard, whispered; **opp** audible

inaugural adj first, initial, introductory, maiden, opening

inaugurate v begin, commence, get off the ground, initiate, institute, introduce, launch, originate, set up, start

inauspicious adj bad, black, discouraging, ill-fated, ill-starred, ominous, unfortunate, unlucky, unpromising, untimely; **opp** auspicious

incapable adj feeble, helpless, inadequate, incompetent, ineffective, inept, powerless, unfit, unqualified, useless, weak; **opp** capable

incapacitated adj disabled, disqualified, immobilized, indisposed, laid up inf, out of action inf, unfit

incarnation n bodily form, embodiment, life, manifestation

incentive n bait, carrot inf, encouragement, impetus, impulse, inducement, lure, motivation, motive, reward, spur, stimulus, sweetener inf

incessant adj ceaseless, constant, continual, endless, interminable, never-ending, nonstop, persistent, relentless, unbroken, unrelenting

incident n 1 adventure, affair, episode, event, experience, happening, matter, occasion, occurrence. 2 brush, clash, confrontation, disturbance, fight, row, scene, skirmish

incidental adj accidental, chance, fortuitous, odd, random, unplanned

incisive adj acute, biting, clear, clever, cutting, decisive, direct, keen, penetrating, piercing, precise, sarcastic, sharp, shrewd, telling

incite v drive, egg on, encourage, excite, goad, inflame, provoke, rouse, whip up, work up

inclement adj bitter, blustery, foul, rough, severe, squally, stormy

inclination n 1 aptitude, bent, bias, habit, leaning, tendency. 2 desire, fancy, fondness, liking, partiality, penchant, preference, wish. 3 ascent, descent, gradient, slant, slope

incline n ascent, descent, drop, gradient, hill, ramp, rise, slope

incline v bank, bend, bow, drop, lean, rise, slant, slope, tilt, tip, veer

inclined adj apt, disposed, given to, having a tendency to, in the habit of, liable to, likely to, prone to, willing

include v comprise, contain, cover, embrace, encompass, hold, incorporate, involve, take in; opp exclude

inclusion n incorporation, insertion, introduction; opp exclusion

inclusive adj 1 all-embracing, all in, comprehensive, full, general, overall. 2 including, taking into account

incoherent adj confused, disjointed, garbled, illogical, inarticulate, incomprehensible, muddled, rambling, unintelligible; opp coherent

income n earnings, interest, pay, profit, revenue, salary, takings, wages

incoming adj approaching, arriving, coming in, entering, landing, new, next

incompatible adj clashing, conflicting, contradictory, contrasting, different, incongruous, inconsistent, jarring, mismatched, unsuitable; opp compatible

incompetent adj clumsy, hopeless inf, incapable, ineffectual, inept, inexpert, unable, unqualified, unskillful, untrained, useless; opp competent

incomplete adj fragmentary, imperfect, insufficient, lacking, partial, short, undeveloped, undone, unfinished

incomprehensible adj baffling, beyond comprehension, complicated, deep, illegible, impenetrable, inexplicable, inscrutable, meaningless, mysterious, obscure, opaque, puzzling, strange, unfathomable, unintelligible, unreadable

inconceivable adj impossible, incredible, mind-boggling inf, out of the question, unbelievable, unheard-of, unimaginable, unthinkable; opp conceivable

inconclusive adj ambiguous, indecisive, open, open-ended, uncertain, undecided, unresolved, unsettled, up in the air inf, vague; opp conclusive

incongruous *adj* conflicting, contradictory, inappropriate, incompatible, inconsistent, odd, out of keeping, out of place, surprising

inconsiderate *adj* careless, insensitive, intolerant, rude, self-centered, selfish, tactless, thoughtless, uncaring, unhelpful, unkind, unsympathetic; *opp* considerate

inconsolable *adj* brokenhearted, desolate, despairing, grief-stricken, heartbroken, miserable, sick at heart, unhappy

inconspicuous *adj* camouflaged, discreet, hidden, insignificant, in the background, invisible, low-key *inf*, modest, muted, ordinary, plain, quiet, small, unassuming, unobtrusive, unremarkable; *opp* conspicuous

inconvenient *adj* annoying, awkward, difficult, disrupting, embarrassing, inappropriate, irritating, tiresome, troublesome, unmanageable, unsuitable; *opp* convenient

incorporate *v* absorb, amalgamate, assimilate, blend, combine, comprise, consist of, contain, fuse, include, integrate, meld, merge, mix, take in, unify, unite

incorrect *adj* erroneous, false, faulty, flawed, inaccurate, misleading, mistaken, out, untrue, wide of the mark, wrong; *opp* correct

incorrigible *adj* beyond redemption, confirmed, dyed-in-the-wool *inf*, habitual, hardened, hopeless *inf*, incurable, inveterate, shameless, unrepentant

incorruptible *adj* honest, honorable, moral, straight, trustworthy, upright, virtuous

increase *n* addition, boost, development, enlargement, escalation, expansion, extension, gain, growth, rise, upturn; *opp* decrease

increase *v* 1 (of size) add to, augment, broaden, build up, dilate, enlarge, expand, extend, gain, get bigger, grow, inflate, lengthen, magnify, make bigger, maximize, multiply, mushroom, proliferate, prolong, snowball, spread, strengthen, stretch, swell, widen; *opp* decrease. 2 (of sound) amplify, boost, intensify, swell, turn up; *opp* decrease. 3 (of quality) advance, broaden, develop, enhance, improve, step up *inf*. 4 (of seriousness, tension) build, escalate, grow, heighten, intensify, mount, raise

increasing *adj* developing, escalating, greater than ever, growing, on the increase, spreading; *opp* decreasing

incredible *adj* 1 absurd, beyond belief, far-fetched, highly unlikely, implausible, impossible, improbable, inconceivable, miraculous, preposterous, surprising, unbelievable, unconvincing, unimaginable. 2 (good) amazing, extraordinary, fantastic *inf*, great, wonderful; *opp* dreadful, terrible

incriminate *v* accuse, blame, charge, implicate, involve, point your finger at *inf*, put the blame on

incur *v* 1 (incur sb's anger) arouse, bring upon yourself, draw, provoke. 2 (incur a fine) be liable to, earn, get, lay yourself open to, run up, suffer

incurable *adj* fatal, hopeless, inoperable,

terminal, untreatable; *opp* curable

indebted *adj* grateful, in sb's debt, obliged, thankful, under an obligation

indecent *adj* **1** blue, crude, dirty, filthy, impure, lewd, naughty, obscene, pornographic, risqué, sexy *inf*, smutty, suggestive, vulgar. **2** improper, in bad taste, offensive, outrageous, unbecoming, unseemly, unsuitable

indecipherable *adj* illegible, unclear, unintelligible, unreadable

indecisive *adj* dithering, faltering, hesitating, of two minds *inf*, shilly-shallying, sitting on the fence, tentative, uncertain, undecided, unsettled, up in the air *inf*, wavering; *opp* decisive

indefensible *adj* inexcusable, unforgivable, unjustifiable, unpardonable, wrong

indefinite *adj* **1** (not decided) ambiguous, doubtful, inconclusive, open, uncertain, undecided, undetermined. **2** (not clear) blurred, confused, dim, fuzzy, hazy, indistinct, unclear, vague

indelible *adj* enduring, fast, fixed, indestructible, ingrained, lasting, permanent, unfading

independence *n* **1** (of countries) freedom, home rule, liberty, self-determination, self-government, self-rule, sovereignty. **2** (of people) freedom, individualism, liberty, self-confidence, self-sufficiency

independent *adj* **1** (of countries) free, liberated, neutral, self-governing. **2** (of things) distinct, free-standing, individual, private, self-contained, separate, unconnected, unrelated. **3** (of people) carefree, footloose, free,

free-thinking, individualistic, liberated, open-minded, self-reliant, self-sufficient, self-supporting, unbiased

indescribable *adj* beyond words, indefinable, unspeakable, unutterable

indestructible *adj* durable, enduring, eternal, everlasting, immortal, indelible, lasting, permanent, solid, strong, tough, unbreakable; *opp* breakable, delicate

index *n* catalog, directory, guide, key, table of contents

indicate *v* be a sign of, communicate, convey, denote, imply, manifest, mean, point to, reveal, say, show, signal, signify, stand for, suggest, symbolize

indication *n* clue, evidence, explanation, hint, sign, signal, symptom, token, warning

indicator *n* display, gauge, guide, index, marker, meter, needle, pointer, sign, signal, signpost, symbol

indictment *n* accusation, allegation, charge, prosecution, summons

indifferent *adj* **1** (indifferent to sth) aloof, apathetic, blasé, callous, cold, cool, detached, distant, uncaring, unconcerned, unfeeling, uninterested, unmoved, unresponsive. **2** (not very good) average, fair, mediocre, ordinary, undistinguished, uninspired

indigestion *n* acidity, dyspepsia, heartburn

indignant *adj* angry, annoyed, disgruntled, exasperated, furious, in a huff, incensed, infuriated, irate, miffed *inf*, peeved *inf*, put out *inf*, resentful, vexed; *opp* pleased

indirect *adj* **1** (not straight) circuitous, crooked, meandering, rambling, roundabout, tortuous, wandering, winding, zigzag; **opp** direct. **2** (not intended) accidental, incidental, secondary, unintended. **3** (not open) devious, disguised, euphemistic, implicit, implied, oblique, sneaky *inf*, surreptitious; **opp** open

indiscreet *adj* careless, foolish, ill-considered, imprudent, insensitive, tactless, undiplomatic; **opp** discreet

indiscretion *n* **1** blunder, error, faux pas, gaffe, mistake, slip, slip of the tongue. **2** carelessness, foolishness, lack of diplomacy, tactlessness, thoughtlessness

indiscriminate *adj* **1** (indiscriminate bombing) careless, general, haphazard, random, sweeping, unsystematic, wholesale. **2** (not choosing carefully) aimless, casual, desultory, promiscuous, uncritical, undiscerning, unsystematic; **opp** selective

indispensable *adj* basic, crucial, essential, imperative, important, necessary, needed, required, vital; **opp** dispensable

indistinct *adj* **1** bleary, blurred, dim, faint, fuzzy, hazy, misty, out of focus, shadowy, vague; **opp** clear, distinct. **2** ambiguous, confused, doubtful, indefinite, muffled, slurred, unclear, weak; **opp** clear, distinct

indistinguishable *adj* alike, identical, interchangeable, the same

individual *adj* **1** characteristic, distinct, distinctive, exclusive, idiosyncratic, original, own, particular, personal, specific, unique. **2** (for one person) for one, private, separate, single

individual *n* character, human being, person, type

individualist *n* free spirit, individual, loner, maverick, nonconformist, original

indoctrinate *v* brainwash, drill, instill, reeducate, school, teach, train

induce *v* coax, convince, encourage, get, impel, incite, motivate, persuade, prompt, talk into, tempt, urge

inducement *n* attraction, bait, encouragement, incentive, lure, motive, provocation, reward, stimulus, sweetener *inf*

indulge *v* **1** (indulge sb's wishes) cater to, fulfill, give in to, give way to, gratify, pander to, satisfy, yield to. **2** (indulge in sth) bask, give yourself up to, luxuriate, revel, wallow. **3** (indulge sb) baby, be indulgent to, cosset, mollycoddle, pamper, spoil, treat

indulgence *n* **1** fulfillment, gratification, satisfaction. **2** excess, extravagance, luxury, self-gratification. **3** compassion, fondness, forgiveness, kindness, tolerance, understanding

indulgent *adj* compassionate, doting, easygoing, fond, humane, kind, lenient, liberal, permissive, sympathetic, tolerant, understanding

industrious *adj* active, busy, conscientious, diligent, energetic, hardworking, keen, productive, tireless, unflagging; **opp** lazy

industry *n* **1** business, commerce, manufacturing, production, trade. **2** activity, application, busyness, diligence, effort, energy, industriousness, labor, perseverance, steadiness, tirelessness, toil, zeal

inedible *adj* bad, harmful, indigestible,

not fit to eat, off *inf*, poisonous, rotten, uneatable, unpalatable; *opp* edible

ineffective *adj* **1** (not having any effect) fruitless, futile, ineffectual, unavailing, unsuccessful, vain; *opp* effective. **2** (an ineffective leader) hopeless *inf*, inadequate, incapable, incompetent, inefficient, inept, powerless, unproductive, useless, weak, worthless; *opp* effective

inefficient *adj* **1** extravagant, uneconomical, wasteful; *opp* efficient. **2** (of a person) disorganized, incapable, ineffectual, inept; *opp* efficient

ineligible *adj* disqualified, inappropriate, out of the running *inf*, ruled out, unacceptable, undesirable, unfit, unqualified, unsuitable, unworthy; *opp* eligible

inept *adj* **1** (inept handling of the crisis) awkward, bungling, clumsy, gauche, heavy-handed, incompetent, ineffectual, unskillful. **2** (an inept remark) ill-timed, inappropriate, out of place, tactless, tasteless, unsuitable

inequality *n* bias, discrepancy, discrimination, lack of balance, imbalance, prejudice, unevenness, variation; *opp* equality

inert *adj* comatose, dead, dormant, immobile, inactive, inanimate, lifeless, motionless, passive, stationary, still, torpid, unresponsive; *opp* active

inertia *n* apathy, drowsiness, idleness, inactivity, laziness, lethargy, listlessness, passivity, sloth, stillness, torpor

inevitable *adj* assured, bound to happen, certain, destined, fixed, inescapable, inexorable, ordained, sure, unavoidable

inexcusable *adj* indefensible, outrageous, reprehensible, unforgivable, unjustifiable, unpardonable

inexpensive *adj* bargain, budget, cheap, dirt-cheap *inf*, economical, low-cost, low-priced, modest, reasonable; *opp* expensive

inexperienced *adj* amateur, immature, innocent, naive, new, raw, unpracticed, unqualified, unskilled, unsophisticated, untrained, wet behind the ears *inf*, young; *opp* experienced

inexplicable *adj* baffling, bewildering, incomprehensible, mysterious, mystifying, puzzling, strange, unaccountable, unfathomable, weird

infallible *adj* **1** (of a method) certain, dependable, foolproof, reliable, sound, sure, sure-fire *inf*, trustworthy, unfailing. **2** (of a person) faultless, flawless, perfect, without fault

infamous *adj* **1** (well-known) ill-famed, notorious, renowned, well-known. **2** (bad) disgraceful, dishonorable, disreputable, monstrous, outrageous, scandalous, shameful, shocking, villainous, wicked

infant *n* babe, baby, child, little child, toddler, tot

infatuated *adj* besotted, bewitched, captivated, foolproof, enamored, enchanted, fascinated, in love, obsessed, smitten *inf*, spellbound, swept off your feet, under sb's spell

infatuation *n* crush *inf*, fixation, mania, obsession, passion, thing *inf*

infect *v* **1** blight, contaminate, corrupt, poison, pollute, spoil, taint, touch. **2** pass on, spread, transmit

infection n 1 bacteria, bug *inf*, disease, epidemic, germs, septicemia, virus. 2 contamination, poison, pollution

infectious adj catching, contagious, spreading, transmissible, transmittable

infer v conclude, deduce, draw a conclusion, gather, presume, read between the lines, understand

inference n assumption, conclusion, conjecture, deduction, presumption

inferior adj 1 (in rank) humble, junior, lesser, lower, lowly, minor, secondary, second-class, subordinate, unimportant; *opp* superior. 2 (in quality) cheap, defective, faulty, imperfect, poor, second-rate, shoddy, substandard; *opp* good, superior

infertile adj arid, barren, childless, sterile, unfruitful, unproductive; *opp* fertile

infest v crawl over, flood, invade, overrun, plague, ravage, swarm

infested adj alive, crawling, overrun, plagued, ridden, swarming, teeming

infiltrate v creep in, enter secretly, filter through, insinuate into, intrude, penetrate, pervade, seep in, soak into, spy on, worm into

infinite adj bottomless, boundless, enormous, eternal, huge, immense, incalculable, inexhaustible, limitless, measureless, never-ending, numberless, unbounded, uncounted, unending, untold, vast, wide, without end, without number

infinity n endlessness, eternity, space, vastness

infirm adj decrepit, doddering, doddery, feeble, frail, weak; *opp* healthy, strong

infirmity n ailment, disability, disease, disorder, illness, impairment, sickness, weakness

inflame v anger, arouse, enrage, exasperate, excite, ignite, incense, infuriate, kindle, madden, provoke, rile, stir up, whip up

inflamed adj angry-looking, festering, fevered, hot, infected, red, septic, sore, swollen

inflammable adj combustible, flammable, incendiary, likely to burn, volatile

inflammation n abscess, boil, burning, heat, infection, irritation, painfulness, rash, redness, sore, soreness, swelling, tenderness

inflate v balloon, blow up, boost, dilate, enlarge, expand, increase, puff out, puff up, pump up, swell

inflexible adj 1 (of a person) adamant, firm, obstinate, pig-headed *inf*, strict, stubborn, unbending, uncompromising, unhelpful; *opp* flexible. 2 (of a material) firm, fixed, hard, inelastic, rigid, stiff, unyielding; *opp* flexible

inflict v apply, deal out, deliver, exact, impose, levy, wreak

influence n ascendancy, authority, clout *inf*, control, dominance, hold, importance, power, prestige, standing

influence v affect, bias, change, determine, have an effect, manipulate, persuade, prejudice, pull strings *inf*, put pressure on, sway

influential adj authoritative, important, instrumental, momentous, persuasive, potent, powerful, prestigious, significant, strong

influx n arrival, flood, flow, inflow,

inform v 1 advise, announce, enlighten, fill sb in in *inf*, give information, give sb the lowdown *inf*, leak, let sb know, notify, put sb in the picture *inf*, teach, tell. 2 (inform on sb) blab, blow the whistle *inf*, rat *sl*, sneak *inf*, split *inf*, squeal *inf*, tell *inf*, tell tales *inf*, tip off *inf*

informal adj 1 (of an event) casual, cozy, friendly, relaxed, simple, unceremonious, unofficial; *opp* formal. 2 (of a person) approachable, easygoing, free and easy, friendly, unpretentious. 3 (of language) chatty, colloquial, everyday, slangy *inf*; *opp* formal

information n advice, data, evidence, facts, info *inf*, intelligence, knowledge, news, statistics

informative adj chatty, educational, enlightening, factual, gossipy, helpful, illuminating, instructive, newsy, revealing; *opp* uninformative

informed adj 1 (keep sb informed) posted, primed, up-to-date, well-briefed. 2 (knowing a lot) clued in, enlightened, intelligent, knowledgable, well-informed, well-read

informer n betrayer, informant, sneak, spy, stool pigeon *inf*, tattletale *inf*, traitor

infrequent adj few and far between, irregular, occasional, once in a blue moon *inf*, rare, sporadic, uncommon, unusual; *opp* frequent

infringe v break, defy, disobey, disregard, flout, ignore, overstep

infuriate v aggravate *inf*, anger, bug *inf*, drive sb mad *inf*, enrage, exasperate, incense, irritate, madden, make sb's blood boil, make sb see red, outrage, provoke, rile

infuriating adj aggravating *inf*, annoying, exasperating, galling, irritating, maddening, provoking

ingenious adj brilliant, clever, crafty, cunning, imaginative, inventive, neat, original, smart

ingenuous adj guileless, honest, inexperienced, innocent, naive, simple, sincere, trusting, unsophisticated; *opp* crafty

ingredient n component, constituent, contents, element, factor, part

inhabit v colonize, dwell, live, make your home, occupy, populate, rent, reside, set up home, settle, stay, take up residence in

inhabitable adj habitable, in reasonable condition, livable in, livable, weatherproof; *opp* uninhabitable

inhabitant n dweller, tenant, occupant, householder, citizen, resident, inmate, lodger, native, townsperson

inhale v breathe in, draw in, suck in, take down into your lungs; *opp* exhale

inherent adj basic, built-in, congenital, essential, fundamental, hereditary, inbred, inbuilt, ingrained, inherited, innate, intrinsic, natural

inherit v accede to, be heir to, be left, be willed, come into, succeed to, take over

inheritance n bequest, birthright, endowment, estate, heritage, legacy

inhibit v check, constrain, curb, hold back, interfere with, prevent, repress, restrict, stem, straitjacket, suppress

inhibited adj constrained, embarrassed, guarded, reserved, self-conscious, shy, uptight *inf*; *opp* uninhibited

inhibition n angst, constraint, embarrassment, reserve, reticence, self-consciousness, shyness

inhospitable adj 1 (of a person) aloof, antisocial, cold, cool, hostile, unfriendly, unsociable, unwelcoming. 2 (of a landscape) barren, bleak, desolate, forbidding, godforsaken, hostile, uninviting

inhuman adj barbaric, barbarous, cruel, heartless, inhumane, merciless, pitiless, savage, unfeeling, unnatural

inhumane adj brutal, callous, cold-blooded, cruel, hard-hearted, heartless, inhuman, pitiless, unfeeling; *opp* humane

iniquitous adj corrupt, criminal, evil, immoral, infamous, outrageous, scandalous, unfair, unjust, wicked, wrong; *opp* fair, right

initial adj early, first, inaugural, introductory, opening; *opp* final

initiate v begin, commence, get under way, instigate, launch, originate, pioneer, prompt, set up, start, stimulate, trigger; *opp* terminate

initiation n admission, baptism, debut, enrollment, induction, initiation rite, introduction, investment, ordination, rite of passage

initiative n 1 ambition, creativity, drive, dynamism, enterprise, resourcefulness, self-motivation. 2 plan, program, project, proposal, scheme, suggestion. 3 advantage, first move, first step, lead, opening gambit

inject v 1 inoculate, mainline inf, shoot inf, shoot up inf, squirt in, vaccinate. 2 (inject cash into sth) add, bring in, infuse, insert, instill, introduce, put

injection n 1 booster, fix inf, immunization, inoculation, jab inf, shot inf, vaccination. 2 (an injection of cash) addition, introduction

injure v 1 (wound) cut, damage, disable, disfigure, fracture, harm, hurt, mutilate, wound. 2 (spoil) damage, harm, ruin, spoil, undermine, weaken

injured adj 1 (wounded) disabled, fractured, hurt, sore, wounded. 2 (spoiled) damaged, harmed, spoiled, undermined, weakened. 3 (an injured look) aggrieved, hurt, put out, reproachful, wounded

injury n bruise, cut, fracture, gash, laceration, sore, wound

injustice n bias, discrimination, favoritism, inequity, offense, one-sidedness, prejudice, unfairness, wrong; *opp* justice

inn n bed-and-breakfast, guesthouse, motel

innate adj built-in, inborn, inbuilt, inherent, inherited, instinctive, intrinsic, natural

inner adj 1 central, innermost, inside, interior, internal, middle; *opp* external, outer. 2 intimate, personal, private, secret; *opp* external, outer, public

innocence n 1 honesty, probity, purity, virtue; *opp* guilt. 2 gullibility, inexperience, naivety, simplicity

innocent adj 1 blameless, in the clear, not guilty; *opp* guilty. 2 childlike, credulous, gullible, inexperienced, naive; *opp* experienced

innovation n change, creativity, introduction, invention, new method, novelty, reform

innuendo n allusion, hint, implication, insinuation, rumor, suggestion, whisper

inquest n hearing, inquiry, investigation, probe, study

inquire v ask, explore, investigate, look into, make inquiries, query

inquiry n 1 examination, exploration, investigation, review, study, survey. 2 query, question, request

inquisitive adj curious, interested, interfering, meddlesome, nosy, prying

insane adj 1 crazy, deranged, disturbed, mad, mental, mentally disturbed, mentally ill, not all there, off your rocker inf, out of you mind, senile, unbalanced, unhinged; **opp** sane. 2 (an insane idea) crackpot inf, crazy, daft inf, foolish, harebrained, mad, ridiculous, stupid; **opp** sensible

insanity n 1 dementia, madness, mental disability, mental disorder, mental illness, senility. 2 (stupidity) folly, foolhardiness, lunacy, madness, stupidity

insatiable adj avid, greedy, inordinate, irrepressible, never satisfied, voracious

inscribe v carve, cut, engrave, etch, mark, sign, write

inscription n dedication, engraving, legend, lettering, message, signature, words

inscrutable adj blank, cryptic, deadpan, enigmatic, impenetrable, mysterious, poker-faced

insect n beetle, bug inf, creepy-crawly inf, fly

insecure adj anxious, exposed, lacking confidence, nervous, uncertain, unsafe, vulnerable; **opp** secure

insecurity n anxiety, lack of confidence, nervousness, uncertainty, vulnerability; **opp** security

insensitive adj crass, heartless, impervious, indifferent, oblivious, tactless, thoughtless, unaffected, uncaring, unfeeling, unmoved, unsympathetic, unthinking; **opp** sensitive

inseparable adj close, devoted, indivisible, inextricable, integral, intimate

insert v add, enclose, enter, implant, interject, introduce, pop in, put in, set in, slide in, stick in

inside adj 1 indoor, inner, innermost, interior, internal; **opp** outside. 2 (inside information) classified, confidential, secret

insidious adj furtive, pervasive, sneaking, sneaky, stealthy, subtle, surreptitious

insight n acumen, awareness, grasp, intuition, perception, perceptiveness, understanding, vision

insignificant adj inconsequential, irrelevant, minor, negligible, paltry, petty, trivial, unimportant; **opp** significant

insincere adj deceitful, dishonest, disloyal, evasive, false, feigned, hypocritical, lying, phony inf, put on inf, shifty, two-faced, underhand, untruthful; **opp** honest, open, sincere

insinuate v give the impression, hint, imply, intimate, suggest

insinuation n hint, implication, innuendo, intimation, slur, suggestion

insipid adj 1 anemic, bland, colorless, pale, washed-out, watery, weak, wishy-washy *inf.* 2 boring, dead, dull, flat, humdrum, lifeless, stale, unimaginative, uninteresting

insist *v* assert, be firm, demand, emphasize, persist, put your foot down *inf*, stand firm, stick to your guns *inf*, stress

insistent *adj* demanding, determined, dogged, forceful, incessant, urgent, persistent, unrelenting

insolence *n* cheek, disrespect, impertinence, impudence, insubordination, nerve, rudeness

insolent *adj* bad-mannered, cheeky, disrespectful, impertinent, impudent, offensive, rude

insoluble *adj* impenetrable, incomprehensible, inexplicable, mystifying, obscure, perplexing, puzzling, unanswerable, unsolvable; *opp* simple, straightforward

insolvent *adj* bankrupt, broke, failed, finished, gone bust *inf*, in debt, in the hands of the receivers, in the red, penniless, ruined

insomnia *n* sleeplessness

inspect *v* audit, check out, examine, give sth the once-over *inf*, go over, go through, look at, look over, scrutinize, study

inspection *n* audit, check, examination, once-over *inf*, scrutiny

inspector *n* auditor, checker, examiner, investigator

inspiration *n* 1 brainstorm, brainwave, bright idea, brilliant idea, idea, insight, revelation, thought. 2 creativity, encouragement, imagination, motivation, muse, stimulus

inspire *v* encourage, enthuse, fire sb's imagination, galvanize, motivate, prompt, spur, stimulate, trigger

inspired *adj* brilliant, dazzling, excellent, exciting, impressive, stunning, supreme, thrilling, wonderful

instability *n* 1 precariousness, shakiness, unsteadiness, wobbliness. 2 insecurity, precariousness, uncertainty, unpredictability, variability, volatility

install *v* ensconce, fit, fit in, inaugurate, instate, load, locate, position, put in place, put in, set up

installment *n* chapter, edition, episode, part, section

instance *n* case, example, occasion, occurrence, time

instant *adj* direct, fast, immediate, instantaneous, on-the-spot, quick, rapid, snap

instigate *v* bring about, encourage, incite, prompt, put into action, set in motion, set up, start, stir up, whip up

instill *v* implant, inculcate, infuse, ingrain, inject, teach

instinct *n* aptitude, feel, feeling, gut feeling, hunch, impulse, intuition, natural ability, predisposition, sixth sense

instinctive *adj* automatic, inborn, inbred, innate, intuitive, involuntary, natural, reflex

institute *n* academy, association, establishment, foundation, institution, organization, society

institute *v* bring about, develop, establish, found, initiate, introduce, launch, organize, originate, set in motion, set up, start

institution n 1 (organization) academy, association, establishment, foundation, home, hospital, institute, organization, society. 2 (custom) convention, custom, practice, tradition. 3 (the process of instituting) creation, establishment, formation, foundation, initiation, introduction

institutional adj bureaucratic, clinical, conventional, drab, formal, impersonal, orderly, regimented, unimaginative, unvarying

instruct v 1 (teach) coach, drill, educate, inform, teach, train. 2 (order) brief, direct, order, tell

instruction n 1 (order) brief, command, direction, injunction, order, requirement. 2 (education) classes, coaching, drilling, education, grounding, guidance, lessons, preparation, training, tuition

instructions n 1 brief, directions, orders. 2 directions, instruction booklet, manual, rule book

instructive adj edifying, educational, enlightening, helpful, illuminating, informative, revealing, useful

instructor n coach, guru, lecturer, mentor, teacher, trainer, tutor

instrument n 1 apparatus, appliance, contraption, device, gadget, implement, machine, musical instrument, tool, utensil. 2 dial, meter, gauge

instrumental adj a prime mover in, contributory, helpful, influential, involved, significant

insubordinate adj defiant, disobedient, disorderly, mutinous, rebellious, recalcitrant, undisciplined, unruly; **opp** obedient

insufficient adj inadequate, meager, not enough, pathetic inf, scant, scanty, skimpy; **opp** ample, plentiful

insular adj closed, cut off, independent, isolated, limited, narrow, parochial, remote, self-contained, self-sufficient, solitary

insulate v 1 cover, encase, lag, protect, put insulation in, soundproof. 2 cushion, cut off, protect, shelter, shield

insult n abuse, affront, insolence, libel, rudeness, slander, slight, slur; **opp** compliment

insult v abuse, affront, be rude to, call names, hurt sb's feelings, libel, offend, slander, snub; **opp** compliment, praise

insulting adj abusive, disparaging, insolent, offensive, rude, scurrilous

insurance n assurance, cover, indemnity, protection, provision, safeguard, surety

insure v cover, indemnify, protect, take out insurance, underwrite

insurgent n freedom fighter, guerrilla, rebel, revolutionary, terrorist

insurrection n coup, insurgency, mutiny, rebellion, revolt, uprising

intact adj in one piece, perfect, sound, unbroken, undamaged, unharmed, unscathed, whole

integral adj basic, constituent, essential, fundamental, indispensable, inherent, intrinsic, necessary, requisite

integrate v amalgamate, assimilate, combine, fuse, incorporate, interweave, knit, merge, mesh, unite

integrity n decency, honesty, honor, morality, principle, probity, rectitude, virtue

intellect n brain, intelligence, mind, reason, understanding

intellectual adj academic, bookish, cerebral, mental, scholarly, studious

intellectual n academic, don, egghead inf, member of the intelligentsia, scholar, thinker

intelligence n aptitude, brains, brilliance, cleverness, gumption inf, intellect, IQ, mental capacity, wit

intelligent adj brainy inf, bright, brilliant, clever, educated, gifted, knowledgable, learned, quick, sensible, sharp, smart, well-informed; opp slow, unintelligent

intelligible adj clear, comprehensible, lucid, meaningful, straightforward, unambiguous, understandable; opp incomprehensible, unintelligible

intend v aim, be determined, expect, have in mind, mean, plan

intense adj acute, deep, extreme, fierce, forceful, heavy, keen, passionate, powerful, severe, strong, vehement

intensify v add to, boost, deepen, emphasize, escalate, exacerbate, fuel, increase, inflame, magnify, reinforce, step up, strengthen

intensity n degree, depth, fierceness, force, power, severity, strength

intensive adj all-out, concentrated, detailed, exhaustive, in-depth, total

intent adj absorbed, attentive, concentrated, concentrating, engrossed, fixed, focused, rapt

intention n aim, ambition, goal, idea, objective, plan, purpose, wish

intentional adj calculated, conscious, deliberate, done on purpose, intended, meant, planned, premeditated, willful; opp accidental, unintentional

intercept v block, catch, cut off, head off, stop

interchangeable adj equivalent, exchangeable, identical, standard

intercourse n 1 (sexual) copulation, love-making, sex, sexual intercourse, sexual relations. 2 (social) association, connection, conversation, dealings, interaction

interest n 1 (attention) absorption, attention, curiosity, notice. 2 (be of interest) concern, consequence, note, relevance, significance. 3 (a leisure activity) hobby, leisure activity, pastime, pursuit. 4 (an appealing quality) appeal, attraction, charm, fascination. 5 (in sb's interest) advantage, benefit. 6 (on a loan or investment) charge, dividend, profit, rate, return

interest v amuse, appeal to, arouse sb's curiosity, attract, captivate, divert, fascinate, hold sb's attention, intrigue; opp bore

interested adj 1 absorbed, attracted, captivated, curious, engrossed, enthusiastic, fascinated, intent, into inf, keen; opp bored. 2 (an interested party) concerned, involved, partial

interesting adj absorbing, appealing, compelling, curious, entertaining, fascinating, intriguing, thought-provoking; opp dull, boring

interfere v 1 butt in, fiddle with, intrude, meddle, poke your nose in inf, pry. 2 interfere with frustrate, get in the way of, hamper, hinder, hold up, impede, inhibit, prevent

interference n intervention, intrusion,

meddling, nosiness inf, prying

interim adj acting, makeshift, pro tem, provisional, stopgap, temporary

interior adj central, core, inland, inner, inside, internal; **opp** exterior, outside

interlude n break, breather inf, breathing space, delay, intermission, interval, pause, recess, respite

intermediary n arbitrator, broker, go-between, mediator, negotiator

intermediate adj halfway, in-between, mid, midway, transitional

interminable adj constant, continual, endless, incessant, innumerable, long-winded, never-ending, perpetual, rambling, tedious, unending

intermission n break, interlude, interval, letup, lull, pause, respite

intermittent adj erratic, fitful, irregular, occasional, on-and-off, periodic, spasmodic, sporadic; **opp** regular

internal adj 1 central, core, inland, inner, inside, interior; **opp** external. 2 civil, domestic, home, in-house, national

international adj cosmopolitan, global, intercontinental, worldwide

interpret v clarify, crack, decipher, decode, elucidate, explain, expound, gloss, make sense of, read, translate, understand

interpretation n analysis, explanation, meaning, reading, sense, translation, understanding, version

interpreter n commentator, exponent, translator

interrogate v cross-examine, debrief, give sb the third degree, grill, put sb through the mill, question, quiz

interrogation n cross-examination,

debriefing, grilling, inquisition, investigation, probing, questioning, third degree

interrupt v 1 barge in inf, break in, butt in inf, chime in inf, disturb, heckle, interject, intervene, muscle in inf. 2 block, break off, break, bring to a standstill, cut off, obstruct, postpone, punctuate, suspend

interruption n break, delay, disruption, disturbance, gap, hitch, interval, intrusion, pause, postponement, stoppage, suspension

interval n 1 break, delay, gap, intermission, interlude, lull, pause, recess. 2 interim, intervening, time, meantime, period, space, spell, time

intervene v 1 (intervene in sth) butt in inf, get in the way, get involved, intercede, step in. 2 (sth intervenes) come between, happen, occur

interview n 1 (for a job or award) assessment, evaluation procedure, oral examination. 2 (discussion with sb) audience, consultation, dialogue, discussion, exchange, face-to-face, one-to-one, press conference, question and answer session

interview v cross-examine, grill, interrogate, put questions to, question, see, talk to, vet

interviewer n 1 assessor, examiner, interrogator, questioner. 2 (in the media) reporter, talk-show host

intimate adj 1 affectionate, close, familiar, informal, loving, sexual, warm. 2 confidential, personal, private, secret

intimate v communicate, hint, impart, imply, indicate, insinuate, let it be known, signal, suggest

intimidate v browbeat, bulldoze, bully, coerce, cow, frighten, lean on *inf*, menace, overawe, pressur, push around, put pressure on, scare, subdue, terrify, terrorize, threaten, twist sb's arm *inf*, tyrannize

intimidation n arm-twisting *inf*, browbeating, bullying, coercion, pressure, terror, threatening behavior

intolerable adj 1 impossible to bear, more than you can stand, unbearable, unendurable. 2 (of behavior) insupportable, offensive, unacceptable

intolerant adj bigoted, chauvinistic, dogmatic, narrow-minded, one-sided, prejudiced, racist, sexist, small-minded, uncharitable, xenophobic; *opp* tolerant

intransigent adj die-hard, hard-line, immovable, implacable, inflexible, intractable, obdurate, obstinate, stubborn, tough, uncompromising

intrepid adj adventurous, bold, brave, courageous, daring, fearless, game, plucky, resolute, stalwart

intricate adj complex, complicated, convoluted, detailed, elaborate, entangled, involved, tangled; *opp* simple

intrigue n 1 collusion, conspiracy, double-dealing, plot, scheme. 2 affair, liaison, love affair, romance

intrigue v 1 appeal to, arouse sb's curiosity, attract, beguile, captivate, capture sb's interest, charm, fascinate, interest, rivet. 2 connive, conspire, plot, scheme

intriguing adj appealing, captivating, exciting, fascinating, interesting,

riveting, tantalizing

intrinsic adj basic, built-in, central, congenital, essential, fundamental, inborn, inherent, native, natural, real

introduce v 1 acquaint, bring together, familiarize, make acquainted, make known, present. 2 begin, bring in, establish, found, inaugurate, initiate, introduce, institute, launch, organize, originate, pioneer, set in motion, set up, start, usher in. 3 announce, begin, lead into, lead up to, preface

introduction n 1 foreword, lead-in, opening, preamble, preface, preliminaries, prelude, prologue. 2 (first experience of sth) baptism, debut, inauguration, induction, initiation, launch, presentation. 3 (the start of sth) beginning, establishment, inauguration, institution, launch, start

introductory adj 1 first, inaugural, initial, opening, prefatory, preliminary. 2 basic, fundamental, preparatory, rudimentary

introspective adj brooding, contemplative, introverted, inward-looking, meditative, pensive

introverted adj introspective, inward-looking, reserved, self-absorbed, shy, withdrawn; *opp* extroverted

intrude v barge in, break in, butt in, crash, encroach, enter uninvited, interfere, interrupt, invade sb's privacy, invade sb's space, poke your nose in, stick your nose in, trespass

intruder n 1 burglar, housebreaker, invader, prowler, stalker, trespasser. 2 crasher, infiltrator, interloper, uninvited guest, unwelcome visitor

intrusion n encroachment, infringement, interference, interruption, invasion, trespass, violation

intrusive adj impertinent, interfering, meddlesome, nosy, officious, pushy inf, uncalled-for, unwanted

intuition n feeling, hunch, insight, instinct, perception, presentiment, sixth sense

invade v 1 (a place) assail, assault, attack, march into, occupy, overrun, penetrate, raid, storm, take over. 2 (sb's privacy) encroach, infringe, interfere, intrude, trespass on, violate

invader n aggressor, assailant, attacker, occupying force, raider, trespasser

invalid adj 1 ailing, bedridden, chronically sick, disabled, feeble, frail, ill, infirm, sick, weak. 2 (of an agreement) null and void, unusable, void, worthless; *opp* valid. 3 (of criticism) baseless, false, spurious, unfounded, unreasonable, wrong; *opp* valid

invalid n chronic patient, convalescent, patient, sick person, sufferer, valetudinarian

invalidate v annul, cancel, negate, nullify, overrule, overthrow, quash, repeal, rescind, revoke, terminate

invaluable adj beyond price, indispensable, irreplaceable, precious, priceless, worth its weight in gold

invasion n 1 (of a place) assault, attack, foray, incursion, inroad, offensive, onslaught, raid. 2 (of sb's privacy) breach, infringement, interference, intrusion, trespass, violation

invent v 1 coin, come up with, conceive,

contrive, create, design, devise, formulate, frame, improvise, originate, think up. 2 (a story) come up with, concoct, cook up inf, dream up, fabricate, make up, think up

invention n 1 (the act of inventing) coinage, contrivance, creation, design, devising, innovation, origination. 2 (sb's invention) brainchild, coinage, contraption, contrivance, construction, design, device. 3 (the ability to invent) creativeness, creativity, genius, imagination, ingenuity, inventiveness, resourcefulness. 4 (sth made-up) cock and-bull story, fabrication, falsehood, fiction, figment of sb's imagination, lie, story, tall tale

inventive adj creative, imaginative, ingenious, innovative, original, resourceful

inventor n architect, author, creator, designer, initiator, innovator, maker, originator, prime mover, producer

inventory n account, catalog, checklist, description, list, record, register, schedule, statement

inverse adj 1 opposite, reverse, transposed. 2 flip side inf, obverse, opposite side, other side, reverse

invert v capsize, overturn, reverse, transpose, turn upside down, upset, upturn

invest v 1 (in a business) buy shares, endow, fund, provide capital for, put money into, sink money into. 2 (money) expend, lay out, play the market, put in, put to work, speculate, spend, use profitably, venture

investigate v analyze, conduct an

inquiry, conduct a survey, consider, inquire into, examine, explore, go into *inf*, hold an inquiry, inspect, look into, make inquiries, probe, research, search, study, weigh up

investigation *n* analysis, inquiry, examination, exploration, inquest, inquiry, inspection, probe, research, review, scrutiny, search, study, survey

investigator *n* 1 examiner, inquirer, researcher. 2 detective, private detective, private eye, sleuth *inf*

investment *n* 1 risk, speculation, venture. 2 capital, finance, funding, stake money

invigorate *v* brace, energize, enliven, quicken, pep up, perk up, put new strength into, refresh, rejuvenate, stimulate, strengthen

invigorating *adj* bracing, enlivening, exhilarating, refreshing, rejuvenating, revitalizing, strengthening, tonic

invincible *adj* impregnable, indestructible, indomitable, insuperable, invulnerable, unassailable, unbeatable, unconquerable, unstoppable; *opp* vulnerable

invisible *adj* camouflaged, concealed, disguised, hidden, indiscernible, obscured, out of sight, unseen; *opp* visible

invitation *n* 1 asking, call, invite *inf*, request, summons. 2 encouragement, enticement, incitement, overture, provocation, temptation, welcome

invite *v* 1 ask, request sb's company, summon. 2 appeal for, ask for, request, seek, solicit. 3 (invite disaster) bring sth on yourself, make sth liable to

happen, provoke

inviting *adj* alluring, attractive, captivating, delightful, engaging, enticing, pleasing, seductive, tempting, warm, welcoming, winning

invoice *n* account, bill, statement of charges

invoke *v* 1 appeal to, beg, call for, call upon, entreat, implore, pray, solicit, supplicate. 2 (invoke a law) apply, implement, put into effect, resort to, use

involuntary *adj* 1 automatic, knee-jerk *inf*, instinctive, mechanical, spontaneous, unintentional, unthinking. 2 against sb's will, compulsory, obligatory, reluctant, unwilling

involve *v* 1 entail, imply, mean, necessitate, require. 2 comprise, bring in, draw in, hold, include, incorporate, take in. 3 affect, concern, interest, touch

involved *adj* 1 complex, complicated, confused, confusing, convoluted, intricate, knotty, mixed up, tangled; *opp* simple. 2 (involved in sth) busy, concerned, interested, participating, taking part. 3 (involved in a crime) associated, implicated, incriminated

involvement *n* association, commitment, concern, connection, interest, participation

ironic *adj* 1 derisive, double-edged, mocking, sarcastic, sardonic, satirical, wry. 2 paradoxical

irony *n* 1 double meaning, mockery, sarcasm, satire. 2 paradox

irrational *adj* 1 (of an idea) absurd, crackpot *inf*, groundless, illogical, implausible, ridiculous, senseless, unreasonable, unsound, wild, without foundation; *opp* sensible. 2 (of a person) confused, crazy, demented, illogical, insane, mad, muddled, muddle-headed, unintelligent, unstable, unthinking

irreconcilable *adj* 1 (of ideas) at odds, clashing, conflicting, contrary, diametrically opposed, incompatible. 2 (of enemies) hard-line, implacable, inflexible, intransigent, uncompromising

irrefutable *adj* beyond doubt, certain, conclusive, incontestable, incontrovertible, indisputable, indubitable, sure, unanswerable, undeniable

irregular *adj* 1 abnormal, eccentric, extraordinary, odd, peculiar, quirky, unusual. 2 (in shape) asymmetric, bumpy, crooked, craggy, jagged, lumpy, ragged, rough, uneven; *opp* regular. 3 erratic, fitful, fluctuating, haphazard, intermittent, occasional, patchy, random, shaky, spasmodic, sporadic, uneven, unsteady, varying; *opp* regular. 4 (not honest) against the rules, illegal, improper, out of order, unconventional, unofficial, unorthodox. 5 (of troops) guerrilla, mercenary, partisan, resistance, underground

irregularity *n* 1 aberrance, abnormality, deviation, eccentricity, oddity, peculiarity. 2 (an irregularity on a surface) asymmetry, bump, bumpiness, hole, lump, pothole, roughness, unevenness. 3 fluctuation, inconsistency, inconstancy, patchiness, shakiness, unevenness, unsteadiness, variability; *opp* regularity. 4 (dishonest behavior) breach, malpractice,

unconventionality, unorthodoxy

irrelevant *adj* beside the point, extraneous, immaterial, inapplicable, inappropriate, neither here not there, nothing to do with it, out of place, unconnected, unrelated; *opp* relevant

irreparable *adj* beyond repair, incurable, irremediable, irreversible, irretrievable, past mending, unalterable

irresistible *adj* 1 compelling, imperative, inevitable, inexorable, overpowering, overwhelming, powerful, unavoidable. 2 alluring, enticing, fascinating, seductive, tempting

irresponsible *adj* careless, feckless, flighty, immature, negligent, reckless, shiftless, thoughtless, unreliable, untrustworthy, wild; *opp* responsible

irreverent *adj* 1 blasphemous, heretical, impious, irreligious, profane, sacrilegious, ungodly. 2 cheeky, derisive, disrespectful, flippant, impertinent, impudent, rude; *opp* respectful

irrigate *v* flood, spray, sprinkle, water, wet

irritable *adj* bad-tempered, cantankerous, crabby *inf*, cross, crotchety, fractious, grumpy, impatient, irascible, peevish, petulant, querulous, short-tempered, tetchy, touchy

irritate *v* 1 anger, annoy, bother, drive sb mad, drive sb up the wall *inf*, exasperate, get on sb's nerves, get sb's back up, nettle, pester, provoke, ruffle, try sb's patience, vex. 2 (irritate the skin) chafe, cause irritation, itch, rub, tickle

irritated *adj* 1 annoyed, cross, exasperated, nettled, ruffled, vexed. 2 (of skin) inflamed, itchy

irritating *adj* annoying, irksome,

maddening, nagging, provoking, troublesome, trying, upsetting

irritation *n* 1 anger, annoyance, exasperation, impatience, irritability, vexation. 2 (on the skin) inflammation, itch, rash

island *n* isle, islet

isolate *v* cloister, cordon off, cut off, detach, disconnect, exclude, insulate, keep apart, quarantine, segregate, separate, sequester, shut out, single out

isolated *adj* 1 (of a person) alone, excluded, forlorn, lonely, segregated, separated, solitary. 2 (of a place) cut off, hidden, lonely, off the beaten track, out of the way, remote, secluded. 3 (of an incident, example) abnormal, anomalous, exceptional, freak, single, solitary, unique

issue *n* 1 affair, argument, bone of contention, controversy, matter, point, problem, question, subject, topic. 2 edition, impression, installment, number, printing, version. 3 conclusion, consequence, effect, end, outcome, result, upshot *inf*. 4 children, descendants, offspring

issue *v* 1 circulate, distribute, emit, give out, publish, put out, release. 2 come out, emanate, emit, exude, flow, gush, ooze, pour out, seep. 3 appear, come out, emerge, leave

itch *n* 1 irritation, itchiness, prickling, tickling, tingle. 2 craving, desire, hankering, hunger, longing, thirst, yearning, yen

itch *v* 1 be itchy, irritate, prickle, tickle, tingle. 2 (be itching to do sthg) ache, burn, crave, hanker, hunger, long,

wish, yearn

item *n* 1 account, article, bit, feature, piece, report, story. 2 aspect, component, consideration, detail, element, ingredient, matter,. 3 (on a list) entry, record. 4 (for sale) article, lot, object, thing

itinerary *n* journey, plan, program, schedule, timetable, travel arrangements, travel plan

jab n 1 dig, nudge, poke, prod, punch, stab. 2 injection, inoculation, vaccination

jab v dig, elbow, nudge, poke, prod, punch, stab, thrust

jacket n 1 (garment) anorak, blazer, cardigan, sports jacket. 2 case, casing, covering, envelope, folder, sheath, wrapper

jagged adj angular, barbed, chipped, craggy, indented, irregular, notched, ragged, rough, serrated, sharp, spiky, toothed, uneven, zigzag

jail n can, cooler inf, inside, jailhouse, lockup, pen inf, penitentiary, prison, slammer inf

jail v confine, detain, immure, imprison, incarcerate, intern, lock up, send down, send to jail, send to prison

jailer n guard, keeper, prison officer, warden

jam n 1 conserve, jelly, marmalade, preserve. 2 blockage, bottleneck, congestion, gridlock, hold-up, obstruction, stoppage, traffic jam. 3 crowd, crush, press, squeeze, swarm, throng. 4 (be in a jam) dilemma, fix, hole, hot water, plight, predicament, quandary, straits, tight spot, trouble

jam v 1 block, clog, congest, cram, fill, obstruct, overcrowd, pack, stop up, stuff. 2 (people jam into a place) cram, crowd, crush, pack, pack, ram, squash, squeeze. 3 (jam sth in) force, press, ram, thrust, wedge. 4 become stuck, stall, stick, stop

jangle v 1 clang, clank, clash, clatter, clink, jingle, rattle, vibrate. 2 (on sb's nerves) disturb, grate on, irritate, jar

jar n bottle, container, crock, pot, tub, urn

jar v 1 jerk, jog, jolt, rattle, shake, shock, vibrate. 2 be at odds with, clash, conflict, oppose. 3 annoy, disturb, grate, grate on, irritate, jangle, offend, upset

jargon n 1 argot, cant, dialect, idiom, language, patois, slang, vernacular. 2 (of a profession) buzz words, language, slang, specialized language, technical terms, usage

jaundiced adj bitter, cynical, distrustful, envious, pessimistic, resentful, skeptical, suspicious

jaunt n airing, excursion, expedition, outing, ramble, stroll, trip

jealous adj 1 bitter, covetous, envious, green with envy, grudging, jaundiced, resentful. 2 distrustful, possessive. 3 careful, on guard, protective, vigilant, watchful, wary

jeer v boo, deride, gibe, heckle, hiss, laugh, make fun of, mock, ridicule, scoff, scorn, sneer, taunt

jeopardize v chance, endanger, gamble with, imperil, put at risk, put in jeopardy, risk, take a chance with, threaten

jeopardy n in jeopardy at risk, compromised, endangered, imperiled, in danger, in peril, jeopardized, threatened, under threat

jerk v 1 pull, shake, snatch, tug, wag, waggle, wrench, yank. 2 (move unevenly) jolt, jump, lurch, rattle, shake, twitch

jerky adj disjointed, fitful, irregular, jumpy, lurching, spasmodic, staccato, twitchy

jest n gag, joke, lampoon, laugh inf, prank, practical joke

jest v banter, clown, crack a joke, joke, kid inf, pull sb's leg, quip, tease

jester n buffoon, clown, comedian, comedienne, comic, entertainer, fool, funny man, joker

jet n cascade, flow, fountain, rush, spurt, stream

jetty n breakwater, landing stage, marina, mole, mooring, pier, wharf

jewel n 1 gem, gemstone, item of jewelry, ornament, piece of jewelry, precious stone, semi-precious stone, stone. 2 (types of jewel) diamond, emerald, lapis lazuli, onyx, pearl, ruby

jewelry n 1 adornments, costume jewelry, jewels, regalia, trinkets, valuables. 2 (item of jewelry) anklet, bracelet, brooch, earring, medallion, necklace, pendant, ring, tiara

jingle v chime, chink, clink, jangle, ping, ring, sound, tinkle

jinx n bad luck, curse, evil eye, gremlin, malediction, spell

job n 1 (paid employment) appointment, employment, opening, position, post, situation, vacancy, work. 2 (type of work) career, duties, occupation, business, line, profession, trade, vocation. 3 (thing to be done) chore, commission, errand, matter, mission, odd job, piece of work, project, task, undertaking

jobless adj at a loose end, between jobs, idle, on the dole inf, out of a job, out of work, redundant, seeking employment, unemployed, unoccupied, workless

jog v 1 canter, run, run-walk, shuffle, toddle, trot, waddle, warm up. 2 (hit sth lightly) agitate, brush, bump, jar, jolt, jostle, knock, nudge, prod, push, set in motion, shake, tap

join n boundary, connection, dividing line, edge, joint, junction, meeting point, seam

join v 1 (join two things) attach, bind, bring together, connect, join up, merge, put together, tie, unify, unite; opp separate. 2 (two things join) come together, connect, converge, join up, meet, merge, unite; opp separate.

3 (join a club, the army) become a member of, enlist, enroll, join up, register, subscribe; *opp* leave

joint *adj* collective, common, communal, concerted, cooperative, mutual, shared

joint *n* **1** angle, articulation, binding, connection, join, junction. **2** (in the body) ankle, elbow, hip, knee, knuckle, shoulder, wrist

joke *n* crack *inf*, funny story, gag, jape, jest, laugh *inf*, one-liner, practical joke, prank, punch line, quip, riddle, shaggy-dog story, sketch, spoof, story, wisecrack, witticism

joke *v* banter, clown, crack a joke, jest, josh, kid *inf*, laugh, pull sb's leg, quip, tease, wisecrack

joker *n* clown, comedian, comedienne, comic, funny man, jester, satirist, wit

jolly *adj* bright, cheerful, cheery, happy, hearty, jovial, joyful, laughing, merry, pleasant

jolt *v* agitate, bump, jar, jerk, jog, knock, nudge, push, shake, shock, shove

jostle *v* brush, crowd, elbow, manhandle, push, push out of the way, shove

journal *n* bulletin, diary, newsletter, newspaper, magazine, periodical, record, review

journalist *n* broadcaster, columnist, critic, correspondent, cub reporter, editor, feature writer, hack *slang*, newshound, press man, reporter, reviewer, writer

journey *n* crossing, drive, excursion, expedition, flight, hike, holiday, odyssey, passage, pilgrimage, ride, trek, trip, voyage, walk

joy *n* bliss, delight, ecstasy, elation, euphoria, happiness, joie de vivre, jubilation, pleasure, rapture, rejoicing; *opp* dismay

joyful *adj* blissful, cheerful, delighted, ecstatic, elated, euphoric, glad, happy, in seventh heaven, jolly, jovial, joyous, jubilant, merry, on cloud nine *inf*, on top of the world, rapturous; *opp* miserable

jubilee *n* anniversary, celebration, centenary, centennial, festival, festivities, royal occasion

judge *n* **1** circuit judge, jurist, justice, magistrate, your Honor. **2** (in a competition) adjudicator, arbiter, assessor, official, referee, umpire

judge *v* **1** appraise, assess, calculate, consider, decide, estimate, evaluate, form an opinion, gauge, guess, weigh, weigh up. **2** (judge a competition) adjudge, adjudicate, arbitrate, decide, referee, umpire. **3** (in law) find, hear, pass sentence, preside, pronounce, rule, sentence, sit in judgment, try

judgment *n* **1** (official) adjudication, arbitration, award, decision, finding, ruling, sentence, verdict. **2** (sb's judgment of sth) appreciation, appraisal, assessment, calculation, consideration, estimate, estimation, evaluation, guess, opinion, view. **3** (ability to make the right decision) common sense, discretion, discrimination, good sense, level-headedness, maturity, objectivity, sense of proportion, sensitivity, sobriety, tact. **4** (mental ability) awareness, balance of your mind, clear head, control, co-ordination, faculties, mind, perception, self-control, senses, sobriety

judicial *adj* constitutional, institutional, juridical, legal, official, statutory

jug *n* carafe, ewer, pitcher, pot, urn, vase, vessel

juggle *v* (juggle your responsibilities) combine, keep all your balls in the air, manipulate, play off, prioritize, reorder, shuffle, swap, switch

juice *n* cordial, crush, essence, gravy, liquid, mineral, sap, squash

juicy *adj* dripping, moist, ripe, sappy, squashy, squelchy *inf*, succulent, watery

jumble *n* chaos, confusion, heap, mixture, muddle, randomness

jumble *v* confuse, entangle, mix, mix up, muddle, shuffle, tangle

jump *n* 1 bounce, bound, dive, hop, leap, skip, spring, takeoff, vault. 2 high jump, long jump, pike, pole vault, ski-jump, straddle, triple jump, parachute jump. 3 (thing jumped over) bar, barrier, ditch, fence, hurdle, obstacle, wall

jump *v* 1 bounce, bound, dive, hop, leap, prance, rise, skip, soar, spring, take off, vault. 2 (over an obstacle) clear, cross, jump over, leap, leapfrog, straddle, traverse. 3 (with fright) flinch, jump out of your skin *inf*, recoil, shiver, start, twitch

jumpy *adj* agitated, edgy *inf*, fidgety, jittery, nervy *inf*, nervous, on edge, on tenterhooks, restless, twitchy *inf*

junction *n* crossroads, fork, intersection

juncture *n* moment, moment in time, occasion, point, position, present time, situation, stage

jungle *n* bush, forest, rain forest, tropical forest, vegetation

junior *adj* inferior, lowly, low-ranking, second, subordinate, young, younger; *opp* senior

junk *n* antiques, bric-a-brac, odds and ends, refuse, rubbish, scrap, trash

jurisdiction *n* authority, brief, command, competence, control, department, orbit, power, remit

just *adj* 1 (of a decision) equitable, fair, justifiable, justified, legitimate, right; *opp* unjust. 2 (of a person) equitable, evenhanded, fair, fair-minded, honest, honorable, impartial, objective, respectful, righteous, unbiased, upright; *opp* unjust

justice *n* 1 (legal concept) constitutionality, jurisprudence, law, lawfulness, legality, legitimacy, right. 2 (quality of being just) decency, equity, fairness, fair play, impartiality, plain dealing, rectitude, respect; *opp* injustice. 3 (after being wronged) amends, compensation, expiation, redress, reparation, retribution, revenge

justifiable *adj* defensible, fair, just, justified, legitimate; *opp* unjustifiable

justify *v* account for, defend, excuse, exonerate, explain, legitimize, vindicate

jut *v* jut out, overhang, poke out, project, protrude, stick out

juvenile *adj* 1 adolescent, immature, underage, young, youthful.

2 (juvenile attitude) adolescent,
childish, immature, infantile,
puerile, silly

juvenile *n* adolescent, child, minor,
young person, youngster, youth

juxtapose *v* compare, contrast, draw
parallels, place side by side

keen *adj* 1 ardent, avid, crazy about *inf*, desirous, eager, earnest, enthusiastic, fervent, mad *inf*, passionate.
2 (a keen sense of smell) acute, astute, penetrating, sensitive, sharp, shrewd, strong

keep *n* 1 castle, fort, inner sanctum, stronghold, tower. 2 (pay for your keep) bed and board, living, maintenance, means, survival

keep *v* 1 conserve, detain, guard, have, hold, own, possess, preserve, retain.
2 (keep a person) care for, feed, look after, maintain, pay for, nurture, provide for, subsidize, sustain, take care of.
3 (keep doing sth) carry on, continue, go on, keep on, persevere, persist.
4 (keep a promise) abide by, adhere to, fulfill, honor, observe, realize, respect.
5 **keep up** conserve, hold, maintain, look after, persevere with, preserve

keeper *n* caretaker, curator, guard, guardian, jailer, warden

key *adj* crucial, essential, important, indispensable, major, vital

key *n* acid test, answer, clue, criterion, explanation, solution

kick *v* 1 boot *inf*, drive, pass, shoot, strike. 2 (kick a habit) beat *inf*, forswear, give up, quit, renounce. 3 **kick out** banish, chuck out *inf*, dismiss, eject, exclude, exile, expel, send out, throw out, vote out

kidnap *v* abduct, capture, hold to ransom, seize, snatch, take hostage

kill *v* assassinate, butcher, cut down, destroy, do sb in, electrocute, eliminate, execute, exterminate, gas, gun down, hang, massacre, murder, poison, slaughter, put down, put out of its misery, put to death, put to sleep, shoot, slay, smother, stone, strangle, suffocate

killer *n* assassin, butcher, executioner, gunman, hangman, murderer, murderess, poisoner, strangler

killing *n* 1 assassination, atrocity, butchery, capital punishment, death, death penalty, electrocution, elimination, euthanasia, execution, extermination, hanging, homicide, manslaughter, massacre, mercy killing, murder, shooting, slaying, strangulation, suffocation. 2 (make a killing) bonanza, fortune, gain, profit, success, windfall

kin *n* blood, family, kindred, kinsfolk, kinsmen, kinswomen, kith, relations, relatives, you and yours

kind *adj* benevolent, compassionate, considerate, fair, friendly, generous, helpful, kindhearted, kindly, obliging, sympathetic, understanding, warm, welcoming, well-meaning; *opp* cruel, unkind

kind *n* category, class, sort, species, type

kindle *v* 1 (kindle a fire) get going, ignite, light, set fire to, set light to, start. 2 (kindle emotions) excite, inspire, rouse, stimulate, stir, stir up

kindness *n* benevolence, compassion, consideration, fairness, friendliness, generosity, kindheartedness, sympathy, warmth; *opp* cruelty, unkindness

king *n* crown, head of state, His Majesty, liege, lord, monarch, ruler, sire

kingdom *n* country, domain, fiefdom, land, monarchy, realm, territory

kiosk *n* booth, box, office, pavilion, stall, window

kiss *v* neck *inf*, peck, smooch *inf*

kit *n* 1 (items for making or doing sth) apparatus, implements, outfit, set, tools, utensils. 2 (items carried or worn) belongings, clothes, equipment, gear *inf*, stuff *inf*, tackle, things

knack *n* ability, aptitude, gift, habit, instinct, talent, trick

knead *v* manipulate, massage, press, pummel, roll, squeeze, work

kneel *v* be on your knees, fall to your knees, genuflect, get down on your knees, kneel down

knife *n* blade, carving knife, cutter, dagger, penknife, sheath knife, stiletto

knit *v* bind, intertwine, make, purl, sew, stitch, weave

knob *n* 1 button, doorknob, handle, lever, switch. 2 boss, bulge, bump, lump, nub, protuberance, protrusion

knock *v* 1 bump, collide, hit, jog, push, strike, tap. 2 **knock down** cut down, demolish, fell, floor, pull down, push over, raze, run over. 3 **knock out** (make sb lose consciousness) anesthetize, chloroform, floor, knock unconscious, KO *inf*, put to sleep. 4 **knock out** (from a competition) beat, defeat, eliminate, overcome, put out, vanquish

knot *n* 1 bow, granny knot, loop, nexus, reef knot, tangle. 2 (knot of people) bunch, circle, cluster, gaggle, gathering, group, huddle, ring

knot *v* bind, entangle, tangle, tie, tie up

know *v* 1 (know a fact) be aware, be certain, be conscious, be familiar with, be informed, be sure, comprehend, understand. 2 (know a person, place) be a friend of, be acquainted with, be familiar with, be friends with, get to know, have been introduced to, have met

knowing *adj* 1 (a knowing grin, remark) conspiratorial, meaningful, sardonic, self-satisfied, sly, superior, worldly-wise, wry. 2 calculated, conscious, deliberate, intended, intentional, purposeful, willful

knowledgable *adj* aware, brainy *inf*, clever, informed, learned, intelligent, scholarly, well-informed; *opp* ignorant

knowledge *n* 1 awareness, certainty, cognition, comprehension, consciousness, erudition, intelligence, learning, understanding. 2 (things that are known) data, facts, findings, information, learning, lore, observations, scholarship, science

label *n* **1** brand, flag, marker, stamp, sticker, tab, tag, ticket. **2** category, classification, designation, epithet, heading, name, pigeonhole, stigma, term

label *v* **1** brand, flag, mark, stamp, tag. **2** brand, categorize, classify, designate, name, pigeonhole, stigmatize, term

labor *n* **1** (work) chores, drudgery, effort, grind *inf*, hard labor, hard work, manual work, strain, toil, work. **2** (workers) hands, laborers, manpower, workers, workforce, workmen. **3** (giving birth) birth pangs, childbirth, contractions, delivery

labor *v* **1** exert yourself, slave, strain, strive, sweat, toil, work, work your fingers to the bone, work your socks off *inf* . **2** (labor a point) behavior, dwell on, elaborate, emphasize, get bogged down on, get stuck on, overdo, over-elaborate, overemphasize, repeat, stress

laborer *n* blue-collar worker, hand, manual worker, unskilled worker, worker, workman

laborious *adj* difficult, hard, labored, painstaking, tedious, wearisome; *opp* easy

lace *n* crochet, embroidery, filigree, net, string

lace *v* **1** (lace a shoe) attach, bind, close, do up, fasten, secure, strap, string, thread, tie. **2** (lace a drink) add to, blend, fortify, mix, spike

lack *n* absence, dearth, deficiency, insufficiency, need, scarceness, scarcity, shortage, want; *opp* abundance

lack *v* be lacking in, be short of, be without, have need of, miss, need, require, want

lacking *adj* **1** (the system is sadly lacking) defective, flawed, impaired, inadequate, unsatisfactory, weak; *opp* satisfactory. **2** (be lacking in social skills) missing, needing, wanting, without

laden *adj* burdened, charged, encumbered, hampered, heavily laden, loaded, piled high, weighed down, weighted

lady *n* **1** female, girl, lass *inf*, wife *inf*, woman; *opp* gentleman. **2** baroness, countess, dame, duchess, marchioness, noblewoman, peeress, viscountess; *opp* lord

ladylike *adj* courtly, cultivated, dainty, decorous, elegant, genteel, gracious, modest, polished, polite, proper, refined, respectable, well-bred, well-mannered; *opp* coarse

lag *v* bring up the rear, dawdle, delay, dilly dally *inf*, drag your feet, drop behind, fall behind, go slow, hang about, hang back, idle, linger, loiter, saunter, straggle, trail; *opp* lead

laid-back *adj* at ease, calm, casual, easy-going, nonchalant, relaxed, unflappable, unhurried; *opp* anxious

lair *n* burrow, covert, den, earth, hideout, hole, nest, refuge, resting place, retreat, shelter

lake *n* lagoon, lido, loch, pool, pond, reservoir, sea, tarn, water

lame *adj* 1 crippled, disabled, handicapped, hobbling, limping. 2 (a lame excuse) feeble, flimsy, inadequate, pathetic, poor, tame, thin, unconvincing, weak; *opp* convincing

lament *v* 1 (lament sth) bemoan, bewail, complain, deplore, regret; *opp* praise. 2 (lament sb's death) beat your breast, cry, grieve, mourn, shed tears, sorrow, wail, weep; *opp* rejoice

lamp *n* lantern, light, nightlight, streetlight, table lamp, torch

land *n* 1 (back on land) coast, dry land, earth, ground, shore, solid ground, terra firma; *opp* sea, space. 2 (fertile land) dirt, earth, ground, loam, soil. 3 (own a lot of land) acres, estate, grounds, property, realty. 4 (a distant land) country, district, nation, province, region, state, territory, tract

land *v* alight, arrive, berth, come ashore, come in to land, debark, disembark, dismount, dock, touch down; *opp* set off

landlord *n* 1 host, hostess, hotelier, innkeeper, landlady, restaurateur; *opp* customer. 2 landowner, manager, manageress, owner, proprietor; *opp* tenant

landmark *n* 1 feature, guidepost, identification, monument. 2 (landmark in sth's history) critical point, milestone, new era, turning point, watershed

landscape *n* aspect, countryside, outlook, panorama, prospect, rural scene, scene, scenery, view, vista

landslide *n* avalanche, landslip, rockfall

language *n* 1 communication, conversation, discourse, expression, parlance, speaking, speech, talk, talking, verbal expression, vocalization, words. 2 (a particular language) argot, dialect, idiom, jargon, lingo *inf*, patois, tongue, vernacular, vocabulary. 3 (the language of a novel) expression, phraseology, phrasing, style, terminology, vocabulary, wording

languish *v* decline, droop, fade, fail, faint, flag, go downhill *inf*, stagnate, suffer, waste, weaken, wilt, wither; *opp* flourish

lank *adj* 1 (of hair) drooping, dull, lifeless, limp, long, lusterless, straggling, straight; *opp* bouncy. 2 (of a person) bony, emaciated, gangling, gaunt, lanky, lean, scraggy, scrawny, skinny, slender, slim, tall, thin; *opp* chubby

lanky *adj* awkward, gangling, lank, lean, scrawny, skinny, tall, thin, ungraceful; *opp* chubby

lap *n* 1 circle, circuit, coarse, loop, orbit, revolution, round, tour. 2 (sit on sb's lap) knee

lap *v* 1 (waves lapping the shore) ripple, slap, slosh, splash, swish, wash. 2 (a cat lapping milk) drink, gulp, guzzle, lick, sip, sup

lapse *v* 1 decline, deteriorate, diminish, drop, fail, fall, go downhill *inf*, go to pot *inf*, sink, slide, slip; *opp* improve. 2 (a passport lapses) become invalid, become void, end, expire, finish, run out, stop, terminate

lapse n blunder, error, failing, fault, indiscretion, mistake, omission, oversight, slip, slip-up inf

large adj ample, big, broad, bulky, colossal, considerable, elephantine, enormous, extensive, generous, giant, gigantic, grand, great, huge, immense, jumbo inf, king-size, liberal, lofty, massive, mighty, monumental, roomy, sizable, spacious, sweeping, substantial, vast, wide; **opp** small

lash n blow, hit, strike, stripe, stroke, thwack inf, wallop inf, whack inf, whip

lash v 1 (lash one thing to another) bind, fasten, hitch, join, leash, rope, secure, strap, tether, tie. 2 (rain lashing the windows) batter, beat, buffet, dash, drum, hammer, hit, knock, pound, smack, strike. 3 (lash sb) beat, birch, flog, horsewhip, strike, thrash, wallop inf, whack inf, whip

last adj 1 closing, concluding, final, terminal, ultimate; **opp** first. 2 latest, most recent; **opp** first. 3 (last in a line) back, end, final, hindmost, rearmost; **opp** front

last v abide, carry on, continue, endure, go on, hold, keep, linger, live, persist, remain, survive; **opp** end

lasting adj abiding, ceaseless, constant, continuing, durable, enduring, eternal, long-lasting, long-term, ongoing, permanent, perpetual, unceasing, undying, unending; **opp** temporary

late adj 1 behind, behind schedule, behind time, belated, delayed, overdue, slow, tardy; **opp** early. 2 (the late Mr. Smith) dead, deceased,

defunct, departed

lately adv latterly, of late, recently; **opp** previously

latitude n carte blanche, elbow-room inf, freedom, free play, indulgence, leeway, liberty, license; **opp** restriction

latter adj 1 last-mentioned, later, second; **opp** former. 2 (the latter part) closing, concluding, end, final, last; **opp** opening

laugh n 1 belly laugh inf, chortle, chuckle, giggle, guffaw, roar of laughter, snigger, titter. 2 (sb is a laugh) card inf, case inf, hoot, scream. 3 (sth is a laugh) fun, lark, scream

laugh v 1 be in stitches, burst out laughing, chortle, chuckle, crack up inf, giggle, guffaw, roll about, snigger, split your sides, titter. 2 **laugh at** deride, jeer, lampoon, make fun of, mock, ridicule, scoff, send up, taunt, tease

laughable adj absurd, derisory, derisive, ludicrous, outrageous, preposterous, ridiculous, risible; **opp** reasonable

laughing stock n butt, dupe, everybody's fool, fair game, fall guy inf, figure of fun, target, victim

laughter n 1 chortling, chuckling, giggling, guffawing, laughing, laughs, sniggering, tittering. 2 amusement, entertainment, glee, hilarity, hysterics, light-heartedness, merriment, mirth

launch v 1 (launch a new business) begin, commence, embark, establish, get going, inaugurate, initiate, instigate, introduce, open, set up, start. 2 (launch a rocket) cast, catapult, discharge, dispatch, fire, hurl, let fly, project, propel, send off, set off, shoot, throw

lavatory n bathroom, convenience,

john *inf*, latrine, little boy's room *inf*,
little girl's room *inf*, powder room, the
gents, the ladies, toilet, urinal,
washroom

lavish *adj* exuberant, lush, luxuriant,
luxurious, opulent, sumptuous;
opp simple. 2 (lavish with sth)
bountiful, extravagant, free, generous,
liberal, munificent, open-handed,
unselfish, unstinting; *opp* mean

law *n* act, bill, bylaw, code,
commandment, covenant, decree,
directive, edict, enactment, injunction,
mandate, order, ordinance, regulation,
rule, statute

law-abiding *adj* compliant, decent,
dutiful, good, honest, lawful, obedient,
peaceable, respectable, upright, well-
behaved; *opp* criminal, trouble-making

lawful *adj* allowable, allowed, authorized,
constitutional, just, legal, legalized,
legitimate, permissible, permitted,
prescribed, proper, rightful, sanctioned,
valid; *opp* unlawful

lawsuit *n* action, case, dispute,
indictment, industrial tribunal,
litigation, proceedings, prosecution,
suit, trial

lawyer *n* advocate, attorney, counsel,
legal advisor, legal practitioner,
member of the bar

lax *adj* careless, casual, neglectful,
negligent, remiss, slack, slipshod,
unreliable, vague

lay *adj* 1 (lay preacher) nonclerical,
non-ordained, part-time, secular;
opp ordained. 2 (lay person) amateur,
inexpert, nonprofessional;
opp professional

lay *v* 1 (lay sth somewhere) deposit,
leave, place, plant, put, rest, set, settle.
2 (lay sth out) arrange, dispose,
organize, position, set out. 3 (lay eggs)
bear, deposit, produce. 4 (lay blame)
allot, ascribe, assign, attribute, charge,
impose, impute. 5 (lay plans) arrange,
concoct, contrive, create, design, devise,
make, plan, plot, prepare, set up, work
out. 6 lay down (a law) command,
formulate, ordain, order, prescribe,
proclaim, set down, stipulate.
7 lay on furnish, give, provide, supply

layabout *n* good-for-nothing, idler,
laggard, loafer, shirker

layer *n* 1 (of rock) bed, row, seam,
stratum, thickness, tier. 2 (of paint)
coat, coating, covering, film, skin

layman *n* amateur, lay person,
nonprofessional, nonspecialist;
opp professional

layout *n* 1 (of a place) arrangement,
design, geography, plan. 2 (of a page)
arrangement, design, format, outline

laze *v* do nothing, idle, lie around, loaf,
lounge, relax, sit around, unwind

laziness *n* idleness, inactivity, indolence,
lax, slackness *inf*, sloth

lazy *adj* idle, inactive, indolent, laxity,
slack *inf*, slothful; *opp* hard-working

lead *n* 1 (the lead) advantage, edge, first
place, precedence, priority, supremacy,
vanguard. 2 (follow sb's lead) direction,
example, guidance, leadership. 3 (get a
lead) clue, guide, hint, indication, line,
suggestion, tip-off. 4 (lead role) hero,
heroine, leading role, pointer, principal,
protagonist, starring role, title role.
5 (extension lead) cable, wire

lead v 1 (lead sb somewhere) conduct, draw, escort, guide, pilot, show the way, steer, usher. 2 (lead sb to think sth) cause, dispose, draw, incline, induce, influence, move, persuade, prevail, prompt. 3 (lead an army) be in charge of, captain, command, direct, govern, head, manage, rule, supervise. 4 (be in the lead) be ahead, be first, be in the lead, exceed, excel, head, leave behind, outdo, outstrip, surpass; *opp* trail. 5 (lead an exciting life) experience, have, live, pass, spend. 6 **lead on** deceive, delude, dupe, hoodwink, mislead, string along *inf*, trick

leader n boss, captain, chief, commander, conductor, director, foreman, guide, head, number one *inf*, principal, ruler, skipper *inf*, supremo *inf*

leading adj best, chief, first, foremost, greatest, highest, major, main, number one *inf*, premier, principal, ruling, senior, top; *opp* minor

leaf n 1 blade, foliage, frond, greenery, needle. 2 (in a book) folio, flyleaf, page, sheet

leaflet n booklet, circular, flyer, handout, notice, pamphlet

league n alliance, association, band, coalition, compact, confederacy, confederation, consortium, corporation, fellowship, fraternity, group, guild, order, partnership, society, syndicate, union

leak n 1 discharge, drip, emission, leakage, seepage, trickle. 2 (of information) disclosure, divulgence, revelation

leak v 1 discharge, drip, escape, exude, issue, ooze, seep, spill, trickle. 2 (leak information) disclose, divulge, give away, let out, let slip, let the cat out of the bag, make known, reveal, spill the beans

lean adj bony, emaciated, gaunt, lanky, scrawny, skinny, slender, slim, thin, wiry; *opp* fat

lean v 1 be propped, be supported, recline, repose, rest. 2 be at an angle, bend, incline, slant, slope, tilt, tip

leaning n aptitude, bend, bias, fondness, inclination, instinct, liking, partiality, penchant, predilection, preference, propensity, taste, tendency

leap v bounce, bound, caper, cavort, frisk, gambol, hop, jump, skip, spring

learn v 1 acquire, assimilate, attain, grasp, imbibe, master, pick up. 2 (learn your lines) commit sth to memory, get off pat, learn by heart, memorize. 3 (learn that sth is true) ascertain, discover, find out, gather, hear, understand

learned adj academic, cultured, erudite, expert, intellectual, knowledgable, scholarly, skilled, versed, well-educated, well-read; *opp* uneducated

learner n apprentice, beginner, cadet, novice, pupil, student, trainee

learning n education, knowledge, letters, scholarship, schooling, study, tuition, wisdom

lease v charter, hire, let, loan, rent

leave n 1 (leave to do sth) authorization, consent, dispensation, freedom, liberty, permission, sanction. 2 (on leave) break, holiday, sabbatical, time off, vacation

leave v 1 (leave a place) be off *inf*, check out, depart, disappear, exit, go, move, quit, retire, split *inf*, withdraw; **opp** arrive. 2 (leave your wife) abandon, break up with, desert, dump *inf*, finish with, split with. 3 (leave your job) cease, chuck it, desist, drop out, give up, pull out, relinquish, resign, stop, walk out. 4 (leave sth to sb) bequeath, endow, hand down, transmit, will. 5 **leave out** disregard, exclude, ignore, miss out, neglect, omit, overlook, reject, skip; **opp** include

lecture *n* 1 (a history lecture) address, class, lesson, paper, seminar, speech, talk. 2 (telling off) chiding, rebuke, remonstrance, reprimand, reproof, scolding, sermon, talking to, telling-off

lecture *v* 1 (lecture in history) address, expound, hold forth, instruct, speak, talk, teach. 2 (lecture a child) admonish, castigate, censure, chide, read the riot act, reprimand, reprove, scold, tear into, tell off

ledge *n* mantle, overhang, projection, protrusion, ridge, shelf, sill, step

left *adj* communist, leftist, left-wing, liberal, progressive, radical, red, socialist

leftover *adj* excess, extra, remaining, surplus, uneaten, unused, unwanted

leftovers *n* excess, extra, remainder, remains, remnants, scraps, surplus

leg *n* 1 (of a person) limb, member, peg *inf*, pin *inf*. 2 (of a piece of furniture) column, pillar, prop, support, upright. 3 (leg of a journey) bit, lap, part, portion, section, segment, stage, stretch

legacy *n* bequest, endowment, estate, gift, heirloom, inheritance

legal *adj* aboveboard, allowed, approved, authorized, decriminalized, lawful,

legalized, legitimate, licensed, permissible, proper, sanctioned, valid; **opp** illegal

legalize *v* allow, approve, authorize, decriminalize, legitimize, license, make legal, permit, sanction, validate; **opp** ban

legend *n* epic, fable, fairy tale, fiction, folk tale, myth, narrative, saga, story, tale

legendary *adj* acclaimed, celebrated, famed, famous, glorious, great, immortal, proverbial, world-famous; **opp** unknown

legible *adj* clear, decipherable, distinct, easy to read, intelligible, neat, plain, readable; **opp** illegible

legislate *v* authorize, decree, enact, establish, ordain, order, prescribe

legislation *n* 1 authorization, codification, enactment, law-making, prescription. 2 (a piece of legislation) act, bill, charter, code, constitution, law, measure, regulation, rule, statute

legitimate *adj* aboveboard, allowed, approved, authorized, decriminalized, lawful, legal, legalized, licensed, permissible, sanctioned, valid; **opp** illegal

legitimize *v* allow, approve, authorize, legalize, license, make legal, permit, sanction, validate; **opp** ban

leisure *n* holiday, recreation, relaxation, relief, rest, spare time, time off, vacation; **opp** work

leisurely *adj* comfortable, easy, gentle, laidback, lazy, relaxed, relaxing, restful, slow, unhurried; **opp** frantic

lend *v* 1 advance, give sb the loan of, loan; **opp** borrow. 2 add, afford, bestow, contribute, endow, furnish, give, grant, impart, provide, supply

length n 1 distance, extent, footage, measure, mileage, reach, span. 2 duration, period, span, stretch, time

lengthen v continue, drag out, draw out, elongate, expand, extend, increase, prolong, protract, stretch; *opp* shorten

lengthy adj extended, interminable, long, long-drawn-out, long-winded, protracted

lenient adj charitable, clement, forbearing, forgiving, gentle, humane, indulgent, kind, lax, magnanimous, merciful, mild, soft, sparing, tolerant

lessen v 1 assuage, curtail, decrease, diminish, ease, lighten, lower, mitigate, reduce, relieve, tone down; *opp* intensify. 2 abate, decline, decrease, die down, diminish, ease off, ebb, let up, moderate, slacken, subside, tail off, weaken; *opp* intensify

lesson n 1 class, coaching, drill, instruction, period, schooling, seminar, session, teaching, tutoring. 2 admonition, deterrent, example, exemplar, message, model, moral, warning

let v 1 agree to, allow, authorize, consent, give leave, give permission, give the go-ahead, grant, permit, sanction, tolerate. 2 contract out, hire, lease, rent, sublet. 3 let down disappoint, disillusion, fail, fall short. 4 let off detonate, discharge, explode, fire, launch, set off, trigger. 5 let off (forgive) absolve, acquit, discharge, excuse, exempt, forgive, let sb go, pardon, release, reprieve, spare. 6 let out (information) betray, disclose, leak, let slip, make known, reveal, tell. 7 let out (a person) free, discharge, let

sb go, liberate, release, set sb free

letdown n anticlimax, disappointment, disillusionment, failure, flop *inf*, washout *inf*

lethal adj deadly, devastating, fatal, mortal, murderous, virulent

lethargic adj apathetic, drowsy, dull, enervated, fatigued, heavy, inactive, indolent, inert, languid, languorous, lazy, listless, passive, sleepy, slothful, slow, sluggish, somnolent, torpid, weary; *opp* energetic

lethargy n apathy, drowsiness, dullness, fatigue, heaviness, indolence, inertia, lack of energy, languor, lassitude, laziness, listlessness, passivity, sleepiness, sloth, slowness, sluggishness, somnolence, torpor, weariness; *opp* energy

letter n 1 card, communication, dispatch, epistle, line, missive, note. 2 character, consonant, initial, sign, symbol, vowel

level adj 1 even, flat, flush, horizontal, smooth, straight, true, uniform; *opp* uneven. 2 aligned, balanced, comparable, equal, equivalent, identical, in line, matching, on a par, proportionate, the same

level n 1 degree, echelon, grade, plane, position, rank, rung, stage, standing, status. 2 altitude, depth, elevation, height. 3 floor, layer, story, stratum

level v 1 even out, flatten, plane, smooth. 2 bulldoze, demolish, destroy, flatten, knock down, lay low, pull down, raze, tear down

lever n crowbar, jimmy, handle, grip

lever v crowbar, force, jimmy, raise, wrench

levy n charge, dues, duty, excise, imposition, tariff, tax, toll

levy v charge, collect, demand, exact, gather, impose, tax

liability n 1 accountability, blame, culpability, duty, obligation, onus, responsibility. 2 (sth is a liability) burden, disadvantage, drag, drawback, encumbrance, handicap, hindrance, impediment, millstone, nuisance

liable adj 1 (liable for sth) accountable, answerable, bound, culpable, obligated, responsible. 2 (liable to do sth) apt, disposed, inclined, in the habit of, likely, predisposed, prone, susceptible, tending, vulnerable

liaison n 1 communication, connection, cooperation, contact, interchange, linkage, link-up, tie. 2 affair, amour, entanglement, intrigue, relationship, romance

liar n deceiver, false witness, fibber inf, perjurer

libel n aspersion, calumny, defamation, denigration, lie, obloquy, slander, slur, smear, vilification

libel v blacken sb's name, calumniate, cast aspersions, defame, denigrate, malign, misrepresent, slander, smear, traduce, vilify

libelous adj calumnious, damaging, defamatory, false, injurious, malicious, scurrilous, slanderous, untrue

liberal adj 1 broad-minded, easygoing, enlightened, lenient, libertarian, moderate, openminded, permissive, progressive, reformist, tolerant, unprejudiced. 2 (a liberal amount) abundant, ample, bountiful, copious, generous, lavish, magnanimous, munificent, plentiful, profuse, unstinting

liberalize v broaden, ease, expand, extend, free up, loosen, moderate, open up, relax, slacken, soften, stretch; **opp** tighten

liberate v deliver, discharge, emancipate, free, let go, let out, redeem, release, rescue, set free, unchain, untie

liberation n deliverance, discharge, emancipation, freedom, liberty, release, unchaining

liberty n autonomy, emancipation, freedom, independence, release, self-determination, sovereignty

license n 1 (permission) authorization, authority, dispensation, entitlement, leave, liberty, permission, privilege, right. 2 (document giving permission) certificate, charter, credentials, permit, warrant. 3 (in behavior) abandon, anarchy, decadence, disorder, dissipation, dissoluteness, excess, immorality, indulgence, laxity, licentiousness, unruliness

license v accredit, allow, authorize, certify, empower, entitle, grant a license to, permit, sanction, warrant

lick v brush, flick, lap, taste, tongue

lid n cap, cover, covering, stopper, top

lie n bluff, deceit, deception, equivocation, fabrication, falsehood, fib inf, fiction, invention, mendacity, misrepresentation, perjury, pretense, story, untruth, whopper inf; **opp** truth

lie v 1 bear false witness, bluff, deceive, dissemble, equivocate, fabricate, falsify, fib inf, invent, make up, misrepresent, perjure, pretend, tell a falsehood, tell a lie. **2** be horizontal, be lying, be prone, be prostrate, be recumbent, be supine, lean back, lounge, recline, repose, rest, sprawl, stretch out

life n **1** animation, being, breath, entity, existence, living; **opp** death. **2** activity, animation, dynamism, energy, enthusiasm, exuberance, liveliness, oomph inf, spark, sparkle, spirit, sprightliness, verve, vigor, vitality, vivacity, zest; **opp** dullness. **3** (sb's life) career, days, lifespan, lifetime, time on earth. **4** autobiography, biography, history, life story, memoir

lifeless adj **1** cold, dead, deceased, defunct, extinct, inanimate, inert, insensate; **opp** living. **2** colorless, dull, flat, heavy, lackluster, unexciting, uninspired, wooden; **opp** lively

lifelike adj authentic, convincing, exact, faithful, graphic, natural, real, realistic, true-to-life, vivid

lifelong adj abiding, constant, enduring, lasting, long-standing, long-term, perennial, permanent, persistent

lift n **1** amelioration, boost, enhancement, fillip, improvement, promotion, shot in the arm inf. **2** (give sb a lift) drive, ride, run, transport, transportation

lift v **1** carry, elevate, hoist, pick up, raise. **2** ameliorate, boost, buoy up, cheer, enhance, improve, promote

light adj **1** airy, delicate, flimsy, gossamer, lightweight, portable, slight; **opp** heavy. **2** bright, full of light, glowing, illuminated, lit-up, sunny, well-lit; **opp** dark. **3** (of a knock, touch) delicate, faint, gentle, indistinct, mild, soft, weak;

opp heavy. **4** amusing, easy, entertaining, diverting, fun, frivolous, lighthearted, simple, superficial, trivial, undemanding; **opp** serious

light n **1** beam, blaze, brightness, brilliance, flare, flash, glare, gleam, glint, glitter, glow, illumination, incandescence, luminescence, luminosity, luster, phosphorescence, radiance, ray, scintillation, shaft, shine, sparkle, twinkle. **2** beacon, bulb, candle, lamp, lantern, taper, torch

light v fire, flame, ignite, kindle, put a match to, set alight

lighten v **1** brighten, cast light on, illuminate, irradiate, light up, make sth bright, shed light on, shine on. **2** allay, alleviate, assuage, ease, lessen, mitigate, reduce, relieve

likable adj agreeable, amiable, appealing, charming, congenial, endearing, engaging, friendly, genial, lovable, nice, personable, pleasant, pleasing, sympathetic, winning

like adj/prep akin, alike, allied, analogous, corresponding, equal, equivalent, identical, matching, parallel, relating, resembling, same, similar

like v admire, appreciate, approve of, be fond of, be keen on, be partial to, cherish, delight in, enjoy, esteem, have a soft spot for inf, love, prize, relish, revel in, take pleasure in; **opp** dislike, hate

likelihood n chance, hope, liability, possibility, probability, prospect

likely adj **1** anticipated, expected, feasible, in the cards, plausible, probable. **2** (likely to do sth) apt, disposed, inclined, liable, prone, tending

liken v compare, draw an analogy between, equate, link, match, relate

likeness n 1 affinity, congruity, correspondence, link, match, resemblance, similarity. 2 depiction, drawing, effigy, image, model, painting, picture, portrait, representation, sketch, statue, study

liking n admiration, affinity, appreciation, approval, bent, esteem, fondness, keenness, love, partiality, penchant, predilection, preference, soft spot *inf*, taste, weakness

limb n appendage, arm, extension, extremity, leg, member, offshoot, projection, wing

limelight n attention, celebrity, fame, prominence, public eye, publicity, recognition, spotlight, stardom

limit n 1 border, bound, boundary, brim, brink, confines, edge, end, extent, frontier, perimeter, periphery. 2 cap, ceiling, curb, cutoff, deadline, limitation, maximum, restraint, restriction

limit v cap, check, circumscribe, confine, control, curb, delineate, demarcate, fix, put a limit on, ration, restrain, restrict

limitation n 1 cap, ceiling, check, curb, cutoff, deadline, limit, maximum, restraint, restriction. 2 defect, deficiency, fault, inadequacy, shortcoming, weakness

limited adj 1 capped, checked, circumscribed, confined, controlled, curbed, delineated, demarcated, fixed, rationed, restrained, restricted. 2 basic, inadequate, insufficient, minimal, restricted, scanty, sparse; *opp* unlimited

limitless adj boundless, countless, endless, everlasting, immeasurable, incalculable, inexhaustible, infinite, innumerable, never-ending, numberless, unbounded, unconfined, unending, unlimited

limp adj drooping, flabby, flaccid, floppy, loose, relaxed, sagging, slack, soft, wilting; *opp* firm, stiff

limp v be lame, falter, hobble, shamble, shuffle, totter

line n 1 band, bar, border, boundary, contour, dash, hyphen, mark, rule, streak, striation, strip, stripe, stroke, trail, underscore. 2 channel, corrugation, crease, fold, furrow, groove, wrinkle. 3 cable, cord, filament, lead, rope, strand, string, thread, wire. 4 (of people) chain, column, cordon, crocodile, file, parade, procession, queue, rank, row, series. 5 approach, avenue, course, direction, drift, method, tack, track, way

line v 1 crease, furrow, inscribe, mark, rule, score, wrinkle. 2 border, edge, fringe, hem, rim. 3 **line up** (form a line) get in line, form a line, form a queue, queue up. 4 **line up** (put into a line) align, arrange in a line, marshal, place in line, straighten up

lines n 1 configuration, contour, delineation, figure, form, outline, shape. 2 part, script, speech, words

linger v 1 dally, dawdle, hang around, hover, lag, loiter, pause, remain, stay, stop, take your time, tarry, wait; *opp* hurry. 2 abide, continue, endure, persist, remain

lingering adj abiding, continuing,

enduring, long, long-drawn-out,
persistent, protracted, remaining

link n 1 affiliation, association,
attachment, bond, connection,
relationship, tie. 2 (joining two things
together) connection, connector,
coupling, join, joint, loop, ring

link v 1 attach, bind, connect, couple,
fasten, join, tie, yoke. 2 associate,
attach, bracket, connect, join, put
together, relate, tie up

lip n brim, brink, edge, margin, rim, verge

liquid adj flowing, fluid, liquefied, melted,
molten, running, runny, sloppy

liquid n fluid, juice, liquor, solution

liquidate v annihilate, bump off inf,
destroy, dispatch, do away with inf,
eliminate, exterminate, get rid of inf,
kill, murder, obliterate, remove, silence,
wipe out

list n catalog, directory, file, index,
inventory, listing, record, register, roll,
schedule, table, tally

list v catalog, enter, enumerate, file,
index, itemize, make a list, make an
inventory, note, record, register,
tabulate, write down

listen v attend, concentrate, hark, hear,
heed, mind, note, observe, pay
attention, take notice

listless adj apathetic, enervated, feeble,
heavy, inactive, indolent, inert, languid,
lethargic, limp, passive, sluggish, supine,
torpid, weary; **opp** energetic

literal adj 1 actual, authentic, genuine,
real, true, unexaggerated. 2 (a literal
translation) accurate, close, exact,
faithful, strict, verbatim, word-for-word

literary adj bookish, cultivated, cultured,

educated, erudite, highbrow, learned,
literate, scholarly, well-read, widely read

literate adj able to read, cultivated,
educated, informed, lettered, schooled,
well-read; **opp** illiterate

literature n 1 books, fiction, letters,
writing. 2 booklet, brochure, circular,
handout, information, leaflet, pamphlet

litigation n action, case, dispute, lawsuit,
legal proceedings, suit

litter n clutter, debris, detritus, garbage,
jetsam, junk, mess, refuse, rubbish, trash,
waste

litter v clutter, make untidy, mess up,
scatter, strew

little adj 1 baby, compact, diminutive,
dinky inf, dwarf, infinitesimal,
Lilliputian, microscopic, midget, mini
inf, miniature, minuscule, minute,
petite, short, small, teeny inf, tiny, wee
inf; **opp** big. 2 (a little child) infant,
junior, small, young; **opp** big.
3 (not much) inadequate, insufficient,
meager, mean, measly inf, miserly,
negligible, paltry, piddling inf, scant,
skimpy, sparse

live adj 1 active, actual, alive, animate,
breathing, existing, living, sentient,
vital; **opp** dead. 2 (a live issue) burning,
current, hot, important, pertinent,
pressing, relevant, topical, vital.
3 (a live broadcast) as it happens, in real
time, unedited; **opp** prerecorded

live v 1 be, be alive, breathe, draw breath,
exist, have life. 2 abide, dwell, have
your home, inhabit, lodge, occupy,
reside, settle. 3 (of a custom) abide,
continue, endure, last, persist, prevail,
remain, stay alive, survive. 4 exist, get

by *inf*, make a living, make ends meet, subsist, support oneself, survive

ivelihood *n* daily bread, job, keep, living, means of support, occupation, subsistence, sustenance, trade, work

ively *adj* active, alert, animated, bouncy, bubbly *inf*, buoyant, bustling, cheerful, chirpy *inf*, energetic, enthusiastic, exuberant, frisky, high-spirited, irrepressible, jolly, nimble, perky *inf*, quick, spirited, sprightly, spry, vigorous, vital, vivacious; *opp* dull, lethargic

ivid *adj* 1 angry, boiling *inf*, enraged, fuming, furious, hopping mad *inf*, incensed, infuriated, mad *inf*, outraged, seething. 2 (of a bruise) black-and-blue, bluish, bruised, discolored, purplish. 3 (of sb's face) ashen, deathly, ghastly, ghostly, gray, pale, pallid, white

iving *adj* active, actual, alive, animate, breathing, existing, live, sentient, vital; *opp* dead

iving *n* daily bread, employment, income, job, keep, livelihood, means of support, occupation, subsistence, sustenance, wage, work

oad *n* 1 bale, cargo, charge, consignment, freight, shipment. 2 burden, cross, duty, encumbrance, millstone, pressure, responsibility, strain, trouble, weight, worry

oad *v* 1 cram, fill, heap, pack, pile, stack, stuff. 2 burden, charge, oppress, pressure, saddle, trouble, weigh down, worry

oan *n* advance, credit, mortgage

oath, loth *adj* averse to, disinclined, opposed, reluctant, resistant, shy, unenthusiastic, unwilling; *opp* eager

oathe *v* abhor, abominate, despise,

detest, execrate, hate, have an aversion to, recoil from, revile, shrink from, shudder at; *opp* love

lobby *n* 1 anteroom, entrance hall, foyer, hall, hallway, reception, waiting room. 2 (pressure group) campaign, campaigners, interest group, lobbyists, pressure group

lobby *v* campaign for, petition, pressurize, promote, push for, try to influence

local *adj* 1 community, neighborhood, parish, provincial, regional, district; *opp* central, national. 2 adjoining, nearby, neighboring

local *n* native, neighbor, resident, villager

locality *n* area, community, district, locale, neighborhood, vicinity

localize *v* confine, contain, limit, restrain, restrict

locate *v* 1 discover, find, pin down, pinpoint, put your hands on, track down, unearth. 2 establish, place, put, set up, site, situate

location *n* place, position, setting, site, situation, spot, venue, whereabouts

lock *n* bolt, catch, clasp, fastening, latch, padlock

lock *v* 1 bolt, fasten, padlock, secure, shut. 2 entangle, entwine, fix, jam, join, mesh. 3 **lock up** detain, imprison, incarcerate, put behind bars, remand, take away sb's freedom, throw sb in jail

lodge *n* cabin, chalet, cottage, gatehouse, house, hut

lodge *v* 1 (lodge an appeal) enter, file, make, put in, register, submit. 2 (get stuck) become embedded, embed, get caught, get stuck, jam, stick. 3 (live) have digs, have lodgings, have rooms, live, stay

lodger n boarder, paying guest, resident, tenant

lodgings n accommodation, apartment, a roof over your head, boarding house, digs *inf*, pad *inf*, rooms, somewhere to live

log n 1 block of wood, branch, chunk of wood, fuel, timber, trunk, twig, wood. 2 account, diary, journal, logbook, record, register

logic n argument, deduction, rationale, reasoning, sense

logical *adj* cogent, coherent, consistent, plausible, rational, reasonable, sensible, sound, structured, valid, well-organized; *opp* illogical

loiter v hang about, hang around, linger, loaf about, stand about, wait around

loll v flop, languish, lean, lie, lounge, slouch, slump, sprawl

lone *adj* isolated, single, solitary, unaccompanied

lonely *adj* abandoned, alone, deserted, desolate, forlorn, forsaken, isolated, lonesome, solitary

long *adj* 1 drawn out, elongated, endless, extended, interminable, lengthy, long-winded, never-ending, prolonged, protracted. 2 (four miles long) in length, lengthways

long v covet, crave, dream of, hanker after, have a craving for, want, yearn for

longing n ambition, craving, desire, hunger, urge, wish

look n 1 examination, gaze, glance, glare, glimpse, glower, inspection, peek, scan, stare. 2 appearance, expression, face, impression

look v 1 browse through, cast your eye over, examine, eye, eyeball *inf*, gaze, glance, have a look, peep, peer, scan, see, stare, study, watch. 2 (seem) appear give the appearance of being, seem, strike you as being. 3 (look everywhere for sth) hunt, search, scour. 4 **look after** care for, keep an eye on, mind, nurse, nurture, take care of, tend, watch. 5 **look forward to** anticipate, count the days until, long for. 6 **look into** check out, inquire about, examine, explore, go into, investigate, make some inquiries, research, study. 7 **look out** be careful, be on the watch for, beware, keep an eye out, mind yourself, watch out. 8 **look up** (look up sth in a reference book) consult, locate, refer to, search for, track down. 9 **look up** (visit sb) call on, drop in on, go and see, visit. 10 **look up** (improve) get better, improve, look rosy, pick up, shape up

lookout n guard, sentry, watch

loom v appear, dominate, hang over, materialize, overshadow, take shape, threaten, tower over

loop n circle, coil, curl, curve, hoop, noose, ring, spiral, turn, twist, whorl

loop v bend, coil, curl, spiral, twist, wind

loophole n excuse, flaw, pretext, way of avoiding sth, way out

loose *adj* 1 baggy, floppy, free, hanging, slack, straggling, trailing, unattached, wobbly. 2 at large, escaped, free, out, untethered. 3 approximate, ballpark *inf*, general, rough, vague

loose v free, let out, liberate, release, set free, let go, set loose, slacken, turn loose, undo, untether, untie

loosen v ease off, relax, release, slacken, undo, unfasten, untie; **opp** tighten

loot n bounty, goodies inf, haul, plunder, spoils

lopsided adj awry, crooked, skewed, tilting, uneven; **opp** straight

lord n 1 aristocrat, baron, count, duke, earl, noble. 2 chief, leader, master, ruler

lordly adj 1 arrogant, condescending, disdainful, haughty, imperious, patronizing. 2 aristocratic, noble

lose v 1 be unable to find, mislay, misplace; **opp** find. 2 be defeated, get beaten, get hammered inf, get thrashed inf; **opp** win

loser n also-ran, failure, runner-up

loss n bereavement, cost, damage, defeat, deficit, deprivation, disappearance, failure, harm, hurt, impairment, privation

lost adj 1 (sth is lost) disappeared, misplaced, missing, vanished. 2 (sb is lost) adrift, disoriented, off course. 3 (feel lost) baffled, bewildered, confused, mystified, puzzled. 4 (from the past) dead, extinct, forgotten, past, vanished, wiped out

lot n 1 **a lot** a good deal, loads inf, lots, many, masses, piles inf, plenty, scores, stacks inf, tons inf. 2 **a lot** a good deal, frequently, often, regularly. 3 batch, bunch, bundle, crowd, group

lotion n cream, liquid, milk, ointment

lottery n 1 draw, raffle, sweepstake. 2 gamble, game, the luck of the draw

loud adj 1 blaring, booming, deafening, ear-splitting, noisy, raucous, rowdy, shrill, thudding, thundering, tumultuous; **opp** quiet. 2 (of a color) flashy inf,

garish, gaudy, lurid, ostentatious, showy; **opp** subdued, subtle

lounge v flop, laze, lie about, lie back, loll, relax, sprawl

lout n hoodlum, hooligan, oaf, slob, thug

lovable adj adorable, appealing, attractive, cuddly, cute, endearing, gorgeous, lovely, sweet

love n 1 adoration, affection, devotion, fondness, infatuation, liking, partiality, passion, soft spot, tenderness, weakness. 2 darling, dear, sweetheart, sweetie

love v 1 (be in love with) adore, be devoted to, be fond of, be in love with, be infatuated with, be keen about, be soft on inf, dote on, fancy inf, have a crush on, have a thing about inf, idolize, think the world of, worship. 2 (love strawberries, a song, dancing) adore, be keen about, be partial to, enjoy, get a kick out of, go for, have a weakness for, really like

lovely adj 1 (a lovely holiday) fabulous, gorgeous, great, marvelous, superb, terrific, wonderful. 2 (good-looking) attractive, beautiful, cute, good-looking, handsome, pretty, sweet

lover n another man, another woman, bit on the side inf, boyfriend, fiancé, fiancée, girlfriend, mistress, old flame, partner

loving adj adoring, affectionate, amorous, ardent, caring, close, devoted, passionate, tender, warm; **opp** cold

low adj 1 (short) dwarf, low-growing, low-lying, shallow, short, small, squat, stunted, sunken; **opp** tall. 2 (stocks are low) cut, deficient, depleted, inadequate, insufficient, meager, modest,

poor, reduced, scant, scarce; **opp** high.
3 (low volume, light) gentle, hushed,
muffled, muted, pianissimo, quiet, soft,
subdued; **opp** bright, loud, strong.
4 (bass) bass, deep; **opp** high-pitched,
soprano. **5** (unhappy) depressed,
despondent, dispirited, down, down in
the dumps inf, downhearted, fed up inf,
gloomy, miserable, sad, unhappy;
opp happy, on a high inf

lower adj **1** inferior, junior, lesser,
secondary, subordinate; **opp** higher.
2 (lower prices) cut, decreased, reduced,
slashed; **opp** higher, increased

lower v **1** drop, let down, take down.
2 (lower prices) bring down, cut,
decrease, discount, mark down, reduce,
slash; **opp** put up. **3** (lower the volume)
reduce, turn down; **opp** turn up

low-key adj casual, downbeat, laid-back,
muted, played down, restrained,
understated

loyal adj committed, dependable,
devoted, dutiful, faithful, reliable,
staunch, true, trusted, trustworthy;
opp disloyal

loyalty n allegiance, dedication,
dependability, devotion, faithfulness,
fidelity, reliability, trustworthiness;
opp disloyalty

lubricate v grease, moisturize, oil

lucid adj **1** (a lucid explanation) clear,
comprehensible, distinct, explicit,
logical, plain, simple, straightforward,
understandable. **2** (clearheaded) all
there inf, clearheaded, compos mentis,
in your right mind, rational, sane,
thinking straight

luck n **1** chance, destiny, fate, fluke,

fortune, serendipity, the stars. **2** (good
luck) best of luck, break inf, good luck,
prosperity, stroke of luck, success,
windfall

lucky adj auspicious, charmed, fortuitous,
fortunate, handy, opportune, timely;
opp unlucky

lucrative adj beneficial, fruitful, high-
income, juicy inf, profitable, well-paid,
worthwhile

ludicrous adj absurd, comic, crazy, daft
inf, farcical, incongruous, preposterous,
ridiculous, silly, stupid; **opp** sensible

luggage n baggage, bags, belongings,
cases, gear inf, possessions, things

lukewarm adj **1** at room temperature,
tepid. **2** half-hearted, indifferent,
unenthusiastic, uninterested;
opp enthusiastic

lull n calm, hush, letup, pause, quiet,
quiet period, stillness, tranquillity

lull v calm down, die down, dwindle, let
up, pacify, quiet down, soothe

luminous adj bright, fluorescent,
glowing, lustrous, phosphorescent,
radiant, shining, vivid; **opp** dull

lump n **1** (swelling) bulge, bump, growth,
swelling, tumor. **2** (piece) blob, chunk,
clump, hunk, piece, wad, wedge

lump v bunch, clump, combine,
consolidate, fuse, group, merge, mix,
pool, put

lunatic adj absurd, crackpot inf, crazy, daft
inf, foolish, idiotic, insane, mad, stupid;
opp sensible

lunatic n insane person, madman,
maniac, nut case inf, psychopath

lunge v dive, fall on, jump, leap, lurch,
plunge, pounce, thrust

lurch *v* list, lunge, pitch, reel, roll, stagger, stumble, sway, weave

lure *n* attraction, carrot, decoy, inducement, invitation, magnet, temptation

lure *v* attract, beckon, draw, ensnare, entice, invite, lead on, seduce, tempt

lurid *adj* **1** bright, garish, gaudy, glaring, loud, vivid. **2** disgusting, gory, grisly, gruesome, nasty, repulsive, revolting, shocking, unpleasant

lurk *v* hide, lie in wait, linger, skulk, sneak, snoop

luscious *adj* appetizing, delicious, juicy, mouth-watering, succulent, yummy *inf*

lush *adj* dense, flourishing, green, luxuriant, prolific, rich, thick

lust *n* craving, desire, lechery, longing, passion

lust after *v* crave, desire, fancy *inf*, need, want

luxurious *adj* affluent, comfortable, deluxe, expensive, extravagant, grand, lavish, opulent, plush, rich, ritzy *inf*; sumptuous, swanky *inf*; **opp** poor, spartan

luxury *n* **1** comfort, extravagance, grandeur, indulgence, opulence, richness, splendor, sumptuousness. **2** (a luxury) extra, extravagance, optional extra, treat, trimmings

lyrical *adj* emotional, expressive, impassioned, poetic, romantic

lyrics *n* libretto, text, words

M

macabre *adj* eerie, frightening, grisly, gruesome, horrible, morbid, sick *inf*

machine *n* apparatus, appliance, contraption, device, gadget, mechanism, robot, tool

machinery *n* 1 apparatus, equipment, gear, plant, tools. 2 channels, organization, procedure, set-up *inf*, structure, system, workings

mad *adj* 1 crazy *inf*, demented, insane, mentally handicapped, mentally ill, mentally unstable, nuts *inf*, out of your mind, senile, unbalanced, unhinged; *opp* sane. 2 (idiotic) crackpot *inf*, crazy, daft *inf*, foolish, idiotic, insane, lunatic, ridiculous, silly, stupid; *opp* sensible

madden *v* anger, annoy, enrage, exasperate, gall, get sb's back up *inf*, infuriate, irritate, make angry, make sb's blood boil, upset; *opp* please

made-up *adj* 1 fabricated, false, fictional, imaginary, invented, spurious; *opp* true. 2 prebuilt, readymade

madman *n* head case *inf*, loony *inf*, madwoman, mentally handicapped person, nut case *inf*, psychopath

madness *n* 1 dementia, insanity, mania, mental illness, psychosis. 2 absurdity, craziness, folly, foolishness, stupidity

magazine *n* journal, monthly, periodical, weekly

magic *adj* 1 brilliant, excellent, marvelous, terrific, wonderful. 2 charmed, enchanted, magical.

magic *n* 1 black magic, conjuring, enchantment, illusion, sleight of hand, sorcery, the occult, the supernatural, voodoo, witchcraft. 2 charm, fascination, magnetism, spell

magician *n* conjuror, illusionist, sorcerer, warlock, witch, wizard

magnanimous *adj* benevolent, big-hearted, big, charitable, generous, kind

magnetic *adj* appealing, attractive, captivating, charismatic, enchanting, fascinating, gripping, inviting, irresistible, mesmerizing, seductive, tantalizing, tempting

magnetism *n* appeal, attraction, charm, draw, fascination, lure, magic, pull, spell, temptation

magnificent *adj* brilliant, excellent, fine, glorious, gorgeous, grand, magic, marvelous, out of this world, splendid, sumptuous, superb, tremendous, wonderful

magnify *v* amplify, blow up, boost, build up, enhance, enlarge, exaggerate, expand, heighten, increase, inflate, make bigger; *opp* reduce

magnitude *n* degree, enormity, extent, greatness, immensity, importance, significance, size, vastness

maid n 1 domestic servant, domestic, girl, housemaid, lady-in-waiting, lady's maid, servant. 2 girl, lass, young woman

mail n collection, delivery, letters, parcels, post, postal service

mail v a-mail, send, send off, transfer

maim v disable, handicap, damage permanently, injure, mutilate, wound

main adj basic, central, chief, critical, crucial, essential, first, foremost, key, major, most important, number one, paramount, predominant, primary, prime, principal, top, vital

main n cable, channel, conduit, line, pipe, water main

maintain v 1 (keep up) continue, keep up, keep, retain, sustain. 2 (maintain a building) carry out repairs, keep in good order, look after, preserve, repair, take care of. 3 (say that sth is true) allege, argue, assert, believe, claim, contend, profess, state

majestic adj grand, imperial, imposing, impressive, magnificent, noble, regal, splendid, stately

majesty n grandeur, magnificence, nobility, pomp, royalty, splendor, stateliness

major adj chief, considerable, crucial, extensive, great, important, key, leading, main, outstanding, principal, significant; *opp* minor

majority n best part, bulk, greater part, largest part, lion's share, main body, more than half, most; *opp* minority

make n brand, sort, type, variety

make v 1 (produce) assemble, bake, build, cook, create, draw up, fashion, fix inf,

form, manufacture, prepare, produce, put together, synthesize. 2 (cause) bring about, cause, generate, give rise to. 3 (compel) coerce, compel, force, oblige, push sb into, require. 4 (earn) bring home, bring in, clear, earn, gain, net. 5 (one and one makes two) add up to, come to, constitute, equal, total. 6 (make a statement, speech) deliver, give, say, utter. 7 **make off** bolt, clear off inf, decamp, escape, get away, run off. 8 **make out** (be able to see or hear) detect, discern, distinguish, hear, pick out, recognize, see. 9 **make out** (understand) decipher, figure out, follow, get inf, grasp, see, understand, work out. 10 **make out** (make out a receipt) complete, fill in, fill out, write out. 11 **make up** compose, concoct, create, dream up, fabricate, hatch, invent. 12 **make up** comprise, constitute, form

make-believe n dream, fantasy, fiction, imagination, invention, play-acting, pretense, role-play; *opp* reality

make do v cope, get by, improvise, manage, put up with, survive

maker n architect, author, builder, composer, creator, manufacturer, originator, producer, writer

makeshift adj emergency, improvised, make-do, provisional, rough-and-ready, stopgap, temporary; *opp* permanent

makeup n cosmetics, face-paint, grease-paint, war paint

makings n beginnings, capability, ingredients, potential, promise, qualities, talent

maladjusted adj disturbed, neurotic,

unbalanced, unstable, with behavioral problems; *opp* well-adjusted

male *adj* boyish, manlike, manly, masculine; *opp* female

malevolent *adj* cruel, evil, fierce, hostile, malicious, malign, spiteful, unfriendly, venomous, vindictive; *opp* good

malice *n* animosity, bitchiness *inf*, bitterness, enmity, hatred, hostility, ill will, rancor, spite, venom, vindictiveness

malicious *adj* bitchy *inf*, bitter, hostile, hurtful, malignant, pernicious, spiteful, venomous, vicious, vindictive

malignant *adj* 1 hostile, malicious, pernicious, spiteful, venomous, vicious. 2 dangerous, destructive, life-threatening; *opp* benign

man *n* 1 chap *inf*, gentleman, guy *inf*, human being, individual, lad, male, young man. 2 Homo sapiens, human race, humankind, humans, men and women, people

man *v* crew, operate, staff, work

manacle *n* chain, fetter, handcuffs, irons, shackle

manage *v* 1 accomplish, bring off, cope, crack it *inf*, deal with, get by, handle, succeed, survive. 2 administer, be in charge of, control, direct, head, lead, organize, oversee, pilot, run, supervise

manageable *adj* 1 attainable, doable, feasible, possible, viable. 2 accommodating, amenable, compliant, controllable, docile, submissive

management *n* 1 administration, board, bosses, directors, employers, executive, managers, owners, top brass *inf*.

2 administration, command, control, direction, handling, organization, overseeing, running, supervision

manager *n* administrator, boss, controller, director, employer, executive, foreman, governor, head of department, head, owner, person in charge, proprietor, superintendent, supervisor

mandate *n* approval, authority, authorization, command, decree, direction, edict, order, power, ruling, sanction, support

maneuver *n* action, dodge, intrigue, machination, plan, plot, ploy, ruse, scheme, subterfuge, tactic, trick

maneuver *v* 1 contrive, engineer, intrigue, manage, manipulate, plan, plot, pull strings, scheme. 2 direct, drive, guide, move, steer

maneuvers *n* deployment, exercise, military exercise, movement, training

mangle *v* crush, destroy, distort, hack, maul, twist, wreck

mangy *adj* moth-eaten, scruffy, shabby, threadbare, wretched

manhandle *v* haul, heave, hump, push, shove

mania *n* 1 derangement, insanity, madness, mental illness. 2 addiction, craving, craze, obsession, passion

maniac *n* deranged person, idiot, loony *inf*, lunatic, madman, madwoman, nut case *inf*, psychopath

manifest *adj* clear, conspicuous, glaring, obvious, patent, plain, unmistakable

manifestation *n* demonstration, display, embodiment, evidence, expression, indication, sign, symbol, testimony

manipulate *v* 1 handle, maneuver,

operate, use, work. 2 (people) exploit,
influence, misuse, take advantage of, use

mankind *n* Homo sapiens, human race,
humanity, humans, men and women,
people

manly *adj* 1 macho, male, masculine,
virile; *opp* effeminate. 2 brave,
chivalrous, gallant, strong, vigorous

man-made *adj* artificial, imitation,
manufactured, simulated, synthetic,
synthesized; *opp* natural

manner *adj* 1 approach, means, method,
procedure, process, style, technique,
way. 2 air, appearance, attitude, bearing,
behavior, demeanor, look, mien, way.
3 **all manner of** all kinds of, a mixture
of, an assortment of, assorted, different,
various, varying

mannerism *n* characteristic, gesture,
foible, habit, idiosyncrasy, peculiarity,
quirk

manners *n* 1 bearing, behavior, conduct,
deportment. 2 civility, correct behavior,
courtesy, decorum, etiquette, good form,
politeness, protocol, propriety, social
graces

manual *adj* 1 by hand, hand-operated.
2 (manual work) laboring, physical,
with your hands

manufacture *v* 1 build, construct, create,
fabricate, forge, form, make, mass-
produce, process, produce, shape, turn
out. 2 (a story) concoct, cook up *inf*,
dream up, invent, think up

manure *n* compost, droppings, dung,
fertilizer, guano, muck

many *adj* abundant, a lot of, copious,
countless, frequent, heaps of *inf*,
innumerable, loads of *inf*, lots of,

myriad, numerous, oodles of *inf*, plenty
of, profuse, tons of *inf*, umpteen *inf*

map *n* chart, guide, plan, street guide,
road map, town plan

march *n* 1 parade, tramp, trek, walk.
2 demonstration, parade, procession,
protest

march *v* file, parade, stride, tramp

margin 1 border, boundary, brink, edge,
perimeter, periphery, rim, side, verge.
2 allowance, latitude, leeway, room,
room for maneuver, scope, space

marginal *adj* 1 borderline, peripheral.
2 doubtful, insignificant, low, minimal,
negligible, slight, small, unimportant

marginalize *v* decrease the influence
of, exclude, make marginal, make
unimportant, push out, push to the
margins

marital *adj* conjugal, married,
matrimonial, nuptial, wedded

mark *n* 1 blemish, blot, blotch, dent, dot,
impression, pockmark, scar, scratch,
smear, smudge, smut, speck, spot, stain,
streak. 2 badge, brand, device, emblem,
hallmark, seal, signature, symbol,
trademark. 3 evidence, indication,
proof, sign, symbol, token. 4 aim, goal,
intention, objective, purpose, target.
5 **below the mark** below par, below the
norm, below the standard, inadequate,
inferior, not up to scratch, substandard.
6 **leave its mark** affect, have an effect,
have an impact, impress, influence,
make an impression. 7 **wide of the mark**
erroneous, fallacious, inaccurate,
incorrect, wrong

mark *v* 1 blemish, blot, damage, deface,
disfigure, dent, dirty, draw on, make a

mark on, scar, scrawl on, scribble on, smudge, spot, stain, streak, write on. **2** brand, label, put a mark on, tag. **3** (mark sb's work) appraise, assess, correct, evaluate, grade. **4** (mark sb's words) attend to, heed, listen to, mind, note, notice, observe, pay attention to, see, take notice of, take seriously, take to heart, watch. **5** (mark an occasion) celebrate, commemorate, honor, observe

marked *adj* apparent, blatant, clear, conspicuous, decided, distinct, evident, notable, obvious, patent, pronounced, remarkable, striking

market *n* **1** bazaar, fair, marketplace, mart. **2** call, demand, desire. **3** business, buying and selling, commerce, dealing

market *v* advertise, peddle, promote, push *inf*, put on the market, retail, sell, trade in, vend

marketable *adj* desirable, in demand, salable, sought after, wanted

marksman *n* crack shot *inf*, good shot, markswoman, sharpshooter

maroon *v* abandon, desert, forsake, leave, leave behind, leave stranded, put ashore, strand

marriage *n* **1** matrimony, union, wedlock. **2** marriage ceremony, nuptials, wedding. **3** alliance, association, combination, link, merger, union

married **1** (of people) hitched *inf*, joined, united, wed, wedded. **2** conjugal, connubial, marital, matrimonial, wedded

marry *v* **1** become man and wife, be married, get hitched *inf*, get married, join in matrimony, tie the knot *inf*, unite, walk down the aisle *inf*, wed.

2 ally, combine, join, link, merge, unite

marsh *n* bog, fen, marshland, mire, morass, quagmire, quicksand, swamp, wetland

marshy *adj* boggy, miry, muddy, quaggy, soft, squelchy, swampy

marvel *v* admire, applaud, be amazed by, be astonished by, be surprised by, praise, wonder at

marvelous *adj* amazing, astounding, breathtaking, brilliant, extraordinary, fantastic, out of this world *inf*, remarkable, sensational, stupendous, superb, terrific, wonderful

masculine *adj* **1** macho, male, manly, virile; *opp* feminine. **2** (of a woman) butch *inf*, manly, unfeminine, unwomanly; *opp* feminine

mash *v* crush, mangle, pound, pulp, pulverize, purée, smash, squash

mask *n* camouflage, cover, disguise, facade, false colors, front, guise, pretense, screen, shield, smokescreen, veil

mask *v* cloak, conceal, cover up, disguise, hide, obscure, screen, veil

mass *adj* extensive, general, indiscriminate, large-scale, popular, universal, wholesale, widespread

mass *n* **1** accumulation, collection, concentration. **2** body, crowd, horde, host, lot, mob, multitude, throng. **3** body, bulk, greater part, lion's share, main body, majority, preponderance. **4** bulk, magnitude, size

mass *v* **1** accumulate, amass, assemble, bring together, collect, gather. **2** assemble, collect, flock together, gather, gather together, meet, marshal, rally, swarm, throng

massacre n annihilation, blood bath, butchery, carnage, genocide, mass execution, mass murder, slaughter

massacre v annihilate, butcher, kill, kill off, mow down, slaughter, slay, wipe out

massage v knead, manipulate, rub, rub down

masses n 1 an abundance, bags inf, heaps inf, hundreds, loads, lots, millions, oodles inf, thousands. 2 **the masses** the common people, the mob, the hoi polloi, the proletariat, the rabble

massive adj colossal, enormous, gigantic, huge, immense, large, mammoth, vast, whopping inf; **opp** tiny

master adj chief, main, most important, predominant, principal

master n 1 boss, chief, controller, director, employer, governor, head, lord, lord and master, ruler, top dog inf. 2 (of a ship) captain, commander, skipper. 3 head, headmaster, head teacher, instructor, schoolmaster, schoolteacher, teacher, tutor. 4 (a master at sth) ace inf, authority, expert, genius, maestro, virtuoso, wizard

master v 1 become expert in, become proficient in, get the hang of inf, grasp, know, learn, learn thoroughly. 2 control, dominate, govern, overcome, overpower, quell, subdue, subjugate, tame

masterly adj accomplished, ace inf, adept, consummate, deft, dexterous, excellent, expert, first-rate, masterful, proficient, skillful, skilled

mastermind n 1 brains, expert, genius, intellect, intellectual. 2 architect, author, brains behind sth, creator,

director, initiator, organizer, originator, planner

mastermind v be the brains behind inf, conceive, devise, direct, initiate, manage, organize, plan, think up

masterpiece n best work, chef d'oeuvre, magnum opus, masterwork, pièce de résistance, tour de force

match n 1 bout, competition, contest, game, tournament. 2 counterpart, equal, equivalent, peer, rival. 3 copy, double, duplicate, look-alike, spitting image inf, twin. 4 complement, counterpart, mate, pair, twin. 5 affiliation, alliance, marriage, pairing, partnership, union

match v 1 agree with, be a pair, be compatible with, be similar to, be the same as, blend with, complement, coordinate with, correspond to, fit, go with, harmonize, make a set, suit; **opp** contrast. 2 be a match for, be equal to, be in the same category as, be on a level with, compare with, compete with, keep pace with, keep up with, measure up to, rival. 3 bring together, combine, link, marry, pair off, pair up, put together, team up

matching adj 1 alike, identical, just like, the same, twin. 2 blending, complementing, coordinating, equivalent, harmonizing, identical, like, parallel, similar, twin

mate n 1 better half inf, husband, other half inf, partner, spouse, wife. 2 colleague, co-worker, fellow-worker, workmate. 3 buddy inf, chum inf, companion, comrade, friend, pal inf

mate v 1 breed, couple, copulate. 2 bring together, marry, match, join, pair, wed

material *adj* 1 concrete, palpable, physical, solid, substantial, tangible. 2 essential, grave, important, key, meaningful, pertinent, relevant, serious, significant, weighty

material *n* 1 element, matter, medium, stuff, substance. 2 cloth, fabric, stuff, textiles. 3 data, details, evidence, facts, info *inf*, information, notes

materialize *v* 1 come about, come into being, happen, occur, take place. 2 appear, become visible, come to light, emerge, present itself, show itself, turn up *inf*

maternal *adj* 1 motherly. 2 (maternal relations) on the distaff side, on your mother's side

matter *n* 1 material, medium, stuff, substance. 2 affair, business, episode, event, incident, issue, occurrence, question, situation, subject, topic. 3 consequence, import, importance, note, significance, weight

matter *v* be important, be relevant, be significant, carry weight, count, make a difference, make any difference, signify

matter-of-fact *adj* deadpan, down-to-earth, dull, factual, flat, literal, mundane, plain, prosaic, straightforward, unvarnished

mature *adj* 1 adult, full-grown, fully developed, fully grown, grown-up, of age, well-developed. 2 experienced, responsible, sensible, wise. 3 mellow, ready, ripe, ripened, seasoned

mature *v* 1 become adult, come of age, develop, grow up, reach adulthood. 2 become responsible, become sensible, become wise. 3 become ripe, grow ripe, mellow, ripen

maturity *n* 1 adulthood, coming-of-age, majority, manhood, womanhood. 2 sense, sense of responsibility, wisdom. 3 mellowness, ripeness

maul *v* 1 claw, lacerate, mangle, mutilate, savage, tear to pieces. 2 abuse, handle roughly, manhandle, molest, paw

maxim *n* adage, aphorism, axiom, motto, proverb, rule, saying

maximum *adj* biggest, extreme, full, fullest, greatest, highest, largest, most, supreme, top, topmost, utmost; *opp* minimum

maximum *n* acme, apex, ceiling, crest, height, highest point, peak, summit, top, upper limit, utmost, zenith; *opp* minimum

maybe *adv* conceivably, could be *inf*, perhaps, possibly, who knows? *inf*, you never know *inf*; *opp* certainly, definitely

maze *n* confusion, jungle, labyrinth, mesh, network, puzzle, tangle, web

meadow *n* field, grassland, paddock, pasture

meager *adj* deficient, inadequate, measly, paltry, poor, scanty, short, skimpy, sparse, stingy; *opp* generous

mean *adj* 1 close-fisted, illiberal, mingy *inf*, miserly, niggardly, parsimonious, stingy, tight, tight-fisted, ungenerous; *opp* generous. 2 bad-tempered, callous, disagreeable, hard-hearted, obnoxious, spiteful, surly, uncharitable, unfriendly, unkind, unpleasant. 3 (of an action) base, contemptible, despicable, ignoble, nasty, odious, shameful, vile. 4 (of a place) humble, miserable, poor, seedy, shabby, squalid, wretched

mean n average, balance, median, middle, midpoint, norm

mean v 1 convey, denote, drive at inf, express, imply, indicate, insinuate, represent, say, signify, spell, stand for, suggest, symbolize. 2 aim, have in mind, intend, plan, propose, set out. 3 bring about, cause, engender, entail, give rise to, involve, lead to, necessitate, produce

meander v 1 bend, curve, loop, snake, twist and turn, wind, zigzag. 2 ramble, stray, stroll aimlessly, wander, wander about

meaning n 1 drift, essence, explanation, gist, implication, import, message, sense, significance, substance, thrust, upshot. 2 consequence, effect, point, purpose, significance, value, worth. 3 aim, design, end, goal, intention, object, plan

meaningful adj 1 important, material, relevant, serious, significant, valid, worthwhile; opp meaningless. 2 eloquent, expressive, pointed, significant

meaningless adj 1 aimless, empty, futile, hollow, insignificant, pointless, trifling, trivial, useless, vain, worthless; opp important. 2 inane, incoherent, incomprehensible, nonsensical, senseless, unintelligible

means n 1 avenue, course, expedient, method, process, way. 2 affluence, capital, finance, fortune, funds, money, property, resources, riches, wealth

measure n 1 amount, capacity, degree, expanse, extent, proportion, quantity, range, reach, scope, size. 2 allotment, allowance, division, part, percentage, portion, quota, ration, share. 3 scale, standard, unit. 4 gauge, measuring spoon, measuring cup, meter, ruler, scale, tape measure. 5 benchmark, criterion, litmus test, test, yardstick. 6 action, course, course of action, expedient, procedure, proceeding, step. 7 act, bill, law, resolution, statute

measure v 1 assess, calculate, calibrate, compute, count, determine, evaluate, judge, mark out, meter, quantify, rate, reckon, size, survey, take measurements, value, weigh. 2 **measure out** allocate, allot, deal out, distribute, divide, dole out, share out. 3 **measure up** be adequate, be as good as, be equal to, be good enough, be on a level with, be suitable, come up to, come up to scratch inf, fit the bill, fulfill expectations, make the grade, match, meet, pass muster

measurement n 1 amount, capacity, depth, dimensions, extent, height, length, proportions, quantity, range, size, weight, width. 2 assessment, calculation, evaluation, judgment, quantification, quantifying, sizing, weighing

meat n 1 animal flesh, flesh, offal. 2 (meat and drink) food, grub inf, nosh inf, nourishment, provisions, rations, sustenance, victuals

mechanical adj 1 automated, automatic, machine-driven, motor-driven, technological. 2 automatic, cursory, habitual, instinctive, involuntary, knee-jerk inf, machinelike, perfunctory, reflex, routine, soulless, unconscious, unthinking

mechanism n 1 apparatus, appliance, contraption, contrivance, device,

gadget, machine, system, tool.
2 components, innards *inf*, machinery, workings, works. 3 agency, channel, means, method, operation, procedure, proceeding, system

mechanize *v* automate, bring up to date, equip with machines, make automatic, modernize

medal *n* award, decoration, honor, medallion, prize, reward, trophy

meddle *v* be a busybody, butt in, interfere, intervene, intrude, poke your nose in *inf*, pry, stick your nose in *inf*, tamper

mediate *v* act as go-between, act as mediator, act as middleman, act as peacemaker, arbitrate, conciliate, intercede, intervene, liaise, make peace, negotiate, reconcile, referee, umpire

medicinal *adj* curative, healing, remedial, restorative, therapeutic

medicine *n* 1 cure, drug, medication, medicament, remedy, panacea.
2 healing, medical science, therapy, treatment

mediocre *adj* average, fair, indifferent, middling, no great shakes *inf*, nothing to write home about *inf*, ordinary, passable, pedestrian, run-of-the-mill, second-rate, so-so, undistinguished, uninspired

meditate *n* 1 be lost in thought, cogitate, deliberate, muse, ponder, reflect, study, think. 2 brood over, chew over *inf*, contemplate, consider, mull over, ponder, reflect on, think over

medium *adj* 1 average, fair, intermediate, mean, median, mediocre, middle, middling, moderate,

medium *n* 1 average, center, compromise, mean, median, middle,

middle way. 2 agency, approach, channel, form, means, means of communication, means of expression, method, vehicle, way. 3 conditions, element, environment, habitat, milieu, setting. 4 clairvoyant, seer, spiritualist

medley *n* assortment, hotchpotch, jumble, miscellany, mishmash, mixed bag, mixture

meek *adj* 1 docile, forbearing, gentle, humble, long-suffering, mild, modest, patient, peaceable, resigned, self-effacing, unassuming, unpretentious.
2 acquiescent, compliant, deferential, docile, soft, spineless, submissive, timid, tractable, weak, weak-kneed *inf*, wimpish *inf*; *opp* aggressive

meet *v* 1 (meet sb) bump into, chance upon, come across, come face to face with, come upon, encounter, happen upon, join, make contact with, meet with, rendezvous with, run into.
2 (people meet) assemble, come together, congregate, gather, mingle, rendezvous. 3 (lines, roads meet) come together, connect, converge, intersect, join, link up, touch. 4 (one line, road meets another) abut, adjoin, reach.
5 (meet certain conditions) answer, comply with, correspond to, fulfill, measure up to, observe, satisfy

meeting *n* 1 (to discuss business) assembly, conclave, conference, convention, discussion, gathering, get-together *inf*, session. 2 (between two people) appointment, assignation, confrontation, contact, encounter, rendezvous. 3 (of roads, lines, rivers) confluence, convergence, crossroads, intersection, junction

melancholy *adj* dejected, depressed, disconsolate, doleful, down *inf*, down in the dumps *inf*, down in the mouth, gloomy, glum, inconsolable, melancholic, miserable, nostalgic, sad, somber, sorry for yourself, tearful, unhappy, wistful

mellow *adj* 1 (of food, taste) fruity, full-bodied, juicy, matured, rich, ripe, smooth, soft, tender. 2 (of a voice, sound) baritone, contralto, deep, mellifluous, resonant, rich, smooth, sweet. 3 (of colors) autumnal, golden, rich, soft, warm. 4 (of a person) calm, gentle, mature, indulgent, relaxed, serene, warm

mellow *v* 1 age, improve with age, mature, ripen, soften. 2 (of a person) chill out *inf*, lighten up *inf*, relax, relent, warm to sth

melodramatic *adj* dramatic, exaggerated, histrionic, sensational, sentimental, theatrical

melody *n* air, descant, music, song, strain, theme, tune

melt *v* 1 defrost, dissolve, liquefy, soften, thaw, unfreeze; *opp* freeze, solidify. 2 (of fears, anger) abate, die down, disappear, disperse, evaporate, fade, fade away, vanish

member *n* 1 adherent, associate, fellow, initiate, subscriber. 2 (of a set) component, constituent, element, part

memoirs *n* autobiography, diary, journal, life story, memories, recollections, reminiscences

memorable *adj* extraordinary, distinctive, historic, impressive, momentous, not to

be forgotten, notable, noteworthy, remarkable, striking, unforgettable; *opp* unmemorable

memorial *adj* celebratory, commemorative, in celebration of sb/sth, in commemoration of sb/sth, in honor of sb/sth, in memory of sb/sth, monumental, in remembrance of sb/sth

memorial *n* cairn, cenotaph, homage, monument, plaque, shrine, statue, time capsule, tribute

memorize *v* absorb, commit to memory, learn, learn by heart, learn by rote, make a mental note of, remember, take in

memory *n* 1 (ability to remember) attention span, mind, powers of recall, recall, remembrance, retention. 2 (sth remembered) impression, recollection, reminiscence. 3 (in computing) bits, bytes, cache, capacity, data bank, data storage, gigabytes, hard disk, kilobytes, megabytes, RAM, random access memory, read-only memory, ROM

menace *n* 1 (dangerous thing, person) bane, danger, evil, hazard, nuisance, peril, risk, sword of Damocles, thorn in sb's side, threat. 2 (an atmosphere of menace) danger, evil, fear, foreboding, intimidation, peril, threat. 3 (naughty child) devil, hooligan, imp, mischief-maker, pest, rapscallion, rascal, scamp *inf*, terror *inf*, troublemaker

menace *v* 1 alarm, browbeat, bully, cow, frighten, intimidate, scare, terrify, terrorize, threaten. 2 (the dangers that menace our society) beset, endanger, hang over, imperil, threaten

menacing *adj* 1 frightening, glowering,

intimidating, lowering, ominous, terrifying, threatening. 2 (of future threats) dangerous, forbidding, impending, looming, ominous, threatening

mend v darn, fix, patch up *inf*, rebuild, reconstruct, renew, repair, restore, sew up

menial *adj* demeaning, dirty, domestic, humble, laboring, low-grade, lowly, low-status, routine, unglamorous, unskilled

mental *adj* cerebral, cognitive, emotional, in the mind, intellectual, psychological; *opp* physical

mentality *n* attitude, cast of mind, character, make-up, mind, mode of thought, personality, psyche, psychology

mentally *adv* cognitively, emotionally, in your mind, in your mind's eye, intellectually, psychologically, silently; *opp* physically

mention *n* acknowledgment, allusion, citation, comment, disclosure, indication, notice, quotation, reference, remark, report, statement

mention v acknowledge, allude to, cite, comment on, declare, disclose, divulge, indicate, quote, refer to, remark on, report, say, speak of, state, talk about, talk of

mercenary *adj* acquisitive, avaricious, covetous, grasping, greedy, in it for the money *inf*, materialistic, money-grubbing *inf*, selfish, venal

merchandise *n* articles, commodities, goods, items, products, wares

merchant *n* businessman, capitalist, entrepreneur, exporter, importer, seller, supplier, trader, tradesman, tradesperson, vendor

merciful *adj* compassionate, forgiving, indulgent, kind, lenient, pitying, soft-hearted, tender-hearted; *opp* merciless

merciless *adj* cruel, hard, pitiless, remorseless, ruthless, severe, without pity; *opp* merciful

mercy *n* 1 charity, clemency, compassion, forgiveness, indulgence, kindness, lenience, pity. 2 **at the mercy of** exposed to, in the clutches of, in the power of, threatened by, under the control of, vulnerable to

merge v 1 (of companies, organizations) ally, amalgamate, be absorbed, be incorporated, be taken over, combine, form a coalition, form an alliance, join forces, join together, team up, unite. 2 (of substances, colors, feelings) be absorbed, be assimilated, be submerged, be swallowed up, blend, converge, fade into, fuse, intermingle, mingle, mix, seep into

merger *n* absorption, alliance, amalgamation, coalition, combination, conglomeration, incorporation, takeover

merit *n* 1 advantage, bonus, credit, good point, pro, quality; *opp* demerit. 2 ability, excellence, praiseworthiness, skill, talent, value, worth

merry *adj* 1 celebrating, cheerful, festive, happy, jolly, joyful, joyous, laughing, lively, rejoicing, reveling. 2 drunk, inebriated, intoxicated, tipsy

mesh *n* lattice, net, netting, network, tangle, web

mesh v agree, be in harmony, be on the same wave length, coincide, combine, connect, dovetail, fit, fit in, fit together, go together, harmonize, interlock, match, tally

mess n 1 chaos, confusion, debris, dirt, disorder, filth, jumble, muddle, pigsty *inf*, rubbish, untidiness. 2 (unsatisfactory situation) calamity, crisis, debacle, disarray, disaster, foul-up *inf*, hole, pickle *inf*, trouble. 3 (place where soldiers eat) bar, cafeteria, canteen, club, dining hall, mess hall

mess v 1 **mess about** act up, have a laugh *inf*, joke, fool about, fool around, misbehave, tease. 2 **mess with sth** fiddle with, fuss, meddle, play with, tinker with, trifle with. 3 **mess up** botch, bungle, get sth wrong, make a mess of, make a pig's ear of *inf*

message n 1 cable, communication, E-mail, fax, letter, memo, memorandum, missive, note, telegram, telephone call, signal, transmission, wire. 2 (of a literary work) idea, import, interpretation, meaning, moral, purport, significance, theme

messenger n bearer, carrier, courier, emissary, envoy, errand-boy, go-between, harbinger, herald, runner

messy adj chaotic, complicated, confused, dirty, filthy, jumbled, untidy

metaphorical adj allegorical, emblematic, figurative, nonliteral, proverbial, symbolic

meteoric adj brilliant, dazzling, fast, irresistible, overnight, quick, rapid, spectacular, speedy, sudden, swift

method n approach, arrangement, manner, means, methodology, mode, modus operandi, plan, practice, procedure, process, rule, style,

system, technique, way

methodical adj careful, deliberate, logical, meticulous, orderly, precise, step-by-step, systematic

meticulous adj accurate, careful, conscientious, correct, detailed, exact, methodical, painstaking, punctilious; *opp* sloppy

microbe n amoeba, bacillus, bacterium, bug *inf*, germ, microorganism, virus

middle adj 1 central, halfway, intermediate, mean, medial, median, mid-. 2 (between two extreme qualities) average, medium, middling

middle n center, core, halfway mark, heart, kernel, midpoint, midst, nucleus

might n energy, force, forcefulness, power, strength, sturdiness, vigor

mighty adj 1 (of person) all-powerful, almighty, forceful, great, powerful, strong, sturdy. 2 (of sound, force) extreme, great, heavy, intense, powerful, severe, strong, vigorous, violent

migrant adj globe-trotting, itinerant, migrating, migratory, traveling, wandering

migrant n asylum seeker, emigrant, exile, globe-trotter, guest worker, gypsy, immigrant, itinerant, nomad, refugee, traveler, voyager, wanderer

migrate v emigrate, flee, fly away, go away, journey, move, relocate, travel, trek, voyage, wander

migration n emigration, flight, immigration, journey, relocation, travel, trek, voyage, wandering

mild adj 1 (of taste, smell) bland, gentle, insipid, inoffensive, soft, subtle, sweet, unobtrusive, weak; *opp* harsh, strong.

2 (of a person) docile, gentle, inoffensive, kind, meek, mild-mannered, placid, unassertive; *opp* aggressive.
3 (of weather) balmy, clement, moderate, temperate, warm, warmish

milieu *n* background, environment, location, setting, social circle, surroundings

militant *adj* aggressive, campaigning, combative, committed, extreme, extremist, hardline, radical, strident, uncompromising; *opp* moderate

military *adj* armed, martial, naval, service, soldierly, warlike

military *n* armed forces, army, forces, militia, services

milk *v* (milk sb) bleed, drain, exploit, extort, extract, siphon, soak, squeeze, suck dry

mill about *v* circulate, hang about, hang around, loiter, mill around, move about, move around, saunter, stroll, walk, wander

mimic *n* chameleon, copycat *inf*, impersonator, impressionist, mime, mime artist

mimic *v* ape, caricature, copy, do an impression of, imitate, impersonate, mime, parody, resemble

mind *n* brain, head, imagination, intellect, intelligence, memory, mental capacity, mental health, mentality, opinion, psyche, psychology, sanity, soul, thinking, thought, will

mind *v* 1 guard, keep, keep an eye on, look after, protect, take care of, watch, watch over. 2 (mind the step) avoid, be aware, be careful, be mindful, beware, look out, pay attention, take care,

watch, watch out. 3 (not mind sth) be bothered, be offended, be upset, care, disapprove, give a damn *inf*, object, take offense

mindful *adj* 1 attentive, aware, careful, conscious, thoughtful, wary, watchful.
2 **be mindful of** be alert to, be alive to, beware of, make allowances for, heed, pay attention to, take account of, take into account, take into consideration, think about

mindless *adj* brainless *inf*, cretinous, daft, hare-brained, idiotic, moronic, stupid, thoughtless, vacuous

mine *n* 1 colliery, deep mine, excavation, pit, quarry, shaft, supply, tunnel, working. 2 bomb, booby trap, detonator, explosive charge, landmine

mine *v* 1 bore, dig, drill, excavate, extract, hew, quarry, tunnel, work.
2 booby-trap, lay mines, plant mines

mingle *v* 1 blend, combine, confuse, fold, intermingle, melt, merge, mix.
2 (talk to people) associate, chat, circulate, fraternize, hobnob *inf*, join in, move around, socialize

minimal *adj* 1 basic, essential, indispensable, minimum. 2 little, nominal, low, meager, slight, small, tiny, token

minimize *v* 1 curtail, cut back, cut down, decrease, keep down, keep to a minimum, prune, reduce, shrink; *opp* maximize. 2 (think sth is unimportant) dismiss, downgrade, laugh off, play down, shrug off, underestimate, underplay, understate

minimum *adj* barest, least, lowest, minimal, smallest, slightest

minimum n least, low point, lowest level, nadir, smallest amount, trough; *opp* maximum

minion n aide, assistant, attendant, bodyguard, flunky, helper, henchman, hireling, lackey, menial, servant, sidekick, subordinate, underling

minister n 1 ambassador, consul delegate, diplomat, emissary, envoy. 2 clergyman, man of the cloth, moderator, parson, pastor, preacher, priest, rector, vicar

minor adj inconsequential, inferior, insignificant, lesser, negligible, slight, small, trivial, unimportant; *opp* major

mint adj new, perfect, pristine, unblemished, unsullied, untarnished, unused, virgin

mint v cast, coin, issue, press, print, produce, stamp, strike

minute adj diminutive, microscopic, mini-, miniature, miniaturized, minuscule, small, tiny; *opp* enormous, huge

minute n instant, jiffy *inf*, moment, second, short time, tick *inf*

minutes n notes, proceedings, record, transactions, transcript

miracle n marvel, mystery, phenomenon, prodigy, wonder

miraculous adj 1 inexplicable, magical, mysterious, paranormal, supernatural. 2 (extremely impressive) fantastic, incredible, marvelous, phenomenal, prodigious, stunning, superb, unbelievable, wonderful, wondrous

mirage n chimera, delusion, hallucination, illusion, image, optical illusion, trick of the light, vision

mirror n glass, looking-glass, reflector

mirth n comedy, fun, hilarity, joking, laughing, laughter, merriment

misapprehension n aberration, error, false impression, misreading, mistake, mistaken impression, misconception, misinterpretation, misjudgment, misunderstanding

misbehave v act up, be cheeky, be impolite, be naughty, be rude, be unruly, behave badly, break the rules, bully, fool about, fool around, make a scene, make mischief, mess about, mess around, play up, show off; *opp* behave

misbehavior n bad behavior, bullying, cheek, delinquency, disobedience, fooling about, fooling around, hooliganism, impoliteness, messing about, messing around, mischief, misconduct, naughtiness, rudeness, showing off, tantrum, tomfoolery, trouble, unruliness

miscalculate v err, get sth wrong, go wrong, make a mistake, misjudge, slip up

miscarriage n 1 abortion, stillbirth. 2 (miscarriage of justice) failure, injustice, mistake, travesty, unsafe conviction, wrongful conviction

miscarry v 1 abort, have a miscarriage, lose a baby. 2 (of a plan) come to nothing, fail, fall through, fall flat, flop, founder, go amiss, go awry, go up in smoke, go wrong, misfire

miscellaneous adj assorted, different, disparate, diverse, jumbled, mixed, motley, odd, sundry, various

mischief n 1 delinquency, misbehavior, misconduct, monkey business *inf*, naughtiness, pranks, shenanigans, trickery, unruliness. 2 damage, deception, dishonesty, evil, harm, hurt, lies, malice, scheming, trouble, vindictiveness, wickedness

mischievous adj 1 bad, badly behaved, cheeky, disobedient, impish, misbehaving, naughty, playful, unruly. 2 deceitful, dishonest, evil, injurious, libelous, malicious, slanderous, spiteful, untrue, vindictive, vicious, wicked

misconception n error, fallacy, false impression, misapprehension, misinterpretation, mistaken impression, misunderstanding

miser n cheapskate inf, hoarder, money-grubber inf, penny-pincher, scrooge, skinflint inf

miserable adj 1 blue inf, brokenhearted, crestfallen, cut-up inf, dejected, depressed, despondent, down inf, down in the dumps inf, downcast, downhearted, forlorn, gloomy, glum, low, melancholy, mournful, sad, sorrowful, unhappy, wretched; *opp* cheerful. 2 churlish, contemptible, cross, despicable, disagreeable, grumpy, ill-natured, low, mean, sour, sulky, sullen, surly, taciturn, unfriendly, unhelpful, unsociable; *opp* pleasant. 3 (of a place) awful, dilapidated, filthy, foul, seedy, shabby, sordid, sorry, squalid, uncomfortable, wretched; *opp* luxurious

misery n 1 anguish, depression, desolation, despair, despondency, distress, gloom, grief, hardship, heartache, hell inf, hopelessness, melancholy, pain, sadness, sorrow, suffering, torment, torture, unhappiness, woe; *opp* happiness. 2 (an unfortunate

event) adversity, blow, hardship, load, misfortune, ordeal, trial, tribulation, trouble, woe; *opp* fortune

misfire v fail, fall through, flop, founder, go amiss, go awry, go up in smoke, go wrong

misfit n eccentric, fish out of water, maverick, nonconformist, oddball inf, square peg in a round hole, weirdo inf

misfortune n accident, adversity, bad luck, blow, calamity, catastrophe, disaster, hardship, harm, loss, misadventure, mishap, setback, tragedy, trial, tribulation, trouble, woe

misguided adj deluded, erroneous, foolish, ill-advised, imprudent, inappropriate, misled, misplaced, mistaken, unreasonable, unsound, unwise, wrong; *opp* well-advised

misjudge v be wrong about, get the wrong end of the stick, get the wrong idea, jump to the wrong conclusion, make a mistake, miscalculate, misconstrue, misinterpret, misread, overestimate, overrate, underestimate, underrate, undervalue

mislay v be unable to find, lose, lose track of, misplace, miss; *opp* find

mislead v beguile, bluff, confuse, deceive, delude, fool, give sb the wrong idea, give sb the wrong impression, hoodwink, lead sb up the garden path, misdirect, misguide, misinform, take sb for a ride, take sb in, throw sb off the scent, trick

misleading adj ambiguous, confusing, deceitful, deceptive, false, spurious, unreliable; *opp* clear

miss n blunder, botch, bungle, error, failure, fault, loss, mistake, omission, oversight, slip, slip-up

miss v 1 (miss a lesson) be too late for, forego, omit, play truant, skip inf. 2 (not include) fail to include, fail to mention, omit, overlook. 3 (narrowly miss being hit) avoid, dodge, escape, evade, sidestep, steer clear of. 4 (miss a target) blunder, botch, bungle, err, fail, fall short, lose, slip up. 5 (miss a person) grieve for, lament, long for, need, pine for, want, yearn for

misshapen adj bent, contorted, crooked, crumpled, deformed, disfigured, distorted, gnarled, grotesque, knotted, malformed, out of shape, screwed up, tangled, twisted, warped

missile n bomb, grenade, projectile, rocket, shell, torpedo, weapon

missing adj absent, astray, gone, lost, mislaid, misplaced, nowhere to be found, unaccounted for; **opp** present

mission n 1 aim, assignment, charge, duty, function, goal, job, objective, purpose, task, undertaking, work. 2 delegation, deputation, task force

missionary n crusader, evangelist, minister, preacher, priest

misspent adj dissipated, misapplied, squandered, thrown away, wasted

mist n cloud, condensation, fog, haze, smog, spray, steam, vapor

mistake n blunder, boob inf, botch, error, fault, faux pas, gaffe, inaccuracy, miscalculation, misjudgment, misprint, misspelling, misunderstanding, omission, oversight, slip, slip-up

mistake v 1 (mistake one thing for another) confuse, mix up, take sth for sth else. 2 (understand sth wrongly) get

the wrong end of the stick, get wrong, misapprehend, misconstrue, misinterpret, misjudge, misread, misunderstand; **opp** understand

mistaken adj erroneous, false, inaccurate, incorrect, inexact, misguided, misinformed, wide of the mark, wrong; **opp** correct

mistress n concubine, girlfriend, kept woman, lover, paramour

mistrust v be skeptical, be suspicious, be unsure, be wary, disbelieve, doubt, fear, have doubts, have misgivings, have suspicions, question, suspect; **opp** trust

misty adj 1 (of weather) cloudy, foggy, hazy, murky; **opp** clear. 2 (of an image) bleary, blurred, dim, faint, fuzzy, indistinct, obscure, smoky, steamy, vague; **opp** distinct

misunderstand v be barking up the wrong tree inf, get the wrong end of the stick, get the wrong idea, get wrong, misapprehend, misconceive, misconstrue, mishear, misinterpret, misjudge, miss the point, mistake; **opp** understand

misunderstanding n error, misapprehension, misconception, misjudgment, misreading, mistake, mix-up

misuse n abuse, corruption, misapplication, squandering, waste

mitigate v allay, alleviate, appease, assuage, calm, check, decrease, diminish, dull, ease, extenuate, lessen, lighten, moderate, mollify, pacify, placate, quiet, reduce, relieve, soothe, subdue, take the edge off inf, temper, weaken; **opp** worsen

mitigating adj exonerating, extenuating,

justifying, qualifying, vindicating

mix *n* amalgam, assortment, blend, combination, compound, mixture, range, union, variety

mix *v* **1** amalgamate, blend, coalesce, combine, cross, fuse, incorporate, intermingle, interweave, join, jumble up, merge, mingle, muddle, unite; *opp* separate. **2** (mix with people) associate, fraternize, go out with, hobnob, keep company, mingle, socialize. **3 mix up** confuse, mistake, muddle up

mixed *adj* **1** (a mixed bunch) assorted, diverse, heterogeneous, miscellaneous, motley, varied; *opp* similar. **2** (mixed feelings) ambiguous, ambivalent, confused, muddled, uncertain, unsure; *opp* clear-cut

mixed-up *adj* **1** at sea, bewildered, confused, muddled, perplexed, puzzled. **2** (a crazy mixed-up kid) disturbed, ill-adjusted, maladjusted, screwed-up *inf*; *opp* together

mixture *n* amalgam, amalgamation, association, blend, brew, collection, compound, cross, fusion, hotchpotch *inf*, medley, mishmash *inf*, mix, union, variety

mix-up *n* confusion, disorder, mistake, misunderstanding, muddle

moan *n* **1** (complaint) beef *inf*, complaint, grouch *inf*, grouse, grumble, whine; *opp* praise. **2** (a moan of pain) cry, groan, sigh, wail, whimper, whine

moan *v* **1** (complain) beef *inf*, carp, complain, grouch *inf*, grouse, grumble, whine. **2** (moan in pain) cry, groan, sigh, wail, whimper, whine

mob *n* body, bunch, collection, crowd, drove, flock, gang, gathering, herd, hoard, host, mass, pack, press, rabble, swarm, throng

mob *v* besiege, crowd, hem in, jostle, overrun, surround, swarm

mobile *adj* **1** (of an object) movable, portable, transportable; *opp* fixed. **2** (of people) itinerant, migrant, nomadic, peripatetic, traveling, wandering. **3** (of a face) animated, changeable, ever-changing, expressive, flexible; *opp* inexpressive

mobilize *v* activate, assemble, call up, gather, get together, marshal, muster, organize, prepare, rally, ready

mock *adj* artificial, bogus, counterfeit, dummy, fake, false, feigned, forged, imitation, pretend *inf*, sham, simulated, spurious; *opp* real

mock *v* deride, insult, jeer, laugh at, make fun of, parody, poke fun at, rib *inf*, ridicule, satirize, scoff, scorn, send up *inf*, sneer, taunt, tease

mockery *n* contempt, derision, disdain, jeering, laughter, parody, ribbing *inf*, ridicule, satire, scoffing, scorn, sending up *inf*, sneering, taunting, teasing

model *n* **1** copy, facsimile, image, imitation, miniature, mock-up, replica, representation. **2** (a model of excellence) archetype, byword, epitome, example, ideal, paradigm, paragon, standard

model *adj* **1** imitation, miniature, mock-up, replica. **2** (a model student) exemplary, ideal, perfect; *opp* terrible

model *v* **1** carve, cast, design, fashion, form, mold, sculpt, shape. **2** (model clothes) display, show off, wear

moderate adj 1 average, light, limited, medium, middle, mild, steady, temperate; *opp* extreme. 2 (of a person) balanced, calm, cautious, cool, fair, gentle, middle-of-the-road, peaceable, reasonable, sober; *opp* extreme

moderate v 1 (become less) abate, calm, decrease, diminish, ease, lessen, lighten, reduce, weaken. 2 (make sth less) alleviate, appease, assuage, calm, check, pacify, placate, quiet, soothe, subdue, take the edge off *inf*

moderation n calmness, composure, control, coolness, fairness, justice, mildness, reasonableness, restraint, temperance

modern adj 1 avant-garde, contemporary, current, fresh, new, newfangled, novel, present, recent. 2 fashionable, in *inf*, in vogue, latest, modish, progressive, stylish, trendy *inf*, up to date, up to the minute, with it *inf*; *opp* old-fashioned

modernize v bring up to date, do up *inf*, refurbish, regenerate, rejuvenate, remake, renew, renovate, revamp, update

modest adj 1 bashful, coy, demure, diffident, discreet, humble, meek, quiet, reserved, restrained, reticent, retiring, self-effacing, shy, unassuming, unpretentious; *opp* brash. 2 (a modest amount) limited, medium, moderate, normal, ordinary, small; *opp* huge

modesty n bashfulness, coyness, demureness, diffidence, discretion, humility, meekness, quietness, reticence, self-effacement, shyness, unpretentiousness; *opp* brashness

modification n adaptation, adjustment, alteration, change, conversion, refinement, reorganization, revision, transformation, variation

modify v adapt, adjust, alter, change, convert, recast, refine, reorganize, revise, transform, vary

moist adj clammy, damp, dank, dewy, humid, runny, steamy, watery, wet; *opp* dry

moisten v damp, dampen, soak, sponge, spray, water, wet; *opp* dry

moisture n damp, dew, humidity, liquid, spray, water, wet, wetness; *opp* dryness

mold n 1 (for making sth) cast, die, form, model, pattern, shape, stamp, template. 2 blight, fungus, growth, mildew, rot

mold v carve, cast, construct, fashion, forge, form, model, sculpt, shape, stamp, work

moldy adj blighted, decayed, decaying, fusty, mildewed, moldering, musty, rotten, rotting

molest v 1 abuse, accost, assault, attack, ill-treat, interfere with, mistreat, rape. 2 annoy, badger, bother, bug *inf*, disturb, harass, harry, hassle, hector, interfere with, irk, irritate, persecute, pester, torment, upset, vex, worry

moment n 1 (in a moment) flash, instant, jiffy *inf*, minute, second, ttwinkling of an eye *inf*. 2 (at that moment) instant, juncture, point, stage, time

momentary adj brief, ephemeral, fleeting, hasty, passing, quick, short, short-lived, transient, transitory; *opp* drawn-out

momentum n drive, energy, force,

impulse, power, propulsion, push, thrust

monarch n emperor, empress, king, potentate, prince, princess, queen, ruler, sovereign

monetary adj budgetary, capital, cash, financial, fiscal

money n bread inf, capital, cash, coin, currency, dough inf, finance, funds, income, means, resources, revenue, savings

mongrel n cross, cross-breed, hybrid, mixed breed; **opp** purebred

monitor n 1 (person) examiner, observer, overseer, prefect, supervisor, watchdog. **2** (device) detector, recorder, scanner, security camera

monitor v check, examine, follow, keep an eye on, keep track of, observe, oversee, record, supervise, survey, trace, track, watch

monk n abbot, brother, friar, hermit

monkey n 1 ape, primate, simian. **2** (you little monkey) devil, imp, rascal, rogue, scamp, terror

monopolize v control, corner, dominate, hog inf, take over

monotonous adj boring, colorless, dreary, droning, dull, flat, humdrum, mindnumbing, plodding, repetitive, soporific, tedious, tiresome, toneless, unchanging, unexciting, uninteresting; **opp** exciting

monster n barbarian, beast, bogey-man, brute, demon, devil, fiend, ghoul, ogre, savage, troll, villain

monstrosity n eyesore, horror

monstrous adj 1 (a monstrous act) abhorrent, abominable, atrocious, awful, brutal, cruel, diabolical, disgraceful, evil,

foul, heinous, horrific, horrifying, inhuman, intolerable, loathsome, odious, outrageous, repulsive, scandalous, shocking, vicious, vile, villainous. **2** (a monstrous building) colossal, enormous, giant, gigantic, great, huge, hulking, immense, mammoth, massive, mighty, prodigious, tremendous, vast; **opp** tiny

monument n cenotaph, gravestone, mausoleum, memorial, obelisk, relic, shrine, statue, tombstone

monumental adj 1 awe-inspiring, awesome, classic, enduring, exceptional, extraordinary, great, historic, immortal, important, impressive, lasting, memorable, outstanding, significant, unforgettable

mood n disposition, frame of mind, humor, inclination, spirit, temper

moody adj abrupt, bad-tempered, cantankerous, crabby, cross, crotchety, curt, doleful, dour, frowning, grumpy, huffy inf, ill-tempered, irritable, miserable, morose, petulant, sulky, sullen, temperamental, testy, touchy, unpredictable; **opp** cheerful

moor v anchor, berth, dock, fasten, fix, lash, secure, tie up

moot adj arguable, contestable, controversial, debatable, disputable, questionable; **opp** uncontroversial

mope v brood, despair, fret, grieve, languish, pine, sulk

moral adj decent, ethical, fair, good, honest, irreproachable, just, law-abiding, noble, principled, proper, pure, respectable, responsible, righteous, upright, upstanding, virtuous; *opp* immoral

morale *n* cheerfulness, confidence, determination, heart, hope, hopefulness, mettle, self-confidence, self-esteem, spirit, zeal

morality *n* decency, fairness, goodness, honesty, integrity, justice, principle, righteousness, uprightness, virtue; *opp* immorality

moralize *v* lecture, pontificate, preach

morals *n* ethics, ideals, manners, mores, principles, scruples, standards

morbid *adj* brooding, ghastly, ghoulish, gloomy, grim, grisly, gruesome, hideous, horrid, macabre, sick *inf*, somber, unhealthy, unwholesome

more *adj* added, additional, extra, fresh, further, increased, new, other, renewed, spare, supplementary; *opp* less

morose *adj* bad-tempered, churlish, depressed, dour, gloomy, glum, grim, humorless, melancholy, moody, mournful, pessimistic, somber, sour, sulky, sullen, taciturn; *opp* cheerful

morsel *n* bit, bite, crumb, fragment, grain, mouthful, nibble, piece, scrap, segment, slice, titbit

mortal *adj* 1 earthly, ephemeral, fleshly, human, temporal, transient, worldly; *opp* immortal. 2 (a mortal injury) deadly, fatal, killing, lethal, terminal; *opp* minor

mortality *n* 1 earthliness, humanity, impermanence, transience, worldliness; *opp* immortality. 2 (infant mortality) deaths, dying, fatalities, loss of life

mortified *adj* ashamed, crushed, deflated, embarrassed, filled with shame, humiliated, shamed; *opp* proud

mortify *v* crush, deflate, embarrass, fill with shame, humiliate, put down, shame

mostly *adv* as a (general) rule, chiefly, commonly, customarily, for the most part, generally, in general, in the main, largely, mainly, normally, on the whole, ordinarily, particularly, predominantly, primarily, principally, typically, usually

mother *n* female parent, ma *inf*, mama, mom *inf*, mommy *inf*, old lady *inf*

mother *v* care for, cherish, fuss over, indulge, look after, nourish, nurse, nurture, pamper, protect, raise, rear, spoil, take care of

motherly *adj* affectionate, caring, fond, kind, loving, maternal, nurturing, protective, tender, warm

motion *n* 1 action, activity, agitation, flow, move, movement, progress, shift, stirring, travel. 2 gesticulation, gesture, movement, signal, wave

motion *v* beckon, direct, gesticulate, gesture, nod, signal, sign, wave

motionless *adj* at rest, frozen, halted, immobile, inert, lifeless, paralyzed, static, stationary, still, stopped, unmoving; *opp* moving

motivate *v* activate, arouse, cause, drive, egg on, encourage, galvanize, goad, impel, incite, induce, influence, inspire, instigate, lead, move, persuade, prod, prompt, provoke, push, set, spur, stimulate, stir, urge

motivated *adj* ambitious, ardent, committed, dedicated, driven, eager, enthusiastic, fervent, galvanized, industrious, inspired, intent, keen

motivation *n* 1 (desire to do sth) ambition, desire, drive, eagerness, enthusiasm, fervor, hunger, inspiration, keenness. 2 (the thing that motivates sth) cause, encouragement, goading, incitement, inducement, inspiration, persuasion, prodding, prompting, pushing, spur

motive n basis, cause, grounds, incentive, inducement, influence, inspiration, intention, lure, motivation, occasion, prompting, provocation, purpose, push, rationale, reason, spur, stimulus

motley adj assorted, diverse, heterogeneous, ill-matched, mingled, miscellaneous, mixed, rag-bag, varied, various

mottled adj blotched, blotchy, dappled, flecked, freckled, marbled, marked, patchy, piebald, speckled, splotchy, spotted, stippled, streaked, variegated

motto n adage, catch-phrase, dictum, epigram, maxim, precept, proverb, rule, saying, slogan, watchword

mound n bank, dune, heap, hill, hillock, hummock, knoll, pile, rise, stack

mount n 1 backing, base, fixture, frame, setting, stand, support. 2 elevation, hill, mound, mountain, peak, summit

mount v 1 ascend, climb, go up, rise, scale. 2 climb on, get astride, get on, jump on. 3 (tension mounts) accumulate, build, escalate, expand, grow, increase, intensify, multiply, pile up, swell. 4 (mount an exhibition) display, exhibit, prepare, produce, put on, stage

mountain n alp, crest, elevation, height, mount, peak, pinnacle, range, sierra, summit

mountainous adj alpine, craggy, high,

highland, rocky, rugged, soaring, steep, towering, upland

mourn v bemoan, bewail, cry for, feel the loss of, grieve, lament, miss, pine for, regret, sorrow, wail, weep

mournful adj depressing, dismal, distressing, doleful, gloomy, heart-breaking, heartrending, melancholy, miserable, painful, piteous, pitiful, plaintive, sad, sorrowful, tragic, unhappy, woeful

mouth n 1 jaws, lips, muzzle.
2 aperture, door, entrance, gateway, inlet, opening, orifice, portal, way in

mouthful n bit, bite, drop, forkful, gulp, morsel, sample, sip, spoonful, swallow, taste

movable adj bendable, detachable, flexible, mobile, moving, plastic, portable, transportable;
opp immovable

move n 1 action, agitation, change, motion, movement, shift, stirring.
2 act, action, deed, gambit, maneuver, measure, play, step, stratagem, stroke, tactic, turn. 3 change, relocation, shift, transfer

move v 1 (sth or sb moves) budge, change places, change position, go, shift, stir. 2 (move sth) carry, transport, shift, take. 3 (move forward) advance, go, head, journey, make headway, make progress, pass, proceed, travel.
4 (move house) go away, leave, migrate, move away, move house, relocate. 5 (make sb feel moved) affect, arouse, fire, impassion, incite, induce, inspire, lead, motivate, persuade, prompt, provoke, push, rouse, spur,

stimulate, stir, touch

movement n 1 action, activity, advance, agitation, change, gesture, motion, move, progress, shift, stirring. 2 carrying, moving, shifting, transfer, transferral, transport, transportation. 3 campaign, coalition, crusade, drive, faction, front, group, lobby, organization, party, pressure group

moving adj 1 affecting, emotional, emotive, heartrending, heartwarming, inspiring, pathetic, poignant, powerful, rousing, stirring, touching. 2 active, dynamic, in motion, mobile, movable

mow v 1 clip, crop, cut, scythe, shear, trim. 2 **mow down** butcher, cut down, massacre, slaughter, slay

mud n clay, dirt, mire, ooze, silt, slime, sludge, soil

muddle n chaos, clutter, confusion, disarray, disorder, jumble, mess, mix-up, shambles inf, tangle

muddle v 1 clutter, disarrange, disorder, disorganize, get sth mixed up, jumble, mess up, mix up, scramble, tangle. 2 bemuse, bewilder, confound, confuse, daze, disorient, disorientate, perplex, puzzle

muddy adj 1 caked, dirty, filthy, messy, mucky. 2 boggy, marshy, slimy, sludgy, soft, spongy, waterlogged

muffle v 1 cloak, cover, enfold, hood, shroud, swathe, wrap up. 2 (muffle a sound) dampen, deaden, disguise, dull, hush, mask, mute, quieten, silence, smother, soften, stifle, suppress

muffled adj dampened, deadened, dull, faint, hushed, indistinct, muted, smothered, stifled,

suppressed, unclear

mug n beaker, cup, flagon, jug, pot, tankard

mugger n assailant, attacker, bag-snatcher, robber, thief, thug

muggy adj clammy, close, damp, humid, oppressive, steamy, sticky, stuffy, sultry

multiple adj collective, many, numerous, several, sundry, various

multiply v accumulate, breed, expand, extend, increase, proliferate, propagate, reproduce, spread

multitude n army, assembly, congregation, crowd, horde, host, legion, mass, mob, sea, swarm, throng

mumble v grumble, murmur, mutter, speak indistinctly

munch v champ, chew, chomp, crunch, eat, gnaw, masticate

mundane adj banal, commonplace, dull, everyday, humdrum, ordinary, pedestrian, prosaic, quotidian, routine, unexciting, uninteresting, workaday; *opp* extraordinary

municipal adj borough, city, civic, civil, community, district, local, metropolitan, public, town, urban

murder n assassination, bloodshed, butchery, carnage, homicide, killing, manslaughter, massacre, slaughter, slaying

murder v assassinate, bump off inf, butcher, destroy, dispatch, do away with inf, do in inf, kill, massacre, put to death, slaughter, slay

murderer n assassin, butcher, cutthroat, gunman, killer, slaughterer, slayer

murderous adj barbaric, barbarous, bloodthirsty, bloody, butchering, death-dealing, homicidal, massacring, psychopathic, savage, slaughtering

murmur n 1 (sound) buzz, drone, hum, rumble, rumbling. 2 (way of speaking) grumble, mumble, mumbling, mutter, muttering, undertone, whisper

murmur v breathe, grumble, mumble, mutter, purr, rumble, speak in an undertone, whisper

muscle n 1 biceps, ligament, sinew, tendon. 2 brawn, clout inf, force, might, potency, power, strength

muscular adj athletic, beefy inf, brawny, burly, hefty, hunky inf, lusty, mighty, powerful, robust, sinewy, stalwart, strapping, strong, sturdy, tough, vigorous, well-built

muse v brood, cogitate, consider, contemplate, daydream, deliberate, dream, meditate, mull over, ponder, reflect, ruminate, speculate, think, weigh, wonder

musical adj dulcet, harmonious, lilting, melodic, melodious, sweet-sounding, tuneful

muster v assemble, call up, collect, congregate, convene, gather, group, marshal, mobilize, rally, round up, summon

musty adj airless, damp, dank, decaying, fusty, mildewed, moldy, smelly, stale, stuffy, unused

mutation n alteration, change, evolution, metamorphosis, modification, transformation, transmutation, variation

mute adj dumb, silent, speechless, unspoken, voiceless, wordless

mutilate v butcher, cripple, damage, deface, disable, disfigure, dismember, hack, lame, maim, mangle

mutinous adj defiant, disobedient, insubordinate, rebellious, restive, revolutionary, riotous, seditious, subversive, uncontrollable, ungovernable, unmanageable, unruly

mutiny n defiance, disobedience, insubordination, insurgence, insurrection, rebellion, resistance, revolt, revolution, riot, rising, sedition, subversion, uprising

mutiny v defy, disobey, rebel, resist, revolt, riot, rise up

mutter v complain, grumble, mumble, murmur, rumble, talk under your breath

mutual adj common, joint, reciprocal, reciprocated, requited, returned, shared

muzzle v censor, curb, gag, restrain, silence, stifle, suppress

mysterious adj abstruse, arcane, baffling, bizarre, cryptic, curious, dark, enigmatic, furtive, hidden, impenetrable, inexplicable, inscrutable, mystifying, obscure, perplexing, puzzling, secret, strange, uncanny, unexplained, unfathomable, unknown, weird

mystery n conundrum, enigma, paradox, problem, puzzle, riddle, secret

mystical adj arcane, hidden, metaphysical, mysterious, occult, otherworldly, paranormal, preternatural, spiritual, supernatural, transcendental

mystify v baffle, bemuse, bewilder, confound, confuse, elude, escape, flummox, nonplus, perplex, puzzle, stump inf

myth *n* 1 allegory, fable, fairy-tale,
legend, parable, saga, story, tale.
2 delusion, fabrication, falsehood,
fiction, figment of sb's imagination,
invention, misconception, untruth
mythical *adj* 1 allegorical, fabled,
fabulous, fairy-tale, fantastical,
legendary, mythic, mythological.
2 fabricated, false, fantasy, imaginary,
invented, made-up, nonexistent,
pretended, unreal, untrue

nadir n bottom, depths, low point, rock bottom

nag n harpy, pest, scold, shrew, virago

nag v annoy, badger, be on sb's back *inf*, carp, goad, go on at *inf*, harass, harp on, hassle *inf*, hector, henpeck, pester, plague, worry

nagging adj continuous, ever-present, irritating, painful, persistent, worrying

nail v attach, fasten, fix, hammer, join, pin, secure, tack

naive adj artless, childlike, credulous, green *inf*, guileless, gullible, inexperienced, ingenuous, innocent, open, simple, trusting, unsophisticated, unsuspicious, unwary, unworldly; *opp* knowing

naked adj bare, exposed, in your birthday suit *inf*, in the altogether *inf*, in the buff *inf*, in the nude, in the raw *inf*, nude, stark-naked, stripped, unclothed, uncovered, undressed; *opp* clothed, dressed

name n 1 appellation, epithet, label, nickname, tag, term, title. 2 (make your name in sth) distinction, eminence, esteem, fame, honor, note, prestige, prominence, reputation, repute, renown

name v 1 baptize, call, christen, designate, dub, entitle, label, nickname, style, tag, term. 2 (name a new chairman) appoint, choose, commission, delegate, designate, elect, identify, nominate, pick, select, specify

nameless adj 1 anonymous, incognito, obscure, unidentified, unknown, unsung. 2 abominable, appalling, dreadful, horrible, indescribable, unmentionable, unspeakable, unutterable

nap n doze, forty winks *inf*, rest, siesta, sleep, snooze *inf*

nap v doze, drowse, have a nap, nod off *inf*, rest, sleep, snooze *inf*

narrate v chronicle, describe, detail, recite, recount, rehearse, relate, repeat, report, tell, unfold

narration n commentary, description, explanation, reading, recital, relation, reporting, storytelling, telling

narrative n account, chronicle, description, history, report, statement, story, tale

narrator n author, chronicler, commentator, reporter, storyteller, writer

narrow adj close, confined, cramped, fine, limited, meager, pinched, restricted, scanty, slender, slim, squeezed, straitened, thin, tight; *opp* wide

narrow v diminish, limit, reduce, shrink, straiten, tighten; *opp* widen

narrow-minded *adj* biased, bigoted, conservative, hidebound, inflexible, insular, intolerant, mean-spirited, old-fashioned, parochial, petty, prejudiced, reactionary, rigid, small-minded, strait-laced; *opp* broad-minded

nasty *adj* **1** awful, disgusting, filthy, foul, horrible, horrid, nauseating, odious, repellent, repugnant, repulsive, revolting, sickening, unpleasant, vile, yucky *inf*; *opp* nice. **2** (be nasty to sb) bitchy *sl*, catty, cruel, disagreeable, horrible, horrid, malicious, mean, spiteful, unkind, unpleasant, vicious; *opp* nice

nation *n* country, domain, kingdom, land, people, population, power, realm, republic, society, state

national *adj* **1** (not local) countrywide, federal, general, nationwide. **2** (not international) domestic, internal, patriotic, popular

nationalism *n* chauvinism, jingoism, loyalty, patriotism, xenophobia

native *adj* **1** (native to a place) aboriginal, domestic, indigenous, local, original. **2** (native intelligence) congenital, hereditary, inborn, inbred, inherited, innate, instinctive, intuitive, natural

native *n* citizen, countryman, dweller, inhabitant, local, resident

natural *adj* **1** authentic, genuine, real, sincere, spontaneous, unaffected, unfeigned; *opp* artificial. **2** (normal) common, logical, ordinary, normal, predictable, regular, routine, standard, typical, understandable, unsurprising, usual; *opp* unnatural. **3** (a natural ability) characteristic, congenital, god-given, hereditary, inborn, inbred, inherited, innate, instinctive, intuitive, native; *opp* learned

naturally *adv* **1** (behave naturally) candidly, ingenuously, unpretentiously. **2** as you would expect, certainly, of course

nature *n* **1** ecology, landscape, Mother Nature, natural history, scenery, the countryside, the earth, the environment, the universe, the world, wildlife. **2** (sth of that nature) description, kind, sort, species, style, type, variety. **3** (sb's nature) character, disposition, make-up, mood, outlook, personality, temperament, traits. **4** (the nature of a thing) character, essence, features, properties, quality

naught *n* nil, nothing, zero

naughty *adj* bad, badly behaved, defiant, delinquent, disobedient, disruptive, impolite, mischievous, rascally, rude, stubborn, undisciplined, unmanageable, unruly, wicked, willful

nausea *n* **1** biliousness, faintness, queasiness, seasickness, sickness, vomiting. **2** disgust, loathing, repugnance, revulsion

nauseate *v* disgust, horrify, make sb sick, make sb want to throw up *inf*, offend, repel, repulse, revolt, sicken, turn sb's stomach

nautical *adj* boating, marine, maritime, naval, sailing, seafaring, seagoing, yachting

navigate *v* **1** cross, cruise, journey, sail, sail across, voyage. **2** (navigate a ship) captain, drive, handle, maneuver, pilot, skipper, steer. **3** (find the way) direct, find the way, guide, plan the route

navigation n **1** directing, maneuvering, steering. **2** (the skills of navigation) sailing, seamanship

navigator n helmsman, mariner, pilot, seaman

navy n armada, convoy, fleet, flotilla

near adj **1** (near in space) accessible, adjacent, adjoining, at close quarters, beside, bordering, close, close by, connected, handy, nearby, neighboring, next-door, touching, within reach. **2** (near in time) approaching, coming, forthcoming, imminent, impending, in the offing, looming, next, round the corner inf

nearly adv about, all but, almost, approaching, approximately, around, as good as, just about, not quite, practically, roughly, virtually

neat adj **1** accurate, clean, dapper, fastidious, methodical, meticulous, orderly, organized, precise, shipshape, smart, spick and span, spruce, straight, systematic, tidy, trim, uncluttered, well-groomed, well-kept, well-turned-out; opp untidy. **2** (neat movements) agile, dainty, deft, dexterous, elegant, graceful, nimble, practiced, precise, skillful, stylish; opp clumsy. **3** (neat whisky) pure, straight, undiluted

necessary adj compulsory, essential, imperative, important, indispensable, mandatory, needed, obligatory, required, vital

necessitate v call for, demand, entail, involve, make necessary, require

necessity n (sth is a necessity) essential,

must inf, need, prerequisite, requirement

need n **1** (need for affection) desire, lack, longing, shortage, wish, yearning. **2** (children in need) deprivation, destitution, distress, poverty. **3** (the need to do sth) call, necessity, obligation. **4** (a basic human need) demand, essential, requirement, want

need v **1** (need sth) be short of, be without, call for, demand, lack, require, want. **2** (need sb) depend on, desire, miss, rely on, want. **3** (need to do sth) be compelled, be obliged, have to

needless adj excessive, gratuitous, groundless, pointless, redundant, superfluous, uncalled for, unnecessary, unwanted

needy adj badly off, deprived, destitute, disadvantaged, hard up inf, penniless, poor, poverty-stricken, underprivileged

negate v cancel, contradict, deny, disprove, invalidate, neutralize, oppose, repeal, reverse, revoke, wipe out

negative adj **1** (negative outlook) complaining, cynical, gloomy, jaundiced, pessimistic, unenthusiastic, unhelpful; opp positive. **2** (saying no) anti inf, contradicting, contradictory, contrary, denying, disagreeing, opposing, refusing, resisting

neglect n carelessness, forgetfulness, inattention, indifference, lack of concern, negligence

neglect v **1** (leave sb or sth) abandon, forget, forsake, ignore, leave alone, pay no attention to. **2** (neglect to do sth) fail, forget, not remember, omit, overlook, shirk, skimp, skip

neglected adj **1** (of a place) abandoned,

derelict, forgotten, overgrown, run-down. **2** (of a child) abandoned, ignored, left alone, mistreated, uncared for

negligent adj careless, forgetful, irresponsible, neglectful, reckless, remiss, slack, slapdash, sloppy, thoughtless, unthinking; opp careful

negligible adj inconsequential, insignificant, minor, petty, slight, small, tiny, trifling, trivial, unimportant

negotiate v agree, bargain, deal, discuss, haggle, hold talks, settle, work out

negotiation n arbitration, bargaining, diplomacy, discussion, mediation, talks

neighborhood n area, community, district, locality, part, place, region, vicinity, zone

neighboring adj adjacent, adjoining, bordering, close, closest, near, nearby, nearest, next, next-door, surrounding

neighborly adj amiable, friendly, helpful, hospitable, kind, obliging, sociable

nerve n **1** (bravery) bravery, coolness, courage, daring, determination, fearlessness, guts inf, resolve, spirit, willpower. **2** (cheek) audacity, brazenness, cheek, impertinence, impudence, insolence, presumptuousness, rudeness

nerve-racking adj anxious, difficult, distressing, frightening, harrowing, nail-biting inf, stressful, tense, worrying

nerves n anxiety, butterflies in your stomach inf, jitters inf, nervousness, strain, stress, tension

nervous adj afraid, agitated, anxious, apprehensive, edgy, fearful, highly strung, impatient, insecure, jumpy, on

edge, on tenterhooks inf, restless, shaky, strained, tense, timid, trembling, uneasy, unnerved, uptight inf, worried; opp calm

nestle v cuddle, curl up, huddle, nuzzle, snuggle

net n lattice, mesh, netting, web

net v capture, catch, enmesh, entangle, snare, trap

network n **1** crisscross inf, grid, labyrinth, lattice, maze, mesh, net, tangle, web. **2** arrangement, interconnection, organization, structure, system

neurosis n anxiety, depression, fixation, obsession, phobia

neurotic adj anxious, compulsive, disturbed, mentally ill, nervous, obsessive, overwrought, unstable

neuter v castrate, geld, spay, sterilize

neutral adj **1** (neutral in an argument) disinterested, fair, impartial, objective, open-minded, unbiased, uncommitted, undecided, uninvolved, unprejudiced. **2** (neutral colors) colorless, dull, indeterminate, pale, vague

neutralize v cancel, cancel out, compensate for, counteract, make ineffective, negate, undo, wipe out

never-ending adj boundless, constant, continual, endless, eternal, everlasting, incessant, infinite, limitless, nonstop, perpetual, relentless, unbroken, uninterrupted, without end

new adj advanced, brand-new, contemporary, current, different, fashionable, fresh, futuristic, latest, modern, newfangled, novel, original, recent, revolutionary, state-of-the-art, topical, trendy inf, unfamiliar, unknown, unused, unusual, up-to-date; **opp** old

newcomer n immigrant, new arrival, outsider, settler, stranger

newfangled adj gimmicky, modern, new, novel, state-of-the-art, ultra-modern

news n 1 (a news report) announcement, bulletin, dispatch, exposé, facts, headlines, leak, release, report, statement, story. 2 (catching up on the news) gossip, information, rumor, scandal, talk, the latest inf, word

newspaper n daily inf, gazette, journal, paper, rag inf, tabloid, weekly

next adv after, afterwards, later, subsequently, then

nibble v bite, eat, gnaw, munch, nip, peck at, pick at, snack on inf

nibble n bite, crumb, morsel, piece, snack, taste

nice adj 1 (of a person) agreeable, amiable, charming, courteous, friendly, kind, likeable, pleasant, polite, understanding; **opp** horrible, nasty. 2 (of the weather) dry, fine, pleasant, sunny, warm; **opp** awful, dreadful. 3 (a nice time) enjoyable, exciting, good, interesting, marvelous, pleasant, pleasurable; **opp** awful, horrible. 4 (of behavior) appropriate, cultivated, polite, proper, refined, respectable, seemly; **opp** bad

niche n alcove, corner, cranny, hollow, nook, opening, recess

nick n chip, cut, dent, mark, notch, scratch

nick v 1 (nick the edge of sth) chip, cut, mark, notch, scratch. 2 (steal) filch, lift, pilfer, pinch, pocket, shoplift, steal,

swipe, take, walk off with

nickname n alias, family name, pet name

niggle n complaint, concern, misgiving, objection, worry

niggle v 1 criticize, find fault, fuss, nag, nitpick inf. 2 (sth niggles you) annoy, irritate, rankle, trouble, worry

niggling adj 1 finicky, fussy, nit-picking inf, picky inf. 2 insignificant, minor, petty, trifling, unimportant. 3 (niggling doubts) gnawing, irritating, persistent, troubling, worrying

night n dark, darkness, nighttime

nightfall n dusk, evening, sundown, sunset, twilight

nimble adj acrobatic, active, agile, deft, graceful, lithe, lively, quick, skillful, sprightly, spry

nip n 1 bite, nibble, pinch, tweak. 2 (nip of whisky) dram, drop, sip, taste

nip v 1 catch, clip, grip, hurt, pinch, snag, squeeze, tweak, twitch. 2 bite, sink your teeth into, snap at

nobility n aristocracy, elite, gentry, high society, l upper class

noble adj 1 (of noble birth) aristocratic, blue-blooded, born with a silver spoon in your mouth, distinguished, highborn, princely, titled, upper-class. 2 (a noble gesture) brave, gallant, generous, heroic, honorable, magnanimous, self-sacrificing, virtuous, worthy. 3 (a noble oak tree) awesome, great, imposing, impressive, splendid

noble n aristocrat, lady, lord, nobleman, noblewoman, peer

nocturnal adj night, nightly, nighttime

nod v 1 bob your head, bow your head, incline your head. 2 (as a signal)

gesture, indicate, motion, sign, signal.
3 nod off doze, drop off, drowse, fall
asleep, nap, nod off, slumber

noise n babble, blare, cacophony, clamor,
clatter, commotion, din, hubbub,
hullabaloo *inf*, racket, row, screaming,
shouting, sound, talk, uproar

noiseless adj hushed, inaudible, mute,
muted, quiet, silent, soft, soundless, still;
opp noisy

noisy adj blaring, blasting, boisterous,
deafening, ear-splitting, loud, piercing,
raucous, riotous, rowdy; *opp* quiet, silent

nomad n migrant, rambler, roamer, rover,
traveler, wanderer

nomadic adj migrant, roaming, roving,
traveling, wandering

nominal adj **1** (the nominal leader of the
country) formal, in name only,
ostensible, puppet, self-styled, so-called,
supposed. **2** (a nominal fee) minimal,
minor, small, symbolic, token; *opp* large

nominate v appoint, assign, choose,
designate, elect, name, propose, put
forward, put up *inf*, recommend, select,
submit

nonchalant adj blasé, calm, casual,
composed, cool, indifferent, laid-back
inf, offhand, self-possessed, unconcerned,
unemotional; *opp* tense, uptight

noncommittal adj careful, cautious,
discreet, evasive, giving nothing away,
guarded, neutral, tactful, unrevealing,
vague, wary

non compos mentis adj crazy, insane,
mad, mentally ill, mentally unbalanced,
of unsound mind

nondescript adj characterless, dull,
featureless, indeterminate, ordinary,

undistinguished, uninteresting,
unmemorable, unremarkable;
opp special

nonentity n lightweight *inf*, nobody,
nothing *inf*, person of no account

nonexistent adj fantasy, fictional,
fictitious, hypothetical, illusory,
imaginary, imagined, legendary,
made-up, mythical, unreal; *opp* real

nonplussed adj astonished, astounded,
amazed, baffled, disconcerted,
dumbfounded, flummoxed, mystified,
speechless, stunned, taken aback

nonsense n **1** balderdash, baloney *inf*,
drivel, gibberish, gobbledegook *inf*,
hogwash *inf*, rubbish, stuff and nonsense,
twaddle. **2** clowning, foolishness, idiocy,
joking, madness, silliness, stupidity

nonstop adj ceaseless, constant,
continuous, endless, incessant, never-
ending, steady, unbroken, unending,
uninterrupted

norm n average, benchmark, mean,
measure, par, pattern, rule, scale,
standard, type, yardstick

normal adj accepted, average, common,
customary, established, everyday,
familiar, general, natural, ordinary,
predictable, regular, routine, run-of-the
mill *inf*, standard, typical, usual;
opp abnormal

normality n naturalness, ordinariness,
regularity, routine, usualness

normally adv as a rule, as usual,
commonly, in general, mostly, naturally,
ordinarily, regularly, routinely, typically,
usually

nose v **1** detect, scent, smell out, sniff
out. **2** interfere, look around, meddle,

poke your nose in *inf*, pry, search, snoop *inf*

nostalgia *n* homesickness, longing, memory, pining, regret, reminiscence, sentiment, sentimentality, wistfulness, yearning

nostalgic *adj* emotional, homesick, longing, pining, regretful, remembering, romantic, sentimental, wistful, yearning

nosy *adj* curious, eavesdropping, inquisitive, interfering, intrusive, meddlesome, prying, snooping *inf*

notable *adj* 1 extraordinary, famous, impressive, memorable, noteworthy, noticeable, obvious, outstanding, rare, remarkable, singular, uncommon, unforgettable, unusual. 2 celebrated, distinguished, eminent, famous, great, noted, prominent, renowned, well-known

notation *n* characters, code, script, signs, symbols, system

note *n* 1 comment, correspondence, explanation, footnote, inscription, jotting, letter, memo *inf*, memorandum, message, minute, record, reference, reminder. 2 (a note of sarcasm in his voice) element, feeling, hint, intonation, quality, tone

note *v* detect, enter, indicate, jot down, make a note, mark, mention, notice, observe, record, register, remark, see, take note, take notice, write down

noted *adj* acclaimed, celebrated, distinguished, eminent, famous, great, illustrious, notable, of note, prominent, recognized, renowned, well-known

noteworthy *adj* exceptional, extraordinary, important, rare,

remarkable, significant, striking, unique, unusual; *opp* ordinary

nothing *n* 1 nil, zero. 2 vacuum, void, blankness, naught, not anything, not a thing, nothingness, zilch *inf*

notice *n* 1 (a notice on the bulletin board) advertisement, announcement, bulletin, handout, leaflet, message, note, poster, sign, warning. 2 (come to sb's notice) attention, awareness, consciousness, observation, regard. 3 (receive notice of sth) advice, information, news, notification, warning. 4 (be given your notice) dismissal, marching orders *inf*, redundancy, the boot *inf*, the sack *inf*

notice *v* be aware, detect, discern, discover, distinguish, feel, find, make out, note, observe, pay attention, perceive, register, see, spot, take note

noticeable *adj* apparent, clear, conspicuous, discernible, distinct, evident, marked, obvious, plain, prominent, pronounced, salient, striking, unmistakable, visible

notify *v* advise, declare, inform, let sb know, make known, proclaim, publish, report, tell, warn

notion *n* assumption, belief, concept, idea, impression, opinion, theory, thought, understanding, view

notional *adj* abstract, conceptual, hypothetical, illusory, imaginary, theoretical, unreal

notoriety *n* bad reputation, dishonor, disrepute, ill repute, infamy, scandal

notorious *adj* disgraceful, dishonorable, disreputable, ill-famed, infamous, of ill repute, outrageous, scandalous, well-known

nourish v care for, feed, maintain, nurture, provide for, strengthen, support, sustain

nourishing adj good for you, healthy, nutritious, sustaining, wholesome

nourishment n diet, food, goodness, nutrition, sustenance

novel adj different, fresh, ground-breaking, imaginative, innovative, new, original, trail-blazing, uncommon, unconventional, unfamiliar, unique, unusual; **opp** old

novel n best-seller, book, fiction, narrative, romance, story, work of fiction

novelty n 1 (the novelty of his plan) difference, freshness, newness, originality, strangeness, unusualness. 2 (cheap novelties) curiosity, gadget, gimmick, knickknack, memento, souvenir, trinket

novice n amateur, apprentice, beginner, learner, newcomer, new recruit, probationer, pupil, rookie inf, student, trainee

now adv at once, at present, at the moment, for the time being, immediately, instantly, just now, nowadays, promptly, right away, right now, straightaway; **opp** later

nowadays adv at present, at the moment, in this day and age, now, these days, today

noxious adj corrosive, foul, harmful, nasty, poisonous, polluting, toxic, unhealthy, unwholesome; **opp** harmless

nucleus n center, core, heart, kernel, middle, nub.

nude adj bare, exposed, in your birthday

suit inf, in the altogether inf, in the buff inf, naked, in the raw inf, stark-naked, stripped, unclothed, uncovered, undressed; **opp** clothed, dressed

nudge v bump, dig, dig sb in the ribs, elbow, jog, poke, prod, push, shove, touch

nuisance n annoyance, bore, bother, drag inf, hassle inf, inconvenience, irritation, pain inf, problem, trouble, worry

nullify v abolish, annul, cancel, declare null and void, do away with, invalidate, negate, neutralize, quash, repeal, revoke, set aside

numb adj anesthetized, asleep inf, cold, dead, deadened, frozen, paralyzed, stunned, stupefied, without feeling

numb v anesthetize, deaden, desensitize, dull, freeze, immobilize, make numb, paralyze

number n 1 digit, figure, integer, numeral, unit. 2 (of a magazine) copy, edition, imprint, issue, printing

number v add up, calculate, compute, count, reckon, total, work out

numberless adj countless, endless, infinite, innumerable, many, more than you can count, myriad, numerous, untold

numeral n Arabic numeral, character, digit, figure, integer, number, Roman numeral, symbol

numerous adj abundant, copious, countless, lots inf, many, multitudinous, myriad, plentiful, several, untold, various; **opp** few

nurse v care for, look after, minister to, take care of, tend, treat

nurture v bring up, cultivate, educate,

feed, nourish, nurse, provide for, rear,
sustain, tend, train

nut *n* 1 kernel, pip, seed, stone.
2 crackpot *inf*, crank *inf*, eccentric,
loony *inf*, lunatic, madman, maniac,
nut case *inf*, psycho *sl*, psychopath,
weirdo *inf*

nutritious *adj* good for you, health-
giving, healthy, nourishing, wholesome

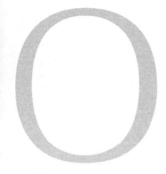

oasis *n* 1 spring, watering-hole, well. 2 haven, hiding-place, island, refuge, retreat, sanctuary

oath *n* 1 (oath of allegiance) affirmation, avowal, bond, pledge, promise, sworn statement, undertaking, vow, word of honor. 2 blasphemy, curse, expletive, obscenity, profanity, swear word

obedient *adj* acquiescent, amenable, compliant, docile, dutiful, law-abiding, manageable, respectful, submissive, well-behaved, well-trained; *opp* disobedient

obese *adj* corpulent, fat, fleshy, heavy, overweight, podgy, portly, stout, tubby; *opp* thin

obey *v* 1 (obey a rule) abide by, accept, adhere to, agree to, comply with, follow, keep, observe, respect, stick to *inf*. 2 (obey sb) be obedient to, be ruled by, bow to, defer to, heed, honor, submit to, take orders from, yield to. 3 (you must obey) be dutiful, be obedient, do what you are told, follow orders. 4 (obey the instructions) act upon, carry out, fulfill, perform

object *n* 1 (a useful object) article, item, thing. 2 (the object of the game) aim, goal, idea, intention, motive, objective, point, purpose, reason. 3 (the object of abuse/frustration) butt, focus, recipient, target, victim

object *v* argue, beg to differ, be opposed, complain, grumble, mind *inf*, oppose, protest, raise objections, take a stand against, take exception to

objection *n* argument, challenge, complaint, disapproval, dissatisfaction, doubt, grievance, opposition, protest, query, quibble

objectionable *adj* abhorrent, deplorable, disgusting, distasteful, foul, horrible, insufferable, intolerable, nasty, obnoxious, offensive, repugnant, revolting, unacceptable, undesirable, unpleasant, vile

objective *n* aim, ambition, aspiration, design, desire, end, goal, hope, intent, intention, object, plan, point, purpose, target

objective *adj* detached, disinterested, dispassionate, evenhanded, fair, impartial, just, neutral, open-minded, rational, unbiased, unemotional, uninvolved, unprejudiced; *opp* biased

obligation *n* commitment, compulsion, constraint, demand, duty, liability, necessity, need, requirement, responsibility

obligatory *adj* binding, compulsory, essential, imperative, mandatory, necessary, required, unavoidable; *opp* optional, voluntary

oblige *v* **1** (make sb do sth) bind, coerce, compel, constrain, force, leave sb no choice, make, put sb under an obligation, require. **2** (do sb a favor) accommodate, help, indulge, please, serve

obliged *adj* **1** (feel obliged to sb) appreciative, grateful, indebted, thankful. **2** (obliged to do sth) bound, compelled, constrained, duty-bound, forced, made, required

obliging *adj* agreeable, amiable, considerate, cooperative, courteous, eager to please, friendly, generous, good-natured, helpful, kind, polite, willing; *opp* difficult, unhelpful

oblique *adj* **1** (oblique line) angled, aslant, at an angle, diagonal, inclined, slanted, slanting, sloped, sloping. **2** (oblique mention) back-handed, implicit, implied, indirect, roundabout; *opp* direct

obliterate *v* blot out, cancel, delete, demolish, destroy, efface, eradicate, erase, leave no trace, remove, rub out, wipe out

oblivion *n* **1** absent-mindedness, abstraction, amnesia, forgetfulness, unawareness, unconsciousness. **2** (consigned to oblivion) anonymity, disuse, extinction, neglect, obscurity. **3** blackness, darkness, senselessness, stupor, unconsciousness

oblivious *adj* absent-minded, absorbed, blind, careless, deaf, forgetful, heedless, ignorant, neglectful, regardless, unaware, unconcerned, unheeding; *opp* aware

obnoxious *adj* disgusting, foul, horrid, insufferable, loathsome, nasty, nauseating, objectionable, odious, offensive, repellent, repugnant, repulsive, revolting, unpleasant; *opp* nice, pleasant

obscene *adj* blue, coarse, crude, depraved, dirty, disgusting, filthy, foul, foul-mouthed, immoral, indecent, lewd, offensive, perverted, pornographic, rude, shocking, sick *inf*, suggestive, vulgar

obscenity *n* **1** (shout an obscenity) curse, dirty word, expletive, four-letter word, naughty word, swear word. **2** (prosecuted for obscenity) blasphemy, evil, filth, immorality, indecency, lewdness, offensiveness, perversion, pornography, vulgarity

obscure *adj* **1** (not obvious) ambiguous, concealed, confusing, cryptic, deep, enigmatic, hidden, mysterious, puzzling, secret, unclear; *opp* obvious. **2** (not clear) blurred, cloudy, dark, dim, faint, fuzzy, gloomy, hazy, indistinct, masked, misty, murky, shadowy, shady, shrouded, unlit, vague; *opp* clear, distinct. **3** (not known about) forgotten, hidden, insignificant, remote, undistinguished, unheard-of, unknown

obscure *v* block, blur, cloak, cloud, conceal, cover, darken, dim, disguise, eclipse, hide, mask, overshadow, screen, shade, shroud, veil

observant *adj* alert, attentive, aware, eagle-eyed, having your eyes peeled, on the ball *inf*, on the lookout, perceptive, sharp, sharp-eyed, vigilant, watchful; *opp* unobservant

observation *n* **1** (watching sth or sb) attention, examination, inspection, monitoring, review, scrutiny, study,

surveillance, watch, watching.
2 (sth that you notice) conclusion,
finding, information, result. 3 (sth that
you say or write) opinion,
reflection, remark, statement, thought

observe v 1 (notice) detect, discern,
discover, note, notice, perceive, see,
spot, witness. 2 (observe sth or sb)
check out inf, keep an eye on inf, keep
tabs on inf, keep under observation, keep
under surveillance, monitor, scrutinize,
spy on, stare at, study, view, watch.
3 (observe a religious custom) celebrate,
follow, honor, keep, mark, obey,
remember. 4 (make an observation)
announce, comment, mention,
remark, say

observer n bystander, commentator, eyewitness, onlooker, spectator, viewer,
watcher, witness

obsess v become an obsession, be on your
mind, consume, control, dominate, grip,
haunt, plague, possess, preoccupy, prey
on, take hold of, torment

obsessed adj gripped, haunted, hung up
on inf, in the grip of, preoccupied

obsession n addiction, bee in your
bonnet inf, complex, compulsion, fetish,
fixation, hang-up inf, infatuation, mania,
phobia, preoccupation, thing inf

obsessive adj addictive, compulsive,
consuming, gripping, passionate

obsolete adj antiquated, antique, archaic,
bygone, dated, discarded, extinct, old,
old-fashioned, outmoded, out of date,
passé, unfashionable

obstacle n bar, barrier, block, blockage,
check, difficulty, hindrance, hitch,
hurdle, interruption, obstruction,

problem, snag, stumbling block

obstinate adj defiant, determined,
dogged, firm, headstrong, inflexible,
persistent, pigheaded, self-willed,
single-minded, stubborn, tenacious,
unbending, unreasonable, willful

obstreperous adj boisterous, disorderly,
loud, naughty, noisy, out of control, out
of hand, rampaging, rough, rowdy,
uncontrolled, undisciplined, unruly, wild

obstruct v block, bring to a standstill,
check, choke, clog, curb, cut off, delay,
frustrate, halt, hamper, hinder, hold up,
impede, interrupt, prevent, restrict, shut
off, slow, stop, thwart

obstruction n bar, barrier, block,
blockage, deterrent, hurdle, obstacle,
restriction, snag, stumbling block

obstructive adj awkward, difficult,
uncooperative, unhelpful, unwilling;
opp cooperative, helpful

obtain v achieve, acquire, buy, come by,
earn, find, gain, get, get hold of, get your
hands on, pick up inf, secure, win

obtrusive adj blatant, conspicuous,
intrusive, noticeable, obvious, out of
place, prominent; *opp* unobtrusive

obvious adj apparent, blatant, clear,
conspicuous, evident, glaring, manifest,
noticeable, open, patent, plain,
pronounced, self-evident, straightforward, transparent, unmistakable,
visible

occasion n 1 (special occasion) affair,
celebration, do inf, event, function,
party. 2 (happy occasion) episode,
event, experience, happening, incident,
occurrence. 3 (a different occasion)
circumstance, instance, situation, time

occasional *adj* casual, incidental, infrequent, intermittent, irregular, odd, rare, sporadic; *opp* regular

occupant *n* householder, inhabitant, inmate, occupier, renter, resident, tenant

occupation *n* 1 business, employment, job, profession, trade, work. 2 activity, craft, diversion, hobby, interest, pursuit, recreation. 3 (occupation of a country) capture, colonization, conquest, invasion, overthrow, possession, seizure, takeover

occupied *adj* 1 (doing sth) active, at work, busy, employed, hard at it *inf*, tied up *inf*, working; *opp* idle. 2 (being used) engaged, full, in use, taken, unavailable; *opp* free

occupy *v* 1 (occupy sb) amuse, divert, engage, engross, entertain, interest, keep busy. 2 (occupy a country) capture, colonize, conquer, invade, overrun, seize, take over. 3 (occupy a house) inhabit, live in, move into, reside in, take up residence in. 4 (occupy your time) fill, fill up, preoccupy, take up, use up

occur *v* 1 appear, arise, come about, crop up, develop, happen, materialize, result, take place, turn up. 2 occur to sb come to mind, cross your mind, dawn on you, enter your head, strike you

occurrence *n* affair, circumstance, development, episode, event, happening, incident, matter, occasion, phenomenon

odd *adj* 1 abnormal, bizarre, curious, different, eccentric, extraordinary, freak, funny, idiosyncratic, incongruous, irregular, outlandish, peculiar, puzzling, rare, remarkable, strange, uncommon, unconventional, unexpected, unusual, weird; *opp* normal. 2 extra, leftover, lone, remaining, single, solitary, spare, surplus, uneven, unmatched, unpaired, unused

oddity *n* aberration, abnormality, anomaly, curiosity, freak, irregularity, peculiarity, phenomenon, quirk, rarity, strangeness, uniqueness

odds *n* (the odds of sth happening) chance, likelihood, probability, prospect

odious *adj* disgusting, foul, hateful, horrible, loathsome, offensive, repellent, repugnant, repulsive, revolting, unpleasant; *opp* lovely, nice, pleasant

odor *n* aroma, bouquet, fragrance, perfume, pong *inf*, scent, smell, stench, stink

offend *v* 1 (offend sb) anger, annoy, displease, embarrass, give offense, humiliate, hurt sb's feelings, insult, irritate, outrage, pain, provoke, repel, revolt, sicken, slight, snub, upset, wound. 2 (commit a crime) break the law, commit a crime, do wrong, sin

offended *adj* affronted, annoyed, disgusted, embarrassed, hurt, insulted, miffed *inf*, outraged, put out, resentful, revolted, sickened, stung, upset, wounded

offender *n* criminal, culprit, delinquent, felon, lawbreaker, outlaw, villain, wrongdoer

offense *n* 1 (commit an offense) breach, crime, felony, illegal act, misdemeanor, sin, transgression, wrong. 2 (cause offense) anger, annoyance, disapproval, disgust, displeasure, hurt, irritation, outrage, resentment, upset *inf*

offensive adj 1 (of behavior) abusive, annoying, antisocial, disgusting, embarrassing, hurtful, indecent, insolent, insulting, irritating, provocative, objectionable, outrageous, rude, tasteless, uncivil, unpleasant, vulgar, yucky sl; **opp** inoffensive. 2 (of a smell) disgusting, distasteful, nasty, nauseating, obnoxious, odious, repellent, revolting, sickening, unsavory, vile, yucky sl; **opp** pleasant. 3 (invading a country) aggressive, attacking, belligerent, hostile, invading, on the warpath inf, threatening, warlike; **opp** defensive

offensive n assault, attack, drive, incursion, onslaught, push, raid, strike

offer n approach, bid, chance, incentive, invitation, opportunity, proposal, proposition, suggestion, tender

offer v bid, give, make an offer, make available, propose, provide, put forward, submit, suggest, tender, volunteer

offering n contribution, donation, gift, hand-out

offhand adj abrupt, brusque, casual, cavalier, cool, curt

office n 1 base, place of work, study, workplace. 2 (have the office of chairman) appointment, business, duty, job, place, position, post, responsibility, role, situation, work

officer n 1 administrator, agent, bureaucrat, committee member, dignitary, officeholder, official. 2 (police officer) police officer

official adj accredited, approved, authorized, bona fide, certified, formal, kosher inf, legitimate, licensed, recognized, sanctioned, valid, validated; **opp** unofficial

official n administrator, agent, authorized person, bureaucrat, civil servant, committee-member, dignitary, officeholder, officer, public servant

officiate v be in charge, be responsible, conduct, lead, preside, referee, run, take charge, take the chair, umpire

officious adj bossy, bumptious, dictatorial, domineering, interfering, obtrusive, opinionated, overbearing, pushy inf, self-important

off-putting adj daunting, demoralizing, disconcerting, discouraging, formidable, intimidating, unnerving, unsettling, upsetting; **opp** encouraging

offset v balance out, cancel out, compensate for, counteract, counterbalance, make up for, neutralize, set off

offshoot n arm, branch, by-product, derivative, limb, spin-off, splinter group

offspring n brood, children, descendants, family, heirs, issue, kids inf, litter, progeny, successors, young

often adv again and again, all the time, constantly, frequently, generally, many times, much, regularly, repeatedly, time after time, time and again; **opp** seldom

oil v anoint, grease, lubricate, wax

ointment n cream, liniment, lotion

okay adj acceptable, adequate, all right, convenient, fine, good, not bad, O.K., passable, reasonable

okay v agree, approve, authorize, consent to, endorse, give sth the go-ahead, give sth the green light, give sth the thumbs up, O.K., pass, rubber-stamp, sanction;

opp block, prevent

old *adj* 1 (of a person) aged, aging, ancient, doddery, elderly, geriatric, getting on, gray, in your dotage, mature. 2 (of objects) aged, ancient, antiquated, antique, early, prehistoric, veteran, vintage. 3 (dilapidated) crumbling, decrepit, dilapidated, past it, threadbare, worn-out, worn. 4 (old-fashioned) antiquated, dated, obsolete, old-fashioned, out of the ark, outdated, passé, stale, time-worn. 5 (traditional) age-old, original, time-honored, traditional. 6 erstwhile, former, previous

old-fashioned *adj* antiquated, dated, obsolescent, obsolete, old-hat *inf*, outdated, outmoded, out of fashion, passé, stale, time-worn, unfashionable

omen *n* bad sign, foreboding, harbinger, portent, sign, warning, writing on the wall

ominous *adj* bad, black, dark, dire, gloomy, inauspicious, menacing, sinister, unfavorable, unpromising; *opp* auspicious

omission *n* error, exclusion, gap, neglect, oversight

omit *v* drop, exclude, forget, leave out, miss, miss out, neglect, overlook

omnipotent *adj* all-powerful, almighty, supreme

onerous *adj* burdensome, difficult, exacting, hard, heavy, taxing, troublesome, unpleasant; *opp* easy, simple

one-sided *adj* biased, partial, partisan, unbalanced, unequal, uneven, unfair; *opp* balanced, impartial; *opp* balanced, fair, unbiased

onlooker *n* bystander, observer, passerby, spectator, viewer, witness

onslaught *n* assault, attack, bombardment, offensive, raid, thrust

onus *n* burden, duty, obligation, responsibility

ooze *v* bleed, drain, dribble, emit, escape, flow, leak, percolate, secrete, seep, trickle, weep

opaque *adj* 1 cloudy, dirty, filmy, hazy, muddy, murky; *opp* clear, transparent. 2 difficult, impenetrable, incomprehensible, obscure; *opp* clear, obvious, straightforward, understandable

open *adj* 1 ajar, uncovered, undone, unfastened, unlocked. 2 spread out, unfolded. 3 (of countryside) broad, clear, exposed, free, rolling, spacious, sweeping, treeless, unenclosed, unrestricted. 4 (of information) available, free, public, unrestricted; *opp* classified, secret. 5 (open aggression) blatant, clear, evident, flagrant, manifest, obvious, overt, plain, undisguised. 6 (the matter is still open) undecided, unresolved, unsettled, up for grabs *inf*

open *v* 1 unbolt, uncork, uncover, undo, unfasten, unlock, untie, unwrap; *opp* close, do up, fasten, shut, wrap up. 2 spread out, unfold, unfurl, unroll; *opp* close, fold up. 3 (open a meeting) begin, commence, get going, initiate, kick off *inf*, launch, set in motion, set up, start; *opp* close

opening *adj* first, inaugural, initial, introductory, preliminary; *opp* closing

opening *n* 1 aperture, chink, crack, doorway, gap, hatch, hole, orifice, slot, split, way in. **2** beginning, birth, dawn, launch, outset, start. **3** break *inf*, chance, opportunity

open-minded *adj* detached, dispassionate, enlightened, impartial, liberal, objective, open to suggestions, receptive, unbiased; *opp* narrow-minded

operate *v* **1** function, go, run, work. **2** (operate a machine) control, drive, handle, use, work. **3** (operate on sb) cut sb open *inf*, do an operation, perform surgery, put sb under the knife *inf*

operation *n* **1** control, management, performance, use, working. **2** (undertaking) business, campaign, effort, enterprise, process, project, task, undertaking, venture. **3** (surgery) biopsy, laparoscopy, surgery, transplant

operational *adj* functioning, going, in operation, in use, in working order, ready, up and running, viable, working

opinion *n* assessment, belief, estimation, feeling, idea, impression, judgment, stance, view, viewpoint, way of thinking

opinionated *adj* arrogant, dictatorial, doctrinaire, dogmatic, inflexible, pigheaded *inf*, pompous, single-minded, uncompromising

opponent *n* adversary, antagonist, competitor, contender, contestant, enemy, player, rival

opportune *adj* advantageous, appropriate, apt, favorable, good, right, suitable, timely, well-timed

opportunity *n* break *inf*, chance, moment, opening, possibility, time

oppose *v* attack, be hostile to, campaign against, combat, counter, defy, fight, obstruct, stand up to, take a stand against, take issue with, take on; *opp* support

opposed *adj* **1** against, antagonistic, anti, hostile, in opposition, on the other side. **2** conflicting, incompatible, opposing, opposite

opposite *adj* **1** facing, on the other side, overlooking. **2** conflicting, contradictory, converse, different, hostile, irreconcilable, opposed, rival, unlike; *opp* similar

opposite *n* antithesis, converse, inverse, reverse, the other side of the coin

opposition *n* **1** enemy, opponent, other side, rival. **2** antagonism, competition, defiance, disapproval, hostility, objection, resistance; *opp* support

oppress *v* **1** crush, intimidate, persecute, put down, subjugate, suppress, terrorize, tyrannize. **2** (make sb unhappy) afflict, depress, torment, weigh down

oppressed *adj* **1** browbeaten, crushed, downtrodden, enslaved, persecuted, subjugated, tyrannized. **2** (unhappy) depressed, desolate, despondent, downhearted, weighed down

oppressive *adj* **1** harsh, repressive, tyrannical, unjust. **2** burdensome, onerous. **3** airless, close, humid, muggy, stifling, stuffy, suffocating

oppressor *n* autocrat, bully, despot, dictator, tormentor, tyrant

opt for *v* choose, decide on, go for *inf*, pick, prefer, settle on

optimistic *adj* buoyant, cheerful, confident, hopeful, looking on the bright side, looking through rose-tinted spectacles, positive, sanguine; *opp* pessimistic

optimum *adj* best, ideal, maximum, optimal, peak, prime, top; *opp* worst

option *n* alternative, choice, possibility, route

optional *adj* discretionary, extra, up to you, voluntary; *opp* compulsory

oral *adj* by mouth, spoken, verbal, vocal

orator *n* lecturer, public speaker, speaker, speechmaker

orbit *n* circuit, course, path, revolution, track

orbit *v* circle, go round

orchestrate *v* arrange, organize, plan, put together, set up, stage-manage

ordeal *n* distress, hardship, misery, nightmare, suffering, tribulation, trouble

order *n* 1 command, court order, directive, injunction, instruction, regulation, requirement. 2 (sth you have ordered) booking, choice, commission, request, requirement, requisition, selection. 3 (way things are arranged) arrangement, categorization, grouping, method, pattern, plan, sequence, structure. 4 (restore order) calm, control, discipline, harmony, law and order, peace, symmetry; *opp* chaos, disorder, disruption

order *v* 1 (tell sb to do sth) decree, direct, give orders to, instruct, require, tell. 2 (put things in order) arrange, categorize, classify, organize, put in order, sort out. 3 (order goods) ask for, book, choose, commission, put in an order for, request, reserve, send off for

orderly *adj* 1 businesslike, efficient, methodical, neat, organized, systematic, tidy; *opp* chaotic, disorganized. 2 controlled, disciplined, quiet, well-

behaved; *opp* rebellious, undisciplined

ordinary *adj* common, common-or-garden, customary, everyday, familiar, humdrum, normal, plain, regular, run-of-the-mill, standard, unexceptional, unremarkable

organic *adj* 1 chemical-free, natural, organically grown. 2 animate, biological, living

organism *n* animal, being, creature, living thing, plant, structure

organization *n* 1 (group) association, body, business, club, combine, company, confederation, consortium, corporation, federation, firm, group, institution, league, society. 2 (structure) arrangement, composition, configuration, construction, design, make-up, order, pattern, structure. 3 (the organizing of sth) logistics, management, operation, planning, regulation, running, setting up

organize *v* 1 (put in order) arrange, categorize, classify, configure, order, put in order, structure. 2 (organize a campaign) arrange, coordinate, design, establish, form, look after, manage, orchestrate, plan, run, see to, set up, sort out, take care of

orgy *n* 1 (wild party) binge *inf*, revel, wild party. 2 (an orgy of sth) binge, bout, fling, splurge, spree

orient *v* 1 design for, direct at, intend for, orientate, make sth suitable for. 2 align, get your bearings, locate, orientate, position, turn

origin *n* 1 basis, derivation, provenance, root, source, starting point. 2 ancestry, background, extraction, family, heritage, lineage, parentage, pedigree, stock

original adj 1 fresh, ground-breaking, imaginative, innovative, new, novel, unusual, untried. 2 earliest, first, initial, primary

originality n creativity, freshness, imagination, individuality, innovation, invention, new ideas, novelty

originate v 1 (create) bring about, coin, create, develop, establish, give birth to, institute, introduce, invent, launch, pioneer, set up, start. 2 (come from) arise, begin, come from, derive from, flow from, spring from, start, stem from

ornament n bauble, decoration, knick-knack, trimming, trinket

ornamental adj attractive, decorative, elaborate, fancy, intricate, nonessential, showy

ornate adj busy, elaborate, fancy, flashy inf, flowery, fussy, grandiose, ornamental, pretentious, rococo, showy; opp plain

orthodox adj accepted, authorized, conformist, conservative, conventional, established, mainstream, official, standard, traditional; opp nonconformist, revolutionary, unconventional, unorthodox

orthodoxy n conformity, conservatism, conventionality, propriety, traditionalism

ostensible adj outward, pretended, professed, purported, seeming, so-called, stated, superficial, supposed

ostentatious adj affected, flamboyant, flashy inf, garish, gaudy, loud, overdone, pretentious, showy; opp quiet, restrained

ostracize v cold-shoulder inf, exclude, isolate, reject, shun, shut out, snub

oust v depose, dislodge, displace, drive out, expel, force out, kick out inf, overthrow, push out, replace, throw out, topple, unseat

outbreak n epidemic, eruption, explosion, flare-up, occurrence, rash, upsurge

outburst n burst, eruption, explosion, fit, flare-up, flood, outbreak, outpouring, storm, surge

outcast n exile, outsider, pariah, persona non grata, refugee, reject

outcome n consequence, effect, result, upshot

outcry n clamor, complaints, cries of indignation, fuss, howls of protest, hue and cry, hullaballoo, objections, opposition, row, uproar

outdated adj antiquated, dated, dead, fuddy-duddy inf, obsolete, old-fashioned, out, out of date, outmoded, out of fashion, passé, unfashionable

outdo v beat, eclipse, excel, get the better of, go one better than, outclass, outshine, outsmart, overshadow, run rings around inf, show up, surpass

outdoor adj alfresco, exterior, external, open-air, out of doors, outside; opp indoor

outer adj 1 exposed, exterior, external, outermost, outside, outward, surface, top; opp inner. 2 distant, far, fringe, outlying, peripheral, remote; opp inner

outfit n 1 clothes, costume, gear inf, get-up inf, rig inf, togs inf. 2 (organization) crew, enterprise, group, organization, set-up, team, unit

outgoing adj 1 (the outgoing president) departing, ex, former, leaving, old,

previous, retiring; **opp** incoming.
2 (friendly) approachable, bubbly, extrovert, friendly, genial, gregarious, lively, sociable

outing n day-trip, excursion, expedition, jaunt, tour, trip, visit

outlaw n bandit, criminal, fugitive, highwayman, robber

outlaw v ban, bar, criminalize, forbid, make illegal, prohibit, proscribe

outlay n charge, cost, disbursement, expenditure, expense, investment, outgoings, spending

outlet n 1 market, retail outlet, retailer, shop, store. 2 channel, discharge, duct, escape valve, mouth, opening, release, vent; **opp** inlet

outline n 1 abstract, bare bones, draft, resume, rough idea, sketch, summary, synopsis. 2 contour, framework, perimeter, profile, shape, sketch, skeleton, tracing

outline v 1 draft, give a rough idea of, rough out, sketch out, sketch, summarize. 2 sketch, trace

outlook n 1 (outlook on life) attitude, opinion, perspective, position, standpoint, view. 2 (forecast) expectations, forecast, future, prognosis, prospect. 3 (a building with a pleasant outlook) aspect, panorama, view, vista

out of date adj antiquated, dated, dead, fuddy-duddy inf, obsolete, old-fashioned, out, outdated, outmoded, out of fashion, passé, unfashionable; **opp** modern, new

output n crop, efficiency, manufacture, performance, product, production figures, production, productivity, result, yield

outrage n 1 anger, disgust, fury, horror, indignation, rage, revulsion, shock. 2 affront, atrocity, crime, disgrace, evil, insult, offense, scandal

outrage v anger, disgust, horrify, incense, infuriate, offend, shock, upset

outrageous adj 1 disgraceful, disgusting, heinous, horrifying, infuriating, offensive, scandalous, shocking, terrible, upsetting. 2 crazy, excessive, mad, preposterous, unreasonable, wild

outright adj absolute, categorical, complete, definite, downright, out-and-out, thorough, total, unmitigated, unqualified, utter

outright adv 1 (frankly) candidly, explicitly, frankly, openly, plainly, straight. 2 (in one go) at once, directly, immediately, in one fell swoop, in one go, instantaneously, there and then. 3 (completely) categorically, completely, entirely, lock, stock, and barrel, totally

outset n beginning, birth, dawn, inception, kick-off inf, launch, start

outside adj 1 exterior, external, open-air, out of doors, outdoor, outer, outermost, outward, surface, top; **opp** inside. 2 (an outside possibility) faint, improbable, marginal, remote, slight, slim, unlikely

outsider n alien, exile, foreigner, incomer, misfit, odd one out, oddball, stranger

outskirts n edge, fringe, margin, outlying areas, periphery, suburbs

outspoken adj blunt, direct, explicit, forthright, frank, mouthy inf, tactless, undiplomatic; **opp** quiet, reserved

outstanding adj 1 excellent, exceptional, great, impressive, magnificent, memorable, notable, remarkable, special, stunning, superb, supreme, world class. **2** (unresolved) ongoing, pending, remaining, to be dealt with, unpaid, unresolved, unsettled

outward *adj* **1** exterior, external, outer, outside, surface. **2** (visible) apparent, discernible, external, noticeable, visible; *opp* inward. **3** (ostensible) apparent, ostensible, professed, superficial, supposed

outweigh *v* be more important than, cancel out, have the edge on, override, prevail, take precedence over

outwit *v* beat, deceive, dupe, get the better of, outmaneuver, outsmart, pull the wool over sb's eyes, put one over on *inf*

ovation *n* acclaim, accolade, applause, clapping, standing ovation, tribute

overall *adj* all-embracing, blanket, broad, complete, comprehensive, general, global, inclusive, total, umbrella

overcast *adj* cloudy, dark, dull, gray, leaden, murky; *opp* clear

overcome *v* conquer, defeat, get the better of, master, quash, rise above, subdue, surmount, triumph over

overcritical *adj* carping, fussy, hard to please, hypercritical, pernickety, quibbling

overcrowded *adj* chock-a-block *inf*, congested, crammed full, full, heaving, jam-packed, overloaded, overrun, packed, swarming, teeming

overdue *adj* behind schedule, delayed, in arrears, late, outstanding, unpaid, unsettled

overeat *v* be greedy, binge, eat like a horse, eat too much, gorge, make a pig of yourself *inf*, overindulge, pig out *inf*, stuff your face *inf*, stuff yourself *inf*; *opp* diet, starve yourself

overflow *v* brim over, flood, pour over, run over, spill over

overgrown *adj* overrun, tangled, thick with weeds, unkempt, untidy, weedy, wild

overhang *v* droop over, jut out, loom over, project, protrude, stick out

overhaul *v* check over, fix, inspect, maintain, mend, recondition, refurbish, renovate, repair, restore, service

overheads *n* everyday expenditure, expenditure, expenses, operating costs, running costs

overjoyed *adj* delighted, ecstatic, euphoric, in raptures, jubilant, on cloud nine *inf*, on top of the world *inf*, thrilled; *opp* depressed, miserable

overlook *v* **1** forget, leave out, miss, not notice, omit. **2** excuse, ignore, let sth pass, let sth ride, turn a blind eye to *inf*, write off. **3** be opposite, face, front onto, have a view of, look out onto

overpower *v* crush, defeat, get the upper hand, get under control, immobilize, overwhelm, pin down, restrain, trounce

overpowering *adj* intolerable, oppressive, overwhelming, powerful, strong, suffocating, unbearable

overrule *v* cancel, countermand, disallow, invalidate, override, overturn, reject, reverse, revoke, set aside, veto

oversee *v* administer, control, keep an eye on, look after, preside over, supervise

overshadow *v* cloud, dwarf, eclipse, obscure, outshine, put in the shade, spoil

oversight *n* blunder, error, gaffe, mistake, omission, slip-up

overt *adj* blatant, evident, explicit, obvious, open, patent, plain, unconcealed, undisguised, visible; *opp* covert, secret

overtake *v* 1 go past, leave behind, outdistance, outstrip, pass, pull ahead of. 2 (events overtake you) befall, catch up with, engulf, hit, overwhelm

overthrow *v* beat, defeat, depose, displace, oust, remove from office, throw out, topple, unseat

overtone *n* connotation, feeling, hint, intimation, sense, suggestion, undercurrent

overturn *v* 1 capsize, keel over, knock over, tip over, topple over, upset, upturn. 2 (overturn a decision) annul, countermand, overrule, quash, reject, repeal, reverse, revoke, set aside, veto

overweight *adj* chubby, corpulent, fat, gross, heavy, massive, obese, outsize, plump, portly, pudgy, roly-poly, stout, tubby, well-padded *inf*; *opp* thin

overwhelm *v* 1 engulf, flood, inundate, snow under, swamp. 2 conquer, crush, defeat, overcome, overpower, quell, subjugate, vanquish. 3 bowl over *inf*, daze, devastate, leave speechless, move deeply, shake, prostrate, stagger, stun

overwhelming *adj* 1 (of an emotion) crushing, devastating, overpowering, shattering, staggering, stunning, uncontrollable. 2 (too many or too much) enormous, huge, immense, inordinate, mind-boggling *inf*, staggering, stupendous

overwrought *adj* agitated, beside yourself, distracted, frantic, frenzied, hysterical, in a state *inf*, tense, uptight *inf*

owe *v* 1 (owe money) be in arrears, be in debt, be in the red, be overdrawn. 2 (owe a favor) be indebted to, be obliged to, be under an obligation to

owing *adj* 1 due, in arrears, outstanding, overdue, owed, payable, unpaid. 2 **owing to** as a result of, because of, due to, thanks to

own *v* 1 be the owner of, have, have in your possession, hold, keep, retain, possess. 2 **own up** admit, come clean, confess, make a clean breast of it, put your hand up to *inf*

owner *n* 1 holder, keeper, possessor. 2 (of land or a business) homeowner, landlady, landlord, proprietor. 3 (of an animal) keeper, master, mistress

P

pace *n* 1 step, stride. 2 (way of walking) gait, tread, walk. 3 (speed) lick *inf*, rate, speed, tempo, velocity

pace *v* 1 pad, patrol, pound, stride, tread, walk. 2 give a lead to, set the pace for

pacifist *n* conscientious objector, dove, passive resistor, peace-lover, peacemaker; *opp* warmonger

pacify *v* calm, calm down, conciliate, placate, quieten, soothe, tranquilize

pack *n* 1 bale, bundle, package, parcel, truss. 2 backpack, haversack, knapsack, rucksack. 3 box, carton, container, package, packet, parcel. 4 (of animals) drove, flock, herd, troop. 5 (of people) band, gang, group, horde, mob, set, troop

pack *v* 1 (pack things) bale, box, bundle up, package, parcel up, place, put, store, stow, wrap, wrap up. 2 (pack a suitcase) cram, fill, fill up, load, stuff. 3 (pack people in) cram, crowd, fill, jam, press into, squeeze into. 4 pack down

compact, compress, press down, press together. 5 **pack off** dismiss, dispatch, send away, send off, send packing *inf*. 6 **pack up** (put things away) clear up, put away, tidy away, tidy up. 7 **pack up** (give up) call it a day *inf*, cease, finish, give up, leave off, pack it in *inf* stop. 8 **pack up** (stop working) break down, come to a halt, conk out *inf*, fail, stop working

package *n* 1 box, carton, container, packet, parcel. 2 combination, lot, package deal, package holiday, whole, whole shebang *inf*

package *v* box, pack, pack up, parcel up, wrap, wrap up

packed *adj* chock-a-block, congested, crowded, filled, filled to capacity, full, full up, jammed, jam-packed, overflowing; *opp* empty

packet *n* box, carton, container, pack, package

pact *n* agreement, alliance, arrangement, bargain, contract, deal, settlement, treaty, understanding

pad *n* 1 cushion, padding, wadding, wad. 2 jotter, notebook, notepad, writing pad. 3 foot, paw, sole

pad *v* 1 cushion, line, pack, protect, stuff, upholster. 2 amplify, augment, eke, elaborate, fill out, flesh out, protract, spin out, stretch

padding *n* 1 filling, packing, protection, stuffing, wadding. 2 verbiage, verbosity, waffle *inf*, wordiness

paddle *n* oar, scull

paddle *v* 1 propel, pull, row, scull. 2 dabble, splash, splash about, wade

pagan *adj* atheistic, godless, heathen,

idolatrous, infidel, polytheistic

page n 1 folio, leaf, sheet, side.
2 attendant, bellboy, pageboy,
servant

pageant n parade, procession, show,
spectacle, tableau

pageantry n ceremony, grandeur,
magnificence, pomp, ritual, show,
spectacle, splendor

pain n 1 ache, cramp, discomfort,
hurt, irritation, pang, smart, soreness,
spasm, sting, tenderness, twinge.
2 agony, anguish, suffering, torment,
torture. 3 (mental) anguish, distress,
grief, heartache, misery, suffering,
torment, torture, unhappiness, woe

pain v 1 (hurt) ache, be painful, be sore,
cause pain, chafe, hurt, smart, sting,
throb. 2 (make sb unhappy) afflict,
aggrieve, distress, grieve, hurt, make
miserable, sadden, torment, torture

painful adj 1 aching, excruciating,
hurting, inflamed, smarting, sore,
stinging, tender, throbbing. 2
disagreeable, distressing, harrowing,
hurtful, nasty, traumatic, trying,
unpleasant, upsetting. 3 arduous,
difficult, hard, laborious, strenuous,
tough; **opp** painless

painkiller n anesthetic, analgesic,
anodyne, palliative

painless adj 1 pain-free, without pain;
opp painful. 2 easy, effortless, simple,
trouble-free; **opp** difficult

painstaking adj assiduous, careful,
conscientious, diligent, meticulous,
punctilious, thorough

paint n color, coloring, dye, pigment,
stain, tint

paint v 1 apply paint to, color, cover,
daub, decorate, dye, spray, stain, tint,
touch up, varnish, whitewash.
2 (show sth) delineate, depict, describe,
picture, portray, represent

painter n artist, decorator, illustrator

pair n brace, couple, duo, match, twins,
twosome

pair v 1 pair up (put things together)
arrange in pairs, couple, join up, link up,
match, match up, put together, twin,
yoke. 2 pair off, pair up (of people)
double up, find a partner, get together,
join up, make a twosome, marry, team
up, wed

palatable adj appetizing, delicious,
mouthwatering, savory, scrumptious,
tasty, yummy inf; **opp** disgusting

palatial adj grand, imposing, luxurious,
magnificent, majestic, opulent,
posh inf, plush inf, spacious, splendid,
stately, sumptuous; **opp** miserable,
tiny

pale adj 1 anemic, ashen, as white
as a sheet, colorless, deathly pale,
drained, like death, like death warmed
up inf, pallid, pasty, peaky inf, wan,
washed-out inf, white, white-faced.
2 (of colors) bleached, faded, light,
pastel, washed-out, wishy-washy inf.
3 (of light) dim, faint, inadequate,
weak

pall v become boring, become tedious,
become tiresome, cloy, lose its
attraction, lose its interest, get boring,
get/grow tedious, get/grow tiresome

palpable adj 1 apparent, blatant, clear,
conspicuous, evident, glaring, manifest,
obvious, patent, plain, unmistakable.

2 concrete, solid, tangible

palpitate v beat rapidly, flutter, pound, pulsate, throb, thud, thump

paltry adj 1 (too small) derisory, insignificant, meagre, miserly, piddling inf, small, trifling, unimportant, worthless; *opp* generous.
2 contemptible, despicable, low, mean, miserable, sorry

pamper v cosset, humor, indulge, make a fuss of, mollycoddle, overindulge, pet, spoil, wait on hand and foot

pamphlet n booklet, brochure, circular, leaflet, tract

pan n 1 casserole, pot, saucepan.
2 container, receptacle, vessel

panacea n cure-all, cure for all ills, elixir, nostrum, universal remedy

panache n dash, élan, flair, flamboyance, pizzazz inf, style, verve

pandemonium n Babel, bedlam, chaos, commotion, hullabaloo, tumult, turmoil, uproar

panel n 1 insert, pane. 2 board, committee, jury

pang n 1 ache, pain, sharp pain, sting, twinge. 2 (pang of conscience) misgiving, qualm, remorse, scruple

panic n alarm, dismay, fear, horror, hysteria, terror

panic-stricken adj aghast, frightened, frightened to death inf, hysterical, panicky, petrified, scared out of your wits inf, scared stiff, scared to death inf, terrified; *opp* calm

panorama n aerial view, bird's-eye view, landscape, scene, view, vista

panoramic adj commanding, extensive, scenic, sweeping, wide

pant v blow, breathe heavily, gasp, gasp for breath, huff and puff, puff, wheeze

pants n jeans, slacks, trousers

paper n 1 (newspaper) broadsheet, daily, newspaper, rag inf, tabloid.
2 (give a paper) dissertation, monograph, record, study, treatise

papers n 1 contract, deed, deeds, document, documents, form, forms, legal papers. 2 ID, identification documents, identification papers, identity card, passport.
3 correspondence, diaries, files, letters, personal papers, records

parable n allegory, fable, moral tale, story with a moral

parade n 1 cavalcade, cortège, demonstration, march, motorcade, pageant, procession. 2 display, exhibition, show, spectacle

parade v 1 file past, march, march past.
2 (show sth off) air, display, exhibit, flaunt, make a show of, show, show off, vaunt. 3 show off, strut, swagger, swank inf

paradise n 1 Eden, Elysian Fields, Elysium, fairyland, Garden of Eden, heaven, heavenly kingdom, kingdom of heaven, Shangri-La, utopia, Valhalla.
2 bliss, delight, ecstasy, joy, seventh heaven

paradox n anomaly, contradiction, inconsistency, oxymoron, self-contradiction

paradoxical adj anomalous, contradictory, inconsistent

paragon n archetype, exemplar, example, ideal, model, model of excellence, pattern, perfect example, standard

parallel *adj* 1 equidistant, side by side.
2 analogous, comparable, corresponding,
equivalent, like, matching, resembling,
similar

parallel *n* 1 corollary, counterpart,
duplicate, equal, equivalent, match,
twin. 2 analogy, comparison,
correspondence, likeness, resemblance,
similarity

paralyze *v* 1 cripple, disable, immobilize,
incapacitate, make powerless. 2 bring to
a halt, bring to a standstill, bring to a
stop, freeze, halt, immobilize, put out of
action, put out of commission, stop.
3 deaden, desensitize, freeze, numb.
4 (with fear) freeze, petrify, stagger,
stop, stun, transfix

paralyzed *adj* 1 crippled, disabled,
immobilized, paraplegic, unable to
move. 2 at a standstill, frozen, halted,
immobile, immobilized, rigid, unable to
move, unusable. 3 dead, deadened,
frozen, numb. 4 (with fear) petrified,
stunned, stupefied, transfixed

paramount *adj* cardinal, chief,
foremost, main, most important, pre-
eminent, primary, principle, supreme,
uppermost

paraphernalia *n* 1 baggage, belongings,
bits and pieces, effects, impedimenta,
luggage, odds and ends, personal
belongings, possessions, stuff, things.
2 (things needed for sth) accessories,
apparatus, equipment, gear, kit, material,
tackle, tools

paraphrase *v* explain, gloss, interpret,
put into other words, rephrase, reword

parasite *n* bloodsucker, cadger, drone,
freeloader *inf*, hanger-on, leech,
scrounger, sponger

parcel *n* 1 bale, box, bundle, carton,
pack, package. 2 (of land) lot, patch,
piece, plot

parcel *v* 1 box, bundle up, do up, pack,
package, pack up, parcel up, tie up,
wrap, wrap up. 2 parcel out allocate,
allot, carve up, deal out, distribute,
divide, share out

parch *v* bake, burn, dehydrate, dessicate,
dry, dry up, scorch, shrivel, wither

parched *adj* 1 arid, baked, burned,
dessicated, dehydrated, dried out,
dried up, dry, scorched, shriveled,
waterless, withered. 2 dry *inf*,
dehydrated, thirsty

pardon *n* 1 forgiveness, indulgence,
mercy. 2 (an official pardon) amnesty,
exoneration, free pardon, release,
reprieve

pardon *v* 1 condone, excuse, forgive,
forgive and forget, let off, overlook.
2 (pardon sb officially) absolve,
exonerate, grant a pardon to,
release, reprieve

pardonable *adj* allowable, excusable,
forgivable, minor, slight,
understandable; *opp* unpardonable

parent *n* dad *inf*, father, mom *inf*,
mother, old dear *inf*, old man *inf* old lady
inf, old woman *inf*, procreator,
progenitor, sire

parentage *n* ancestry, birth, descent,
extraction, family, lineage, origin,
pedigree, race, stock

park *n* 1 green, playground, public
garden, public park, recreation ground.
2 estate, gardens, grounds, parkland

parliament *n* assembly, congress,

convocation, council, legislative
assembly, legislature, senate

parody n burlesque, caricature, imitation,
lampoon, satire, send-up inf, spoof inf,
take off inf

parody v caricature, imitate, lampoon,
mimic, satirize, send up inf, take off inf

parry v 1 (parry blows) avert, block,
deflect, fend off, rebuff, repel, stave off,
turn aside, ward off. 2 (parry awkward
questions) avoid, dodge, duck inf, evade,
elude, sidestep inf

part n 1 bit, fraction, fragment,
percentage, piece, portion, scrap,
section, segment, share, slice.
2 component, constituent, element,
ingredient. 3 (part of an organization)
branch, department, division, section,
unit. 4 (theatrical) character, lines, role,
words. 5 (your part in an undertaking)
capacity, duty, function, job,
responsibility, role, task. 6 (part of
a town) area, district, neighborhood,
quarter, region, sector, zone. 7 **for the
most part** all in all, by and large,
generally, mostly, to all intents and
purposes, usually. 8 **take part** be
involved, contribute, do your share,
engage in, have a hand in, have
something to do with, join in,
participate, play a part

part v 1 (part things that are joined)
break, break up, cleave, divide, separate,
sever, split, tear. 2 (people part) break
up, divorce, get a divorce, get a
separation, get divorced, go their
separate ways, part company, separate,
split up. 3 **part from** go away from,
leave, say farewell to, say good-bye to,

say your good-byes, separate, split inf,
take your leave. 4 **part with** cede,
give away, give up, let go, let go of,
relinquish, sacrifice, sell, yield

partake v 1 contribute to, engage in,
have a hand in, have sth to do with,
participate in, play a part in, share in,
take part in. 2 (partake of food, drink)
consume, drink, eat, share in

partial adj 1 imperfect, incomplete,
in part, limited, part, unfinished.
2 biased, discriminatory, having an
interest, inequitable, one-sided,
partisan, prejudiced, unfair, unjust;
opp impartial, unbiased. 3 **be partial to**
be fond of, be keen on, care for, have a
liking for, have a taste for, have a
weakness for, like

partially adv fractionally, half, in part,
moderately, not completely, not fully,
not wholly, partly, slightly, to a certain
extent, to a limited extent, to some
degree, to some extent

participant n competitor, contributor,
member, party, shareholder

participate v be involved in, contribute
to, engage in, join in, have a hand in,
have sth to do with, play a part in, take
part in

particle n 1 bit, crumb, fragment,
grain, morsel, scrap, smidgen inf, speck,
spot, tiny bit, tiny piece. 2 atom,
molecule

particular adj 1 distinct, individual,
precise, individual, specific, unique;
opp general. 2 exceptional, outstanding,
remarkable, singular, special, unusual.
3 choosy inf, discriminating, exacting,
fastidious, finicky, fussy, pernickety inf,

selective. **4 in particular** especially,
particularly, specifically

parting n 1 adieu, departure, farewell,
good-bye, leave-taking, leaving.
2 breaking up, divorce, separation,
splitting up. 3 breaking up, detachment,
dividing, division, partition, separating,
separation, severance, splitting up

partisan adj biased, bigoted, doctrinaire,
factional, one-sided, partial, prejudiced,
sectarian, unbalanced, unfair;
opp impartial

partisan n 1 adherent, backer, devotee,
disciple, follower, supporter, sympathizer,
upholder. 2 freedom fighter, guerrilla,
insurgent, member of the resistance,
terrorist

partition n 1 barrier, room divider,
screen, wall. 2 (act of separating)
division, partitioning, segregation,
separation, split; *opp* unification

partition v divide, section off, segregate,
separate, split, split up, wall off

partner n 1 (in business, sport)
accomplice, ally, associate, collaborator,
colleague, comrade, companion, co-
worker, fellow worker, sleeping partner,
teammate. 2 (in a couple) boyfriend,
common-law husband, common-law
wife, companion, girlfriend, husband,
live-in lover *inf*, mate, significant other
inf, spouse, wife

partnership n 1 alliance, association,
brotherhood, collaboration, fellowship,
fraternity, joint effort, union.
2 (in business) cartel, company,
confederation, conglomerate, coop *inf*,
cooperative, joint venture, syndicate

party n 1 bash *inf*, do *inf*, get-together *inf*,

orgy, reception, social, social gathering,
soirée. 2 (political) bloc, faction,
fraction, grouping. 3 (the parties
involved) individual, person. 4 (to a
dispute, conspiracy) accomplice,
litigant, participant, third party.
5 be a party to approve of, condone, get
involved in, participate in, support, take
part in

pass n 1 (make a pass at sb) advance,
approach, assault, fumble, lunge,
proposition, harassment. 2 (between
mountains) canyon, channel, cutting,
gap, gorge, gully, opening, passage,
path, ravine, valley. 3 (an official
pass) authorization, identification,
identity card, license, passbook,
passport, permit, proof of identity,
safe conduct, swipe card, ticket,
warrant, visa

pass v 1 drive by, drive past, go by,
go past, move past, overtake, pass by,
run by, run past, walk by, walk past. 2
(pass a level, amount) break, exceed, go
above, go beyond, outstrip, surpass,
transcend. 3 (pass an exam) be
successful, get through, graduate,
qualify; *opp* fail. 4 (pass a law) accept,
agree, approve, confirm, enact, establish,
promulgate, ratify, validate, vote
through; *opp* reject. 5 (pass sth to sb)
circulate, deal, deliver, give, hand,
hand over, pass on, present, proffer,
transfer. 6 (in a quiz) fail to answer, give
in, make no bid, miss a turn, opt out, say
nothing. 7 (pass the time) fill, occupy,
spend, while away. 8 (time passes)
advance, continue, elapse, flow, fly, go
on, tick by. 9 **pass away** breathe your

last, depart this world, die, expire, go to
meet your Maker, kick the bucket *inf*,
pass on, perish. **10 pass out** black out,
collapse, faint, lose consciousness, swoon

passable *adj* adequate, average, fair,
satisfactory, tolerable

passage *n* **1** (from a book) excerpt,
extract, paragraph, part, quotation,
reading, section, text, verse. **2** (narrow
lane) alley, arcade, catwalk, channel,
corridor, covered way, hall, hallway,
lane, tunnel, passageway, walkway.
3 (on a ship) crossing, journey, transit,
voyage

passenger *n* commuter, customer, tourist,
traveler

passerby *n* bystander, passing motorist,
pedestrian

passing *adj* brief, fleeting, incidental,
momentary, short, short-lived,
temporary, transient, transitory

passion *n* **1** (strong feeling) animation,
ardor, devotion, emotion, enthusiasm,
excitement, fervor, fire, heat, keenness,
vehemence, zeal. **2** (strong sexual
feeling) arousal, desire, craving,
fondness, infatuation, love, lust

passionate *adj* **1** animated, ardent,
burning, devoted, eager, emotional,
enthusiastic, excitable, excited,
fervent, fiery, heartfelt, hot,
hot-headed, impassioned, intense,
tempestuous, vehement, wild, zealous.
2 (sexually) amorous, aroused, hot,
loving, lustful, randy *inf*, sensual, sexy,
turned-on *inf*

passive *adj* inactive, inert, patient,
quiescent, unassertive, unresisting,
submissive; *opp* active

past *adj* **1** ancient, bygone, earlier,
erstwhile, ex-, former, historical, old,
onetime, preceding, previous, prior,
yesterday's; *opp* future. **2** done, finished,
forgotten, gone, in the past, over,
over and done with; *opp* continuing,
present, ongoing

past *n* **1** antiquity, bygone days, bygones,
days gone by, former times, old times,
olden days, history, mists of time,
yesterday, yesteryear, yore; *opp* future.
2 (sb's past) background, experiences,
former life, life history, origins, record;
opp future

paste *n* adhesive, cement, glue, gum,
putty

paste *v* affix, cement, fasten, fix, glue,
gum, stick

pastiche *n* burlesque, copy, imitation,
parody, satire, take-off *inf*

pastime *n* amusement, distraction,
diversion, entertainment, hobby,
interest, leisure activity, pursuit,
recreation, sport

pastoral *adj* **1** agrarian, agricultural,
Arcadian, bucolic, country, farming,
rural, rustic. **2** (pastoral care) fatherly, in
loco parentis, nurturing, parental,
paternal

pasture *n* field, grass, grassland, grazing
land, meadow, pastureland

pat *v* dab, hit, slap, tap, touch

patch *n* **1** area, blotch, mark, marking,
shape, spot, stain. **2** (patch of land)
area, lot, parcel, piece, plot, strip, tract

patch *v* **1** darn, mend, repair. **2 patch up**
(patch up a quarrel) reconcile, repair,
resolve, restore, settle

patchy *adj* erratic, good in parts,

inconsistent, intermittent, irregular, sketchy, uneven, variable, varying

patent adj apparent, blatant, clear, conspicuous, definite, evident, flagrant, glaring, manifest, obvious, palpable, plain, unmistakable

path n 1 alley, avenue, bridle path, bridleway, footpath, lane, pathway, pavement, road, route, track, trail, walkway, way. 2 (of a moving object) arc, course, curve, direction, orbit, trajectory

pathetic adj 1 abject, abysmal, bad, dismal, feeble, hapless, hopeless, ineffectual, miserable, pitiable, pitiful, poor, sad, sorry, weak, wretched. 2 (upsetting) affecting, heartbreaking, moving, piteous, pitiful, plaintive, poignant, sad, sentimental, sorry, tear-jerking, touching, upsetting

pathos n emotion, poignancy, sadness, sentimentality

patience n calm, calmness, endurance, forbearance, fortitude, passivity, resignation, stoicism, tolerance; *opp* impatience

patient adj 1 calm, long-suffering, passive, resigned, stoical, tolerant, waiting; *opp* impatient. 2 (of a piece of work) assiduous, diligent, indefatigable, meticulous, painstaking, persevering, persistent, thorough, unhurried, untiring; *opp* hurried

patient n case, client, inmate, invalid, resident, subject, sufferer, victim

patriot n chauvinist, loyalist, nationalist

patriotic adj chauvinistic, flag-waving, gung-ho *inf*, jingoistic, loyal, loyalist, my-country-right-or-wrong, nationalistic

patrol n garrison, guard, guards, posse, rangers, scouts, squad, vigilantes, watch

patrol v be on the beat, cruise, do the rounds, guard, inspect, keep vigil, monitor, police, watch

patron n 1 backer, benefactor, contributor, donor, friend, protector, sponsor, supporter. 2 client, customer, habitué, regular, visitor

patronage n 1 assistance, backing, endorsement, protection, sponsorship, support. 2 (of an unfair, illegal kind) back-scratching, jobs for the boys, nepotism, old school tie

patronize v 1 be condescending, look down on, look down your nose at, sneer at, talk down to. 2 (patronize a shop. restaurant) buy from, do business with, drink at, eat at, frequent, shop at, visit

patronizing adj condescending, disdainful, haughty, high-handed, overbearing, scornful, sneering, snobbish, snooty *inf*; *opp* respectful

pattern n 1 arrangement, decoration, design, device, figure, marking, motif, ornamentation, shape. 2 (for making sth) blueprint, guide, instructions, model, plan, sample, specimen, stencil, template. 3 (events following a pattern) order, plan, shape, structure, system

paunch n abdomen, beer belly *inf*, beer gut *inf*, belly, gut, middle-aged spread, pot *inf*, potbelly *inf*, stomach, spare tire *inf*, tummy *inf*

pause n abeyance, break, cessation, delay, gap, halt, hesitation, interlude, interruption, interval, rest, silence

pause v break off, cease, delay, hesitate, interrupt, rest, stop, wait

pave v pave the way for allow, enable, foreshadow, make possible, permit, precede, prepare

pay n allowance, commission, earnings, emoluments, honorarium, income, payment, take home pay, remittance, remuneration, reward, salary, stipend, wage, wages

pay v 1 buy, cough up inf, fork out inf, foot the bill, hand over, lay out, part with, shell out inf, pay out, pay up, remit, settle up, spend. 2 (produce a profit, benefit) be advantageous, be profitable, be rewarding, be worthwhile, make a profit, make money, pay off. 3 (pay sb to do sth) employ, engage, hire, remunerate, reward, take on. 4 (pay sb for damage, expenses) compensate, defray, indemnify, pay back, recompense, refund, reimburse. 5 pay for (suffer as a result of) atone for, be penalized for, be punished for, compensate for, do penance for, expiate, make amends for, make good, make reparations for, make up for, suffer for. 6 pay off cancel, clear, close, discharge, liquidate, meet, repay, settle, square

payable adj due, outstanding, owed, owing, to be paid, unpaid

payment n amount, award, compensation, deposit, installment, premium, refund, reimbursement, repayment, reward, sum

peace n 1 armistice, concord, harmony, pacification, peacetime, reconciliation, truce; opp war. 2 calm, calmness, peacefulness, quiet, repose, rest, serenity, tranquillity

peaceable adj amicable, conciliatory, peaceful, peace-loving

peaceful adj 1 (wanting, seeking peace) amicable, conciliatory, peaceable, peace-loving; opp warlike. 2 (free of conflict) at peace, calm, harmonious, untroubled. 3 (without noise, movement) at peace, at rest, calm, placid, quiet, restful, serene, still, tranquil

peak n 1 brow, crest, hilltop, mountain top, pinnacle, point, summit, tip, top. 2 acme, apex, climax, height, high, high point, high-water mark, maximum, pinnacle, top, zenith; opp trough

peak v 1 climax, culminate, reach a crescendo, reach a peak. 2 have peaked be in decline, be on the downward slide, be on the way down, be past your best, decline, fall off

peal n carillon, chime, clang, ring, ringing, toll, tolling

peal v chime, clang, resound, ring, ring out, toll

peasant n country dweller, countryman, country cousin inf, farm laborer, farm worker, farmer, farmhand, rustic, serf, smallholder, yokel inf

peck v bite, nibble, nip

peculiar adj 1 bizarre, eccentric, extraordinary, funny, odd, out of the ordinary, queer, singular, strange, unusual, weird; opp normal. 2 (peculiar to sth) characteristic, distinctive, distinguishing, exclusive, individual, own, particular, proper, special, specific, unique

peculiarity n 1 eccentricity, foible,

idiosyncrasy, oddity. **2** attribute, characteristic, feature, hallmark, property

pedantic *adj* academic, bookish, didactic, doctrinaire, dogmatic, donnish, nit-picking, over-literal, scholarly, scholastic

pedestrian *adj* boring, commonplace, dull, mediocre, plodding, prosaic, run-of-the-mill, unimaginative, uninspired, unoriginal

pedestrian *n* foot passenger, hiker, passerby, rambler, walker

pedigree *n* ancestry, background, descent, family, family tree, genealogy, heritage, lineage

peel *v* pare, skin, strip, uncover

peep *v* glance, glimpse, look, peek, sneak a look, snoop, take a butcher's *inf*

peer *n* **1** aristocrat, baron, baroness, count, duke, earl, lady, lord, marquis, noble, nobleman, viscount. **2** associate, colleague, companion, equal

peer *v* gaze, look, look closely, squint *inf*, stare

peevish *adj* bad-tempered, cantankerous, churlish, complaining, crabby *inf*, cross, crotchety *inf*, crusty *inf*, disagreeable, discontented, fractious, fretful, grouchy *inf*, grumbling, grumpy, ill-natured, irritable, petulant, querulous, rude, sulky, sullen, surly, testy

peg *v* fix, keep, maintain, pin, secure, stabilize

pelt *v* batter, beat, bombard, riddle, shower, sprinkle, stone

pen *n* **1** ballpoint, ballpoint pen, cartridge pen, felt-tip, felt-tip pen, fountain pen, quill. **2** cage, coop, corral, enclosure,

fold, pound, sheep fold, pigsty, stall, stockade, sty

pen *v* **1** author, compose, draft, draw up, write. **2** pen in box in, corral, enclose, enfold, fence in, hem in, imprison, pin down, restrict

penal *adj* corrective, criminal, disciplinary, prison, punitive

penalize *v* **1** book, caution, discipline, fine, punish. **2** (a situation which penalizes sb) disadvantage, place at a disadvantage, handicap

penalty *n* caution, endorsement, fine, forfeit, punishment, sentence

penance *n* amends, atonement, expiation, penitence, punishment, repentance

pending *adj* **1** on the table, outstanding, undecided, unfinished. **2** approaching, coming, imminent, impending, in store, in the offing, on the cards, on the way

penetrate *v* bore, enter, go in, go into, go through, perforate, permeate, pervade, pierce, stab

penitent *adj* apologetic, contrite, guilty, remorseful, repentant, sheepish, sorry

pen name *n* alias, assumed name, nom de guerre, nom de plume, pseudonym, stage name

penniless *adj* bankrupt, broke *inf*, cleaned out *inf*, destitute, impecunious, impoverished, indigent, poor, poverty-stricken, without a penny, without a penny to your name

pension *n* allowance, annuity, benefit, income support, private income

pensioner *n* old age pensioner, retired person, senior citizen, veteran

pensive *adj* contemplative, day-dreaming, deep in thought, meditative, reflective, ruminating, thinking, thoughtful, withdrawn, wistful

pent-up *adj* accumulated, built-up, frustrated, repressed

people *n* 1 folk, folks *inf*, human beings, human race, humanity, humankind, man, mankind, men, mortals, individuals. 2 (the people) citizenry, citizens, common people, commoners, electorate, hoi polloi, lower orders, masses, ordinary people, plebs *inf*, populace, population, proletariat, public, society, subjects, voters. 3 clan, community, ethnic group, nation, race, tribe

people *v* colonize, inhabit, live in, occupy, populate, settle, stock

perceive *v* apprehend, appreciate, be aware of, be conscious of, detect, discern, distinguish, experience, hear, note, notice, observe, recognize, register, see, sense

perceptible *adj* apparent, appreciable, audible, detectable, discernible, observable, noticeable, palpable, perceivable, recognizable, visible; *opp* imperceptible

perception *n* awareness, consciousness, discernment, experience, knowledge, grasp, insight, perceptiveness, recognition, understanding

perceptive *adj* acute, alert, astute, attentive, aware, bright, clever, discerning, intelligent, keen-eyed, observant, on the ball *inf*, penetrating, perspicacious, quick, sensitive, sharp, sharp-eyed, smart

perch *n* position, roost, seat, station, vantage point

perch *v* alight, balance, land, poise, position yourself, rest, roost, settle, sit, station yourself

percussion *n* bass drum, bongos, drum, kettledrum, glockenspiel, maracas, tambourine, snare drum, timpani, tom-tom, triangle, xylophone

perennial *adj* 1 constant, continuing, durable, enduring, eternal, everlasting, lasting, permanent, unceasing. 2 continual, cyclical, recurrent, recurring, regular, seasonal

perfect *adj* 1 consummate, faultless, flawless, ideal, immaculate, impeccable, incomparable, irreproachable, matchless, pure, spotless, sublime, unbeatable, unblemished, unmarred, untarnished; *opp* imperfect. 2 (a perfect circle) entire, finished, full, whole; *opp* imperfect. 3 (perfect nonsense) absolute, complete, downright, out-and-out, sheer, total, unadulterated, unmitigated, utter

perfect *v* accomplish, achieve, bring to fruition, carry out, complete, consummate, effect, execute, finish, fulfill, perform, realize, see through

perfection *n* 1 completeness, faultlessness, flawlessness, incomparability, integrity, precision, purity, spotlessness, wholeness; *opp* imperfection. 2 (the perfection of a technique) accomplishment, achievement, completion, consummation, end, execution, finishing, fruition, fulfillment, realization

perforate v bore, drill, penetrate, pierce, prick, punch, puncture, stab

perform v 1 (perform a task) accomplish, achieve, carry out, complete, discharge, do, effect, execute, finish, fulfill, pull off inf, satisfy, transact, work. 2 (perform a play) act, depict, enact, play, present, produce, put on, render, represent, stage

performance n 1 (a gala performance) act, appearance, entertainment, exhibition, gig inf, play, portrayal, presentation, production, show. 2 (the performance of a task) accomplishment, achievement, completion, conduct, discharge, effect, execution, finishing, fulfilment, satisfaction, transaction

performer n actor, actress, artist, artiste, dancer, entertainer, musician, player, singer, thespian

perfume n 1 after-shave, cologne, eau de cologne, fragrance, scent, toilet water. 2 (the perfume of flowers) aroma, bouquet, fragrance, odor, scent, smell

perhaps adv conceivably, feasibly, it could be, maybe, possibly; **opp** definitely

peril n danger, hazard, insecurity, jeopardy, menace, risk, susceptibility, uncertainty, vulnerability; **opp** safety

perilous adj dangerous, hazardous, insecure, precarious, risky, threatening, uncertain, unsafe; **opp** safe

perimeter n border, boundary, bounds, circumference, confines, edge, fringe, frontier, limit, margin, periphery, verge

period n interval, phase, season, session, space, span, spell, stage, stint, stretch, term, time, while

periodical adj cyclical, every once in a while, every so often, intermittent, occasional, periodic, recurrent, recurring, regular, repeated, spasmodic, sporadic

perish v 1 be killed, bite the dust inf, die, expire, fall, kick the bucket inf, lose, your life, pass away, snuff it sl; **opp** live. 2 collapse, crumble, decline, disappear, fall, vanish; **opp** survive. 3 decay, decompose, disintegrate, go bad, go off, go sour, rot, waste, wither

perishable adj biodegradable, decaying, destructible, unstable

perjure v bear false witness, commit perjury, give false testimony, lie under oath

perjury n false testimony, false witness, lying under oath, oath breaking, violation of oath

permanent adj abiding, constant, continual, continuous, durable, endless, enduring, eternal, everlasting, fixed, immutable, indestructible, invariable, irreparable, lasting, life-long, never-ending, nonstop, perpetual, persistent, steadfast, unchanging; **opp** temporary

permeate v diffuse, filter through, imbue, infiltrate, impregnate, penetrate, percolate, pervade, saturate, soak

permissible adj acceptable, allowable, authorized, lawful, legal, legitimate, permitted, sanctioned, within the law, within the rules; **opp** forbidden

permission n agreement, allowance, approval, assent, authorization, consent, dispensation, franchise, freedom, go-ahead inf, green light, leave, liberty, license, sanction, thumbs-up *inf*

permissive *adj* broad-minded, easygoing, indulgent, lenient, liberal, tolerant; *opp* strict

permit *n* authority, authorization, license, pass, passport, permission, sanction, ticket, visa, warrant

permit *v* agree, allow, approve, assent, authorize, consent, countenance, enable, endorse, entitle, grant, legalize, let, license, sanction, tolerate; *opp* forbid

perpendicular *adj* at 90 degrees, at right angles, erect, plumb, straight, upright, vertical

perpetrate *v* bring about, carry out, commit, do, effect, execute, inflict, perform, pull off *inf*

perpetual *adj* abiding, constant, continual, continuous, durable, endless, enduring, eternal, everlasting, fixed, immutable, indestructible, invariable, irreparable, lasting, life-long, never-ending, nonstop, permanent, persistent, steadfast, unchanging; *opp* temporary

perpetuate *v* continue, eternalize, immortalize, keep going, maintain, preserve, sustain; *opp* end

perplex *v* baffle, bamboozle *inf*, bewilder, dumbfound, confound, confuse, flummox, mystify, nonplus, puzzle, stump, throw *inf*

perplexing *adj* 1 baffling, bewildering, confounding, confusing, enigmatic, inexplicable, mysterious, mystifying, puzzling, strange, weird; *opp* normal. 2 complex, complicated, difficult, hard, intricate, involved, knotty; *opp* simple

perquisite *n* advantage, benefit, bonus, dividend, extra, freebie *inf*, gratuity, perk, plus

persecute *v* abuse, afflict, distress, harass, hound, hunt, ill-treat, maltreat, mistreat, oppress, pursue, torment, torture, victimize

persevere *v* carry on, continue, endure, go on, hammer away *inf*, hang on, hold on, hold out, keep at it *inf*, keep going, keep it up *inf*, maintain, persist, pursue, remain; *opp* give up

persist *v* carry on, continue, endure, go on, hammer away *inf*, hang on, hold on, hold out, keep at it *inf*, keep going, keep it up *inf*, maintain, persevere, pursue, remain; *opp* give up

persistent *adj* 1 (of a person) assiduous, determined, dogged, hard-working, immovable, insistent, obstinate, patient, persevering, relentless, resolute, steadfast, stubborn, tenacious, tireless, unflagging, untiring, unwavering. 2 (of a noise) ceaseless, constant, continual, continuous, endless, eternal, everlasting, incessant, interminable, lasting, long-lasting, never-ending, permanent, perpetual, relentless, unending, unrelenting, unrelieved; *opp* intermittent

person *n* being, body, character, figure, human, human being, individual, mortal, soul

personal *adj* 1 characteristic, distinctive, exclusive, idiosyncratic, individual, own, particular, peculiar, personalized, unique. 2 (a personal phone call) confidential, intimate, private

personality *n* 1 (sb's personality)

character, disposition, individuality, make-up, nature, persona, temperament. 2 (a TV personality) big name, celebrity, famous name, household name, idol, star, superstar, VIP

personnel n employees, helpers, human resources, labor, labor force, manpower, members, people, staff, workers, workforce

perspective n 1 (sb's perspective on sth) angle, approach, attitude, opinion, outlook, point of view, position, slant, stance, stand, standpoint, vantage point, view, viewpoint. 2 (in perspective) context, proportion, relation, relativity

perspiration n beads of sweat, moisture, sweat, wetness

perspire v drip with sweat, glow, pour with sweat, secrete, sweat, swelter

persuade v allure, cajole, coax, coerce, convince, entice, impel, induce, influence, press, prevail upon, prompt, sway, talk into, tempt, urge, wheedle inf, win over; opp dissuade

persuasion n 1 cajoling, coaxing, coercing, convincing, enticement, inducement, influencing, persuading, pressing, prompting, urging, wheedling. 2 (your political persuasion) attitude, belief, conviction, opinion, position, slant, stance, stand, standpoint, view, viewpoint

persuasive adj 1 (of evidence) compelling, conclusive, convincing, credible, impressive, plausible, sound, strong, telling, unarguable, watertight; opp unconvincing. 2 (of a person) effective, eloquent, forceful, impressive, influential, strong

pertinent adj admissible, applicable, apposite, appropriate, apt, fit, fitting, material, relevant, suitable, to the point; opp irrelevant

perturb v agitate, alarm, bother, disconcert, disquiet, distress, disturb, fluster, frighten, ruffle, scare, trouble, unnerve, unsettle, upset, worry

perturbed adj agitated, alarmed, anxious, bothered, disconcerted, disquieted, distressed, disturbed, flustered, ill at ease, nervous, restless, ruffled, scared, shaken, troubled, uncomfortable, uneasy, unnerved, unsettled, upset, worried; opp unconcerned

peruse v browse, check, examine, have a look at, inspect, look over, read, run your eye over, scan, scrutinize, study

pervade v diffuse, extend, fill, filter through, imbue, infuse, penetrate, percolate, permeate, saturate, spread through

pervasive adj common, extensive, inescapable, omnipresent, pervading, prevalent, rife, ubiquitous, universal, widespread; opp rare

perverse adj awkward, contrary, difficult, headstrong, inflexible, intractable, obstinate, pig-headed, rebellious, stubborn, uncooperative, unruly, wayward; opp reasonable

perversion n 1 aberration, abnormality, debauchery, depravity, deviance, deviation, immorality, unnaturalness, vice, wickedness. 2 (the perversion of sth) corruption, distortion, falsification, misrepresentation, twisting

pervert n degenerate, deviant, weirdo sl

pervert v abuse, bend, distort, falsify, misapply, misconstrue, misrepresent, misuse, twist, warp

perverted adj abnormal, amoral, corrupt, debased, debauched, depraved, deviant, immoral, sick, twisted, unhealthy, unnatural, warped; **opp** natural

pessimistic adj bleak, cynical, defeatist, fatalistic, gloomy, negative, resigned; **opp** optimistic

pest n 1 annoyance, bother, inconvenience, irritation, nuisance, pain, pain in the neck, trial. 2 (on plants) bug, creepy-crawly inf, insect, parasite

pester v annoy, badger, bother, disturb, harass, harry, hassle, hound, irk, nag, plague, torment, trouble, worry

pestilence n affliction, blight, cancer, curse, disease, epidemic, plague, scourge

pet n apple of your eye, blue-eyed boy, blue-eyed girl, darling, favorite, idol, jewel

pet v caress, fondle, pat, stroke

petition n 1 (sign a petition) list of signatures, protest document. 2 (file a petition) appeal, application, entreaty, plea, request, suit, supplication

petition v appeal, apply, ask, beg, beseech, entreat, plead, press, solicit, urge

petrify v 1 fill sb with fear, frighten, horrify, panic, paralyze, scare, scare sb out of his wits/skin, scare sb to death, stun, stupefy, terrify. 2 calcify, fossilize, turn to stone

petty adj 1 (petty squabbling) inconsequential, insignificant, little, minor, negligible, paltry, slight, small, trifling, trivial, unimportant; **opp** important, major. 2 (don't be so petty) grudging, mean, nit-picking, small-minded, spiteful, stingy, ungenerous; **opp** generous

phantom n apparition, ghost, phantasm, specter, spirit, spook

phase n chapter, period, part, point, season, spell, stage, step, time

phenomenal adj amazing, astonishing, astounding, exceptional, extraordinary, fabulous, fantastic, incredible, marvelous, mind-blowing inf, mind-boggling inf, miraculous, outstanding, remarkable, sensational, singular, staggering, stunning, unbelievable, unique, wondrous; **opp** unremarkable

phenomenon n 1 (a natural phenomenon) circumstance, event, happening, incident, occurrence, sight. 2 (a musical phenomenon) marvel, miracle, prodigy, rarity, sensation, wonder

philanthropist n altruist, humanitarian, giver, good Samaritan, provider

philistine n barbarian, ignoramus, lout; **opp** intellectual

philosopher n logician, metaphysician, sage, scholar, theorist, thinker

philosophical adj 1 (a philosophical discussion) abstract, erudite, learned, theoretical, thoughtful. 2 (be philosophical about sth) accepting, calm, collected, composed, cool, patient, rational, realistic, reasonable, resigned, stoical

philosophy n 1 (study philosophy) ideology, logic, metaphysics, rationalism, reason, thinking, thought.

2 (your philosophy on sth) attitude, belief, conviction, ideology, opinion, outlook, point of view, principle, thinking, view, viewpoint

phlegmatic *adj* 1 (physical things) calm, cool, composed, imperturbable, philosophical, placid, serene, stoical, undemonstrative, unemotional; *opp* excitable. 2 apathetic, impassive, indifferent, unenthusiastic, unresponsive; *opp* enthusiastic

phobia *n* antipathy, aversion, dislike, distaste, dread, fear, hang-up *inf*, hatred, horror, loathing, neurosis, obsession, repulsion, terror

phone *n* car phone, mobile phone, telephone

phone *v* call, call up, dial, give sb a buzz, give sb a call, give sb a ring, make a phone call, ring, ring up, telephone

phony *adj* artificial, assumed, bogus, counterfeit, fake, false, fictitious, forged, fraudulent, imitation, mock, pretend, pseudo, put-on *inf*, sham, spurious, trick; *opp* real

photocopy *n* copy, duplicate, photostat

photocopy *v* copy, duplicate, photostat, reproduce, run off

photograph *n* enlargement, exposure, image, likeness, photo, picture, print, shot, snap *inf*, snapshot

photograph *v* capture on film, film, record, shoot, take a picture

photographic *adj* (a photographic memory) accurate, exact, pictorial, precise, retentive, visual

phrase *n* 1 catchphrase, expression, idiom, proverb, remark, saying, statement, utterance. 2 clause, group of words, sentence

phrase *v* express, formulate, frame, present, put, say, term, utter, voice, word

physical *adj* 1 (physical things) concrete, material, palpable, real, substantial, tangible, visible; *opp* intangible. 2 (physical activity) bodily, corporal, corporeal, physiological; *opp* mental

physician *n* consultant, doc *inf*, doctor, general practitioner, GP, medic *inf*, medical practitioner, quack *inf*, specialist

physique *n* body, build, figure, form, frame, shape

pick *n* best, cream, elite, favorite, flower, pride; *opp* worst

pick *v* 1 choose, decide, elect, favor, make a choice, opt for, plump for, prefer, select, settle on, single out, vote for; *opp* discard. 2 (pick flowers) collect, cut, gather, harvest, pluck, pull. 3 **pick on** browbeat, bully, give sb a hard time, harass, hector, persecute, push sb around *inf*; *opp* favor

picture *n* 1 drawing, illustration, image, likeness, painting, photograph, portrait, print, representation, sketch. 2 (a picture of what sth is like) account, depiction, description, image, impression, report. 3 (take a picture) photo, shot, snapshot. 4 (a motion picture) blockbuster, film, flick *inf*, movie, video

picture *v* call to mind, conceive, conjure up, envisage, evoke, imagine, see, think up, visualize

picturesque *adj* attractive, beautiful, charming, idyllic, lovely, pretty, quaint, scenic, striking; *opp* ugly

piece *n* 1 bit, bite, chunk, dollop *inf*,

fraction, fragment, hunk, length, lump, morsel, part, portion, quantity, scrap, section, segment, share, shred, slab, slice, sliver, unit. **2** (a piece in the newspaper) article, column, composition, item, report, review. **3** (a piece by a famous sculptor) creation, specimen, study, work, work of art

pier *n* breakwater, dock, jetty, landing stage, quay, wharf

pierce *v* bore, drill, impale, jab, penetrate, perforate, prick, puncture, spike, stab

piercing *adj* **1** (a piercing sound) ear-splitting, high-pitched, loud, sharp, shrieking, shrill; *opp* gentle, soft. **2** (a piercing wind) arctic, biting, bitter, cold, freezing, keen, numbing, wintry; *opp* warm

pigment *n* color, colorant, dye, stain, tincture, tint

pile *n* **1** accumulation, agglomeration, bundle, collection, heap, mass, mound, mountain, stack, stock, store, tower. **2** abundance, heaps *inf*, load, loads *inf*, mass, masses *inf*, lots *inf*, stacks *inf*

pile *v* accumulate, amass, assemble, collect, gather, heap, hoard, load, pile up, stack up, stockpile, stock up, store up

pile-up *n* accident, collision, crash, smash, smash-up

pilgrim *n* crusader, devotee, seeker, traveler, wanderer, wayfarer, worshiper

pilgrimage *n* crusade, expedition, journey, mission, quest, search

pill *n* capsule, drug, lozenge, medicine, pastille, pellet, tablet

pillage *n* looting, marauding, plunder,

plundering, raiding, ransacking, rifling, robbery, robbing, sack

pillage *v* despoil, loot, plunder, raid, ransack, ravage, raze, rifle, rob, sack, strip

pillar *n* **1** column, pier, pilaster, pole, post, prop, shaft, stanchion, support, upright. **2** (pillar of society) backbone, mainstay, rock, supporter, upholder, worthy

pilot *n* **1** airman, aviator, captain, commander, director, driver, flier, helmsman, navigator. **2** experiment, model, prototype, test, trial

pilot *v* **1** conduct, convey, direct, drive, fly, guide, lead, navigate, point, shepherd, steer. **2** model, test, try out

pimple *n* acne, blackhead, boil, pustule, spot, swelling, zit *sl*

pin *n* bolt, brooch, clip, fastener, nail, peg, rivet, spike, staple, tack

pin *v* **1** affix, attach, clip, fasten, fix, join, nail, peg, rivet, secure, staple, stick, tack. **2 pin down** constrain, hold down, immobilize, pinion, restrain

pinch *v* **1** compress, grasp, nip, press, squeeze, tweak. **2** chafe, confine, cramp, crush, hurt, rub, squeeze. **3** filch *inf*, lift *inf*, make off with *inf*, nick *inf*, plunder, poach, rob, shoplift, steal, swipe *inf*, walk off with

pine *v* ache, crave, hanker, hunger, long, miss, mourn, mope, sicken, yearn

pinnacle *n* acme, apex, apogee, cap, crest, crown, height, high point, peak, summit, top, zenith

pinpoint *v* define, discover, distinguish, find, home in on, identify, locate, specify, spot

pioneer n 1 colonist, discoverer, explorer, frontiersman, frontierswoman, settler. 2 architect, developer, discoverer, founder, frontrunner, groundbreaker, innovator, inventor, leader, originator, trailblazer, trendsetter

pioneer v begin, create, develop, discover, experiment with, found, initiate, instigate, institute, introduce, invent, lead the way, launch, originate, set up, start

pious adj 1 dedicated, devoted, devout, God-fearing, godly, holy, religious, reverent, righteous, saintly, spiritual, virtuous; *opp* impious. 2 goody-goody *inf*, holier-than-thou, hypocritical, sanctimonious, self-righteous, self-satisfied

pipe n channel, conduit, cylinder, duct, hose, line, main, passage, pipeline, tube

pipe v 1 channel, conduct, siphon, transmit. 2 cheep, chirp, flute, peep, shrill, squeak, trill, twitter, warble, whistle

piquant adj hot, peppery, pungent, salty, savory, sharp, spicy, tart, tasty; *opp* bland

pirate n 1 buccaneer, corsair, freebooter, hijacker, marauder, raider, rover. 2 copier, plagiarist

pirate v appropriate, copy, infringe copyright, plagiarize, poach, reproduce

pit n 1 abyss, cavity, chasm, crater, dent, depression, ditch, excavation, gulf, hole, hollow, indentation, pothole, trench. 2 coal-mine, colliery, mine, quarry, shaft, working

pitch n 1 arena, field, ground, park, playing field, stadium. 2 degree, extent, height, intensity, level, point. 3 angle, dip, gradient, incline, slant, slope, steepness, tilt

pitch v 1 bowl, cast, chuck *inf*, fling, heave, hurl, lob *inf*, sling, throw, toss. 2 (pitch a tent) erect, put up, raise, set up. 3 pitch in assist, chip in *inf*, contribute, do your bit, help, join in, lend a hand, participate, play a part

pitch-black adj coal-black, ebony, jet-black, pitch-dark, raven

piteous adj affecting, distressing, grievous, heartbreaking, heartrending, lamentable, miserable, moving, pathetic, pitiable, pitiful, plaintive, poignant, sad, touching, upsetting, woeful, wretched

pitfall n catch, danger, difficulty, drawback, hazard, peril, snag, stumbling-block, trap

pitiful adj 1 affecting, distressing, grievous, heartbreaking, heartrending, lamentable, miserable, moving, pathetic, piteous, pitiable, plaintive, poignant, sad, touching, upsetting, woeful, wretched. 2 contemptible, hopeless, inadequate, laughable, mean, measly, miserable, paltry, pathetic *inf*, poor, ridiculous, risible, shabby, sorry, useless, worthless; *opp* good

pitiless adj brutal, callous, cold-blooded, cold-hearted, cruel, hard, hard-hearted, harsh, heartless, implacable, inexorable, inhuman, merciless, relentless, ruthless, sadistic, uncaring, unfeeling, unmerciful, unsympathetic; *opp* merciful

pittance n chicken-feed *inf*, drop, mite, peanuts *inf*, scrap, trifle

pity n 1 charity, clemency, commiseration, compassion,

compunction, condolence, fellow-feeling, forbearance, kindness, mercy, quarter, sympathy, tenderness, understanding. 2 (a pity) bad luck, crime *inf*, crying shame *inf*, misfortune, shame

pity *v* commiserate, feel for, feel sorry for, show compassion, show mercy, sympathize, weep for; *opp* envy

pivot *n* 1 axis, axle, fulcrum, hinge, pin, spindle, swivel. 2 center, focus, heart, hub

pivot *v* revolve, rotate, swing, swivel, turn

placard *n* advertisement, bill, notice, poster, sign

placate *v* appease, assuage, calm, conciliate, humor, mollify, pacify, propitiate, satisfy, soothe

place *n* 1 area, location, point, position, scene, setting, site, situation, spot, station, venue, whereabouts. 2 city, country, county, district, locale, locality, neighborhood, quarter, region, state, town, vicinity, village. 3 (sb's home) abode, apartment, domicile, dwelling, house, flat, property, residence, rooms. 4 (second place in a race) grade, position, rank, role, standing, station, status. 5 (a job) employment, job, office, position, post, situation

place *v* 1 deposit, dump *inf*, lay, leave, locate, plant, position, put, rest, settle, situate, stand, station, stick *inf*. 2 arrange, categorize, class, classify, grade, group, order, put in order, rank, sort

placid *adj* calm, collected, composed, cool, easy-going, equable, even-tempered, gentle, imperturbable, mild, peaceful, phlegmatic, quiet, serene, steady, still, tranquil, unexcitable, unruffled; *opp* excitable

plagiarize *v* copy, crib *inf*, lift *inf*, pirate, reproduce, steal

plague *n* 1 disease, epidemic, infection, outbreak, pestilence. 2 affliction, bane, blight, blot, calamity, cancer, curse, evil, scourge, torment, trial

plague *v* afflict, annoy, badger, bedevil, bother, bug *inf*, disturb, harass, hassle *inf*, hound, molest, nag, persecute, pester, tease, torment, torture, trouble, vex

plain *adj* 1 apparent, audible, clear, comprehensible, distinct, evident, legible, lucid, manifest, obvious, patent, transparent, unambiguous, unmistakable, visible. 2 average, common, commonplace, everyday, homely, lowly, modest, ordinary, simple, typical, unaffected, unpretentious; *opp* sophisticated. 3 austere, bare, basic, discreet, modest, muted, pure, restrained, severe, simple, stark, unadorned, spartan; *opp* decorated, fancy. 4 (of sb's appearance) ordinary-looking, ugly, unattractive, unprepossessing; *opp* pretty. 5 artless, bluff, blunt, candid, frank, guileless, honest, open, outspoken, straightforward, unvarnished, upfront *inf*

plain *n* flatland, grassland, lowland, pampas, plateau, prairie, savannah, steppe, veld

plain-spoken *adj* artless, bluff, blunt, candid, direct, explicit, forthright, frank, guileless, honest, open, outspoken, straightforward, unvarnished, upfront *inf; opp* indirect

plaintive *adj* doleful, melancholy, mournful, pathetic, piteous, pitiful, plangent, rueful, sad, sorrowful, unhappy, wistful, woebegone, woeful; *opp* cheerful

plan *n* 1 aim, course, design, device, formula, idea, intention, method, plot, policy, procedure, program, project, proposal, proposition, scenario, scheme, strategy, suggestion, system. 2 bird's-eye view, blueprint, chart, diagram, drawing, layout, map, representation, sketch

plan *v* 1 arrange, concoct, contrive, design, devise, draft, draw up, formulate, map out, mastermind, organize, outline, plot, prepare, project, scheme, think up, work out. 2 aim, contemplate, envisage, foresee, intend, mean, propose, purpose, think of

plane *adj* even, flat, flush, horizontal, level, regular, smooth, uniform

plane *n* 1 flat surface, level, surface. 2 degree, footing, level, position, rank, stratum. 3 aeroplane, aircraft, airplane, jet, jumbo

planet *n* globe, orb, satellite, sphere, world

plant *n* 1 bush, flower, greenery, herb, shrub, vegetable, weed. 2 factory, foundry, mill, shop, works, workshop, yard. 3 apparatus, equipment, gear, machinery, machines, tools

plant *v* 1 implant, scatter, seed, sow, transplant. 2 locate, place, put, set, situate, station

plaster *n* 1 gypsum, mortar, plasterwork, stucco. 2 bandage, dressing, sticking-plaster

plaster *v* coat, cover, daub, overlay, smear, spread

plastic *adj* ductile, flexible, malleable, pliable, pliant, soft, supple, workable; *opp* rigid

plate *n* 1 dish, platter, salver. 2 illustration, lithograph, photo, photograph, picture, print

platform *n* 1 dais, podium, rostrum, stage, stand. 2 manifesto, objectives, plan, policy, program, proposals

platitude *n* banality, cliché, commonplace, stock phrase, truism

plausible *adj* believable, conceivable, credible, imaginable, likely, logical, persuasive, possible, probable, rational, reasonable, sensible, tenable; *opp* implausible

play *n* 1 comedy, drama, performance, piece, show, tragedy. 2 amusement, diversion, entertainment, frivolity, frolics, fun, games, horse-play, leisure, merry-making, playing, recreation, revelry, sport

play *v* 1 amuse yourself, caper, cavort, enjoy yourself, frisk, frolic, have a good time, have fun, gambol, romp, sport, trifle. 2 (in a game, match) compete, join in, participate, take part. 3 (play a character) act, impersonate, perform, play the part of, portray, represent, take the part of. 4 **play down** belittle, downplay, gloss over, make light of, make little of, minimize, underplay, underrate, understate. 5 **play on** abuse, capitalize on, exploit, impose on, make the most of, profit by, take advantage of, trade on. 6 **play up** accentuate, emphasize, exaggerate, highlight, overstate, spotlight, stress, talk up, underline

playboy n hedonist, ladies' man, man-about-town, philanderer, pleasure-seeker, rake, roué, socialite, sybarite, womanizer

player n 1 competitor, contestant, participant, sportsman, sportswoman, team member. 2 (theater) actor, actress, artiste, entertainer, performer, thespian, trouper. 3 (music) artist, artiste, instrumentalist, musician, performer, soloist, virtuoso

playful adj cheerful, frisky, frolicsome, fun-loving, high-spirited, humorous, impish, jokey, kittenish, light-hearted, lively, merry, mischievous, puckish, roguish, spirited, sportive, sprightly, teasing, vivacious; **opp** serious

plea n 1 appeal, entreaty, petition, prayer, request, suit, supplication. 2 argument, claim, excuse, explanation, justification

plead v 1 appeal, beg, beseech, entreat, implore, petition, pray, solicit, supplicate. 2 allege, argue, assert, claim, declare, maintain, put forward, reason

pleasant adj 1 agreeable, amusing, delightful, enjoyable, fine, good, gratifying, lovely, nice, pleasing, pleasurable, satisfying, welcome; **opp** unpleasant. 2 (of a person) affable, agreeable, amiable, charming, cheerful, congenial, engaging, friendly, genial, good-humoured, likable, nice, sympathetic, winning; **opp** unpleasant

pleasantry n badinage, banter, greeting, jest, joke, quip, remark

please v 1 amuse, appeal, charm, cheer, content, delight, divert, entertain, give

pleasure, gladden, gratify, indulge, make happy, satisfy, suit, tickle inf; **opp** displease. 2 (do as you please) choose, desire, like, prefer, see fit, want, will, wish

pleased adj charmed, content, contented, delighted, elated, euphoric, glad, gratified, happy, satisfied, thrilled, tickled inf; **opp** annoyed, unhappy

pleasing adj agreeable, amusing, attractive, beautiful, charming, delightful, enjoyable, fine, good, gratifying, lovely, nice, pleasant, pleasurable, satisfying

pleasure n amusement, bliss, comfort, contentment, delectation, delight, diversion, enjoyment, entertainment, ecstasy, euphoria, fulfillment, gratification, happiness, joy, recreation, satisfaction

pledge n 1 assurance, covenant, oath, promise, undertaking, vow, warrant, word. 2 bail, bond, collateral, deposit, gage, guarantee, security, surety

pledge v commit yourself, contract, covenant, give your word, guarantee, promise, swear, undertake, vouchsafe, vow, warrant

plentiful adj abounding, abundant, bounteous, bountiful, copious, generous, inexhaustible, lavish, liberal, overflowing, plenteous, profuse; **opp** rare

plenty n 1 abundance, loads inf, lots inf, masses inf, mountains, plethora, profusion, quantity, stacks inf, sufficiency, tons inf, wealth.
2 abundance, affluence, bounty, fruitfulness, luxury, opulence, plenitude, prosperity, wealth; **opp** scarcity

pliable adj **1** bendable, ductile, elastic, flexible, malleable, plastic, pliant, soft, stretchable, supple, workable; *opp* rigid. **2** (of a person) amenable, compliant, docile, flexible, impressionable, manageable, pliant, receptive, tractable, yielding; *opp* stubborn

plight n case, condition, difficulty, dilemma, hot water *inf*, jam *inf*, pickle *inf*, problem, predicament, scrape *inf*, situation, spot *inf*, state, straits, trouble

plod v clump, drag, lumber, plough, slog, stomp, tramp, tread, trudge

plot n **1** cabal, conspiracy, intrigue, machination, plan, scheme, stratagem. **2** (of a story) action, narrative, outline, scenario, story, story-line, thread. **3** (plot of land) acreage, allotment, garden, lot, parcel, patch, smallholding, tract

plot v **1** collude, conspire, cook up *inf*, devise, hatch, intrigue, maneuver, plan, scheme. **2** calculate, chart, compute, draft, draw, locate, map, mark, outline, record, sketch

plow v cultivate, dig, furrow, ridge, till, turn over, work

pluck v clutch, grab, grasp, jerk, pull, seize, snatch, tug, tweak, yank

plug n **1** bung, cork, seal, spigot, stopper. **2** advertisement, hype *inf*, mention, promotion, publicity, push

plug v **1** block, bung, close, cork, seal, stop, stopper, stuff. **2** advertise, hype *inf*, mention, promote, publicize, push

plume n feather, plumage, quill

plump adj **1** ample, buxom, chubby, corpulent, dumpy, fat, fleshy, full, obese, portly, pudgy, roly-poly, rotund, round, stout, tubby; *opp* thin

plunder n **1** booty, contraband, ill-gotten gains, loot, pickings, prize, spoils, stolen goods, swag *inf*. **2** looting, marauding, pillage, plundering, raiding, ransacking, rifling, robbery, robbing, sack

plunder v despoil, lay waste, loot, pillage, raid, ransack, ravage, rifle, rob, sack, spoil, steal, strip

plunge v **1** descend, dip, dive, drop, fall, hurtle, nosedive, plummet, pitch, sink, swoop, tumble. **2** dip, douse, immerse, sink, submerge, thrust

ply v carry on, engage in, exercise, follow, practice, pursue, work at

poach v filch *inf*, lift *inf*, make off with *inf*, nick *inf*, pinch *inf*, plagiarize, plunder, rob, steal, swipe *inf*, thieve

pocket n bag, compartment, hollow, pouch, receptacle, sack

pocket v appropriate, filch *inf*, nick *inf*, pinch *inf*, steal, take, walk off with

pod n case, hull, husk, shell

poem n ditty *inf*, haiku, limerick, lyric, ode, rhyme, song, sonnet, verse

poet n bard, lyricist, rhymer, sonneteer, versifier

poetic adj flowery, imaginative, lyric, lyrical, musical, rhythmical

poetry n poems, rhymes, rhyming, verse

poignant adj affecting, bitter, distressing, emotional, evocative, heartbreaking, intense, moving, painful, pathetic, pitiful, sad, sentimental, tender, touching, tragic, upsetting

point n **1** (meet at a certain point) location, place, position, site, spot. **2** (a sharp point) apex, end, nib, prong, sharp end, spike, spur, tine, tip, top.

3 (point in time) instant, juncture, moment, second, stage, time. **4** (the point of doing sth) aim, goal, intention, motive, purpose, reason, use. **5** (the point of what sb is saying) crux, drift, essence, gist, meaning, relevance, significance, theme, thrust. **6** (sb's good points) attribute, characteristic, facet, feature, quality, trait

point v **1** (point sth at sb) aim, direct, level, train. **2** (point at sth) call attention to, draw attention to, indicate, point out, show, signal. **3** (point sb in the right direction) guide, lead, steer

pointed adj barbed, edged, sharp, spiky

pointer n **1** arrow, hand, indicator, needle. **2** advice, hint, recommendation, suggestion, tip, warning

pointless adj aimless, fruitless, futile, ineffective, in vain, irrelevant, meaningless, senseless, silly, stupid, unproductive, useless, worthless; **opp** useful

poise n aplomb, assurance, calmness, composure, cool, coolness, dignity, equanimity, sang-froid, self-assurance, self-possession

poised adj **1** calm, collected, composed, dignified, self-confident, self-possessed, unflappable inf. **2** balanced, hovering, in equilibrium, steady, teetering, wavering. **3** (poised for sth) all set, keyed up, prepared, ready, standing by, waiting

poison n toxin, venom

poison v **1** (poison sth) adulterate, blight, contaminate, infect, pollute, spoil. **2** (poison sb) give poison to, kill, murder. **3** (poison sb's mind) corrupt, deprave, pervert, subvert, warp

poisonous adj deadly, fatal, lethal, noxious, toxic, venomous, virulent

poke v dig, elbow, hit, jab, nudge, prod, punch, push, stab, stick, thrust

poky adj confined, cramped, narrow, small, tiny; **opp** spacious

pole n bar, column, mast, post, prop, rod, shaft, spar, stake, stick, upright

polarize v diverge, divide, separate, split

police n constabulary, police force, the fuzz inf, the law inf

police v control, guard, keep in order, oversee, patrol, protect, regulate, supervise, watch over

policeman n cop inf, copper inf, detective, inspector, officer, policeman, policewoman

policy n approach, code, course, guidelines, line inf, manifesto, plan, practice, procedure, program, protocol, rules, scheme, strategy, theory

polish n **1** brightness, brilliance, finish, glaze, gleam, gloss, luster, sheen, shine, sparkle, veneer. **2** beeswax, oil, shellac, varnish, wax. **3** (sb has polish) class inf, elegance, grace, refinement, sophistication, style

polish v brighten, buff, burnish, clean, rub, shine, smooth, wax

polished adj **1** (a polished surface) bright, gleaming, glossy, lustrous, shining, shiny, slippery, smooth. **2** (polished manners) civilized, classy inf, cultivated, elegant, polite, posh, refined, sophisticated, well-bred; **opp** rough. **3** (a polished performance) accomplished, expert, flawless, impeccable, masterly, perfect, proficient, skillful; **opp** bad, poor

polite *adj* 1 (of a person) attentive, chivalrous, civil, considerate, courteous, gracious, respectful, thoughtful, well-behaved, well-mannered, well-spoken; *opp* rude. 2 diplomatic, discreet, euphemistic, formal, proper, tactful

political *adj* administrative, civic, diplomatic, governmental, legislative, parliamentary, public, state

politician *n* congressman, legislator, senator, statesman

politics *n* affairs of state, civics, diplomacy, government, political science, public affairs, statesmanship

poll *n* 1 ballot, count, election, referendum, vote, voting. 2 canvass, census, market research, sampling, show of hands, survey

poll *v* ballot, canvass, interview, question, sample, survey

pollute *v* adulterate, contaminate, dirty, foul, infect, make dirty, poison, soil, spoil, stain, taint

pollution *n* adulteration, contamination, dirt, dirtiness, filth, filthiness

pomp *n* ceremony, display, glitter, glory, grandeur, magnificence, majesty, ostentation, pageantry, ritual, spectacle, splendor, show

pompous *adj* affected, arrogant, boastful, bombastic, conceited, grandiose, imperious, inflated, ostentatious, overbearing, pretentious, self-important, showy, smug, snooty *inf*, stuck-up *inf*, vain; *opp* modest

pond *n* lake, millpond, pool, puddle, tarn

ponder *v* brood, consider, contemplate, deliberate, meditate, mull over, muse, reflect, ruminate, study, think

ponderous *adj* 1 awkward, bulky, cumbersome, heavy, huge, massive, slow, unwieldy; *opp* light. 2 (a ponderous speech) boring, dreary, dull, humorless, labored, long-winded, plodding, slow, tedious, tiresome

pool *n* lagoon, lake, oasis, paddling pool, pond, puddle, swimming pool, tarn

pool *v* amalgamate, combine, merge, put together, share

poor *adj* 1 (of a person) badly off, broke *inf*, deprived, destitute, hard up *inf*, impoverished, needy, penniless, poverty-stricken, skint *inf*; *opp* rich. 2 (a poor amount) deficient, inadequate, insufficient, meager, miserable, reduced, scanty, sparse. 3 (poor quality) bad, cheap, defective, faulty, imperfect, inferior, rubbishy, shoddy, substandard; *opp* good. 4 (unlucky) ill-fated, luckless, miserable, pathetic, pitiable, unfortunate, unhappy, unlucky, wretched; *opp* lucky. 5 (a poor home) humble, lowly, mean, modest, simple. 6 (poor soil) arid, bare, barren, depleted, infertile, unproductive; *opp* rich

pop *v* bang, burst, crack, detonate, explode, go off, snap

populace *n* crowd, general public, masses, mob, multitude, people, public, rabble

popular *adj* 1 (liked by many people) accepted, approved, celebrated, famous, fashionable, favorite, in, in demand, liked, sought-after, well-known, well-liked; *opp* unpopular. 2 (believed by many people) common, conventional, current, general, predominant, prevailing, standard, universal, widespread

popularity n acceptance, acclaim, approval, currency, demand, fame, favor, renown, vogue

popularize v give credence to, give currency to, make accessible, make available, make popular, promote, spread

populate v colonize, dwell in, fill, inhabit, live in, occupy, overrun, people, settle

population n citizens, community, folk, inhabitants, people, populace, public, residents, society

populous adj crowded, densely populated, heavily populated, overpopulated, packed

porch n doorway, entrance, lobby, vestibule

pore over v 1 (pore over a book) examine, peruse, read, scrutinize, study. 2 (pore over a question) brood on, contemplate, dwell on, go over, meditate on, mull over, muse on, ponder, reflect on, think about

pornographic adj blue, dirty, erotic, explicit, filthy, indecent, obscene, porn inf, sexual, titillating

porous adj absorbent, cellular, penetrable, permeable, spongelike, spongy

port n dock, harbor, haven, seaport

portable adj compact, convenient, easy to carry, handy, light, lightweight, manageable, mobile, movable, pocket, pocket-sized, small, transportable

porter n caretaker, concierge, door-keeper, doorman, gatekeeper, janitor, security-guard, watchman

portion n 1 bit, chunk, helping, piece, section, segment, serving, slice, sliver,

wedge. 2 (sb's portion) allocation, allowance, cut inf, measure, percentage, quantity, quota, ration, share, whack inf

portrait n drawing, image, likeness, painting, photograph, picture, portrayal, representation, self-portrait, study

portray v 1 delineate, depict, draw, illustrate, paint, render, represent, sketch. 2 characterize, depict, describe, represent, show

pose n 1 attitude, bearing, position, posture, stance. 2 act, affectation, facade, front, masquerade, posture, pretense, role

pose v 1 (pose for your picture) model, sit, strike a pose. 2 act, be a poser inf, put on airs, put on an act, show off. 3 (pose a question) ask, put, submit, suggest. 4 (pose a problem) cause, create, present

poseur n fraud, poser inf, posturer, show-off

posh adj 1 (of a person) aristocratic, genteel, rich, snobbish, stuck-up inf, upper-class; opp common. 2 (of a restaurant, shop) classy inf, elegant, expensive, fancy, fashionable, swanky inf, swish inf, up-market inf, upscale inf; opp cheap

position n 1 (position on a map) bearings, location, reference, whereabouts. 2 (a house in a good position) area, locale, location, place, setting, site, situation, spot. 3 (a comfortable position for driving) angle, pose, posture, stance, way of sitting. 4 (put sb in an awkward position) plight, predicament, situation, state.

5 (opinion) attitude, belief, opinion, point of view, stance, view. 6 (position in society) caste, class, importance, place, rank, station, status. 7 (applying for a position in the company) job, post, situation. 8 (position in a league) grade, level, place, rank

position v arrange, array, lay out, locate, place, put, set, site, situate, stand, station

positive adj 1 absolute, actual, affirmative, categorical, certain, clear, clear-cut, decided, definite, emphatic, firm, incontrovertible, indisputable, real, undeniable, unmistakable. 2 certain, confident, convinced, sure; *opp* doubtful. 3 (some positive advice) constructive, helpful, practical, productive, useful, worthwhile; *opp* unhelpful. 4 (a positive approach) confident, hopeful, idealistic, optimistic; *opp* negative

possess v 1 be the owner of, enjoy, have, hold, own. 2 (possess a sense of humor) be blessed with, be endowed with, have. 3 (take by force) acquire, invade, occupy, seize, take over, take possession of. 4 (possess sb's mind) bewitch, captivate, cast a spell over, charm, control, dominate, enchant, enthrall, haunt, hypnotize, influence, obsess

possessions n assets, belongings, effects, property, things, worldly goods

possessive adj 1 clinging, controlling, dominating, domineering, jealous, overprotective, proprietorial, protective. 2 acquisitive, covetous, grasping, greedy, selfish; *opp* generous

possibility n chance, danger, likelihood, odds, potential, probability, prospect, risk

possible adj able to be done, attainable, conceivable, credible, feasible, imaginable, likely, plausible, potential, practicable, probable, realizable, reasonable, viable, within reach; *opp* impossible

possibly adv God willing, hopefully *inf*, if possible, maybe, perhaps

post n 1 (wooden post) column, pillar, pole, shaft, stake, support, upright. 2 (job) appointment, job, position, situation, vacancy. 3 (catch the mail) collection, delivery, mail, postal service. 4 (deal with your mail) correspondence, letters, mail

post v dispatch, mail, send, transmit

poster n advertisement, flyer, notice, placard, sign

posterity n 1 future, future generations. 2 children, descendants, offspring, heirs, successors

postpone v adjourn, defer, delay, hold over, put back, put off, put on ice *inf*, put on the back burner *inf*, shelve, suspend

postscript n addition, afterthought, appendix, codicil, PS

postulate v advance, assume, hypothesize, posit, propose, suppose

posture n attitude, bearing, carriage, deportment, pose, stance

pot n bowl, cauldron, container, dish, jar, pan, urn, vessel

potent adj effective, forceful, influential, mighty, overwhelming, powerful, strong, vigorous; *opp* weak

potential adj budding, developing,

embryonic, future, likely, possible, promising, would-be *inf*

potion *n* brew, concoction, dose, draft, drink, drug, elixir, liquid, mixture

potter *v* 1 (potter in the garden) dabble, do odd jobs, fiddle, mess about, tinker. 2 (potter along) dawdle, dilly-dally, move slowly

pottery *n* ceramics, china, crockery, earthenware, porcelain, stoneware, terracotta

pouch *n* bag, pocket, purse, sack, wallet

pounce *v* ambush, attack, drop, jump, lunge, snatch, spring, strike, swoop, take sb by surprise

pound *n* compound, corral, enclosure, pen, yard

pound *v* 1 batter, beat, knead, press, pummel, thump. 2 crush, grind, mash, powder, pulverize, smash. 3 (pounding along) clump, stamp, stomp, tramp. 4 (heart began to pound) bang, beat heavily, bump, palpitate, pulse, throb, thump

pour *v* 1 (liquid pouring) cascade, course, flood, flow, gush, jet, run, rush, spew, spill, splash, spout, spurt, stream. 2 (rain) rain hard, teem. 3 (pour the wine) decant, serve

poverty *n* destitution, distress, hardship, insolvency, need, penury, want; *opp* wealth

powder *n* dust, fine particles, talc

powder *v* crush, granulate, grind, pound, pulverize

power *n* 1 drive, energy, force, might, muscle, potency, powerfulness, strength, vigor. 2 (the power to do sth) ability, capability, competence, potential.

3 (power over sb) ascendancy, authority, clout *inf*, command, control, dominance, domination, influence, mastery, rule, sovereignty, supremacy, sway. 4 (power to grant sth) authority, authorization, license, prerogative, right

powerful *adj* 1 mighty, robust, strapping, strong, sturdy, tough; *opp* weak. 2 (a powerful ruler) authoritative, commanding, dominant, invincible, mighty, omnipotent, sovereign, strong, supreme; *opp* weak. 3 (a powerful argument) compelling, convincing, effective, eloquent, forceful, persuasive, telling; *opp* weak

powerless *adj* debilitated, defenseless, dependent, disabled, feeble, frail, helpless, impotent, incapable, incapacitated, ineffectual, paralyzed, unable, unarmed, vulnerable, weak; *opp* strong

practicable *adj* achievable, attainable, doable *inf*, feasible, possible, realistic, sensible, viable, workable; *opp* impracticable

practical *adj* 1 (a practical person) capable, competent, efficient, expert, hands-on, no-nonsense *inf*, practiced, proficient, skilled, trained. 2 (be practical about sth) businesslike, down-to-earth, hard-headed, hard-nosed *inf*, matter-of-fact, pragmatic, realistic, sensible. 3 (practical shoes) functional, sensible, utilitarian

practice *n* 1 drill, exercise, preparation, rehearsal, repetition, study, training. 2 (it's only a practice) rehearsal, run-through *inf*. 3 (a common practice) custom, habit, tradition, way.

4 (standard practice) method, procedure, tradition. 5 (put sth into practice) action, effect, operation

practice v 1 drill, exercise, go over, go through, polish, prepare, refine, rehearse, repeat, run through, study, train, warm up, work out. 2 (practice a religion) follow, observe

pragmatic adj businesslike, efficient, matter-of-fact, practical, realistic, sensible

praise n 1 acclaim, accolades, applause, approval, commendation, compliments, congratulations, ovation, thanks, tributes. 2 (praise of God) adoration, devotion, exaltation, glory, worship

praise v 1 (praise sb) acclaim, admire, applaud, cheer, clap, commend, compliment, congratulate, pay tribute to, rave about inf; opp criticize. 2 (praise God) adore, exalt, glorify, honor, offer praise to, worship

praiseworthy adj admirable, commendable, creditable, deserving, excellent, good, laudable

prance v bound, caper, cavort, dance, frisk, gambol, jump, leap, play, romp, skip

prank n jape, practical joke, stunt, trick

prattle v chatter, gabble, jabber, twitter, waffle inf

pray v 1 ask, beg, beseech, entreat, implore, petition, plead, request, urge. 2 (pray to God) commune with God, offer a prayer, say your prayers

prayer n communion, devotion, litany

preach v 1 evangelize, give a sermon, spread the gospel, teach. 2 advise, exhort, give advice, harangue, lay down the law, lecture, pontificate, urge

preacher n clergyman, cleric, evangelist, minister, missionary, parson, pastor, televangelist

preamble n foreword, introduction, opening remarks, overture, preface, prelude

precarious adj dangerous, dicey, dodgy inf, doubtful, dubious, hairy inf, hazardous, insecure, perilous, risky, treacherous, uncertain, unreliable, unsafe, unstable, unsure, vulnerable, wobbly; opp safe

precaution n 1 anticipation, care, caution, foresight, forethought, prudence, wariness. 2 preventive measure, protection, provision, safeguard, safety measure

precede v be in front, come before, come first, go ahead, go before, go in front, head, herald, introduce, lead, lead into, lead up to, preface, start, usher in

precedent n criterion, example, instance, model, patter, prototype, standard, yardstick

precious adj 1 (his precious baby) adored, beloved, cherished, darling, dear, favorite, irreplaceable, loved, treasured. 2 (precious stones) invaluable, priceless, prized, rare, valuable

precipice n bluff, brink, cliff, cliff face, crag, drop, escarpment, height, rock face

precipitate adj 1 abrupt, breakneck, brief, headlong, hurried, plunging, rapid, speedy, sudden, swift, unexpected, violent. 2 hasty, heedless, hurried, impetuous, impulsive, rash, reckless

precipitate v accelerate, advance, bring on, encourage, expedite, further, hasten, hurry, quicken, spark off, speed up, trigger

precise adj 1 accurate, clear, exact, explicit, specific, unambiguous.
2 (the precise meaning) actual, correct, faithful, literal, right, strict. 3 (at a precise time) definite, exact, fixed, particular, specific. 4 (precise movements) accurate, careful, exact, meticulous, scrupulous

preclude v debar, exclude, forestall, make impossible, prevent, prohibit, rule out, stop, thwart

precocious adj advanced, ahead, bright, developed, forward, gifted, intelligent, mature, quick

preconception n assumption, bias, expectation, notion, preconceived idea, prejudice, presumption

precursor n forerunner, harbinger, herald, predecessor

predatory adj hunting, marauding, pillaging, plundering, preying, rapacious, voracious

predecessor n ancestor, antecedent, forebear, forefather, forerunner, precursor

predetermined adj agreed, fixed, prearranged, set, settled

predicament n corner, crisis, difficult situation, dilemma, emergency, fix inf, hole inf, mess, pickle inf, plight, quandary, scrape inf, tight spot inf

predict v augur, divine, forebode, forecast, foresee, foreshadow, foretell, portend, presage, prophesy

predictable adj anticipated, certain, expected, foreseeable, foreseen, in the cards inf, likely, reliable, sure, unsurprising; **opp** unpredictable

prediction n forecast, prognosis, prophecy

predominant adj 1 ascendant, controlling, dominant, in control, leading, most powerful, principal, ruling, superior. 2 chief, main, most obvious, most noticeable, prevailing

predominate v be dominant, be in the majority, be most noticeable, be predominant, carry weight, have the upper hand, hold sway, outnumber, outweigh, overrule, prevail, rule

preeminent adj distinguished, excellent, famous, foremost, important, incomparable, outstanding, prominent, renowned, superior, unrivaled, unsurpassed

preempt v 1 acquire, appropriate, assume, commandeer, seize, take over, usurp. 2 anticipate, forestall, prevent

preen v 1 (of animals) arrange, clean, plume, smooth. 2 (of people) array, beautify, deck out, doll up inf, dress up, groom, prettify, primp, spruce up, titivate

preface n foreword, introduction, preamble, prelude, prologue

preface v begin, introduce, launch, lead into, open, precede, prefix, start

prefer v be partial to, choose, desire, elect, fancy, favor, go for inf, incline towards, like, like better, opt for, pick, select, vote for, want, wish

preferable adj advantageous, best, better, chosen, favored, more desirable, more suitable, nicer, preferred, superior, wanted

preference n 1 choice, desire, favorite, first choice, option, pick, selection, wish. 2 advantage, favoritism, partiality, precedence, preferential treatment, priority

preferential adj advantageous, better, biased, favorable, favored, partial, privileged, special, superior

pregnant adj carrying a child, expecting inf, having a baby, with child

prejudge v anticipate, presume, presuppose

prejudice n 1 agism, bigotry, chauvinism, discrimination, favoritism, intolerance, jingoism, narrow-mindedness, racism, sexism, unfairness, xenophobia. 2 bias, leaning, partiality, preconceived idea

prejudice v 1 (make sb prejudiced) bias, color, distort, influence, interfere with, jaundice, poison, predispose, slant, sway, warp. 2 (prejudice your case) be disadvantageous, be prejudicial, damage, harm, hurt, spoil, undermine

prejudiced adj biased, bigoted, discriminatory, intolerant, narrow-minded, unfair, unjust; opp impartial

prejudicial adj damaging, deleterious, detrimental, harmful, unfavorable

preliminary adj 1 first, initial, introductory, opening, prefatory, preparatory, prior. 2 early, experimental, exploratory, pilot, qualifying, tentative, test, trial

prelude n 1 introduction, introductory movement, overture, preface, prologue. 2 beginning, curtain-raiser inf, herald, precursor, start, warm-up inf

premature adj 1 early, immature, incomplete, raw, too early, too soon, undeveloped, unripe, untimely. 2 hasty, ill-considered, impulsive, rash

premeditated adj calculated, considered, deliberate, intended, intentional, planned, willful; opp spontaneous

premise n argument, assertion, assumption, basis, grounds, hypothesis, supposition

premises n building, establishment, place, property, site

premium n bonus, fee, payment, prize, remuneration, reward, surcharge

premonition n 1 apprehension, fear, feeling, foreboding, funny feeling, hunch inf, idea, intuition, misgiving, presentiment, suspicion. 2 indication, omen, portent, sign, warning

preoccupied adj absentminded, absorbed, distracted, engrossed, far-away, immersed, intent, lost in thought, oblivious, pensive, rapt, taken up, thoughtful, unaware

preparation n 1 arrangements, briefing, development, gearing up inf, getting ready, groundwork, making ready, making provision, organization, plans, practice, preparing, setting up, spadework, training. 2 (preparation for an exam) coaching, reading, revising, revision, study, studying, working

preparatory adj introductory, opening, prefatory, preliminary

prepare v 1 (prepare sth) arrange, assemble, draw up, get ready, make ready, put together. 2 (prepare to do sth) brace yourself, exercise, gear up inf, make preparations, plan, practice, psych

yourself up *inf*, steel yourself, take steps, train, warm up. **3** (prepare for an exam) cram *inf*, practice, revise, study.
4 (prepare sb for sth) brief, coach, drill, educate, equip, groom, rehearse, teach, train, tutor. **5** (prepare a meal) cook, fix *inf*, get ready, make, put together

prepared *adj* **1** (prepared to do sth) able, disposed, inclined, minded, of a mind, predisposed, ready, willing.
2 (everything was prepared) arranged, in order, in readiness, ready, set

preposterous *adj* absurd, bizarre, crazy, excessive, impossible, incredible, ludicrous, monstrous, out of the question, outrageous, ridiculous, shocking, unbelievable, unthinkable

prerequisite *n* condition, must *inf*, necessity, precondition, qualification, requirement

prescribe *v* advise, commend, decree, direct, impose, instruct, lay down, order, recommend, specify, stipulate, suggest

presence *n* **1** (your presence is required) attendance, company. **2** (aware of sb's presence) closeness, nearness, proximity.
3 (sb has presence) charisma, magnetism, personality, poise, self-assurance, self-confidence, self-possession

present *adj* **1** contemporary, current, existing, immediate, instant, present-day, up-to-date. **2** accounted for, at hand, available, here, in attendance, nearby, ready, there, to hand

present *n* **1** (the present) here and now, now, the time being, today. **2** (a present) contribution, donation, gift, offering

present *v* **1** (present sb to people)

announce, introduce, make known.
2 (present a gift) award, bestow, confer, donate, give, hand over, offer. **3** (present a proposal) advance, put forward, set forth, submit, suggest, tender. **4** (present a different side of your character) demonstrate, display, exhibit, reveal, show. **5** (present a TV show) host, introduce. **6** (present a show) act, give, mount, perform, put on, stage

presentable *adj* acceptable, all right, becoming, decent, fit to be seen, good enough, okay *inf*, passable, respectable, suitable, tidy, up to scratch *inf*, well-groomed

presentation *n* demonstration, display, exhibition, launch, performance, production, show

preserve *v* **1** care for, conserve, defend, guard, keep, look after, maintain, perpetuate, protect, safeguard, save, secure, uphold. **2** (preserve food) bottle, can, cure, dry, freeze, pickle, salt, smoke

preside *v* administer, be in charge, chair, conduct, control, direct, govern, head, lead, manage, officiate, run, take charge, take the chair

press *n* journalism, newspapers, magazines, papers, reporters, the media

press *v* **1** compress, condense, crush, jam, mash, push, reduce, squeeze, stuff.
2 (press sb close) clasp, crush, embrace, enfold, hold, hug, squeeze. **3** (press sb to do sth) ask, beg, compel, constrain, enjoin, entreat, exhort, implore, insist, persuade, put pressure on, urge.
4 (people press into a place) cluster, crowd, flock, gather, push, surge, swarm, throng. **5** (press clothes) flatten, iron,

make flat, smooth

pressing adj critical, crucial, high priority, imperative, important, serious, urgent, vital; **opp** nonurgent, unimportant

pressure n 1 compression, crushing, force, heaviness, load, squeezing, stress, weight. 2 (pressure in your job) constraints, demands, difficulties, hassle inf, problems, strain, stress, tension. 3 (using pressure to make sb do sth) coercion, compulsion, duress, force, power

prestige n cachet, credit, distinction, eminence, esteem, fame, good name, honor, importance, influence, kudos slang, reputation, standing, status

prestigious adj acclaimed, celebrated, distinguished, eminent, famed, famous, glamorous, highly regarded, high-ranking, illustrious, important, influential, respected, well-known

presume v 1 assume, believe, conjecture, guess, imagine, infer, suppose, surmise, take for granted, take it, think. 2 be presumptuous, dare, go so far as, have the effrontery, have the temerity, make bold, take the liberty, venture

presumptuous adj arrogant, audacious, bold, cheeky, cocksure, forward, insolent, overconfident, pushy inf, too big for your britches inf; **opp** modest

presuppose v assume, imply, presume, suppose, take as read, take for granted

pretend v 1 affect, allege, bluff, deceive, dissemble, fake it, falsify, feign, impersonate, make out, pose, put on an act, simulate, trick. 2 (children like to pretend) act, fantasize, imagine, make

believe, play, play-act, suppose

pretense n 1 act, affectation, appearance, artifice, charade, deceit, deception, dissembling, excuse, facade, falsehood, front, hypocrisy, insincerity, lying, mask, masquerade, pose, posing, posturing, pretext, ruse, sham, show, simulation, trickery, veneer. 2 fantasy, imagination, invention, make-believe, unreality

pretentious adj affected, conceited, exaggerated, flamboyant, grandiose, ostentatious, pompous, showy, snobbish, superficial; **opp** unpretentious

pretext n cover, excuse, lie, ploy, pretense, reason, red herring, ruse, wile

pretty adj 1 (of a person) appealing, attractive, beautiful, cute, fair, good-looking, lovely, nice-looking; **opp** ugly. 2 (of a place) attractive, charming, delightful, pleasant; **opp** ugly; **opp** unattractive

prevail v be victorious, conquer, overcome, overrule, prove superior, succeed, triumph, win, win out, win through

prevailing adj common, current, customary, established, fashionable, general, ordinary, popular, prevalent, usual, widespread

prevalent adj accepted, common, commonplace, current, established, extensive, frequent, rampant, rife, ubiquitous, universal, usual, widespread; **opp** rare

prevaricate v beat about the bush, be evasive, cavil, dodge, equivocate, evade, fence, fib, hedge, lie, quibble, shilly-shally, sidestep

prevent v avert, avoid, block, check, curb, deter, fend off, foil, forestall, frustrate, hamper, hinder, impede, nip in the bud, obstruct, put a stop to, restrain, stave off, stop, thwart, ward off; *opp* encourage

preventative adj deterrent, obstructive, precautionary, preemptive, preventive, protective

previous adj earlier, erstwhile, ex-, former, one-time, past, preceding, prior

prey n game, kill, quarry, victim

price n amount, bill, charge, cost, damage inf, estimate, expenditure, expense, fee, figure, offer, outlay, payment, quotation, rate, sum, terms, valuation, value, worth

priceless adj 1 costly, dear, expensive, invaluable, irreplaceable, precious, valuable, worth its weight in gold; *opp* worthless. 2 (hilarious) a scream inf, comic, funny, hilarious, killing inf

prick v 1 jab, nick, perforate, pierce, puncture, spike, stab. 2 (prickle) hurt, itch, prickle, smart, sting, tickle, tingle

prickle n barb, spike, spine, thorn

prickle v hurt, itch, prick, smart, sting, tickle, tingle

prickly adj 1 (with prickles) brambly, scratchy, sharp, spiky, spiny, thorny, vicious. 2 (of a person or situation) awkward, difficult, irritable, tetchy, thorny, touchy, tricky, waspish

pride n 1 dignity, ego, feelings, honor, self-esteem, self-respect. 2 arrogance, big-headedness inf, conceit, snobbery, vanity

priest n chaplain, clergyman, clergywoman, curate, deacon, ecclesiastic, father, member of the clergy, minister, padre, parson, pastor, priestess, rector, shaman, vicar

priggish adj goody-goody inf, moralistic, prim, sanctimonious, smug, strait-laced, stuffy inf

prim adj demure, fastidious, formal, prissy, proper, starchy, strait-laced

primarily adv basically, chiefly, essentially, first and foremost, in the main, largely, mainly, mostly, particularly, predominantly, principally

primary adj 1 earliest, elementary, first, initial, primitive. 2 chief, essential, foremost, main, most important, paramount, prime, principal

prime adj 1 best, choice, class-one, first-class, grade A, leading, superior, top-quality, top. 2 chief, essential, main, most important, paramount, primary, principal

prime n best part, height, heyday, peak, zenith

prime v brief, coach, get ready, groom, inform, prepare, train

primitive adj basic, crude, early, elementary, naive, rough, rudimentary, simple, uncivilized, unsophisticated

prince n monarch, ruler, sovereign

principal adj chief, first, foremost, fundamental, key, leading, main, major, most important, paramount, prime, top; *opp* minor

principal n boss inf, dean, director, head teacher, head, lead, leader, manager, star, top dog inf

principle n 1 axiom, canon, creed, doctrine, law, maxim, rule, theory. 2 decency, honor, integrity, morality, morals, probity, scruples, standards

print *n* 1 copy, engraving, etching, painting, photo, photograph, picture, reproduction, woodcut. 2 fingerprint, footprint, impression, indentation, mark. 3 characters, font, lettering, letters, text, type, typeface

print *v* 1 issue, publish, reproduce, run off, send to press, write. 2 engrave, etch, imprint, mark, stamp

priority *n* first place, first thing, main concern, main thing, most important thing, precedence, preference, prerogative

prison *n* 1 cell, cooler *inf*, detention center, dungeon, goal, jail, lock-up, penitentiary, place of detention. 2 confinement, custodial sentence, custody, detention, incarceration

prisoner *n* captive, convict, detainee, hostage, inmate, jailbird *inf*, POW

privacy *n* confidentiality, freedom from interference, isolation, peace and quiet, right to be left alone, seclusion, secrecy, solitude

private *adj* 1 (confidential) closed, confidential, off the record, restricted, secret, top secret, unofficial. 2 (secluded) concealed, hidden, isolated, secluded, solitary, withdrawn. 3 (personal) exclusive, intimate, own, personal, privately owned, secret

privilege *n* advantage, benefit, concession, entitlement, exemption, honor, license, perk *inf*, prerogative, right

privileged *adj* advantaged, elite, exempt, fortunate, immune, lucky, special

prize *adj* best, champion, prize-winning, special, top, winning

prize *n* accolade, award, cup, jackpot, medal, purse, reward, trophy, winnings

prize *v* cherish, idolize, revere, set great store by, treasure, value, worship

probability *n* chance, expectation, likelihood, odds, prospect

probable *adj* anticipated, apparent, expected, in the cards *inf*, likely, odds-on *inf*, plausible, very possible

probably *adv* doubtless, in all likelihood, in all probability, it is likely that, it is to be expected that, presumably

probe *n* examination, exploration, inquiry, investigation, study

probe *v* 1 examine, explore, feel, investigate, poke, prod. 2 check out, examine, investigate, look into, research, search

problem *adj* difficult, intractable, problematic, troublesome, unruly; *opp* easy

problem *n* brainteaser, can of worms *inf*, conundrum, difficulty, dilemma, headache *inf*, predicament, puzzle, quandary, snag, trouble

problematic *adj* awkward, complicated, delicate, thorny, tricky; *opp* simple

procedure *n* approach, drill, formula, means, method, operation, plan of action, policy, process, routine, step, system, technique, way

proceed *v* begin, carry on, continue, get going *inf*, go ahead, make progress, move on, press on, start; *opp* stop

proceedings *n* 1 affairs, business, events, goings-on *inf*, legal action, matters, measures, moves, steps. 2 account, annals, archives, minutes, report, transactions

proceeds n earnings, income, profit, receipts, revenue, takings

process n action, activity, method, operation, procedure, stages, steps, system, technique, way

process v administer, convert, deal with, handle, manufacture, prepare, produce, refine

procession n column, convoy, cortège, file, line, march, parade, string, succession

proclaim v 1 announce, declare, decree, make known, pronounce, publish. 2 be a sign of, herald, indicate, prove, reveal, show

proclamation n announcement, declaration, decree, edict, notice, publication

procrastinate v defer, dither, drag your feet, hesitate, play for time, prevaricate, put sth off, stall, vacillate

procure v acquire, buy, come by, get hold of, lay your hands on, obtain, pick up, secure, wangle inf

prod v 1 dig, jab, poke. 2 egg on inf, encourage, goad, motivate, rouse, spur, stimulate, urge

prodigal adj excessive, extravagant, imprudent, irresponsible, profligate, reckless, wanton, wasteful; opp careful, thrifty

prodigious adj enormous, gigantic, huge, immense, impressive, magnificent, massive, phenomenal, staggering, tremendous, vast

prodigy n genius, marvel, phenomenon, sensation, talent, wonder

produce n crops, fruit and vegetables, goods, groceries, merchandise, products, stock, stuff

produce v 1 (make) compose, construct, create, develop, form, generate, make, manufacture, put together, turn out. 2 (cause) bring about, cause, create, deliver, evoke, generate, give birth to, give rise to, give, initiate, result in, spark off, trigger, yield. 3 (produce information or evidence) disclose, present, provide, put forward, reveal, supply. 4 (produce a play) direct, do, mount, present, put on, stage

producer n 1 creator, grower, maker, manufacturer. 2 administrator, backer, director, impresario

product n 1 commodity, goods, item, merchandise, produce, wares. 2 by-product, consequence, effect, legacy, outcome, result, upshot

productive adj beneficial, effective, efficient, fertile, fruitful, profitable, prolific, rich, useful, worthwhile; opp fruitless, unproductive

productivity n capacity, efficiency, output, production rate, rate of work

profess v announce, assert, claim, declare, express, maintain, own, proclaim, state

profession n business, career, job, line of work, occupation, trade, vocation, work

professional adj 1 businesslike, competent, efficient, excellent, experienced, fine, polished, skillful; opp incompetent, unprofessional. 2 qualified, white-collar; opp unskilled. 3 doing sth for a living, paid; opp amateur

proficient adj accomplished, capable, competent, effective, efficient, experienced, expert, good, skillful, skilled, talented

profile n 1 outline, shape, side view, silhouette. 2 account, biography, CV, description, outline, portrait, review, sketch, study, summary, vignette

profit n 1 bottom line, dividend, earnings, gain, proceeds, receipts, return, revenue, takings, yield. 2 advantage, benefit, gain, good, return, value

profit v 1 (sth profits you) be an advantage to, be of use to, benefit, do sb good, help. 2 **profit from** benefit from, cash in on, exploit, use

profitable adj 1 cost-effective, lucrative, money-making, money-spinning, rewarding, successful; *opp* unprofitable. 2 advantageous, beneficial, constructive, useful, worthwhile; *opp* useless, worthless

profiteer n extortionist, racketeer, speculator, wheeler-dealer

profligate adj 1 excessive, extravagant, wasteful; *opp* careful. 2 degenerate, dissolute, immoral, shameless, unprincipled, wild

profound adj 1 (intense) deep, great, intense, keen, marked, passionate, sincere, strong. 2 (learned) difficult, erudite, impenetrable, intellectual, learned, scholarly, weighty

profuse adj abundant, copious, lavish, luxuriant, plentiful, prolific, unstinting

profusion n abundance, glut, loads inf, masses, mountain inf, plenty, superfluity, surplus, vast quantities, wealth; *opp* scarcity

program n 1 broadcast, edition, production, series, show, transmission.

2 agenda, bill, curriculum, listing, menu, order of events, order of the day, plan, schedule, scheme, syllabus

program v 1 arrange, line up, organize, plan, put together, schedule. 2 (program a video) adjust, set

progress n advance, advancement, development, evolution, growth, headway, improvement, movement, progression, step forward

progress v advance, come on, develop, get better, get on, forge ahead, improve, make headway, make progress, make strides, move, move forward, proceed

progression n 1 (headway) advancement, course, development, headway, progress. 2 (succession) chain, series, stream, string, succession

progressive adj advanced, avant-garde, contemporary, enlightened, go-ahead, innovative, liberal, modern, radical, trendy inf, up-to-date; *opp* old-fashioned

prohibit v ban, forbid, make illegal, make impossible, outlaw, preclude, prevent, proscribe, rule out, stop, veto; *opp* allow, permit

prohibition n ban, banning, embargo, injunction, outlawing, prevention, proscription, restriction

prohibitive adj 1 discouraging, preventive, restrictive. 2 (a prohibitive price) excessive, exorbitant, impossible, unreasonable; *opp* reasonable

project n enterprise, idea, job, operation, plan, program, proposal, scheme, task, undertaking, venture

project v 1 (stick out) bulge, extend, jut out, overhang, protrude, stick out. 2 (propel) cast, direct, fire, hurl, launch,

propel, shoot, throw out, throw.
3 (forecast) calculate, compute,
estimate, extrapolate, forecast, plan,
predict

projectile *n* bullet, missile, rocket, shell,
shot

projection *n* **1** bulge, ledge, overhang,
protrusion, protuberance, shelf.
2 calculation, computation, estimate,
extrapolation, forecast, prediction

proliferate *v* escalate, expand, flourish,
grow, increase, multiply, mushroom,
reproduce, rocket, snowball

prolific *adj* abundant, lush, luxuriant,
plentiful, productive, profuse, riotous,
vigorous

prolong *v* drag out, extend, lengthen,
make longer, spin out, stretch, string
out; *opp* shorten

prominent *adj* **1** bulging, conspicuous,
jutting out, noticeable, obtrusive,
protruding, sticking out. **2** distinguished,
eminent, foremost, important, leading,
main, major, top, well-known

promiscuous *adj* dissolute, fast, free,
immoral, loose, sleeping around *inf*,
wanton, wild

promise *n* **1** assurance, commitment,
guarantee, oath, pledge, undertaking,
vow. **2** hint, sign, suggestion.
3 (sb shows promise) ability, flair,
potential, talent

promise *v* **1** give your word, guarantee,
pledge, swear, undertake, vouch, vow.
2 (show signs of) augur, hint at,
indicate, show signs of, suggest

promising *adj* **1** bright, encouraging,
favorable, good, hopeful, optimistic,
rosy; *opp* discouraging. **2** budding,

gifted, rising, talented, up-and-coming

promote *v* **1** (encourage) back, boost,
encourage, foster, further, nurture, push
inf, stimulate, support; *opp* discourage.
2 (advertise) advertise, champion,
endorse, market, plug *inf*, publicize,
recommend, sell. **3** (give sb promotion)
advance, give sb promotion, upgrade;
opp demote

promotion *n* **1** backing, boost,
encouragement, furtherance, nurturing,
support. **2** advertising, advertising
campaign, hype *inf*, marketing, publicity.
3 advancement, elevation, preferment,
upgrading; *opp* demotion

prompt *adj* direct, early, immediate,
instant, on time, punctual, quick, rapid,
speedy, swift, timely; *opp* late, slow,
sluggish

prompt *n* cue, hint, nudge, prod,
reminder

prompt *v* **1** cause, encourage, induce,
inspire, make, motivate, move, urge.
2 give sb a cue, help out, jog sb's
memory, prod, remind

promulgate *v* advertise, announce,
circulate, issue, make known, publicize,
put about, spread

prone *adj* **1** (prone to sth) apt, disposed,
given, inclined, liable, likely, subject,
susceptible, tending, vulnerable.
2 (lying prone) face down, full-length,
horizontal, prostrate, recumbent,
stretched out

prong *n* branch, pin, point, spike, tine

pronounce *v* **1** articulate, enunciate,
express, say, vocalize, voice.
2 announce, assert, declare, decree,
proclaim, state

pronounced adj clear, definite, distinct, distinctive, evident, marked, noticeable, obvious, strong

pronouncement n announcement, declaration, decree, edict, judgment, proclamation, statement, verdict

pronunciation n accent, articulation, delivery, diction, enunciation, inflection, intonation, speech, stress, way of saying sth

proof n authentication, confirmation, corroboration, demonstration, evidence, facts, substantiation, verification

prop n brace, buttress, post, shaft, stanchion, stay, strut, support, truss

prop v 1 brace, buttress, hold up, shore up, support, underpin. 2 lean, rest, stand

propaganda n brainwashing, disinformation, hype inf, indoctrination, misinformation, promotion campaign, public relations exercise, publicity

propagate v 1 breed, generate, grow, increase, produce, reproduce, take cuttings. 2 (information) circulate, disseminate, promote, spread, transmit

propel v fling, hurl, launch, move, project, push, send, shoot, thrust

propensity n disposition, leaning, liability, proclivity, susceptibility, tendency

proper adj 1 acceptable, accepted, appropriate, conventional, correct, decent, decorous, fitting, respectable, right, seemly, suitable. 2 genuine, real, right, true; opp false

property n 1 (possessions) belongings, effects, gear inf, possessions, things. 2 building, land, real estate. 3 attribute, characteristic, feature, power, quality

prophecy n forecast, fortune-telling, prediction, prognosis, second sight

prophesy v forecast, foresee, foretell, predict

prophet n clairvoyant, oracle, seer, sibyl, soothsayer

prophetic adj far-seeing, inspired, prescient

propitious adj advantageous, auspicious, favorable, fortunate, lucky, opportune, promising, timely; opp inauspicious, unfavorable

proportion n 1 amount, distribution, fraction, part, percentage, portion, ratio, share. 2 balance, harmony, symmetry

proportional adj commensurate, comparable, corresponding, in proportion to, proportionate, relative

proposal n bid, offer, plan, project, proposition, recommendation, suggestion, tender

propose v 1 (suggest) offer, put forward, recommend, suggest, table. 2 (propose to do sth) aim, have in mind, intend, mean, plan. 3 (propose a motion or candidate) nominate, put forward, put up, sponsor

proposition n 1 (suggestion) offer, plan, proposal, recommendation, suggestion. 2 (undertaking) job, prospect, task, undertaking, venture

proprietor n landlady, landlord, landowner, owner

propriety n correctness, courtesy, decency, decorum, delicacy, etiquette, good form, good manners, politeness, protocol, rectitude, respectability, seemliness

prosaic adj dull, flat, lifeless, mundane,

pedestrian, stale, trite, unimaginative, uninteresting; *opp* interesting, novel

proscribe v ban, bar, forbid, make illegal, outlaw, prevent, prohibit; *opp* allow, permit

prosecute v accuse, bring an action against, bring before the courts, charge, haul up before the bench *inf*, indict, prefer charges against, put on trial, take to court, try

prospect n chance, expectation, future, hope, idea, likelihood, odds, outlook, possibility, probability, promise, thought

prospect v examine, explore, search, survey

prospective adj aspiring, expected, future, likely, possible, potential, probable, would-be

prospectus n advertising material, booklet, brochure, catalog, particulars, promotional material

prosper v blossom, boom, do well, flourish, get on, go from strength to strength, grow, succeed, thrive

prosperity n affluence, boom, plenty, prosperousness, success, wealth, well-being; *opp* adversity, bust *inf*, failure, poverty, recession

prosperous adj affluent, booming, comfortable, doing well, rich, thriving, wealthy, well-heeled, well-off, well-to-do; *opp* deprived, poor, struggling

prostitute n callgirl, courtesan, hooker *inf*, whore, woman of ill repute

prostitute v cheapen, debase, demean, lower, sell

protagonist n 1 advocate, champion, chief player, exponent, leader, leading light, prime mover, principal, proponent, standard-bearer.
2 competitor, contender, contestant, player

protect v conserve, cover, defend, guard, keep safe, look after, preserve, shelter, shield, take care of, watch over

protection n care, conservation, custody, defense, guard, guardianship, preservation, safe-keeping, security, shelter, shield

protective adj 1 fireproof, safety, waterproof. 2 overprotective, possessive, solicitous, vigilant, watchful

protector n bodyguard, champion, defender, guard, guardian, shield

protest n 1 complaint, dissent, objection, opposition, outcry. 2 demonstration, protest march, rally. 3 avowal, claim, declaration, protestation

protest v 1 appeal, argue, complain, kick up a fuss *inf*, make a stand against, object, take exception to. 2 campaign, demonstrate, lobby, march. 3 (protest your innocence) assert, declare, maintain, profess, state

protester n activist, campaigner, demonstrator, dissident, objector

protocol n 1 code of behavior, courtesies, custom, etiquette, formalities, good form, procedure, propriety. 2 agreement, concordat, convention, pact, treaty

prototype n model, original, precursor

protracted adj endless, extended, interminable, lengthy, long-winded, long, never-ending, prolonged; *opp* brief, short

protrude v bulge out, come through, extend, jut, jut out, poke out, project, stick out

protruding adj bulbous, bulging out, distended, jutting out, projecting, prominent, protuberant

proud adj 1 delighted, glad, gratified, happy, honored, pleased, satisfied, well pleased; *opp* ashamed. 2 arrogant, big-headed *inf*, boastful, cocky *inf*, conceited, disdainful, haughty, high-and-mighty *inf*, imperious, overbearing, self-important, snobbish, snooty *inf*, stuck up *inf*, supercilious, vain; *opp* modest. 3 distinguished, glorious, grand, honorable, illustrious, magnificent, noble, splendid, worthy. 4 dignified, independent, self-respecting. 5 (proud day) glorious, gratifying, happy, marvelous, satisfying

prove v 1 authenticate, bear out *inf*, confirm, corroborate, demonstrate, determine, establish, find proof, produce proof, show, substantiate, verify; *opp* disprove. 2 check, put to the test, test, try out. 3 (prove to be) emerge, end up, be found, turn out

proverb n adage, axiom, maxim, old saw, saying

proverbial adj 1 famous, infamous, legendary, notorious, renowned, well-known. 2 axiomatic, traditional, typical

provide v 1 endow, equip, fix up with *inf*, provision, stock up, supply. 2 contribute, donate, give, grant, lay on, present. 3 give, offer, produce, yield. 4 provide for care for, keep, maintain, make provision for, support. 5 provide for/against anticipate, be prepared for, guard against, get ready for, make arrangements, make plans, make

preparations, make provisions, plan ahead, plan for, prepare for, take precautions

providence n 1 destiny, divine intervention, fate, fortune, God's will. 2 care, discretion, economy, foresight, good management, prudence, thrift; *opp* improvidence

provident adj careful, economical, farsighted, prudent, shrewd, thrifty; *opp* improvident

providential adj chance, fortuitous, happy, fortunate, lucky, opportune; *opp* unfortunate

province n 1 district, region, section, state, territory. 2 area of activity, area of responsibility, business, concern, field, part, responsibility, role, sphere

provincial adj 1 local, regional, state; *opp* national. 2 country, outlying, rural, rustic, small-town. 3 backward, insular, inward-looking, limited, narrow, narrow-minded, parochial, small-minded, unsophisticated; *opp* cosmopolitan

provision n 1 (the provision of sth) equipping, providing, supply, supplying. 2 (make provision for sth) arrangement, plan, precaution, precautionary measure, preparation. 3 (the provisions of a contract) condition, limitation, proviso, qualification, requirement, restriction, stipulation, term

provisional adj conditional, contingent, interim, limited, qualified, stopgap, temporary, tentative, transitional

provisions n food, food and drink, foodstuffs, food supplies, groceries, ration, stores, supplies

proviso n condition, exception, limitation, provision, qualification, requirement, restriction, stipulation

provocation n 1 affront, aggravation, annoyance, harassment, insult, irritation, offense, taunt, taunting, teasing. 2 goading, incitement, justification, motive, prompting, rousing, stimulus, stirring

provocative adj 1 aggravating, annoying, exasperating, goading, infuriating, insulting, offensive, provoking, stimulating. 2 alluring, erotic, raunchy inf, seductive, sexy, suggestive, titillating

provoke v 1 arouse, awaken, bring about, cause, elicit, evoke, excite, give rise to, incite, induce, inspire, kindle, occasion, produce, prompt, rouse, stimulate, stir up, work up. 2 (provoke sb) aggravate, anger, annoy, exasperate, gall, get on your nerves inf, harass, infuriate, insult, irritate, madden, make your blood boil inf, offend, outrage, pique, rile, rouse, tease, torment, upset, wind up inf

prowess n 1 ability, aptitude, competence, expertise, mastery, proficiency, skill, talent. 2 boldness, bravery, courage, gallantry, grit inf, guts inf, mettle, nerve, pluck, spirit, steadfastness, valor

prowl v creep, move stealthily, slink, sneak, stalk, steal

proximity n 1 closeness, nearness. 2 locality, neighborhood, vicinity

prudent adj 1 careful, cautious, circumspect, judicious, sagacious, sensible, shrewd, wary, wise; **opp** imprudent, unwise. 2 (prudent use of sth) canny, careful, economical, farsighted, provident, thrifty; **opp** wasteful

prudish adj easily shocked, goody-goody inf, old-fashioned, puritanical, priggish, prim, straitlaced, Victorian

prune v 1 clip, cut back, lop, shape, thin, thin out, trim. 2 curtail, cut, cut back, make cutbacks, make cuts, make reductions, pare down, reduce, retrench, shorten, trim

pry v be a busybody, be inquisitive, be nosy, interfere, intrude, meddle, nose about inf, poke your nose in inf, search, snoop, stick your nose in inf

prying adj curious, inquisitive, interfering, intrusive, meddlesome, meddling, nosy inf, snooping, spying

pseudonym n alias, assumed name, pen name, professional name, stage name

psyche n anima, individuality, inner being, personality, self, soul, spirit

psychiatrist n analyst, psychoanalyst, psychotherapist, shrink inf

psychic adj clairvoyant, extrasensory, mystic, occult, paranormal, preternatural, supernatural, supernormal, telepathic

psychological adj 1 cerebral, mental; **opp** physical. 2 emotional, in the mind, mental, irrational, subconscious, unconscious; **opp** physical

psychology n 1 science of the mind, study of the mental processes, study of personality. 2 (sb's psychology) attitude, mental processes, mind, mind-set inf, thought processes, way of thinking

psychopath n lunatic, madman, maniac, psycho inf

pub n bar, inn, saloon, tavern, wine bar

puberty n adolescence, pubescence, sexual maturity, teenage years, teens

public adj 1 (a public place) accessible, communal, open to all, open to the public, unrestricted. 2 (a public institution) civic, communal, community, national, nationalized, social, state. 3 (public awareness) collective, common, democratic, general, majority, popular, universal, widespread. 4 (make sth public) acknowledged, known, notorious, obvious, open, overt, plain, published, well-known, widely known.
5 (public figure) eminent, important, in the public eye, prominent, well-known

public n 1 citizens, community, electorate, everyone, ordinary people, people, people in general, populace, society, the country, the hoi polloi, the masses, the nation, the people.
2 (do sth to please your public) admirers, audience, clientele, fans, followers, patrons, supporters.
3 in public for all to see, in full view, openly, publicly

publication n 1 book, booklet, brochure, leaflet, magazine, newspaper, pamphlet, periodical, title. 2 (the publication of information) announcement, broadcasting, declaration, disclosure, dissemination, notification, publicizing, reporting. 3 (the publication of a book) issuing, printing, production, publishing

publicity n 1 advertising, ballyhoo inf, hype inf, marketing, plug inf, promotion. 2 attention, limelight, public interest

publicize v 1 advertise, give publicity to, hype inf, market, plug inf, promote, push. 2 announce, broadcast, make known, make public, publish, spotlight

publish v 1 bring out, issue, print, produce, put out, release. 2 advertise, announce, break the news about, broadcast, circulate, declare, disclose, divulge, leak inf, make known, make public, publicize, report, reveal

puerile adj adolescent, childish, immature, infantile, juvenile

puff n blast, breath, draft, flurry, gust, whiff

puff v 1 blow, breathe heavily, exhale, gasp, pant, wheeze. 2 (a cigarette) drag inf, draw, inhale, inhale, pull on, smoke. 3 puff up bloat, blow out, blow up, distend, inflate, swell

puffy adj bloated, distended, enlarged, puffed up, swollen

pugnacious adj aggressive, bellicose, belligerent, combative, irascible, quarrelsome; opp gentle, passive

pull n 1 jerk, tug, twitch, yank.
2 attraction, draw, force, lure, magnetism, power. 3 clout inf, influence, power

pull v 1 drag, draw, haul, tow, trail, tug, yank; opp push. 2 (pull flowers, vegetables) collect, cull, extract, pick, pluck, pull out, pull up, uproot. 3 (pull a muscle) sprain, strain, tear, wrench.
4 (pull the crowds) attract, bring in, draw, entice, lure. 5 pull down demolish, destroy, knock down, level, raze. 6 pull through come through, pull round, rally, recover, survive

pulp n 1 flesh, soft part. 2 mash, mush,

paste, puree

pulse n beat, beating, drumming, heartbeat, pounding, pulsation, rhythm, throb, throbbing, vibration

pump v 1 drive, force, inject, push, send. 2 (pump sb for information) cross-examine, give sb the third degree inf, grill inf, interrogate, question. 3 pump up blow up, inflate

pun n double entendre, play on words

punch n bash, blow, bop inf, clout, hit, hook, jab, smack, thump, wallop, whack

punch v 1 bash, belt inf, box, clout, hit, pound, pummel, slug, sock inf, strike, thump, wallop. 2 (punch a hole) bore, drill, hole, make a hole in, perforate, pierce, prick, puncture

punctual adj early, in good time, on the dot, on time, prompt, when expected; opp late

punctuate v 1 break, interrupt, intersperse, pepper, sprinkle. 2 insert punctuation, put in punctuation marks

puncture n 1 hole, leak, nick, opening, perforation, pin-prick, rupture. 2 blow out, burst tire, flat inf, flat tire

puncture v bore, deflate, hole, let down, make a hole in, penetrate, perforate, pierce, punch, rupture

pungent adj 1 (of a smell) acid, acrid, bitter, caustic, rank, sharp; opp gentle. 2 (of a taste) aromatic, hot, peppery, piquant, spicy, tangy; opp mild

punish v 1 castigate, chasten, chastise, correct, discipline, exact retribution from, inflict punishment on, make sb pay for sth, penalize, rap sb over the knuckles inf, take disciplinary action

against, teach sb a lesson inf. 2 beat, cane, flog, scourge, spank, thrash, whip

punishable adj criminal, culpable, indictable

punishing adj arduous, backbreaking, exhausting, grueling, hard, strenuous, taxing, tiring, tough, wearing; opp easy, light

punishment n 1 chastening, chastisement, correction, disciplinary action, discipline, penalty, punitive measure, retribution, sanction. 2 beating, caning, flogging, hiding, pain, scourging, spank, spanking, thrashing, whipping

punitive adj 1 castigating, disciplinary, penal, penalizing, punishing. 2 cruel, harsh, savage, severe, stiff

puny adj feeble, frail, sickly, small, stunted, underdeveloped, undersized, weak, weakly; opp strong

pupil n 1 schoolboy, schoolgirl, scholar, student. 2 beginner, learner, novice, trainee. 3 apprentice, disciple, follower, protégé, protégée, student

puppet n 1 doll, dummy, marionette. 2 dupe, mouthpiece, pawn, stooge, tool

purchase n 1 acquisition, buy, investment. 2 foothold, grasp, grip, leverage, toehold

purchase v acquire, buy, get, invest in, obtain, pay for, pick up, procure, secure

pure adj 1 (pure gold) flawless, genuine, perfect, real, unadulterated, unalloyed, undiluted, true. 2 (pure air, water) clean, clear, germ-free, immaculate, spotless, sterile, uncontaminated, unpolluted, untainted, wholesome;

opp polluted. **3** (of a person) blameless, chaste, decent, good, immaculate, impeccable, innocent, irreproachable, uncorrupted, unsullied, virginal, virtuous. **4** (pure malice) absolute, downright, complete, out-and-out, perfect, sheer, total, utter. **5** (pure science) abstract, theoretical

purge *n* **1** cleansing, purging, purification. **2** clear out, dismissal, expulsion, ousting, rooting out, weeding out. **3** dose of salts, laxative, purgative

purge *v* **1** clean out, cleanse, purify, wash out. **2** clear out, depose, dismiss, eliminate, liquidate, expel, get rid of, oust, root out, weed out

purify *v* clean, cleanse, decontaminate, disinfect, fumigate, make pure, refine, sanitize, sterilize, wash

purist *n* dogmatist, pedant, stickler

puritanical *adj* ascetic, austere, goody-goody *inf*, narrow-minded, prim, prudish, self-denying, straitlaced, strict

purpose *n* **1** (have a purpose) aim, ambition, design, end, goal, intention, motivation, motive, object, objective, plan, target. **2** (sth lacks purpose) determination, direction, firmness, persistence, resoluteness, resolution, steadfastness, tenacity. **3** (the purpose of sth) point, reason, use, usefulness, value. **4 on purpose** by design, consciously, deliberately, intentionally, knowingly, willfully, with intent; *opp* accidentally

purposeful *adj* determined, dogged, firm, resolute, persistent, single-minded, steadfast, tenacious

purposeless *adj* aimless, meaningless, motiveless, pointless, senseless, useless

purse *n* **1** pocketbook, pouch, wallet. **2** coffers, exchequer, funds, means, money, resources, treasury, wealth. **3** award, prize, reward

pursue *v* **1** chase, dog, follow, give chase, go after, harry, hound, hunt, hunt down, run after, shadow, stalk, tail, track. **2** (pursue a goal) aim for, aspire to, been intent on, have as a goal, seek, strive for, work for, work towards. **3** (pursue a career, way of life) apply yourself to, carry on, conduct, continue, continue with, engage in, go for *inf*, go on with, persist in, proceed with, stick with

pursuit *n* **1** (the pursuit of a person, animal) chase, hue and cry, hunt, inquiry, pursuing, trail. **2** (leisure pursuits) activity, enthusiasm, hobby, interest, line, occupation, pastime, pleasure. **3** (the pursuit of knowledge) hunt, inquiry, quest, search, seeking after, striving for

push *n* **1** (give sb a push) butt, jolt, jostle, nudge, poke, prod, shove, thrust. **2** (military) advance, assault, attack, charge, offensive, sortie, thrust. **3** (have a lot of push) ambition, drive, energy, enterprise, enthusiasm, get-up-and-go, gumption *inf*, initiative

push *v* **1** (push sth) drive, press, propel, ram, shove, thrust. **2** (push past people) barge, bustle, elbow, hustle, jostle, manhandle, nudge, shoulder, shove, squeeze. **3** (push sth into a place) cram, force, jam, press in, ram, squash, squeeze, stuff. **4** (push sb into doing sth) browbeat, coerce, encourage, force, impel, incite, lean on *inf*, motivate, persuade, press, prompt, put pressure on, urge. **5** (push a product) advertise, hype *inf*, plug *inf*, promote, publicize, recommend. **6 push around** boss around, browbeat, bully, intimidate, lean on *inf*, tyrranize

pushed *adj* **1** busy, hurried, in a hurry, pressed, rushed, under pressure, up against it. **2 pushed for** feeling the need of, lacking, not having enough of, running short of, short of, without

pushover *n* **1** (a person) easy mark, easy prey, mug *inf*, soft touch, sucker *inf*, weakling, wimp. **2** (a task) breeze *inf*, child's play, cinch, doddle *inf*, easy task, piece of cake *inf*, walkover

pushy *adj* ambitious, assertive, brash, forceful, overbearing, presumptuous

put *v* **1** fix, install, locate, park, place, position, set, settle, situate, stand. **2** allocate to, assign to, consign, deploy, dispose, impose, station. **3 put down** (put sth down somewhere) deposit, lay, lay down, set down, settle. **4 put down** (put sb down) belittle, criticize, denigrate, deprecate, disparage, find fault with, knock, pick holes in, run down. **5 put down** (put down a rebellion) crush, defeat, put a stop to, quash, quell, repress stamp out, stop, suppress. **6 put down** (write down) enter, inscribe, jot down, log, make a note of, note, record, set down, take down, write down. **7 put down** (put an animal down) destroy, put out of its misery, put to sleep, kill. **8 put down to** ascribe, attribute, blame, chalk up to, impute, put the blame on. **9 put forward** advance, introduce, move, nominate, present, propose, recommend,

submit, suggest. **10 put off** (put sth off) defer, delay, postpone, put back, put on ice, put on the back burner, reschedule, shelve. **11 put off** (put sb off an idea) discourage, dissuade, dishearten, offend, repel. **12 put off** (put sb off when they are working) distract, divert, divert the attention of, sidetrack. **13 put off** (put off the light) switch off, turn off. **14 put on** (put on clothes) change into, dress in, don, slip into. **15 put on** lay on, make available, provide, supply. **16 put on** (put on a play, an exhibition) do, mount, present, produce, stage. **17 put on** (pretend) affect, fake, feign, pretend, sham, simulate. **18 put on** (put on the light) switch on, turn on. **19 put on** (**put on weight**) gain, increase. **20 put up** (put up a building) build, construct, erect. **21 put up** (put sb up) accommodate, allow sb to stay, give sb a bed, give sb a place to stay, provide sb with accommodations, take sb in. **22 put up** (put up money) advance, donate, give, pledge, provide, supply. **23 put up to** (put sb up to sth) egg on, encourage, incite, persuade, talk sb into sthg, urge on. **24 put up with** accept, bear, endure, stand, swallow, take, tolerate

putrid *adj* bad, decayed, decomposed, fetid, foul, off, putrefied, rancid, rotten, rotting, spoiled, stale, stinking; *opp* fresh

puzzle *n* brainteaser, conundrum, dilemma, enigma, mystery, poser *inf*, quandary, question, riddle

puzzle *v* **1** baffle, bewilder, confuse, flummox *inf*, mystify, perplex, stump *inf*. **2** (puzzle over sth) brood, consider,

muse, ponder, study, think about, think
over, wonder about. **3 puzzle out** crack
inf, decipher, figure out, find the answer
to, solve, think out, unravel, work out
puzzled *adj* at a loss, at sea, baffled,
bewildered, confused, flummoxed *inf*,
mystified, perplexed, stumped
puzzling *adj* abstruse, baffling,
bewildering, confusing, cryptic,
enigmatic, incomprehensible, involved,
mind-boggling *inf*, mysterious,
mystifying, perplexing, unclear;
opp clear

quail v back away, cower, cringe, falter, flinch, quake, recoil, shake, shrink, shy away, tremble, waver

quaint adj charming, curious, droll, eccentric, fanciful, odd, offbeat, olde worlde inf, old-fashioned, peculiar, queer, strange, sweet, unusual, whimsical

quake v quiver, rock, shake, shiver, shudder, tremble, vibrate

qualification n 1 ability, aptitude, capability, competence, eligibility, fitness, proficiency, skill, suitability, training. 2 condition, exception, limitation, modification, provision, proviso, restriction, stipulation

qualified adj 1 able, capable, certificated, competent, experienced, fit, proficient, skilled, trained. 2 (qualified acceptance) cautious, conditional, guarded, half-hearted, limited, modified, provisional, reserved, restricted; **opp** wholehearted

qualify v 1 be eligible, be entitled, have/gain the right, get through, go through, make the grade inf, meet the requirements, pass, reach the required standard, succeed. 2 (sth qualifies sb for a particular responsibility) authorize, empower, entitle, equip, fit, make eligible, make suitable, prepare, suit. 3 (qualify a statement) add a rider to, limit, mitigate, moderate, modify, modulate, nuance, restrict, soften, temper, tone down, weaken

quality n 1 (extent to which sth is good) caliber, excellence, merit, rating, standard, standing, status, value, worth. 2 (what sth is like) character, description, essence, kind, nature. 3 (the qualities of sth or sb) advantage, aspect, attribute, characteristic, feature, good point, hallmark, mark, property, trait

qualms n anxiety, apprehension, conscience, disinclination, disquiet, doubt, guilt, hesitancy, hesitation, misgivings, pangs, reluctance, remorse, reservations, reticence, scruples, second thoughts, uncertainty, uneasiness

quandary n difficulty, dilemma, fix inf, impasse, plight, predicament, problem, puzzle, uncertainty

quantity n aggregate, amount, lot, number, sum, total

quarrel n altercation, argument, battle, break, conflict, confrontation, difference of opinion, disagreement, dispute, falling-out, feud, fight, rivalry, row *inf*, squabble, tiff *inf*, vendetta, war, wrangle *inf*

quarrel *v* argue, battle, be estranged, be in conflict, bicker, cross, cross swords, dispute, fall out, feud, fight, row *inf*, spar, squabble, tangle, wrangle *inf*

quarrelsome *adj* aggressive, angry, argumentative, bad-tempered, bloody-minded, cantankerous, choleric, confrontational, contrary, disagreeable, disputatious, explosive, fractious, impatient, irascible, irritable, obstructive, pugnacious, querulous, quick-tempered, testy, truculent, unfriendly, vengeful, volatile

quarry *n* 1 excavation, hole in the ground, mine, open-cast mine, pit. 2 goal, objective, prey, prize, target, victim

quarter *n* 1 area, district, locality, neighborhood, part of town. 2 (advice from a particular quarter) direction, person, source

quarters *n* abode, accommodation, apartments, barracks, billet, digs *inf*, dwelling, home, house, lodgings, residence, rooms

quash *v* annul, cancel, nullify, invalidate, overrule, overthrow, overturn, rescind, reverse, revoke, suppress; *opp* uphold

quaver *v* falter, fluctuate, quake, shake, tremble, vibrate, waver

queasy *adj* bilious, ill, nauseous, queer *inf*, seasick, sick, unwell, woozy *inf*

queen *n* 1 Crown, head of state, Her Majesty, lady, matriarch, monarch, ruler, sovereign. 2 consort, dowager queen

queer *adj* aberrant, abnormal, bizarre, curious, deviant, eccentric, funny, inexplicable, odd, outlandish, peculiar, singular, strange, suspicious, unusual, weird

quell *v* allay, beat down, conquer, defeat, eliminate, extinguish, overcome, pacify, quash, stifle, subdue, suppress, vanquish

quench *v* end, extinguish, gratify, relieve, sate, satisfy, slake

query *n* 1 inquiry, problem, question. 2 (a query over sb's future) doubt, hesitation, problem, question, question mark, suspicion, uncertainty

query *v* call into question, challenge, contest, dispute, doubt, mistrust, question, suspect

quest *n* crusade, expedition, journey, mission, pursuit, search

question *n* 1 brainteaser *inf*, conundrum, demand, inquiry, query, riddle; *opp* answer. 2 (sth to be considered or decided) affair, controversy, debate, issue, mystery, point, problem, puzzle, situation

question *v* 1 ask, cross-examine, debrief, grill *inf*, inquire, interrogate, interview, poll, probe, pump *inf*, quiz. 2 (question whether sth is true) argue over, call into question, challenge, contest, dispute, doubt, impugn, object to, oppose, quarrel with, query

questionable *adj* arguable, borderline, contestable, controversial, debatable, disputable, doubtful, dubious, open to challenge, problematic, uncertain

queue n file, line, string, waiting line

queue v file, form a line, line up, queue up, stand in line, wait in line

quibble n argument, complaint, criticism, dispute, nit-picking, objection, pettifogging, point of contention, query

quibble v argue, carp, dispute, part company, nit-pick, pettifog, split hairs, take issue

quick adj 1 brisk, fast, fast-moving, fleet of foot, headlong, high-speed, nippy inf, rapid, speedy, swift; **opp** slow. 2 (not lasting long) abrupt, hasty, hurried, lightning, momentary, rapid, swift. 3 (not delayed) immediate, instant, instantaneous, prompt, rapid, spur-of-the-moment, swift. 4 (quick to do sth) hasty, in a hurry, precipitate, prompt. 5 (thinking quickly) alert, astute, bright, clever, intelligent, keen, perceptive, quick-thinking, quick-witted, sharp, shrewd, smart

quicken v 1 (sth quickens) accelerate, gather pace, gather speed, go faster, speed up; **opp** slow down. 2 (quicken sth) accelerate, expedite, hasten, hurry, speed up; **opp** slow down

quiet adj 1 calm, noiseless, peaceful, placid, restful, serene, silent, sleepy, soundless, still, tranquil, unexciting; **opp** noisy. 2 (of sb's voice) breathy, inaudible, hushed, low, muffled, murmuring, muted, small, soft, subdued, tiny, whispering; **opp** loud. 3 (of a person) docile, inactive, introverted, meek, passive, phlegmatic, placid, quiescent, reserved, retiring, silent, taciturn, uncommunicative,

withdrawn; **opp** noisy. 4 (have a quiet word with sb) confidential, discreet, on the quiet inf, private, secret

quiet n calm, calmness, hush, peace, peacefulness, placidity, quietness, repose, rest, silence, stillness, tranquillity; **opp** noise

quip n bon mot, crack inf, epigram, gag inf, jest, joke, one-liner, wisecrack, witticism

quirk n 1 caprice, eccentricity, foible, idiosyncrasy, kink, oddity, peculiarity, whim. 2 (quirk of fate, nature) aberration, anomaly, exception, freak, reversal, turn, twist

quit v 1 depart, give notice, go away, hand in your notice, leave, resign, vacate, withdraw; **opp** stay on. 2 (stop doing sth) abandon, abstain, cease, cut out, desist, discontinue, drop, give up, refrain, renounce, stop; **opp** continue

quite adv 1 fairly, moderately, pretty inf, rather, relatively, somewhat. 2 absolutely, altogether, completely, entirely, fully, totally, wholly

quits adj equal, even, level, on equal terms, square

quiver v oscillate, palpitate, pulsate, shake, shiver, shudder, throb, tremble, vibrate

quiz n competition, contest, game show, questionnaire

quiz v cross-examine, fire questions at, grill inf, interrogate, interview, poll, pump, question

quota n allocation, allowance, amount, assignment, consignment, cut inf, measure, percentage, portion, proportion, quantity, ratio, ration, share, supply

quotation *n* 1 citation, excerpt, extract, line, verse, passage, quote *inf*, reference. 2 (a price) bid, estimate, figure, price, rate, tender

quote *v* 1 cite, instance, mention, recite, refer to, repeat, reproduce. 2 bid, cost, estimate, price, tender

rabble *n* **1** band, crowd, gang, horde, mob, rioters, troublemakers. **2** (lowest ranks of society) common people, commoners, hoi polloi, lower classes, masses, plebs *inf*, riff-raff

race *n* **1** chase, competition, contest, event, heat, match, pursuit, run. **2** (in particular sports) handicap, marathon, rally, sprint, stakes, steeplechase. **3** ethnic group, nation, nationality, people, tribe

race *v* **1** (in sport) be pitted against sb, chase, compete, contest, pursue, sprint. **2** (run, move quickly) bowl, career, dash, gallop, hasten, hurry, run, rush, scamper, speed, sprint, whizz *inf*

racial *adj* anthropological, communal, ethnic, ethnological, folk, national, tribal

rack *n* frame, framework, holder, pallet, stand, structure

rack *v* **1** (racked by pain, uncertainty) afflict, assail, besiege, crucify, harass, harrow, oppress, persecute, plague, torment, torture. **2 rack your brains** search your memory, think hard, turn sth over in your mind, try to remember

racket *n* **1** cacophony, din, disturbance, fracas, noise, sound, tumult, uproar. **2** corruption, extortion, fraud, graft, scam *inf*, scheme

radiant *adj* **1** (giving off light) bright, brilliant, dazzling, glittering, luminous, resplendent, shining, shiny, sparkling. **2** (of a person) beaming, delighted, expansive, happy, serene, smiling, warm

radiate *v* **1** (radiate heat, energy) emanate, emit, exude, generate, give off, produce, send forth, shed, send out, shine, spread. **2** (lines radiating from a central point) branch, diverge, fan out, spread, spread out

radical *adj* **1** campaigning, left-of-center, left-wing, militant, progressive, revolutionary, socialist; **opp** conservative, reactionary. **2** (radical change) complete, extreme, fundamental, great, major, severe, thorough, thoroughgoing; **opp** minor

radio *n* **1** receiver, transistor radio, tuner, wireless. **2** (for sending and receiving messages) CB, transmitter, walkie-talkie

rage *n* anger, bile, frenzy, fulmination, fury, rampage, violence, vituperation

rage *v* **1** be angry, be beside yourself, be enraged, be furious, be hopping mad *inf*, be in a frenzy, be in a fury, be incensed, be infuriated, be mad, blow a fuse *inf*, blow a gasket *inf*, blow your top *inf*, boil over, explode *inf*, flip your lid *inf*, foam at the mouth, fume, go berserk, hit the roof *inf*, lose your temper, rail, rant, rave, roar, seethe, shout, swear, thunder. **2** (of a storm, controversy) be at its height, continue, continue unabated; *opp* abate

ragged *adj* **1** frayed, in ribbons, in shreds, in tatters, old, patched, ripped, shabby, tattered, tatty *inf*, threadbare, torn, worn through. **2** (not straight) irregular, jagged, serrated, uneven, untidy, wavy, zigzag

rags *n* castoffs, old clothes, remnants, shreds, tatters

raid *n* **1** assault, attack, foray, incursion, invasion, sally, sortie. **2** (by police) inspection, search, seizure, spot check

raid *v* **1** assault, attack, foray, invade, storm. **2** (involving robbery) loot, pillage, plunder, rob. **3** (police) descend on, inspect, search, spot-check

raider *n* **1** assailant, attacker, invader. **2** bandit, brigand, looter, marauder, robber, predator, thief

rain *n* cloudburst, deluge, downpour, drizzle, flood, precipitation, raindrops, rainfall, shower, storm, thunderstorm, torrent

rain *v* bucket *inf*, drizzle, pour, pour down, rain cats and dogs *inf*, spit

raise *v* **1** elevate, hoist, hold up, jack up, lift, lift up, pick up, pull up, push up, rear; *opp* lower. **2** augment, boost, increase, inflate, jack up *inf*, mark up, push up, put up, up *inf*; *opp* lower. **3** (raise the quality, status of sth) enhance, exalt, heighten, improve, promote, upgrade. **4** (sth raises fears, doubts, questions) activate, arouse, awaken, breed, cause, create, engender, evoke, excite, foment, foster, generate, incite, instigate, kindle, provoke, rouse, set off, spark, stimulate, trigger. **5** (sb raises a question, problem) ask, bring up, broach, express, introduce, mention, moot, pose, present, propose, put forward, state, suggest. **6** (raise cattle, children) breed, bring up, look after, nurture, rear. **7** (raise funds) amass, collect, generate, make, solicit

rally *n* **1** drive, race. **2** (large meeting) assembly, conference, congress, convention, convocation, gathering, mass meeting, meeting, public meeting, reunion. **3** (of stock prices) improvement, increase, recovery, resurgence, revival

rally *v* **1** be revitalized, be revived, bounce back, improve, make a comeback, recover, regroup, reorganize, resist, revive. **2** (rally the troops) inspire, mobilize, revitalize, revive, revivify, spur on, steel, stir up. **3 rally round** be supportive, come to the rescue, help, support

ram *v* batter, buffet, bump, butt, collide with, cram, crush, hit, impact, pound, strike

ramble *n* hike, stroll, walk

ramble *v* **1** (talk) chatter, digress, drone on, wander. **2** (walk) amble, hike, range, roam, rove, stroll, walk, wander

rampage *n* **on the rampage 1** (in an angry mood) angry, berserk, breathing

fire, furious, on the warpath, raging.
2 looting, marauding, out of control,
pillaging, rampaging, stampeding,
violent

rampage v charge, go berserk, loot,
pillage, run amok, run riot,
stampede, storm

rampant adj out of control, raging,
rampaging, riotous, stampeding,
unbridled, uncontrollable, uncontrolled,
unrestrained, wanton, wild

ramshackle adj decrepit, dilapidated,
flimsy, jerry-built, rickety, shaky,
unstable, unsteady, tumbledown

rancid adj curdled, festering inf, off,
rank, putrid, rotting, sour, spoiled,
stale

random adj accidental, arbitrary, casual,
chance, disorganized, fortuitous,
haphazard, hit-or-miss, indiscriminate,
irregular, sporadic, spot, stray,
unplanned, unsystematic

range n 1 (of sb's interests,
responsibilities) area, breadth,
compass, diversity, extent, gamut,
scale, scope, span, spectrum, sphere,
spread, sweep, variety. 2 (of vision,
weapon) area, distance, extent,
field, limit, reach

range v comprise, consist of, encompass,
extend, include, reach, span, spread,
stretch, vary

rank adj disgusting, fetid, foul, foul-
smelling, putrid, rancid, revolting,
smelly inf, stinking

rank n class, grade, level, place, position,
ranking, rating, seniority, standing,
station, status

rank v categorize, class, classify, grade,

order, place, rate

ransack v plunder, rifle, rummage, scour,
search, trash inf, turn upside-down

ransom n bribe, compensation,
deliverance, liberation, pay-off,
redemption

ransom v buy back, deliver, liberate,
recover, redeem, rescue

rant v bawl, bellow, bluster, go on and
one, harangue, rage, rail, rave, roar,
shout, spout, swear, thunder,
vociferate, yell

rape n abuse, assault, attack, indecent
assault, molestation, sexual abuse,
sexual assault, violation

rape v abuse, assault, attack, defile,
deflower, force yourself on, indecently
assault, molest, ravish, sexually abuse,
sexually assault, violate

rapid adj 1 breakneck, brisk, fast,
fast-moving, headlong, high-speed,
lightning, nippy inf, quick, speedy,
swift. 2 (not lasting long) hasty,
hurried, momentary, quick, swift.
3 (not delayed) immediate, instant,
instantaneous, lightning, prompt,
quick, spur-of-the-moment, swift

rare adj 1 few and far between,
infrequent, occasional, scarce,
scattered, sporadic, **opp** common.
2 (having unusual qualities) atypical,
exceptional, extraordinary, singular,
uncommon, untypical, unique,
unusual; **opp** common

rascal n 1 devil, imp, jackanapes,
mischief-maker, rapscallion inf,
scallywag inf, scamp inf, terror inf.
2 (wicked, criminal) blackguard,
bounder, cad, rat, reprobate, rogue,

scoundrel, villain

rash *adj* devil-may-care, foolhardy, harebrained, hasty, headlong, headstrong, heedless, hot-headed, hurried, ill-advised, ill-considered, impetuous, imprudent, impulsive, incautious, injudicious, madcap, overadventurous, precipitate, premature, reckless, spur-of-the-moment, unguarded, unthinking

rash *n* 1 allergic reaction, dermatitis, eczema, eruption, inflammation, irritation, psoriasis, redness, skin irritation, spots. 2 (a rash of burglaries) flood, outbreak, plague, rush, series, spate, wave

rate *n* 1 (rate of change, increase) degree, intensity, level, pace, ratio, scale, speed, tempo. 2 (money to be paid) amount, band, charge, cost, fare, fee, figure, payment, price, scale, sum, tariff, wage. 3 at any rate anyhow, anyway, in any case, in any event, nevertheless, whatever the case may be

rate *v* 1 adjudge, appraise, assess, class, classify, estimate, evaluate, gauge, grade, judge, measure, put a value on, rank, regard, value. 2 be worth, be worthy of, deserve, merit

ratify *v* accredit, approve, certify, confirm, countersign, endorse, pass, sanction, sign, underwrite, validate

rating *n* category, class, classification, designation, grade, level, placing, rank, ranking, position, standard, standing, status, tariff, type, value

ratio *n* comparison, fraction, frequency, proportion, quotient, rate

ration *n* allocation, allowance, amount, assignment, dose, helping, measure, portion, provision, quantity, quota, share, supply

ration *v* allot, apportion, distribute, eke out, mete out, parcel out, share, share out

rational *adj* enlightened, intelligent, logical, lucid, reasonable, sane, sensible, sound; *opp* irrational

rationale *n* argument, case, grounds, justification, logic, motivation, philosophy, reason, reasoning, theory

rationalize *v* account for, clarify, elucidate, excuse, explain, justify, resolve, think through, vindicate

rattle *v* 1 (rattle sth) bang, clang, clank, clatter, jangle. 2 (rattle sb) alarm, disconcert, disturb, fluster, frighten, perturb, put off, scare, shake, unnerve, upset, worry; *opp* calm

raucous *adj* grating, harsh, hoarse, husky, jarring, loud, noisy, piercing, rasping, rough, shrill, squawking, strident; *opp* quiet

ravage *v* 1 demolish, destroy, devastate, lay waste, level, raze, ruin, spoil, wreak havoc on, wreck. 2 loot, pillage, plunder, raid, ransack

rave *v* 1 fume, go crazy, go mad, rage, rant, roar, splutter, storm, thunder. 2 (rave about sb) enthuse, go into raptures *inf*, gush *inf*

raving *adj* crazed, crazy, delirious, demented, deranged, frenzied, hysterical, insane, irrational, mad, rabid, raging, unbalanced, wild; *opp* sane

raw *adj* 1 (raw food) fresh, rare,

uncooked, underdone, unprepared;
opp cooked, prepared. **2** (raw materials)
basic, coarse, crude, natural, rough,
unfinished, unprocessed, unrefined,
untreated. **3** (a raw wound) bloody,
chafed, grazed, inflamed, open,
scraped, scratched, sensitive, sore,
tender, unhealed; ***opp*** healed

ray *n* **1** (a ray of light) bar, beam, flash,
gleam, glint, laser, shaft, streak, stream.
2 (a ray of hope) flicker, glimmer, hint,
spark, trace

reach *n* **1** (beyond your reach) distance,
extension, extent, grasp, spread, stretch.
2 (the reach of an organization) area,
authority, command, control, influence,
jurisdiction, power, range, scope, sphere,
sway, territory

reach *v* **1** (reach a high standard)
accomplish, achieve, arrive at, attain,
gain, get, make. **2** (reach a place, an
object) contact, extend to, get as far as,
stretch to, touch. **3 reach for** extend,
outstretch, put out your hand, stretch,
try to get

react *v* **1** answer, reciprocate, reply,
respond, retaliate, retort. **2** act, behave,
function, operate, proceed, work

reaction *n* answer, reply, response,
retaliation, retort, riposte

reactionary *adj* conservative, die-hard,
old-fashioned, rightist, right-wing,
traditionalist; ***opp*** progressive, radical

read *v* **1** (read a book) dip into, look at,
peruse, pore over, scan, skim, study.
2 (read the news) announce, deliver,
recite, speak, utter. **3** (read sth into sth)
assume, comprehend, construe,
infer, interpret, see, take sth to

mean, understand

ready *adj* **1** (prepared) all set *inf*,
arranged, completed, equipped, fit,
organized, prepared, primed, set,
waiting; ***opp*** unprepared. **2** (available)
accessible, at hand, at your disposal,
at your fingertips *inf*, available,
convenient, handy, near, on call,
present; ***opp*** unavailable. **3** (willing)
agreeable, consenting, disposed, eager,
game *inf*, glad, happy, pleased, willing;
opp unwilling

real *adj* **1** (real leather) authentic, bona
fide, genuine, true; ***opp*** artificial, fake.
2 (a real person) actual, corporeal,
existing, genuine, ordinary, non-
fictitious; ***opp*** fictitious

realistic *adj* **1** (of a person) clear-sighted,
common-sense, down-to-earth,
levelheaded, matter-of-fact,
objective, practical, pragmatic,
rational, sensible; ***opp*** unrealistic.
2 (a realistic copy) convincing,
faithful, lifelike, true to life, truthful;
opp unrealistic

reality *n* actuality, experience, fact, life,
practice, real life, the real world, truth;
opp theory

realize *v* **1** appreciate, catch on to *inf*,
comprehend, conceive, grasp, imagine,
recognize, take in, understand.
2 (realize a plan) accomplish, achieve,
bring off, complete, do, effect, fulfill,
implement, make happen

realm *n* country, domain, empire,
kingdom, land, monarchy, principality,
province, state

reap *v* **1** (reap rewards) acquire, collect,
derive, gain, gather, get, obtain, realize,

receive, win. 2 (reap a harvest) cut, gather in, harvest; **opp** sow

rear *adj* back, end, following, hind, hindmost, last, posterior; **opp** front

rear *n* back, back end, end, hind, rear end, stern, tail, tail end; **opp** front

reason *n* 1 (your reason for doing sth) aim, basis, cause, end, explanation, goal, grounds, impetus, incentive, intention, justification, motive, object, objective, pretext, purpose, rationale. 2 (a man of reason) brains, common sense, intellect, judgment, logic, reasonableness, sanity, sense, understanding, wisdom, wit

reason *v* calculate, conclude, consider, deduce, figure out, infer, judge, reckon, surmise, think, work out

reasonable *adj* 1 (of a person) calm, fair, intelligent, impartial, just, logical, practical, realistic, sane, sensible, sober, sound, thinking, unbiased, wise; **opp** irrational. 2 (quite good) average, fair, moderate, ordinary, passable, tolerable. 3 (of a price) acceptable, appropriate, cheap, competitive, fair, inexpensive, low, modest; **opp** high

reasoning *n* 1 (learn sth through reasoning) analysis, deduction, logic, rationalization, theorizing, thinking, thought. 2 (sb's reasoning) argument, case, hypothesis, line of thought, rationale

reassure *v* calm, cheer, comfort, encourage, hearten, put sb at ease, restore sb's confidence, set sb's mind at rest, support, uplift; **opp** worry

rebel *n* anarchist, dissenter, heretic, insurgent, nonconformist, revolutionary

rebel *v* defy, disobey, dissent, resist, revolt, rise up, take a stand; **opp** obey

rebellion *n* 1 mutiny, resistance, revolt, revolution, riot, rising, uprising. 2 (a mood of rebellion) defiance, disobedience, dissent, heresy, nonconformity; **opp** obedience

rebellious *adj* defiant, difficult, disloyal, disobedient, disorderly, insurgent, intractable, mutinous, nonconformist, obstinate, rebel, recalcitrant, revolutionary, turbulent, unruly, wild; **opp** obedient

rebound *n* boomerang, bounce, recoil, return, ricochet, spring back

rebound *v* boomerang, bounce, recoil, return, ricochet, spring back

rebuild *v* overhaul, reassemble, recondition, reconstruct, recreate, redevelop, refashion, regenerate, remake, renovate, restore

rebuke *v* blame, castigate, censure, chide, give sb a (good) talking to *inf*, haul sb over the coals, lecture, read sb the riot act, reprehend, reprimand, reproach, reprove, scold, take sb to task, tell off *inf*, tick off *inf*

rebuke *n* blame, censure, lecture, reprimand, reproach, reproof, scolding, talking-to *inf*, telling-off *inf*, ticking-off *inf*

recall *v* 1 (recall sb's name) recollect, remember, summon up, think of. 2 (recall a product) call in, summon, take back, withdraw

recede *v* 1 (a tide recedes) ebb, fall back, go back, regress, retreat, shrink back, subside, withdraw;

opp advance. **2** (a threat recedes) decline, decrease, dwindle, fade, lessen, peter out, subside, wane; *opp* increase

receipt *n* **1** (a train ticket receipt) acknowledgment, bill, proof of payment, sales slip, stub, voucher. **2** (on receipt of sth) acceptance, delivery, getting, obtaining, receiving, taking

receive *v* **1** acquire, be given, be sent, collect, gain, get, obtain, pick up, take; *opp* give, send. **2** (receive some news) apprehend, be informed, be notified, be told, find out, gather, hear, learn of; *opp* tell. **3** (receive bad treatment) be subjected to, encounter, endure, experience, go through, meet with, suffer, sustain, undergo; *opp* give. **4** (receive guests) entertain, greet, let in, meet, show in, welcome

recent *adj* brand new, contemporary, current, fresh, late, latest, modern, new, novel, up-to-date, up-to-the-minute, young; *opp* old

reception *n* **1** (get an enthusiastic reception) acknowledgment, greeting, reaction, response, treatment, welcome. **2** (attend a reception) bash *inf*, do *inf*, function, gathering, get-together *inf*, party, social

receptive *adj* amenable, flexible, interested, open, open-minded, sympathetic, responsive, well-disposed, willing; *opp* hostile

recess *n* **1** alcove, cavity, hollow, niche, nook. **2** adjournment, break, breather *inf*, closure, holiday, respite, rest, time off, time out, vacation

recession *n* decline, depression, downturn, drop, hard times, slump; *opp* boom

recipe *n* directions, formula, instructions, method, prescription, procedure, process, system, technique

reciprocal *adj* alternate, common, complementary, correlative, corresponding, equivalent, exchanged, give-and-take, interchangeable, mutual, returned, shared; *opp* one-way

reciprocate *v* do the same, give back, match, reply, requite, respond, return

recital *n* **1** concert, performance, program, show. **2** (a recital of sth you did) account, description, narration, narrative, recounting, relation, report, statement, telling

recite *v* articulate, deliver, narrate, perform, present, rattle off *inf*, recount, reel off *inf*, relate, repeat

reckless *adj* careless, crazy *inf*, daredevil, foolhardy, hasty, heedless, impetuous, imprudent, impulsive, irresponsible, mad *inf*, rash, thoughtless, wild; *opp* careful, cautious, prudent

reckon *v* (sb is reckoned to be the best) believe, consider, deem, hold, judge, rate, regard. **2** (reckon that sth is true) assume, believe, conjecture, fancy, guess, imagine, suppose, surmise, think

reclaim *v* get back, recapture, recover, regain, reinstate, retrieve, take back

recline *v* lean, lie, loll, lounge, rest, stretch out

recluse *n* hermit, loner, monk, nun

recognition *n* (in recognition of sb's

bravery) acceptance, admission, appreciation, avowal, endorsement, notice, respect. 2 (act of recognizing) identification, recollection, remembrance

recognize v 1 identify, know, place, recall, recollect, remember, spot. 2 (recognize sb's bravery) accept, admit, appreciate, avow, endorse, notice, respect

recoil v 1 fly back, rebound, return, ricochet, spring back. 2 (of a person) draw back, falter, flinch, jump, shrink, shy away, start, wince

recollect v recall, remember, summon up, think of

recollection n impression, memory, remembrance, reminiscence

recommend v 1 (recommend a course of action) advise, advocate, counsel, propose, put forward, suggest, urge. 2 (recommend sb for a job) back inf, commend, endorse, favor, push inf, put in a good word for, speak favorably/highly/well of, support, vouch for

recommendation n 1 advice, counsel, hint, proposal, suggestion, tip. 2 approval, backing, blessing, commendation, endorsement, reference, support

reconcile v 1 (reconcile yourself to sth) accept, get used to, make the best of, resign, submit, yield; *opp* resist. 2 (reconcile people) appease, bring together, conciliate, pacify, placate, restore harmony, reunite; *opp* divide

reconnaissance n examination,

exploration, inspection, investigation, observation, patrol, reconnoitering, scrutiny, spying

reconnoiter v examine, explore, inspect, investigate, observe, patrol, scan, scrutinize, survey

reconsider v change your mind, have a change of heart, reassess, re-examine, rethink, review, revise, think again, think better of, think twice

record n 1 (a record of proceedings) account, chronicle, documentation, dossier, file, journal, log, register, report. 2 (have a good record in sales) background, career, curriculum vitae, history, performance. 3 (play a record) album, disk, LP, recording, release, single. 4 off the record confidential, private, secret, unofficial; *opp* public

record v 1 catalog, chronicle, document, enter, file, log, minute, note, put down, note down, register, report, set down, transcribe, write down. 2 tape, tape-record, video

recording n album, cassette, CD, compact disc, disk, record, tape, video, videotape

recount v communicate, depict, describe, impart, narrate, portray, recite, relate, repeat, report, tell

recover v 1 be on the mend, convalesce, get back on your feet, get back to normal, get better, get well, improve, perk up inf, pick up, pull through, rally, recuperate, revive; *opp* deteriorate. 2 (recover property) get back, reclaim, recoup, redeem, regain, repossess, retrieve, salvage, win back

recovery n 1 convalescence,

improvement, progress, rally, recuperation, revival. 2 (recovery of property) reclaiming, recouping, redeeming, regaining, repossession, retrieval, salvage

recreation n amusement, distraction, diversion, enjoyment, exercise, fun, hobby, leisure, pastime, play, pleasure, relaxation, relief, sport; *opp* work

recrimination n accusation, comeback *inf*, counterattack, countercharge, reprisal, retaliation, retort, retribution, vengeance

recruit n apprentice, beginner, convert, initiate, learner, new boy *inf*, newcomer, new girl *inf*, novice, trainee

recruit v draft, employ, engage, enlist, enroll, sign on, sign up, take on

rectify v correct, cure, fix, improve, put right, redress, remedy, repair, right, square

recuperate v be on the mend, convalesce, get back on your feet, get back to normal, get better, get well, improve, perk up *inf*, pick up, pull through, rally, recover, revive; *opp* deteriorate

recur v come back, happen again, persist, reappear, return

recurrent adj continued, frequent, habitual, intermittent, periodic, persistent, recurring, repeated, returning; *opp* one-off

recycle v reclaim, reprocess, retrieve, reuse, salvage, save, use again

red adj crimson, rosy, ruby, ruddy, scarlet, vermilion

redden v blush, flush, glow, go red

redeem v 1 (redeem a voucher) cash in,

exchange for cash, use. 2 (redeem property) get back, reclaim, recoup, recover, regain, repossess, retrieve, salvage, win back. 3 (redeem sb) deliver, emancipate, free, liberate, release, rescue, save, set free

reduce v contract, cut, decrease, diminish, lessen, limit, lower, minimize, moderate, shorten, shrink, slash, truncate; *opp* increase

reduction n contraction, cut, cutback, decline, decrease, drop, lessening, limit, lowering, minimizing, moderation, shortening, shrinking, slashing, truncating; *opp* increase

redundant adj 1 nonessential, superfluous, supernumerary, surplus, unnecessary, unneeded, unwanted; *opp* essential. 2 (be made redundant) dismissed, jobless, laid-off, sacked, unemployed; *opp* employed

reel v falter, lurch, pitch, rock, roll, stagger, stumble, sway, totter, wobble

refer v 1 (refer to sth) allude, cite, hint, make reference to, mention, speak of. 2 (refer sb to sth) direct, guide, pass on, point, recommend, send. 3 (refer to a dictionary) consult, go to, look at, study, turn to

referee n adjudicator, arbiter, arbitrator, judge, ref *inf*, umpire

reference n 1 (make reference to) allusion, mention, note, remark. 2 (in reference to) concern, connection, consideration, regard, relation, respect. 3 (write a reference) endorsement, recommendation, testimonial

refine v 1 decontaminate, distill, filter, process, purify, treat. 2 civilize, cultivate, elevate, improve, perfect, polish, temper

refined adj civilized, courteous, cultivated, cultured, dignified, discerning, discriminating, elegant, genteel, gracious, ladylike, polished, polite, sophisticated, urbane, well-bred; *opp* common

refinement n 1 breeding, civility, courtesy, cultivation, culture, dignity, discernment, elegance, finesse, gentility, graciousness, polish, politeness, sophistication, taste. 2 (make a refinement) alteration, change, enhancement, improvement, modification

reflect v 1 echo, mirror, reproduce, return, send back, scatter, throw back. 2 (reflect on sth) consider, contemplate, deliberate, meditate, mull over, muse, ponder, ruminate, think, wonder

reflection n 1 echo, reproduction, image. 2 consideration, contemplation, deliberation, meditation, musing, pondering, thought, wondering

reform n change, conversion, correction, improvement, rebuilding, reconstruction, regeneration, remodeling, renovation, reorganization, repair, restoration, revision

reform v change, convert, correct, improve, mend, rebuild, reclaim, reconstruct, refashion, regenerate, remodel, renovate, reorganize, repair, restore, revamp, revise

refrain v abstain, avoid, cease, desist, do without, eschew, forbear, give up, leave off, quit *inf*, renounce, stop

refresh v 1 brace, cheer, cool, energize, enliven, fortify, freshen, invigorate, perk up *inf*, pick up, reanimate, renew, restore, revitalize, revive, revivify, stimulate. 2 (refresh sb's memory) activate, awaken, jog, prod, prompt, renew, rouse, stimulate

refreshing adj 1 bracing, cheering, cooling, energizing, fortifying, fresh, invigorating, restorative, revitalizing, reviving, stimulating, tonic. 2 different, fresh, original, new, novel, stimulating, welcome

refreshments n drinks, eatables, food, nibbles *inf*, snacks, titbits

refuge n 1 asylum, haven, hideaway, hideout, hiding place, protection, retreat, safety, sanctuary, security, shelter, stronghold. 2 expedient, recourse, resort, stratagem, strategy, tactic

refugee n displaced person, émigré, escapee, exile, fugitive, runaway

refund n rebate, reimbursement, repayment, return

refund v give back, make good, pay back, reimburse, repay, restore, return

refurbish v do up *inf*, fix up *inf*, make over, overhaul, recondition, redecorate, refit, remodel, renovate, restore, revamp, spruce up

refuse n debris, detritus, dregs, dross, garbage, junk, litter, rubbish, trash, waste

refuse v decline, deny, rebuff, reject, repudiate, say no, spurn, turn down, withhold

refute v counter, discredit, disprove, negate, overthrow, prove wrong, rebut, silence

regain v find, get back, recapture, reclaim, recoup, recover, recuperate, retake, retrieve, win back

regard n 1 attention, consideration, heed, interest, mind, notice, thought. 2 admiration, affection, appreciation, deference, esteem, honor, love, respect. 3 gaze, look, observation, scrutiny, stare

regard v adjudge, believe, consider, deem, esteem, hold, imagine, judge, look upon, perceive, rate, reckon, see, suppose, think, treat, value, view. 2 (watch) eye, keep an eye on, look at, observe, scrutinize, stare at, study, watch, view

regarding prep about, apropos, as regards, as to, concerning, in regard to, in respect of, in the matter of, on the subject of, pertaining to, re, respecting, with reference to, with regard to

regime n dictatorship, government, junta, leadership, order, reign, rule, system

regiment v bring into line, control, discipline, order, organize, regulate, systematize

region n area, county, department, district, division, locality, part, place, province, quarter, section, sector, state, territory, tract, zone

regional adj district, local, parochial, provincial, sectional

register n annals, archives, catalog, chronicle, diary, directory, file, index, inventory, journal, ledger, list, log, record, roll

register v 1 archive, catalog, chronicle, enter, file, index, inscribe, list, log, note,

record, take down, write down. 2 (register an emotion) betray, display, exhibit, express, indicate, manifest, reflect, reveal, show

regress v backslide, degenerate, deteriorate, go back, lapse, lose ground, recede, relapse, retreat, retrogress, return, revert, slip back; **opp** improve

regret n 1 compunction, conscience, contrition, guilt, penitence, remorse, repentance, ruefulness, self-reproach, sorrow. 2 bitterness, disappointment, grief, sadness, sorrow

regret v 1 accuse yourself, feel guilty, feel remorse, feel sorry, repent, reproach yourself, rue. 2 bemoan, bewail, deplore, deprecate, grieve, lament, miss, mourn, weep over

regrettable adj deplorable, disappointing, disgraceful, reprehensible, sad, shameful, unfortunate; **opp** fortunate

regular adj 1 (a regular pattern) consistent, constant, equal, even, fixed, measured, ordered, periodic, predictable, recurring, repeated, rhythmic, set, steady, symmetrical, systematic, uniform, unvarying. 2 (a regular route, procedure) common, conventional, customary, daily, established, everyday, familiar, frequent, habitual, known, normal, ordinary, orthodox, prevailing, routine, standard, typical, usual. 3 (a regular job) dependable, reliable, safe, steady

regulate v adjust, administer, arrange, balance, control, direct, govern, guide, handle, manage, monitor, order, oversee, rule, run, settle, steer, superintend, supervise

regulation n 1 bylaw, commandment, decree, dictate, directive, edict, law, order, ordinance, precept, requirement, restriction, rule, ruling, statute. 2 (the regulation of sth) adjustment, administering, administration, control, controlling, directing, direction, government, handling, management, monitoring, ordering, overseeing, running, steering, supervising, supervision

rehearsal n drill, dry run, practice, preparation, reading, run-through, try-out

rehearse v drill, go over, go through, practice, prepare, read through, repeat, run through, try out

reign n administration, command, control, dominion, empire, government, monarchy, power, rule, sovereignty

reign v administer, be in power, be on the throne, command, govern, rule

reincarnation n rebirth, transmigration

reinforce v back up, bolster, brace, buttress, emphasize, fortify, harden, prop, shore up, stiffen, strengthen, stress, support, toughen, underline

reinforcements n auxiliaries, back-up, help, reserves, support

reinstate v recall, rehabilitate, replace, restore, return, take back

reject n cast-off, discard, failure, second

reject v 1 (reject a person, thing) cast out, discard, dismiss, disown, eliminate, exclude, jettison, jilt, rebuff, renounce, repudiate, scrap, send back, send packing inf, shun, spurn, throw away, throw out. 2 (reject a request, offer) decline, deny, refuse, say no, turn

down, veto; **opp** accept

rejection n 1 brush-off inf, casting out, discarding, dismissal, disowning, elimination, exclusion, jilting, renunciation, repudiation, scrapping, spurning, throwing away, throwing out. 2 denial, no, refusal, thumbs down inf, veto; **opp** acceptance

rejoice v celebrate, delight, exult, glory, revel, triumph

rejoicing n celebration, delight, elation, euphoria, exultation, gladness, happiness, jubilation, merry-making, revelry, triumph

relapse n degeneration, deterioration, lapse, regression, retrogression, reversion, setback, weakening, worsening

relapse v backslide, degenerate, deteriorate, fail, have a relapse, lapse, regress, revert, sink, weaken, worsen

relate v 1 communicate, describe, detail, impart, make known, narrate, present, recount, report, set forth, tell. 2 (establish a connection) ally, associate, connect, correlate, couple, join, link. 3 relate to (be relevant) apply, be relevant, concern, have to do with, pertain, refer to

related adj affiliated, akin, allied, associated, connected, correlated, coupled, interconnected, linked, relevant, similar

relation n 1 association, bearing, bond, connection, correlation, interconnection, link, relevance, similarity. 2 family member, kin, kith and kin, relative

relations n 1 affairs, communication,

connections, contact, dealings, interaction, liaison, links. 2 family, kin, kindred, kinsfolk, relatives

relationship n 1 affinity, association, bond, conjunction, connection, correlation, interconnection, kinship, link. 2 affair, alliance, friendship, intrigue, liaison, partnership, romance

relative adj comparable, comparative, parallel, respective

relative n family member, kin, kith and kin, relation

relax v 1 calm down, chill out sl, cool down, laze around, loosen up, put your feet up inf, slow down, take it easy, unwind. 2 (relax a control) diminish, ease, lessen, let up, loosen, reduce, slacken, soften, weaken; opp tighten

relaxation n 1 amusement, diversion, enjoyment, fun, leisure, pleasure, recreation, refreshment, repose, rest. 2 (relaxation of a control) diminishing, easing, lessening, letting up, loosening, slackening, softening, weakening; opp tightening

relaxed adj at ease, at home, calm, carefree, casual, comfortable, cool, easy, easygoing, informal, insouciant, laid-back inf, leisurely, light-hearted, nonchalant, peaceful, serene, tranquil, unconcerned, untroubled; opp uptight

relay n 1 relief, shift, turn. 2 broadcast, dispatch, program, transmission

relay v broadcast, carry, communicate, hand on, pass on, send, spread, televise, transmit

release n 1 acquittal, deliverance, discharge, emancipation, freeing,

liberating, setting free, unchaining, unfastening, unshackling, untying. 2 (a press release) announcement, bulletin, communication, proclamation, publication

release v 1 acquit, deliver, discharge, emancipate, extricate, free, let go, let out, liberate, loose, set free, unchain, unfasten, unshackle, untie. 2 (release news) announce, break, circulate, communicate, disseminate, distribute, issue, make available, make known, make public, present, publish, put out, send out

relent v be merciful, capitulate, forbear, give way, melt, show mercy, soften, yield

relentless adj harsh, implacable, inexorable, merciless, pitiless, remorseless, ruthless, unbending, unrelenting, unyielding

relevant adj applicable, apposite, appropriate, apt, connected, germane, material, pertinent, related, salient, significant, to the point; opp irrelevant

reliable adj certain, consistent, constant, dependable, faithful, loyal, predictable, proven, regular, responsible, safe, secure, solid, sound, stable, staunch, sure, true, trusty, trustworthy, unfailing; opp unreliable

relic n fragment, keepsake, memento, remains, reminder, remnant, scrap, token, trace, vestige

relief n aid, alleviation, assistance, balm, comfort, cure, deliverance, diversion, ease, help, letup inf, remedy, remission, rescue, respite, solace, succour, support

relieve v 1 aid, allay, alleviate, assist, assuage, calm, comfort, deliver, ease, help, lessen, lift, lighten, mitigate, moderate, palliate, reduce, release, remedy, rescue, soothe, succour, support. **2** (relieve sb at work) fill in for, stand in for, substitute for, replace, take over from, take the place of

religion n belief, creed, denomination, divinity, doctrine, dogma, faith, sect, theology

religious adj devotional, devout, faithful, God-fearing, godly, holy, pious, pure, reverent, righteous, spiritual

relish v appreciate, delight in, enjoy, like, love, revel in, savor, take pleasure in

reluctant adj averse, disinclined, grudging, hesitant, loath, slow, unenthusiastic, unwilling; *opp* keen, willing

rely v **rely on** bank on, be sure of, bet on, count on, depend on, have confidence in, lean on, put your trust in, reckon on, swear by, trust

remain v abide, be left, carry on, continue, endure, keep on, last, linger, live on, persist, prevail, stand, stay, survive

remainder n balance, excess, leavings, leftovers, remains, remnants, residue, rest, surplus

remaining adj left, lingering, outstanding, persisting, surviving, unfinished

remains n **1** balance, crumbs, debris, dregs, leavings, leftovers, pieces, relics, remnants, residue, rest, scraps, traces, vestiges. **2** ashes, body, bones, cadaver, carcass, corpse

remark n assertion, comment, declaration, observation, pronouncement, reflection, statement, utterance

remark v **1** assert, comment, declare, mention, note, observe, pass comment, reflect, say, state. **2** discern, espy, heed, mark, note, notice, observe, perceive, regard, see

remarkable adj amazing, astonishing, astounding, considerable, distinctive, distinguished, exceptional, extraordinary, impressive, notable, noteworthy, outstanding, phenomenal, preeminent, rare, singular, strange, striking, surprising, uncommon, unforgettable, unusual; *opp* ordinary, unremarkable

remedy n antidote, corrective, counter-measure, cure, drug, medication, medicine, palliative, panacea, relief, therapy, treatment

remedy v alleviate, assuage, control, correct, counter, counteract, cure, ease, heal, help, rectify, relieve, soothe, treat

remember v be mindful of, call up, keep in mind, recall, recognize, recollect, reminisce, retain

remind v bring to mind, call up, give a reminder, jog your memory, prompt

reminder n **1** cue, hint, memo *inf*, memorandum, mnemonic, note, nudge, prompt. **2** keepsake, memento, relic, remembrance, souvenir

reminiscent adj evocative, redolent, similar, suggestive

remiss adj careless, forgetful, heedless, inattentive, lax, neglectful, negligent, slack, slipshod, sloppy *inf*, thoughtless, unmindful, unthinking

remission n **1** absolution, amnesty, discharge, exemption, exoneration, forgiveness, parole, pardon, release, repeal, reprieve. 2 abatement, alleviation, lull, moderation, reduction, relaxation, respite, suspension

remittance n allowance, fee, payment, transfer

remnant n bit, crumbs, debris, dregs, fragment, leavings, leftovers, relic, remnant, residue, rest, scrap, trace, vestige

remonstrate v argue, challenge, complain, dispute, dissent, expostulate, object, oppose, protest, take exception, take issue

remorse n compunction, conscience, contrition, guilt, mortification, penitence, regret, repentance, self-reproach, shame, sorrow

remorseful adj ashamed, conscious-stricken, contrite, guilt-ridden, guilty, mortified, penitent, regretful, repentant, sorry

remorseless adj cruel, harsh, implacable, inexorable, inhumane, merciless, pitiless, relentless, ruthless, unrelenting, unremitting

remote adj 1 cut off, distant, far, faraway, far-off, inaccessible, in the middle of nowhere, isolated, lonely, off the beaten track, out of the way, secluded. 2 aloof, chilly, cool, detached, distant, haughty, removed, reserved, standoffish, unapproachable, unfriendly, withdrawn; opp friendly

removal n 1 carrying away, moving, relocating, removing, taking away, transfer, transportation. 2 abolition, deletion, effacing, elimination, eradication, erasure, extermination,

liquidation, obliteration, withdrawal. 3 (of a person) deposition, dislodging, dismissal, ejection, expulsion, eviction, firing, ousting, replacement, sacking

remove v 1 carry away, convey, move, relocate, take away, transfer, transport. 2 abolish, banish, delete, do away with, eliminate, efface, eradicate, erase, excise, expunge, exterminate, get rid of, kill, liquidate, obliterate, withdraw. 3 (remove a person) depose, dislodge, dismiss, eject, expel, evict, fire, oust, replace, sack. 4 (remove clothes) doff, peel off, shed, slip off, strip off, take off

render v 1 cause to be, get, leave, make. 2 (give) cede, contribute, deliver, furnish, give, hand over, make available, offer, present, provide, submit, supply, surrender, tender, turn over, yield. 3 (give a performance of) act, depict, do, execute, interpret, perform, present, portray, represent

renege v back out, break your promise, cop out inf, default, go back on your word, pull out

renew v 1 modernize, overhaul, recondition, refit, refurbish, regenerate, rejuvenate, remodel, renovate, repair, replace, restore, resurrect, revamp, revitalize, revive, transform. 2 (renew efforts) come back to, continue, pick up, recommence, restart, resume, return to. 3 (renew a pledge) confirm, reaffirm, reiterate, repeat, restate

renounce v abandon, abstain, cast off, deny, discard, disown, eschew, forgo, forsake, forswear, give up, quit, reject, relinquish, repudiate, spurn, waive

renovate v fix up inf, modernize,

overhaul, recondition, refit, refurbish, remake, remodel, repair, restore, revamp

renowned *adj* acclaimed, celebrated, distinguished, eminent, famed, famous, illustrious, known, noted, prominent, well-known

rent *n* fee, hire, lease, payment, rental, tariff

rent *v* charter, lease, let

repair *n* darn, fixing, mending, overhaul, patch, restoration

repair *v* darn, fix, heal, mend, patch, patch up, put right, renovate, restore

repay *v* 1 (repay money) compensate, pay back, recompense, refund, reimburse, settle up, square. 2 (repay a wrong) avenge, get back at, get even, get your own back *inf*, hit back, reciprocate, retaliate, revenge, settle the score

repeal *v* (repeal a law) abolish, annul, cancel, invalidate, rescind, revoke, withdraw

repeat *n* recap *inf*, repetition, replay, reproduction, rerun

repeat *v* 1 (say sth again) echo, parrot, quote, recap *inf*, recite, reiterate, retell, say again. 2 (do sth again) copy, do again, duplicate, rehearse, replay, replicate, reproduce, rerun, show again

repel *v* 1 (repel invaders) beat back, confront, drive back, fend off, fight, force back, hold off, keep at bay, resist, ward off. 2 (sth repels you) be repellent, disgust, make your flesh creep, make you sick, nauseate, offend, put off *inf*, revolt, shock, sicken, turn your stomach. 3 (repel water) be impermeable to, keep out, resist; *opp* attract

repellent *adj* abhorrent, disgusting, distasteful, foul, horrid, loathsome, nauseating, obnoxious, obscene, odious, offensive, off-putting, repugnant, repulsive, revolting, sickening, vile

repent *v* atone, be contrite, be penitent, be sorry, feel remorse, regret, reproach yourself, rue

repentance *n* compunction, contrition, grief, guilt, penitence, regret, remorse, self-accusation, self-reproach, shame, sorrow

repentant *adj* apologetic, ashamed, chastened, conscience-stricken, contrite, guilt-ridden, penitent, remorseful, sorry; *opp* unrepentant

repercussion *n* backlash, consequence, effect, result, sequel

repetition *n* 1 (too much repetition) copying, duplication, redundancy, repeating, repetitiousness. 2 (a repetition) duplication, echo, recurrence, repeat, restatement, retelling

repetitive *adj* boring, dull, mechanical, monotonous, recurrent, repeated, tedious, unchanging

replace *v* 1 (replace sth) change, make good, put back, renew, restore, substitute. 2 (replace sb) come after, cover for, fill in for, follow, oust, stand in for, succeed, supersede, take the place of, understudy

replacement *n* double, locum, proxy, stand-in, substitute, successor, surrogate, understudy

replenish *v* fill, refill, renew, replace, restock, stock up

replica *n* carbon copy, clone, copy, duplicate, facsimile, imitation, likeness, model, reproduction

reply n acknowledgement, answer, comeback *inf*, reaction, rejoinder, response, retort, riposte

reply v 1 (reply to what sb says) answer, counter, rejoin, respond, retort, riposte. 2 (reply to a letter) acknowledge, answer, write back. 3 (reply to what sb does) react, reciprocate, respond, retaliate

report n 1 account, announcement, article, description, message, news, note, paper, piece, statement, story, write-up. 2 (a loud report) backfire, bang, blast, boom, crack, crash, discharge, echo, explosion, noise, sound

report v 1 (tell people about sth) announce, broadcast, circulate, communicate, describe, disclose, document, publish, recount, reveal, tell, write about, write up. 2 (report sb) accuse, complain about, denounce, inform against, inform on, rat on *inf*, squeal on *inf*, tell on *inf*. 3 (report for duty) announce yourself, arrive, be present, check in, come, present yourself, sign in, turn up

reporter n correspondent, journalist, newscaster, newsman, newspaperman, newspaperwoman, newswoman, presenter, writer

repose n calmness, ease, peace, peacefulness, quietness, relaxation, rest, serenity, sleep, slumber, stillness, tranquillity

reprehensible adj bad, blameworthy, culpable, delinquent, deplorable, disgraceful, inexcusable, shameful, unpardonable, wicked, wrong

represent v 1 correspond to, embody, exemplify, express, mean, stand for, symbolize, typify. 2 (sb must represent the people) act for, be the representative of, be the spokesperson for, speak for. 3 (represent sb in a picture) depict, draw, evoke, illustrate, paint, portray, render, show, sketch. 4 (represent sb on stage) act out, assume the guise of, enact, impersonate, personify, pose as, pretend to be, show

representation n account, depiction, description, figure, icon, illustration, image, likeness, model, painting, picture, portrait, portrayal, statue

representative adj 1 (of a sample) archetypal, average, characteristic, illustrative, indicative, normal, symbolic, typical. 2 (of a government) authorized, chosen, delegated, democratic, elected, elective, official, popular

representative n 1 ambassador, consul, councillor, delegate, deputy, emissary, envoy, ombudsman, spokesman, spokesperson, spokeswoman, stand-in, substitute. 2 (a representative for a company) agent, rep *inf*, salesman, salesperson, saleswoman

repress v 1 (repress people) control, crush, dominate, intimidate, keep down, oppress, overpower, quash, quell, restrain, subdue, subjugate. 2 (repress feelings) bottle up *inf*, control, inhibit, hold in, keep in, smother, stifle, suppress; *opp* show

repressed adj 1 (of people) frustrated, inhibited, restrained, tense, unbalanced, uptight *inf*, withdrawn. 2 (of feelings) hidden, subconscious, suppressed, unconscious

repression *n* control, domination, oppression, subjugation, totalitarianism, tyranny

repressive *adj* absolute, authoritarian, brutal, despotic, dictatorial, fascist, harsh, oppressive, tyrannical, undemocratic; *opp* liberal

reprieve *n* amnesty, pardon, postponement, stay of execution

reprieve *v* forgive, let off, pardon, rescue, save, set free, spare

reprimand *n* condemnation, criticism, dressing-down *inf*, lecture *inf*, rebuke, reproach, scolding, slap on the wrist *inf*, talking-to *inf*, telling-off *inf*, ticking-off *inf*

reprimand *v* castigate, criticize, lecture *inf*, rebuke, reproach, scold, tell off *inf*, tick off *inf*

reprisal *n* redress, retaliation, retribution, revenge, vengeance

reproach *n* blame, contempt, criticism, disapproval, discredit, disgrace, scorn, shame, stigma

reproach *v* blame, censure, condemn, criticize, find fault, reprimand, scold, show disapproval; *opp* praise

reproachful *adj* censorious, critical, disappointed, disapproving, disparaging, reproving, scolding, scornful

reproduce *v* 1 clone, copy, echo, forge, imitate, match, mirror, parallel, recreate, redo, remake, repeat, replicate. 2 copy, duplicate, make a copy of, photocopy, print, reprint. 3 bear young, breed, give birth, increase, multiply, procreate, produce offspring, spawn

reproduction *n* copy, duplicate, facsimile, fake, fax, forgery, imitation, photocopy, picture, print, replica

repudiate *v* contradict, deny, disagree with, disclaim, dispute, rebuff, reject

repugnant *adj* abhorrent, disagreeable, disgusting, distasteful, hateful, horrible, nauseating, objectionable, offensive, repellent, revolting, sickening, unpleasant

repulsive *adj* abominable, disgusting, distasteful, foul, gross *slang*, hateful, hideous, loathsome, nasty, nauseating, odious, off-putting *inf*, repellent, repugnant, revolting, sick *inf*, sickening, ugly, vile

reputable *adj* (a reputable company) aboveboard, excellent, good, highly regarded, honorable, legitimate, of good repute, prestigious, reliable, respectable, respected, trustworthy, upright, well-thought-of; *opp* disreputable

reputation *n* character, good name, name, position, prestige, recognition, renown, repute, respectability, standing, status

reputed *adj* alleged, believed, considered, deemed, judged, reckoned, regarded, rumored, said, supposed, thought

request *n* appeal, call, demand, desire, entreaty, petition, plea, prayer, question

request *v* apply for, ask, ask for, beg, beseech, call for, claim, demand, desire, implore, invite, pray, seek

require *v* 1 (need) be missing, be short of, crave, desire, lack, miss, need, want, wish. 2 (require sb to do sth) ask, bid, command, compel, force, insist upon, instruct, oblige, order, put pressure on, request. 3 (require a lot of strength) call for, demand, depend on, necessitate, need, take

requirement n condition, demand, essential, necessity, need, precondition, qualification, stipulation

requisite adj called for, compulsory, essential, indispensable, mandatory, necessary, needed, obligatory, required, vital

rescue n deliverance, freeing, liberation, recovery, release, rescuing, salvage, saving

research nrescue v deliver, free, get back, get out, liberate, recover, redeem, release, retrieve, salvage, save, set free
analysis, enquiry, examination, experimentation, exploration, fact-finding, inquiry, investigation, study, tests

research v analyze, examine, experiment, explore, investigate, look into, review, study, test

resemblance n analogy, comparison, conformity, congruity, correspondence, kinship, likeness, similarity

resemble v bear a resemblance to, be like, duplicate, echo, look like, mirror, put you in mind of, sound like, remind you of, take after

resent v begrudge, be resentful about, dislike, envy, feel aggrieved at, feel bitter about, grudge, grumble at, object to, take exception to, take offense at, take umbrage at

resentful adj aggrieved, angry, bitter, disgruntled, in a huff inf, indignant, irate, irked, irritated, jealous, miffed inf, offended, peeved inf, piqued, put out inf,

spiteful, vindictive

resentment n anger, animosity, bitterness, displeasure, fury, hard feelings, hurt, ill-will, indignation, malice, pique, rancor, spite

reservation n 1 (have reservations about sth) doubt, hesitation, misgiving, qualm, reluctance, skepticism, scruple. 2 (live on a reservation) enclave, homeland, preserve, reserve, sanctuary, territory, tract. 3 (a reservation at a restaurant) appointment, arrangement, booking

reserve adj auxiliary, extra, fall-back, in reserve, spare, substitute

reserve n 1 (kept a reserve for emergencies) fund, hoard, savings, stock, stockpile, store, supply. 2 (known for his reserve) aloofness, coolness, detachment, formality, modesty, remoteness, restraint, reticence, self-effacement, shyness. 3 (animals on a reserve) area, game park, park, protected area, reservation, sanctuary, tract. 4 (an extra person) backup inf, reinforcements, replacement, stand-in inf, substitute

reserve v 1 (reserve a ticket) book, order, pay in advance for, prearrange. 2 (reserve sth for later) conserve, earmark, hang on to inf, hoard, keep, keep back, lay aside, put away, save, set aside, stockpile, store up, withhold

reserved adj 1 (of a person) aloof, cautious, cold, cool, demure, diffident, modest, quiet, remote, restrained, reticent, self-effacing, shy, silent, undemonstrative, unfriendly, unsociable. 2 (of a table, seat) booked, engaged, held, kept, retained, taken

reside v abide, dwell, inhabit, live, lodge, occupy, settle, stay

residence n address, dwelling, flat, home, house, lodgings, quarters

resident n citizen, householder, inhabitant, local, lodger, occupant, occupier, tenant

residue n dregs, excess, extra, leftovers, remainder, remains, remnant, rest, surplus

resign v abdicate, give notice, give up, hand in your notice, hand over, leave, quit, retire, step down *inf*

resigned adj 1 compliant, forbearing, long-suffering, passive, patient, philosophical, stoical, subdued, tolerant, unresisting. 2 (resigned to sth) accepting, acquiescent, reconciled, submitting, yielding

resilient adj 1 (of materials) bouncy, elastic, firm, flexible, plastic, pliable, pliant, rubbery, springy, supple; *opp* brittle. 2 (of a person) adaptable, buoyant, irrepressible, quick to recover, strong, tough, unstoppable

resist v 1 (stop sth) block, check, counteract, curb, frustrate, halt, hinder, inhibit, keep at bay, obstruct, prevent, rebuff, stop. 2 (resist an enemy) battle against, combat, confront, defy, fight, oppose, repel, stand up to, thwart. 3 (resist moisture) be resistant to, repel, withstand. 4 (try to resist a cake) abstain from, avoid, desist from, do without, refrain from

resistant adj 1 immune to, impervious to, proof against, strong, tough, unaffected by; *opp* susceptible to. 2 (resistant to change) antagonistic, defiant, hostile,

intransigent, obstinate, opposed, recalcitrant, stubborn, uncooperative, unyielding

resolute adj adamant, bold, committed, decided, decisive, determined, dogged, immovable, obstinate, persistent, resolved, set, singleminded, staunch, steadfast, stubborn, tenacious, unbending, undaunted, unwavering

resolution n 1 boldness, commitment, courage, dedication, determination, persistence, purpose, resolve, staying power, steadfastness, willpower. 2 (a resolution) aim, decision, declaration, intent, intention, judgment, motion, plan, pledge, promise, resolve, undertaking, verdict, vow

resolve v 1 (resolve to do sth) agree, decide, determine, intend, make up your mind, undertake. 2 (resolve a difficulty) clear up, figure out, settle, sort out, solve, unravel, work out

resort n haunt, refuge, retreat, spot, vacation spot

resort to v employ, exercise, fall back on, make use of, turn to, use, utilize

resource n 1 fund, reserve, stock, stockpile, supply. 2 course, device, expedient, means, way

resourceful adj able, bright, capable, clever, creative, enterprising, imaginative, ingenious, inspired, inventive, quick-witted, skillful, talented

resources n assets, capital, funds, holdings, money, possessions, reserves, supplies, wealth

respect n 1 (respect for sb) admiration, approval, awe, consideration, esteem,

honor, recognition, regard, reverence.
2 (in this/that respect) aspect, attribute, characteristic, detail, feature, matter, particular, point, quality, sense, trait, way. **3** (show respect) consideration, courtesy, deference, politeness, thoughtfulness. **4** (with respect to your letter) reference, regard

respect v **1** (respect sb) admire, adore, defer to, esteem, have a high opinion of, honor, look up to, revere, think highly of, venerate. **2** (respect rules) abide by, adhere to, comply with, follow, heed, obey, observe; **opp** break. **3** (respect sb's views) recognize, show consideration for, take into account, value

respectable adj **1** (of a person) decent, dignified, genteel, good, honest, honorable, law-abiding, of good repute, proper, reputable, trustworthy, upright, venerable, virtuous, worthy. **2** (of an amount) adequate, ample, appreciable, considerable, decent, fair, goodly, presentable, reasonable, satisfactory, sizable, substantial, tolerable

respectful adj admiring, civil, considerate, courteous, deferential, dutiful, humble, polite, reverential, subservient; **opp** disrespectful

respective adj individual, own, particular, personal, relevant, special, specific, various

respite n break, breather inf, cessation, halt, hiatus, holiday, interval, letup inf, lull, pause, relief, rest, time off, time out

respond v **1** (respond to a letter) acknowledge, answer, reply, write back. **2** (respond to speech or action) answer, counter, react, reciprocate,

reply, retort, return

response n answer, comeback inf, feedback, reaction, reply

responsibility n **1** (have a responsibility) accountability, answerability, authority, duty, importance, liability, obligation, onus, power, trust. **2** (responsibility for sth going wrong) accountability, blame, burden, fault, guilt, liability

responsible adj **1** (having responsibility) accountable, in charge, in control, liable. **2** (responsible for sth wrong) accountable, answerable, at fault, culpable, guilty, to blame; **opp** innocent. **3** (behaving in a responsible way) adult, conscientious, dependable, levelheaded, mature, reasonable, reliable, sensible, steady, trustworthy; **opp** irresponsible. **4** (a responsible job) decision-making, executive, front-line inf, high, important, managerial, powerful; **opp** menial

rest n **1** (stop for a rest) break, breather inf, halt, interlude, intermission, interval, lull, pause, respite, time off, time out. **2** (a well-earned rest) break, vacation. **3** (a sleep) forty winks inf, nap, siesta, sleep. **4** (need plenty of rest) calmness, ease, hush, inactivity, peace, quiet, relaxation, repose, sleep, tranquillity. **5** (throw away the rest) balance, excess, leftovers, others, remainder, remnants, residue, surplus

rest v **1** be still, catnap, doze, have a nap, have a rest, have a sleep, lie down, nod off, put your feet up, snooze inf, take it easy inf, unwind. **2** (rest on a surface) lean, lie, place, prop, set, sit, stand, steady, support. 3 (everything rests on your answer) depend, hang, hinge, rely, turn

restful adj calm, calming, leisurely, peaceful, placid, quiet, relaxed, relaxing, serene, sleepy, soothing, still, tranquil

restless adj 1 (not staying in one place) itinerant, nomadic, roaming, roving, transient, traveling, unsettled, wandering; **opp** settled. 2 (constantly moving) active, busy, changable, changing, in motion, moving, on the move, turbulent; **opp** still. 3 (not getting much sleep) disturbed, fitful, fretful, sleepless, uncomfortable, uneasy, wakeful; **opp** restful. 4 (not patient or calm) agitated, edgy, excitable, fidgeting, fidgety, ill at ease, impatient, jittery inf, jumpy, nervous, restive, uneasy, unruly, unsettled, worked up, worried; **opp** calm, relaxed

restore v 1 (restore sth old) clean, fix, fix up inf, mend, recondition, redecorate, refurbish, renew, renovate, repair, revamp. 2 (restore a person) build up, refresh, rejuvenate, revive, revitalize, strengthen. 3 (restore stolen property) bring back, give back, hand back, recover, replace, return, send back

restrain v 1 (restrain feelings) control, curb, hold in check, inhibit, rein in, repress, stifle, subdue, suppress; **opp** show. 2 (restrain a prisoner) chain up, confine, detain, handcuff, imprison, lock up, manacle, tie up; **opp** let loose. 3 (restrain sb from doing sth) hinder, hold back, keep, obstruct, prevent,

save, stop; **opp** encourage

restrained adj 1 (of a person) calm, controlled, mild, moderate, reticent, undemonstrative, unemotional. 2 (of colors) discreet, muted, soft, subtle, tasteful, understated, unobtrusive

restraint n 1 (show restraint) inhibition, moderation, prudence, self-control, self-discipline. 2 (a restraint on sth) ban, check, constraint, curb, deterrent, embargo, limit, rein, restriction

restrict v circumscribe, confine, contain, control, hamper, handicap, hinder, impede, imprison, limit, moderate, regulate, restrain

restriction n ban, check, condition, control, curb, handicap, limit, limitation, proviso, qualification, regulation, restraint, rule, stipulation

result n 1 (the result of sth happening) conclusion, consequence, effect, outcome, repercussion, sequel, upshot. 2 (the wrong result) answer, decision, judgment, solution, verdict

result v appear, arise, come about, derive, develop, emerge, ensue, follow, happen, occur, proceed, spring, stem, take place, turn out

resume v begin again, carry on, continue, proceed, recommence, reopen, restart, take up

resurrect v breathe new life into, bring back, raise from the dead, reawaken, reintroduce, renew, restore to life, revive

resuscitate v bring round, give the kiss of life to, revive, save

retain v 1 absorb, contain, hang on to inf, hold, keep, keep hold of, keep in, maintain, preserve, reserve, save, soak up; *opp* lose. 2 keep in mind, learn, memorize, recall, recollect, remember; *opp* forget

retaliate *v* avenge yourself, get even *inf*, get your own back, give as good as you get, hit back, reciprocate, repay, settle a score, strike back, take revenge

retard *v* arrest, delay, handicap, hinder, hold back, impede, obstruct, set back, slow down

reticent *adj* quiet, reserved, retiring, secretive, shy, silent, tight-lipped, uncommunicative

retire *v* 1 give up work, leave, quit, stop working. 2 depart, exit, go away, go out, leave, withdraw. 3 call it a day, go to bed, go to sleep, turn in *inf*

retiring *adj* bashful, coy, demure, diffident, meek, modest, quiet, reserved, reticent, shrinking, shy, timid, unassertive; *opp* outgoing

retort *n* answer, rejoinder, reply, response, riposte

retort *v* answer, answer back, come back at, counter, reply, riposte, say in reply

retract *v* 1 draw in, pull back, pull in, sheathe. 2 backtrack on, cancel, deny, disclaim, disown, renounce, repudiate, reverse, revoke, take back, withdraw

retreat *n* 1 asylum, den, haunt, haven, hideaway, hideout, hiding place, refuge, sanctuary, shelter. 2 departure, evacuation, exit, flight, withdrawal

retreat *v* 1 back away, back down, back off, depart, draw back, evacuate, fall back, flee, give way, go away, go back, leave, move back, pull back, recoil, retire, run away, take flight, take to your heels *inf*, turn tail, withdraw;

opp advance. 2 ebb, flow back, recede, shrink back; *opp* advance

retribution *n* compensation, justice, punishment, reckoning, recompense, redress, reparation, repayment, reprisal, retaliation, revenge, reward, vengeance

retrieve *v* bring back, fetch, find, get back, recall, recapture, recover, regain, repossess, rescue, salvage, trace, track down, win back

retrospective *adj* backward-looking, looking back, with hindsight

return *n* 1 arrival, coming home, homecoming, reappearance. 2 (a good return on your investment) earnings, gain, income, interest, profit, revenue, yield

return *v* 1 come again, come back, go back, reappear. 2 (return to look for sth) backtrack, double back, go back, retrace your steps. 3 (return a library book) give back, put back, replace, restore, send back, take back. 4 (return a favor) pay back, reciprocate, repay

reveal *v* 1 (reveal a secret) announce, betray, broadcast, confess, disclose, divulge, give away, leak, let on, let out, let slip, make known, publicize, tell. 2 (show sth) bare, display, expose, show, uncover, unmask, unveil

revel *v* 1 celebrate, have fun, live it up *inf*, make merry, paint the town red *inf*, party. 2 (revel in sth) bask, delight, gloat, luxuriate, relish, savor, take pleasure, wallow

revelation *n* admission, betrayal, confession, disclosure, discovery, leak *inf*, publishing, revealing, telling

revelry *n* celebrations, festivities, fun,

gaiety, jollification, jollity, living it up *inf*, merrymaking, party

revenge *n* 1 (get your revenge) redress, reprisal, retaliation, retribution, vengeance. 2 (feelings of revenge) hate, hatred, hostility, malice, spite, spitefulness, vindictiveness

revenue *n* gain, income, interest, money, proceeds, profits, receipts, returns, takings, rewards, yield

reverberate *v* boom, echo, rebound, resonate, resound, ring, thunder, vibrate

revere *v* adore, exalt, glorify, honor, idolize, pay homage to, praise, respect, venerate, worship

reverent *adj* adoring, awed, deferential, devout, humble, pious, religious, respectful, reverential, solemn, submissive, worshipful

reverse *adj* back-to-front, backward, backwards, contrary, converse, inverted, opposite, transposed

reverse *n* 1 contrary, converse, inverse, opposite. 2 back, other side, rear, wrong side

reverse *v* 1 (in a vehicle) back, go backwards, move backwards. 2 (reverse a judgment) annul, cancel, change, countermand, invalidate, overrule, overturn, quash, repeal, revoke, set aside, undo, upset. 3 (reverse an image) invert, put back to front, transpose, turn over, turn round, turn upside down, up-end

review *n* 1 analysis, assessment, fresh look, reassessment, reconsideration, re-examination, rethink. 2 (write a review) appreciation, commentary, criticism, critique, evaluation, judgment,

report, study, write-up

review *v* 1 (review a decision) look again at, reassess, reconsider, reexamine, rethink, think over. 2 (review a performance) analyze, appraise, assess, criticize, evaluate, judge, write a review of. 3 (review the year) look back on, look back over, recall, recollect, reflect on, remember, survey

reviewer *n* commentator, critic, judge

revise *v* 1 (revise your opinion) alter, amend, change, modify, reconsider, review. 2 (revise your work) correct, edit, improve, redraft, rephrase, rewrite, update. 3 (revise for a test) brush up, cram *inf*, learn, read, reread, study

revision *n* 1 alteration, amendment, change, correction, modification, rewriting, updating. 2 homework, reading, studying

revival *n* reawakening, rebirth, renaissance, renewal, resurgence, resurrection, return, upsurge

revive *v* 1 (revive a person) bring round, give the kiss of life to *inf*, resuscitate, rouse. 2 (sb revives) come back to life, come round, come to, rally, recover, regain consciousness. 3 (a drink to revive you) cheer, invigorate, refresh, revitalize, strengthen. 4 (revive memories) awaken, call forth, rekindle, stir up

revolt *n* civil war, coup, insurgency, insurrection, mutiny, rebellion, revolution, rising, uprising

revolt *v* 1 defect, disobey, mutiny, rebel, resist, riot, rise up, take to the streets. 2 (sth revolts you) appall, disgust, make your flesh creep, make you sick,

nauseate, offend, repel, sicken,
turn your stomach

revolting adj abhorrent, disgusting,
distasteful, foul, horrible, nasty,
nauseating, obnoxious, obscene,
offensive, repellent, repugnant,
repulsive, shocking, sickening, vile

revolution n 1 coup, coup d'état,
insurgency, mutiny, putsch, rebellion,
revolt, rising, uprising. 2 change,
reorganization, shift, transformation,
upheaval, U-turn inf. 3 circle, circuit,
cycle, gyration, orbit, rotation, round,
spin, turn

revolutionary adj 1 (revolutionary
methods) avant-garde, different, drastic,
experimental, groundbreaking,
innovative, new, novel, progressive,
radical; opp conservative.

2 (revolutionary forces) extremist,
insurgent, mutinous, rebel, subversive

revolve v circle, go round, gyrate, orbit,
rotate, spin, swivel, turn, turn round,
twist, wheel, whirl

revulsion n abhorrence, aversion,
disgust, distaste, hate, hatred,
loathing, repugnance

reward n award, bonus, decoration, gift,
honor, medal, payment, present, prize,
remuneration, tribute

reward v compensate, decorate, give a
reward to, honor, pay, recompense,
remunerate, tip

rewarding adj beneficial, fulfilling,
gratifying, productive, profitable,
satisfying, useful, valuable, worthwhile;
opp unrewarding

rhetoric n eloquence, expressiveness, gift
of the gab inf, oratory, rhetorical

language, speechifying, verbosity

rhetorical adj bombastic, extravagant,
flamboyant, florid, flowery, high-flown,
insincere, longwinded, ostentatious,
pretentious, showy, verbose, wordy

rhyme n ditty, doggerel, jingle, ode,
poem, poetry, song, verse

rhythm n accent, beat, cadence, flow, lilt,
meter, movement, pattern, pulse, stress,
swing, tempo, time

rhythmic adj flowing, harmonious,
lilting, measured, melodious, metrical,
musical, pulsating, regular, repeated,
rhythmical, steady, throbbing

rich adj 1 affluent, flush inf, loaded inf,
made of money inf, moneyed,
prosperous, wealthy, well-heeled inf,
well-off, well-to-do; opp poor. 2 (rich
furnishings) costly, elaborate, elegant,
expensive, exquisite, fine, gorgeous,
grand, lavish, opulent, palatial, precious,
splendid, sumptuous, valuable;
opp simple. 3 (rich ground) abundant,
ample, copious, fertile, fruitful, lush,
luxurious, plentiful, productive, prolific;
opp poor. 4 (an area rich in wildlife)
abounding, full, overflowing, replete,
rife, teeming, well-provided, well-
stocked, well-supplied. 5 (rich food)
cloying, creamy, delicious, fattening,
fatty, full-flavored, heavy, savory, spicy,
succulent, sweet, tasty; opp light.
6 (rich sounds) deep, full, mellow,
melodious, resonant; opp thin.
7 (a rich red) brilliant, deep, intense,
strong, vivid, warm

riches n affluence, assets, fortune, gold,
money, possessions, property, resources,
treasure, wealth; opp poverty

rid v **1** cleanse, clear, deliver, free, purge, purify, relieve, rescue, save, unburden. **2 get rid of** destroy, dispose of, do away with, dump, eject, eliminate, expel, jettison, remove, throw away, unload

riddle n brainteaser inf, conundrum, enigma, mystery, poser, problem, puzzle, question

ride n drive, journey, joyride inf, lift, outing, spin inf, trip

ride v **1** float, gallop, go, journey, move, progress, travel, trot. **2** (ride a bicycle) be mounted on, control, handle, manage, mount, pedal, sit on, steer

ridicule n derision, irony, laughter, mockery, sarcasm, satire, scorn, sneering, teasing, taunting

ridicule v be sarcastic about, caricature, deride, humiliate, jeer at, laugh at, make jokes about, mock, parody, poke fun at, satirize, sneer at, taunt, tease

ridiculous adj **1** (a ridiculous story) amusing, crazy, droll, farcical, funny, humorous, illogical, incredible, ludicrous, nonsensical, preposterous, surreal, unbelievable. **2** (you look ridiculous) absurd, comical, foolish, funny, hilarious, silly, weird. **3** (a ridiculous price) crazy, derisory, laughable, ludicrous, outrageous, shocking, stupid, unreasonable; **opp** reasonable

rife adj abundant, common, general, predominant, prevalent, rampant, ubiquitous, universal, widespread; **opp** rare

rift n **1** (a physical rift) breach, break, chink, cleft, crack, crevice, fault, fissure, opening, split. **2** (a rift in a family) breach, difference, disagreement, division, feud, quarrel, separation

rig v **1** equip, fit, fit out, furnish, provide, set up, supply. **2** (rig the results) arrange, engineer, fake, falsify, fix inf, manipulate, tamper with. **3 rig up** assemble, build, cobble together, construct, improvise, knock up, throw together

right adj **1** (what you did was right) correct, decent, equitable, fair, good, honest, honorable, just, lawful, moral, proper, virtuous; **opp** wrong. **2** (the right time) accurate, correct, exact, precise, true; **opp** wrong. **3** (at the right moment) appropriate, convenient, ideal, opportune, proper; **opp** wrong. **4** (the right thing to wear) appropriate, decent, fit, proper, seemly, suitable; **opp** inappropriate. **5** (do sth the right way) best, good, normal, preferable, preferred, recommended, sensible, usual; **opp** wrong

right n **1** (fight for your rights) claim, due, entitlement, freedom, interest, privilege. **2** (have the right to do sth) authority, license, permission, power, prerogative. **3** (have right on your side) decency, good, goodness, honor, justice, lawfulness, morality, reason, truth, virtue; **opp** wrong

right v **1** (make sth right) amend, correct, fix, make amends for, put right, put to rights, rectify, redress, remedy, repair, settle, sort out, straighten out. **2** (right a fallen chair) pick up, set upright, stand upright, straighten up

right adv **1** directly, in a straight line, straight. **2** directly, immediately,

promptly, quickly, straightaway.
3 (it fell right off the table) all the way, altogether, completely, quite, totally, utterly. **4** (right on the nose) exactly, slap-bang *inf*, precisely, squarely.
5 (not doing it right) appropriately, correctly, properly, satisfactorily, suitably.
6 (treating her right) equitably, fairly, honestly, honorably, justly.
7 (work out right) advantageously, favorably, for the best, fortunately, to your advantage, well

righteous *adj* blameless, ethical, fair, God-fearing, good, honest, honorable, just, law-abiding, moral, pure, sanctimonious, upright, upstanding, virtuous; *opp* immoral

rightful *adj* authorized, bona fide, correct, lawful, legal, legitimate, proper, real, true

rigid *adj* **1** (rigid ideas) firm, fixed, hard and fast, harsh, inflexible, rigorous, set, strict, unalterable, unrelenting; *opp* flexible. **2** (rigid materials) hard, inelastic, inflexible, solid, stiff, strong, taut, unbending; *opp* flexible

rigor *n* **1** hardship, harshness, rigidity, severity, sternness, strictness, toughness. **2** (do sth with rigor) accuracy, meticulousness, precision, thoroughness

rigorous *adj* challenging, demanding, exacting, hard, harsh, meticulous, painstaking, scrupulous, severe, strict, stringent, thorough, tough

rim *n* border, brim, brink, circumference, edge, lip, margin, perimeter, verge

rind *n* crust, husk, outer layer, peel, skin

ring *n* **1** band, circle, circlet, disk, halo, loop, round. **2** arena, enclosure, rink.

3 alliance, band, clique, gang, gathering, group, knot, league, mob, organization, syndicate. **4** (telephone call) bell *inf*, buzz *inf*, call, phone call *inf*, telephone call. **5** (sound of bells) buzz, chime, clang, clink, jangle, jingle, peal, ping, ringing, tinkle, tolling

ring *v* **1** buzz, chime, clang, clink, ding-dong, jangle, jingle, peal, ping, sound, toll. **2** echo, resonate, resound, reverberate. **3** (telephone) call, phone *inf*, telephone. **4** (make a ring around sth) circle, encircle, enclose, fence in, hem in, put a ring around, surround

rinse *v* bathe, clean, cleanse, dip, flush, sluice, swill, wash, wash out, wet

riot *n* **1** anarchy, chaos, confusion, disorder, lawlessness, pandemonium, rioting, tumult, turbulence, upheaval, uproar, violence. **2** brawl, demonstration, fight, fracas, free-for-all, mutiny, protest, scuffle, rebellion, revolt, uprising

riot *v* brawl, fight, go berserk, go wild, mutiny, rampage, rebel, revolt, rise up, run amok, run wild, take to the streets

riotous *adj* **1** (a riotous crowd) anarchic, disorderly, lawless, mutinous, rebellious, rowdy, uncontrollable, unruly, violent. **2** (a riotous evening) boisterous, hilarious, loud, noisy, unrestrained, uproarious, wild

rip *n* gash, hole, opening, slit, split, tear

rip *v* **1** (rip sth to shreds) cut, gash, lacerate, pull apart, rupture, shred, slit, split, tear. **2** (rip sth out of sb's hands) grab, pull, snatch, wrench, yank

ripe *adj* **1** full-grown, mature, mellow, ready, ready to eat. **2** auspicious, favorable, ideal, opportune, right, suitable, timely

ripen v age, become ripe, come to maturity, develop, grow ripe, mature, mellow

rise n 1 advance, escalation, improvement, increase, jump, leap, upsurge, upswing, upturn; *opp* drop, fall. 2 ascent, bank, elevation, hill, incline, ramp, ridge, upward slope. 3 increment, pay increase

rise v 1 get to your feet, get up, leap up, stand up, surface *inf*, wake up. 2 (go upward) ascend, climb, come up, go up, levitate, lift, mount, move up, take off; *opp* descend. 3 (of prices) escalate, go up, increase, rocket, soar, spiral; *opp* fall. 4 (of sounds) become louder, grow, increase, intensify, soar, swell; *opp* fall. 5 (rise in the firm) advance, be promoted, do well, progress, prosper. 6 (of a road) climb, get steeper, go uphill, slope upward; *opp* descend. 7 (of a tower) loom, soar, stand out, tower. 8 (of water) come up, get deeper, get higher, swell; *opp* fall. 9 (of a river) begin, flow from, issue from, originate, spring

risk n 1 chance, danger, likelihood, possibility. 2 danger, hazards, jeopardy, peril, speculation, uncertainty. 3 (it's a risk) gamble, venture

risk v 1 (risk losing) chance, dare, hazard, take the risk of, venture. 2 (risk your life) endanger, gamble with, imperil, jeopardize, put at risk

risky adj chancy *inf*, dangerous, fraught with danger, hazardous, perilous, precarious, touch-and-go, tricky,

uncertain, unsafe; *opp* safe

rite n ceremony, custom, observance, practice, ritual, service, tradition

ritual adj 1 ceremonial, customary, formal, prescribed, traditional. 2 (habitual) customary, habitual, prescribed, regular, routine, set

ritual n 1 ceremony, custom, observance, practice, rite, tradition. 2 (routine) ceremony, habit, procedure, routine

rival adj competing, conflicting, enemy, opposing, opposite, warring; *opp* friendly

rival n adversary, antagonist, challenger, competitor, contender, contestant, enemy, opponent, opposition; *opp* friend, helper, teammate

rival v be as good as, challenge, compete with, equal, match up to, measure up to, oppose, parallel, vie with

rivalry n adversary, competition, competitiveness, conflict, contention, hostility, opposition; *opp* cooperation, friendliness

road n avenue, bypass, drive, expressway, freeway, highway, lane, roadway, route, street, thoroughfare

roam v prowl, ramble, range, tramp, travel, walk, wander

roar v 1 bawl, bellow, blare, boom, crash, cry, rumble, shout, thunder, yell. 2 (laugh) guffaw, hoot, howl with laughter, kill yourself laughing, laugh, split your sides *inf*

rob v 1 break into, burgle, hold up, loot, mug, pick sb's pocket, raid, ransack, rifle, steal from, steal, thieve. 2 cheat, con, rip off *inf*, swindle

robber n bandit, burglar, cat burglar, housebreaker, looter, mugger, pickpocket, shoplifter, thief

robbery n breakin, burglary, embezzlement, fraud, holdup, housebreaking, larceny, looting, misappropriation, mugging, pilfering, raid, shoplifting, stealing, theft

robe n attire, ceremonial dress, costume, gown, vestment

robot n android, automaton, computer-controlled machine, humanoid, machine

robust adj 1 hardy, powerful, rugged, strong, sturdy, tough, vigorous, well-made. 2 practical, pragmatic, realistic, sensible, sound, strong

rock n boulder, crag, outcrop, reef, stone

rock v 1 lurch, move to and fro, pitch, sway, teeter, totter, wobble. 2 astound, shake, shock, stagger, startle, stun, take by surprise

rocky adj 1 bumpy, craggy, pebbly, rough, rugged, stony. 2 iffy inf, shaky, uncertain, unstable, unsteady, wobbly

rod n bar, baton, pole, shaft, stick, wand

rogue n cheat, con-man, crook, fraud, rascal, scoundrel, sharper

role n 1 capacity, contribution, function, job, position, task. 2 (in a play) character, part

roll n 1 ball, bobbin, cylinder, furl, round, scroll, spool, tube, tube, twist. 2 (rolling movement) cycle, revolution, rotation, spin, turn, twirl. 3 (register) census, directory, inventory, list, listing, record, register, schedule. 4 (rumble) boom, reverberation, roar, rumble

roll v 1 coil, curl, furl, go round, revolve, rotate, somersault, spin, tumble, turn, twirl, wheel, wind. 2 (of a ship) lurch,

pitch, reel, rock, toss. 3 (flatten) compact, compress, flatten, level out, press down, press, smooth

romance n 1 intrigue, love affair, love, passion, relationship. 2 love story, romantic fiction. 3 adventure, fascination, glamour

romantic adj 1 affectionate, amorous, emotional, lovey-dovey inf, loving, passionate, sentimental, soppy inf, tender; *opp* unromantic. 2 dreamy, exciting, fabulous, fairy-tale, glamorous, idealistic, impractical, starry-eyed; *opp* down-to-earth, practical

room n 1 capacity, elbow-room, space, volume. 2 (scope) capacity, freedom, latitude, leeway, margin, opportunity, scope. 3 accommodation, bedroom, place to stay

roomy adj baggy, big, extensive, large, sizable, spacious, voluminous; *opp* small

root n 1 rhizome, taproot, tuber. 2 (the root of a problem) basis, bottom, cause, core, crux, germ, origin, seat, source, starting point

root v 1 germinate, sprout, take root. 2 (search) forage, root around, rummage, scrabble, search. 3 root out cut out, destroy, dig out, discover, eliminate, eradicate, get rid of, remove, search out, unearth, uproot, weed out

rope n cable, cord, guy, halter, hawser, line, tether, towrope

rot n 1 canker, decay, decomposition, mold, putrefaction. 2 (nonsense) drivel inf, garbage inf, gibberish, nonsense, rubbish, tripe inf

rot v crumble, decay, decompose, disintegrate, fester, go bad, go off, go sour, mold, perish, putrefy

rota n list, roster, schedule, timetable

rotate v 1 go round, pivot, revolve, spin, swirl, swivel, turn, twirl, wind.
2 alternate, come round, do in turn, recur, share, take turns at

rotten adj 1 (decaying) addled, bad, decaying, foul, moldering, off inf, perished, putrid, rotting, sour; **opp** fresh.
2 (terrible) awful, bad, disappointing, dismal, foul inf, inferior, lousy inf, miserable, nasty, poor, terrible; **opp** terrific, wonderful. 3 (ill) bad, ill, off color, poorly, rough inf, sick, under the weather, unwell; **opp** fine, well

rough adj 1 bumpy, coarse, jagged, rocky, rugged, scratchy, stony, uneven; **opp** smooth. 2 (a rough estimate) approximate, crude, estimated, general, quick, raw, rudimentary, sketchy, vague; **opp** detailed, exact, precise. 3 (of a person) badly behaved, brusque, curt, ill-mannered, loutish, rowdy, rude, surly; **opp** refined. 4 (of work, conditions) arduous, hard, heavy-handed, severe, spartan, tough, unfair, unjust, violent. 5 (of a voice) grating, gruff, harsh, hoarse, husky, rasping; **opp** smooth, soft. 6 (of the sea) choppy, heavy, stormy, wild; **opp** calm. 7 (ill) bad, ill, off color, poorly, rotten inf, sick, under the weather, unwell; **opp** fine, well

round adj ball-shaped, bulbous, circular, curved, cylindrical, disk-shaped, globular, rounded, spherical, spheroid

round n 1 ball, band, circle, disk, globe, ring, sphere. 2 (in sport or competitions) bout, cycle, game, heat, level, series, session, stage. 3 (of a doctor or guard) beat, circuit, lap, route, tour, turn

round v (go round) circle, circumnavigate, come round, go round, skirt, turn

roundabout adj circuitous, devious, evasive, indirect, longwinded, meandering, oblique, rambling, tortuous; **opp** direct

rouse v 1 (stir up) arouse, awaken, egg on inf, galvanize, incite, inflame, kindle, provoke, rally, stimulate, stir up, whip up, work up; **opp** calm, discourage.
2 (rouse sb) awaken, wake up, waken

rousing adj electrifying, energetic, exciting, fervent, lively, moving, spirited, stimulating, stirring, vigorous; **opp** dull, flat, lifeless, uninspiring

rout n conquest, defeat, drubbing, overthrow, thrashing; **opp** victory

rout v conquer, crush, defeat, drive off, hammer inf, overthrow, thrash, trounce

route n course, crossing, itinerary, journey, path, run, way

routine adj 1 common, everyday, familiar, habitual, ordinary, regular, standard, usual; **opp** special, unusual.
2 (dull) boring, dull, monotonous, predictable, run-of-the-mill, tedious, unexciting; **opp** exciting

routine n 1 custom, drill, formula, habit, pattern, procedure, program, system.
2 act, patter, performance, piece, set

row n (line) chain, column, file, line, procession, queue, rank, series, string, tier

row n 1 (argument) altercation, argument, controversy, disagreement, dispute, quarrel, scrap, spat, squabble, tiff, wrangle. 2 (noise) commotion, din, fracas, hubbub, hullabaloo, noise, racket, rumpus, uproar

row v argue, bicker, quarrel, squabble, wrangle

rowdy adj badly behaved, boisterous, loutish, noisy, rough, unruly, wild; **opp** quiet, well-behaved

royal adj imperial, majestic, princely, regal, sovereign, stately

rub v 1 buff, clean, polish, scour, scrub, shine, smooth, wipe. 2 (stroke) caress, fondle, massage, stroke. 3 (chafe) abrade, chafe, scrape, wear away. 4 apply, put on, smear, spread. 5 **rub out** cancel, delete, efface, erase, remove, rub off, wipe out

rubbish adj 1 (nonsense) balderdash, claptrap, drivel, gobbledegook, nonsense, rot inf. 2 (refuse) debris, detritus, dross, garbage, junk, litter, rubble, scrap, trash, waste, refuse

ruddy adj blushing, crimson, florid, flushed, healthy, pink, red, rosy, scarlet

rude adj 1 abusive, bad-mannered, cheeky, discourteous, disrespectful, impertinent, impolite, insolent, insulting, offensive, offhand, short, uncivil, uncouth; **opp** polite. 2 (of a joke) blue, coarse, crude, dirty, naughty, obscene, risqué, smutty, vulgar; **opp** clean

rudeness n bad manners, cheek, cheekiness, coarseness, discourtesy, disrespect, impertinence, impudence, insolence, offensiveness, vulgarity; **opp** courtesy, good manners, politeness

rudimentary adj basic, crude, early, elementary, primitive, simple;

opp sophisticated

rudiments n basic principles, basics, essentials, foundations, fundamentals, nuts and bolts

ruffian n bully, hooligan, lout, rowdy, scamp, thug, tough

ruffle v 1 disturb, mess up, ripple, rumple, stir, tousle. 2 agitate, annoy, disconcert, disturb, fluster, irritate, nettle inf, put out, rattle inf, unsettle, upset

rugged adj barren, craggy, hard, harsh, rocky, rough, tough, weatherbeaten, weathered

ruin n bankruptcy, collapse, defeat, destitution, destruction, downfall, end, failure, havoc, insolvency, undoing, wreck, wreckage

ruin v bankrupt, bring down, defeat, demolish, destroy, devastate, mess up, shatter, smash, spoil, wreck

ruined adj bankrupt, crumbling, derelict, destroyed, dilapidated, in ruins, insolvent, ramshackle, spoiled, uninhabitable, wrecked

ruinous adj catastrophic, crippling, crushing, devastating, dire, disastrous, fatal, injurious, shattering

rule n 1 axiom, code, direction, formula, guideline, law, maxim, order, principle, regulation, ruling, standard, statute, tenet. 2 (control) administration, authority, command, control, dominion, government, management, power, regime, reign, sovereignty, supervision

rule v 1 decide, decree, determine, find, judge, lay down, order, pronounce. 2 (govern) administer, be in power, be on the throne, control, govern, hold the reigns, lead, manage, reign, run.

3 rule out disallow, discount, dismiss, disqualify, eliminate, exclude, preclude, prohibit, reject

ruler n chief, dictator, emperor, governing body, government, governor, head of state, king, leader, monarch, potentate, president, queen, regent, sovereign

ruling adj controlling, dominant, in power, leading, reigning, supreme

ruling n adjudication, decision, decree, finding, judgment, pronouncement, verdict

rumor n dirt inf, gossip, grapevine, hearsay, lowdown inf, news, scandal, story, talk, the latest

run n **1** canter, gallop, jog, sprint, trot. **2** (a journey) drive, journey, outing, ride, route, spin inf, trip. **3** (a series) period, round, series, spell, stretch, succession. **4** enclosure, pen

run v **1** bolt, charge, dash, gallop, hotfoot it inf, hurry, jog, race, scurry, sprint, tear. **2** (run a company) administer, control, direct, govern, head, lead, manage, operate, supervise. **3** (function) behave, function, go, operate, perform, work. **4** (trains run every hour) go, move, operate, pass, travel. **5** (extend) continue, extend, go, last, lie, reach, stretch. **6** (run for office) apply, be a candidate, compete, go in for, put your name forward, stand, take part. **7** (flow) cascade, discharge, dribble, flow, gush, pour, spill, spout, stream, trickle. **8** (drip) dissolve, drip, go soft, melt. **9 run away** abscond, escape, leave home, bolt, run off, make off. **10 run over** (look at sth again) go through, look through, recap, recapitulate, repeat, run through.

11 run over (knock down) hit, knock down, knock over, run down. **12 run over** (of liquid) overflow, spill over

runner n **1** athlete, harrier, jogger, sprinter. **2** shoot, sprout, sucker, tendril

running adj **1** consecutive, continual, continuous, in a row, incessant, on the trot, ongoing, perpetual, successive, uninterrupted. **2** (running water) flowing, moving; **opp** still

rupture n **1** breach, break, cleft, fracture, split, tear. **2** hernia. **3** (disagreement) break, disagreement, division, feud, quarrel, rift, schism

rupture v breach, break, burst, divide, fracture, separate, sever, split, tear

rural adj agrarian, agricultural, countrified, country, countryside, pastoral, rustic; **opp** urban

rush n bustle, charge, dash, flood, haste, hurry, panic, race, scramble, speed, sprint, stampede, surge, urgency

rush v bolt, charge, dart, dash, flood, fly, get a move on, hotfoot it inf, hurry, move fast, race, run, scramble, shoot, speed, sprint, stampede, surge, tear, zoom

rust n corrosion, oxidation

rust v corrode, oxidize

rustic adj agrarian, agricultural, countrified, country, countryside, pastoral, rural

rustle n crackle, hiss, swish, whisper

rustle v crackle, hiss, swish, whisper

rusty adj **1** corroded, oxidized, rusted. **2** (out of practice) below par, neglected, not up to scratch inf, out of practice, poor, stale, weak. **3** brick-red, chestnut, coppery, reddish-brown, rust-colored

rut *n* 1 furrow, gouge, groove, gutter, hollow, track, trough, wheel mark.
2 **in a rut** at a dead end, bored, in a routine, on the treadmill, stuck in the daily grind

ruthless *adj* brutal, callous, cold, cruel, harsh, heartless, inhuman, merciless, pitiless, savage, severe, unfeeling, unrelenting, violent

sabotage *n* damage, destruction, subversion, vandalism, wrecking

sabotage *v* attack, damage, destroy, disable, put out of action, thwart, vandalize, wreck

sack *n* 1 dismissal, notice, redundancy, the ax, the boot *inf*, your cards. 2 bag, totebag

sack *v* ax, discharge, dismiss, downsize, fire, give sb the boot *inf*, give sb the push *inf*, give sb the sack, give sb his marching orders *inf*, lay off, make redundant, terminate sb's contract

sacred *adj* blessed, consecrated, devotional, divine, godly, hallowed, heavenly, holy, inviolate, religious, revered, sacrosanct, sanctified, spiritual

sacrifice *n* 1 loss, relinquishment, renunciation, surrender. 2 offering

sacrifice *v* forfeit, forego, give up, lose, offer, relinquish, renounce, surrender

sacrilege *n* blasphemy, desecration, disrespect, godlessness, heresy, irreverence, profanity, violation

sacrosanct *adj* inviolable, non-negotiable, protected, sacred, untouchable

sad *adj* 1 (unhappy) brokenhearted, crestfallen, dejected, depressed, desolate, despondent, disappointed, distressed, down in the dumps *inf*, down *inf*, grief-stricken, heartbroken, low, miserable, tearful, unhappy, upset; *opp* cheerful, happy. 2 (a sad story) depressing, distressing, heartbreaking, heartrending, moving, poignant, touching, tragic, upsetting; *opp* cheerful, heartwarming. 3 (unsatisfactory) bad, deplorable, disastrous, disgraceful, miserable, pitiful, regrettable, sorry, unfortunate, unsatisfactory, wretched; *opp* excellent

sadden *v* break sb's heart, depress, disappoint, dishearten, dismay, distress, make unhappy, upset; *opp* cheer

sadistic *adj* barbarous, brutal, cruel, heartless, inhuman, perverted, savage

sadness *n* dejection, depression, despondency, disappointment, grief, heartache, misery, regret, sorrow, unhappiness; *opp* happiness

safe *adj* 1 (unharmed) all right, in one piece, intact, out of danger, safe and sound, unharmed, unhurt, uninjured. 2 (of a place) impregnable, protected, secure; *opp* dangerous. 3 (harmless) fit for human consumption, good, harmless, healthy, nontoxic, pure, tried and tested, uncontaminated, wholesome; *opp* dangerous, harmful. 4 (reliable) careful, cautious, conservative, dependable, prudent, reliable, trustworthy, unadventurous

safe n repository, safety deposit box, strongbox, vault

safeguard n defense, guarantee, insurance, precaution, protection, security, shield, surety

safeguard v foster, guard, keep safe, look after, preserve, protect, secure, watch over

safety n dependability, protection, reliability, sanctuary, security, shelter

sag v bend, dip, droop, drop, fall, flop, give, hang down, sink, slump, wilt

sail v 1 cruise, go sailing, put to sea, set sail, steam, tack. 2 captain, navigate, pilot, skipper. 3 (sail into the room) drift, float, fly, glide, skim, soar, sweep, waltz

sailor n marine, mariner, seafarer, seaman, skipper

saintly adj angelic, blessed, devout, God-fearing, godly, good, holy, pious, pure, religious, righteous, virtuous

sake n account, advantage, benefit, good, interest, purpose, reason

salary n earnings, fee, income, pay, remuneration, stipend, take-home pay, wage

sale n auction, deal, marketing, retailing, selling, trade, traffic, transaction

salient adj chief, conspicuous, important, main, noticeable, obvious, principal, prominent, striking; **opp** irrelevant, minor

sallow adj pale, pallid, pasty, sickly, unhealthy-looking, wan, yellowish; **opp** rosy, ruddy

salt adj brackish, saline, salted, salty

salute n acknowledgment, greeting, homage, recognition, salutation, tribute

salute v acknowledge, greet, honor, pay tribute to, praise, take your hat off to inf

salvage v reclaim, recover, redeem, rescue, restore, resurrect, retrieve, save

salvation n reclamation, recovery, redemption, rescue, saving

same adj 1 alike, corresponding, duplicate, equal, equivalent, identical, interchangable, like, matching, parallel, similar, twin; **opp** different. 2 changeless, consistent, constant, unchanging, uniform, unvarying

sample n example, foretaste, specimen, swatch, taster, trailer, trial pack

sample v taste, try out, try

sanctify v 1 anoint, bless, canonize, consecrate, dedicate, make holy, purify. 2 approve, authorize, legitimize, license, permit, sanction, support; **opp** forbid

sanctimonious adj goody-goody inf, holier-than-thou, pious, self-righteous, smug, superior

sanction n 1 agreement, approval, authority, authorization, backing, consent, endorsement, the go-ahead, permission, seal of approval, support, the green light inf, the thumbs up inf. 2 penalty, punishment, sentence. 3 ban, boycott, embargo, penalty, restriction

sanction v allow, approve, authorize, back, endorse, give sth the thumbs up inf, give the go-ahead to, give sth the green light inf, okay inf, permit, support; **opp** forbid, prevent

sanctity n devotion, godliness, holiness, righteousness, sacredness, saintliness, spirituality, virtue

sanctuary n 1 asylum, cover, haven, protection, refuge, safety, shelter.

2 animal sanctuary, conservation area, nature reserve, protected area, reservation, reserve. 3 altar, chapel, church, holy place, sanctum, temple

sane adj all there inf, balanced, in possession of all your faculties, in your right mind, lucid, of sound mind, rational, reasonable, right-minded, stable; **opp** insane, mad

sanitary adj clean, germfree, healthy, hygienic, pure, salubrious, sterile, uncontaminated; **opp** dirty, unhealthy, unhygienic

sanity n common sense, good sense, level-headedness, normality, rationality, reason

sap n life force, life-blood, vigor, vitality

sarcasm n derision, irony, mockery, satire, scoffing, scorn

sarcastic adj caustic, derisive, ironic, mocking, sardonic, satirical, scoffing, scornful

satire n burlesque, caricature, irony, mockery, parody, ridicule, sarcasm, skit, spoof inf, take-off inf

satirical adj caustic, ironical, irreverent, mocking, sarcastic, sardonic

satirize v caricature, make fun of, mock, parody, poke fun at, take off inf

satisfaction n 1 comfort, contentment, enjoyment, fulfillment, gratification, pleasure, pride; **opp** dissatisfaction. 2 compensation, justice, redress, reparation, vindication

satisfactory adj acceptable, adequate, all right, average, fair, good enough, not bad, okay, passable, quite good, reasonable, sufficient, suitable, up to scratch inf; **opp** poor,

unacceptable, unsatisfactory

satisfy v 1 (satisfy a need or requirement) answer, comply with, fulfill, meet, resolve, supply. 2 (satisfy sb's hunger or thirst) assuage, gratify, quench, satiate, suffice. 3 (convince sb) convince, make happy, persuade, placate, put sb's mind at rest, reassure

saturate v douse, drench, permeate, soak, steep, suffuse, wet

sauce n dressing, coulis, condiment, gravy

saucy adj cheeky, nervy, sauciness

savage adj 1 (wild) fierce, primitive, uncivilized, untamed, wild; **opp** tame. 2 (vicious) barbaric, brutal, cruel, ferocious, ruthless, vicious, violent

save v 1 (keep) collect, conserve, hoard, hold on to, invest, keep, put aside, put away, put back, reserve, stash away, stockpile, store. 2 (economize) cut costs, cut expenditures, economize, find savings, make cuts, make economies. 3 (rescue) bail out, conserve, defend, deliver, free, preserve, protect, rescue, safeguard, salvage, screen, shield. 4 (save you from having to do sth) make unnecessary, prevent, spare, stop

savings n capital, funds, investments, nest egg, piggy bank inf, reserves

savior n champion, fairy godmother, friend in need, Good Samaritan, guardian angel, knight in shining armor, rescuer

savor v appreciate, enjoy, luxuriate in, relish, revel in, wallow in

savory adj 1 piquant, salty, spicy, tangy. 2 appetizing, delicious, mouthwatering, scrumptious inf, tasty

say *n* 1 (have your say) chance to speak, opinion, right to speak, two cents' worth. 2 (have no say) authority, influence, input, part, sway, voice, vote

say *v* 1 (refuse to say the word) enunciate, mention, mouth, pronounce, utter, voice. 2 (say that sth is true) affirm, allege, announce, assert, claim, come out with *inf*, declare, maintain, put about *inf*, report, state, suggest. 3 (say how you feel) articulate, communicate, convey, enunciate, express, intimate, make known, put into words, tell. 4 answer, comment, declare, exclaim, remark, reply, respond, retort. 5 (say a prayer) deliver, read, read out, recite, repeat

saying *n* 1 adage, axiom, dictum, maxim, motto, precept, proverb. 2 catchphrase, cliché, expression, formula, slogan

scale *n* 1 calibration, gradation, graduation, measuring system, steps. 2 hierarchy, ladder, order, pecking order *inf*, ranking, spectrum, spread. 3 (on a large/small/grand scale) degree, extent, range, scope, way. 4 (in music) octave, sequence, series. 5 (rough skin) dandruff, flake, plate, scurf

scale *v* ascend, clamber up, climb, climb up, go up, mount, scramble up

scamper *v* dart, dash, frisk, frolic, gambol, romp, run, scoot, scuttle

scan *v* 1 check, examine, gaze at, investigate, look at, pore over, scrutinize, search, stare at, study, survey, sweep. 2 (look at writing) flick through, flip through, have a look at, leaf through, glance over, look over, read, read through, run your eye over, skim, skim through

scandal *n* 1 crime, impropriety, misconduct, offense, sin, transgression. 2 (a political scandal) outrage, sensation. 3 (cause a scandal) disgrace, dishonor, disrepute, embarrassment, ignominy, infamy, notoriety, reproach, shame. 4 (gossip) backbiting, defamation, dirt, gossip, muckraking, rumor, slander, slur, talk, tittle-tattle

scandalize *v* affront, appall, cause raised eyebrows, disgust, horrify, offend, outrage, shock, upset

scandalous *adj* 1 disgraceful, disgusting, odious, immoral, indecent, outrageous, shameful, shocking, sordid. 2 defamatory, libelous, scurrilous, slanderous

scanty *adj* inadequate, insufficient, limited, meager, measly, paltry, poor, restricted, scant, skimpy

scar *n* 1 blemish, brand, discoloration, disfigurement, mark. 2 (emotional scar) damage, injury, trauma

scar *v* 1 blemish, brand, discolor, deface, disfigure, mark. 2 (mentally) affect, damage, injure, leave its mark, leave scars, traumatize, upset

scarce *adj* at a premium, few and far between, hard to come by *inf*, hard to find *inf*, inadequate, infrequent, in short supply, insufficient, lacking, rare, scanty, seldom seen, short, sparse, uncommon, unusual, wanting

scarcely *adv* barely, hardly, only just

scare *n* alarm, alert, fright, horror, shock, terror

scare v alarm, daunt, frighten, give sb a fright, intimidate, make sb afraid, make sb jump inf, panic, petrify, put the fear of God into sb inf, startle, terrify, terrorize, unnerve

scared adj alarmed, fearful, frightened, nervous, panicky, panicstricken, petrified, shaken, startled, terrified

scary adj alarming, frightening, hairraising, horrifying, petrifying, terrifying

scathing adj biting, caustic, critical, cutting, harsh, sarcastic, scornful, severe, stinging, trenchant, withering

scatter v 1 (scatter things) diffuse, disseminate, fling, litter, shower, sow, spread, sprinkle, strew, toss about. 2 (people scatter) break up, disband, disperse, go off in all directions, separate

scene n 1 area, locality, location, place, position, setting, site, spot. 2 landscape, panorama, prospect, scenery, view, vista. 3 backdrop, background, location, set, setting. 4 (make a scene) carry-on inf, commotion, disturbance, furor, fuss, row, tantrum, to-do, upset. 5 picture, sight, spectacle. 6 (not my scene) area of interest, field, interest, milieu, sphere, world. 7 (of a play or film) act, clip, episode, part, section, sequence

scenery n 1 landscape, panorama, surroundings, terrain, view, vista. 2 backdrop, set, stage set, setting

scenic adj beautiful, breathtaking, lovely, picturesque, pretty, spectacular

scent n 1 aroma, bouquet, fragrance, odor, perfume, smell. 2 (an animal's scent) spoor, track, trail. 3 (perfume) cologne, fragrance, perfume, toilet water

scent v 1 be on the trail of, follow the scent of, nose out, smell, sniff, sniff out. 2 become aware of, detect, discern, get wind of, recognize, sense, sniff out

schedule n 1 agenda, calendar, diary, itinerary, plan, program, timetable. 2 catalog, inventory, list, register

schedule v arrange, arrange a time, book, fix a time, organize, plan, program, slot in, time, timetable

scheme n 1 course of action, plan, procedure, program, project, strategy, system, tactics. 2 blueprint, design, draft, layout, outline, plan, project, proposal. 3 arrangement, organization, system. 4 conspiracy, intrigue, machinations, plot, ploy, racket inf, ruse, stratagem

scheme v collude, conspire, intrigue, maneuver, plan, plot

scheming adj artful, calculating, conniving, cunning, Machiavellian, sly, underhand, wily

scholar n 1 academic, egghead inf, intellectual, learned person, man of letters, pundit, woman of letters. 2 pupil, schoolboy, schoolgirl, student

scholarly adj 1 (of a person) academic, bookish, erudite, intellectual, learned, lettered, studious, well-read. 2 (of a piece of work) academic, rigorous, scientific, well-documented, well-argued, well-researched

scholarship n 1 academic achievement, education, erudition, knowledge, learning, letters. 2 bursary, endowment, exhibition, fellowship, grant

school n 1 academy, college, educational establishment, educational institution, seminary. **2** adherents, circle, devotees, disciples, followers, group, movement, pupils, set. **3** (school of thought) belief, creed, faith, outlook, persuasion, opinion, point of view, school of thought, way of thinking

schooling *n* **1** education, formal education, instruction, learning, teaching, tuition. **2** coaching, drill, grounding, instruction, preparation, training

science *n* **1** branch of knowledge, discipline, organized knowledge, systematic study. **2** art, skill, technique

scientific *adj* analytical, controlled, methodical, rational, regulated, rigorous, systematic

scintillating *adj* bright, brilliant, dazzling, flashing, flickering, lively, sparkling, stimulating, vivacious

scoff *v* **1** be sarcastic, be scornful, gibe, jeer, sneer. **2** (eat) bolt, devour, finish off, guzzle, polish off *inf*. **3** scoff at belittle, deride, despise, disparage, flout, laugh at, mock, poke fun at, pooh-pooh *inf*, ridicule, scorn

scold *v* bawl out *inf*, berate, blame, castigate, chide, give sb a talking-to, haul over the coals, lecture, nag, rap over the knuckles, read the riot act to, rebuke, reprimand, reproach, reprove, tell off, tick off

scoop *v* bail, dig, excavate, gouge, hollow, ladle, scrape, shovel, spoon

scoop *n* **1** dipper, ladle, spoon. **2** (in a newspaper) exclusive, exposé, inside story, revelation

scope *n* **1** area, compass, competence, extent, field, limit, range, reach, span,

sphere, terms of reference. **2** capacity, chance, elbow-room, freedom, latitude, leeway, liberty, opportunity, room, room to maneuver

scorch *v* blacken, blister, burn, char, dry up, parch, sear, singe, shrivel

scorching *adj* baking, boiling, fiery, flaming, red-hot, roasting, searing, sizzling, sweltering, very hot; *opp* freezing

score *n* **1** count, marks, points, result, sum, tally, total **2** (on a surface) gash, gouge, groove, mark, scrape, scratch. **3** (a score to settle) a bone to pick, grievance, grudge. **4** know the score be aware of the situation, know the facts, know what's what

score *v* **1** achieve, chalk up, gain, gain a point, get a goal, notch up, win. **2** add up, count, keep count, keep a record, keep score, record. **3** (score the surface of sth) gash, gouge, mark, scrape, scratch

scorn *n* contempt, derision, disdain, disparagement, mockery, sarcasm

scorn *v* **1** be above, deride, disdain, disparage, flout, look down on, mock, scoff at, slight, treat with contempt; *opp* admire. **2** (scorn sb) rebuff, refuse, reject, spurn, turn down, turn your nose up at *inf*; *opp* accept

scornful *adj* contemptuous, derisive, disdainful, haughty, insolent, mocking, sarcastic, slighting, sneering, snide *inf*, superciliou, superior; *opp* respectful

scoundrel *n* good-for-nothing, heel *slang*, miscreant, rascal, reprobate, rogue, ruffian, villain

scour *v* **1** abrade, clean, rub, scrub, wash.

2 (search) comb, go over, hunt through, ransack, rummage through, search, turn upside down *inf*

scourge *n* affliction, bane, burden, curse, evil, infliction, misery, misfortune, plague, punishment, terror, torment, visitation

scout *n* advance guard, escort, lookout, outrider, spy, vanguard

scowl *v* frown, glare, glower, grimace

scramble *v* 1 clamber, climb, crawl, scurry, struggle. 2 compete, contend, jockey, jostle, push, rush, strive, struggle, vie

scrap *n* 1 bit, fragment, grain, offcut, part, particle, piece, remnant, snippet, trace. 2 (of food) bit, bite, crumb, grain, morsel, mouthful, scraping. 3 (scrap merchant) junk, rejects, rubbish, waste. 4 (fight) argument, brawl, clash, fight, quarrel, row, scuffle, set-to, squabble, tiff

scrap *v* 1 chuck *inf*, demolish, discard, drop, get rid of, jettison, shed, throw away, throw on the scrap heap, write off. 2 (fight) argue, bicker, fall out *inf*, fight, quarrel, scuffle, squabble

scrape *n* 1 abrasion, graze, laceration, scratch, wound. 2 grating, grinding, rasping, scratch, scratching, squeak. 3 mark, scuff, scratch. 4 (awkward situation) escapade, mischief, prank, trouble. 5 difficulty, fix *inf*, mess, plight, predicament, tight corner, tight spot, trouble

scrape *v* 1 abrade, bark, graze, lacerate, rub, scratch, scuff, skin. 2 grate, grind, rasp, scratch, squeak. 3 clean, erase, file, remove, rub, scour, scrub

scratch *v* 1 abrade, bark, claw, cut, graze, mark, score, scrape, wound. 2 delete, eliminate, pull out, withdraw

scratch *n* 1 abrasion, cut, graze, wound. 2 line, mark, scrape. 3 **up to scratch** acceptable, adequate, competent, good enough, okay *inf*, satisfactory, up to standard

scream *v* bawl, cry, howl, screech, shriek, squall, squeal, wail, yell, yowl

scream *n* 1 cry, howl, screech, shriek, squeal, wail, yell, yowl. 2 (a real scream) barrel of laughs *inf*, hoot *inf*, laugh, riot

screen *n* 1 awning, blind, canopy, curtain, shade. 2 guard, protection, shelter, shield. 3 camouflage, cloak, cover, disguise, facade, front, shield, veil. 4 divider, partition

screen *v* 1 guard, protect, shade, shelter, shield. 2 camouflage, conceal, disguise, hide, mask, veil. 3 (of people) check, examine, investigate, test, vet

screw *v* rotate, tighten, turn, twist, work

scribble *v* dash off, doodle, jot down, scrawl

script *n* 1 (of a play or film) book, libretto, lines, screenplay, text, words. 2 hand, handwriting, writing

scripture *n* Bible, good book, gospel, holy writ, sacred writings, word of God

scrounge *v* beg, cadge, sponge

scrounger *n* beggar, cadger, freeloader, parasite, sponger

scrub *v* 1 clean, rub, scour, wash. 2 abandon, call off, cancel, do away with, drop, give up

scruffy *adj* 1 (of a person) disheveled, ragged, shabby, slovenly, tattered,

unkempt, untidy. **2** (of a place)
disreputable, rundown, shabby, squalid,
untidy

scruples *n* compunction, conscience,
doubt, hesitation, misgiving, qualm,
second thought, twinge of conscience

scrupulous *adj* **1** ethical, fair, honest,
honorable, moral, principled, proper,
upright. **2** careful, conscientious,
diligent, fastidious, finicky, meticulous,
painstaking, precise, punctilious,
rigorous, strict, thorough

scrutinize *v* check, examine, explore,
inspect, investigate, look at closely,
peruse, scan, search, study

scrutiny *n* check, checking,
examination, exploration, inspection,
investigation, perusal, search, study

scum *n* **1** dross, film, froth, grime.
2 dregs of society, rabble, riffraff

scurrilous *adj* **1** abusive, defamatory,
insulting, libelous, slanderous.
2 coarse, foul, gross, indecent, low,
obscene, offensive, vile, vulgar

sea *n* **1** ocean, the briny, the deep,
the waves. **2** (a sea of people) expanse,
host, mass, multitude, plethora,
profusion, sheet. **3** **at sea** at a loss,
baffled, bewildered, confused, lost,
mystified, perplexed

seal *v* **1** close up, cork, fasten, make
airtight, make watertight, plug, secure,
stick down, stop, stopper, stop up.
2 (decide sth) clinch, decide, finalize,
secure, settle. **3** **seal off** close off, cordon
off, isolate, quarantine, segregate

seal *n* **1** badge, crest, emblem, insignia,
mark, sign, symbol. **2** (seal of approval)
assurance, authentication, confirmation,

guarantee, ratification, warrant,
warranty

seam *n* **1** stitching. **2** layer, lode,
stratum, thickness, vein

search *n* **1** check, examination,
inspection, look, probe, scrutiny.
2 hunt, inquiry, investigation, pursuit,
quest. **3** **in search of** hunting for, in
pursuit of, looking for, on the lookout
for, on the track of, seeking

search *v* **1** comb, examine, explore, go
over, go over with a fine-tooth comb,
go through, hunt through, investigate,
poke about, pry, ransack, rummage
through, sift through, turn inside out,
turn upside down. **2** (search sb) check,
examine, frisk, inspect, scrutinize.
3 **search for** ferret about for, hunt
for, look for, seek, try to find

searching *adj* **1** (a searching look)
discerning, intense, intent, keen,
penetrating, piercing, sharp.
2 (searching questions) analytic,
close, penetrating, probing, thorough

season *n* period, phase, spell, term, time,
time of year

season *v* **1** add flavoring to, add
seasoning to, flavor, salt, spice.
2 add spice to, add zest to, color,
enliven, leaven, liven up, pep up

seasonable *adj* appropriate, opportune,
suitable, timely, well-timed

seasoning *n* condiment, dressing,
flavoring, herbs, herbs and spices,
pepper, salt, salt and pepper, spice

seat *n* **1** bench, chair, pew, settle, stool.
2 (place where sth is based) capital,
center, headquarters, heart, hub,
location, place, site, situation

seat v 1 place, put, settle. 2 (the room seats 50) accommodate, have room for, have seating for, hold, take

seating n accommodation, chairs, places, room, seats

secluded adj 1 concealed, cut off, hidden, inaccessible, isolated, lonely, off the beaten track, out of the way, remote, solitary, tucked away. 2 cloistered, private, sequestered, sheltered, shut away

second adj 1 (in time, sequence) added, additional, duplicate, extra, following, further, later, next, other, repeated, subsequent, succeeding. 2 (in importance) assistant, deputy, inferior, junior, lesser, lower, secondary, second-best, second-class, subordinate, supporting, vice-

second n 1 flash, instant, jiffy *inf*, minute *inf*, moment, split second, twinkling of an eye, wink of an eye. 2 assistant, backer, helper, right-hand man, supporter

second v 1 approve, back, endorse, side with, support, take sb's side. 2 assign, move, post, relocate, transfer

secondary adj 1 inferior, less important, lesser, minor, subordinate, subsidiary. 2 (not happening or experienced directly) auxiliary, by-, at one remove, derivative, derived, indirect, second-hand; *opp* primary. 2 (of schools) high, senior; *opp* primary

secret adj clandestine, concealed, confidential, covert, esoteric, hidden, mysterious, private, undercover, undisclosed, unknown

secret n coded message, confidence, mystery, skeleton in the closet

secretary n administrative assistant, clerk, gofer *inf*, PA, personal assistant, typist

secrete v 1 discharge, exude, generate, produce. 2 conceal, hide, hoard, palm, put away, salt away *inf*, sequester, spirit away, tuck away

secretive adj enigmatic, furtive, mysterious, reticent, sly, sneaky *inf*, surreptitious, suspicious, uncommunicative; *opp* open

sect n 1 cult, denomination, faith, religion. 2 camp, caucus, clique, faction, grouping, party, splinter group

sectarian n bigot, extremist, partisan, racist, segregationist, zealot

section n 1 area, division, part, portion, region, segment, sector, unit. 2 (of an organization) branch, department, division, group, subdivision, unit. 3 (of text) paragraph, part, passage, stretch, subsection

sector n 1 area, district, division, section, territory, ward, zone. 2 (sector of industry) area, branch, division, part, section, subdivision, type

secular adj 1 civil, humanist, lay, non-religious, profane, temporal, worldly; *opp* religious

secure adj 1 (of objects, goods) fastened, locked, locked up, secured, tight, unbreakable. 2 (in a particular position) fast, firm, fixed, held in place, stable, supported; *opp* insecure. 3 (of a person, place) impregnable, invulnerable, protected, safe, unassailable, untouchable; *opp* insecure

secure v 1 (secure an object) anchor,

batten down, bind, bolt, fasten, fix, fortify, lock, make safe, padlock, reinforce, tie, tighten. 2 (keep a place secure) defend, guard, protect, safeguard. 3 (get sth) achieve, acquire, gain, get, get hold of, insure, make certain, obtain, procure

security n asylum, defense, protection, refuge, safety, shelter

sedate adj calm, composed, decorous, deliberate, dignified, majestic, slow, solemn, staid, stately, unhurried; *opp* frantic

sedative adj anodyne, calming, hypnotic, narcotic, relaxing, sleep-inducing, soothing, tranquilizing

sedentary adj desk-bound, inactive, seated, sitting, stationary; *opp* active

sediment n alluvium, deposit, dregs, grounds, lees, residue, silt

seduce v 1 (attract sb) attract, charm, entice, flirt with, flutter her eyelashes at inf, tempt. 2 (sexually) bed, corrupt, debauch, deflower, get sb into bed, have your evil way with inf, lead sb astray

seductive adj alluring, appealing, attractive, bedroom, charming, come-hither, enticing, erotic, flirtatious, ravishing, sexy, tempting

see v 1 behold, catch sight of, descry, discern, distinguish, espy, glimpse, have before your eyes, look, make out, note, notice, observe, perceive, sight, spot, spy, view, watch, witness. 2 (have an image, idea in your mind) conceive, foresee, imagine, picture, visualize. 3 (understand) appreciate, apprehend, comprehend, fathom, follow, grasp,

perceive, realize, understand. 4 (see many things during your life) bear witness to, encounter, experience, go through, meet, meet with. 5 (have a meeting with sb) consult, go out with, go to, have a date with, have an appointment with, interview, meet, rendezvous with, spend time with, visit. 6 (see sb somewhere) accompany, come with, conduct, drive, escort, go with, run inf, take. 7 **see about** consider, inquire, investigate, look into, think about. 8 **see through** (see through sb) be wise to, have no illusions about, not be deceived by, not be taken in by, penetrate, unmask. 9 **see through** (see sth through) complete, endure, finish, go all the way, keep at, persevere with, persist with, see out, stick out inf. 10 **see to** attend to, busy yourself with, concern yourself with, concentrate on, deal with, occupy yourself with, organize, see about, turn your attention to

seed n 1 ear, germ, grain, pip, stone. 2 (the seeds of sth) beginning, cause, germ, origin, root, source

seedy adj decaying, dilapidated, faded, disreputable, dubious, gone to seed, grubby, rundown, shabby, sleazy inf, squalid

seek v be after, be on the lookout for, chase after, go in search of, hunt, look for, pursue, search for, want

seem v appear, feel, give the impression, look, sound

seethe v be agitated, be angry, be furious, be in a rage, be incensed, be livid, boil, foam at the mouth, fume, rage, simmer

segment n chunk inf, part, portion, section, sector, share

segregate v divide, keep apart, isolate, quarantine, separate, sort; **opp** mix

seize v 1 grab, lay hands on, pick up, snatch, take hold of. 2 (seize a criminal) apprehend, arrest, capture, catch, nab inf, take, take away. 3 (seize goods) confiscate, sequestrate, take, take away. 4 seize up crash, freeze, get stuck, give out, grind to a halt, stick, stiffen

seizure n 1 (of a criminal) arrest, capture. 2 (of goods) confiscation. 3 (medical) apoplexy, attack, convulsion, fit, paroxysm, spasm, stroke, turn inf

select v choose, cull, draw, elect, pick, pick out, prefer, sample

selection n assortment, choice, collection, range, sample, set

selective adj 1 careful, choosy, discriminating, discerning, fastidious, finicky inf, fussy inf, particular, picky inf. 2 (a selective account of events) biased, discriminatory, edited, incomplete, misleading, unbalanced; **opp** balanced

self-centered adj egoistic, egotistical, selfish, self-absorbed, self-interested, self-obsessed, self-regarding, self-seeking, smug, vain

self-confident adj assured, brash, cocky inf, confident, self-assured, sure of yourself, swaggering

self-conscious adj discomfited, embarrassed, ill at ease, shy, uncomfortable

self-esteem n confidence, dignity, pride, self-confidence, self-image, self-respect

self-evident adj axiomatic, clear, natural, obvious, plain, self-explanatory

selfish adj egoistic, egotistical, greedy, mean, mercenary, miserly, self-centered, self-interested, self-seeking; **opp** altruistic, generous

selfless adj altruistic, generous, heroic, magnanimous, modest, self-effacing, self-sacrificing; **opp** selfish

self-respect n confidence, dignity, pride, self-confidence, self-esteem, self-image

self-righteous adj holier-than-thou, pious, pompous, pontificating, sanctimonious, sententious, vain

sell v 1 cash in, dispose of, export, find a buyer for, get rid of, offload inf; **opp** buy. 2 (have sth to sell) advertise, deal in, dispense, have for sale, hawk inf, put on sale, offer, stock, trade in, vend

seller n commercial traveler, hawker, merchant, sales rep inf, sales representative, salesman, shopkeeper, vendor; **opp** buyer

send v 1 (send a letter, parcel) consign, despatch, export, forward, mail, post, put in the mail, relay, send off, ship; **opp** receive. 2 (send sth into the air) drive, force, kick, propel, throw. 3 (send sb somewhere) assign, force, order, post, second, throw. 4 (send a signal, electronic message) beam, broadcast, emit, send out, transmit; **opp** receive. 5 send for ask for, call, call in, call up, order, request, summon; **opp** send away

senile adj confused, demented, doddering, forgetful, gaga inf, in their dotage, in their second childhood, old, soft in the head inf, rambling, raving, suffering from Alzheimer's disease

senior adj elder, first, high, outranking,

ranking, superior, top; *opp* junior

sensation *n* 1 experience, feeling, impression, perception, sense. 2 animation, commotion, controversy, excitement, shock, stir, surprise

sensational *adj* 1 amazing, astonishing, extraordinary, incredible, surprising, unexpected. 2 brilliant *inf*, excellent, exciting, fabulous *inf*, fantastic *inf*, great, magnificent, marvelous, stupendous *inf*, thrilling, wonderful. 3 (sensational journalism) exaggerated, lurid, melodramatic, over-the-top, sensationalist, tabloid, titillating

sense *n* 1 (physical, mental attribute) ability, faculty, feel, feeling, instinct, gift, perception, reflex, sensitivity, talent. 2 (a sense of sth about to happen) awareness, feeling, gut feeling, hunch, instinct, intuition, perception, sensation, sixth sense. 3 (have the sense to do sth) common sense, foresight, gumption *inf*, intelligence, judgment, understanding, wisdom, wit. 4 (the sense of a word) connotation, denotation, implication, import, meaning, reference

sense *v* be aware of, be conscious of, detect, experience, feel, intuit, perceive

senseless *adj* 1 asleep, comatose, out cold *inf*, unconscious. 2 absurd, crazy, daft *inf*, fatuous, foolish, futile, half-witted, idiotic, illogical, inane, irrational, ludicrous, mad, meaningless, mindless, nonsensical, pointless, ridiculous, silly, stupid, useless; *opp* sensible

sensibility *n* delicacy, emotions, feelings, finer feelings, sensitivity

sensible *adj* intelligent, judicious, logical, meaningful, practical, rational, sober, wise; *opp* foolish, stupid

sensitive *adj* 1 (feeling emotions deeply) delicate, easily hurt, emotional, feeling, highly strung, touchy. 2 (sensitive to the problems involved) alert, attuned, aware, conscious, in tune, perceptive, responsive, sympathetic; *opp* insensitive. 3 (of a measuring instrument) accurate, delicate, finely tuned, reactive, responsive

sensual *adj* 1 (of pleasure) bodily, carnal, fleshly, material, physical, sexual, tactile; *opp* intellectual. 2 (arousing pleasure) arousing, attractive, exciting, sensuous, sexy, titillating, voluptuous. 3 (seeking pleasure) debauched, decadent, hedonistic, lascivious, lustful, pleasure-seeking

sensuous *adj* curvaceous *inf*, curvy, sensual, sinuous, sleek, slinky, smooth, voluptuous, sexy

sentence *n* 1 proposition, question, statement. 2 decree, decision, edict, judgment, order, penalty, punishment, term of imprisonment, verdict

sentence *v* condemn, decree, imprison, judge, order, penalize, pronounce sentence, punish

sentiment *n* 1 attitude, feeling, judgment, opinion, view, way of thinking, wish. 2 compassion, emotion, pathos, pity, sadness, sensibility, sympathy, tenderness

sentimental *adj* emotional, exaggerated, gooey *inf*, gushing, pathetic, sad, sickly, sloppy, tear-jerking

sentry *n* guard, lookout, sentinel,

soldier, watchman

separable *adj* detachable, divisible, removable, separate; *opp* inseparable

separate *adj* 1 (two separate parts) detached, disconnected, discrete, distinct, divided, independent, individual, separable, separated, unattached. 2 (a separate subject) different, in its own right, other, unconnected, unrelated

separate *v* 1 (separate two things) break up, cut off, divide, detach, disconnect, dissociate, divorce, isolate, part, pull apart, segregate, sever, sort, split, sunder, take apart, tear asunder. 2 (sth separates into two) break up, come apart, diverge, divide, fork, split. 3 (of a couple) become estranged, break up, divorce, go their separate ways, lead separate lives, live apart, part, part company, split, split up

separated *adj* divorced, estranged, living apart

separation *n* break, breakup, divorce, estrangement, parting, parting of the ways, rift, split

septic *adj* festering, gangrenous, infected, poisoned, suppurating

sequel *n* aftermath, consequence, continuation, fall-out, follow-up, repercussion

sequence *n* continuation, list, order, procedure, progression, series, succession

serene *adj* calm, content, happy, peaceful, placid, quiet, untroubled

series *n* array, column, group, list, row, sequence, set, succession

serious *adj* 1 (a serious matter, decision) critical, crucial, far-reaching, grave, important, life-and-death, major, momentous, of consequence, pressing, significant, urgent, vital, weighty; *opp* trivial. 2 (a serious illness) acute, bad, chronic, critical, dangerous, grave, grievous, life-threatening, severe; *opp* mild. 3 (not laughing) austere, dour, earnest, grave, humorless, long-faced, pensive, poker-faced *inf*, prim and proper, severe, sober, solemn, somber, stern, thoughtful, unsmiling. 4 (not joking) earnest, genuine, honest, in earnest, sincere, truthful. 5 (serious about doing sth) determined, earnest, firm, in earnest, resolute, resolved

sermon *n* 1 (in church) address, discourse, homily, preaching, speech. 2 admonishment, homily, lecture, lesson, reprimand, scolding, talking-to *inf*

servant *n* assistant, butler, companion, drudge *inf*, employee, factotum, flunkey, footman, housekeeper, lackey, maid, menial, minion, retainer, secretary, slave, valet; *opp* master, mistress

serve *v* 1 (serve a customer) assist, attend to, deal with, help, see to, wait on. 2 (serve food) bring, dole out *inf*, give out, ladle, serve up, spoon. 3 (be a servant to) assist, be employed by, be in sb's employ, help, work for. 4 (serve a purpose) aid, answer, help, be useful for, fulfill, satisfy

service *n* 1 (official, public) authority, body, brigade, bureau, department, force, institution, network, office, organization, unit, utility. 2 (offered by an organization) aid, amenity, assistance, benefit, facility, help, opportunity, product, support, system. 3 (in a shop, restaurant) assistance, attentiveness, help. 4 (in a particular job or cause) assistance, dedication, devotion, duty, employment, help, labor, record, work. 5 (in a church) ceremony, rite, ritual, sacrament. 6 (for a car) adjustment, check, examination, maintenance, overhaul, repairs

service v adjust, check, check over, examine, give sth the once-over inf, maintain, overhaul, repair

serviceable adj adequate, in good repair, practicable, usable, useful

servile adj cringing, groveling, humble, ingratiating, obsequious, slavish, submissive, unctuous

session n 1 period, sitting, spell, stretch, time. 2 assembly, conference, discussion, hearing, meeting, sitting

set adj 1 definite, definitive, determinate, firm, fixed, inflexible, permanent, pre-arranged, pre-ordained, prescribed, rigid, unalterable, unchanging; **opp** vague. 2 (set to do sth) about to, on the point of, prepared to, primed to, ready to, soon to. 3 (set on doing sth) bent, determined, earnest, intent, resolute, resolved, stubborn

set n 1 array, assemblage, assortment, batch, collection, combination, lot, group, series, suite. 2 (type) category, class, genus, group, kind, range, type

set v 1 apply, arrange, locate, lodge, put, place, plant, position, rest, situate, station. 2 (set a clock, machine) adjust, calibrate, prepare, regulate, start, synchronize. 3 (set a time, date) agree, appoint, arrange, decide, determine, fix, schedule, specify. 4 (set sb a task) allocate, assign, designate, give, prescribe, present. 5 (a substance sets) coagulate, congeal, crystallize, gel, harden, solidify, stiffen, thicken. 6 (of the sun, moon) descend, go down, sink; **opp** rise. 7 **set about** approach, begin, deal with, do, get on with, get to grips with, go about, organize, plan, start, tackle. 8 **set in** become established, begin, establish itself, start, take hold, take root. 9 **set off** (start a journey) depart, leave, set forth, set out, set sail, start, start off. 10 **set off** (an explosion, an argument) cause, explode, ignite, initiate, instigate, provoke, spark, spark off, trigger, trigger off. 11 **set out** (set things out) arrange, display, exhibit, lay out, present. 12 **set out** (set out to do sth) aim, aspire, attempt, intend, plan, set your sights on, try. 13 **set up** arrange, construct, equip, establish, install, organize, prepare, put in place

setback n complication, delay, difficulty, disappointment, failure, holdup, obstacle, problem, tribulation, vicissitude

setting n 1 backdrop, background, context, decor, location, milieu, scene, scenery, situation, surroundings. 2 (the settings of a machine) adjustment, attribute, calibration, option, property, timing

settle v 1 agree, arrange, conclude, decide, resolve, reconcile, sort inf, sort out. 2 (settle a bill, debt) clear, defray, discharge, liquidate, pay, pay off, redeem, repay, square. **3** (settle in a place) camp, colonize, ensconce yourself *inf*, establish yourself, go to live, install yourself, occupy, people, populate, put down roots, set up home. **4** (of snow) be precipitated, come to rest, lie, stick. **5 settle down** calm down, make yourself at home, make yourself comfortable, relax. **6 settle for** accept, agree to, be content with, be satisfied with

settlement *n* **1** agreement, compact, concordat, pact, reconciliation, resolution. **2** colony, community, encampment, habitation, hamlet, township, village

sever *v* break, chop, cut, cut off, disconnect, dissociate, part, pull apart, separate, snip, split

severe *adj* **1** bad, bitter, dangerous, drastic, extreme, fierce, great, heavy, intense, serious, violent; *opp* mild, minor. **2** (severe test) arduous, demanding, difficult, exacting, hard, rigorous, stringent, taxing, tough. **3** (of punishment) cruel, hard, harsh, oppressive, pitiless, rigid, rigorous, strict, stringent; *opp* lenient. **4** (of sb's character, appearance) austere, cold-hearted, dour, forbidding, grim, humorless, intimidating, serious, sober, solemn, stern, unsmiling; *opp* friendly

sew *v* crochet, embroider, darn, knit, mend, stitch

sex *n* **1** femininity, masculinity, gender, sexuality. **2** coitus, copulation, fornication, hanky-panky *inf*, intercourse, intimacy, it *inf*, love-making, mating, penetration,

physical love, roll in the hay *inf*, sexual activity, sexual intercourse, sexuality

sexual *adj* erotic, genital, marital, physical, reproductive, sensual, sex-related

sexuality *n* **1** eroticism, libido, lust, sensuality, sex, sex drive. **2** inclinations, proclivities, sexual orientation, sexual preference, tastes

sexy *adj* alluring, arousing, attractive, enticing, erotic, ravishing, seductive, sensual, sensuous

shabby *adj* **1** dilapidated, dingy, dirty, dowdy, drab, faded, frayed, gone to seed, grubby, moth-eaten, ragged, rundown, old, scruffy, seedy, tatty *inf*, threadbare, worn; *opp* neat, smart. **2** base, contemptible, deceitful, despicable, discreditable, dishonest, dishonorable, disreputable, grubby, ignoble, lowdown *inf*, mean, nasty, shameful, shoddy, sordid, squalid, treacherous, unfair, ungenerous, unkind, unscrupulous, unworthy; *opp* noble

shade *n* **1** dark, darkness, gloom, penumbra, shadow, shelter; *opp* light. **2** (of color) degree, intensity, nuance, tinge, tint, variation

shade *v* cloud, conceal, cover, darken, dim, hide, mask, obscure, screen, shadow, shield, shroud, veil; *opp* expose

shadow *n* **1** outline, shape, silhouette. **2** (in the shadows) darkness, dimness, gloom, obscurity, shade; *opp* daylight. **3** (no shadow of a doubt) hint, suggestion, suspicion, touch, trace. **4** (cast a shadow over sb) cloud, gloom, sadness, unhappiness

shadowy adj 1 dark, dim, dusky, gloomy, murky, obscure, shaded; **opp** well-lit. 2 (a shadowy figure) dreamlike, faint, ghostly, nebulous, obscure, phantom, unreal, vague; **opp** distinct

shady adj 1 cool, leafy, shaded, sheltered; **opp** sunny. 2 (a shady character) crooked, disreputable, dubious, fishy inf, shifty, slippery, suspicious, untrustworthy; **opp** trustworthy

shaft n 1 (a mine shaft) duct, flue, mine, passage, pit, tunnel, well. 2 (shaft of light) beam, gleam, laser, pencil, ray, streak. 3 (shaft of a golf club) handle, pole, post, rod, shank, stem, upright

shaggy adj bushy, disheveled, hairy, hirsute, long-haired, tousled, unkempt, unshorn, woolly; **opp** clean-shaven

shake v 1 agitate, bump, convulse, jar, quiver, rattle, rock, shiver, shudder, sway, totter, tremble, vibrate, waver, wobble. 2 (shake your fist) brandish, flourish, wave. 3 **shake up** alarm, distress, disturb, frighten, perturb, rattle, ruffle, shock, throw inf, unnerve, unsettle, upset; **opp** comfort, reassure

shaky adj 1 (take your first shaky steps) doddering, faltering, feeble, insecure, precarious, quivery, shaking, staggering, teetering, tottering, trembling, unstable, unsteady, weak, wobbly; **opp** confident. 2 decrepit, dilapidated, flimsy, precarious, ramshackle, rickety, rocky, unstable, unsteady, weak, wobbly; **opp** robust

shallow adj empty-headed, facile, foolish, frivolous, glib, ignorant, insincere, puerile, silly, simple, superficial,

unintelligent, unthinking; **opp** thinking

sham n counterfeit, fake, forgery, fraud, hoax, imitation, pretense

shambles n chaos, confusion, disarray, disorder, disorganization, mess, muddle; **opp** order

shame n condemnation, discredit, disgrace, dishonor, disrepute, humiliation, ignominy, infamy, loss of face, reproach, scandal, smear, stigma, vilification; **opp** pride

shame v condemn, discredit, disgrace, dishonor, humiliate, lose face, reproach, smear, stigmatize, vilify

shamefaced adj ashamed, embarrassed, guilty, humiliated, mortified, penitent, red-faced inf, remorseful, repentant, shamed, sorry; **opp** proud

shameful adj atrocious, base, contemptible, deplorable, despicable, disgraceful, indecent, low, mean, outrageous, reprehensible, scandalous, wicked; **opp** noble

shameless adj audacious, brash, brazen, corrupt, depraved, immodest, improper, indecent, unabashed, unashamed, undisguised, unprincipled, unself-conscious, wanton; **opp** modest

shape n 1 configuration, contours, cut, figure, form, format, formation, lines, model, mold, outline, pattern. 2 (of a person) body, build, figure, physique, profile, silhouette. 3 (in good shape) condition, fettle, health, kilter, state

shape v 1 (shape an object) carve, cast, create, cut, fashion, form, make, model, mould, produce. 2 (shape a plan) define, develop, devise, organize, plan, prepare

shapeless *adj* amorphous, formless, irregular, nebulous, undeveloped, unshaped, unstructured, vague; *opp* well-defined

share *n* allocation, allotment, allowance, assignment, cut, division, helping, part, percentage, portion, proportion, quota, ration, serving

share *v* allocate, allot, apportion, assign, deal out, distribute, divide, halve, quarter, split

sharp *adj* 1 (of a knife) jagged, pointed, serrated, spiky; *opp* blunt. 2 (a sharp bend) abrupt, acute, angular, hairpin, sudden, tight; *opp* wide. 3 (of a person) alert, astute, bright, clever, incisive, intelligent, observant, perceptive, quick, quick-witted, shrewd, smart; *opp* slow. 4 (a sharp pain) acute, cutting, intense, piercing, severe, shooting, stabbing, stinging, violent; *opp* nagging, slight. 5 (a sharp image) clear, crisp, distinct, focused, well-defined; *opp* unclear. 6 (a sharp tongue) bitter, critical, curt, cutting, harsh, hurtful, sarcastic, sardonic, scathing, severe, venomous, vitriolic; *opp* kind. 7 (a sharp taste) acid, acrid, caustic, hot, piquant, pungent, tangy, tart; *opp* bland

sharpen *v* file, grind, hone; *opp* blunt

shatter *v* blast, break, burst, crack, crush, demolish, disintegrate, explode, fracture, smash, splinter, split, wreck

shed *v* 1 (shed leaves, skin) cast off, discard, drop, molt, slough; *opp* grow. 2 (shed workers) dismiss, fire *inf*, get rid of, make redundant, sack *inf*; *opp* take on

sheen *n* brightness, glaze, gleam, glint, gloss, luster, polish, reflection, shimmer, shine, sparkle; *opp* dullness

sheepish *adj* bashful, coy, embarrassed, guilty, meek, reticent, self-conscious, shy, timid, uncomfortable; *opp* brazen

sheer *adj* 1 (a sheer drop) abrupt, perpendicular, precipitous, sharp, steep, vertical; *opp* gradual. 2 (sheer stupidity) complete, downright, out-and-out, plain, pure, total, unqualified, utter. 3 (sheer material) filmy, fine, flimsy, gauzy, see-through, thin, translucent, transparent; *opp* thick

sheet *n* 1 (a sheet of snow) blanket, coat, covering, film, layer, veneer. 2 (a sheet of glass) pane, panel, piece, plate, slab. 3 (a sheet of paper) folio, leaf, page, piece

shell *n* 1 case, casing, covering, husk, pod. 2 (of a ship) chassis, framework, hull, structure

shell *v* attack, barrage, blitz, bomb, bombard, strike, torpedo

shelter *n* 1 (a shelter for the homeless) haven, refuge, retreat, sanctuary. 2 (look for shelter) defense, protection, refuge, safety, sanctuary, security

shelter *v* conceal, defend, enclose, guard, harbour, hide, keep safe, protect, safeguard, shield

sheltered *adj* 1 (of a place) protected, screened, secluded, shaded, shady, shielded,; *opp* exposed. 2 (of sb's life) cloistered, protected, quiet, unadventurous, unexciting, withdrawn; *opp* full

shelve *v* defer, delay, postpone, put off, put on ice, put on the back burner, suspend; *opp* continue

shield n barrier, cover, defense, guard, protector, safeguard, screen

shield v cover, defend, guard, keep safe, protect, safeguard, screen; *opp* expose

shift n 1 (in your opinion) about-turn, adjustment, alteration, change, modification, reversal, sea change, switch, transfer, variation. 2 (the night shift) crew, gang, group, team, workforce

shift v 1 budge, displace, move, relocate, reposition; *opp* remain. 2 (shift your opinion) adjust, alter, change, modify, reverse, switch, transfer, vary; *opp* maintain

shifty adj crooked, disreputable, dodgy *inf*, dubious, fishy *inf*, shady, slippery, suspicious, untrustworthy; *opp* trustworthy

shimmer v flicker, gleam, glint, glisten, glow, sparkle, twinkle

shine n brightness, glare, gleam, glisten, glitter, glow, shimmer, sparkle, twinkle; *opp* dullness

shine v 1 beam, blaze, dazzle, flash, glare, gleam, glisten, glitter, glow, radiate, shimmer, sparkle, twinkle. 2 (shine at sth) be excellent, be exceptional, be outstanding, do well, excel, stand out

shiny adj bright, burnished, gleaming, glistening, glittering, glossy, lustrous, polished, shimmering, shinning, sparkling, twinkling; *opp* dull

ship n boat, craft, cruiser, destroyer, ferry, frigate, liner, steamer, tanker, trawler, vessel, yacht

ship v carry, convey, deliver, ferry, send, transport

shirk v avoid, dodge, duck, evade, get out of, play truant, shun, sidestep, skive

shiver v quake, quiver, shake, shudder, tremble

shock n 1 (come as a shock) blow, bombshell, thunderbolt, trauma, upset. 2 (a feeling of shock) astonishment, distress, fright, offense, outrage, revulsion

shock v astonish, astound, daze, disquiet, distress, frighten, give sb a turn *inf*, horrify, jar, jolt, offend, outrage, revolt, shake, sicken, stagger, startle, stun, stupefy, traumatize, unsettle

shocking adj appalling, astounding, atrocious, awful, disgraceful, distressing, foul, ghastly, hideous, horrific, obscene, offensive, outrageous, revolting, scandalous, sickening, terrible, upsetting

shoddy adj cheap, inferior, poor, rubbishy *inf*, second-rate, shabby, slipshod, tacky *inf*, trashy *inf*; *opp* quality

shoot v 1 (shoot sb) bag, bring down, gun down, hit, injure, kill, shell, snipe at, wound. 2 (shoot a gun) aim, discharge, fire, launch. 3 (shoot out of the room) bolt, charge, dart, dash, fly, hurtle, leap, race, rush, speed, streak, tear; *opp* saunter

shop n boutique, chain store, department store, outlet, retailer, seller, store, supermarket, wholesaler

shore n bank, beach, coast, oceanfront, oceanside, sands, water's edge, waterside

short adj 1 (a short speech) abbreviated, abridged, brief, compact, compressed, concise, pithy, succinct, summarized, terse, truncated; *opp* long. 2 (of a person) diminutive, little, midget, petite, pint-sized *inf*, slight, small, squat; *opp* tall. 3 (a short break) brief, cursory, fleeting, momentary, passing, quick, short-lived, transitory; **opp** long. **4** (in short supply) deficient, inadequate, insufficient, lacking, low, scarce, sparse, tight, wanting; **opp** plentiful

shortage n dearth, deficiency, deficit, inadequacy, insufficiency, lack, scarcity, shortfall, want; **opp** excess

shortcoming n bad thing, defect, drawback, failing, fault, flaw, frailty, imperfection, limitation, weakness, weak point; **opp** strength

shorten v abbreviate, abridge, compress, condense, contract, curtail, cut, decrease, dock, lessen, prune, reduce, shrink, summarize, trim, truncate; **opp** lengthen

short-sighted adj **1** myopic, near-sighted; **opp** long-sighted. **2** careless, ill-advised, ill-considered, imprudent, injudicious, rash, unthinking, unwary, unwise; **opp** sensible

short-tempered adj crabby inf, fiery, hot-tempered, impatient, irascible, irritable, quick-tempered, touchy; **opp** patient

shot n **1** (take a shot) fling, hurl, lob, pot shot, throw. **2** (fire a shot) ammunition, bullet, lead, missile, pellet, slug inf. **3** (hear a shot) blast, crack, explosion, gun fire. **4** (have a shot at sth) attempt, bash inf, crack inf, effort, endeavor, go inf, guess, stab inf, try, turn

shout v ball, bellow, call, cheer, clamor, cry, holler inf, rant, roar, scream, screech, shriek, yell; **opp** whisper

shove v barge, drive, elbow, force, nudge, press, prod, push, shoulder, thrust

shovel v clear, dig, excavate, ladle, scoop, shift, spoon

show n **1** (go to see a show) concert, drama, gig inf, pageant, parade, performance, play, production. **2** (a car show) demonstration, display, exhibition, expo inf, exposition, fair, presentation. **3** (for show) affectation, appearance, display, facade, illusion, ostentation, pose, pretense

show v **1** (sth shows) appear, be in view, be seen, be visible, catch the eye, make an appearance, materialize, stand out, stick out. **2** (show sth is true) demonstrate, divulge, explain, expose, express, indicate, make known, make plain, prove, reveal, teach, uncover. **3** (show symptoms) display, exhibit, manifest, present. **4** (show sb to their seat) accompany, conduct, direct, escort, guide, lead, steer, usher. **5 show off** be full of yourself inf, boast, blow your own horn inf, brag, crow, swagger around. **6 show up** embarrass, humiliate, let down, mortify, shame

showdown n clash, climax, confrontation, crisis, face-off, moment of truth inf

shower n **1** (of rain) deluge, downpour, fall, flurry, rainstorm, sprinkling, torrent. **2** (of bullets) barrage, stream, volley

shower v deluge, heap, inundate, lavish, load, overwhelm, pour

show-off n big-head, braggart, egotist, exhibitionist, poser inf

showy adj conspicuous, elaborate, fancy, flamboyant, flashy, fussy, garish, gaudy, lavish, loud inf, lurid, ornate, ostentatious, pretentious,

shred n 1 bit, fragment, piece, rag, scrap, sliver, tatter. 2 (a shred of evidence) grain, iota, jot, scintilla, scrap, speck, trace

shred v cut, grate, rip, scrap, tear

shrewd adj astute, canny, clever, crafty, cunning, intelligent, keen, knowing, observant, perceptive, quick-witted, sharp, sly, smart, wily; **opp** ignorant

shriek v cry, holler inf, howl, scream, screech, squawk, squeal, wail, whoop, yell; **opp** whisper

shrill adj acute, ear-splitting, high, jarring, penetrating, piercing, screeching, sharp, shrieking; **opp** soft

shrink v 1 contract, decrease, diminish, dwindle, lessen, reduce; **opp** grow. 2 (shrink from sth) back off, cower, draw back, flinch, recoil, retreat, shy away, wince, withdraw

shrivel v curl, dehydrate, droop, dry out, dry up, wilt, wither, wizen, wrinkle

shroud n blanket, cloak, cloud, cover, mantle, mask, screen, swathe, veil

shroud v blanket, cloak, cloud, conceal, cover, envelop, hide, mask, screen, swathe, veil, wrap

shudder n convulsion, jerk, quake, quiver, rattle, shake, shiver, spasm, tremble, tremor, vibration

shudder v convulse, jerk, quake, quiver, rattle, shake, shiver, tremble, vibrate

shuffle v 1 (shuffle somewhere) drag your feet, hobble, limp, scrape your feet, slide; **opp** stride. 2 (shuffle cards) confuse, disarrange, intermix, jumble, mix, rearrange, reorganize

shun v avoid, elude, evade, flee, give sb a wide berth inf, give sb the cold shoulder inf, rebuff, reject, spurn, turn away from; **opp** welcome

shut v 1 bolt, close, draw, fasten, lock, seal, secure, slam; **opp** open. 2 shut up gag, hush, keep quiet, make silent, muzzle, silence

shy adj bashful, coy, diffident, hesitant, inhibited, introverted, nervous, reserved, reticent, retiring, self-conscious, self-effacing, sheepish, shrinking, timid, wary, withdrawn; **opp** self-confident

sick adj 1 (feel sick) nauseated, nauseous, queasy. 2 (ill) ailing, bedridden, diseased, feeble, ill, indisposed, infirm, poorly, sickly, under the weather inf, unwell, weak; **opp** well. 3 (sick humor) black, ghoulish, grim, macabre, morbid, perverted, sadistic, unhealthy

sicken v appall, disgust, gross out inf, make you sick, nauseate, offend, repel, revolt, turn your stomach

sickening adj abhorrent, disgusting, distasteful, foul, gross, hideous, loathsome, nauseating, objectionable, offensive, repugnant, repulsive, revolting, vile

sickly adj ailing, delicate, feeble, frail, ill, infirm, languid, puny, unhealthy, weak; **opp** healthy

side n 1 (a side of a field) border, boundary, division, edge, fringe, limit, margin, perimeter, periphery, rim, verge. 2 (a side of a cube) aspect, face, facet, flank, part, surface, view. 3 (be on opposing sides) camp, faction, group, party, sect, team, wing

side with v ally with, back, be on the

side of, form an alliance with, join up with, partner, prefer, support, take the side of, team up with; *opp* oppose

sidestep *v* avoid, bypass, circumvent, dodge, duck *inf*, elude, evade, find a way around, skirt, steer clear of; *opp* confront

sidetrack *v* deflect, distract, divert, send off track

sieve *v* filter, screen, separate, sift, strain

sift *v* 1 filter, screen, separate, sieve, strain. 2 (sift evidence) analyze, examine, investigate, probe, screen, scrutinize, sort out, study, pore over, work over

sigh *n* breath, exhalation, murmur

sight *n* 1 (have good sight) eyes, eyesight, seeing, vision. 2 (a wonderful sight) appearance, display, scene, spectacle, view, vista

sight *v* behold, discern, distinguish, glimpse, make out, notice, observe, perceive, recognize, see, spot

sign *n* 1 clue, evidence, hint, indication, manifestation, mark, proof, suggestion, symptom, token, trace. 2 board, marker, notice, placard, signpost. 3 gesticulation, gesture, indication, motion, movement, signal. 4 cipher, code, device, emblem, hieroglyph, insignia, logo, mark, symbol

signal *n* 1 cue, gesticulation, gesture, indication, motion, movement, sign. 2 evidence, hint, indication, mark, proof, token

signal *v* beckon, gesticulate, gesture, give a signal, indicate, motion, nod, sign, wave

signature *n* autograph, mark, name

significance *n* 1 idea, import, meaning, message, point, purpose, sense, signification. 2 consequence, importance, magnitude, moment, seriousness, value, weight

significant *adj* considerable, important, meaningful, momentous, noteworthy, of consequence, of note, serious, valuable, weighty; *opp* insignificant

signify *adj* be a sign of, betoken, connote, denote, imply, indicate, mean, point to, portend, represent, stand for, suggest, symbolize

silence *n* calm, hush, lull, peace, quiet, quietness, soundlessness, stillness, tranquillity; *opp* noise

silent *adj* 1 calm, hushed, noiseless, peaceful, quiet, soundless, still, tranquil; *opp* noisy. 2 dumb, mum, mute, speechless, taciturn, tight-lipped, tongue-tied, voiceless, wordless; *opp* talkative

silhouette *n* contour, form, outline, profile, shape

silly *adj* absurd, asinine, brainless, childish, crazy, daft *inf*, fatuous, foolish, frivolous, giddy, idiotic, immature, inane, infantile, meaningless, mindless, pointless, puerile, ridiculous, simple-minded, stupid; *opp* sensible

similar *adj* akin, alike, analogous, close, comparable, corresponding, equivalent, like, matching, parallel, related, resembling, the same, uniform; *opp* different

similarity *n* affinity, agreement, closeness, correspondence, equivalence, kinship, likeness, match, relation, resemblance, similitude, uniformity;

opp difference

simmer v 1 boil, bubble, cook, poach, stew. 2 fume, rage, seethe, smart, smolder

simple *adj* 1 clear, comprehensible, easy, intelligible, lucid, obvious, plain, straightforward, uncomplicated, understandable; *opp* complicated. 2 austere, basic, classic, clean, modest, natural, plain, pure, restrained, unadorned, unfussy; *opp* elaborate. 3 artless, candid, childlike, frank, guileless, gullible, ingenuous, innocent, naive, natural, sincere, unaffected, unsophisticated; *opp* sophisticated

simplicity *n* 1 clarity, clearness, comprehensibility, ease, intelligibility, lucidity, obviousness, straightforwardness. 2 austerity, cleanness, modesty, naturalness, plainness, purity, restraint. 3 artlessness, candor, frankness, gullibility, ingenuousness, innocence, naiveté, naturalness, sincerity

simplify v abridge, clarify, cut, make simpler, edit, prune, shorten, streamline

simplistic *adj* facile, glib, inadequate, naive, oversimplified, shallow, superficial

simultaneous *adj* at the same time, coinciding, concurrent, contemporaneous, parallel, synchronized, synchronous

sin *n* corruption, crime, depravity, error, evil, guilt, immorality, iniquity, misdeed, misdemeanor, offense, peccadillo, transgression, trespass, vice, wickedness, wrong, wrongdoing

sin v do wrong, err, fall, go astray, lapse,

offend, stray, transgress, trespass

sincere *adj* candid, earnest, frank, genuine, guileless, heartfelt, honest, open, real, serious, truthful, unaffected, unfeigned, wholehearted; *opp* insincere

sincerity *n* candor, earnestness, frankness, genuineness, good faith, honesty, openness, seriousness, truth, truthfulness; *opp* insincerity

sinful *adj* bad, corrupt, criminal, depraved, erring, evil, fallen, guilty, immoral, iniquitous, wicked, wrong; *opp* virtuous

sing v chant, chirp, croon, hum, pipe, serenade, trill, warble, yodel

singe v blacken, burn, char, scorch, sear

single *adj* 1 distinct, individual, isolated, lone, one, only, separate, sole, solitary, singular, unique. 2 bachelor, celibate, free, lone, unattached, unmarried, unwed; *opp* married

single-handed *adj* alone, by yourself, independent, on your own, solitary, solo, unaided, unassisted

single-minded *adj* dedicated, determined, dogged, fixed, focused, persevering, purposeful, resolute, set, steadfast, stubborn, tireless, unswerving, unwavering

singular *adj* 1 distinct, individual, isolated, lone, one, only, separate, sole, solitary, single, unique. 2 abnormal, curious, different, distinctive, exceptional, extraordinary, notable, noteworthy, odd, outstanding, peculiar, rare, remarkable, strange, striking, unique, unusual; *opp* normal, usual

sinister *adj* dark, dire, disquieting, disturbing, evil, forbidding, foreboding, frightening, malevolent, malign, malignant, menacing, nefarious, ominous, threatening, villainous

sink v 1 collapse, decline, descend, diminish, dip, droop, drop, ebb, fade, fall, flag, founder, lapse, lessen, lower, plummet, plunge, sag, slip, subside, weaken, worsen. 2 be engulfed, be submerged, founder, go down, go under, plummet

sip v drink, lap, sample, sup, taste, try

sit v 1 be seated, perch, rest, settle, squat, take a seat. 2 (a court sits) assemble, be in session, convene, gather, meet

site n area, ground, location, place, plot, position, setting, situation, spot

site v install, locate, place, position, put, set, situate

situate v install, locate, place, position, put, set, site

situation n 1 background, case, circumstances, condition, position, state of affairs. 2 environment, locale, location, place, plot, position, setting, site, spot. 3 employment, job, place, position, post

sizable adj ample, big, considerable, decent, generous, large, significant, substantial, worthwhile; **opp** small

size n 1 amount, area, capacity, dimensions, extent, gauge, measurements, proportions, range, scale, scope, volume. 2 (large size) bulk, expanse, hugeness, immensity, largeness, magnitude, mass, vastness, volume

skeptic n agnostic, cynic, doubter, doubting Thomas, unbeliever

skeptical adj cynical, disbelieving, distrustful, doubting, dubious, hesitant, incredulous, mistrustful, suspicious, uncertain, unconvinced, unsure

sketch n depiction, doodle, draft, drawing, outline, plan, representation

sketch v delineate, depict, doodle, draft, draw, indicate, outline, plot, portray, represent, rough out

sketchy adj cursory, patchy, provisional, imprecise, inadequate, incomplete, inexact, perfunctory, rough, skimpy, superficial, undeveloped, vague; **opp** detailed

skill n ability, accomplishment, adeptness, adroitness, aptitude, artistry, cleverness, competence, craft, deftness, dexterity, efficiency, expertise, facility, finesse, flair, gift, knack, mastery, proficiency, prowess, quickness, talent, technique, workmanship

skilled adj able, accomplished, adept, adroit, clever, competent, consummate, deft, dexterous, efficient, experienced, expert, handy, masterful, masterly, nimble, practiced, proficient, qualified, quick, skillful, trained; **opp** unskilled

skillful adj able, accomplished, adept, adroit, clever, competent, consummate, deft, dexterous, efficient, expert, handy, masterful, masterly, nimble, practiced, proficient, quick, skilled, trained

skim v 1 coast, fly, glide, graze, plane, sail, skate, slide, soar. 2 flick through, flip through, glance at, leaf through, scan, skip

skimp v be economical with, be mean with, be sparing with, cut corners, economize, pinch, scrimp, save, stint

skin n 1 epidermis, fleece, fur, hide, pelt. 2 casing, coat, coating, covering, crust, exterior, film, husk, membrane, outside, peel, rind, shell, surface

skin v flay, pare, peel, shell, strip

skip v 1 bob, bound, caper, cavort, dance, frisk, gambol, hop, jump, leap, prance, romp, spring, trip. 2 avoid, bypass, forget, ignore, leave out, miss, miss out, omit, overlook, pass over, skim through

skirmish n affray, battle, brush, clash, combat, conflict, confrontation, contest, engagement, fight, fracas, fray, incident, melee, set-to, spat, tussle

skirmish v battle, clash, confront, contend, fight, tussle

skirt v avoid, border, bypass, circle, circumvent, dodge, evade, go around, pass round, sidestep, steer clear of

sky n air, atmosphere, blue, firmament, heavens, space, stratosphere

slab n block, chunk, hunk, lump, piece, slice, wedge

slack adj 1 baggy, drooping, droopy, limp, loose, sagging, saggy, soft, relaxed; opp tight. 2 careless, disorganized, idle, inattentive, indolent, lax, lazy, neglectful, negligent, remiss, slapdash, slipshod, sloppy, undisciplined. 3 (business is slack) inactive, quiet, slow, sluggish; opp busy

slack n excess, leeway, play, room

slacken v 1 (a rope) droop, loosen, sag, soften, relax. 2 (pressure) abate, decrease, diminish, drop, ease off, lessen, loosen, moderate, reduce, relax, release

slam v 1 bang, crash, dash, fling, hurl, smash, throw, thump. 2 attack, blast inf, criticize, lambast, pillory, vilify

slander n calumny, defamation, libel, misrepresentation, muckraking,

slur, smear

slander v blacken the name of, calumniate, defame, disparage, libel, malign, misrepresent, muckrake, slur, smear, traduce, vilify

slanderous adj calumnious, damaging, defamatory, disparaging, false, libelous, malicious, scurrilous, untrue, vicious

slant n 1 angle, camber, diagonal, gradient, incline, list, pitch, rake, ramp, slope, tilt. 2 angle, approach, attitude, perspective, point of view, standpoint, take, view, viewpoint. 3 bias, distortion, emphasis, leaning, prejudice, twist, weight

slant v 1 be at an angle, be skewed, incline, lean, list, slope, tilt. 2 angle, bias, color, distort, prejudice, skew, twist, weight

slanting adj angled, aslant, at an angle, diagonal, inclined, leaning, listing, oblique, shelving, skewed, sloping, tilted, tilting; opp straight

slap v clout, cuff, hit, smack, spank, strike, whack

slapdash adj careless, clumsy, disorganized, hasty, hurried, inattentive, lax, messy, neglectful, negligent, remiss, slack, slipshod, sloppy, slovenly, undisciplined, untidy; opp careful

slash n cut, gash, hack, incision, laceration, rent, rip, slit

slash v 1 cut, gash, hack, knife, lacerate, rend, rip, score, slit. 2 (slash prices) cut, decrease, drop, lower, mark down, reduce

slaughter n bloodshed, butchery, carnage, extermination, killing, massacre, murder, slaying

slaughter v butcher, exterminate, kill, massacre, murder, slay

slave n drudge, serf, servant, vassal

slave v drudge, labor, slog, sweat, toil, work your fingers to the bone

slavery n bondage, captivity, enslavement, serfdom, servitude, subjugation, thralldom

slavish adj 1 abject, cringing, deferential, fawning, groveling, gushing, obsequious, servile, submissive, subservient, sycophantic. 2 (slavish imitation) close, strict, sycophantic, uncritical, unimaginative, unoriginal, unthinking

slay v assassinate, bump off inf, butcher, do away with inf, exterminate, get rid of inf, kill, massacre, murder, put to death, slaughter

sleazy adj cheap, disreputable, dirty, low, seedy, sordid, squalid, unwholesome

sleek adj gleaming, glossy, lustrous, satiny, shiny, silky, smooth, well-groomed

sleep n catnap, doze, forty winks inf, nap, repose, rest, siesta, slumber, snooze

sleep v be asleep, catnap, doze, drop off inf, drowse, fall asleep, nap, nod off inf, slumber, snooze, snore

sleepless adj awake, conscious, insomniac, restless, wakeful, wide awake

sleepy adj dopey, drowsy, dull, heavy, lethargic, sluggish, somnolent, tired, torpid, weary

slender adj 1 fine, graceful, lean, narrow, slight, slim, svelte, sylph-like, willowy; **opp** fat. 2 (slender means) inadequate, insubstantial, insufficient, little, meager, paltry, scanty, slight, small. 3 (a slender hope) faint, feeble, flimsy, fragile, frail, slight, slim, tenuous, thin, weak; **opp** strong

slice n layer, piece, portion, segment, share, shaving, sliver, wedge

slice v carve, cut, divide, segment

slick adj 1 glib, oily, plausible, polished, smooth, specious, suave, unctuous. 2 (doing sth well) adroit, deft, dexterous, efficient, polished, skillful, smooth, streamlined, well organized

slide v coast, glide, plane, skate, skid, skim, slip, slither, veer

slight adj 1 imperceptible, inconsequential, insignificant, meager, minor, minute, modest, negligible, small, tiny; **opp** large. 2 delicate, frail, petite, slender, slim, small; **opp** big

slight n affront, discourtesy, disregard, disrespect, insult, neglect, rebuff, rudeness, snub

slight v affront, disdain, disregard, disrespect, ignore, insult, neglect, put down, rebuff, scorn, snub

slightly adv a bit, a little, moderately, somewhat, to a small extent

slim adj 1 fine, lean, narrow, slender, slight, svelte, sylph-like, trim, willowy; **opp** fat. 2 (slim hope) faint, feeble, flimsy, fragile, frail, remote, slight, slim, tenuous, thin, weak; **opp** strong

slimy adj 1 clammy, glutinous, greasy, mucous, muddy, oily, slippery, slithery, squishy inf, viscous, wet. 2 (of a person) creepy inf, gushing, obsequious, oily, smooth, sycophantic, unctuous

sling v cast, chuck inf, fling, heave, hurl, lob, pelt, pitch, throw, toss

slink v creep, prowl, skulk, slide, slip, sneak, steal

slinky adj clinging, close-fitting,

sexy *inf*, sinuous, sleek

slip *v* 1 coast, glide, plane, skate, skid, skim, slide, slither. 2 creep, edge, slide, sneak, steal

slip *n* blunder, boob *inf*, bungle, error, failure, lapse, miscalculation, mistake, oversight, slip-up

slippery *adj* 1 glassy, greasy, icy, oily, perilous, slimy, smooth, wet. 2 (of a person) crafty, cunning, devious, dishonest, evasive, shifty, sneaky, tricky, two-faced, unreliable, wily

slit *n* aperture, cleft, crack, cut, gash, hole, incision, opening, rent, slash, slot, split, tear, vent

slit *v* cut, cut open, gash, knife, lance, pierce, rip, slash, slice, tear

slither *v* creep, glide, slide, slink, slip, snake, undulate, worm

slog *n* 1 (hard work) effort, exertion, hard task, struggle. 2 (hard going) hike, trek, trudge. 3 (a hard hit) hit, slug *inf*, sock *inf*, stroke, wallop *inf*, whack *inf*

slog *v* 1 (hit sth) hit, punch, slug, sock *inf*, strike, thump, wallop *inf*, whack. 2 (slog away at sth) labor, persevere, plod, plow, slave. 3 (slog through the mud) plod, tramp, trek, trudge

slogan *n* catchphrase, catchword, jingle, motto, saying

slope *n* angle, ascent, camber, descent, dip, drop, fall, gradient, incline, hill, mountain, pitch, ramp, rise, slant, tilt

slope *v* dip, drop away, fall, incline, lean, pitch, rise, slant, tilt, tip

sloping *adj* angled, diagonal, dipping, inclined, inclining, leaning, listing, oblique, slanted, slanting, tilting

sloppy *adj* 1 liquid, runny, sludgy, slushy, soggy, splashy, watery, wet; *opp* firm. 2 (of work) careless, clumsy, disorganized, hurried, lax, messy, slapdash, untidy, weak; *opp* careful. 3 (a sloppy film) mawkish, schmaltzy *inf*, sentimental, soppy *inf*, trite

slot *n* 1 aperture, crack, gash, groove, hole, notch, opening, slit, vent. 2 opening, period, place, position, space, spot, time, vacancy

slouch *v* droop, hunch, loll, sag, slump, stoop

slovenly *adj* careless, dirty, disheveled, disorderly, lax, loose, messy, negligent, slack, slapdash, slatternly, slipshod, sloppy *inf*, unmethodical, untidy; *opp* careful

slow *adj* 1 (slow movement) careful, cautious, creeping, dawdling, lazy, leaden, leisurely, measured, painstaking, ponderous, sluggish, snail-like, steady, unhurried, unwilling; *opp* fast. 2 (a slow death) gradual, lingering, long-drawn-out, prolonged, protracted; *opp* quick. 3 (a slow learner) backward, behind, late, retarded, with special needs. 4 dense, dim, dull, stupid

slow *v* decelerate, ease up *inf*, go slower, put the brakes on, reduce speed, slow down

sluggish *adj* drowsy, dull, heavy, inactive, inert, languid, lazy, lethargic, listless, slothful, slow, torpid, unresponsive; *opp* lively

slump *v* collapse, crash, drop, fall, go down, nosedive, plummet, plunge, sink, slip, subside

slump *n* collapse, crash, depression,

devaluation, dip, downturn, drop, failure, fall, falling-off, low, nosedive, recession, trough; *opp* boom

slur *n* affront, aspersion, disgrace, insinuation, insult, libel, slander, slight, smear, stain, stigma

sly *adj* artful, crafty, cunning, deceitful, devious, foxy, furtive, mischievous, scheming, secret, secretive, shifty, shrewd, sneaky, stealthy, surreptitious, tricky, underhand, wily

smack *v* belt *inf*, clout, cuff, hit, pat, slap, spank, strike, swipe

small *adj* 1 baby *inf*, dwarf, little, microscopic, mini, miniature, minute, pocket-sized *inf*, teeny, teeny-weeny, tiny, wee, young; *opp* big. 2 (of a person) petite, pint-sized *inf*, puny, short, slender, slight, thin, undersized; *opp* big. 3 (a small problem) inconsequential, insignificant, minor, petty, trivial, unimportant; *opp* big. 4 (a small amount) inadequate, insufficient, meager, mean, measly, scanty, stingy, unsatisfactory; *opp* large

small-minded *adj* bigoted, grudging, intolerant, mean, narrow-minded, petty, prejudiced, selfish, ungenerous

smart *adj* 1 chic, dapper, dashing *inf*, elegant, fashionable, neat, snazzy *inf*, stylish, tidy, well-dressed, well-groomed, well turned-out; *opp* scruffy. 2 (clever) astute, bright, clever, gifted, intelligent, quick, quick-witted, sharp

smart *v* burn, hurt, sting, throb, tingle

smash *n* accident, car crash, collision, crash, pile-up *inf*

smash *v* 1 break, crack, demolish, shatter. 2 (smash into sth) bash, bump, collide,

crash, knock, pound, slam, strike

smashing *adj* brilliant, excellent, fabulous, first-class, great, marvelous, out of this world, sensational, super, terrific, wonderful; *opp* awful

smattering *n* bit, dash, small amount, sprinkling

smear *n* 1 blot, blotch, daub, mark, smudge, splotch, spot, streak. 2 (a smear on sb's name) blot, slur, stain, stigma

smear *v* 1 (smear sth with paint) bedaub, coat, cover, dirty, mark, soil, stain, streak. 2 (smear paint on sth) dab, daub, plaster, slap, smudge, wipe. 3 (smear sb's reputation) blacken, sully, tarnish, vilify

smell *n* 1 (the smell of roses) aroma, bouquet, fragrance, odor, perfume, redolence, scent. 2 (the smell of old socks) reek, stench, stink, whiff

smell *v* 1 (be able to smell sth) get a whiff of, scent, sniff out. 2 (sth smells) reek, stink, whiff

smelly *adj* foul-smelling, high *inf*, malodorous, rank, reeking, stinking

smile *n* beam, grin, laugh, smirk, sneer

smile *v* beam, grin, laugh, leer, simper, smirk

smirk *v* grin, leer, look smug, simper, sneer

smitten *adj* 1 (smitten with a disease) affected, afflicted, laid low, plagued, struck down, suffering. 2 (smitten with sb) beguiled, bewitched, bowled over *inf*, captivated, charmed, entranced, infatuated, swept off your feet, taken

smoke *n* exhaust, fumes, pollution, smog, steam, vapor

smoke *v* 1 (give off smoke) burn, emit

smoke, smolder. 2 (smoke a cigarette) have a cigarette, inhale, puff

smooth adj 1 even, flat, flush, horizontal, level, plane, unwrinkled; *opp* bumpy. 2 burnished, glossy, polished, satiny, shiny, silken, silky, sleek, soft, velvety; *opp* rough. 3 (smooth surface of a lake) calm, glassy, mirrorlike, peaceful, still, tranquil, unbroken, undisturbed, unruffled. 4 (a smooth person) debonair, glib, insincere, persuasive, slick, smug, suave, urbane. 5 (smooth movements) comfortable, easy, effortless, flowing, fluent, fluid, regular, rhythmic, steady; *opp* jerky. 6 (smooth sounds) agreeable, bland, mellow, mild, pleasant, soft, soothing; *opp* harsh

smooth v brush, buff up, burnish, comb, even out, file, flatten, iron, level, plane, polish, press, press down, roll out, sand down

smother v 1 (smother a person) asphyxiate, choke, stifle, suffocate. 2 (smother a sound) hide, keep back, muffle, stifle, suppress. 3 (smother flames) damp down, extinguish, put out, stamp out

smudge n blotch, mark, smear, smut, spot, streak

smudge v blur, dirty, mark, soil, smear, streak

smug adj complacent, conceited, pleased with yourself, priggish, self-important, self-righteous, self-satisfied, superior

snack n bite, light meal, nibbles, nosh, refreshments

snag n catch, complication, disadvantage, drawback, hitch, obstacle, problem, setback, stumbling block

snap n 1 click, crack, crackle, pop. 2 (a cold snap) interval, period, spell, time. 3 (a holiday snap) photo, photograph, picture, snapshot

snap v 1 break, come apart, crack, fracture, give way, separate, split. 2 (of a dog) bite, catch, nip, seize, snatch. 3 (snap at sb) bark, flash, growl, jump down sb's throat *inf*, retort, snarl, speak sharply

snare n ambush, net, noose, trap

snare v capture, catch, ensnare, entrap, net, seize, trap

snatch n (a snatch of a tune) bit, fragment, part, piece, snippet

snatch v 1 catch, clutch, grab, grasp, grip, pluck, pull, seize, take, win, wrench. 2 abduct, hold ransom, kidnap, make off with, nab *inf*, steal, take as a hostage

sneak n informer, snitch *inf*, telltale

sneak v 1 (sneak through the bushes) cower, creep, lurk, pad, prowl, sidle, skulk, slink, stalk, steal. 2 (sneak sth in) slip, smuggle, spirit, whisk. 3 (sneak on sb) inform against, report, snitch *inf*, tell *inf*, tell tales

sneaky adj deceitful, furtive, mean, shady, shifty *inf*, sly, stealthy, surreptitious, treacherous, underhand

sneer v be contemptuous, be scornful, deride, hiss, jeer, laugh, mock, ridicule, scoff, smirk, snigger, taunt

sniff v breathe, breathe in, get a whiff of, inhale, scent, smell, snuffle

snigger v chuckle, giggle, laugh, sneer, titter

snip n bit, clipping, cutting, fragment, piece, scrap, shred, tatter

snip v clip, crop, cut, dock, nick, notch, prune, shave, trim

snivel v blubber, cry, grizzle, moan, sniff, sniffle, snuffle, sob, whimper, whine

snobbish adj arrogant, condescending, haughty, hoity-toity, patronizing, pompous, posh inf, proud, smug, snobby, snooty inf, stuck-up inf, superior

snoop v interfere, meddle, nose about inf, poke your nose in inf, pry, sneak, spy

snub n affront, insult, rebuff, slap in the face inf, slight

snub v be rude to, give the cold shoulder to, humiliate, ignore, insult, rebuff, shun, slight, spurn

snug adj comfortable, comfy inf, cozy, intimate, sheltered, soft, warm

snuggle v cuddle, curl up, nestle, nuzzle

soak v 1 drench, saturate, wet through. 2 (soak sth) immerse, marinate, steep. 3 (soak into sth) infuse, penetrate, permeate

soaking adj drenched, dripping, saturated, soaked, soaked to the skin, sodden, sopping, waterlogged, wringing wet; **opp** dry

soar v 1 (of a bird) ascend, fly, hover, rise, take flight, take off. 2 (of prices) climb, escalate, go up, increase, rise, shoot up, spiral; **opp** plummet, tumble

sob v bawl, cry, gasp, howl, shed tears, snivel, weep

sober adj 1 abstinent, moderate, teetotal. 2 (sober clothing) dark, drab, dull, plain, restrained, somber, subdued. 3 (a sober expression) grave, serious, solemn, thoughtful. 4 (a sober look at sth) calm, clear-headed, level-headed, rational, sensible

sociable adj affable, companionable, convivial, cordial, extroverted, friendly, gregarious, outgoing, social, warm, welcoming; **opp** unsociable

social adj 1 collective, communal, community, general, group, popular, public. 2 civilized, organized. 3 communicative, friendly, gregarious, outgoing, sociable; **opp** antisocial

social n do inf, gathering, get-together inf, party

socialize v be sociable, entertain, get together, go out, join in, mix

society n 1 civilization, community, culture. 2 mankind, people, the community, the public. 3 (club) association, circle, club, group, guild, league, union

sodden adj boggy, drenched, saturated, soaked, soggy, sopping, swampy, waterlogged; **opp** dry

soft adj 1 doughy, elastic, flexible, gelatinous, gooey inf, malleable, mushy, plastic, pliable, pulpy, spongy, springy, squashy, supple, tender, yielding; **opp** hard. 2 (a soft coat) downy, feathery, fleecy, fluffy, furry, silky, smooth, velvety; **opp** rough. 3 (soft light) diffuse, dim, faint, gentle, low, restful, subdued; **opp** harsh. 4 (soft sounds) dulcet, faint, gentle, hushed, inaudible, low, mellow, murmured, muted, quiet, soothing, subdued, whispered. 5 (soft colors) light, muted, pale, pastel; **opp** vivid. 6 (a soft breeze) balmy, gentle, light, mild, pleasant; **opp** strong. 7 (of a person) compassionate,

easygoing, feeble, forgiving, gentle,
kind, lenient, loving, sensitive, soft-
hearted, sympathetic, tender-hearted,
tolerant, weak. **8** (soft ground) boggy,
marshy, muddy, swampy, waterlogged;
opp firm

soften *v* alleviate, calm down, cushion,
deaden, decrease, diminish, lower, make
softer, moderate, muffle, quell, quiet,
subdue, tone down, turn down

soggy *adj* boggy, sodden, soft, sopping,
swampy, waterlogged, wet; *opp* dry

soil *n* clay, dirt, dust, earth, ground,
loam, topsoil

soil *v* contaminate, dirty, foul, make dirty,
muddy, pollute, smear, smudge, spatter,
spot, stain, tarnish

soldier *n* commando, fighter, gunner,
officer, paratrooper, private, serviceman,
servicewoman, warrior

sole *adj* **1** (the sole survivor) lone, only,
single, solitary. **2** (for your sole use)
exclusive, individual

solemn *adj* **1** (looking solemn) earnest,
grave, grim, long-faced, serious, sober,
thoughtful, unsmiling. **2** (a solemn
ceremony) ceremonial, ceremonious,
dignified, formal, grand, holy, important,
imposing, impressive, religious, stately.
3 (a solemn vow) genuine, honest,
serious, sincere, wholehearted

solicit *v* (solicit advice) appeal for, ask
for, request, seek

solid *adj* **1** compact, compressed,
concrete, dense, firm, hard,
impermeable, rigid, thick, unmoving.
2 durable, robust, sound, stable, strong,
sturdy, substantial, well-made;
opp flimsy. **3** (solid gold) genuine,

pure, real, unalloyed, unmixed.
4 (a solid shape) cubic, rounded,
spherical, three dimensional; *opp* flat.
5 (solid support) complete, dependable,
effective, reliable, stalwart, trustworthy,
undivided, united, unwavering

solidarity *n* accord, camaraderie,
cohesion, harmony, like-mindedness,
stability, team spirit, unanimity, unity

solidify *v* become hard, clot, coagulate,
congeal, crystallize, go hard, harden, jell,
set, thicken; *opp* liquefy

solitary *adj* **1** (of a thing) alone, by itself,
lone, one, single, sole. **2** (of a person)
friendless, isolated, lonely, lonesome,
unsociable. **3** (of a place) desolate,
hidden, lonely, out-of-the-way, private,
remote, secluded

solitude *n* isolation, loneliness, privacy,
remoteness, retirement, seclusion

solo *adj, adv* alone, by yourself,
individually, on your own,
unaccompanied

soluble *adj* (soluble in water) dispersing,
dissolving, melting

solution *n* **1** answer, clarification,
conclusion, explanation, key, result,
solving, working out. **2** blend,
compound, emulsion, infusion, mixture,
solvent, suspension

solve *v* **1** (solve a mystery) clear up,
explain, figure out, find the solution
to, unravel. **2** (solve your problems)
find the answer to, resolve, sort out.
3 (solve a clue) crack *inf*, decipher,
interpret

solvent *adj* creditworthy, debt-free, in
credit, in the black, solid, sound, viable

somber *adj* black, bleak, cheerless, dark,

dim, dismal, doleful, funereal, gloomy, joyless, melancholy, morose, mournful, sad, sepulchral

song *n* anthem, ballad, carol, ditty, hymn, lullaby, pop song, tune

soon *adv* any minute now *inf*, before long, before you know it *inf*, in a minute, in a moment, in a while, in the near future, in two shakes of a lamb's tail *inf*, quickly, shortly, straightaway

soothe *v* 1 alleviate, appease, assuage, calm, ease, relieve, soften. 2 (soothe a baby) calm, comfort, lull, pacify, quiet, settle

sophisticated *adj* 1 (of people) cool *inf*, cosmopolitan, cultivated, cultured, grown-up *inf*, mature, refined, suave, urbane, worldly, worldly wise; *opp* unsophisticated. 2 (of technology) advanced, complex, complicated, elaborate, highly developed, intricate, involved; *opp* simple

soppy *adj* 1 (a soppy film) corny *inf*, mawkish, schmaltzy, sentimental, slushy *inf*. 2 (a soppy person) daft *inf*, foolish, overemotional, sentimental, silly, soft *inf*, wet

sorcerer *n* enchanter, enchantress, magician, sorceress, warlock, witch, wizard

sorcery *n* black magic, charms, incantations, magic, spells, voodoo, witchcraft, witchery, wizardry

sordid *adj* 1 dingy, dirty, filthy, foul, mean, miserable, seedy, shabby, sleazy, slovenly, squalid, ugly, unpleasant, vile, wretched. 2 corrupt, dishonorable, disreputable, immoral, mercenary, shabby *inf*, unethical

sore *adj* 1 aching, angry, bruised, burning, inflamed, irritated, painful, raw, red, sensitive, smarting, tender, wounded. 2 (feel sore about sth) aggrieved, annoyed, hurt, irritated, peeved *inf*, put out *inf*, resentful, upset

sorrow *n* anguish, dejection, desolation, disappointment, distress, grief, heartache, melancholy, misery, regret, sadness, tearfulness, unhappiness, woe, wretchedness; *opp* happiness, joy

sorrowful *adj* brokenhearted, dejected, grief-stricken, heartbroken, melancholy, miserable, sad, saddened, tearful, unhappy, upset, woebegone; *opp* happy

sorry *adj* 1 apologetic, ashamed, contrite, penitent, remorseful, repentant, shamefaced; *opp* unrepentant. 2 distressed, grieved, sad, sorrowful, unhappy, upset; *opp* glad. 3 (sorry for sb) compassionate, concerned, full of pity, moved, pitying, sympathetic; *opp* uncaring

sort *n* 1 brand, kind, make, type. 2 breed, family, kind, race, species, strain, type, variety. 3 category, class, classification, description, genre, kind, nature, style, type

sort *v* 1 (put things into groups) class, divide, grade, put in groups, rank, select. 2 (put things in order) arrange, catalog, categorize, classify, group, put in order, systematize, tidy. 3 (sort papers) file, organize, tidy. 4 sort out (put in order) organize, tidy up. 5 sort out (sort out a problem) deal with, find a solution to, handle, resolve

soul *n* 1 being, body, creature, individual, mortal, person. 2 inner self, spirit, true being

sound adj 1 complete, entire, firm, fit, hale and hearty, healthy, in good health, in good shape, intact, perfect, unhurt, uninjured, whole. 2 (strong) robust, solid, strong, sturdy, substantial, tough, undamaged; **opp** flimsy. 3 (sound reasoning) convincing, correct, logical, plausible, proper, reasonable, right, sane, sensible, true, valid, wise

sound n bang, blare, crash, creak, cry, din, hoot, music, noise, scream, shout, squeak, thud, yelp, voice

sound v 1 be heard, echo, make a noise, resonate, resound, reverberate. 2 (you sound desperate) appear, look, seem. 3 (sound the words carefully) articulate, pronounce, say, utter, voice. 4 **sound out** canvass, examine, inquire into, investigate, look into, probe, research, test

soup n bouillon, broth, consommé, stock

sour adj 1 (a sour taste) acid, bitter, lemony, pungent, sharp, tangy, tart, vinegary. 2 (sour milk) bad, curdled, off, rancid, turned; **opp** fresh. 3 (of a person) bad-tempered, bitter, cross, crotchety, discontented, grouchy inf, grumpy, irritable, jaundiced, nasty, unpleasant; **opp** pleasant

source n 1 author, beginning, cause, creator, origin, starting point. 2 (source of a river) head, spring, start, wellhead, wellspring

souvenir n keepsake, memento, memorabilia, relic, reminder

sovereign adj absolute, all-powerful, chief, dominant, highest, imperial, predominant, principal, royal, ruling, supreme, unlimited

sovereign n crowned head, emperor, empress, king, monarch, prince, princess, queen, ruler, tsar

sow v 1 (sow seeds) plant, scatter, strew. 2 (sow confusion) instigate, promote, spread

space n 1 emptiness, infinity, nothingness, vacuum, void. 2 (fired a rocket into space) outer space, the galaxy, the solar system, the stratosphere, the universe. 3 (need more space) capacity, elbow room inf, freedom, leeway, margin, room, scope, spaciousness. 4 (a large space) area, expanse, volume. 5 (gap) blank, empty space, gap, hole, opening

spacious adj ample, broad, capacious, comfortable, extensive, huge, large, open, roomy, sizable, vast, wide; **opp** small

span n distance, extent, length, reach, spread, stretch, width

span v arch over, bridge, cover, cross, extend across, go over, straddle, stretch over, vault over

spank v belt, cuff, give a hiding to inf, put over your knee, slap, smack, wallop

spare adj additional, emergency, extra, free, in reserve, leftover, odd, remaining, surplus, unoccupied, unused, unwanted

spare v 1 afford, do without, manage, sacrifice. 2 (spare some change) donate, give, provide. 3 (spare sb or sth) be merciful, free, have mercy, let off inf, pardon, release, reprieve, save

sparing adj careful, economical, frugal, miserly, parsimonious, prudent, stingy inf, thrifty, tight-fisted inf; **opp** lavish

spark n flare, flash, flicker, gleam, glint, sparkle

spark v ignite, kindle, provoke, set off, touch off, trigger

sparkle v 1 beam, flash, gleam, glint, glisten, glitter, glow, shimmer, shine, twinkle, wink. 2 bubble, effervesce, fizz

sparse adj light, meager, scanty, scarce, slight, thin

spasm n attack, bout, contraction, convulsion, cramp, fit, jerk, outburst, seizure, twitch

spasmodic adj convulsive, erratic, fitful, intermittent, irregular, jerky, occasional, periodic, sporadic

spate n deluge, flood, flow, rush, torrent

spatter v daub, pepper, shower, splash, splatter, spray, sprinkle

speak v 1 argue, communicate, converse, express yourself, give a lecture, have a chat, have a word, hold forth, pipe up inf, recite, say sth, talk, tell sth, use your voice. 2 (speak Spanish) converse in, pronounce, talk in. 3 speak out have your say, make yourself heard, raise your voice, sound off, speak up, speak your mind

speaker n lecturer, orator, public speaker, spokesperson

spearhead v initiate, launch, lead, pioneer, set in motion

special adj 1 different, distinctive, exceptional, extraordinary, noteworthy, odd, out-of-the-ordinary, peculiar, strange, unique, unmistakable, unusual; opp ordinary. 2 (a special day) festive, gala, important, memorable, momentous, red-letter, significant, unique, unusual; opp ordinary

specialist n authority, buff inf, connoisseur, consultant, expert, professional

specialize v be a specialist in, be best at, concentrate on, focus on, have a reputation for, have special knowledge in

specialty n claim to fame inf, field, forte, gift, special skill, strength, strong point, talent

species n breed, class, genus, kind, sort, type, variety

specific adj 1 definite, especial, exact, individual, particular, special, specified. 2 (be specific about what you want) definite, detailed, explicit, firm, particular, precise, unambiguous, unequivocal

specification n conditions, description, details, instructions, particulars, requirements

specify v define, detail, enumerate, indicate, list, mention, name, set out, spell out, state, stipulate

specimen n example, illustration, instance, model, pattern, representative sample, sample

speck n dot, fleck, smudge, speckle, spot

speckled adj dappled, dotted, flecked, freckled, mottled, patchy, spotted, stippled

spectacle n 1 display, event, extravaganza, pageant, parade, performance, scene, show, sight. 2 (make a spectacle of yourself) curiosity, fool, laughing-stock

spectacular adj beautiful, breathtaking, daring, dazzling, dramatic, eye-catching, impressive, magnificent, sensational, striking

spectator n beholder, bystander, eyewitness, observer, onlooker, viewer, watcher, witness

specter n apparition, ghost, phantom, spirit, wraith

speculate v conjecture, consider, hypothesize, make a guess, meditate, muse, reflect, suppose, think, wonder

speech n 1 (make a speech) address, discourse, lecture, monologue, oration, sermon, soliloquy, talk. 2 (human speech) communication, conversation, dialogue, discussion, talk. 3 (way of speaking) articulation, delivery, diction, elocution, pronunciation, way of speaking

speechless adj 1 dumb, inarticulate, mum, mute, silent, struck dumb, tongue-tied, wordless. 2 (too shocked to speak) aghast, amazed, astounded, dazed, dumbstruck, shocked, thunderstruck

speed n 1 briskness, haste, hurry, quickness, rapidity, speediness, swiftness, velocity. 2 pace, rate, tempo

speed v 1 flash, hurtle, race, streak, tear, whizz, zoom. 2 (run) career, dash, fly, gallop, hurry, race, run, rush, scamper, sprint. 3 break the speed limit, exceed the speed limit, go too fast. 4 speed up accelerate, gather momentum, get moving inf, hurry up, increase speed, put on speed, put your foot down inf, rush, step on it inf

speedy adj fast, hasty, hurried, immediate, prompt, quick, rapid, swift

spell n 1 charm, enchantment, incantation, magic formula, sorcery, witchcraft. 2 (a spell of wintry weather) interval, patch, period, time

spellbound adj bewitched, captivated, charmed, enthralled, entranced, fascinated, gripped, hooked inf, mesmerized, overcome, rapt, riveted, transported, under a spell

spend v 1 (spend money) fork out inf, fritter away, pay out, shell out inf, splurge inf, squander, use up, waste. 2 (spend time) fill, occupy, pass, while away

sphere n 1 ball, circle, globe, globule, orb. 2 area, department, domain, field, jurisdiction, province, realm, specialty, subject, territory

spherical adj ball-shaped, globe-shaped, globular, round

spice n 1 flavor, flavoring, kick inf, piquancy, punch inf, relish, savor, seasoning, spiciness. 2 (in life) color, excitement, interest, zest, zing inf

spicy adj aromatic, flavorsome, fragrant, highly flavored, hot, peppery, pungent, seasoned, sharp, well-seasoned; opp bland

spike n barb, nail, pin, point, prong, skewer, spine, stake

spill v 1 (spill a drink) knock over, overturn, slop, splash, tip over, upset. 2 (spill the contents of sth) drop, scatter, shed, upset. 3 (spill over) brim over, discharge, disgorge, overflow, pour, slop over, spill over

spin n gyration, revolution, roll, rotation, turn, twist, whirl

spin v 1 circle, gyrate, pirouette, reel, revolve, rotate, swivel, turn, twirl, twist, wheel, whirl. 2 (your head spins) be giddy, go round, grow dizzy, reel, swim

spine n 1 backbone, spinal column, vertebrae. 2 barb, bristle, needle, quill, spike

spine-chilling adj bloodcurdling, creepy inf, eerie, frightening, hair-raising, horrifying, scary inf, spooky inf, terrifying

spineless adj cowardly, faint-hearted, feeble, gutless inf, soft inf, timid, weak, weak-willed, wimpish inf, yellow inf, yellow-bellied inf; **opp** courageous

spiral adj circular, coiled, corkscrew, helical, scrolled, twisting, winding

spirit n 1 apparition, ghost, phantom, poltergeist, specter, vision. 2 (admire sb's spirit) attitude, bravery, courage, determination, enterprise, enthusiasm, guts inf, mettle, optimism, pluck, resolution, vigor, willpower

spirited adj animated, assertive, brave, daring, energetic, enthusiastic, gutsy inf, heroic, lively, passionate, vigorous

spiritual adj devotional, devout, divine, heavenly, holy, pure, religious, sacred

spit n dribble, drool, saliva, slaver, slobber, spittle

spit v dribble, hiss, salivate, slobber, splutter

spite n animosity, bitterness, envy, hate, hatred, ill-feeling, malice, maliciousness, pique, resentment, spitefulness, vindictiveness

spiteful adj barbed, catty inf, cruel, cutting, hurtful, ill-natured, malevolent, malicious, snide, venomous, vicious, vindictive

splash n 1 (splash of color) burst, dash, patch, spattering, spot, streak. 2 (making a splash) impact, sensation. 3 (having a splash in the pool) dip, paddle, plunge, swim, wallow

splash v 1 (splash sb with water) shower, slop, slosh, spatter, splatter, spray, sprinkle, squirt, wash, wet. 2 (splash around) bathe, dabble, paddle, wallow. 3 (splash the news over all the papers) blazon, broadcast, headline, plaster, publicize, trumpet

splendid adj 1 admirable, awe-inspiring, glorious, grand, heroic, magnificent, outstanding, sublime, superb. 2 beautiful, costly, dazzling, elegant, fabulous, gorgeous, impressive, lavish, magnificent, opulent, rich, sumptuous. 3 beautiful, excellent, fantastic inf, fine, glorious, great inf, marvelous, super inf, wonderful

splendor n beauty, brightness, brilliance, dazzle, glitter inf, grandeur, luxury, magnificence, pomp, radiance, richness, sumptuousness

splice v braid, entwine, intertwine, interweave, join, overlap, plait, tie together

splinter n chip, flake, fragment, needle, shard, shaving, sliver

splinter v break, chip, crack, fracture, shatter, smash, split

split n 1 breach, cleft, crack, division, fissure, gap, gash, opening, rip, slash, slit, tear. 2 (between people) breakup, difference of opinion, division, divorce, estrangement, rift, separation

split v 1 break, burst, crack, disintegrate, rip, separate, snap, splinter. 2 (split sth) bisect, break, chop, cleave, cut, divide, rip, separate, slash, slice, slit, tear (split the proceeds) distribute, divide, dole out, parcel out, share out. 3 (split into

two) branch, diverge, divide, fork.
4 split up break up, disband, divorce, go your separate ways, part, separate

spoil v **1** blemish, blight, damage, deface, destroy, disfigure, harm, impair, injure, mar, mess up, ruin, undermine, undo, upset, wreck. **2** (spoil sb) baby, coddle, cosset, indulge, make a fuss of, mollycoddle, overindulge, pamper. **3** (of food) addle, curdle, decay, go bad, go off inf, go sour, rot, turn

sponsor n backer, benefactor, patron, promoter, supporter

sponsor v back, finance, fund, promote, subsidize, support, underwrite

spontaneous adj automatic, impromptu, impulsive, instinctive, off-the-cuff, reflex, spur-of-the-moment, unhesitating, unplanned, unrehearsed, voluntary; **opp** planned

spooky adj creepy, eerie, frightening, ghostly, hair-raising, scary, spine-chilling, supernatural, uncanny, unearthly, weird

sporadic adj erratic, every now and then, intermittent, irregular, occasional, on and off, patchy, periodic, random, scattered, spasmodic

sport n athletics, ball games, games, hunting, PE, physical activity, physical exercise, team games, water sports, winter sports

sport v carry, display, flaunt, show off, wear

sporting adj decent, fair, generous, gentlemanly, honorable; **opp** unsporting

sportsman n athlete, competitor, contestant, participant, player, sportswoman, team member

sporty adj active, athletic, energetic, fit, healthy, muscular, outdoor

spot n **1** blackhead, freckle, mole, pimple, pockmark, pustule, rash, whitehead, zit inf. **2** blob, blotch, dot, drop, fleck, mark, patch, speck, splash, stain. **3** area, location, place, position, site, situation. **4** bit, drop, little, smidgen, touch

spot v **1** catch sight of, glimpse, make out, notice, recognize, see. **2** mark, spatter, splash, stain

spotless adj **1** clean, gleaming, hygienic, immaculate, shining, spick and span, sterile; **opp** dirty. **2** (of sb's reputation) above reproach, faultless, flawless, squeaky-clean inf, unsullied, untarnished; **opp** tarnished

spotty adj **1** blotchy, dappled, dotty, flecked, mottled, polka-dot, speckly, spotted. **2** acned, pimply

spouse n husband, mate, missis inf, old man inf, other half inf, partner, wife

spout v **1** erupt, flow, gush, jet, pour, shoot, spew, spurt, squirt, stream. **2** expound, go on, harangue, hold forth, rabbit on inf, rant, rattle on inf

sprawl v **1** flop, languish, loll, lounge, recline, slouch, slump, spread out, stretch out. **2** be scattered, ramble, spill over, spread, straggle, tumble over

spray n **1** droplets, fountain, mist, shower, spatter. **2** aerosol, atomizer, pump, sprinkler, vaporizer

spray v mist, shower, spatter, splash, sprinkle, wet

spread n **1** (the spread of sth) advance, expansion, growth, increase, proliferation. **2** (span) expanse, extent, range, reach, span. **3** (in a newspaper) article, feature, piece, story. **4** (sth to put on bread) butter, conserve, jam, margarine, paste, pâté, preserve. **5** feast, meal

spread v **1** (open out) expand, extend, fan out, open out, stretch, unfold, unfurl. **2** (grow) broaden, develop, disperse, distribute, expand, get bigger, grow, increase, multiply, mushroom, proliferate, swell. **3** (reach) cover, extend, reach, sprawl, stretch. **4** (lay out) arrange, distribute, lay out, scatter. **5** (spread butter) apply, coat, cover with, plaster on *inf*, put on, rub over, smear on. **6** (spread news) advertise, broadcast, circulate, disseminate, give out, make known, pass round, promulgate, publicize

spree n bender *inf*, binge, bout, day out, fling, junket *inf*, night out, splurge *inf*

sprightly adj active, agile, alert, brisk, chipper *inf*, energetic, jaunty, lively, nimble, perky *inf*, spry

spring n **1** bounce, bound, hop, jump, leap, vault. **2** elasticity, flexibility, give, springiness. **3** springtime. **4** geyser, spa, water source, well

spring v **1** bounce, bound, jump, leap, pounce, recoil, vault. **2** (spring from) come from, derive, emanate, originate, spring from, start, stem from. **3** (spring up) appear, develop, emerge, grow, mushroom, pop up, shoot up, spring up, sprout

sprinkle v dribble, drizzle, pepper, scatter, shower, spatter, spray, strew

sprinkling n dribble, dusting, few, handful, scattering, splash, trickle

sprint v charge, dash, hotfoot it *inf*, race, run, rush, tear

sprout v come into bud, come up, germinate, grow, put out shoots, shoot

spur n encouragement, impetus, incentive, inducement, motivation

spur v drive, encourage, give sb the incentive, goad, incite, motivate, pressurize, prod, prompt, stimulate, urge

spurious adj artificial, bogus, false, insincere, mock, phony *inf*, pretended, pseudo, sham; *opp* genuine, real

spurn v give sb the cold shoulder, rebuff, reject, repulse, shun, turn away; *opp* encourage

spy n agent, double agent, foreign agent, informer, member of the secret service, mole *inf*, secret agent, snooper, undercover agent, 007 *inf*

spy v **1** catch sight of, discover, glimpse, notice, see, spot. **2** follow, gather intelligence, keep an eye on, keep under observation, trail, keep under surveillance, snoop *inf*, tail *inf*, watch

squabble n argument, difference of opinion, disagreement, fight, row, spat, tiff, wrangle

squabble v argue, bicker, fall out, fight, have a tiff, row, wrangle

squalid adj **1** deprived, dingy, dirty, filthy, foul, nasty, neglected, rundown, seedy, slovenly, wretched; *opp* smart. **2** corrupt, disreputable, indecent, shameful, sleazy, sordid

squalor n decay, deprivation, dilapidation, dirt, filth, neglect, seediness, wretchedness

squander v blow *inf*, fritter away, misuse, pour down the drain *inf*, splurge *inf*, throw away, waste

square adj 1 quadrilateral, rectangular, right-angled, true. 2 (honest) above board, decent, fair, honest, on the level, straight

squash v 1 compress, crush, flatten, mash, pound, press, pulp, pulverize, squeeze. 2 (squash things in) cram, crowd, jam, pack, ram, squeeze, wedge

squawk v call, caw, croak, screech, shriek, squeak, squeal

squeak v cheep, cry, peep, pipe, scream, screech, shrill, squeal, yelp

squeal v cry, howl, scream, screech, shout, shriek, squawk, wail, yelp

squeamish adj delicate, faint, funny inf, groggy inf, nauseated, queasy, sick

squeeze v 1 (press) clasp, compress, crush, grip, mash, nip, pinch, press, pulp, squash. 2 (squeeze things in) cram, crowd, force, jam, pack, ram, squash, stuff, wedge. 3 (squeeze sth to get out water) extract, press, twist, wring

squirm v fidget, flounder, thrash about, twist, wriggle, writhe

squirt v eject, gush, jet, shoot, shower, spew out, spray, spurt

stab v cut, gash, gore, jab, knife, pierce, run through, skewer, slash, spear, spike

stability n equilibrium, firmness, permanence, reliability, security, solidity, soundness, steadiness, strength, sturdiness; opp insecurity, shakiness, unsteadiness

stabilize v balance, keep steady, make stable, settle, steady

stable adj balanced, constant, established, fast, firm, lasting, on a firm footing, permanent, reliable, secure, solid, sound, steadfast, steady, sturdy, unchanging, unvarying, well founded; opp shaky, unstable

stack n heap, hoard, mass, mound, mountain, pile, tower

stack v heap, load, pile up, pile, put, stow

staff n 1 baton, cane, crook, mace, scepter, stave, stick, walking stick, wand. 2 crew, employees, members of staff, personnel, workers, workforce

stage n 1 (phase) juncture, lap, leg, level, phase, point, step. 2 (platform) dais, platform, podium, proscenium, rostrum. 3 (the stage) acting, footlights, repertory, show business, theater

stagger v 1 careen, lurch, pitch, reel, rock, roll, totter. 2 amaze, astound, flabbergast, overwhelm, shake, stun, surprise, take sb's breath away. 3 alternate, interlace, vary

stagnant adj brackish, foul, lethargic, sluggish, stale, standing, static, still; opp flowing, fresh

stagnate v decay, deteriorate, fester, go nowhere, become stagnant, languish, rot, vegetate

staid adj demure, fuddy-duddy inf, prim, proper, quiet, reserved, sedate, serious, solemn, stiff, straitlaced, stuffy inf, unadventurous; opp adventurous

stain n 1 blotch, discoloration, mark, spot. 2 coloring, dye, varnish

stain v 1 dirty, discolor, make dirty, mark, splash, spot. 2 blacken, damage, disgrace, spoil, taint, tarnish. 3 color, dye, varnish

stair n escalator, flight of stairs, riser, rung, staircase, stairway, steps, tread

stake n 1 pole, post, rod, shaft, spike,

stave, stick, support. **2** bet, money, wager. **3** claim, concern, interest, investment, share

stake v **1** brace, hold up, prop up, support. **2** bet, chance, gamble, risk, wager

stale adj **1** dry, hard, musty, off inf, old, past its expiration date, sour; opp fresh. **2** clichéd, dry-as-dust, dull, hackneyed, jaded, tedious, tired, worn-out; opp fresh, new

stalk v **1** follow, hound, hunt, pursue, shadow, tail, track, trail. **2** flounce, march, prance, stride, strut

stall n booth, kiosk, stand, table

stall v delay, drag your feet, hedge, hesitate, hold off, play for time, prevaricate, put off, stonewall

stamina n dynamism, endurance, energy, fortitude, go inf, guts inf, resilience, staying power, strength, vigor

stammer v fumble your words, hesitate, splutter, stumble, stutter, trip over your tongue

stamp n authorization, brand, die, impression, mark, print, seal

stamp v **1** (stamp on sth) crush underfoot, squash, step on, trample, tread on. **2** brand, emboss, impress, label, mark, mark, print. **3 stamp out** abolish, destroy, eliminate, eradicate, exterminate, get rid of, put an end to, quash, suppress

stampede n charge, dash, headlong dash, rout, rush

stance n **1** angle, approach, attitude, line, position, stand, standpoint. **2** attitude, bearing, carriage, pose, posture

stand n **1** base, holder, pedestal, rack, support, tripod. **2** (stall) booth, kiosk, stall, table. **3** grandstand, terraces. **4** (take a stand) angle, approach, attitude, line, position, stance

stand v **1** (stand sth somewhere) erect, lean, place, position, put, set. **2** (stand up) get to your feet, get up, rise. **3** (be situated) be, be found at, be located, be situated, lie, sit. **4** (tolerate) abide, bear, cope with, endure, handle, put up with, stomach, take, tolerate, withstand

standard adj average, basic, normal, orthodox, regular, set, staple, typical, usual

standard n **1** benchmark, criterion, example, guideline, ideal, level, measure, model, norm, principle, quality, requirement, spec inf, specification, yardstick. **2** banner, colors, ensign, flag, pennant

standardize v bring into line, equalize, make consistent, regularize, regulate, systematize

standpoint n angle, approach, attitude, line, opinion, perspective, philosophy, point of view, position, school of thought, stance, stand, way of seeing things

staple adj basic, essential, key, main, normal, primary, standard, usual

star adj brilliant, leading, principal, prominent, well known

star n **1** celebrity, film star, leading actor, leading light, name, personality, pop star, rock star, superstar. **2** celestial body. **3** asterisk

star v appear, feature, take the lead

stare v gape, gawp, gaze, glare, look, peer, scrutinize, watch

stark adj 1 (bleak) austere, barren, bleak, desolate, drab, grim, harsh, plain, severe. 2 (stark contrast) clear, glaring, obvious, sharp. 3 (stark terror) absolute, complete, downright, pure, sheer, total, unmitigated, utter

start n 1 beginning, birth, commencement, creation, dawn, early stages, foundation, inception, introduction, launch, onset, opening, origin, outset, root, source. 2 advantage, edge, head start, lead. 3 jerk, jump, spasm, wince

start v 1 (start doing sth) begin, commence, get cracking inf, get down to it, get going, get the show on the road inf, kick off inf, make a start, set the ball rolling, set out, take the plunge. 2 (set sth up) create, establish, form, found, get off the ground, inaugurate, initiate, instigate, introduce, launch, open, pioneer, set up, start up, trigger. 3 (sth starts) appear, arise, begin, come into being, start up. 4 (start a journey) depart, get going, get the show on the road inf, get under way, hit the road inf, leave, push off inf, set off, set out. 5 (start a machine) activate, boot, get going, start up, switch on, turn on. 6 (jump) flinch, jerk, jump, jump out of your skin inf, shy away, wince

startle v alarm, frighten, give sb a fright, give sb a turn, make sb jump out of hisskin, make sb jump, shock, surprise

starvation n famine, hunger, lack of food, malnutrition, undernourishment

starve v deprive of food, die of hunger, die of starvation, fast, go hungry, go on hunger strike, refuse food

starving adj could eat a horse inf, dying of hunger inf, famished, hungry, malnourished, ravenous, starved, undernourished

state n 1 circumstances, condition, mode, position, shape, situation, status. 2 (in a real state) chaos, condition, fluster, frame of mind, mess, mood, panic, plight, predicament, tizzy inf. 3 country, kingdom, land, nation, republic, territory. 4 (the state) civil authorities, establishment, government

state v affirm, announce, articulate, assert, declare, express, proclaim, pronounce, put into words, say, specify, voice

stately adj ceremonial, dignified, formal, grand, imperial, imposing, magnificent, majestic, regal, royal

statement n account, announcement, assertion, bulletin, comment, communiqué, declaration, disclosure, explanation, press release, proclamation, report, testimony

static adj 1 (still) immobile, inert, motionless, stationary, still, unmoving; **opp** active, in motion. 2 (of pressure or costs) constant, fixed, frozen, level, stable, steady, unvarying; **opp** changeable, fluctuating, varying

station n 1 (for trains or buses) bus station, depot, railroad station, stop, terminus. 2 (TV or radio station) channel, company, radio station, TV station. 3 base, center, depot, headquarters, post

station v install, locate, place, post,

put, send, set, situate

stationary adj at a standstill, fixed, moored, motionless, parked, standing, static, still, stockstill, unmoving; **opp** moving

statistics n data, facts and figures, figures, numbers, records

status n 1 class, grade, importance, level, position, prestige, rank, standing. 2 condition, position, state

staunch adj faithful, firm, loyal, steadfast, strong, true, unswerving

stay n holiday, stop, stopover, vacation, visit

stay v 1 (wait) hang on, linger, remain, wait. 2 (persist) continue, go on, keep, last, persist, remain. 3 (stay with friends) be put up, crash inf, live, lodge, move in with, sleep at, stop over, stop, visit

steadfast adj dependable, faithful, firm, loyal, reliable, stalwart, staunch, unswerving; **opp** fickle

steady adj 1 balanced, firm, safe, secure, solid, stable, still, sure; **opp** shaky, unstable, wobbly. 2 consistent, constant, continuous, even, nonstop, perpetual, regular, rhythmic, round-the-clock, unbroken, unfaltering, uniform, uninterrupted, unvarying. 3 (a steady climb) gentle, gradual; **opp** steep

steady v 1 balance, brace, hold steady, keep still, secure, stabilize, support. 2 calm, compose, control

steal v 1 burglarize, embezzle, hijack, lift, misappropriate, nick inf, pilfer, pinch inf, pirate, poach, pocket, rob, shoplift, snatch, swipe inf, take, walk off with. 2 creep, glide, pussyfoot, slink, slip, sneak, tiptoe

stealth n cunning, furtiveness, secrecy, sleight of hand, slyness

stealthy adj clandestine, concealed, covert, cunning, furtive, inconspicuous, secretive, sly, sneaky, surreptitious, undercover

steep adj 1 abrupt, perpendicular, precipitous, sharp, sheer, sudden, vertical. 2 (of a price) excessive, extortionate, high, unreasonable

steer v 1 be at the wheel, be in the driving seat, direct, drive, guide, navigate, pilot. 2 (steer to the left of sth) direct, drive, go, head, turn, veer

stem n branch, shoot, stalk, trunk, twig

stem v check, contain, cut off, halt, staunch, stop

step n 1 footfall, footstep, gait, pace, print, stride, tramp, tread, walk. 2 (stair) doorstep, rung, stair, threshold, tread. 3 level, point, position, rank

step v move, pace, stamp, stride, tramp, trample, tread, walk

stereotype n conventional idea, formula, model, mold, pattern

stereotype v label, pigeonhole, typecast

sterile adj 1 antiseptic, aseptic, clean, disinfected, germ-free, hygienic, pure, spotless, sterilized, uncontaminated. 2 barren, infertile, sterilized, unproductive; **opp** fruitful, productive. 3 fruitless, futile, pointless, unimaginative, unproductive, useless

sterilize v 1 clean, disinfect, make sterile. 2 castrate, give a man a vasectomy, make infertile, make sterile, neuter, spay

stern adj austere, cruel, forbidding, grave, grim, hard, harsh, serious, severe, somber, strict

stew n casserole, goulash

stick n baton, branch, cane, crook, piece of wood, pole, rod, staff, stake, twig, walking stick, wand

stick v 1 (stick sth in) insert, jab, poke, push, stab, thrust. 2 (stick things together) attach, bond, cement, fasten, fix, fuse, glue, join, paste, secure, tape. 3 be unable to move, get bogged down, get clogged up, get stuck, jam, seize up. 4 (stick sth somewhere) chuck, drop, dump, put. 5 (stick sth out) endure, linger, persist, remain, stay

sticky adj 1 adhesive, glutinous, gooey, gummed, self-adhesive, tacky, viscous. 2 clammy, close, humid, moist, muggy, oppressive, steamy, sultry. 3 (a sticky situation) awkward, delicate, difficult, embarrassing, tricky

stiff adj 1 arthritic, firm, hard, rheumatic, rigid, solid, solidified, taut, tense, unbending; **opp** bendable, supple. 2 challenging, determined, difficult, hard, resolute, rigorous, strict, strong, tough

stiffen v become stiff, brace, clot, coagulate, congeal, harden, gel, make rigid, reinforce, set, solidify, tense, thicken

stifle v 1 asphyxiate, choke, muffle, smother, suffocate. 2 check, control, crush, curb, keep back, quash, quell, repress, silence, suppress

stigma n blemish, blot, disgrace, dishonor, scar, shame, stain

still adj at rest, calm, flat, motionless, peaceful, quiet, restful, serene, silent, stagnant, static, stationary, tranquil, undisturbed, unmoving

still v calm, hush, lull, quiet, settle, soothe, subdue

stilted adj artificial, forced, labored, stiff, unnatural, wooden; **opp** flowing, fluent, fluid, smooth

stimulant n antidepressant, pick-me-up inf, restorative, tonic; **opp** depressant, downer inf

stimulate v animate, arouse, encourage, excite, fire up, foment, induce, inflame, instigate, invigorate, motivate, prompt, provoke, stir up, trigger; **opp** discourage

stimulating adj arousing, challenging, dynamic, exciting, exhilarating, inspiring, invigorating, motivating, stirring, thought-provoking; **opp** dull

stimulus n encouragement, goad, incentive, inducement, provocation, shot in the arm inf, spur

sting v 1 (of an insect) bite, hurt, nip, prick. 2 (hurt) burn, hurt, prickle, smart

stink v be high, reek, smell bad, smell

stint n session, share, shift, spell, stretch, time, turn

stipulate v demand, insist on, lay down, require, specify, state

stir n commotion, disturbance, excitement, flurry, furor, fuss, to-do, tumult, uproar

stir v 1 (with a spoon) agitate, blend, churn, mingle, mix. 2 (move) budge, come round, move, show signs of life, wake up. 3 (stir feelings) arouse, excite, fire up, inflame, inspire, kindle, provoke, rouse, touch

stirring adj dramatic, electrifying, emotive, exciting, gripping, heady, invigorating, moving, rousing, spirited, thrilling

stock n 1 (merchandise) goods,
merchandise, range, supply, variety,
wares. 2 (reserve) cache, fund, hoard,
reserve, reservoir, store, supply.
3 (family) ancestry, blood, descent,
extraction, family, line, lineage,
parentage, pedigree, race, strain.
4 (farm animals) animals, beasts,
farm animals, livestock. 5 (of a gun)
handle, shaft, grip

stock v carry, deal in, handle, have
available, have on sale, keep in stock,
keep, sell, supply

stock adj 1 banal, clichéd, conventional,
formulaic, hackneyed, ready, routine,
set-piece, set, standard, traditional, trite;
opp original. 2 average, basic, common,
regular, standard; *opp* special

stocky adj chunky, dumpy, solid, squat,
sturdy, thickset; *opp* slender

stodgy adj 1 (of food) filling, heavy,
indigestible, solid, substantial, thick;
opp light. 2 (of writing) dry, dull,
heavy-going, stuffy, tedious, turgid,
unimaginative; *opp* lively

stoical adj accepting, cool, dispassionate,
impassive, imperturbable, long-suffering,
phlegmatic, resigned, self-disciplined,
unemotional

stolid adj bovine, impassive, slow,
unemotional, unimaginative,
unresponsive, wooden

stomach n 1 abdomen, belly, guts *inf*,
insides *inf*, paunch, tummy. 2 (desire)
appetite, desire, hunger, inclination,
liking, taste

stomach v 1 abide, bear, endure, put
up with, stand, take, tolerate. 2 digest,
eat, swallow

stone n 1 boulder, pebble, rock.
2 gem, jewel, precious stone, rock *inf*.
3 gravestone, headstone, memorial
stone, monument, obelisk, tombstone

stony adj 1 gravelly, pebbly, rocky,
shingly. 2 adamant, callous, hard,
hardhearted, harsh, indifferent, pitiless,
severe, unfeeling, unforgiving,
unsympathetic. 3 blank, chilly, cold,
expressionless, fixed, frigid, frosty, icy

stoop v 1 bend, bend down, bow, lean
down. 2 be round-shouldered, hunch
your shoulders. 3 (stoop to sth)
condescend, deign, demean yourself,
descend to, humble yourself, lower
yourself to, resort to, sink to

stop n 1 cessation, conclusion,
discontinuation, end, finish, halt,
termination. 2 ban, bar, block, check,
control, curb, hindrance, impediment.
3 break, pause, rest. 4 break, sojourn,
stay, stop-off, stopover, visit. 5 depot,
station, terminal, terminus

stop v 1 (stop moving) come to a halt,
come to a standstill, come to a stop,
draw up, halt, pause, pull up, stop
moving. 2 (stop sth happening)
abolish, ax, ban, bring to an end,
call off, crack down on, cut short,
discontinue, end, finish, interrupt,
nip in the bud, put a stop to, put down,
quell, suppress, terminate, wind up.
3 (sth stops happening) be over, cease,
come to an end, conclude, finish, pause,
peter out. 4 (stop for lunch) break off,
cease, desist, knock off *inf*, leave off,
quit *inf*, refrain from. 5 (prevent) block,
check, curb, foil, frustrate, hamper,
hinder, hold back, impede, obstruct,

prevent, repress, restrain, thwart.
6 (the police stop sb) arrest, capture, catch, detain, hold, intercept, seize.
7 (stop the flow of sth) block, bung up, plug, seal, stem, staunch, stop up.
8 (stop off somewhere) interrupt your trip, lodge, put up, stay, stop off, stop over, visit

stoppage n close, closure, halt, pause, interruption, shutdown, standstill, strike, walkout

store n **1** cache, fund, hoard, provision, reserve, reservoir, stock, stockpile, supply. **2** depository, repository, storehouse, storeroom, warehouse. **3** chain store, department store, emporium, outlet, retail outlet, shop, supermarket, superstore

store v hoard, keep, lay in, preserve, put away, put by, reserve, save, set aside, squirrel away inf, stash inf, stockpile, stock up

storm n **1** cyclone, gale, hurricane, tempest. **2** clamor, commotion, furor, outcry, row, rumpus, to-do inf, tumult, turmoil

storm v **1** attack, charge, make a raid on, rush, take by storm. **2** blow your top inf, bluster, complain, fly off the handle inf, fume, rage, rant, rave, scold, thunder

stormy adj blustery, gusty, rainy, squally, tempestuous, thundery, turbulent, wild, windy

story n **1** allegory, anecdote, fable, legend, myth, narrative, parable, romance, tale, yarn. **2** account, chronicle, history, record, report, saga. **3** (a news story) article, dispatch, feature, news item, piece, report.

4 plot, story-line. **5** falsehood, fib inf, lie, tall tale, untruth, white lie.
6 (in a building) floor, level

stout adj **1** big, beefy inf, burly, corpulent, fat, heavy, overweight, plump, portly, rotund, thickset, tubby; opp slender, slim. **2** robust, solid, strong, sturdy, substantial, thick, tough; opp flimsy. **3** brave, courageous, determined, firm, gallant, resolute, staunch, steadfast, tough, unswerving, valiant; opp cowardly

straight adj **1** direct, unbending, unswerving. **2** aligned, erect, even, in line, level, square, symmetrical, true, upright. **3** in order, neat, orderly, organized, put to rights, shipshape, sorted out. **4** consecutive, in a row, one after another, successive, unbroken, uninterrupted. **5** decent, fair, honest, honorable, right-minded, upright. **6** (straight talking) blunt, candid, direct, forthright, frank, honest, plain-speaking, sincere, straightforward. **7** (of alcoholic drinks) neat, pure, unadulterated, undiluted. **8** conventional, orthodox

straightaway adv at once, immediately, instantly, now, pronto inf, right away, without delay

straighten v **1** make straight, neaten, put straight, tidy, unbend, uncurl, untwist.
2 straighten out clear up, disentangle, put in order, put right, resolve, settle, sort out

straightforward adj **1** blunt, candid, direct, forthright, frank, honest, plain-speaking, sincere. **2** easy, intelligible, simple, uncomplicated; opp complicated, difficult

strain n 1 tautness, tension. 2 sprain, wrench. 3 anxiety, burden, demands, pressure, stress, tension, worry. 4 exertion, exhaustion, overwork. 5 breed, species, variety

strain v 1 distend, draw tight, extend, pull tight, stretch, tighten. 2 (a muscle) pull, sprain, tear, twist, wrench. 3 (strain sb) be too much for, overtax, overwork, push to the limit, tax, tire, tire out, wear out, weary. 4 (strain to do sth) bend over backwards inf, do your utmost, drive yourself to the limit, exert yourself, give your all, knock yourself out inf, labor, make every effort, strive, struggle. 5 filter, purify, separate, sieve, sift

strained adj 1 artificial, awkward, embarrassed, false, forced, labored, put-on, self-conscious, stiff, uncomfortable, unnatural, wooden. 2 drawn, stressed, tense, troubled, weary. 3 (of relations) hostile, tense, troubled, uneasy, under a strain

strand n 1 fiber, filament, thread. 2 lock, tress, wisp. 3 beach, coast, seashore, shore, waterfront

stranded adj 1 aground, beached, high-and-dry, stuck. 2 abandoned, forsaken, left high and dry, marooned, stuck, unable to leave

strange adj 1 abnormal, bizarre, curious, funny, mystifying, odd, peculiar, perplexing, puzzling, quaint, queer, remarkable, surreal. 2 eerie, grotesque, sinister, uncanny, weird. 3 (strange lands) alien, exotic, foreign, remote, unexplored, unknown. 4 (of a person) crazy, eccentric, funny, odd, unconventional, way out inf, zany

stranger n alien, foreigner, new arrival, newcomer, outsider, visitor

strangle v 1 asphyxiate, choke, garrote, throttle. 2 check, curb, gag, repress, restrain, silence, stifle, suppress

strap n band, belt, leash, thong, tie

strap v bind, buckle, fasten, lash, secure, tie, truss

stratagem n maneuver, plan, plot, ploy, ruse, scheme, subterfuge, tactic, trick

strategic adj 1 calculated, deliberate, planned, politic, tactical. 2 critical, crucial, important, key, vital

strategy n approach, design, game plan, master plan, plan, plan of action, policy, program

stray adj 1 abandoned, homeless, lost, wandering. 2 casual, chance, haphazard, isolated, odd, random

stray v 1 drift, meander, move aimlessly, ramble, range, roam, wander. 2 deviate, digress, err, get lost, go astray, go wrong, wander

streak n 1 band, bar, line, striation, strip, stripe. 2 mark, smear, smudge. 3 (mean streak) dash, element, touch, trace, vein. 4 (winning streak) period, run, series, stretch, time

streak v 1 mark with streaks, smear, smudge, striate. 2 dart, dash, flash, fly, gallop, hurtle, rush, speed, sprint, tear, whiz, zoom

stream n 1 brook, channel, creek, rill, rivulet, tributary, watercourse. 2 flow, gush, jet, rush, surge, torrent

stream v 1 cascade, course, flood, flow, gush, pour, run, spill, spout. 2 (of people) flood, pour, surge, swarm. 3 (in the wind) flap, float, flutter, swing

streamlined *adj* 1 aerodynamic, sleek, smooth. 2 efficient, organized, rationalized, slick, well-run

street *n* avenue, crescent, cul-de-sac, drive, lane, row, road, terrace

strength *n* 1 brawn, might, muscle, power, robustness, stamina, staying power, sturdiness, toughness, vigor. 2 effectiveness, efficacy, force, intensity, potency, power, validity, weight. 3 backbone *inf*, commitment, courage, determination, firmness, fortitude, grit, resolution, resolve, spirit, tenacity. 4 (strength of feeling) ardor, fervency, force, forcefulness, intensity, vehemence. 5 (the strengths of sth) advantage, asset, forte, strong point

strengthen *v* 1 (give more strength to) bolster, brace, buttress, consolidate, fortify, make stronger, prop up, reinforce, toughen. 2 (make sth more successful) boost, build up, encourage, make stronger, stiffen, support. 3 (sth strengthens) become strong, build up, gain strength, get stronger, grow stronger, heighten, intensify. 4 (strengthen a belief) authenticate, back up, bear out, confirm, corroborate, reinforce, substantiate, support. 5 (strengthen a person) build up, invigorate, make healthy, make strong, nourish, tone up, toughen up

strenuous *adj* 1 arduous, backbreaking, demanding, grueling, hard, heavy, laborious, taxing, tiring, tough; *opp* easy, light. 2 active, determined, energetic, forceful, resolute, spirited,

tenacious, vigorous, zealous

stress *n* 1 anxiety, pressure, strain, tension, worry. 2 difficulty, distress, trauma. 3 emphasis, importance, significance, weight. 4 accent, beat, emphasis

stress *v* 1 accentuate, dwell on, emphasize, harp on, lay stress on, point up, rub in, spotlight, underline. 2 accentuate, emphasize, place the accent on, put the stress on. 3 (stress sb) overtax, overwork, pressurize, push too far, subject to stress, subject to strain

stressful *adj* anxious, difficult, taxing, tiring, traumatic, worrying

stretch *v* 1 distend, draw out, elongate, expand, extend, inflate, lengthen, pull out, pull taut, pull tight. 2 be elastic, be stretchy, enlarge, expand, get bigger, get loose. 3 extend, range, spread, unfold. 4 (stretch sb's mind) challenge, overtax, push to the limit, strain, tax. 5 **stretch out** (offer sth to sb) extend, hold out, offer, reach out. 6 **stretch out** (lie) lie down, lie flat, recline, sprawl

stretch *n* 1 area, expanse, extent, spread, sweep, tract. 2 period, spell, stint, term, time

strict *adj* 1 authoritarian, firm, harsh, inflexible, rigid, severe, stern, stringent; *opp* lenient, soft. 2 accurate, close, exact, faithful, meticulous, precise, scrupulous, true. 3 absolute, complete, total, utter

strident *adj* discordant, grating, harsh, jarring, raucous, shrill

strife *n* animosity, bickering, conflict, contention, disagreement, discord, dissension, friction, hostility, quarreling, wrangling

strike n 1 industrial action, stoppage, walkout. 2 assault, attack, bombardment

strike v 1 beat, clout inf, hit, punch, slap, smack, smite, sock inf, thump, wallop, whack. 2 bang into, bump into, collide with, dash against, hit, run into, smash into. 3 (disaster strikes) affect, afflict, hit, reach, smite. 4 (attack sb) assault, attack, fall upon, launch an attack on, set upon, storm. 5 (strike a ball) drive, force, hit, impel, propel, swipe. 6 (strike a bargain) achieve, arrive at, attain, reach. 7 (go on strike) go on strike, mutiny, stop work, walk off job, walk out, walk picket line. 8 (sth strikes you) appear, come to, dawn on, impress, occur to, seem

striking adj 1 arresting, dazzling, extraordinary, impressive, memorable, outstanding, splendid, stunning. 2 conspicuous, evident, noticeable, obvious, prominent, visible

string n 1 cord, line, rope, twine, yarn. 2 chain, sequence, series, succession. 3 column, file, line, row, queue, stream

stringent adj exacting, inflexible, rigid, rigorous, severe, strict, tight; opp loose

strip n band, bar, belt, piece, ribbon, shred, slip

strip v 1 disrobe, get undressed, strip off, take sb's clothes off, take your clothes off, undress, unclothe. 2 (strip sb of sth) confiscate, deprive, divest, take away. 3 (strip a place) clean out, clear out, empty, gut, loot, plunder, ransack, rob. 4 (strip sth off) pare, peel, peel off, remove, skin, take off

striped adj banded, barred, striated

strive v attempt, bend over backwards inf, do everything you can, do your utmost, endeavor, give it your best shot inf, labor, make a real effort, strain, struggle, toil, try, try your hardest. 2 compete, contend, fight, grapple with, struggle

stroke n 1 blow, clout inf, hit, slap, smack, swipe, thump, wallop, whack. 2 achievement, coup, feat. 3 (pen stroke) flourish, line, mark, sweep. 4 (medical) apoplexy, cardiovascular accident, CVA, embolism, seizure, thrombosis

stroke v caress, fondle, massage, pet, run your hand over, rub, soothe

stroll n airing, amble, ramble, turn, walk

stroll v amble, dawdle, go for a stroll, go for a walk, ramble, saunter, stretch your legs, take a walk, wander

strong adj 1 athletic, brawny, burly, hardy, mighty, muscular, powerful, resilient, robust, rugged, sturdy, tough, vigorous. 2 hale and hearty, healthy, sound, vigorous, well. 3 brave, courageous, decisive, dependable, determined, firm, forceful, formidable, resolute, strong-minded, tough. 4 durable, hard-wearing, heavy, impenetrable, indestructible, long-lasting, solid, sturdy, tough, well-made, well-built. 5 (a strong supporter) dedicated, eager, enthusiastic, fervent, fierce, keen, loyal, passionate, staunch, steadfast, vehement, zealous. 6 (a strong argument) cogent, compelling, convincing, persuasive, plausible, powerful, valid, weighty. 7 (strong measures) draconian, drastic, extreme, firm, forceful, harsh, severe, tough. **8** (a strong light) bright, brilliant, dazzling, glaring, gleaming, intense, radiant, vivid. **9** (a strong flavor) full, highly flavored, pungent, savory, spicy, sharp, well-flavored. **10** (a strong solution) concentrated, undiluted. **11** (strong drink) alcoholic, intoxicating

structure n **1** arrangement, configuration, conformation, constitution, design, form, formation, makeup, organization. **2** building, construction, edifice, erection, framework, pile

structure v arrange, build, construct, design, form, frame, organize, put together, shape

struggle n **1** brush, clash, conflict, contest, encounter, fight, scrap, skirmish, tussle. **2** battle, difficulty, effort, fight, grind, hassle, labor, problem, trouble. **3** competition, contention, fight, rivalry

struggle v **1** bend over backward inf, do everything you can, do your utmost, endeavor, give it your best shot inf, labor, make a real effort, strain, toil, try, try your hardest. **2** clash, compete, contend, fight, vie. **3** brawl, fight, grapple, scuffle, wrestle

strut v parade, swagger, walk proudly

stubborn adj **1** (of a person) adamant, defiant, determined, dogged, headstrong, inflexible, intractable, obdurate, obstinate, pig-headed, rigid, uncompromising, unreasonable, unyielding, willful. **2** (of a stain) hard to get rid of, long-lasting, persistent, tenacious

stuck adj **1** bogged down, fast, fixed, immovable, rooted, unable to move. **2** fastened, fixed, glued. **3** at a loss, baffled, beaten, stumped, stymied inf, up against a brick wall inf

student n **1** pupil, scholar, undergraduate. **2** apprentice, learner, trainee

studied adj affected, artificial, calculated, conscious, contrived, deliberate, false, feigned, planned

studious adj **1** academic, attentive, bookish, earnest, hard working, industrious, serious, scholarly, thoughtful. **2** assiduous, attentive, careful, diligent, meticulous, painstaking, thorough

study n **1** analysis, examination, inquiry, investigation, review, scrutiny, survey. **2** academic work, education, learning, lessons, reading, research, scholarship, schoolwork. **3** essay, paper, review

study v **1** analyze, consider, contemplate, inquire into, investigate, look into, research, survey, think about. **2** examine, inspect, look closely at, peruse, pore over, read carefully, scrutinize. **3** (study a subject) learn, learn about, major in, read, read about, read up on, take a course in, take lessons in. **4** (study hard) burn the midnight oil inf, cram inf, read up on, revise

stuff n **1** baggage, fabric, material, raw material, substance. **2** baggage, belongings, bits and pieces, effects, gear, impedimenta, junk, paraphernalia, possessions, things. **3** articles, bits and pieces, garbage, items, junk, objects, things

stuff v 1 cram, crowd, fill, force, jam, load, pack, push, ram, shove, squeeze, stow, wedge. 2 fill, line, pack, pad

stuffy adj 1 airless, close, muggy, oppressive, stifling, suffocating, sultry. 2 conventional, dreary, dull, formal, fuddy-duddy *inf*, priggish, prim, sedate, staid, starchy, stiff, stodgy

stumble v 1 fall, flounder, lose your balance, lurch, reel, slip, stagger, trip. 2 blunder, falter, flounder, hesitate, stutter. 3 **stumble on** come across, discover, encounter, find, run across, turn up

stun v 1 astonish, astound, devastate, dumbfound, flabbergast *inf*, overcome, overwhelm, shock, stagger. 2 daze, knock out, paralyze, stupefy

stunning adj 1 beautiful, brilliant, dazzling, fabulous, gorgeous, lovely, marvelous, ravishing, sensational, smashing *inf*, wonderful. 2 astonishing, extraordinary, impressive, incredible, remarkable, spectacular, splendid, striking, stupendous

stunt n act, deed, exploit, feat, trick

stunted adj diminutive, dwarf, dwarfish, little, small, tiny, undersized

stupendous adj 1 amazing, astounding, breathtaking, marvelous, overwhelming, phenomenal, prodigious, sensational, staggering, superb, wonderful. 2 colossal, enormous, gigantic, huge, massive, vast; *opp* tiny

stupid adj 1 (of a person) brainless, clueless, daft, dense, dim, foolish, gullible, half-witted, moronic, naive, silly, simple, thick *inf*, unintelligent; *opp* clever, intelligent. 2 (of an idea) absurd, asinine, crackpot, crazy, futile, half-baked, idiotic, ill-advised, inane, irrational, ludicrous, mindless, pointless, rash, senseless, silly, unwise; *opp* good, sensible

stupidity n 1 (of a person) brainlessness, foolishness, gullibility, lack of intelligence, naivety; *opp* intelligence. 2 (of an idea) absurdity, folly, foolishness, futility, idiocy, inanity, lunacy, madness, mindlessness, pointlessness, silliness; *opp* cleverness

stupor n coma, daze, oblivion, torpor, trance, unconsciousness

sturdy adj 1 (of a person) brawny, healthy, husky, muscular, powerful, powerfully built, robust, strapping, strong, tough, vigorous, well built; *opp* slight. 2 (of an object) durable, solid, substantial, tough, well made; *opp* delicate, flimsy

stutter v falter, hesitate, stammer, stumble

style n 1 (sb has style) dash, élan, elegance, flair, panache, polish, smartness, sophistication, stylishness. 2 approach, custom, habit, manner, method, way. 3 (a style of sth) design, kind, pattern, type, variety. 4 (fashion) cut, design, fashion, look, mode, pattern, shape, vogue. 5 (literary style) diction, language, mode of expression, sentence structure, wording. 6 (live in style) affluence, comfort, elegance, luxury

style v design, fashion, make, produce, tailor

stylish adj chic, classy *inf*, elegant, fashionable, modish, smart, snazzy *inf*, sophisticated, trendy; **opp** unfashionable

subconscious adj hidden, inner, intuitive, latent, repressed, subliminal; **opp** conscious

subdue v 1 conquer, crush, defeat, dominate, humble, master, overcome, overpower, quell, subjugate, tame, trample, vanquish. 2 (a feeling) check, control, curb, hold back, keep under control, repress, restrain, suppress. 3 mellow, moderate, quiet, restrain, tone down

subdued adj 1 chastened, crestfallen, dejected, down in the mouth, quiet, sad, serious, solemn; **opp** vivacious. 2 dim, hushed, low-key, muted, quiet, restrained, sober, soft, subtle, toned down, unobtrusive; **opp** bright, loud

subject n 1 affair, business, gist, issue, matter, point, question, subject matter, substance, theme, topic. 2 area of study, branch of knowledge, course, discipline, field. 3 (in an experiment) case, client, guinea pig, participant, patient. 4 (of a country) citizen, national. 5 (of a king) liege, subordinate, underling, vassal

subject v expose to, lay open to, put through, submit to

subjective adj biased, emotional, individual, personal, prejudiced; **opp** objective

subjugate v beat down, break, bring to heel, bring sb to his knees, conquer, crush, defeat, enslave, gain ascendancy over, gain control over, gain mastery over, humble, overcome, quell, subdue, suppress, tame, vanquish

sublime adj awe-inspiring, exalted, excellent, exquisite, fine, ideal, lofty,

magnificent, majestic, marvelous, out of this world inf, rarefied, refined, subtle, superb, superior, wonderful

submerge v 1 (sth submerges) dive, go down, go under, plunge, sink; **opp** surface. 2 (submerge sth) dip, dunk inf, engulf, immerse, plunge, sink

submission n 1 acquiescence, capitulation, compliance, surrender. 2 (submissive attitude) boot-licking inf, deference, docility, meekness, obedience, passivity, self-effacement, servility, subjection, submissiveness, subservience, unassertiveness. 3 (a document submitted) application, bid, paper, presentation, proposal, tender

submissive adj acquiescent, boot-licking inf, deferential, docile, groveling, humble, masochistic, meek, obedient, passive, self-effacing, servile, subservient, unassertive; **opp** dominant

submit v 1 bend the knee, bow, capitulate, cede, concede, give in, give way, knuckle under, lay down your arms, succumb, surrender, wave the white flag, yield; **opp** resist. 2 (submit a piece of work) give in, hand in, present, put in, put forward, register, send in, surrender, tender

subordinate adj 1 inferior, lesser, junior, lower, lower-ranking; **opp** superior. 2 dependent, less important, low priority, secondary, subsidiary

subordinate n assistant, deputy, inferior, junior, minion, underling; **opp** superior

subscribe v 1 enlist, enroll, join, register, sign up, take out a subscription. 2 **subscribe to** (a magazine) buy, have sth delivered, take. **3 subscribe to** (a belief, principle) agree with, approve of, back, be in favor of, believe in, endorse, favor, hold, hold to, sign up to *inf*, support; *opp* oppose

subscription *n* 1 enrollment, membership, registration. 2 (money paid) charge, contribution, dues, fee

subsequent *adj* 1 consequent, ensuing, following, further, later, resulting, succeeding; *opp* preceding, prior. **2 subsequent to** after, as a result of, following, further to, in the wake of; *opp* prior to

subside *v* 1 cave in, collapse, crumble, fall down, settle, sink. 2 abate, calm down, die down, diminish, lessen, let up, quiet down, slacken off, peter out, recede

subsidence *n* collapse, crumbling, sinking

subsidiary *adj* additional, ancillary, auxiliary, less important, lesser, minor, secondary, subordinate, supplementary; *opp* main

subsidize *v* bail out, contribute to, finance, financially support, foot the bill for, fund, invest in, pay for, pick up the tab for *inf*, prop up *inf*, underwrite

subsidy *n* aid, contribution, financial support, finance, funding, grant, investment, loan

substance *n* chemical, gas, fluid, liquid, material, matter, mineral, ore, stuff *inf*

substandard *adj* below par, below standard, inadequate, mediocre, shoddy, unacceptable, unsatisfactory; *opp* satisfactory

substantial *adj* ample, considerable, extensive, great, large, important, marked, meaningful, notable, significant, sizable, valuable, weighty; *opp* insubstantial, negligible

substantiate *v* authenticate, back up, bear out, confirm, corroborate, demonstrate, establish, give substance to, illustrate, prove, support, uphold, validate

substitute *n* 1 replacement, stopgap, surrogate. 2 (person) deputy, locum, proxy, relief, reserve, stand-in, stopgap, surrogate, understudy

substitute *v* 1 exchange, replace, swap, switch. **2 substitute for** cover for, deputize for, fill in for, hold the fort for *inf*, relieve, replace, stand in for, take over from, take the place of

subtle *adj* 1 complex, delicate, elusive, exquisite, fine, intricate, nice, nuanced, refined, sublime, understated; *opp* overstated. 2 adroit, artful, astute, clever, crafty, cunning, devious, diplomatic, discerning, discreet, discriminating, guileful, ingenious, perceptive, sensitive, shrewd, skillful, tactful, wily

subtlety *n* 1 complexity, delicacy, elusiveness, intricacy, nicety, nuance, refinement. 2 adroitness, artfulness, astuteness, cleverness, cunning, deviousness, diplomacy, discernment, discretion, ingenuity, guile, perceptiveness, sensitivity, shrewdness, skill, tact, tactfulness, wiles

subtract *v* deduct, knock off *inf*, remove, take away, take off; *opp* add

suburbs *n* bedroom communities, outlying areas, outskirts, periphery, satellite towns, sprawl, suburbia

subversive adj 1 avant-garde, challenging, mischievous, questioning, radical, revolutionary. 2 corrupting, deceitful, destructive, disruptive, seditious, treasonable, underhand

subvert v corrupt, disrupt, pervert, sabotage, turn, undermine, vitiate, weaken

succeed v 1 achieve success, arrive inf, be successful, come up trumps inf, do well, flourish, get a result inf, get your name in lights inf, hit the jackpot inf, make good inf, make it inf, prosper, score inf, thrive, win, win through; *opp* fail. 2 (in doing or getting sth) accomplish, achieve, attain, be able, be successful, bring off, gain, manage, realize, win; *opp* fail. 3 (of a plan) be successful, come to fruition, do the trick inf, have the desired effect, turn out well, work, work out; *opp* fail. 4 (succeed sb in office) accede, be next in line, come after, come next, follow, follow in sb's footsteps, inherit, replace, take over, take sb's place; *opp* precede

success n 1 fame, fortune, fruition, mastery, prosperity, triumph, victory; *opp* failure. 2 accomplishment, achievement, attainment, gain, hit inf, triumph, victory, win; *opp* failure. 3 (a person) celebrity, somebody inf, star, VIP, winner; *opp* failure

successful adj 1 all-conquering, booming, flourishing, profitable, prosperous, rich, strong, thriving, top, triumphant, victorious. 2 (a successful attempt) effective, fruitful, lucky, lucrative, profitable,

rewarding, victorious, winning; *opp* failed, unsuccessful

succession n 1 catalog, chain, continuation, course, list, litany, sequence, series. 2 (the succession to the throne) accession, descent, inheritance, line, lineage, order of precedence

successive adj consecutive, following, in succession, on the run, one after the other, running, succeeding, unbroken, uninterrupted

successor n heir, inheritor, next in line, replacement; *opp* predecessor

succinct adj brief, clear, compact, concise, condensed, laconic, pithy, short, short and sweet inf, snappy, terse; *opp* long, wordy

succulent adj delicious, juicy, luscious, lush, ripe, sappy, tasty

succumb v capitulate, crumble, die, fall, fall victim, give up, go under, submit, yield; *opp* survive

sudden adj 1 (quick) abrupt, hurried, instant, instantaneous, momentary, quick. 2 (unexpected) impromptu, impulsive, spontaneous, unexpected

sue v drag sb through the courts, proceed against, prosecute, serve a writ on, summons, take legal action against, take sb to court

suffer v 1 ache, ail, be in distress, be in pain, grieve, hurt inf, struggle, writhe. 2 (suffer from an illness) be a victim of, be affected by, be afflicted by, be cursed with, be troubled with, have. 3 (suffer hardship) bear, endure, experience, feel, go through, live through, put up with, sustain, undergo

suffering *n* affliction, agony, anguish, discomfort, distress, grief, hardship, harm, heartache, hurt, misery, pain, torment, torture

suffice *v* be sufficient, do, satisfy, serve

sufficient *adj* adequate, ample, decent, enough, plenty, satisfactory; *opp* insufficient

suffocate *v* asphyxiate, choke, smother, stifle, strangle, throttle

suggest *v* advise, move, propose, recommend. 2 hint, imply, indicate, insinuate, intimate. 3 conjure up, connote, evoke, recall

suggestion *n* 1 idea, motion, plan, proposal, proposition. 2 hint, indication, intimation, remark, whisper

suggestive *adj* 1 evocative, indicative, reminiscent. 2 (sexually suggestive) bawdy, blue *inf*, improper, indelicate, indecent, lewd, ribald, rude, risqué, smutty, titillating

suit *v* 1 (of clothes) become, fit, flatter, go with, match, set off. 2 be suitable for, befit, conform to, please, satisfy

suitable *adj* acceptable, adequate, applicable, apposite, appropriate, apt, befitting, convenient, due, fit, fitting, opportune, pertinent, proper, relevant, right, satisfactory, to your liking; *opp* unsuitable

suitor *n* admirer, beau, swain

sulk *v* brood, fume, pout, seethe

sulky *adj* aloof, angry, bitter, brooding, broody, churlish, cross, fuming, gloomy, glum, grouchy *inf*, grumpy *inf*, in a huff *inf*, huffy *inf*, irascible, irritable, moody, morose, peeved *inf*, peevish, petulant, querulous, resentful, seething,

sour, sullen, surly, truculent, uncommunicative, uncooperative, unhappy, unsociable, vexed; *opp* cheerful

sullen *adj* angry, ashen-faced, brooding, broody, cheerless, depressed, gloomy, hostile, moody, morose, obstinate, peeved *inf*, peevish, resentful, seething, somber, sour, sulky, surly, tight-lipped, uncommunicative, uncooperative, unfriendly, unhappy, unsociable

sultry *adj* close, heavy, humid, muggy, oppressive, sticky, stifling, sweltering

sum *n* 1 addition, aggregate, tally, total. 2 (sum of money) amount, payment, quantity. 3 addition, calculation, division, multiplication, problem, subtraction

summarize *v* abridge, condense, encapsulate, outline, précis, put in a nutshell, round up, sum up

summary *n* abridgment, abstract, digest, outline, précis, resume, round-up, rundown, synopsis

summit *n* 1 brow, crest, peak, pinnacle, top. 2 (of sb's career, achievements) acme, apex, consummation, crowning glory, height, peak, pinnacle, top, zenith; *opp* nadir

summon *v* beckon, bid, call, call for, call up, convene, convoke, invite, send for

sumptuous *adj* de luxe, glorious, gorgeous, grand, lavish, luxurious, magnificent, opulent, rich, splendid, superb; *opp* poor

sundry *adj* assorted, different, diverse, miscellaneous, odd, several, some, varied, various

sunny *adj* bright, brilliant, clear,

cloudless, fine, glorious, radiant, summery, sunlit

sunrise n crack of dawn, dawn, daybreak, first light; **opp** sunset

sunset n dusk, evening, sundown, twilight; **opp** sunrise

superb adj admirable, brilliant, excellent, exquisite, fabulous, fantastic, fine, first-class, first-rate, glorious, gorgeous, magnificent, marvelous, outstanding, splendid, sublime, superior, superlative, unrivaled, wonderful, world-class; **opp** awful, dreadful

superficial adj 1 (done quickly) casual, cursory, desultory, hasty, hurried, perfunctory, quick, rushed, sketchy, slapdash. 2 (without deep thought) facile, shallow, skin deep, silly, slight, trite, trivial; **opp** profound. 3 (on the surface) apparent, external, surface

superfluous adj excess, excessive, extra, left over, needless, redundant, remaining, residual, spare, surplus, unnecessary, unwanted

superhuman adj divine, godlike, heroic, miraculous, mythic, Olympian, supernatural; **opp** subhuman

superior adj 1 better, choice, classy inf, elegant, excellent, exclusive, fine, first-class, first-rate, high-quality, preferable, quality inf, refined, select, sophisticated, superlative, top, top-notch inf, up-scale inf; **opp** inferior. 2 (in hierarchy) chief, commanding, higher, more important, outranking, ranking, senior; **opp** subordinate. 3 (of sb's character, attitude) arrogant, boastful, condescending, contemptuous, disdainful, elitist, haughty, high and mighty, lofty, paternalistic, patronizing, pretentious, scornful, self-important, smug, snobbish, snooty inf, stuck-up inf, supercilious

superior n boss, chief, commander, commanding officer; **opp** subordinate

superlative adj beyond compare, brilliant, excellent, fine, first-class, first-rate, glorious, great, incomparable, magnificent, marvelous, matchless, outstanding, peerless, perfect, second to none, superb, superior, tiptop inf, top-notch inf, unrivaled, unsurpassed, wonderful; **opp** awful, dreadful

supernatural adj eerie, ghostly, inexplicable, magical, miraculous, mysterious, mystic, occult, out of the ordinary, paranormal, phantom, preternatural, psychic, spectral, spiritual, strange but true, uncanny, unearthly, unexplained, unnatural, weird

superstition n belief, folklore, legend, myth, old wives' tale

superstitious adj credulous, irrational

supervise v administer, be in charge of, conduct, control, direct, govern, invigilate, keep an eye on, look after, manage, mind, monitor, organize, oversee, preside over, regulate, run, watch over

supervision n care, charge, control, direction, governance, management, monitoring, organization, regulation, running, surveillance

supervisor n boss, controller, director, foreman, head, inspector, instructor, leader, manager, monitor, organizer, overseer, prefect, regulator, teacher, timekeeper, trainer, tutor, warden

supple adj 1 bendable inf, elastic, flexible, malleable, plastic, pliable, pliant, soft, yielding; opp rigid. 2 (of a person) agile, double-jointed, graceful, lithe, nimble

supplement n 1 addendum, addition, add-on, appendix, continuation, extra, postscript. 2 (payment) bonus, excess, surcharge. 3 (to a newspaper) glossy inf, insert, magazine, pull-out, special issue

supplement v add to, augment, back up, bolster, boost, complement, enhance, extend, increase, reinforce, strengthen, support

supplementary adj accompanying, added, additional, ancillary, auxiliary, backup, complementary, excess, extra, further, subsidiary, supporting

supplier n dealer, distributor, exporter, importer, merchant, provider, purveyor, retailer, seller, shopkeeper, source, trader, vendor, wholesaler

supply n 1 (the supply of goods) donation, delivery, distribution, export, provision, sale. 2 (a supply of sth) amount, quantity, cache, consignment, delivery, hoard, quantity, provision, ration, reserve, reservoir, stock, stockpile, store. 3 **supplies** (for soldiers, explorers) equipment, essentials, food, necessities, provisions, rations

supply v 1 (supply goods) contribute, deal in, deliver, distribute, donate, export, furnish, give, hand over, offer, procure, provide, purvey, retail, sell, trade in. 2 (supply a person) cater to, endow, equip, keep sb in sth

support n 1 aid, assistance, backing, backup, endorsement, help; opp opposition. 2 advocacy,

agreement, approval, backing, endorsement, favor; opp opposition. 3 (financial) aid, assistance, backing, finance, funding, grant, investment, loan, maintenance, provision, relief, sponsorship, subsidy. 4 (an object giving support) brace, bracket, buttress, column, frame, mounting, pillar, prop, strut, truss

support v 1 aid, assist, back, back up, bolster, defend, endorse, get behind, give strength to, help, protect, reinforce, second, speak up for, sponsor, stick up for; opp oppose. 2 advocate, agree with, approve of, back, be in favor of, believe in, endorse, favor, hold to, subscribe to; opp oppose. 3 (support a football team) cheer on, follow, get behind, root for, stick up for inf, worship inf. 4 (evidence that supports a theory) agree with, be consistent with, bear out, bolster, boost, buttress, confirm, corroborate, demonstrate, illustrate, prove, reinforce, strengthen, substantiate, underpin; opp contradict. 5 (financially) back, bail out, contribute to, donate to, finance, fund, invest in, keep, maintain, provide for, sponsor, subsidize, underwrite. 6 (physically) bear, carry, hold, hold up, keep in place, prop, prop up, shore up, withstand

supporter n 1 adherent, advocate, backer, believer, champion, defender, disciple, proponent, seconder, subscriber, voter; opp opponent. 2 (of a voluntary organization) benefactor, contributor, donor, friend, helper, member, patron, subscriber, volunteer. 3 (of a football team) cheerleader, devotee, fan, fanatic, follower. 4 (of a financial venture) backer, benefactor, contributor, donor, funder, investor, patron, sponsor, subscriber, underwriter

supportive adj approving, caring, encouraging, helpful, reassuring, understanding, sympathetic

suppose v assume, conjecture, expect, guess, infer, presume, speculate, surmise, think

supposition n assumption, conjecture, hypothesis, guess, guesswork, presumption, speculation, theory

suppress v 1 beat down, bring to heel, conquer, crush, curb, defeat, destroy, eliminate, eradicate, extinguish, oppress, put down, quell, repress, snuff out, subdue, subjugate, terminate, vanquish, wipe out. 2 (suppress information) bury, censor, conceal, cover up, hide, keep back, keep secret, sit on inf; **opp** disclose. 3 (suppress feelings) conceal, control, hide, mask, repress, stifle; **opp** show

suppression n 1 conquest, defeat, destruction, elimination, eradication, extinction, oppression, repression, subjugation, terminate. 2 concealment, secrecy; **opp** disclosure

supremacy n ascendancy, command, dominance, domination, dominion, hegemony, leadership, mastery, pre-eminence, sovereignty, superiority

supreme adj 1 absolute, best, consummate, excellent, exquisite, extreme, greatest, highest, perfect, pre-eminent, prime, ultimate. 2 most important, overriding, paramount, prime, uppermost

sure adj 1 certain, confident, in no doubt, positive; **opp** uncertain. 2 (be sure of getting sth) assured, certain, destined, guaranteed. 3 (a sure method of doing sth) infallible, reliable, trusty, unerring, unfailing

surface n 1 covering, crust, epidermis tech, exterior, face, skin, top, topsoil, upper layer. 2 **on the surface** apparently, at first glance, on the face of it, outwardly, superficially, to the casual eye, to the untrained eye

surface v appear, break the surface, come to the surface, come up, emerge, rise; **opp** submerge

surfeit n excess, glut, overabundance, profusion, superfluity, surplus

surge v 1 (of water) gush, pour out, rush, stream. 2 (of the ocean) billow, heave, rise, roll, swell, swirl. 3 (of a crowd) drive, force their way, move, press, push, rush. 4 (of emotions) grow, rise up, surge up, well up

surly adj bad-tempered, churlish, crusty inf, gruff, grumpy inf, hostile, ill-natured, irascible, irritable, rude, sulky, sullen, uncivil, unfriendly

surmise v assume, believe, conjecture, deduce, fancy, gather, guess, hypothesize, imagine, infer, judge, postulate, presume, speculate, suppose; **opp** know

surpass v beat, better, do better than, eclipse, exceed, leave behind, leave standing, outclass, exceed, outdo, outshine, outstrip, top

surplus n balance, excess, extra, glut, oversupply, remainder, residue, superfluity, surfeit; **opp** shortage

surprise n 1 (a feeling of surprise)

amazement, astonishment, incredulity, wonder. 2 (be a complete surprise) bolt from the blue *inf*, bombshell, revelation, shock

surprise *v* 1 amaze, astonish, astound, bewilder, dumbfound, faze, flabbergast, nonplus, rock, take sb aback, take sb by surprise, shock, startle, stun, throw *inf*. 2 (surprise a burglar) burst in on, catch, catch sb in the act, catch sb red-handed, detect, discover, spring upon, startle, take sb by surprise, take sb unawares

surprised *adj* amazed, astonished, astounded, bewildered, dumbfounded, fazed, flabbergasted, incredulous, nonplussed, shocked, speechless, staggered, startled, struck dumb, stunned, thrown *inf*, thunderstruck; *opp* unsurprised

surprising *adj* amazing, astonishing, astounding, bewildering, extraordinary, incredible, mind-blowing, remarkable, shocking, staggering, startling, unexpected, unusual; *opp* unsurprising

surrender *n* 1 capitulation, giving in, giving up, submission. 2 abandoning, giving up, handing over, relinquishment, waiving, yielding

surrender *v* 1 capitulate, concede, give in, give up, lay down your arms, submit, throw in the towel *inf*, yield; *opp* fight on. 2 (surrender sth) abandon, give up, hand over, part with, relinquish, waive, yield; *opp* keep

surreptitious *adj* clandestine, covert, crafty, furtive, hidden, secret, sly, shifty, sneaky, stealthy, underhand; *opp* open

surround *v* encircle, enclose, encompass, envelop, go round, girdle, ring, skirt

surrounding *adj* adjacent, adjoining, bordering, nearby, neighboring; *opp* distant

surroundings *n* background, environment, environs, location, milieu, setting, vicinity

surveillance *n* inspection, observation, reconnaissance, scrutiny, vigilance, watch

survey *n* examination, inquiry, inspection, overview, scrutiny, study

survey *v* 1 (survey the view) contemplate, examine, inspect, look at, observe, scan, scrutinize, view. 2 (survey a building) appraise, do a survey of, map out, measure, plan out, plot

survive *v* carry on, continue, endure, keep going, last, live, live on, persist, remain, subsist, succeed; *opp* fail

susceptible *adj* 1 (susceptible to sth) disposed, given, inclined, liable, open, predisposed, prone, subject, vulnerable; *opp* resistant. 2 (susceptible teenagers) gullible, impressionable, innocent, sensitive, suggestible, vulnerable

suspect *adj* doubtful, dubious, iffy *inf*, questionable, shady *inf*, suspicious; *opp* trustworthy

suspect *v* 1 believe, conjecture, consider, fancy, feel, guess, have a feeling, have a hunch, imagine, suppose, surmise, think; *opp* know. 2 (suspect sb) be skeptical about, distrust, doubt, have doubts about, have suspicions about, mistrust; *opp* trust

suspend *v* 1 (suspend sth from the ceiling) attach, dangle, hang, swing. 2 (suspend proceedings) adjourn, cut short, defer, delay, discontinue, freeze, interrupt, postpone, put off, put on ice, put on the back burner, shelve; **opp** continue

suspense n anticipation, anxiety, apprehension, drama, expectancy, expectation, not knowing, tension, uncertainty, waiting

suspicion n 1 caution, distrust, doubt, dubiousness, misgiving, mistrust, wariness; **opp** trust. 2 (have a suspicion) belief, feeling, funny feeling, hunch, idea, impression, notion, supposition

suspicious adj 1 (a suspicious character) dubious, fishy inf, funny, shady inf, shifty, suspect, unreliable, untrustworthy; **opp** trustworthy. 2 (a suspicious husband) doubtful, jealous, unbelieving; **opp** trusting

sustain v 1 continue, keep going, keep up, maintain, prolong; **opp** lose. 2 (sustain the weight of sth) bear, buttress, carry, keep up, prop, reinforce, shore up, support

sustained adj constant, continuous, long-term, nonstop, perpetual, prolonged, steady; **opp** short-term

swallow v down inf, gulp, guzzle, wash down

swamp n bog, fen, marsh, mire, mud, quagmire

swamp v drench, flood, immerse, submerge

swampy adj boggy, marshy, muddy, soggy, spongy, waterlogged; **opp** dry

swap v barter, exchange, interchange, switch, trade

swarm n army, bevy, crowd, drove, flock, herd, horde, mass, multitude, pack, stream, throng

swarm v 1 (people swarm) cluster, congregate, crowd, flock, gather, mass, stream, throng; trickle. 2 (swarming with people) be crowded with, be full of, be overrun with, bristle, crawl, seethe, teem

sway n authority, command, control, government, jurisdiction, power, rule, sovereignty

sway v 1 bend, incline, lean, lurch, oscillate, rock, swing, wave. 2 (sway sb's decision) affect, bias, change sb's mind, control, convert, govern, guide, induce, influence, persuade

swear v 1 blaspheme, curse, use bad language. 2 (swear to do sth) avow, declare, give your word, promise, vouchsafe, vow

swearing n bad language, blasphemy, cursing, foul language

swearword n curse, expletive, four-letter word inf, obscenity

sweat n (in a sweat) fluster, fuss, lather inf, panic, state inf

sweat v 1 break out in a sweat, drip with sweat, glow, have a hot flush, perspire. 2 (sweat over sth) agonize, fret, lose sleep, panic, torture yourself, worry

sweaty adj clammy, damp, moist, perspiring, sticky, sweating; **opp** dry

sweep v 1 (sweep the floor) brush, clean, clear. 2 (sweep past) flounce, fly, glance, glide, sail, stride, tear, zoom

sweeping adj 1 (sweeping changes) across-the-board, all-embracing, all-inclusive, blanket, broad, comprehensive, extensive, far-ranging, far-reaching, global, wide, wide-ranging, universal; **opp** localized. 2 (a sweeping statement) exaggerated, indiscriminate, overstated, superficial, unqualified, wholesale; *opp* considered

sweet *adj* 1 (sweet food) sugared, sugary, sweetened; *opp* savory. 2 (a sweet child) agreeable, amiable, appealing, attractive, charming, cute, endearing, engaging, good-natured, likable, lovable, winning; *opp* disagreeable. 3 (a sweet smell) aromatic, balmy, fragrant, fresh, perfumed, pure; *opp* acrid

sweeten *v* add sugar to, honey, make sweeter, sugar

sweetheart *n* admirer, boyfriend, girlfriend, love, lover, suitor

swell *n* escalation, increase, rise, surge; *opp* reduction

swell *v* 1 balloon, billow, bloat, blow up, bulge, distend, enlarge, expand, extend, inflate; *opp* shrink. 2 (swell the population) add to, augment, boost, escalate, increase, raise; *opp* reduce

swelling *n* bulge, bump, enlargement, inflammation, lump, protrusion, protuberance, tumor

swerve *v* bend, deflect, deviate, diverge, career, dodge, sheer, shift, skew, swing, turn, veer, wander

swift *adj* brisk, fast, flying, hasty, hurried, prompt, quick, rapid, speedy; *opp* slow

swimsuit *n* bathing suit, swimwear

swindle *v* cheat, con *inf*, deceive, defraud, double-cross, dupe, fleece, pull a fast one, rip sb off *inf*, take sb for a ride, trick

swindler *n* cheat, con artist *inf*, con man *inf*, fraud, shark *inf*

swing *n* change, fluctuation, shift, sway, turnaround, variation

swing *v* 1 (swing from the ceiling) dangle, hang, suspend. 2 (swing from side to side) oscillate, rock, sway, veer, wave

swirl *v* churn, circulate, revolve, spin, turn, twirl, twist, whirl

switch *n* button, control, dial, knob

switch *v* 1 (switch brands) change, exchange, replace, substitute, swap, trade. 2 (switch direction) change, deflect, deviate, divert, redirect, reverse, turn

swivel *v* gyrate, pirouette, pivot, revolve, rotate, spin, swing, turn, twirl

swollen *adj* bloated, blown-up, bulging, distended, enlarged, inflamed, puffed-up, puffy

swoop *v* descend, dive, drop down, lunge, plunge, sweep down; *opp* rise

syllabus *n* course, curriculum, program

symbol *n* badge, crest, emblem, insignia, logo, sign, token

symbolic *adj* 1 meaningful, significant; *opp* meaningless. 2 (symbolic of sth) allegorical, figurative, metaphorical, representative

symbolize *v* denote, indicate, mean, represent, signify, stand for, suggest

symmetrical *adj* balanced, even, proportional, regular; *opp* asymmetrical

sympathetic *adj* caring, compassionate, concerned, feeling, friendly, humane, interested, kind, responsive, supportive, understanding, warm; *opp* unsympathetic

sympathize *v* 1 agree, be on the same wave length, empathize, identify, see eye to eye, understand. 2 be sorry for, commiserate, feel pity

sympathizer *n* advocate, ally, backer, partisan, supporter; *opp* opponent

sympathy *n* **1** caring, compassion, concern, friendliness, humanity, kindness, responsiveness, support, understanding; *opp* hostility.
2 (sympathy with sb's point of view) agreement, empathy, understanding; *opp* opposition

symptom *n* characteristic, evidence, indication, manifestation, sign, signal, warning, warning sign

synthesis *n* amalgamation, blend, combination, compound, fusion, union

synthetic *adj* artificial, fake, man-made, manufactured, mock, simulated; *opp* natural

system *n* **1** (a filing system) arrangement, classification, network, setup *inf*, structure. **2** (a system for dealing with complaints) approach, means, method, procedure, process, routine, scheme, technique, way

systematic *adj* efficient, logical, methodical, orderly, organized, precise, structured, well organized; *opp* haphazard, random

table *n* **1** bench, counter, desk, trestle, worktop. **2** (a mathematical table) chart, diagram, figure, graph, index, inventory, list, plan, register, roll, schedule

tablet *n* capsule, drug, medication, medicine, pill

taboo *n* anathema, ban, prohibition, veto

tacit *adj* implicit, implied, inferred, taken for granted, understood, unexpressed, unspoken, unstated, unvoiced; *opp* expressed

taciturn *adj* antisocial, quiet, reserved, reticent, uncommunicative, unforthcoming, unsociable, withdrawn; *opp* chatty

tack *n* **1** nail, pin, pushpin, staple. **2** (change tack) approach, course, direction, line, method, plan, policy, procedure, strategy, tactic, way

tack *v* **1** affix, attach, fasten, fix, nail, pin, staple. **2** (tack cloth) sew, stitch

tackle *n* **1** (fishing tackle) apparatus, equipment, gear *inf*, stuff *inf*, things *inf*, tools. **2** (in sport) block, challenge, grapple, interception

tackle *v* **1** (tackle a job) attempt, begin, have a go at *inf*, have a stab at *inf*, set about, take on, undertake. **2** (tackle a problem) confront, cope with, deal with, face up to, grapple with, handle, sort out. **3** (in sport) block, challenge, grapple with, intercept, take on

tact *n* care, delicacy, diplomacy, discretion, judgment, perception, savoir-faire, sensitivity, tactfulness; *opp* tactlessness

tactful *adj* careful, delicate, diplomatic, discreet, perceptive, sensitive; *opp* tactless

tactic *n* approach, course, line, maneuver, means, method, policy, procedure, scheme, strategy, tack, way

tactical *adj* clever, cunning, planned, shrewd, skillful, smart, strategic

tactless *adj* blundering, blunt, bungling, careless, clumsy, gauche, inconsiderate, indiscreet, insensitive, thoughtless, undiplomatic, unfeeling, unsubtle; *opp* tactful

tail *n* back, brush, end, extremity, rear, train

taint *n* blemish, blot, defect, fault, flaw, smear, spot, stain, stigma

taint *v* adulterate, contaminate, corrupt, dirty, foul, infect, pollute, soil, spoil; *opp* enrich

take *v* **1** (take sth from sb) get, grab, grasp, grip, obtain, receive, seize, snatch; *opp* give. **2** (take sth to sb) carry, cart, convey, ferry, transport. **3** (take sb to the door) accompany, escort, guide, lead, usher. **4** (buy or rent) buy, hire, lease, pay for, pick, purchase, rent, reserve, select. **5** (I can't take it anymore) abide, bear, endure, put up with, stand, stomach, suffer, tolerate, undergo. **6** (take a pill) consume, drink, eat, swallow. **7** (take 3 from 10) deduct, subtract, take away; *opp* add. **8 take down** make a note of, note, record, set down, transcribe, write. **9 take off** (run away) abscond, depart, disappear, go, go off *inf*, leave, run away, split *inf*. **10 take off** (clothing) remove, slip off, throw off; *opp* put on. **11 take on** employ, engage, enlist, enroll, hire, sign; *opp* dismiss. **12 take over** assume control, become leader, come to power, seize control, take command, usurp. **13 take up** adopt, become involved in, embark on, get into, start

takeoff *n* ascent, departure, launch, liftoff; *opp* landing

takeover *n* amalgamation, merger; *opp* sell-off

takings *n* earnings, income, profit, receipts, returns, revenue, yield; *opp* outgoings

tale *n* **1** fable, legend, myth, story. **2** (a tale about sb's exploits) account, anecdote, report, story. **3** (tell tales) fabrication, falsehood, fib, lie, story *inf*, untruth, yarn *inf*; *opp* truth

talent *n* ability, aptitude, brilliance, capacity, expertise, flair, genius, gift, prowess

talented *adj* able, accomplished, brilliant, gifted, skillful

talk *n* **1** chat, chit-chat *inf*, conversation, gossip. **2** conference, consultation,

dialogue, discussion, negotiation, parley. **3** (give a talk) address, lecture, oration, presentation, sermon, speech

talk *v* **1** babble, chat, chatter, converse, gossip, have a conversation, say, speak, tell, utter, verbalize. **2** confer, discuss, hold negotiations, negotiate, parley. **3** blab *inf*, confess, crack, inform, spill the beans *inf*, squeal *inf*, tell all

talkative *adj* chatty, communicative, effusive, expansive, garrulous, gossipy, long-winded, loquacious, open, verbose, vocal, wordy; *opp* taciturn

tall *adj* big, gangling, giant, high, lanky, lofty, soaring, towering

tally *n* addition, count, reckoning, record, score, sum, total

tally *v* **1** accord, agree, coincide, concur, conform, correspond, fit, harmonize, match up, square. **2** add up, calculate, compute, count, reckon, total, work out

tame *adj* **1** amenable, broken, disciplined, docile, domesticated, gentle, house-trained, manageable, obedient, submissive, tamed, tractable. **2** bland, boring, dull, feeble, flat, insipid, safe, uncontroversial, vapid, weak, wishy-washy *inf*

tame *v* break in, discipline, domesticate, house-train, master, pacify, subdue, train

tamper *v* adjust, alter, fiddle, interfere, meddle, mess, tinker

tangible *adj* actual, concrete, corporeal, definite, material, palpable, perceptible, physical, positive, real, solid, substantial, unmistakable

tangle *n* **1** coil, jumble, knot, mass, mat, mesh, mess, scramble, snarl, twist, web. **2** confusion, imbroglio, jumble, labyrinth, maze, mess, mix-up

tangle v catch, enmesh, ensnare, entangle, knot, scramble, snarl, trap, twist

tangled adj 1 caught, enmeshed, ensnared, entangled, jumbled, knotted, matted, scrambled, snarled, twisted. 2 complex, complicated, confused, jumbled, knotty, messy, mixed up, muddled, scrambled; **opp** simple

tank n 1 cistern, container, receptacle, reservoir, vat, vessel. 2 armored car, combat vehicle

tanned adj bronzed, brown, sunburned, suntanned, weather-beaten

tantalize v entice, fascinate, frustrate, keep sb on tenterhooks, lead sb on, make sb's mouth water, provoke, tease, tempt, titillate, torment

tantrum n display of temper, fit, outburst, storm

tap n 1 blow, knock, pat, rap, touch. 2 faucet, spigot, spout, valve

tap v 1 drum, hit, knock, pat, rap, strike, touch. 2 bleed, drain, draw off, siphon off. 3 draw on, exploit, extract, make use of, milk, mine, use, utilize

tape n 1 band, binding, ribbon, strip. 2 audiotape, cassette, recording, tape-recording, video, videotape

tape v 1 bind, fasten, fix, seal, secure, stick. 2 record, tape-record, video, video-record

target n 1 aim, ambition, end, goal, hope, intention, mark, object, objective, purpose. 2 (target of abuse, jokes) butt, object, prey, quarry, scapegoat, victim

tariff n 1 charges, menu, price list, rate, schedule. 2 duty, excise, levy, tax, toll

tarnish v 1 blacken, blemish, corrode, dirty, discolor, rust, soil, spoil, stain, taint. 2 (tarnish sb's reputation) blacken, blemish, blot, disgrace, dishonor, mar, ruin, spoil, stain, sully, taint

tart adj 1 acid, astringent, citrus, piquant, sharp, sour, tangy. 2 (tart remark) acid, astringent, biting, caustic, cutting, mordant, scathing, sharp, stinging, trenchant

task n activity, assignment, charge, chore, duty, enterprise, errand, exercise, job, mission, undertaking, work

taste n 1 flavor, relish, savor, smack, tang. 2 (have a taste of sth) bit, bite, dash, drop, morsel, mouthful, nibble, nip, sample, sip, swallow, touch. 3 (have a taste for sth) appetite, bent, desire, fondness, inclination, leaning, liking, love, partiality, penchant, predilection, preference, relish. 4 (good taste) class inf, cultivation, culture, discernment, discrimination, elegance, judgment, grace, polish, refinement, style, stylishness

taste v bite, nibble, sample, savor, sip, swallow, test, try

tasteful adj artistic, classy inf, cultivated, cultured, decorous, discerning, discriminating, elegant, graceful, in good taste, polished, refined, restrained, subtle, stylish, understated, well judged; **opp** tasteless

tasteless adj 1 cheap, crude, flashy inf, garish, gaudy, graceless, in bad taste, indecorous, inelegant, in poor taste, kitsch, loud, tacky inf, tawdry, uncouth, undiscriminating, vulgar; **opp** tasteful.

2 (of food) bland, dull, flavorless, insipid, mild, uninteresting, vapid, watery; **opp** tasty

tasty adj appetizing, delectable, delicious, flavorful, flavorsome, luscious, mouth-watering, palatable, piquant, savory, scrumptious inf, yummy inf; **opp** tasteless

tattered adj battered, frayed, ragged, raggedy, ripped, shredded, tatty, torn, worn out

tatty adj battered, frayed, old, ragged, raggedy, scruffy inf, shabby, shoddy, tattered, threadbare, worn

taunt n barb, catcall, dig, gibe, insult, jeer, sneer

taunt v deride, gibe, goad, insult, jeer, laugh at, make fun of, mock, poke fun at, revile, ridicule, sneer, tease, torment

taut adj firm, flexed, rigid, strained, stretched, tense, tight; **opp** slack

tawdry adj cheap, common, flashy inf, garish, gaudy, showy, tacky inf, tasteless, tatty, vulgar

tax n charge, due, duty, excise, imposition, levy, tariff, tithe, toll

tax v **1** assess, charge, exact, impose, levy, put duty on. **2** exhaust, make demands on, pressure, pressurize, push, strain, stretch, try, wear out

teach v advise, coach, direct, drill, educate, enlighten, give lessons, guide, impart, inculcate, inform, instill, instruct, lecture, school, show, train, tutor

teacher n adviser, coach, don, educator, governess, guide, guru, instructor, lecturer, master, mentor, mistress, pedagogue, professor, schoolmaster, schoolmistress, schoolteacher, trainer, tutor

team n band, bunch, company, crew, gang, group, lineup, party, set, side, squad, troupe

team up v band together, cooperate, form an alliance, join, get together, unite, work together

tear n gash, hole, laceration, opening, rent, rip, rupture, scratch, slit, split

tear v claw, gash, gore, lacerate, mangle, pull apart, rend, rip, rupture, scratch, shred, split, sunder

tearful adj blubbering inf, crying, emotional, in tears, lachrymose, sniveling, sobbing, weeping, weepy inf

tease v bait, goad, laugh at, make fun of, mock, needle inf, pester, plague, poke fun at, provoke, pull sb's leg inf, rib inf, tantalize, taunt, torment

technical adj complicated, esoteric, expert, scientific, skilled, specialist, specialized, technological

technique n **1** course, manner, means, method, mode, procedure, system, way. **2** ability, art, artistry, craft, facility, knack, proficiency, skill, touch, workmanship

technological adj advanced, automated, computerized, electronic, high-tech inf, scientific

tedious adj banal, boring, drab, dreary, dull, endless, humdrum inf, laborious, long-drawn-out, long-winded, mind-numbing, monotonous, repetitive, prosaic, tiresome, uninteresting, vapid, wearisome; **opp** interesting

tedium n banality, boredom, drabness, dreariness, dullness, laboriousness, monotony, repetitiousness, routine, tediousness; **opp** interest

teem with v alive with, be full of, be infested with, be overrun with, brim with, crawl with, overflow with, seethe with, swarm with

teenager n adolescent, boy, girl, juvenile, minor, pubescent, young person, youth

teetotaler n abstainer, nondrinker

telegram n cable, telex, wire

telephone n mobile, phone

telephone v call, dial, give sb a buzz *inf*, give sb a call, give sb a ring, phone, ring

televise v broadcast, film, relay, send out, show, transmit

television n tube *inf*, TV

tell v 1 (give information) advise, announce, communicate, describe, disclose, divulge, explain, express, impart, inform, let sb know, make known, mention, narrate, notify, recite, recount, relate, reveal, say, speak, state, utter. 2 (tell sb to do sth) bid, call upon, command, direct, enjoin, instruct, order, require. 3 (make known sth secret) blab *inf*, blow the whistle, give the game away, inform, open your mouth *inf*, rat *inf*, snitch *inf*, spill the beans *inf*, squeal *sl*, talk, tell tales. 4 (tell what sth is) appreciate, calculate, comprehend, deduce, differentiate, discern, distinguish, identify, make out, notice, perceive, recognize, see

telling adj considerable, decisive, effective, important, influential, marked, meaningful, potent, powerful, revealing, significant, sizable, solid, striking, substantial, weighty

temper n 1 attitude, character, disposition, humor, makeup, mind,

mood, nature, personality, temperament. 2 anger, annoyance, fury, hot-headedness, ill-humor, irascibility, irritation, passion, peevishness, petulance, rage, tantrum, wrath. 3 **lose your temper** blow up, blow your top *inf*, explode, flip *inf*, fly into a rage, fly off the handle *inf*, get angry, get mad *inf*, go crazy *inf*, go mad *inf*, go nuts *inf*, have a fit *inf*, hit the roof *inf*, lose your composure, lose your cool *inf*, see red

temper v allay, assuage, lessen, mitigate, moderate, modify, modulate, reduce, soften, soothe, tone down

temperament n attitude, character, constitution, disposition, humor, make-up, mind, mood, nature, personality, temper

temperamental adj capricious, changeable, emotional, erratic, excitable, fickle, highly strung, inconsistent, moody, sensitive, touchy, unpredictable, unreliable, volatile

temperance n abstemiousness, abstinence, continence, moderation, self-control, self-discipline, self-restraint, sobriety, teetotalism

temperate adj 1 (of weather) agreeable, balmy, clement, fair, mild, moderate, pleasant. 2 (of a person) abstemious, calm, continent, controlled, disciplined, moderate, reasonable, restrained, sensible, sober; **opp** wild

tempest n cyclone, gale, hurricane, storm, tornado, typhoon, whirlwind

tempestuous adj fierce, furious, heated, intense, passionate, stormy, tumultuous, turbulent, uncontrolled, violent, wild

temple n church, house of god, place of

worship, sanctuary, shrine

tempo n beat, pace, rate, rhythm, pulse, speed, timing

temporary adj brief, ephemeral, fleeting, impermanent, interim, momentary, passing, provisional, short-lived, short-term, transient, transitory; **opp** permanent

tempt v allure, attract, bait, bribe, cajole, coax, dare, decoy, draw, entice, inveigle, invite, lure, persuade, provoke, seduce, tantalize, woo

temptation n allure, appeal, attraction, bait, bribe, decoy, draw, enticement, inducement, lure, provocation, pull, seduction, snare

tempting adj alluring, appetizing, attractive, enticing, inviting, mouth-watering, persuasive, seductive, tantalizing

tenacious adj adamant, determined, dogged, firm, fixed, immovable, inflexible, obstinate, persistent, resolute, set, single-minded, staunch, steadfast, strong, stubborn, unshakable, unswerving, unwavering, unyielding

tenant n inhabitant, leaseholder, lodger, occupant, occupier, renter, resident

tend v 1 be disposed, be inclined, be liable, be prone, gravitate, have a tendency, incline, lean. 2 (look after) attend, care for, cultivate, guard, keep, look after, maintain, manage, minister to, nurse, protect, take care of, wait on, watch over

tendency n bent, bias, disposition, drift, inclination, leaning, partiality, penchant, predilection, predisposition, preference, proclivity, proneness,

propensity, susceptibility, trend

tender adj 1 dainty, delicate, fragile, frail, sensitive, soft, vulnerable, weak; **opp** tough. 2 affectionate, amorous, caring, compassionate, concerned, emotional, fond, gentle, kind, loving, sentimental, solicitous, soft-hearted, sympathetic, tender-hearted, warm. 3 aching, bruised, inflamed, irritated, painful, raw, sensitive, smarting, sore, throbbing

tenderness n affection, caring, compassion, concern, fondness, gentleness, kindness, love, sentiment, solicitude, sympathy, warmth

tense adj 1 anxious, apprehensive, edgy, highly strung, jittery, jumpy, keyed-up inf, nervous, on edge, on tenterhooks, strained, stressed, under pressure, uptight inf, worked up inf, worried; **opp** relaxed. 2 (a tense situation) exciting, fraught, nail-biting inf, nerve-racking, strained, stressful, worrying. 3 (keep a rope tense) firm, flexed, rigid, strained, stretched, taut, tight; **opp** slack

tension n 1 anxiety, apprehension, excitement, nervousness, pressure, stress, suspense, unease, worry. 2 (in a rope) firmness, pull, rigidity, strain, tautness, tightness

tentative adj cautious, diffident, doubtful, experimental, exploratory, faltering, hesitant, indecisive, indefinite, nervous, preliminary, provisional, shy, speculative, timid, uncertain, uncommitted, unsure, wavering; **opp** definite

tenuous adj doubtful, dubious, flimsy, fragile, insubstantial, shaky, sketchy,

slender, slight, slim, uncertain; **opp** clear
tepid adj 1 lukewarm, warmish.
2 apathetic, cool, half-hearted,
indifferent, lukewarm, unenthusiastic
term n 1 appellation, denomination,
designation, epithet, expression, name,
phrase, title, word. 2 duration, period,
season, space, span, spell, time. 3 (in a
school, college) course, semester, session
term v call, denominate, designate, dub,
entitle, express, label, name, style, tag
terminal adj deadly, fatal, final, incurable,
killing, lethal, mortal
terminal n 1 airport, depot, port, station,
terminus. 2 keyboard, monitor,
workstation
terminate v bring to an end, cease,
conclude, cut off, end, discontinue,
finish, interrupt, put an end to, put a
stop to, stop, wind up; **opp** start
terminology n argot, cant, expressions,
jargon, language, lexicon, nomenclature,
phraseology, vocabulary, words
terms n 1 conditions, particulars,
provisions, provisos, qualifications,
specifications, stipulations. 2 charges,
fee, payments, price, rates, schedule,
tariff
terrain n country, ground, land,
landscape, territory, topography, turf
terrible adj 1 abysmal, appalling, awful,
bad, dire, dreadful, no good, poor,
rotten, useless; **opp** brilliant, wonderful.
2 appalling, awful, dreadful, fearsome,
frightful, ghastly, gruesome, harrowing,
hateful, horrible, horrific, horrendous,
horrifying, hideous, loathsome, nasty,
nauseating, outrageous, revolting,
shocking, unbearable, unspeakable,

unthinkable, vile
terrific adj 1 amazing, brilliant, excellent,
fabulous, fantastic, fine, good, great,
marvelous, outstanding, superb,
wonderful; **opp** awful, dreadful.
2 (a terrific noise) considerable,
enormous, extraordinary, extreme, great,
huge, tremendous, vast
terrify v alarm, frighten, horrify, make
sb's blood run cold inf, make sb's hair
stand on end inf, paralyze, petrify, scare
sb to death, shock, terrorize
terrifying adj alarming, appalling,
fearsome, frightening, frightful,
horrendous, horrific, horrifying,
petrifying
territory n area, country, county, district,
enclave, land, neighborhood, patch,
precinct, province, region, space, state,
terrain, zone
terror n alarm, dread, fear, fright, horror,
panic, shock, trepidation
terrorize v browbeat, bully, coerce,
frighten, intimidate, menace, oppress,
persecute, scare, threaten, torment
terse adj 1 (a terse account) brief,
concise, incisive, pithy, short, succinct,
to the point; **opp** lengthy. 2 (a terse
reply) abrupt, blunt, brusque, curt, short
test n analysis, appraisal, assessment,
check, checkup inf, evaluation, exam,
examination, investigation,
questionnaire, quiz, research, trial
test v analyze, appraise, assess, check,
evaluate, experiment, investigate, prove,
put to the test, question, research, study,
try, try out, verify
testament n attestation, demonstration,
evidence, proof, testimony, witness

testify v 1 (testify in a court) be a witness, give evidence, state on oath. 2 (testify that you have done sth) affirm, assert, attest, avow, certify, declare, swear

testimonial n certificate, character reference, commendation, endorsement, recommendation, reference, tribute

testimony n affidavit, attestation, avowal, corroboration, evidence, protestation, statement, submission, sworn statement

text n 1 book, textbook, work. 2 chapter, paragraph, passage, verse. 3 story, words, writing

texture n appearance, composition, consistency, feel, grain, quality, structure, surface, touch, weave

thank v offer thanks, say thank you, show appreciation, show gratitude

thankful adj appreciative, glad, grateful, happy, indebted, obliged, pleased, relieved

thankless adj (a thankless task) futile, unappreciated, unrecognized, unrewarded, unrewarding, useless, vain

thanks n acknowledement, appreciation, credit, gratefulness, gratitude, recognition

thaw v defrost, de-ice, heat up, liquefy, melt, soften, warm, warm up

theater n 1 acting, drama, dramatic art, show business, the stage. 2 auditorium, hall, playhouse

theatrical adj affected, artificial, dramatic, exaggerated, melodramatic, overdone, showy, stagy, unnatural

theft n burglary, embezzlement, fraud, larceny, pilfering, robbery, shoplifting, stealing, swindling, thieving

theme n argument, idea, matter, subject, text, topic

theoretical adj abstract, academic, hypothetical, notional, not practical, speculative, unproven, untested

theorize v conjecture, form a theory, guess, hypothesize, speculate, suppose

theory n argument, assumption, belief, conjecture, explanation, guess, hypothesis, notion, speculation, view

therapeutic adj beneficial, curing, good, healing, health-giving, helpful, medicinal, remedial

therapist n analyst, counselor, healer

therapy n cure, healing, remedy, treatment

thesis n 1 argument, assertion, contention, hypothesis, idea, opinion, proposition, theory, view. 2 (write a thesis) composition, dissertation, essay, paper, treatise

thick adj 1 broad, bulky, chunky, deep, fat, large, solid, stout, wide; *opp* thin. 2 (a thick mixture) clotted, coagulated, concentrated, firm, dense, solid, sticky, stiff, viscous; *opp* thin. 3 (thick fog) dense, heavy, impenetrable, murky. 4 (a thick coat) heavy, padded, quilted, warm; *opp* thin. 5 (thick hair) abundant, bushy, luxuriant, plentiful. 6 (thick forest) close-packed, dense, impassable, impenetrable. 7 (not clever) brainless, dim *inf*, dull, obtuse, slow, stupid, unintelligent; *opp* bright

thicken v cake, clot, coagulate, condense, congeal, firm up, gel, set, solidify

thief n bandit, burglar, cheat, embezzler,

housebreaker, looter, mugger, pickpocket, pirate, robber, shoplifter, stealer, swindler

thieving adj dishonest, light-fingered

thin adj 1 (a thin line) fine, narrow. 2 (thin material) delicate, diaphanous, filmy, fine, flimsy, gauzy, gossamer, see-through, sheer; **opp** thick. 3 (of a person) bony, gaunt, lanky, lean, scraggy, skinny, slender, slight, slim, svelte, underweight, wiry; **opp** fat. 4 (a thin mixture) dilute, diluted, runny, sloppy, watery, weak

thing n 1 apparatus, article, device, gadget, implement, instrument, invention, item, machine, mechanism, object, thingumajig, tool, utensil. 2 (a thing that happens) affair, circumstance, deed, episode, event, happening, incident, occurrence, phenomenon, proceeding. 3 (a thing you think) feeling, idea, notion, theory, thought. 4 (a thing you do) act, action, chore, exploit, job, responsibility, task, undertaking. 5 (have a thing about heights) (inf) aversion, dislike, fear, fixation, hang-up inf, horror, mania, neurosis, obsession, phobia, preoccupation. 6 (have a thing about chocolate) liking, love, partiality, passion, penchant, weakness

think v 1 believe, be under the impression, conclude, consider, feel, guess inf, have an opinion, imagine, judge, presume, reckon, suppose. 2 (have time to think) brood, chew things over, concentrate, daydream, deliberate, meditate, mull things over, muse, ponder, rack your brains, reflect,

reminisce, worry. 3 (try to think what might happen) anticipate, envisage, expect, foresee, imagine, plan, visualize, work out. 4 **think over** consider, contemplate, mull over, ponder, weigh up. 5 **think up** come up with, concoct, create, devise, dream up, imagine, improvise, invent

thinker n innovator, intellect, inventor, philosopher, sage, scholar

thinking adj intelligent, logical, philosophical, rational, reflective, sensible, thoughtful

thirst n 1 dehydration, dryness, thirstiness. 2 (a thirst for sth) appetite, craving, desire, eagerness, hunger, longing, yearning

thirsty adj 1 dehydrated, dry, gasping inf, parched. 2 (wanting sth badly) avid, eager, greedy, hankering, longing, yearning

thorn n barb, needle, prickle, spike, spine

thorny adj 1 (with thorny stems) barbed, pointed, prickly, sharp, spiky, spiny. 2 (a thorny problem) awkward, bothersome, complicated, difficult, tough, troublesome, worrying; **opp** simple

thorough adj 1 (a thorough examination) careful, complete, comprehensive, conscientious, deep, detailed, exhaustive, full, in-depth inf, intensive, methodical, meticulous, painstaking, scrupulous. 2 (a thorough waste of time) absolute, complete, downright, out-and-out, outright, perfect, sheer, thoroughgoing, total, unqualified, utter

thoroughfare n access, highway,

passage, passageway, road, roadway, street, way

thought n 1 (require some thought) concentration, consideration, contemplation, deliberation, meditation, musing, reflection, rumination, thinking, worrying. 2 (have a thought) idea, notion, observation, opinion, plan. 3 (have thought for sb) compassion, concern, consideration, kindness, regard, sympathy, thoughtfulness

thoughtful adj 1 absorbed, contemplative, lost in thought, pensive, reflective, ruminative, serious, solemn, wistful, worried. 2 (a thoughtful person) attentive, caring, compassionate, considerate, helpful, kind, kindly, solicitous, unselfish

thoughtless adj 1 careless, foolish, ill-advised, irresponsible, mindless, rash, reckless, silly, stupid, unthinking, unwise. 2 cruel, impolite, inconsiderate, indiscreet, insensitive, rude, tactless, undiplomatic, unfeeling, unkind

thrash v 1 beat, belt inf, cane, flog, give sb a hiding, lash, punish, spank, whip. 2 (defeat) beat, defeat, hammer sl, lick inf, run rings around inf, trounce, wipe the floor with inf. 3 (thrash around in your bed) squirm, toss and turn, twist, twitch, wriggle, writhe

thread n cotton, fiber, filament, hair, strand, yarn

threadbare adj frayed, holey, old, ragged, scruffy, shabby, tattered, tatty, used, worn, worn-out

threat n danger, foreboding, forewarning, hazard, menace, omen, portent, risk, warning

threaten v 1 endanger, imperil, jeopardize, put at risk, put in jeopardy. 2 (threaten sb) bully, intimidate, issue threats to, lean on inf, make threats to, pressurize, terrorize. 3 (black clouds threatening rain) forebode, foreshadow, forewarn of, give warning of, portend, warn of

threatening adj bullying, intimidatory, menacing, warning

three n threesome, triad, trinity, trio, triumvirate

threshold n 1 door, doorstep, doorway, entrance, entry, sill. 2 (on the threshold of sth) beginning, brink, opening, outset, start, verge

thrift n carefulness, economizing, economy, frugality, miserliness, penny-pinching, saving

thrifty adj careful, economical, economizing, frugal, mean, miserly, parsimonious, penny-pinching, prudent, sparing

thrill n 1 flutter, frisson, quiver, shudder, tingle, tremble, tremor, vibration. 2 delight, joy, pleasure. 3 buzz inf, kick inf

thrill v arouse, electrify, excite, stir, titillate

thrilling adj electrifying, exciting, gripping, hair-raising inf, riveting, rousing, sensational, stimulating, stirring

thrive v 1 be vigorous, bloom, do well, grow, shoot up. 2 develop, flourish, grow, increase, prosper, succeed

thriving adj 1 blooming, doing well, flourishing, growing, healthy, prolific. 2 booming, burgeoning, developing, growing, prospering, prosperous, successful, wealthy

throb v beat, palpitate, pound, pulsate, pulse, thump, vibrate

throng n crowd, flock, horde, host, mass, mob, multitude, swarm

throttle v asphyxiate, choke, smother, stifle, strangle, suffocate

throw n fling, heave, lob, shot, shy, toss

throw v 1 cast, chuck inf, fling, heave, hurl, launch, lob, pitch, project, propel, shy, sling, toss. 2 **throw away** (throw away the garbage) chuck out inf, discard, dispense with, dispose of, dump inf, jettison, reject, scrap, throw out. 3 **throw away** (throw away your chance) blow inf, lose, squander, waste. 4 **throw out** (throw out garbage) chuck out inf, discard, jettison, junk inf, scrap. 5 **throw out** (throw sb out of their home) chuck out inf, evict, kick out inf. 6 **throw out** (throw out light) emit, give off, radiate, send out

thrust n 1 force, impetus, momentum, pressure. 2 drive, jab, lunge, poke, prod, push, shove, stab

thrust v drive, elbow, force, impel, jostle, lunge, plunge, poke, press, prod, push, shove, stab, urge

thud n bang, clunk, crash, smack, thump

thud v bang, clump, crash, knock, smack, thump

thug n assassin, delinquent, gangster, heavy sl, hoodlum, hooligan, killer, murderer, ruffian, tough inf, troublemaker, vandal, yob

thump n bang, clunk, crash, knock, rap, slap, smack, thud

thump v 1 bang, batter, beat, clobber sl, crash, hit, knock, pound, punch, rap,

smack, strike, thrash, thud, whack inf. 2 pound, pulse, throb

thunder n boom, booming, clap, crack, crash, roar, roaring, roll, rumble, rumbling

thunder v bellow, blast, boom, clap, crack, crash, peal, resound, reverberate, roar, rumble, shout, yell

thwart v check, defeat, foil, frustrate, hinder, impede, obstruct, oppose, outwit, prevent, stand in the way of, stop, stump

ticket n card, coupon, docket, label, pass, permit, slip, sticker, tab, tag, token, voucher

tide n course, current, drift, ebb, flow, stream, tidal flow, tidewater, tideway, undertow

tidy adj 1 (a tidy person) careful, house-proud, methodical, neat, organized, presentable, systematic, well-groomed; opp untidy. 2 (a tidy room) clean, in good order, shipshape, spick and span, spruce, trim, uncluttered, well-kept, well-ordered; opp untidy

tie n 1 catch, clip, cord, fastening, link. 2 (have no ties) bond, commitment, obligation, responsibility. 3 (in a game) dead heat, draw, stalemate. 4 (wear a tie) bow tie, cravat, necktie

tie v 1 attach, bind, chain, connect, couple, fasten, hitch, join, knot, lash, link, moor, rope, secure, splice, tether, tie up. 2 (in a game) be even, be equal, be level, be neck and neck, draw

tier n bank, file, layer, level, line, order, rank, row, story

tight adj 1 fast, firm, fixed, rigid, secure, stiff, strained, stretched, taut, tense.

2 (a tight space) compact, constricted, cramped, inadequate, limited, restricted, small. 3 (a tight sweater) close-fitting, figure-hugging, snug, tight-fitting, too small; **opp** loose. 4 (a tight lid) airtight, impermeable, leakproof, sealed, waterproof, watertight. 5 (not generous) mean, miserly, stingy, tight-fisted; **opp** generous. 6 (a tight match) close, even, well-matched

tighten v become tighter, close, close up, constrict, fasten, harden, make taut, make tight, narrow, pull tight, secure, squeeze, stiffen, stretch, tense

tilt n angle, inclination, incline, pitch, slant, slope

tilt v bank, heel over, incline, keel over, lean, list, slant, slope, tip

timber n beams, boards, firewood, forest, logs, planks, trees, tree trunks, wood

time n 1 (in the time of Jefferson) age, days, epoch, era, period. 2 (do sth for a time) interval, period, spell, stretch, term, while. 3 (the right time to do sth) juncture, moment, occasion, opportunity, point. 4 (clap in time) beat, measure, meter, rhythm, tempo

time v 1 (time your arrival) choose a time for, fix a time for, plan, schedule. 2 (time how long sth takes) clock, count, measure

timeless adj ageless, deathless, endless, eternal, everlasting, immortal, lasting, permanent, unchanging, undying

timely adj appropriate, convenient, fitting, judicious, opportune, prompt, punctual, suitable, well-timed; **opp** untimely

timetable n agenda, calendar, diary, list, program, rota, schedule

timid adj afraid, apprehensive, bashful, coy, fearful, nervous, scared, shy, spineless, unadventurous, wimpish inf; **opp** bold

tingle n 1 itch, pins and needles inf, prickling, stinging, tickle, tingling. 2 quiver, sensation, shiver, thrill, tremor

tingle v itch, prickle, sting, tickle

tinker v dabble, fiddle, meddle, mess about, play, potter, tamper, toy

tint n color, coloring, dye, hue, shade, stain, tone, wash

tint v color, dye, rinse, stain, wash

tiny adj diminutive, infinitesimal, insignificant, little, microscopic, mini inf, miniature, minute, negligible, small, teeny-weeny inf, wee; **opp** huge, large

tip n 1 (the end of sth) apex, cap, cover, crown, end, head, nib, peak, pinnacle, point, summit, top. 2 (a useful tip) hint, piece of advice, pointer, recommendation, suggestion, tip-off. 3 (leave a tip) gift, gratuity, money, reward

tip v 1 capsize, incline, keel, lean, list, overturn, slant, spill, tilt, tip over, topple, upend, upset. 2 (tip sth somewhere) dump, empty, pour out, unload. 3 (tip sb) give a tip to, leave a tip for, reward

tire v 1 (tire sb) exhaust, overtire, take it out of inf, wear out, weary. 2 (feel tired) droop, flag, get tired. 3 (tire of sth) be fed up with inf, be sick of inf, be weary of, get bored with

tired adj dead on your feet inf, dog-tired inf, done in inf, drained, drowsy, exhausted, fatigued, shattered inf, sleepy, weary, worn out, zonked *sl*

tireless *adj* determined, dogged, energetic, industrious, unflagging, untiring, vigorous

tiresome *adj* annoying, boring, dull, exasperating, irritating, laborious, maddening, monotonous, tedious, troublesome, trying, wearing

tiring *adj* arduous, exacting, exhausting, fatiguing, strenuous, taxing, tough, wearying

tissue *n* 1 gauze, netting, webbing. 2 paper handkerchief. 3 tissue paper

title *n* 1 caption, credit, heading, headline, inscription, label, name. 2 designation, form of address, name, nickname, position, rank, status. 3 (title to sth) claim, entitlement, ownership, possession, privilege, right. 4 (win a title) championship, crown

titled *adj* aristocratic, noble, upper-class

toast *n* drink, salute, tribute

toast *v* 1 drink a toast to, drink the health of, drink to, raise your glass to, salute. 2 (toast sth under the grill) brown, crisp, cook, grill, heat, warm

together *adv* 1 (work together) closely, collectively, cooperatively, jointly, side by side. 2 (do sth together) all at once, at the same time, in chorus, in unison, simultaneously

toil *n* drudgery, effort, exertion, grind *inf*, hard work, industry, labor, slaving, work

toil *v* drudge, keep at it *inf*, labor, push yourself, slave, slog, strive, struggle, sweat *inf*, work

toilet *n* bathroom, latrine, lavatory, privy, urinal, washroom

token *adj* nominal, notional, superficial, symbolic

token *n* 1 (a token of sth) demonstration, emblem, evidence, expression, indication, keepsake, mark, memento, proof, reminder, sign, symbol. 2 counter, coupon, disk, voucher

tolerable *adj* 1 acceptable, bearable, endurable; *opp* intolerable, unbearable. 2 acceptable, adequate, all right, average, fair, good enough, O.K. *inf*, not bad *inf*, satisfactory

tolerance *n* 1 acceptance, endurance, forbearance, fortitude, resilience, stamina, toughness. 2 fairness, forgiveness, indulgence, lenience, open-mindedness, patience, understanding

tolerant *adj* charitable, easygoing, forbearing, magnanimous, open-minded, patient, sympathetic, understanding, unprejudiced; *opp* intolerant

tolerate *v* accept, allow, bear, condone, countenance, endure, permit, put up with, sanction, stand, stomach, submit to, suffer, swallow, take, undergo

toll *n* 1 (pay a toll) charge, customs, dues, duty, fee, levy, payment, tariff, tax. 2 (a heavy toll) cost, damage, loss, penalty

toll *v* 1 chime, clang, knell, peal, ring, sound, strike. 2 (toll the hour) announce, call, herald, signal

tomb *n* burial chamber, catacomb, crypt, grave, mausoleum, monument, sepulchre, tombstone, vault

tone *n* 1 (of voice) accent, emphasis, force, inflection, intonation, modulation, phrasing, pitch, sound, sound quality, stress, timbre, tone of voice, volume. 2 (mood) air, atmosphere, attitude, character, drift, effect, feel, feeling, manner, mood, note, quality, spirit, style, temper, vein. 3 (color) cast, color, hue, shade, tint

tone v 1 blend, go, go well, harmonize, match, suit. 2 **tone down** dampen, moderate, modulate, play down, reduce, restrain, soften, subdue, temper

tongue n dialect, idiom, language, lingo inf, parlance, patois, speech, talk, vernacular

tongue-tied adj at a loss for words, dumb, dumbfounded, dumbstruck, inarticulate, mute, silent, speechless, struck dumb

tonic n boost, pick-me-up, refresher, shot in the arm inf, stimulant

tool n aid, appliance, contrivance, device, gadget, implement, instrument, machine, utensil

top adj 1 (top score) best, high, highest, maximum, most, winning. 2 (the top step) highest, topmost, uppermost. 3 (a top athlete) ace inf, fine, great, topnotch inf. 4 (top people in society) elite, important, influential, superior. 5 (top quality) best, choicest, first, finest, supreme

top n 1 apex, crest, crown, head, height, highest point, peak, pinnacle, summit, tip, vertex, zenith. 2 (top of a container) cap, cork, cover, covering, lid, stopper. 3 (top of the line) head, lead. 4 (piece of clothing) blouse, shirt, sweater, sweatshirt, T-shirt

top v 1 (top the dish with tomatoes) coat, complete, cover, decorate, finish, garnish, spread. 2 (do better than sth or sb) beat, do better than, eclipse, exceed, excel, outdo, outstrip, surpass, transcend

topic n issue, matter, point, question, subject, text, theme

topical adj contemporary, current, in the news, recent, up-to-date

topple v 1 (topple sth) fell, knock down, knock over, push over, tip over, upset. 2 (sth topples) capsize, collapse, fall, fall over, keel over, overbalance, overturn, totter, tumble. 3 (topple a government) bring down, oust, overthrow, overturn, unseat

torch n brand, flashlight, lamp

torment n 1 agony, anguish, distress, hell, misery, ordeal, pain, persecution, suffering, torture, wretchedness. 2 annoyance, bane, bother, curse, hassle inf, irritation, nuisance, worry

torment v 1 afflict, cause pain to, distress, harrow, hurt, pain, persecute, plague, torture, victimize. 2 aggravate inf, annoy, bother, harass, hassle inf, irritate, nag, persecute, pester, provoke, tease

torn adj 1 cut, lacerated, ragged, slit, split, tattered. 2 (feel torn) of two minds inf, split, uncertain, undecided, unsure, wavering

tornado n cyclone, gale, hurricane, squall, storm, tempest, twister inf, typhoon, whirlwind

turpid adj apathetic, dull, heavy, inert, languid, lethargic, listless, sleepy, slothful, slow, slow-moving, sluggish

torrent n cascade, current, deluge, downpour, flood, flow, gush, rush, spate, stream, tide

tortuous adj circuitous, complicated, convoluted, curling, curvy, indirect, meandering, turning, twisted, twisting, twisty, wandering, winding; **opp** direct

torture n abuse, agony, anguish, cruelty, distress, hell, humiliation, martyrdom, misery, pain, persecution, punishment, suffering, torment

torture v 1 abuse, be cruel to, bully, cause pain to, hurt, ill-treat, inflict pain on, persecute, torment, victimize. 2 afflict, agonize, distress, nag, plague, trouble, worry

toss n 1 (a toss of the head) jerk, jiggle, movement, shake. 2 (the toss of a coin) flip, throw, tossing

toss v 1 chuck inf, fling, hurl, sling, throw. 2 (ships being tossed by the waves) bob, disturb, jolt, lurch, pitch, plunge, rock, roll, shake. 3 (tossing and turning) move restlessly, squirm, wriggle, writhe, thrash, tumble. 4 (toss your head) jerk, throw back. 5 (toss a pancake) flip, throw, turn. 6 (toss a coin) flick, flip, spin, throw

total n amount, answer, mass, sum, sum total, totality, whole

total v 1 add up to, amount to, come to, make, reach. 2 add up, calculate, compute, count up, find the sum of, reckon, work out

totalitarian adj absolute, authoritarian, autocratic, despotic, dictatorial, fascist, one-party, oppressive, tyrannical, undemocratic

totter v be unsteady, dodder, falter, lurch, quiver, reel, rock, shake, stagger, stumble, sway, teeter, walk unsteadily, wobble

touch n 1 blow, brush, caress, contact, hit, pat, pressure, stroke, tap. 2 (a touch of sth) bit, dash, drop, hint, jot, pinch, smattering, speck, spot, suggestion, taste, trace. 3 (do sth by touch) feel, feeling, sense of touch, touching. 4 (sb's touch) ability, artistry, capability, expertise, flair, gift, knack, skill, technique, way

touch v 1 (touch sth) brush, caress, feel, finger, fondle, handle, pat, push, rub, stroke, tap. 2 (things touch) abut, border, come into contact, come together, converge, join, meet. 3 (touch sb emotionally) affect, disturb, get to inf, influence, make sad, move, soften, stir, upset. 4 (don't touch) fiddle with, interfere with, mess about with, move, play with, toy with. 5 **touch up** enhance, finish off, improve, patch up, perfect, put the finishing touches to, repair, retouch

touching adj affecting, emotional, heart-rending, heart-warming, moving, poignant, sad, stirring, tender, upsetting

touchy adj bad-tempered, cross, easily offended, grouchy inf, grumpy, hypersensitive, irritable, oversensitive, quick-tempered, sensitive, short-tempered, thin-skinned

tough adj 1 durable, firm, hard, hard-wearing, indestructible, lasting, leathery, rigid, rugged, solid, sound, stiff, stout, strong, sturdy, substantial, unbreakable, well-made; **opp** delicate, flimsy. 2 (a tough decision) difficult, hard, troublesome; **opp** easy. 3 (a tough climb) arduous, challenging, demanding, difficult, grueling, hard, strenuous; **opp** gentle. 4 (tough meat) chewy, hard, gristly, leathery, rubbery, stringy; **opp** tender. 5 (of a person) hard, macho, rough, rowdy, strong, vicious, violent, wild. 6 (a tough life) grim, hard, harsh, rough, severe, strict; **opp** easy. 7 (be tough with sb) firm, merciless, severe, stern, strict, unbending, unsympathetic; **opp** lenient. 8 (that's tough) regrettable, too bad inf, unfortunate, unlucky

tough n brute, bully, heavy sl, hooligan, ruffian, thug

tour n excursion, jaunt, journey, outing, ride, trip

tour v explore, go around, go sightseeing, journey through, travel around, vacation in, visit

tourist n globetrotter inf, sightseer, traveler, visitor, voyager

tournament n championship, competition, contest, event, match, meeting, series

tow v drag, draw, haul, lug, pull, trail, tug

tower n 1 belfry, bell tower, column, minaret, obelisk, pillar, skyscraper, spire, steeple, turret. 2 castle, citadel, fort, fortress, keep, stronghold

tower v dominate, loom, mount, overlook, rear, rise, soar, stand out, stick up

towering adj 1 (very high) colossal, gigantic, high, huge, lofty, sky-high, soaring. 2 (very intense) extreme, fiery, frenzied, intense, mighty, overpowering, terrible, vehement, violent

town n borough, city, hamlet, settlement, township, village

toxic adj dangerous, deadly, harmful, lethal, noxious, poisonous

toy n game, plaything

trace n 1 evidence, indication, mark,

record, relic, remnant, sign, survival, token, vestige. 2 (a trace of sth) bit, dash, drop, hint, iota, shadow, suggestion, touch, trifle, whiff. 3 footprint, mark, print, spoor, track, trail

trace v 1 detect, dig up, discover, find, get back, recover, retrieve, track down, turn up, uncover, unearth. 2 follow, pursue, track, track down, trail, tail. 3 (trace sth on paper) chart, copy, draw, go over, make a copy of, map, mark out, record, show, sketch

track n 1 footmark, footprint, footstep, mark, path, print, scent, spoor, trace, trail. 2 bridle path, bridleway, footpath, path, road, route, trail, way. 3 course, flight path, orbit, route, slipstream, trajectory, wake. 4 line, rail, rails. 5 circuit, dirt-track, racecourse, racetrack

track v chase, dog, follow, hound, pursue, shadow, stalk, tail, trace, trail

tracks n impressions, imprints, marks, wheel marks

tractable adj amenable, compliant, controllable, docile, dutiful, manageable, obedient, submissive, tame, willing

trade n 1 barter, business, buying and selling, commerce, dealing, exchange, marketing, merchandising, trading, traffic, trafficking, transactions. 2 (learn a trade) business, calling, career, job, line of work, occupation, profession, skill. 3 (arrange a trade) deal, exchange, swap

trade v bargain, barter, buy and sell, deal, do business, exchange, market, peddle, traffic, swap, switch

trader n broker, buyer, dealer, merchant, retailer, salesman, seller, shopkeeper, storekeeper, supplier

tradesman n 1 merchant, retailer, seller, shopkeeper, storekeeper, supplier. 2 craftsman, skilled worker, workman

tradition n 1 belief, folklore. 2 custom, habit, institution, practice, rite, ritual, usage

traditional adj 1 conventional, customary, established, familiar, fixed, habitual, time-honored, usual. 2 (traditional legends) folk, historic, old, oral, popular, unwritten

traffic n 1 cars, vehicles. 2 freight, movement of goods, movement of passengers, shipping, transport, transportation. 3 (traffic in drugs) barter, business, commerce, dealings, peddling, smuggling, trade, trading, trafficking

traffic v deal, do business, peddle, smuggle, trade

tragedy n 1 blow, calamity, catastrophe, disaster, misfortune, shock. 2 adversity, misfortune, sad events, sadness

tragic adj 1 appalling, awful, calamitous, catastrophic, dire, disastrous, dreadful, fatal, ill-fated, ill-starred, miserable, sad, shocking, unfortunate, unlucky; opp fortunate. 2 doleful, grief-stricken, hurt, pathetic, pitiful, sad, sorrowful, unhappy, woeful

trail n 1 evidence, footmarks, footprints, marks, scent, signs, slipstream, spoor, traces, wake. 2 path, pathway, road, route, track

trail v 1 (pull sth behind you) drag, draw, haul, pull, tow. 2 (hang down) dangle, drag, droop, hang, sweep. 3 (go after sb) chase, follow, pursue, shadow, stalk, tail, trace, track, track down. 4 (go along a surface) crawl, creep. 5 (go slowly) dawdle, drag, lag, linger, loiter, plod, straggle

train n 1 carriage, diesel, steam train. 2 caravan, column, convoy, line, file, procession. 3 (sth that follows) path, stream, wake, wash, tail, trail

train v 1 (train sb) coach, drill, educate, guide, indoctrinate, instruct, prepare, school, teach, tutor. 2 (train to do sth) learn, prepare, rehearse, study. 3 (train before a race) exercise, practice, work out. 4 (train a rifle on sb) aim, direct, level, point

trainer n coach, instructor, teacher, tutor

training n 1 exercise, practice, preparation. 2 discipline, education, guidance, instruction, schooling, teaching, upbringing

trait n attribute, characteristic, feature, idiosyncrasy, mannerism, peculiarity, quality, quirk

traitor n back-stabber, betrayer, deceiver, deserter, double-crosser, informer, Judas, renegade

tramp n bag lady, beggar, bum inf, dosser inf, down-and-out, drifter, homeless person, vagrant, wanderer

tramp v 1 (go for a walk) hike, march, ramble, roam, rove, stride, trek, walk. 2 (walk heavily) march, plod, stamp, stomp, stump, toil, traipse, trudge

trample v crush, flatten, squash, squish inf, stamp on, stand on, step on, tread on, walk on

trance n daze, dream, hypnotic state, rapture, reverie, semi-consciousness, spell, stupor

tranquil adj 1 calm, peaceful, placid, quiet, restful, serene, still, undisturbed. 2 (of a person) composed, cool, even-tempered, placid, serene, unemotional, unflappable

tranquilize v calm, calm down, pacify, quieten, relax, sedate, settle, soothe

tranquilizer n barbiturate, downer inf, narcotic, sedative, **opp** stimulant

tranquillity n calm, calmness, composure, coolness, equanimity, peace, peacefulness, placidity, quiet, quietness, restfulness, serenity, stillness

transaction n agreement, arrangement, deal, item, negotiation, purchase, sale, settlement

transcend v exceed, go beyond, leave behind, outdo, rise above, surpass, top

transcribe v copy, record, rewrite, transliterate, write out

transfer n 1 change, changeover, conveyance, delivery, move, relocation, transport, transmission. 2 change of ownership, conveyancing, handover, sale

transfer v 1 carry, change over, convey, ferry, move, relocate, transplant, transport. 2 give, hand over, pass on, pass over, sell

transfix v 1 fix, hold, hypnotize, mesmerize, paralyze, petrify, root to the spot. 2 impale, run through, skewer, spear, spike, stab

transform v alter, change, convert, make over, metamorphose, remodel, reshape, restructure, revolutionize

transformation n change, alteration, conversion, makeover, metamorphosis, remodeling, reshaping, restructuring, revolution, sea change, transition

transgress v 1 break the law, do wrong, misbehave, offend, sin; **opp** behave. 2 breach, break, contravene, defy, disobey, infringe, overstep, violate; **opp** abide by, keep, obey

transgression n 1 crime, disobedience, error, misbehavior, misdemeanor, mistake, offense, sin, wrong, wrongdoing. 2 breach, contravention, infringement, violation

transient adj brief, ephemeral, fleeting, passing, short-lived, short, temporary, transitory; **opp** long-lasting, permanent

transition n change, conversion, development, evolution, progress, progression, shift, transformation

transitional adj 1 (a transitional government) caretaker, provisional, temporary. 2 changeover, changing, conversion, developing, developmental, evolutionary, evolving

transitory adj brief, ephemeral, fleeting, passing, short-lived, short, temporary, transient; **opp** long-lasting, permanent

translate v 1 decipher, decode, explain, interpret, paraphrase, transcribe. 2 alter, change, convert, rephrase, transform, turn

transmission n 1 broadcast, edition, program, repeat, show, showing. 2 broadcasting, carriage, communication, dispatch, dissemination, relaying, sending, shipment, spread, transfer, transport

transmit v broadcast, carry, convey,

dispatch, disseminate, emit, forward, mail, pass on, post, put on air, put out, relay, send, ship, spread, transfer, transport

transparent adj 1 blatant, clear, evident, obvious, open, patent, plain, unambiguous, unequivocal, unmistakable, visible; *opp* obscure. 2 clear, crystal-clear, glassy, see-through, sheer, translucent; *opp* cloudy, opaque

transpire v 1 arise, come about, happen, occur. 2 emerge, become apparent, become known, come to light

transport n carriage, conveyance, dispatch, freight, haulage, movement, moving, shipment, shipping, transfer

transport v bring, carry, convey, fetch, move, shift, ship, take, transfer

transpose v 1 change, exchange, invert, reorder, reverse, swap, switch. 2 convert, rewrite

trap n ambush, booby-trap, pitfall, ploy, ruse, snare, trick

trap v block, catch, catch out, confine, corner, cut off, hold back, imprison, inveigle, lure, shut in, snare, trick, trip up

trapped adj blocked, caught, cornered, cut off, imprisoned, in a tight spot, locked in, shut in, snared, stuck, with your hands tied; *opp* free

trappings n accessories, apparatus, bits and pieces, extras, finery, frills, gear inf, paraphernalia, things, trimmings

trash n 1 garbage, junk, litter, refuse, rubbish, waste. 2 drivel, hot air, nonsense, rot inf, rubbish, tripe inf, twaddle inf

trashy adj cheap, poor, shoddy, tacky, useless, worthless

traumatic adj difficult, distressing, frightening, harrowing, nerve-racking, painful, stressful, upsetting; *opp* easy

travel v backpack, cross, fly, go, go on a trip, go on vacation, journey, move, proceed, sail, tour, trek, vacation, visit, walk

traveler n backpacker, commuter, explorer, gypsy, holidaymaker, itinerant, migrant, nomad, passenger, pilgrim, tourist, vacationer, visitor

traveling adj itinerant, migrant, migratory, mobile, nomadic, touring, wandering

travesty n caricature, distortion, farce, misrepresentation, mockery, parody, perversion, send-up, sham

treacherous adj 1 dangerous, dicey inf, hazardous, perilous, tricky, unsafe; *opp* safe. 2 deceitful, disloyal, double-crossing, double-dealing, faithless, false, unfaithful, untrustworthy; *opp* loyal

treachery n back-stabbing, betrayal, deceit, deception, disloyalty, double-dealing, duplicity, treason; *opp* loyalty

tread n footfall, footstep, step, tramp, walk

tread v 1 go, march, pace, step, stride, tramp, walk. 2 crush underfoot, press, squash, stamp on, stand on, trample, walk on

treason n betrayal, disloyalty, high treason, rebellion, sedition, subversion, treachery

treasure n 1 booty, cache, gold, hoard, jewels, riches, treasure trove, valuables. 2 (a person) darling, gem, star

treasure v cherish, guard, idolize,

treat n amusement, indulgence, luxury, outing, pleasure, present, surprise

treat v 1 consider, deal with, handle, manage, regard, tackle, think of, view. 2 (give treatment to) attend to, care for, cure, dress, give treatment to, minister to, nurse, tend. 3 (give sb a treat) buy sth for sb, entertain, give sb a treat, pay for, take sb out

treatise n article, dissertation, essay, monograph, paper, study, thesis, tract

treatment n 1 conduct, coverage, handling, management, usage, use. 2 care, cure, first aid, healing, medication, medicine, operation, prescription, remedy, surgery, therapy

treaty n agreement, alliance, concordat, contract, convention, deal, pact, protocol, settlement

trek n expedition, hike, journey, march, safari, slog inf, trip, walk

trek v backpack, hike, march, slog inf, traipse, travel, trudge, walk

tremble n judder, quaking, quiver, shaking, shiver, shudder, vibration, wobble

tremble v judder, quake, quiver, shake, shiver, shudder, vibrate, wobble

tremendous adj 1 ace inf, amazing, brilliant, excellent, fantastic, marvelous, sensational, superb, terrific, wonderful; opp awful, dire. 2 colossal, enormous, giant, gigantic, great, huge, massive, vast; opp minute, tiny

tremor n earthquake, judder, quake, quiver, shaking, shiver, tremble, trembling, vibration, wobble

trench n channel, ditch, furrow, hole, trough

trend n 1 bias, development, direction, inclination, movement, shift, tendency. 2 craze, fad inf, fashion, look, style, vogue

trendy adj all the rage, fashionable, in fashion, in vogue, latest, smart, stylish, up-to-date, up-to-the-minute

trespass v encroach, intrude

trial adj experimental, exploratory, pilot, probationary, provisional, test

trial n 1 case, court case, court-martial, court proceedings, hearing, inquiry, lawsuit, legal action, legal proceedings, litigation, prosecution, tribunal. 2 (test) check, dry run inf, probation, test, test run, testing, trial period, trial run. 3 (hardship) adversity, difficulty, hardship, misery, nuisance, ordeal, pain inf, problem, suffering, tribulation, trouble, woe, worry

tribe n clan, ethnic group, family, group, people, race

tribute n accolade, acknowledgment, appreciation, compliment, honor, praise, recognition; opp criticism

trick n 1 cheat, con inf, deception, dodge, hoax, ploy, practical joke, prank, ruse, scam inf, stunt, swindle. 2 art, gift, knack, secret, skill, technique. 3 conjuring, magic, sleight of hand

trick v cheat, con inf, deceive, diddle, double-cross, fool, pull a fast one inf, pull sb's leg, pull the wool over sb's eyes inf, swindle, take sb in

trickery n cheating, con inf, deceit, deception, dishonesty, double-dealing, duplicity, fraud, hoax, sleight-of-hand, swindle

trickle n dribble, drip, leak, leakage, seepage

trickle v dribble, drip, filter, leak, ooze, percolate, run, seep

tricky adj awkward, complicated, delicate, dicey inf, difficult, risky, sticky inf, touch-and-go; **opp** simple, straightforward

trifle n 1 bauble, irrelevance, knick-knack, nothing, rubbish, sth of little consequence, trinket, trivia, triviality. 2 bit, drop, little bit, tad inf, touch

trifle v fiddle, fool, meddle, mess about inf, play, toy, treat lightly

trifling adj frivolous, inconsequential, insignificant, irrelevant, minor, negligible, paltry, petty, silly, trivial, unimportant, worthless; **opp** important, major

trim adj 1 neat, neat and tidy, orderly, smart, spick and span, tidy, well-groomed; **opp** untidy. 2 in good shape, shapely, slender, slim, willowy; **opp** fat, overweight

trim v 1 clip, cut, cut back, even up, lop, pare, peel, prune, shape, snip, tidy up. 2 decorate, dress, garnish

trimmings n accompaniments, decorations, extras, garnish, ornaments, trappings

trip n business trip, day trip, excursion, expedition, holiday, journey, outing, ride, tour, visit

trip v fall, fall over sth, lose your footing, slip, stagger, stumble

trite adj banal, cliched, dull, hackneyed, insincere, overused, stale, tired, unimaginative, uninteresting, uninspired, unoriginal,

worn-out; **opp** original

triumph n 1 (a victory) achievement, coup, feat, sensation, success, victory, win. 2 (joy) elation, exultation, joy, jubilation, pride

triumph v carry the day, come out on top, come through, defeat, overcome, prevail, succeed, vanquish, win; **opp** fail, lose

triumphant adj 1 elated, exultant, gleeful, joyful, joyous, jubilant, pleased, proud. 2 successful, victorious, winning

trivia n minutiae, rubbish, trifles, trivialities

trivial adj inconsequential, insignificant, minor, paltry, petty, trifling, unimportant, worthless; **opp** important

troop n band, bunch, company, contingent, crowd, flock, gang, group, horde, pack, squad, team, unit

troop v crowd, flock, go, march, stream, surge, swarm

trophy n award, cup, prize, shield

tropical adj hot, humid, steamy, sticky, sultry, sweltering, torrid

trot n jog, lope, run, scamper

trot v go, jog, run, scamper, scuttle, toddle, trundle

trouble n 1 (difficulty) affliction, anxiety, difficulty, hassle, heartache, misfortune, nuisance, problem, suffering, tribulation, worry. 2 (unrest) bother, commotion, discontent, disorder, disturbance, fighting, fuss, rioting, row, unrest; **opp** calm, peace. 3 (heart trouble) complaint, condition, defect, disorder, illness, problem

trouble v afflict, bother, concern, distress,

disturb, plague, torment, upset, worry;
opp reassure

troublemaker *n* agitator, hooligan,
mischief-maker, rabble-rouser, rowdy,
stirrer

troublesome *adj* 1 annoying, difficult,
distressing, hard, irritating, problematic,
tiresome, tricky, trying, upsetting,
worrying; *opp* easy, straightforward.
2 (of a person) badly behaved,
disobedient, disorderly, naughty, rowdy,
undisciplined, unruly; *opp* obedient,
placid, well-behaved

trousers *n* chinos, cords, denims, jeans,
pants, slacks

truant *n* 1 absconder, absentee, dodger,
runaway. 2 **play truant** be absent
without leave, go AWOL, play hooky *inf*

truce *n* armistice, ceasefire, cessation,
letup, pact, peace, respite, suspension of
hostilities

trudge *n* haul, hike, march, slog *inf*,
struggle, traipse, tramp, trek, walk

trudge *v* hike, march, plod, slog *inf*,
stomp, struggle, traipse, tramp,
trek, walk

true *adj* 1 (a true story) correct, factual,
honest, legitimate, right, truthful, valid.
2 (genuine) actual, authentic, bona
fide, genuine, proper, real. 3 (the true
meaning) accurate, close, correct, exact,
precise. 4 (loyal) constant, dedicated,
dependable, devoted, faithful, firm,
loyal, staunch, trustworthy

trunk *n* 1 (of a tree) main stem, stalk,
stem. 2 box, case, chest, crate. 3 (of an
animal) nose, snout. 4 body, torso

trust *n* 1 (faith) belief, confidence,
expectation, faith, reliance.

2 (custody) care, charge, custody,
guardianship, protection, responsibility,
safekeeping

trust *v* 1 bank on, be sure of, count on,
depend on, have confidence in, have
faith in, put your faith in, rely on.
2 anticipate, assume, expect, hope,
presume, suppose

trusting *adj* credulous, gullible, innocent,
unquestioning, unsuspecting, unwary;
opp skeptical, suspicious, wary

trustworthy *adj* dependable, honest,
loyal, reliable, responsible, true;
opp dishonest, unreliable

trusty *adj* dependable, faithful, loyal,
reliable, staunch, trusted, trustworthy

truth *n* accuracy, authenticity, candor,
correctness, fact, genuineness, honesty,
legitimacy, reality, truthfulness, validity,
veracity; *opp* falsehood, fallacy

truthful *adj* accurate, candid, correct,
frank, honest, realistic, reliable, right,
sincere, straight; *opp* deceitful

try *n* attempt, bash *inf*, effort, go,
shot *inf*, stab *inf*

try *v* 1 aim, attempt, do your best,
endeavor, have a go, have a stab at *inf*,
make an attempt, make an effort,
undertake. 2 (judge) adjudicate, hear,
judge, put on trial. 3 (test) appraise,
check out, evaluate, sample, test, trial,
try out. 4 annoy, put to the test,
strain, tax

trying *adj* annoying, arduous, demanding,
difficult, exasperating, irritating,
stressful, taxing, tiresome, tiring,
tough; *opp* easy

tub *n* barrel, bath, butt, cask, container,
jar, keg, pot

tube n conduit, cylinder, duct, hose, pipe, roll

tug n haul, heave, jerk, pluck, pull, wrench, yank

tug v drag, haul, heave, jerk, lug, pluck, pull, tow, wrench, yank

tuition n coaching, education, instruction, lessons, teaching, training, tutelage

tumble n 1 fall, somersault. 2 collapse, crash, drop, fall, nosedive, plunge, slump

tumble v 1 fall, fall over, lose your footing, overbalance, pitch, roll, somersault, topple. 2 (of prices or numbers) collapse, crash, dive, drop, fall, nosedive, plummet, plunge, slump; **opp** rise

tumult n bedlam, chaos, commotion, confusion, disorder, free-for-all, hubbub, hullabaloo, noise, pandemonium, racket, rumpus, turmoil, upheaval, uproar; **opp** calm, peace

tumultuous adj chaotic, confused, disorderly, frenzied, hectic, noisy, rowdy, stormy, turbulent, unruly, uproarious, wild; **opp** calm, peaceful

tune n ditty, melody, music, song

tune v adapt, adjust, pitch, regulate, set, suit

tuneful adj attractive, catchy, easy listening, easy on the ear, lilting, lyrical, melodic, melodious, musical, pleasant, sweet; **opp** discordant, harsh

tuneless adj atonal, discordant, dissonant, flat, harsh, monotonous, out of tune, unmusical; **opp** harmonious, melodic

tunnel n burrow, hole, passage, shaft, subway, underpass

tunnel v bore, burrow, dig, mine

turbulent adj confused, disorderly, in turmoil, rough, rowdy, seething, stormy, tempestuous, troubled, tumultuous, unruly, unsettled, unstable, violent, volatile, wild; **opp** calm, orderly, peaceful

turf n 1 grass, grassland, green, lawn, pitch. 2 clod, divot

turgid adj flowery, grand, highfalutin, ornate, pompous, pretentious, wordy; **opp** plain, simple

turmoil n bedlam, chaos, commotion, confusion, disorder, hubbub, pandemonium, tumult, turbulence, upheaval, uproar; **opp** calm, peace

turn n 1 (in a game) go, move, period, round, shot, stint, try. 2 coil, cycle, loop, pirouette, revolution, roll, spin, twist. 3 (change of direction) angle, bend, change of direction, corner, curve, deviation, hairpin, junction, loop, swerve, turning, U-turn. 4 (events have taken a new turn) change, development, direction, drift, shift, tendency, trend, variation. 5 (a comedy turn) act, performance, performer, routine, set

turn v 1 (spin) circle, coil, curl, go around, gyrate, loop, pivot, revolve, roll, rotate, spin, spiral, swivel, twirl, wind. 2 bend, flip, fold, invert, reverse. 3 (change direction) change course, change direction, go, head, move, steer, swerve, swing round, veer, wheel. 4 (turn a corner) go round, negotiate, round, take. 5 (turn a hose on sb) aim, direct, point, train. 6 (change to) alter, become, change to, convert, get, go, mutate, transform. 7 **turn down** (reject) decline, refuse, reject, say no to, throw out, veto. **8 turn down** (turn down the volume) decrease, lower, make softer, make quieter, muffle, mute, reduce, soften; *opp* turn up. **9 turn off** (switch off) disconnect, put off, shut down, shut off, stop, switch off, turn out; *opp* start, switch on, turn on. **10 turn off** (turn off the main road) leave, take a side road, take a turning, turn left, turn right; *opp* join. **11 turn off** (put sb off) alienate, deter from, discourage, disgust, offend, put off, repel, sicken; *opp* attract. **12 turn on** (switch on) activate, boot, get going, start, start up, switch on; *opp* stop, switch off, turn off. **13 turn on** (depend on) be dependent on, depend on, hang on, hinge on, rest on, revolve around. **14 turn on** (attack) assault, attack, lay into, set upon. **15 turn on** (excite) attract, enthuse, excite, interest, stimulate, thrill; *opp* turn off. **16 turn up** (arrive) appear, arrive, attend, come, get here, get there, put in an appearance, show up. **17 turn up** (turn up the volume) amplify, increase, make louder, raise; *opp* turn down . **18 turn up** (discover) come across, dig up, discover, expose, find, uncover, unearth. **19 turn up** (come to light) arise, be found, come to light, crop up, happen, occur, transpire. **20 turn up** (turn up a hem) shorten, take up; *opp* lengthen, let down.

turning *n* crossroads, exit, fork, junction, left turn, right turn, road, side road, turn, turn-off

turning point *n* change, crisis, crossroads, decisive moment, eleventh hour, juncture, key moment, moment of

truth, point of no return, turn of the tide, watershed

turnover *n* business, flow, movement, output, production, profits, revenue, sales figures, takings, thoughput, receipts

tutor *n* coach, guru, instructor, lecturer, mentor, supervisor, teacher

tutor *v* coach, educate, instruct, lecture, supervise, teach, train

twilight *n* dusk, early evening, half-light, sundown, sunset, the end of the day

twin *adj* corresponding, dual, duplicate, identical, matching, symmetrical, twofold

twin *n* clone, counterpart, double, duplicate, match, mate, other half, pair, partner, spitting image, twin brother, twin sister

twine *n* cord, string, thread

twine *v* climb, coil, entwine, intertwine, snake, spiral, twist, weave, wind, worm, wrap

twinkling *n* flash, instant, jiffy, moment, second, split second, trice

twirl *n* coil, pirouette, revolution, rotation, spin, spiral, swirl, turn, twiddle, twist, whirl, whorl

twirl *v* coil, gyrate, pirouette, pivot, revolve, rotate, spin, spiral, turn, twiddle, twist, whirl, wind

twist *n* **1** coil, curl, screw, spin, spiral, swivel, turn, twiddle, twirl, wind, wring. **2** (bend) angle, bend, curve, hairpin, turn, zigzag. **3** (distortion) bend, buckle, contortion, distortion, kink, warp, wrinkle. **4** (turn of events) complication, development, oddity, quirk, revelation, slant, turn of events, variation

twist v **1** coil, corkscrew, curl, meander, screw, snake, spin, spiral, swivel, turn, twine, weave, wind, worm, wrap, wring, zigzag. **2** (contort) bend, buckle, contort, distort, kink, screw up, warp, wrinkle. **3** squirm, wriggle, writhe. **4** (twist your ankle) hurt, pull, sprain, strain, turn, wrench. **5** (twist sb's words) change, distort, falsify, misinterpret, misquote, misrepresent, pervert, warp

twisty adj bendable, contorted, crooked, curving, meandering, rambling, serpentine, sinuous, snaking, tortuous, twisting, winding, zigzag

twit n clot, clown, dimwit inf, dingbat inf, dope inf, fool, idiot, nerd inf, nitwit inf, twerp inf

twitch n **1** convulsion, jerk, jump, spasm, tic, tremor. **2** jerk, pull, tug, tweak, yank

twitch v **1** flutter, go into spasm, jerk, jump, shake, tremble. **2** jerk, pull, snatch, tug, tweak, yank

two n brace, couple, duet, duo, pair, twosome

tycoon n baron, businessperson, capitalist, entrepreneur, fat cat inf, financier, industrialist, magnate, millionaire, mogul, wheeler-dealer

type n **1** category, character, class, genre, group, kind, nature, order, sort, species, variety. **2** characters, font, lettering, letters, print, text, typeface, words

typical adj **1** average, normal, ordinary, regular, routine, run-of-the-mill, usual; **opp** unusual. **2** archetypal, classic, conventional, model, orthodox, representative, quintessential, standard, stock; **opp** unusual. **3** characteristic, in character, normal, predictable, unsurprising, usual, to be expected; **opp** unusual

typify v be a good example of, characterize, epitomize, exemplify, personify, represent, sum up, symbolize

tyrannical adj authoritarian, autocratic, despotic, dictatorial, domineering, high-handed, oppressive, overbearing, severe, totalitarian, undemocratic, unjust

tyranny n **1** absolutism, authoritarianism, autocracy, despotism, dictatorship. **2** coercion, cruelty, harshness, oppression, severity

tyrant n **1** absolute ruler, authoritarian, autocrat, despot, dictator. **2** bully, martinet, oppressor, slavedriver

ugly *adj* 1 (of a person) not much to look at *inf*, plain, unattractive; *opp* good-looking. 2 (of a thing) grotesque, hideous, horrible, inelegant, misshapen, nasty, unprepossessing, unsightly. 3 (an ugly sight) disagreeable, distasteful, foul, frightful, hideous, horrible, monstrous, nasty, nauseating, obnoxious, offensive, repulsive, shocking, sickening, vile. 4 (an ugly situation) dangerous, menacing, nasty, ominous, sinister, threatening. 5 (an ugly mood) angry, hostile, sullen, surly

ulterior *adj* concealed, covert, hidden, private, secret, underlying, undisclosed; *opp* overt

ultimate *adj* 1 closing, concluding, eventual, extreme, final, last, terminal. 2 basic, fundamental, primary, root, underlying. 3 greatest, highest, paramount, supreme, unsurpassed

umpire *n* adjudicator, arbitrator, judge, ref *inf*, referee

unabashed *adj* blatant, bold, brazen, shameless, unconcerned, undismayed

unable *adj* 1 incapable, incompetent, ineffectual, not equal to, not up to, unfit, unqualified; *opp* able. 2 impotent, without the power to, not in a position to, powerless; *opp* able

unabridged *adj* complete, entire, full-length, unexpurgated, whole; *opp* abridged

unacceptable *adj* 1 inadequate, inadmissible, invalid, unsatisfactory; *opp* acceptable. 2 disagreeable, improper, inappropriate, intolerable, objectionable, obnoxious, offensive, taboo, undesirable, unpleasant, unsuitable

unaccompanied *adj* alone, by yourself, lone, on your own, solitary, solo, unescorted, unattended

unaccustomed *adj* 1 new, novel, out of the ordinary, special, unfamiliar, unusual; *opp* accustomed, usual. 2 **unaccustomed to** green, inexperienced, new to, not practiced in, not used to, unfamiliar with, unversed in; *opp* accustomed to

unafraid *adj* bold, confident, daring, fearless, intrepid, undaunted; *opp* afraid

unanimous *adj* 1 collective, common, concerted, united. 2 agreed, at one, in complete agreement, like-minded, of one mind, united, with one voice

unappetizing *adj* flavorless, insipid, not very nice, off-putting *inf*, tasteless, unattractive, uninteresting, unpalatable, unpleasant, yucky *inf*; *opp* appetizing

unapproachable *adj* 1 aloof, chilly, cold, cool, detached, distant, frigid, remote, reserved, standoffish, unfriendly, unsociable, withdrawn; *opp* approachable. 2 inaccessible, out of reach, out of the way, remote; *opp* accessible

unarmed *adj* defenseless, exposed, helpless, unprotected, vulnerable, weaponless; *opp* armed

unassuming *adj* diffident, humble, modest, natural, reticent, retiring, self-effacing, simple, unaffected, unassertive, unpretentious

unattached *adj* 1 available, footloose and fancy free, free, independent, on your own, single, unmarried, without a partner. 2 autonomous, independent, nonaligned. 3 detached, disconnected, loose; *opp* attached

unattended *adj* 1 abandoned, left alone, unguarded. 2 alone, by yourself, on your own, unaccompanied, unescorted

unattractive *adj* 1 (of a person) not much to look at *inf*, plain, ugly; *opp* attractive. 2 (of a thing) inelegant, unprepossessing, ugly, unsightly; *opp* attractive. 3 disagreeable, distasteful, foul, nasty, objectionable, off-putting *inf*, repellent, repulsive, unpleasant, vile. 4 dull, plain, uninteresting, uninviting; *opp* attractive

unauthorized *adj* illegal, illicit, irregular, unlawful, unlicensed, unofficial

unavoidable *adj* 1 bound to happen, certain, destined, fated, inescapable, inevitable, inexorable, predestined, sure, unalterable; *opp* avoidable. 2 compulsory, mandatory, necessary, obligatory

unaware *adj* ignorant, ill-informed,

oblivious, unconscious, uninformed, unknowing, unsuspecting; *opp* aware

unbalanced *adj* 1 asymmetrical, irregular, lopsided, out of balance, unstable, unsteady, wobbly; *opp* balanced. 2 crazy, demented, deranged, eccentric, insane, irrational, mad, mentally ill, out of your mind, out to lunch *inf*, unstable *inf*; *opp* sane. 3 biased, bigoted, one-sided, partial, prejudiced; *opp* balanced, fair

unbearable *adj* insufferable, intolerable, more than flesh and blood can stand *inf*, too much *inf*, unacceptable, unendurable

unbelievable *adj* beyond belief, far-fetched, implausible, impossible, improbably, inconceivable, incredible, preposterous; *opp* believable

unbiased *adj* disinterested, equitable, even-handed, fair, impartial, just, neutral, objective, unprejudiced; *opp* biased

unbreakable *adj* indestructible, shatter-proof, rugged, solid, tough, toughened

uncalled-for *adj* gratuitous, needless, undeserved, unjustified, unnecessary, unwarranted

uncanny *adj* 1 creepy *inf*, eerie, mysterious, queer, spooky *inf*, strange, supernatural, weird. 2 astonishing, astounding, extraordinary, incredible, remarkable, striking

uncertain *adj* 1 ambivalent, distrustful, doubtful, dubious, hesitant, indecisive, not convinced, not sure, of two minds, skeptical, tentative, unconvinced, undecided, unsure, vague, wavering; *opp* certain, sure. 2 chancy, dicey *inf*, doubtful, iffy *inf*, in the balance, precarious, questionable, risky, unclear, undecided, unpredictable, up in the air. **3** changeable, erratic, fitful, inconstant, not dependable, unpredictable, unreliable, unsettled, variable

uncertainty *n* **1** ambivalence, confusion, distrust, doubt, hesitance, indecision, lack of confidence, perplexity, skepticism, vacillation, vagueness; *opp* certainty. **2** doubtfulness, unpredictability, unreliability. **3** doubt, misgiving, qualm

uncharitable *adj* censorious, hard, harsh, insensitive, intolerant, stern, unchristian, uncompromising, unforgiving, unkind, unsympathetic; *opp* charitable

uncharted *adj* not mapped, strange, undiscovered, unexplored, unfamiliar, unknown, unsurveyed

uncivilized *adj* **1** barbarian, barbaric, barbarous, primitive, savage, wild; *opp* civilized. **2** boorish, churlish, coarse, philistine, uncouth, uncultured, uncultivated, uneducated, unsophisticated

unclean *adj* **1** corrupt, defiled, lewd, licentious, sinful, unchaste; *opp* pure. **2** dirty, filthy, foul, impure, polluted, soiled, stained, tainted; *opp* clean

unclear *adj* **1** dim, blurred, faint, fuzzy, hazy, indistinct, out of focus, opaque; *opp* clear. **2** ambiguous, confused, garbled, imprecise, muddled, obscure, vague; *opp* clear. **3** not known, uncertain, unknown, unpredictable; *opp* clear

uncomfortable *adj* **1** cold, comfortless, cramped, hard, lumpy, painful, spartan; *opp* comfortable. **2** anxious, awkward, edgy, embarrassed, ill-at-ease, nervous, self-conscious, troubled, worried; *opp* comfortable. **3** awkward, embarrassing, strained, unpleasant

uncommon *adj* **1** distinctive, exceptional, out of the ordinary, rare, special, strange, unusual. **2** few and far between *inf*, not common, rare, scarce, unusual. **3** extraordinary, outstanding, remarkable, striking

uncommunicative *adj* **1** close, curt, secretive, short, silent, taciturn, tight-lipped, unforthcoming. **2** aloof, reserved, reticent, retiring, shy, standoffish, unsociable, withdrawn

uncomplimentary *adj* deprecatory, derogatory, disparaging, insulting, pejorative, rude, scathing, unfavorable, unflattering; *opp* complimentary

uncompromising *adj* firm, hard-line, implacable, inflexible, intransigent, obstinate, stiff-necked, strict, stubborn, unbending

unconditional *adj* absolute, categorical, complete, entire, full, outright, total, unlimited, unqualified, unreserved, unrestricted, wholehearted, with no strings attached *inf*

unconnected *adj* **1** detached, divided, independent, separate; *opp* connected. **2** disjointed, illogical, incoherent, irrelevant, rambling, unrelated

unconscious *adj* **1** comatose, dead to the world *inf*, in a coma, insensible, knocked out, out cold *inf*, out for the count *inf*, senseless; *opp* conscious. **2** ignorant, insensible, oblivious, unaware, unsuspecting. **3** accidental, inadvertent, unintended, unpremeditated, unwitting; *opp* deliberate. **4** automatic, instinctive, involuntary, reflex, spontaneous, unthinking. **5** repressed, subconscious, subliminal, suppressed; *opp* conscious

uncontrollable *adj* **1** incorrigible, out of control, recalcitrant, undisciplined, ungovernable, unmanageable, unruly, untameable, untamed, wild. **2** frantic, frenzied, furious, ungovernable, violent

uncontrolled *adj* **1** furious, rampant, riotous, undisciplined, untamed, wild. **2** unbridled, unchecked, uninhibited, unrestrained

unconventional *adj* **1** atypical, bizarre, different, idiosyncratic, irregular, odd, offbeat, peculiar, queer, strange, unorthodox, unusual, way-out *inf*, weird, zany; *opp* conventional. **2** bohemian, eccentric, independent, individual, unorthodox, wayward, zany; *opp* conventional. **3** futuristic, new, novel, original, progressive, revolutionary, unorthodox

unconvincing *adj* dubious, far-fetched, hard to believe, implausible, improbable, inconclusive, questionable, specious, unlikely; *opp* convincing

uncooperative *adj* lazy, not lifting a finger *inf*, obstinate, obstructive, recalcitrant, resistant, selfish, self-willed, unhelpful, unruly; *opp* cooperative, helpful

uncoordinated *adj* all thumbs *inf*, awkward, blundering, bungling, clumsy, inept, lumbering, maladroit, ungainly, ungraceful

uncouth *adj* bad-mannered, boorish, churlish, coarse, crude, loutish, rough, rude, uncivilized; *opp* polite

uncover *v* **1** bare, expose, lay bare, show, strip. **2** open, unwrap. **3** bring to light, detect, disclose, discover, reveal, unearth, unmask

undecided *adj* **1** indefinite, in the balance, not decided, not known, not settled, pending, uncertain, unresolved. **2** ambivalent, dithering, doubtful, hesitant, indecisive, in two minds, not convinced, uncertain, unsure

undefined *adj* **1** imprecise, indeterminate, unclear, unexplained, unspecified, vague. **2** blurry, formless, hazy, indefinite, nebulous, shadowy, vague

undeniable *adj* **1** certain, clear, evident, manifest, obvious. **2** indisputable, irrefutable, proven, sound, sure, unquestionable

underclothes *n* lingerie, undergarments, underwear, undies *inf*

undercover *adj* clandestine, concealed, covert, furtive, hidden, hush-hush *inf*, secret, stealthy, surreptitious

undercurrent *n* **1** feeling, hint, murmur, suggestion, tendency, undertone, vibes *inf*. **2** rip, rip tide, undertow

underdog *n* little fellow *inf*, loser, victim, weaker party

underestimate *v* **1** look down on, not appreciate, not do justice to, sell short *inf*, underrate, undervalue; *opp* overestimate. **2** (a cost or price) minimize, miscalculate, misjudge, set too low, undervalue

undergo *v* be subjected to, endure, experience, go through, submit to, suffer

underground adj 1 below ground, below the surface, buried, covered, subterranean sunken. 2 clandestine, concealed, covert, hidden, secret, surreptitious, undercover, unofficial. 3 alternative, revolutionary, subversive

undergrowth n brush, brushwood, ground cover, scrub

underhand adj crafty, crooked, deceitful, devious, dishonest, double-dealing, fraudulent, sly, sneaky, treacherous, unscrupulous

underline v 1 draw a line under, underscore. 2 accentuate, call attention to, emphasize, highlight, stress

underlying adj 1 basic, fundamental, intrinsic, primary, prime, root. 2 concealed, hidden, masked, veiled

undermine v 1 damage, impair, sabotage, sap, subvert, threaten, weaken. 2 burrow under, dig under, excavate, tunnel under. 3 erode, wear away

underrate v not appreciate, not do justice to, sell short inf, underestimate, undervalue; opp overrate

understand v 1 appreciate, apprehend, catch on inf, comprehend, fathom, figure out, follow, get, get sb's drift inf, get the hang of inf, get the message inf, get the picture inf, get to the bottom of, grasp, interpret, see, take in, tumble to, work out. 2 empathize with, feel compassion towards, know how sb feels, sympathize with. 3 assume, believe, conclude, gather, hear, learn, presume, suppose, think

understanding n 1 appreciation, apprehension, comprehension, grasp, interpretation. 2 acumen, awareness,

discernment, insight, judgment, intelligence, knowledge, perceptiveness, percipience, sense, wisdom. 3 compassion, empathy, insight, kindness, sympathy, tolerance. 4 assumption, belief, conclusion, feeling, idea, perception, supposition, view. 5 arrangement, bargain, compact, contract, gentleman's agreement, pact. 6 consensus, harmony, sympathy

understanding adj compassionate, considerate, forgiving, kind, patient, perceptive, sensitive, sympathetic, tolerant

understood adj implicit, implied, inferred, tacit, unspoken, unstated

undertake v accept responsibility for, begin, embark on, give an undertaking, promise to do, set about, shoulder, start, tackle

undertaking n 1 affair, assignment, business, enterprise, operation, project, task, venture. 2 assurance, pledge, promise, vow, word

undertone n 1 low tone, low voice, murmur, whisper. 2 atmosphere, feeling, hint, suggestion, trace, undercurrent

undervalue v not appreciate, think too little of, underestimate, underrate

underwear n lingerie, underclothes, undergarments, undies inf

underweight adj all skin and bones inf, bony, emaciated, half-starved, scrawny, skinny, thin, undernourished; opp overweight

underwrite v 1 back, finance, fund, guarantee, insure, sponsor, subsidize, support. 2 agree to, approve, confirm, consent to, endorse, okay inf, ratify, sanction. **3** countersign, endorse, initial, sign

undesirable adj **1** disagreeable, disliked, nasty, unacceptable, unpleasant, unwanted. **2** disagreeable, nasty, objectionable, obnoxious, offensive, unattractive, unpleasant, unsavory

undisciplined adj **1** anarchic, disobedient, disorderly, naughty, rebellious, uncontrollable, unmanageable, unruly, untrained, wild. **2** capricious, erratic, willful. **3** chaotic, disorderly, disorganized, lax, uncontrolled, unsystematic

undisputed adj accepted, acknowledged, certain, indisputable, recognized, unchallenged, uncontested, undeniable, undoubted

undistinguished adj average, commonplace, everyday, indifferent, mediocre, nothing special inf, nothing to write home about inf, ordinary, unexceptional, unimpressive, unremarkable; opp special

undo v **1** detach, disconnect, disentangle, loosen, open, uncouple, unfasten, unlock, untie, unwrap. **2** annul, cancel, invalidate, nullify, quash, repeal, rescind, reverse, revoke, set aside. **3** defeat, destroy, overthrow, overturn, ruin, shatter, undermine, wreck

undoing n **1** collapse, defeat, destruction, disgrace, downfall, overthrow, reversal, ruin, shame. **2** blight, curse, misfortune, trouble, weakness

undone adj **1** detached, disconnected, free, loose, open, unbuttoned, uncoupled, unfastened, untied. **2** ignored, incomplete, left, neglected,

not attended to, not done, omitted, outstanding, unfinished. **3** defeated, overthrown, ruined, shattered

undoubted adj **1** beyond doubt, certain, incontrovertible, indubitable, irrefutable, proved, proven, sure, undeniable, unquestionable. **2** certain, uncontested, undisputed

undress v **1** change, get changed, get undressed, peel off, strip, strip off, take your clothes off, tear your clothes off. **2** (undress sb) get sb undressed, strip, take sb's clothes off, tear sb's clothes off

undue adj disproportionate, excessive, extreme, inappropriate, inordinate, undeserved, unjustified, unnecessary, unreasonable, unwarranted

unduly adv disproportionately, excessively, inordinately, unnecessarily, unreasonably

undying adj constant, deathless, eternal, everlasting, immortal, perpetual, unceasing, without end

unearth v **1** bring to light, discover, expose, ferret out, find, reveal, uncover. **2** dig up, disinter, dredge up, excavate, exhume

unearthly adj **1** eerie, ghastly, ghostly, spooky inf, strange, uncanny, weird. **2** absurd, preposterous, ridiculous

uneasy adj **1** agitated, anxious, apprehensive, disturbed, edgy, jittery, nervous, on edge, perturbed, tense, troubled, twitchy, upset, worried. **2** awkward, insecure, precarious, strained, tense, uncomfortable, unstable

uneconomic adj inefficient, loss-making, uneconomical, unproductive, unprofitable, wasteful

uneducated adj ignorant, ill-informed, illiterate, lowbrow, nonacademic, uncultivated, uninformed, unschooled, unskilled, untaught, untrained, untutored; **opp** educated

unemotional adj aloof, calm, cold, controlled, cool, deadpan, detached, dispassionate, distant, emotionless, expressionless, frigid, hard-nosed, heartless, icy, impassive, impersonal, indifferent, inscrutable, insensitive, passionless, phlegmatic, poker-faced, reserved, soulless, stoical, stolid, stony-faced, unconcerned, undemonstrative, unfeeling, unmoved, unresponsive, unruffled, unsentimental

unemployed adj idle, jobless, laid off, on the dole inf, out of a job, out of work, redundant, resting, unemployable, unoccupied; **opp** employed

unending adj ceaseless, constant, endless, eternal, everlasting, imperishable, incessant, never-ending, nonstop, perennial, permanent, perpetual, interminable, undying, unrelenting, unremitting, without end

unequal adj 1 asymmetrical, different, differing, disproportionate, dissimilar, uneven, unmatched, unvarying. 2 (of a society) class-ridden, hierarchical, inequitable, prejudiced, undemocratic, unfair, unjust; **opp** egalitarian

unequaled adj best, beyond compare, greatest, highest, incomparable, matchless, peerless, record, record-breaking, second to none, supreme, unbeaten, unique, unparalleled, unrivaled, unsurpassed

unequivocal adj absolute, certain, clear, definite, plain, unambiguous, unmistakable

unethical adj dishonest, dishonorable, unconscionable, unfair, unprincipled, unprofessional, unscrupulous, wrong; **opp** ethical

uneven adj 1 bumpy, jagged, lumpy, pitted, pockmarked, rough, rutted, undulating, up-and-down; **opp** even. 2 erratic, fitful, inconsistent, intermittent, irregular, spasmodic, up-and-down, variable, varying

uneventful adj boring, humdrum, ordinary, quiet, routine, unexciting, uninteresting; **opp** eventful

unexceptional adj average, indifferent, mediocre, middling, ordinary, regular, uneventful; **opp** exceptional

unexpected adj like a bolt from the blue, sudden, surprising, unannounced, unanticipated, unforeseen, unheralded, unpredicted; **opp** expected

unfailing adj absolute, constant, dependable, regular as clockwork, reliable, surefire inf

unfair adj 1 arbitrary, dishonest, sneaky inf, undeserved, unethical, unjust, unjustifiable, unmerited, unreasonable, wrong, wrongful; **opp** fair. 2 (favoring some people and not others) biased, discriminatory, inequitable, one-sided, partial, partisan, prejudiced, unbalanced, unequal, uneven; **opp** fair, just. 3 (victimizing sb) cruel, hard, harsh, unkind

unfaithful adj 1 adulterous, flighty, flirtatious, inconstant, philandering, promiscuous, two-timing; **opp** faithful. 2 deceitful, disloyal, double-crossing, double-dealing, faithless, false, perfidious, traitorous, treacherous; **opp** loyal

unfashionable *adj* behind the times, dated, dowdy, old-fashioned, out of date, out of fashion, out of favor, outdated, outmoded, square *inf*, unhip *inf*, unpopular; **opp** fashionable

unfasten *v* detach, free, loose, release, separate, unclip, uncouple, undo, unhitch, unhook, unlock, untie; **opp** fasten

unfavorable *adj* 1 (of circumstances) adverse, disadvantageous, inauspicious, unfortunate, unpromising. 2 (of comments, opinion) adverse, damning, critical, disapproving, hostile, negative; **opp** favorable

unfeeling *adj* callous, cold, cold-blooded, cold-hearted, cruel, emotionless, hard, impassive, indifferent, insensitive, hard-hearted, heartless, inhuman, inhumane, insensitive, pitiless, uncaring, unconcerned, unemotional, unmoved, unsentimental, unsympathetic; **opp** sympathetic

unfit *adj* 1 below par, ill, injured, out of shape *inf*, sick, unhealthy, unwell, weak; **opp** fit, healthy. 2 ill-adapted, ill-suited, inadequate, inappropriate, incapable, incompetent, unacceptable, unequipped, unsuitable, unsuited, unsatisfactory, useless

unflinching *adj* bold, brave, constant, courageous, determined, nerveless, resolute, steadfast, steady, unflagging, unwavering

unfold *v* 1 extend, open out, spread out, straighten out, unfurl, unroll. 2 (of story,

events) be revealed, become known, continue, develop, evolve, progress, take place, take shape

unforeseen *adj* sudden, surprising, unanticipated, unexpected, unplanned, unscheduled

unfortunate *adj* 1 hapless, ill-fated, ill-starred, luckless, out of luck, unlucky, unsuccessful. 2 annoying, deplorable, regrettable, infelicitous, lamentable, untimely

unfounded *adj* baseless, false, groundless, idle, invalid, unjustified, unproven, unsupported, untenable, untrue, without foundation

unfriendly *adj* aloof, antagonistic, churlish, cold, distant, hostile, impolite, rude, stand-offish *inf*, surly, unkind, unpleasant; **opp** friendly

ungainly *adj* awkward, clumsy, gangling, heavy-footed, hulking, lumbering, shambling, uncoordinated; **opp** graceful

ungodly *adj* 1 blasphemous, corrupted, depraved, evil, heathen, profane, sacrilegious, sinful, unholy, wicked. 2 (at this ungodly hour) improper, inappropriate, indecent, uncivilized, unseemly

ungrateful *adj* churlish, discourteous, impolite, mercenary, rude, ungracious, unthankful; **opp** grateful

unhappy *adj* 1 depressed, disconsolate, distressed, downcast, downhearted, inconsolable, melancholy, miserable, sad; **opp** happy. 2 (unhappy about a decision) aggrieved, annoyed, discontented, disgruntled, dissatisfied, resentful; **opp** happy. 3 (of event, circumstances) deplorable, lamentable, regrettable, sad, tragic, unfortunate; *opp* fortunate

unharmed *adj* intact, safe, safe and sound, undamaged, unhurt, unscathed, untouched, whole

unhealthy *adj* **1** ailing, delicate, frail, ill, in poor health, infirm, invalid, sick, unfit, unwell, weak; *opp* healthy. **2** (unhealthy conditions) detrimental, harmful, insalubrious, insanitary, noxious, unwholesome

unheard-of *adj* inconceivable, original, unknown, unfamiliar, unimaginable, unimagined, unprecedented, without precedent

unidentified *adj* mysterious, nameless, unfamiliar, unknown, unnamed, unrecognized

uniform *adj* **1** common, comparable, consistent, equal, homogeneous, identical, invariable, same, similar, unified, universal. **2** (of speed, rate) constant, even, regular, same, smooth, unchanging, unvarying

uniform *n* costume, dress, livery, outfit, regalia, robes, suit

uniformity *n* consistency, evenness, homogeneity, monotony, regularity, sameness, similarity, utility

unify *v* amalgamate, bind, bring together, combine, fuse, harmonize, join, merge, unite

unimaginable *adj* beyond belief, fantastic, impossible, inconceivable, incredible, unbelievable

unimportant *adj* insignificant, irrelevant, meaningless, minor, obscure, paltry, petty, secondary, trifling, trivial, two-bit *inf*, worthless; *opp* important

uninhabited *adj* barren, desert, deserted, empty, unoccupied, unpopulated, vacant; *opp* inhabited

unintelligent *adj* brainless *inf*, daft *inf*, dim *inf*, foolish, hare-brained *inf*, impractical, mindless, obtuse, senseless, silly, slow, slow-witted, stupid, thoughtless, unimaginative, unwise, witless; *opp* intelligent

unintentional *adj* accidental, casual, chance, coincidental, inadvertent, subconscious, unconscious, unintended; *opp* deliberate, intentional

uninterested *adj* apathetic, bored, distracted, fed up, incurious, indifferent, listless, tired, unconcerned; *opp* interested

union *n* **1** (act of coming together) amalgamation, association, combination, conjunction, fusion, intermingling, marriage, merger, unification, uniting. **2** (organization) alliance, association, brotherhood, coalition, confederacy, confederation, federation, fellowship, fraternity, guild, league, partnership, society

unique *adj* incomparable, inimitable, matchless, one of a kind, original, peerless, unequaled, unparalleled, unprecedented, unrepeatable, unrivaled

unison *n* in unison collectively, in agreement, in concert, in harmony, together, unanimously, with one accord, with one voice

unit *n* **1** agency, corps, department, detachment, detail, group, section, squad, task-force. **2** building block, component, constituent, element, item, member, module, part, piece

unite v 1 (unite things, groups) ally, amalgamate, associate, blend, bring together, combine, fuse, harmonize, join, link, marry, meld, merge, unify, wed; **opp** separate. 2 (people unite) ally, associate, band together, close ranks, collaborate, cooperate, come together, gang up, join forces, pool your resources, work together

united adj 1 (of people) agreed, at one, collaborative, collective, combined, concerted, cooperative, coordinated, in harmony, in unison, together, unanimous. 2 (of organizations) amalgamated, affiliated, allied, combined, in alliance, in association, unified

unity n 1 (within a structure, a text) agreement, coherence, cohesion, completeness, consistency, harmony, oneness, regularity, uniformity. 2 (within a group of people) accord, agreement, collaboration, concord, consensus, cooperation, harmony, like-mindedness, rapport, solidarity, sweetness and light *inf*, togetherness *inf*, unanimity; **opp** disunity

universal adj all-embracing, all-inclusive, common, comprehensive, constant, general, global, ubiquitous, uniform, unvarying, widespread

universe n cosmos, creation, ether, heavens, outer space, space, void

unjust adj immoral, indefensible, inequitable, undeserved, unequal, unfair, unjustifiable, unjustified, unmerited, wrong, wrongful; **opp** fair, just

unjustifiable adj excessive, illegitimate, indefensible, inexcusable, unacceptable, unconscionable, unforgivable, unjust, unjustified, unreasonable, unwarranted; **opp** justifiable

unkind adj beastly *inf*, callous, churlish, cruel, harsh, impolite, inconsiderate, insensitive, malevolent, malicious, mean, nasty *inf*, pitiless, rough, rude, sadistic, savage, severe, sharp, spiteful, uncaring, uncharitable, unchristian, unfair, unfriendly, unpleasant, unsympathetic, vicious; **opp** kind

unknown adj anonymous, mysterious, nameless, obscure, strange, uncharted, undiscovered, unexplored, unheard-of, unfamiliar, unidentified, unnamed, unrecognized, unspecified, unsung; **opp** famous, well-known

unlawful adj against the law, banned, criminal, forbidden, illegal, illicit, outlawed, prohibited, unauthorized, wrongful; **opp** legal

unlike prep **be unlike** be different from, be dissimilar to, bear no resemblance to, have nothing in common with

unlikely adj 1 (sth is unlikely to happen) doubtful, impossible, improbable, inconceivable. 2 (of a story) dubious, farfetched, implausible, improbable, incredible, suspect, unbelievable, unconvincing; **opp** believable, convincing

unlimited adj boundless, endless, immeasurable, infinite, limitless, unbounded

unload v clear out, deposit, empty, remove, set down, take out, unpack

unlock v open, release, unbolt, unfasten; **opp** lock

unloved adj disliked, detested,

emotionally deprived, forsaken, friendless, hated, jilted, loathed, neglected, rejected, shunned, starved of affection, uncared-for, unpopular, unwanted

unlucky adj down on your luck, hapless, ill-fated, ill-starred, luckless, out of luck, star-crossed, unfortunate, unhappy, unsuccessful; opp lucky

unmarried adj 1 bachelor, celibate, divorced, engaged, single, unattached, unwed, widowed; opp married.
2 (of a couple, partner) cohabiting, common-law, living in sin

unmistakable adj blatant, categorical, clear, conspicuous, glaring, indisputable, manifest, obvious, plain, striking, unambiguous, unequivocal

unmitigated adj absolute, complete, downright, out-and-out, thorough, total, unqualified, utter, veritable

unmoved adj aloof, cold, impassive, impervious, indifferent, stony-faced, unaffected, uncaring, unconcerned, unfeeling, unperturbed; opp moved

unnatural adj 1 (unnatural phenomena) abnormal, bizarre, extraordinary, paranormal, strange, supernatural; opp natural. 2 (of feelings, relationships) abnormal, against nature, deviant, perverted, unhealthy, unwholesome; opp natural, normal. 3 (of behavior) affected, artificial, contrived, false, feigned, forced, insincere, mannered, stagy, strained, studied; opp natural

unnecessary adj 1 dispensable, expendable, gratuitous, needless, pointless, redundant, superfluous, surplus to requirements, unwanted,

useless; opp necessary. 2 excessive, gratuitous, inappropriate, injudicious, inopportune, out of place, uncalled-for, undesirable, unhelpful, unseasonable, unsuitable, untimely, untoward, unwelcome

unnerve v agitate, alarm, daunt, demoralize, deter, disconcert, discourage, dishearten, disquiet, frighten, fluster, perturb, put off, rattle inf, scare, shake, stop sb in his tracks, take aback, throw off balance, trouble, unman, unsettle, worry

unobtrusive adj discreet, low-key, low-profile, modest, self-effacing, unassuming, unnoticeable, unostentatious

unoccupied adj deserted, empty, uninhabited, unpopulated, vacant

unofficial adj casual, informal, unauthorized, unconfirmed, unsanctioned, wildcat; opp official

unorthodox adj abnormal, creative, different, irregular, noncomformist, non-standard, original, strange, unconventional, unusual;
opp conventional, orthodox

unpaid adj amateur, free of charge, gratis, honorary, voluntary, volunteer; opp paid

unpleasant adj 1 bad, disagreeable, disgusting, distasteful, foul, nasty, nauseating, offensive, repellent, repugnant, unpalatable, unsavory, unspeakable inf; opp pleasant.
2 (of a person) bad-tempered, churlish, cruel, disagreeable, hostile, ill-natured, insulting, nasty, nauseating, obnoxious, offensive, repulsive, rude, surly, ugly, unattractive, unfriendly, unkind,

unspeakable *inf*; **opp** nice

unpopular *adj* disliked, out of favor, unfashionable, unloved, unwanted, unwelcome; **opp** popular

unpredictable *adj* **1** chance, erratic, haphazard, in the balance, irregular, random, uncertain, unforeseeable, up in the air *inf*. **2** (of a person) capricious, enigmatic, erratic, fickle, full of surprises, inconsistent, mercurial, temperamental, unreliable, unstable, volatile

unproductive *adj* fruitless, futile, idle, ineffective, pointless, time-wasting, unprofitable, unrewarding, useless, vain, wasted, worthless; **opp** productive

unravel *v* disentangle, untangle, straighten out, unpick, untie

unreal *adj* **1** artificial, fabricated, false, fictitious, hypothetical, illusory, imaginary, imagined, invented, made-up, make-believe, nonexistent, untrue; **opp** real. **2** (causing surprise, bewilderment) absurd, bizarre, paradoxical, strange, surreal, topsy-turvy, unnatural

unrealistic *adj* foolish, half-baked *inf*, impossible, impracticable, impractical, improbable, unreasonable, unworkable, wild; **opp** realistic

unreasonable *adj* **1** absurd, illogical, irrational, ludicrous, meaningless, nonsensical, senseless; **opp** reasonable. **2** (of demands, expectations, prices) disproportionate, excessive, exorbitant, extortionate, extreme, inordinate, extravagant, outrageous, preposterous, steep, unconscionable, unfair; **opp** fair, reasonable. **3** (of a person) cruel, harsh,

inflexible, intolerant, obdurate, obstinate, opinionated, pig-headed *inf*, prejudiced, stubborn, unfair; **opp** reasonable

unrelated *adj* coincidental, disparate, independent, separate, unconnected; **opp** related

unreliable *adj* dubious, fallible, questionable, suspect, uncertain, unsafe, unsound, untrustworthy; **opp** reliable

unrest *n* agitation, discontent, discontentment, discord, dissatisfaction, dissension, dissent, protest, rebellion, rioting, strife, trouble, turmoil, violence; **opp** calm, peace

unruly *adj* badly behaved, disobedient, disorderly, insubordinate, misbehaving, mischievous, mutinous, naughty, obstreperous, rebellious, rowdy, uncontrollable, undisciplined, ungovernable, unmanageable, wayward, wild; **opp** quiet, well-behaved

unsafe *adj* **1** (of a person) at risk, in danger, insecure, unprotected, vulnerable; **opp** safe. **2** (of an activity, vehicle, equipment) dangerous, faulty, reckless, risky, unreliable, unsound; **opp** safe. **3** (of a criminal conviction) doubtful, dubious, questionable, unreliable, unsound, wrongful

unsatisfactory *adj* bad, disappointing, inadequate, poor, unacceptable, unfit, unsatisfying; **opp** satisfactory

unsavory *adj* **1** disagreeable, distasteful, disgusting, gross, nasty, offensive, repellent, repulsive, unpleasant; **opp** pleasant. **2** (an unsavory character) criminal, crooked, doubtful, dubious, low-life, questionable, seedy, shady, sleazy *inf*, suspect, suspicious, underworld, untrustworthy

unscrupulous *adj* amoral, bad, corrupt, deceitful, devious, dishonest, evil, exploitative, immoral, ruthless, unconscionable, unethical, unprincipled, untrustworthy, wicked

unsettle *v* agitate, bother, confuse, discomfit, disconcert, disturb, make sb feel uncomfortable, perturb, rattle *inf*, ruffle, shake, throw, throw sb off balance, trouble, unnerve, upset, worry; *opp* reassure

unsettled *adj* 1 agitated, anxious, dissatisfied, edgy *inf*, fidgety, on edge, perturbed, restive, restless, shaken, rattled *inf*, tense, troubled, uneasy. 2 (of weather) changeable, rainy, showery, wet; *opp* settled

unsightly *adj* hideous, obtrusive, out of place, repulsive, ugly, unattractive, unpleasant; *opp* attractive

unsound *adj* defective, doubtful, dubious, erroneous, fallacious, faulty, flawed, ill-founded, illogical, questionable, shaky, specious, spurious, uncertain, unreasonable, unreliable, unsafe, weak

unspoiled *adj* as good as new, conserved, in its natural state, intact, natural, perfect, preserved, unadulterated, unblemished, unchanged, undamaged, unimpaired, undefiled, untouched

unspoken *adj* implicit, implied, tacit, taken for granted, unarticulated, undeclared, understood, unstated

unstable *adj* 1 (of a structure) flimsy, insecure, precarious, rickety, rocky, shaky, tottering, unsafe, unsteady,

wobbly; *opp* stable. 2 (of a situation) changeable, erratic, fitful, fluctuating, inconsistent, shifting, unpredictable, variable, volatile; *opp* stable. 3 (of a person) capricious, irrational, temperamental, unbalanced, unhinged, unpredictable, unreliable; *opp* stable

unsteady *adj* 1 (of a structure) flimsy, insecure, precarious, rickety, rocky, shaky, tottering, unsafe, unstable, wobbly; *opp* steady. 2 (of sb's voice) changeable, erratic, fluctuating, inconstant, irregular, up and down, variable, wavering; *opp* steady

unsuccessful *adj* 1 failed, fruitless, futile, unprofitable, useless, vain; *opp* successful. 2 (in a game) beaten, defeated, hapless, losing, unlucky, vanquished; *opp* successful

unsuitable *adj* ill-chosen, ill-judged, inappropriate, inapt, incompatible, incongruous, out of keeping, out of place, unacceptable, unfitting, unsuited; *opp* suitable

unsure *adj* doubtful, dubious, hesitant, irresolute, of two minds, skeptical, suspicious, unconvinced, undecided, wavering; *opp* sure

unsuspecting *adj* credulous, green *inf*, gullible, naive, off guard, trusting, unwary; *opp* skeptical

untangle *v* 1 (untangle a rope) disentangle, straighten, unravel; *opp* tangle. 2 (untangle a mystery) clear up, explain, solve, sort out

unthinkable *adj* 1 beyond the bounds of possibility, implausible, impossible, inconceivable; *opp* possible. 2 (unthinkable cruelty) incredible, outrageous, terrible, unbelievable, unimaginable

untidy *adj* cluttered, disorderly, in a mess, in a state, in disarray, jumbled, like a pig sty, littered, messy, rumpled; *opp* tidy

untie *v* disentangle, free, loosen, release, undo, unfasten; *opp* fasten

untimely *adj* 1 (untimely death) early, premature. 2 (an untimely visit) ill-timed, inconvenient, inopportune; *opp* well-timed

untold *adj* 1 (untold damage) indescribable, inexpressible, unimaginable, unspeakable, unthinkable, unutterable. 2 (untold millions) countless, immeasurable, incalculable, innumerable, uncountable, uncounted

untoward *adj* improper, inappropriate, indecorous, disloyal, unacceptable, unbecoming, unseemly, unsuitable; *opp* acceptable

untrue *adj* erroneous, fallacious, false, inaccurate, incorrect, mistaken, spurious, wrong; *opp* true

untrustworthy *adj* crooked, deceitful, devious, dishonest, disloyal, shady *inf*, slippery *inf*, tricky, two-faced, undependable, unreliable; *opp* trustworthy

unusual *adj* abnormal, atypical, bizarre, curious, different *inf*, extraordinary, irregular, odd, out of the ordinary, queer, rare, remarkable, strange, surprising, uncommon, unexpected, unfamiliar, weird *inf*; *opp* normal, usual

unwelcome *adj* 1 (make sb feel unwelcome) excluded, rejected, uninvited, unwanted; *opp* welcome. 2 (an unwelcome intrusion)

disagreeable, displeasing, unacceptable, undesirable, uninvited, unpleasant, unwanted; *opp* welcome

unwell *adj* ailing, groggy *inf*, ill, in poor health, not very well, off-color, out of sorts, poorly, sick, sickly, under the weather; *opp* well

unwieldy *adj* 1 (of an object) bulky, cumbersome, hefty, hulking, massive, unmaneuverable. 2 (of a system) awkward, cumbersome, inconvenient, unmanageable; *opp* efficient

unwilling *adj* 1 (an unwilling helper) grudging, reluctant, resistant, uncooperative, unenthusiastic, unhelpful; *opp* willing. 2 (unwilling to do sth) averse, disinclined, indisposed, loath, slow; *opp* willing

unwind *v* 1 disentangle, slacken, uncoil, undo, unravel, unreel, unroll, untwist; *opp* wind. 2 (relax) chill out *inf*, relax, take it easy, wind down

unwise *adj* daft *inf*, foolhardy, foolish, ill-advised, ill-judged, improvident, imprudent, inadvisable, injudicious, irresponsible, rash, reckless, senseless, silly, stupid, thoughtless; *opp* wise

unwitting *adj* 1 innocent, unaware, unknowing, unsuspecting. 2 (an unwitting blunder) accidental, chance, inadvertent, involuntary, unintended, unintentional; *opp* intentional

unworthy *adj* base, contemptible, despicable, disgraceful, disreputable, reprehensible, shameful; *opp* worthy

unyielding *adj* adamant, firm, hardline, inflexible, intransigent, obstinate, pig-headed, resolute, rigid, steadfast, stubborn, tough, uncompromising;

opp flexible

upbringing *n* breeding, cultivation, education, instruction, nurture, raising, rearing, training

upgrade *v* (upgrade sth) enhance, expand, improve, make better, refurbish; *opp* downgrade. 2 (upgrade sb) advance, elevate, promote, raise; *opp* downgrade

upheaval *n* chaos, commotion, confusion, difficulty, disorder, disruption, disturbance, revolution, to-do *inf*, turmoil, upset

uphill *adj* 1 (an uphill climb) ascending, climbing, rising, upward; *opp* downhill. 2 (an uphill struggle) arduous, difficult, exhausting, grueling, hard, laborious, onerous, punishing, strenuous, taxing, tough; *opp* easy

uphold *v* advocate, back, champion, defend, encourage, endorse, maintain, stand by, stick up for *inf*, support; *opp* reject

upkeep *n* care, maintenance, repair, running, support

uplifting *adj* cheering, encouraging, feel-good, heartening, inspiring; *opp* depressing

upper *adj* elevated, high, highest, superior, top, topmost, uppermost; *opp* lower

upright *adj* 1 erect, on end, perpendicular, straight, vertical; *opp* leaning. 2 decent, fair, good, honest, principled, respectable, righteous, straight *inf*, upstanding, virtuous; *opp* dishonest

uprising *n* coup, coup d'état, disturbance, insurgence, insurrection, mutiny, rebellion, revolt, revolution, riot, rising

uproar *n* bedlam, chaos, commotion, hullabaloo *inf*, mayhem, outcry, pandemonium, riot, rumpus *inf*, tumult, turbulence, turmoil

uproarious *adj* 1 chaotic, boisterous, disorderly, loud, noisy, rowdy, riotous, tumultuous, turbulent, unruly, wild; *opp* calm. 2 (an uproarious show) hilarious, hysterical, rip-roaring, side-splitting

upset *adj* anxious, bothered, dismayed, distressed, disturbed, hurt, ruffled, saddened, shaken, troubled, worried

upset *n* 1 bother, dismay, distress, disturbance, hurt, sadness, worry. 2 (a stomach upset) complaint, disturbance, illness, sickness

upset *v* 1 (upset sb) bother, dismay, distress, disturb, hurt, ruffle, sadden, shake, trouble, worry. 2 (upset sb's plans) disrupt, disturb, hinder, interfere with, jeopardize, mess up, spoil. 3 (upset sth) overturn, tip over, topple, turn over, upend

upshot *n* conclusion, culmination, denouement, issue, outcome, result

upside down *adj* inverted, overturned, the wrong way up, topsy-turvy, upended, upturned

upstanding *adj* decent, fair, good, honest, principled, respectable, righteous, straight *inf*, upstanding, virtuous; *opp* dishonest

upward *adj* ascending, climbing, rising, uphill; *opp* downward

urban *adj* built-up, city, civic, inner city, metropolitan, municipal, suburban, town; *opp* rural

urge *n* compulsion, desire, drive, hunger,

impulse, itch, longing, need, thirst, wish, yearning

urge *v* **1** (urge sb to do sth) compel, drive, egg on *inf*, encourage, entreat, force, goad, impel, incite, induce, persuade, prompt, spur, stimulate. **2** (urge restraint) advise, advocate, back, counsel, endorse, recommend, suggest

urgency *n* haste, hurry, importance, necessity, need, seriousness, top priority

urgent *adj* compelling, crucial, high priority, imperative, important, pressing, top priority

use *n* **1** employment, exploitation, operation, usage, utilization. **2** (have several uses) application, function, purpose. **3** (be of no use) advantage, benefit, good, help, point, service, usefulness, value, worth

use *v* **1** employ, exploit, make use of, operate, ply, put into service, utilize, wield, work. **2** (use all of sth) consume, deplete, exhaust, expend, fritter away, get through, spend, waste

used *adj* cast-off, hand-me-down, nearly-new, second-hand, worn; *opp* new

useful *adj* advantageous, beneficial, effective, fruitful, helpful, of help, of use, productive, profitable, rewarding, successful, valuable, worthwhile; *opp* useless

useless *adj* **1** fruitless, futile, hopeless, ineffective, of no help, of no use, pointless, unavailing, unproductive, unprofitable, unrewarding, unsuccessful, vain; *opp* useful. **2** (not good at sth) hopeless, inadequate, incapable, incompetent, inept, no good *inf*, poor; *opp* talented

usual *adj* common, conventional, customary, established, expected, familiar, habitual, normal, ordinary, orthodox, regular, routine, set, standard, stock, traditional, typical; *opp* unusual

utilize *v* employ, have recourse to, make the most of, make use of, put to use, resort to, take advantage of, turn to, use

utmost *adj* extreme, greatest, highest, maximum, paramount, supreme

utmost *n* **1** (do sth to the utmost) extreme, greatest, highest, max *inf*, maximum. **2** (try your utmost) best, hardest

utter *adj* absolute, complete, downright, out-and-out, outright, perfect, sheer, total, unmitigated, unqualified

utter *v* articulate, come out with *inf*, express, put sth into words, say, speak, verbalize. vocalize, voice

utterly *adv* absolutely, completely, entirely, perfectly, thoroughly, totally

vacancy n job, opening, position, post, slot

vacant adj 1 (a vacant room) available, empty, free, idle, unfilled, unused; **opp** occupied. 2 (a vacant expression) absent-minded, blank, dreamy, faraway, inane, inattentive, vacuous; **opp** attentive

vacate v abandon, depart from, desert, evacuate, get out of, leave, quit, withdraw from

vacuum n emptiness, gap, nothingness, space, void

vagabond n beggar, bum inf, tramp, vagrant

vagrant n beggar, bum inf, vagabond

vague adj 1 (a vague image) blurred, dim, fuzzy, hazy, ill-defined, indistinct, misty, nebulous, obscure, out of focus, shadowy, unclear; **opp** clear. 2 (a vague answer) ambiguous, confused, doubtful, hazy, imprecise, inexact, loose, uncertain, unclear, woolly inf, **opp** precise

vain adj 1 (of a person) arrogant, big-headed inf, boastful, cocky inf, conceited, egotistical, narcissistic, proud, self-admiring, swaggering; **opp** modest. 2 (a vain attempt) fruitless, futile, hopeless, ineffective, of no help, of no use, pointless, unavailing, unproductive, unprofitable, unrewarding, unsuccessful, useless; **opp** successful

valiant adj bold, brave, courageous, gallant, heroic, plucky inf, worthy; **opp** faint-hearted

valid adj acceptable, approved, authentic, authorized, bona fide, current, genuine, legitimate, official; **opp** invalid

validate v approve, authenticate, authorize, certify, endorse, legitimize, make valid, ratify, sanction; **opp** invalidate

valley n canyon, chasm, dale, dell, depression, glen, gorge, gully, hollow, ravine, vale; **opp** hill

valuable adj 1 costly, dear inf, expensive, irreplaceable, precious, priceless; **opp** worthless. 2 (valuable advice) advantageous, beneficial, helpful, of help, of use, useful, worthwhile; **opp** useless

value n 1 cost, price, rate, worth. 2 (the value of sb's advice) advantage, benefit, help, importance, merit, profit, use, usefulness, worth

value v 1 (value a house) assess, estimate, evaluate, price, put a figure on inf, rate. 2 (value sb's friendship) appreciate, cherish, hold dear, prize, respect, treasure

vandal n hooligan, looter, raider,

ruffian, thug, troublemaker

vanish v disappear, disperse, dissolve, dwindle, evaporate, fade, go away; **opp** appear

vanity n arrogance, big-headedness *inf*, boastfulness, cockiness *inf*, conceit, egotism, narcissism, pride, self-admiration; **opp** modesty

vanquish v beat, clobber *inf*, conquer, crush, defeat, lick *inf*, master, overcome, overpower, overthrow, put down, quash, quell, triumph over, wipe the floor with *inf*

vapor n fog, fumes, gas, haze, mist, smoke, steam

variable adj changeable, erratic, fickle, fitful, fluctuating, fluid, inconstant, shifting, unpredictable, unstable, unsteady, up and down *inf*, volatile, wavering; **opp** constant

variation n 1 (a variation from the norm) departure, deviation, difference, discrepancy, divergence, variant. 2 (every day without variation) alteration, change, modification

varied adj assorted, different, diverse, heterogeneous, miscellaneous, mixed, sundry, various

variety n 1 (enjoy variety) change, diversity, variation. 2 (a variety of different things) assortment, collection, combination, mixture, range. 3 (a variety of flower) brand, breed, category, class, classification, kind, make, sort, species, strain, type

various adj assorted, different, diverse, heterogeneous, miscellaneous, mixed, sundry, varied

vary v 1 (vary sth) adapt, adjust, alter, change, diversify, modify, transform. 2 (vary in quality) be different, differ

vast adj colossal, enormous, extensive, gigantic, great, huge, immense, infinite, limitless, mammoth, massive, monstrous, unlimited; **opp** tiny

vault n basement, cavern, cellar, crypt, repository

vault v bound, clear, hurdle, jump, leap, spring

veer v change course, change direction, dodge, sheer, shift, swerve, swing, turn

vegetate v go to seed *inf*, idle, languish, laze around, stagnate

vegetation n flora, foliage, greenery, growth, plant life, plants, undergrowth

vehement adj ardent, eager, earnest, enthusiastic, fervent, fierce, intense, keen, passionate, vigorous; **opp** half-hearted

veil n blanket, cloak, cover, covering, curtain, film, mantle, mask, screen, shade, shroud

veil v cloak, conceal, cover, disguise, hide, mask, obscure, screen, shroud

vein n 1 (in a lighter vein) humor, mode, mood, spirit, style, temper, tenor, tone. 2 (a vein of humor) dash, hint, strain, streak, thread. 3 (a vein of coal) bed, deposit, seam, stratum, streak, stripe

vendetta n conflict, feud, quarrel

veneer n 1 (a veneer of respectability) appearance, facade, front, guise, pretense, semblance, show. 2 (a veneer of lacquer) coating, covering, finish, surface

venerable adj esteemed, hallowed, honored, respected, venerated

venerate v adore, esteem, hero-worship,

idolize, pay homage to, respect, revere, reverence, worship

vengeance n an eye for an eye, pay-back *inf*, reprisal, retaliation, retribution, revenge, tit for tat

venom n 1 poison, toxin. 2 acrimony, bitterness, grudge, hate, hatred, malevolence, malice, rancor, spite, viciousness, vindictiveness, virulence

venomous adj 1 deadly, noxious, poisonous, toxic. 2 acrimonious, bitter, grudging, malevolent, malicious, rancorous, savage, spiteful, vicious, vindictive, virulent

vent n aperture, cut, duct, flue, gap, hole, opening, orifice, outlet, passage, slit, slot, split

vent v air, articulate, emit, express, give vent to, let out, make known, pour out, utter, voice

ventilate v aerate, air, air-condition, freshen, oxygenate

venture n chance, endeavor, enterprise, experiment, gamble, project, risk, speculation, undertaking

venture v 1 bet, chance, dare, gamble, risk, speculate, stake, wager. 2 (venture an opinion) advance, dare, hazard, put forward, risk, volunteer

venue n location, place, setting

verbal adj oral, said, spoken, word-of-mouth

verbose adj garrulous, long-winded, loquacious, prolix, talkative, voluble, wordy; *opp* brief, concise

verdict n adjudication, assessment, conclusion, decision, finding, judgment, opinion, ruling

verge n border, boundary, brink, edge,

limit, lip, margin, side, threshold

verge on v approach, border on, come close, come near, tend towards

verify v affirm, attest, authenticate, check, confirm, corroborate, establish, prove, substantiate, support, testify to, validate, vouch for

versatile adj adaptable, all-round, flexible, handy, multipurpose, resourceful, variable

verse n 1 canto, couplet, lines, stanza, strophe. 2 lyric, ode, poem, poetry, rhyme, sonnet

version n account, description, interpretation, portrayal, reading, rendering, rendition, report, translation

vertical adj erect, on end, perpendicular, standing, straight, upright; *opp* horizontal

vertigo n dizziness, giddiness, light-headedness, loss of balance

very adv awfully *inf*, decidedly, deeply, eminently, enormously, especially, exceedingly, extremely, greatly, highly, hugely, most, outstandingly, particularly, really, remarkably, to a great extent, terribly *inf*, truly, unbelievably, unusually, vastly

vessel n 1 boat, craft, ship. 2 container, pot, receptacle, tank, vat

vet v check out, examine, inspect, investigate, review, scan, scrutinize

veteran adj adept, experienced, expert, old, practiced, seasoned

veteran n master, old hand, old soldier, past master, pro *inf*, trouper; *opp* novice

veto n ban, bar, block, boycott, embargo, interdict, prohibition, refusal, rejection, thumbs down *inf*

veto v ban, bar, block, boycott, dismiss, forbid, prohibit, proscribe, refuse, reject, rule out, turn down, vote against; *opp* allow

vex v aggravate, annoy, bother, disturb, exasperate, get on sb's nerves *inf*, harass, hassle *inf*, infuriate, irk, irritate, plague, provoke, rile, torment, trouble, upset, worry

viable adj achievable, feasible, operable, possible, practicable, realistic, reasonable, sound, sustainable, usable, valid, workable; *opp* impossible

vibrant adj alive, animated, colorful, dynamic, electric, energetic, lively, sparkling, spirited, throbbing, vivacious, vivid; *opp* dull

vibrate v oscillate, pulsate, quiver, resonate, reverberate, shake, shiver, throb, tremble, wobble

vibration n oscillation, pulse, quivering, resonance, reverberation, shaking, shivering, throbbing, trembling, wave, wobble

vice n 1 badness, corruption, depravity, evil, immorality, iniquity, sin, turpitude, wickedness, wrongdoing; *opp* virtue.
2 bad habit, defect, failing, flaw, foible, imperfection, peccadillo, shortcoming, weakness; *opp* virtue

vicinity n area, district, environs, locale, locality, neighborhood, proximity, region, territory, zone

vicious adj 1 atrocious, barbaric, barbarous, bloodthirsty, brutal, callous, cruel, diabolical, fiendish, foul, heinous, inhuman, merciless, monstrous, pitiless, ruthless, sadistic, savage, vile, violent.
2 bitchy *inf*, catty, cruel, cutting,

malicious, mean, nasty, poisonous, rancorous, savage, sharp, spiteful, venomous, vindictive, vitriolic; *opp* kind

victim n casualty, fatality, injured party, martyr, prey, scapegoat, sufferer, target

victimize v bully, discriminate against, exploit, intimidate, oppress, persecute, pick on, prey on, single out, take advantage of, terrorize, torment

victor n champion, conqueror, first, number one, prizewinner, vanquisher, winner

victorious adj champion, conquering, first, prizewinning, successful, top, triumphant, vanquishing, winning; *opp* defeated, vanquished

victory n conquest, mastery, success, triumph, win; *opp* defeat

view n 1 aspect, landscape, outlook, panorama, picture, prospect, scene, scenery, sight, vision, vista.
2 attitude, belief, conviction, feeling, idea, notion, opinion, perception, position, sentiment, thought

view v behold, check out *inf*, consider, contemplate, examine, eye, gaze at, inspect, look at, observe, regard, scan, survey, watch, witness

viewer n audience, observer, onlooker, spectator, watcher

viewpoint n angle, attitude, opinion, perception, perspective, point of view, position, slant, stance, standpoint

vigilant adj alert, attentive, careful, cautious, eagle-eyed, observant, on your guard, on your toes *inf*, sharp-eyed, unsleeping, wakeful, wary, watchful

vigor n activity, animation, dash,

dynamism, energy, fitness, force, forcefulness, gusto, health, heartiness, life, liveliness, power, robustness, soundness, spirit, stamina, strength, sturdiness, verve, virility, vitality

vigorous adj active, animated, brisk, dynamic, effective, energetic, fit, flourishing, forceful, full-blooded, hale, hardy, healthy, hearty, intense, lively, lusty, potent, powerful, robust, sound, spirited, strong, sturdy, thriving, virile, vital

vile adj 1 bad, base, contemptible, debased, degenerate, depraved, despicable, detestable, evil, ignoble, immoral, impure, loathsome, low, perverted, shocking, sinful, ugly, vicious, wicked; opp good. 2 disgusting, foul, horrible, horrid, loathsome, nasty, nauseating, repellent, repugnant, repulsive, revolting, unpleasant, yucky inf; opp lovely

villain n criminal, crook inf, evil-doer, malefactor, miscreant, reprobate, rogue, ruffian, scoundrel, wretch, wrong-doer

villainous adj bad, base, corrupt, criminal, debased, dishonest, evil, fiendish, hateful, heinous, infamous, sinful, treacherous, vicious, vile, wicked

vindicate v confirm, corroborate, justify, prove sb right, substantiate, verify

vindication n confirmation, corroboration, justification, proof, substantiation, verification

vindictive adj avenging, bitter, malevolent, malicious, malignant, rancorous, resentful, revengeful, spiteful, unforgiving, vengeful

vintage adj choice, classic, fine, good,

high quality, mature, mellowed, old, prime, quality, seasoned, select, superior, venerable

violate v 1 (violate a law) breach, break, contravene, defy, disobey, disregard, flout, ignore, infringe, transgress. 2 (violate sb) abuse, assault, attack, defile, desecrate, dishonor, force oneself upon, outrage, pollute, rape, ravish

violation n 1 (of a law) abuse, breach, breaking, contravention, defiance, disobedience, disregard, flouting, ignoring, infraction, infringement, offense, transgression. 2 (of a person) abuse, assault, attack, defilement, desecration, dishonoring, outrage, rape

violence n 1 aggression, assault, attack, bloodshed, brutality, fighting, ferocity, force, roughness, savagery. 2 (of feelings) passion, power, ferocity, force, forcefulness, intensity, power, strength, tempestuousness, vehemence, wildness

violent adj 1 aggressive, attacking, bellicose, belligerent, bloodthirsty, brutal, destructive, ferocious, fierce, hot-headed, hot-tempered, intemperate, savage, vicious, warlike. 2 passionate, powerful, fierce, fiery, forceful, intense, powerful, raging, strong, tempestuous, unbridled, uncontrollable, uncontrolled, unrestrained, vehement, wild

VIP n celebrity, dignitary, official, personality, star

virgin adj chaste, immaculate, inexperienced, maidenly, pure, uncorrupted, undefiled, untouched, vestal, virtuous

virgin n girl, maid, maiden

virile adj lusty, macho, male, manly, masculine, potent, red-blooded, rugged, strong, vigorous; **opp** effeminate

virtue n 1 goodness, honesty, honor, innocence, integrity, morality, probity, rectitude, righteousness, uprightness; **opp** vice. 2 advantage, asset, attribute, credit, good point, merit, quality, strength; **opp** weakness. 3 chastity, honor, innocence, purity, virginity; **opp** vice

virtuoso adj bravura, brilliant, dazzling, masterly, outstanding, stunning

virtuoso n artist, genius, maestro, master, prodigy

virtuous adj 1 blameless, decent, ethical, exemplary, good, honest, honorable, incorruptible, moral, principled, pure, righteous, upright, worthy. 2 chaste, innocent, maidenly, pure, uncorrupted, undefiled, untouched, vestal, virginal

virulent adj 1 dangerous, deadly, lethal, life-threatening, noxious, pernicious, poisonous, venomous. 2 acrimonious, bitter, hate-filled, hostile, malevolent, malicious, malignant, savage, vicious, vindictive

visible adj apparent, clear, conspicuous, detectable, discernible, distinct, distinguishable, evident, manifest, noticeable, observable, obvious, open, palpable, perceivable, plain, recognizable, unconcealed, undisguised, unmistakable; **opp** invisible

vision n 1 eyes, eyesight, perception, sight, view. 2 (sth imagined) apparition, daydream, delusion, dream, fantasy, hallucination, illusion, image, mental image, mental picture. 3 (a person with vision) far-sightedness, foresight, imagination, insight, intuition, perception, perceptiveness, prescience, understanding

visionary adj farseeing, farsighted, futuristic, idealistic, imaginative, insightful, intuitive, perceptive, prescient, prophetic, Utopian

visit n call, stay, stopover, visitation

visit v call on, drop in on inf, go to see, look up inf, pay a call on, pay a visit to, pop in on inf, see, stay with, stop by

visitor n 1 caller, company, guest. 2 pilgrim, sightseer, tourist, traveler, vacationer

visual adj 1 optic, optical. 2 discernible, observable, perceivable, perceptible, visible

visualize v conceive, dream up, envisage, have an image of, imagine, picture, think of

vital adj 1 basic, cardinal, critical, crucial, decisive, essential, fundamental, imperative, important, indispensable, key, mandatory, requisite, urgent; **opp** inessential. 2 alive, animated, dynamic, energetic, forceful, lively, sparkling, spirited, vigorous, vivacious; **opp** lifeless

vitality n animation, dynamism, energy, go inf, life, liveliness, sparkle, spirit, stamina, strength, vigor, vivacity, zest

vitriolic adj acerbic, acid, bitchy inf, bitter, caustic, cruel, hostile, malicious, poisonous, sardonic, savage, scathing, spiteful, venomous, vicious, vindictive, virulent, withering

vivacious adj alive, animated, bubbly, cheerful, ebullient, high-spirited, light-hearted, lively, sparkling, spirited, sprightly; **opp** dull

vivid adj 1 bright, brilliant, clear, colorful, dazzling, glowing, intense, rich, strong, vibrant; **opp** dull. 2 detailed, evocative, graphic, lifelike, memorable, powerful, realistic, stirring, striking

vocabulary n 1 lexicon, lexis, words. 2 dictionary, glossary, lexicon, phrase book, word-list

vocal adj 1 oral, said, spoken, verbal, vocalized, voiced. 2 blunt, forthright, loud, noisy, outspoken, strident, vociferous

vocation n calling, career, employment, job, mission, niche, occupation, profession, role, work

vociferous adj blunt, forthright, insistent, loud, noisy, outspoken, strident, vehement, vocal

vogue n craze, fad, fashion, latest thing inf, in thing inf, mode, rage, style, taste, trend

voice n 1 accent, articulation, inflection, intonation, singing, speaking, speech, tone, utterance. 2 (the voice of the people) opinion, say, view, vote, will, wish

voice v air, articulate, assert, communicate, declare, divulge, enunciate, explain, express, give voice to, put into words, speak, tell, utter

void n blank, emptiness, gap, lacuna, nothingness, space, vacuum

volatile adj capricious, changeable, erratic, explosive, fickle, flighty, inconstant, mercurial, moody, temperamental, unpredictable, unstable, unsteady, up and down inf,

variable; **opp** stable

volley n barrage, battery, blast, bombardment, burst, discharge, explosion, fusillade, hail, salvo, shower

volume n 1 amount, body, bulk, capacity, dimensions, mass, quantity, size. 2 book, title, tome, treatise, work

voluntary adj elective, free, optional, noncompulsory, unforced; **opp** compulsory

volunteer n benefactor, helper, voluntary assistant

volunteer v be willing, offer, propose, put yourself forward, step forward

voluptuous adj 1 ample, buxom, curvaceous, curvy inf, plump, rounded, sexy, shapely, well-endowed. 2 carnal, hedonistic, luxurious, pleasure-seeking, self-indulgent, sensual

vomit v be sick, bring sth up, chuck inf, disgorge, heave inf, hurl inf, puke inf, regurgitate, retch, spew inf, throw up inf

voracious adj avid, devouring, eager, famished, gluttonous, greedy, hungry, insatiable, keen, ravenous

vote n 1 ballot, election, plebiscite, poll, referendum. 2 franchise, say, suffrage, voice

vote v cast your vote, choose, elect, have your say, nominate, opt, pick, return, select

vouch for v affirm, answer for, assert, attest to, bear witness, certify, confirm, endorse, guarantee, sponsor, uphold, validate, verify

vow n oath, pledge, promise, undertaking, word of honor

vow v affirm, declare, give your word, guarantee, pledge, promise, swear, take an oath

voyage *n* crossing, cruise, expedition, journey, passage, travels, trip

vulgar *adj* 1 coarse, common, crude, dirty, foul, gross, ill-bred, ill-mannered, impolite, improper, indecent, naughty, offensive, rude, uncouth, unseemly; *opp* polite. 2 flashy, gaudy, in bad taste, inelegant, nasty, showy, tasteless, tawdry; *opp* tasteful

vulnerable *adj* at risk, defenseless, easily hurt, exposed, helpless, open, powerless, sensitive, susceptible, tender, unguarded, unprotected, weak, wide open; *opp* strong

wad *n* ball, bundle, lump, mass, pad, plug, roll

wade *v* 1 paddle, splash. 2 (wade through sth) plow, work your way

waffle *n* evasiveness, padding, prattle, verbiage, wordiness

waffle *v* babble, blather *inf*, jabber, prattle, ramble

waft *v* 1 bear, carry, puff, transport. 2 be borne, be carried, drift, float, glide, travel

wag *v* 1 bob, flap, nod, waggle, wave, wiggle, wobble. 2 rock, shake, sway, swing, twitch, undulate, vibrate

wage *n* allowance, earnings, fee, income, pay, payment, remuneration, salary, stipend, wages

wager *n* bet, gamble, stake

wager *v* bet, chance, gamble, lay odds, place a bet, put money on, stake

waggle *n* shake, wag, wave, wiggle, wobble

waggle *v* flutter, oscillate, shake, sway,

wag, wave, wiggle, wobble

wail *n* complaint, cry, howl, moan, sob

wail *v* bawl, caterwaul, cry, howl, lament, shriek, sob, weep

wait *n* delay, halt, holdup, interval, pause, rest, stop

wait *v* 1 be patient, bide your time, delay, hang fire, hang on *inf*, hesitate, hold back, hold your horses *inf*, linger, pause, sit tight *inf*, stay, stop. 2 **wait on** attend to, minister to, serve

waive *v* forgo, give up, relinquish, renounce, sign away, surrender, yield

wake *v* 1 (wake sb) disturb, rouse, waken, wake up. 2 (sb wakes) get up, rise, stir, wake up

wakeful *adj* 1 restless, sleepless. 2 alert, attentive, observant, on the lookout, vigilant, wary, watchful

waken *v* awaken, stir, wake up

walk *n* 1 hike, promenade, ramble, stroll, trek. 2 (way of walking) gait, step, stride, way of walking. 3 (a tree-lined walk) alley, avenue, drive, footpath, lane, path, pavement

walk *v* 1 go by foot, go walking, hike, ramble. 2 amble, plod, saunter, stroll, traipse, tramp, troop, trudge. 3 (walk on the grass) stand, step, trample, tread. 4 **walk out** (leave) flounce out, get up and go, leave suddenly, storm out. 5 **walk out** (go on strike) go on strike, picket, put down tools, quit, stop work, strike. 6 **walk out on** abandon, desert, leave

walker *n* hiker, pedestrian, rambler

walkout *n* labor action, protest, stoppage, strike

wall *n* 1 panel, partition, room divider,

screen. **2** barricade, embankment,
fortification, parapet, rampart

wallet *n* case, holder, pouch, purse

wallow *v* **1** (wallow in the mud) lie,
roll, splash around, tumble, wade.
2 (wallow in emotions) bask, delight,
enjoy, glory, indulge, luxuriate, revel,
take delight

wan *adj* ashen, bloodless, colorless, pale,
pasty, peaky, tired, washed out, waxen,
white

wand *n* baton, rod, sprig, staff, stick, twig

wander *v* **1** cruise, drift, meander,
ramble, range, roam, rove, saunter, stray,
stroll, walk. **2** curve, wind, zigzag.
3 deviate, digress, drift, go off at a
tangent, swerve, veer

wane *v* decrease, diminish, dwindle,
ebb, fade, fail, grow less, lessen, shrink,
subside, taper off, weaken; *opp* wax

want *n* **1** (sth wanted) craving, demand,
desire, fancy, hankering, longing, need,
requirement, thirst, wish. **2** (sth needed)
absence, dearth, deficiency,
insufficiency, lack, need, scarcity,
shortage. **3** (living in want) destitution,
famine, hunger, need, neediness,
poverty; *opp* plenty, wealth

want *v* **1** aspire to, covet, crave, desire,
fancy, hanker after, like, long for, pine
for, prefer, set your heart on *inf*, wish,
yearn for. **2** (need sth) be in need of,
be short of, call for, demand, lack,
miss, need, require

wanton *adj* **1** (wanton destruction)
gratuitous, malicious, motiveless,
needless, pointless, senseless, spiteful,
unjustified, unprovoked, willful.
2 (having no morals) immoral,

loose, promiscuous, shameless

war *n* **1** battle, campaign, conflict,
crusade, fight, hostilities, military
action. **2** combat, fighting, warfare

ward *n* **1** compartment, cubicle, room.
2 area, district, division, quarter, zone.
3 charge, dependant

warden *n* administrator, caretaker,
curator, guard, guardian, janitor, keeper,
supervisor, watchman

warehouse *n* depository, depot,
stockroom, store, storehouse

wares *n* goods, merchandise, produce,
stock, stuff

warfare *n* armed conflict, combat,
fighting, hostilities, strife

warlike *adj* aggressive, belligerent,
combative, hostile, martial, militant,
militaristic, warmongering, warring;
opp peaceful

warm *adj* **1** (warm weather) balmy,
hot, mild, pleasant, summery, sunny,
temperate; *opp* cold. **2** (warm water)
heated, lukewarm, tepid; *opp* cold.
3 (a warm embrace) effusive, emotional,
enthusiastic, friendly, heartfelt, hearty,
passionate, sincere; *opp* cold, cool.
4 (a warm nature) affectionate, caring,
friendly, genial, happy, loving, warm-
hearted; *opp* cold. **5** (a warm sweater)
cozy, thick, woolly; *opp* thin

warm *v* heat, heat up, make warm, melt,
reheat, thaw, thaw out, warm up;
opp cool

warmth *n* **1** heat. **2** (warmth of feeling)
affection, animation, ardor, eagerness,
enthusiasm, fervor, heartiness,
intensity, love, passion, sincerity,
spirit, tenderness, zeal

warn v admonish, advise, alert, caution, counsel, forewarn, give notice, inform, let sb know, tell, tip off inf

warning n 1 advice, caution, forewarning, notice, notification, threat, tip, tipoff inf. 2 (a warning of what was to come) omen, portent, premonition, sign, signal, token

warrant n authority, authorization, document, license, papers, permission, permit, sanction, written order

warrant v 1 affirm, assure, attest, certify, declare, endorse, guarantee, pledge, swear to, vouch for. 2 be a reason for, deserve, excuse, justify. 3 authorize, commission, empower, entitle, license, permit, sanction

warrior n fighter, soldier

wary adj alert, attentive, careful, cautious, distrustful, guarded, on the lookout, on your guard, prudent, suspicious, vigilant, watchful

wash n bath, clean, cleaning, rinse, scrub, shampoo, shower, washing

wash v 1 bath, bathe, clean, cleanse, flush, launder, moisten, mop, rinse, scrub, shampoo, shower, soap, sponge, swab, swill, wet, wipe. 2 (of waves) beat, break, dash, lap, splash

washout n debacle, disappointment, disaster, failure, fiasco, flop inf

waste adj 1 extra, left over, superfluous, unusable, unused, unwanted, useless, worthless. 2 arid, bare, barren, bleak, derelict, desolate, empty, uncultivated, uninhabited, unproductive, wild

waste n 1 debris, dregs, dross, excess, garbage, junk, leavings, leftovers inf, litter, refuse, remnants, rubbish, scrap, trash. 2 extravagance, loss, misuse, squandering, wastage, wastefulness. 3 (frozen wastes) desert, wasteland, wilderness

waste v 1 be wasteful with, blow inf, fritter away, misspend, misuse, splurge, squander, throw away, use up. 2 (wasting away) become emaciated, grow weak, waste away, weaken, wither

wasteful adj excessive, extravagant, lavish, needless, profligate, spendthrift, thriftless, uneconomical; **opp** economical

watch n 1 chronometer, clock, digital watch, timepiece, wristwatch. 2 (keep a watch) guard, lookout, surveillance, vigil

watch v 1 check out inf, eye, gaze at, look, note, observe, peer at, regard, see, stare at, view. 2 keep tabs on inf, keep watch on, spy on. 3 (watch what you're doing) attend to, be watchful, keep your eyes on, pay attention, take care. 4 (supervise sb) guard, keep an eye on, look after, mind, protect, supervise, take care of. 5 **watch out** be alert, be careful, be on your guard, be vigilant, be watchful, keep your eyes open, look out, mind, take care

watchful adj alert, attentive, eagle-eyed, guarded, observant, sharp-eyed, suspicious, vigilant, wary, wide awake

watchman n caretaker, guard, lookout, security man, sentry

water v dampen, douse, drench, flood, hose, irrigate, moisten, saturate, soak, spray, sprinkle, wet

waterfall n cascade, cataract, falls

waterproof adj damp-proof, water-repellent, water-resistant, watertight, weatherproof

watertight *adj* sealed, sound, waterproof

watery *adj* 1 (like water) aqueous, fluid, liquid. 2 (too thin) dilute, diluted, runny, tasteless, thin, watered down, weak, wishy-washy *inf*. 3 (containing water) boggy, damp, moist, sodden, soggy, squelchy, waterlogged, wet. 4 (full of tears) moist, tear-filled, tearful, weepy, wet

wave *n* 1 (a wave of sth) current, flood, movement, outbreak, rush, stream, surge, tide, trend, upsurge. 2 (in the ocean) billow, breaker, crest, ripple, roller, surf, swell, tidal wave. 3 (a wave of your hand) flourish, gesture, shake, sign, signal

wave *v* 1 (wave a stick) brandish, flourish, shake, swing, wag, waggle, wield. 2 (wave in the wind) billow, flap, flutter, ripple, stir, undulate. 3 (wave to sb) beckon, gesticulate, gesture, indicate, signal

waver *v* 1 be indecisive, be of two minds, dither, falter, hesitate, shilly-shally *inf*, vacillate. 2 become unsteady, flicker, fluctuate, quiver, reel, shake, sway, teeter, totter, tremble, undulate, vary, wave, weave, wobble

wavy *adj* 1 (wavy hair) curling, curly; *opp* straight. 2 (a wavy line) curving, curvy, squiggly, undulating, winding; *opp* straight

wax *v* broaden, develop, expand, get bigger, grow, increase, mount, rise, swell, widen; *opp* wane

way *n* 1 (way of doing sth) approach, manner, means, method, mode, plan, procedure, scheme, system, technique. 2 (the way to a place) access, avenue, channel, course, direction, lane, path, pathway, road, roadway, route, street, track, trail. 3 (sb's way) behavior, conduct, custom, eccentricity, habit, manner, mannerism, nature, personality, routine, style, temperament, trait, wont. 4 (different in some ways) aspect, circumstance, detail, feature, particular, point, respect, sense

waylay *v* accost, ambush, attack, buttonhole, hold up, intercept, lie in wait for, pounce on, surprise

weak *adj* 1 anemic, debilitated, decrepit, delicate, exhausted, faint, feeble, fragile, frail, infirm, puny, sickly, tender, tired, unsteady, wasted, weedy, worn out; *opp* strong. 2 breakable, brittle, fragile, inadequate, insubstantial, rickety, shaky, thin, unsafe; *opp* strong. 3 (a weak position) defenseless, exposed, open, unguarded, unprotected, vulnerable; *opp* strong. 4 (a weak ruler) cowardly, fearful, impotent, indecisive, ineffective, ineffectual, powerless, spineless, timid, unassertive; *opp* powerful. 5 (a weak sound) distant, dull, faint, low, muffled, quiet, small, soft; *opp* loud. 6 (a weak light) dim, fading, faint, poor, small; *opp* bright. 7 (a weak excuse) feeble, flimsy, hollow, lame, pathetic, unconvincing, unsatisfactory; *opp* good. 8 (a weak mixture) diluted, insipid, runny, tasteless, thin, thinned down, watery; *opp* strong

weaken *v* 1 (weaken sth) destroy, dilute, diminish, erode, exhaust, lessen, lower, make weaker, reduce, sap, soften, thin down, tire, undermine, water down, wear out. **2** (sth weakens) abate, become weaker, decline, decrease, dwindle, ease up, ebb, fade, flag, give in, give way, let up, tire, wane

weakling n coward, doormat inf, drip inf, mouse, sissy, wimp inf

weakness n **1** cowardliness, feebleness, frailty, impotence, powerlessness, spinelessness, vulnerability; **opp** strength. **2** Achilles' heel inf, defect, failing, fault, flaw, imperfection, shortcoming, weak point; **opp** strength. **3** (a weakness for sth) fondness, liking, partiality, penchant, soft spot, taste

wealth n **1** affluence, assets, capital, cash, funds, means, money, opulence, prosperity, resources, riches, treasure; **opp** poverty. **2** (a wealth of sth) abundance, bounty, fullness, mine, plenty, profusion, richness, store, treasury

wealthy adj affluent, comfortable, flush inf, loaded inf, prosperous, rich, well-heeled inf, well-off, well-to-do; **opp** poor

weapon n bomb, chemical weapon, firearm, gun, missile, nuclear weapon

wear n **1** (show signs of wear) damage, depreciation, erosion, friction, use. **2** (get more wear out of sth) mileage inf, use. **3** (leisure wear) attire, clothes, clothing, dress, garments, outfit

wear v **1** be clothed in, be dressed in, clothe yourself in, have on, put on, sport inf. **2** (wear glasses) have, need, use. **3** (wear away) become worn, corrode, damage, erode, fray, grind away, injure, mark, scuff, wash away, weaken, wear away, wear out, wear thin. **4 wear off** become weaker, decrease, diminish, fade, lose effect, peter out, subside, wane, weaken. **5 wear out** deteriorate, fray, wear thin. **6 wear out** (wear sb out) drain, exhaust, fatigue, sap, tire, weary

wearing adj draining, exasperating, exhausting, fatiguing, irksome, stressful, tiresome, tiring, trying, wearisome

wearisome adj annoying, boring, bothersome, burdensome, dreary, dull, exhausting, fatiguing, monotonous, repetitive, tedious, trying

weary adj **1** dead on your feet inf, dog-tired inf, exhausted, fatigued, flagging, jet-lagged inf, shattered inf, sleepy, tired, worn out. **2** (weary of sth) bored, fed up, impatient, jaded, lethargic, listless, sick and tired inf

weather n climate, conditions, temperature, the elements

weather v **1** (come through sth successfully) brave, come through, endure, overcome, resist, surmount, survive, withstand. **2** (change because of the weather) be exposed, color, erode, harden, toughen, wear

weave v **1** (weave threads) blend, braid, criss-cross, entwine, interlace, intermingle, intertwine, knit, merge, plait, sew, twist, unite. **2** (weave a web) build, construct, create, make, spin. **3** (weave between the cars) dodge, tack, wind your way, zigzag

web n cobweb, knot, lattice, mesh, net, network, tangle

wedding n marriage, nuptials, union

wedge n block, chock, chunk, lump

wedge v block, cram, crowd, force, jam, pack, squeeze, stick, stuff, thrust

weep v bawl, blubber, cry, lament, moan, mourn, shed tears, sob, wail, whimper

weigh v 1 (weigh sth) measure the weight of, put on the scales. 2 (weigh a certain amount) have a weight of, tip the scales at inf. 3 (weigh things up) assess, balance, compare, consider, contemplate, evaluate, judge, mull over, think about, think over, weigh up

weight n 1 (a heavy weight) burden, load. 2 (the weight of sth) density, heaviness, mass. 3 (what she says carries weight) authority, credibility, force, importance, influence, power, significance, value, worth. 4 (a weight off my mind) burden, load, strain, trouble, worry

weighty adj 1 burdensome, dense, heavy. 2 crucial, important, momentous, serious, substantial, vital; opp trivial. 3 burdensome, onerous, oppressive, stressful, troublesome

weird adj bizarre, creepy inf, eerie, funny, ghostly, grotesque, mysterious, odd, queer, spooky inf, strange, supernatural, uncanny, unearthly, unnatural, unusual, zany

welcome adj 1 (a welcome break) acceptable, agreeable, cheering, delightful, desirable, much-needed, pleasant, pleasurable, refreshing, wanted; opp unwelcome. 2 (make sb feel welcome) appreciated, wanted; opp unwelcome

welcome n greeting, hospitality, reception, salutation

welcome v 1 (welcome sb) give a welcome to, greet, meet, receive. 2 (welcome sth) accept, appreciate,

be pleased by, like, want

welfare n comfort, good fortune, happiness, health, prosperity, success, well-being

well adj 1 (fit and well) fit, healthy, hearty, in good health, sound, strong, thriving; opp unwell. 2 (if all is well) all right, fine, O.K. inf, satisfactory

well n fount, fountain, pool, reservoir, shaft, source, spring, waterhole

well adv 1 (everything went well) nicely, pleasantly, satisfactorily, smoothly, successfully; opp badly. 2 (do sth well) ably, carefully, conscientiously, correctly, effectively, excellently, expertly, proficiently, properly, skillfully, thoroughly, with skill; opp badly. 3 (eat well) abundantly, amply, fully, heartily, sufficiently, very much. 4 (live well) comfortably, in comfort, prosperously. 5 (know sb well) deeply, fully, intimately, personally, thoroughly. 6 (treat sb well) civilly, fairly, generously, hospitably, kindly, nicely, politely; opp badly. 7 (speak well of sb) admiringly, favorably, glowingly, highly, warmly, with praise; opp ill

well-balanced adj balanced, elegant, graceful, harmonious, proportional, symmetrical, well-proportioned

well-behaved adj cooperative, disciplined, dutiful, good, hard-working, law-abiding, obedient, well-trained

well-fed adj 1 healthy, in good condition, well-nourished; opp malnourished. 2 chubby, fat, plump, pudgy, stout; opp thin

well-known adj celebrated, eminent, familiar, famous, illustrious, notable, noted, notorious, popular, prominent, renowned, widely known; *opp* unknown

well-off *adj* 1 affluent, comfortable, prosperous, rich, wealthy, well-to-do; *opp* poor. 2 fortunate, lucky

wet *adj* 1 bedraggled, clammy, damp, dank, dewy, dripping, moist, saturated, soaking, sodden, soggy, sopping, waterlogged, watery, wet through, wringing wet; *opp* dry. 2 (of weather) drizzling, humid, pouring, raining, rainy, showery; *opp* dry. 3 (the paint is still wet) runny, sticky, tacky; *opp* dry

wet *v* dampen, dip, douse, drench, irrigate, moisten, put water on, saturate, soak, splash, spray, sprinkle

wharf *n* dock, jetty, landing stage, pier, quay

wheel *n* circle, disk, hoop, ring

wheel *v* 1 circle, go round, move in circles, pivot, revolve, rotate, spin, swerve, swing, swivel, turn, veer, whirl. 2 (wheel sth along) pull, push, trundle

wheeze *v* breathe noisily, cough, gasp, hiss, pant, puff, rasp, whistle

whiff *n* 1 aroma, blast, hint, odor, scent, smell, stink. 2 (a whiff of air) breath, gust, puff

whim *n* craze, desire, fancy, idea, impulse, notion, urge

whimper *n* cry, groan, moan, sob, whine

whimper *v* cry, moan, sniffle, snivel, sob, weep, whine

whimsical *adj* bizarre, capricious, curious, fanciful, mischievous, odd, peculiar, playful, quaint, unusual

whine *n* cry, groan, moan, sob, wail, whimper

whine *v* bleat, complain, cry, fuss, gripe

inf, groan, grouch *inf*, grumble, moan, sob, wail, whimper

whip *n* birch, bull whip, cane, crop, horsewhip, lash, switch

whip *v* 1 beat, cane, flog, horsewhip, lash, tan *inf*, thrash. 2 (whip sth away) jerk, pull, snatch, yank. 3 (whip cream) beat, stir, whip up, whisk

whirl *n* confusion, daze, dither, flurry, muddle, spin

whirl *v* 1 circle, gyrate, pirouette, pivot, reel, revolve, roll, rotate, spin, swirl, turn, twist, wheel. 2 (my head starting to whirl) go round, reel, spin

whirlwind *n* hurricane, tornado, typhoon

whisper *n* low voice, murmur, quiet voice, undertone

whisper *v* breathe, murmur, mutter, say under your breath, speak softly, talk quietly

white *adj* 1 cream, ivory, off-white, snow-white. 2 (of sb's face) ashen, bloodless, pale, pallid, pasty, wan, white as a sheet. 3 (clean) bright, clean, immaculate, spotless

whiten *v* blanch, bleach, fade, lighten, make pale, make white

whole *adj* 1 complete, entire, full, solid, total, unabbreviated, unabridged, uncut. 2 flawless, good, in one piece, intact, perfect, sound, unbroken, undamaged, unharmed, unhurt, uninjured

wholesale *adj* broad, comprehensive, extensive, far-reaching, global, indiscriminate, mass, sweeping, universal, widespread

wholesome *adj* 1 beneficial, good, good for you, healthy, nourishing, nutritious, strengthening. 2 clean, decent, innocent, nice, pure, respectable, virtuous

wicked *adj* amoral, bad, blasphemous, corrupt, criminal, diabolical, dishonorable, evil, foul, immoral, malicious, mischievous, murderous, naughty, obscene, perverted, scandalous, shameful, sinful, unholy, unscrupulous, vicious, vile, villainous, violent, wrong; *opp* good

wickedness *n* evil, depravity, immorality, sin, sinfulness, villainy, wrong, wrongdoing; *opp* virtue

wide *adj* 1 ample, broad, expansive, full, large, roomy, spacious, vast, yawning. 2 all-embracing, broad, encyclopedic, far-ranging, general, inclusive, wide-ranging. 3 dilated, extended, open, outspread, outstretched. 4 (wide of the mark) off-course, off-target

widen *v* broaden, dilate, enlarge, expand, extend, flare, make wider, open out, open wide, spread, stretch

widespread *adj* common, extensive, far-reaching, general, pervasive, popular, prevalent, rife, sweeping, universal

width *n* breadth, broadness, diameter, extent, girth, range, reach, scope, span, thickness, wideness

wield *v* 1 brandish, employ, flourish, swing, use, wave. 2 (wield power) command, exercise, exert, have, hold, possess

wife *n* bride, mate, partner, spouse

wild *adj* 1 (a wild animal) feral, ferocious, fierce, free, savage, unbroken, untamed; *opp* tame. 2 (wild country) desolate, godforsaken, natural, overgrown,

remote, uncivilized, uncultivated, unpopulated, unsettled, waste; *opp* cultivated. 3 (wild behavior) barbaric, boisterous, disorderly, excited, noisy, out of control, riotous, rough, rowdy, uncivilized, uncontrolled, undisciplined, unmanageable, unruly, violent; *opp* calm. 4 (drive sb wild) angry, berserk, crazy, delirious, demented, deranged, frantic, hysterical, incensed, mad, seething; *opp* calm. 5 (a wild guess) arbitrary, crazy, foolish, ill-considered, impulsive, inaccurate, random, reckless, silly, uninformed; *opp* sensible. 6 (of weather) blustery, rough, stormy, windy; *opp* calm. 7 (wild about sb) crazy *inf*, daft, mad *inf*, nuts *inf*, passionate. 8 (a wild appearance) disheveled, tousled, unkempt, untidy, wind-blown; *opp* neat

wilderness *n* desert, jungle, waste, wasteland, wilds

wile *n* 1 artfulness, cheating, craftiness, cunning, guile, slyness, trickery. 2 gambit, maneuver, ploy, ruse, stratagem, trick

will *n* 1 (the will to succeed) determination, resolve, single-mindedness, willpower. 2 (do sth against sb's will) desire, wish. 3 (make a will) testament

will *v* (to will sth to happen) bid, cause, command, decree, effect, force, influence, order, persuade, wish

willful *adj* 1 determined, dogged, headstrong, inflexible, obstinate, perverse, pigheaded, self-willed, stubborn. 2 calculated, conscious,

willing adj 1 (willing to do sth) happy, pleased, prepared, ready. 2 (a willing volunteer) cooperative, eager, enthusiastic, helpful, keen, obliging

willpower n commitment, determination, drive, nerve, purposefulness, resolution, resolve, self-control, self-discipline, strength of will, will

wilt v 1 (of flowers) become limp, droop, flop, sag, shrivel, wither. 2 (of courage) diminish, fade, fail, lessen, melt away, wane; *opp* grow

wily adj artful, clever, crafty, cunning, deceitful, furtive, scheming, shifty, shrewd, sly, tricky, underhand

win n conquest, success, triumph, victory

win v 1 be the winner, be victorious, come first, overcome, prevail, succeed, triumph. 2 (win sth) achieve, acquire, attain, catch, collect, earn, gain, get, pick up *inf*, receive, secure, walk away with *inf*

wince v blench, cower, cringe, draw back, flinch, grimace, quail, recoil, shrink, start

wind n 1 air, blast, breath, breeze, current, draft, gale, gust, hurricane, monsoon, squall, tornado, whirlwind, zephyr. 2 breath, puff *inf*, respiration

wind v 1 coil, curl, furl, loop, reel, roll, spiral, twine, twist, wrap, wreathe. 2 bend, curve, loop, meander, ramble, snake, turn, twist, zigzag

windfall n bonanza, godsend, jackpot, stroke of good luck

winding adj bending, circuitous, convoluted, crooked, curving, indirect, looping, meandering, rambling, roundabout, spiraling, twisting, wandering

windy adj blowy, blustery, breezy, drafty, fresh, gusting, gusty, squally, stormy, tempestuous, wild, windswept

wing n 1 (of a building) annex, extension. 2 (of a political party) branch, faction, group, grouping, section, side

wink v 1 bat, blink, flutter. 2 flash, gleam, glitter, sparkle, twinkle

winner n champ *inf*, champion, conquering hero, conqueror, prizewinner, title-holder, victor

winning adj 1 conquering, leading, successful, top, triumphant, unbeaten, victorious; *opp* losing. 2 (winning ways) alluring, attractive, beguiling, bewitching, captivating, charming, cute, delightful, disarming, endearing, lovely, sweet

winnings n booty, gains, proceeds, profits, spoils, takings

wintry adj arctic, biting, bleak, cheerless, chilly, cold, desolate, frozen, harsh, icy, snowy; *opp* summery

wipe v 1 brush, clean, dry, dust, mop, polish, rub, sponge, swab, wash. 2 wipe out annihilate, blot out, destroy, eradicate, erase, exterminate, obliterate

wipe n brush, clean, dust, rub, wash

wiry adj 1 (of a person) lean, muscular, sinewy, spare, strong, thin, tough. 2 (wiry hair) bristly, coarse, kinky, stiff

wisdom n cleverness, common sense, good sense, insight, intelligence, judgment, knowledge, learning, perception, sense, understanding

wise *adj* **1** (of a person) clever, deep-thinking, educated, experienced, fair, informed, intelligent, just, knowledgeable, perceptive, philosophical, well-informed, well-read; *opp* stupid. **2** (a wise choice) clever, diplomatic, good, logical, prudent, sensible, smart, thoughtful; *opp* unwise

wish *n* ambition, aspiration, craving, desire, fondness, hope, liking, longing, request, requirement, want, yearning

wish *v* **1** (wish for sth) covet, crave, desire, fancy, hanker after, hope for, hunger for, long for, need, set your heart on, thirst for, want, yearn for. **2** (if you wish) ask, bid, command, desire, direct, order, require, want. **3** (wish them Merry Christmas) bid

wistful *adj* disconsolate, dreaming, longing, melancholy, mournful, nostalgic, pensive, regretful, sad, yearning

wit *n* **1** banter, fun, funniness, humor, jokes, puns, quips, repartee, witticisms, wittiness. **2** (a wit) comedian, comic, funny person, humorist, joker, wag. **3** (have the wit to do sth) common sense, intellect, intelligence, sense, wisdom

witch *n* crone, enchantress, magician, sorceress

witchcraft *n* black magic, charms, enchantment, incantations, magic, sorcery, spells, the occult, voodoo, wizardry

withdraw *v* **1** cancel, extract, pull back, pull out, remove, retract, take back, take out. **2** (withdraw from the contest) back away, back down, back out, drop out, go, leave, pull out, quit, retire, retreat, run away

withdrawal *n* **1** extraction, removal. **2** departure, evacuation, exit, leaving, retreat

withdrawn *adj* aloof, detached, distant, introverted, private, quiet, reserved, shy, silent, taciturn, timid, uncommunicative, unsociable; *opp* outgoing

wither *v* decay, decline, die, disintegrate, droop, dry out, dry up, fade, go limp, languish, perish, shrink, shrivel, waste away, wilt

withering *adj* cruel, cutting, devastating, hurtful, scornful, wounding

withhold *v* check, control, curb, hide, hold back, keep, keep back, refuse, repress, reserve, retain, suppress

withstand *v* bear, brave, cope with, defy, endure, face, hold out against, put up with *inf*, resist, stand up to, survive, take, thwart, tolerate

witness *n* bystander, eyewitness, observer, onlooker, spectator, viewer, watcher

witness *v* behold, be present at, notice, observe, see, view, watch

wits *n* brains, common sense, ingenuity, intelligence, judgment, reason, sense, understanding

witticism *n* clever remark, crack *inf*, joke, one-liner, play on words, pun, quip, wisecrack *inf*, witty remark

witty *adj* amusing, brilliant, clever, comic, droll, facetious, funny, humorous, sarcastic

wizard *n* conjurer, enchanter, magician, sorcerer, warlock

wobble v be unsteady, quake, quaver, quiver, rock, see-saw, shake, stagger, sway, teeter, totter, tremble, vibrate, waver

wobbly adj 1 (a wobbly tooth) insecure, loose. 2 (a wobbly voice) quavering, shaking, shaky, trembling. 3 (feeling wobbly) rocky, teetering, tottering, unstable, unsteady

woe n affliction, anguish, despair, distress, grief, heartache, misery, misfortune, pain, sadness, sorrow, suffering, unhappiness

woeful adj 1 (unhappy) dismal, gloomy, miserable, mournful, remorseful, sad, sorrowful, sorry, unhappy; **opp** cheerful, happy. 2 heart-breaking, piteous, pitiful, sad, tragic, wretched. 3 (deplorable) abysmal, appalling, awful, deplorable, disgraceful, hopeless, miserable, poor, sorry, terrible; **opp** excellent

woman n female, girl, lady

womanizer n Casanova, Don Juan, ladies' man, philanderer

womanly adj female, feminine, ladylike, matronly, motherly

wonder n 1 amazement, astonishment, awe, fascination, reverence, surprise. 2 curiosity, marvel, miracle, mystery, phenomenon, sensation, sight, spectacle

wonder v 1 ask yourself, conjecture, deliberate, ponder, puzzle, reflect, speculate, think. 2 be amazed, be flabbergasted, be surprised, marvel

wonderful adj brilliant, excellent, fantastic, great, incredible, magnificent, marvelous, outstanding, remarkable, sensational, smashing, stunning, superb, terrific; **opp** awful, dreadful

woo v 1 be after, chase, court, pursue, seduce. 2 attract, chase after, cozy up to inf, cultivate, find favor with, pursue, seek the support of

wood n 1 boards, chipboard, hardwood, lumber, planks, plywood, softwood, timber. 2 coppice, copse, forest, grove, jungle, orchard, rain forest, tree plantation, trees, woodland. 3 firewood, fuel, kindling, logs

wooden adj 1 made of wood, timber, wood. 2 awkward, clumsy, dead, deadpan, expressionless, flat, lifeless, stiff, stilted, unnatural; **opp** emotional, lively

wool n 1 coat, fleece, fur, hair. 2 fiber, yarn

woolly adj 1 curly, fleecy, fluffy, frizzy, furry, shaggy, soft, woolen. 2 confused, hazy, ill-defined, muddled, unclear, unfocused, unstructured, vague; **opp** crystal-clear

word n 1 expression, name, term. 2 (have a word with sb) chat, talk, discussion, conversation, brief exchange. 3 (news) comment, information, lowdown inf, message, news, notice, remark, rumor, statement. 4 (give the word to go ahead) command, go-ahead, green light, order, signal. 5 (promise) guarantee, pledge, promise, undertaking, vow

word v couch, express, phrase, put, say, state

wordy adj discursive, long-winded, loquacious, never-ending, rambling, roundabout, verbose, waffly; **opp** brief, concise, succinct

work n 1 business, career, employment,

field, job, line, livelihood, living,
occupation, post, profession, trade.
2 (effort) drudgery, effort, elbow grease
inf, exertion, graft *inf*, grind *inf*, hassle
inf, slog *inf*, trouble. **3** (task) assignment,
charge, chore, duty, housework, job,
project, responsibility, task, undertaking.
4 (composition) book, composition,
creation, oeuvre, opus, piece,
production, writing

work *v* **1** be busy, be employed, earn
a living, go to work, have a job,
labor, make an effort, slave, toil.
2 (the machine won't work) function,
go, operate, perform, run. **3** (to work
a machine) control, drive, handle,
operate, use. **4** (the plan worked) be
effective, have the desired effect,
succeed, be successful, go according to
plan. **5** (maneuver) ease, edge, guide,
maneuver, push, wiggle. **6** (work loose,
work free) become, get. **7** (arrange)
accomplish, achieve, arrange, bring
about, bring off, contrive, fix, produce,
pull off, sort *inf*, swing it *inf*. **8** (work
the soil) cultivate, dig, till. **9 work out**
(work out a sum or total) calculate,
estimate, solve. **10 work out** (the total
works out to be $5) add up to, amount
to, be, come to, total. **11 work out**
(work out why sth happened) clear up,
decide, figure out, puzzle out, resolve,
solve, sort out, understand. **12 work
out** (work out a plan) construct,
develop, devise, formulate, plan, put
together. **13 work out** (it worked out
well/badly) develop, go, pan out *inf*, turn
14 work out (things didn't work out)
be successful, go as planned, go well,

succeed, turn out well. **15 work out**
do exercises, exercise, get fit, train

worker *n* breadwinner, craftsperson,
employee, laborer, member of staff,
operative, staff, trader, troops *inf*,
wage-earner, workaholic

workforce *n* crews, employees, labor
force, labor pool, personnel, staff, team,
troops *inf*

workman *n* laborer, tradesman, worker

workmanship *n* art, craft, craftsmanship,
expertise, finish, handiwork, skill, work

works *n* **1** factory, foundry, industrial
unit, mill, plant, workshop.
2 (of an author or musician) books,
compositions, oeuvre, output, writings.
3 (good works) actions, acts, deeds.
4 (working parts) action, innards,
insides, mechanism, working parts,
workings. **5 the works** the full
treatment, the lot, the whole caboodle,
the whole shebang.

workshop *n* **1** atelier, garage, industrial
unit, production room, studio,
workroom. **2** class, discussion group,
practical session, seminar

world *n* **1** earth, globe, planet.
2 everybody, human race, humanity,
international community, people,
public, whole world. **3** (the academic
world) domain, field, province, realm,
sphere. **4** (the world of steam) age, days,
era, life and times, period, time

worldly *adj* **1** earthly, material,
materialistic, physical, secular,
temporal, terrestrial; *opp* spiritual.
2 cosmopolitan, experienced, shrewd,
smart, sophisticated, streetwise *inf*,
worldly wise; *opp* naive

worldwide *adj* global, international, transnational, ubiquitous, universal, widespread; *opp* local

worn *adj* decrepit, frayed, moth-eaten, old, ragged, scruffy, shabby, tattered, tatty *inf*, threadbare, tired, weary, worn-out; *opp* new

worn-out *adj* 1 all in *inf*, exhausted, ready to drop *inf*, shattered *inf*, tired out, weary. 2 broken-down, decrepit, moth-eaten, on its last legs, shabby, tatty *inf*, threadbare, useless, wrecked

worried *adj* agitated, anxious, apprehensive, bothered, concerned, distraught, distressed, fearful, fretful, nervous, on edge, perturbed, stressed-out *inf*, tense, troubled, uneasy, uptight *inf*, worked-up; *opp* calm, laid-back *inf*, relaxed

worry *n* 1 (anxiety) agitation, anxiety, apprehension, bother, concern, disquiet, distress, nervousness, stress, tension, trouble, uneasiness. 2 (a problem) bother, burden, doubt, irritation, nuisance, pest, problem

worry *v* 1 (worry about sth) agonize, be agitated, be anxious, be concerned, bother, feel uneasy, fret, get worked up. 2 (sth/sb worries you) bother, concern, disturb, hassle, irritate, nag, pester, torment, trouble, unsettle, upset

worsen *v* 1 (get worse) decline, degenerate, deteriorate, get worse, go downhill, go from bad to worse; *opp* improve. 2 (make sth worse) aggravate, damage, exacerbate, make worse; *opp* improve

worship *n* deification, devotion, prayer, reverence, service, veneration

worship *v* 1 idolize, pray to, revere, venerate. 2 go to church, pray. 3 admire, adore, dote on, idolize, look up to, love, put on a pedestal

worth *n* 1 excellence, importance, merit, profit, significance, usefulness, value, virtue. 2 cost, price, value

worthless *adj* 1 futile, ineffective, insignificant, meaningless, not worth the paper it's written on, of no value, pointless, poor, trashy, useless, valueless; *opp* useful, valuable. 2 (good-for-nothing) despicable, good-for-nothing, useless, no-good *inf*

worthwhile *adj* advantageous, beneficial, constructive, fruitful, good, helpful, productive, profitable, rewarding, useful, valuable; *opp* useless

worthy *adj* commendable, deserving, excellent, good, honorable, laudable, praiseworthy, respectable

wound *n* 1 cut, gash, graze, injury, laceration, lesion, scar. 2 anguish, blow, damage, distress, grief, hurt, injury, scar, shock, trauma

wound *v* 1 cut, damage, harm, hurt, injure, lacerate, stab. 2 (distress) damage, distress, hurt, injure, offend, shock, traumatize

wrangle *n* argument, difference of opinion, disagreement, dispute, fight, quarrel, row, spat *inf*, squabble, tiff

wrangle *v* argue, bicker, disagree, fall out, fight, quarrel, row *inf*, squabble

wrap *v* 1 bind, cover, encase, enfold, envelop, fold, lag, muffle, package, shroud. 2 **wrap up** gift-wrap, package, wrap. 3 **wrap up** dress warmly, keep warm, muffle up, put warm things on.

4 wrap up bring to an end, close, conclude, finish off, round off, summarize, wind up. **5 wrap up** be quiet, pipe down, shut up. **6 wrapped up in** engrossed, hooked on, in another world, involved, obsessed, preoccupied

wrath n anger, annoyance, displeasure, fury, indignation, irritation, rage; *opp* delight, pleasure

wreath n 1 bouquet, floral tribute, tribute. 2 band, coronet, crown, garland

wreathe v coil, cover, encircle, envelop, festoon, smother, twist, wind, wrap

wreck n 1 (wreckage) mess, remains, ruin, ruins, shipwreck, wreckage, write-off. 2 (destruction) annihilation, destruction, devastation, loss, ruin, shattering, spoiling, wrecking

wreck v dash, demolish, destroy, devastate, play havoc with, ruin, scuttle, smash, spoil, write off

wreckage n debris, pieces, remains, rubble

wrench v 1 jerk, pull, rip, tear, tug, twist, yank. 2 dislocate, pull, put out, sprain, strain, twist

wrestle v contend with, fight, grapple, struggle, tussle

wretch n 1 down-and-out, miserable creature, poor soul, unfortunate. 2 louse *inf*, pig *inf*, rat *inf*, rogue

wretched adj 1 miserable, poor, sorry, unfortunate. 2 (bad) appalling, atrocious, bad, deplorable, grim, miserable, terrible; *opp* excellent, good, wonderful. 3 (unhappy) dejected, depressed, distressed, down, downcast, gloomy, miserable, sad, unhappy; *opp* cheerful, happy

wriggle n squirm, twist, wiggle

wriggle v snake, squirm, twist, wiggle, worm, writhe

wring v 1 (wring out clothes) squeeze, twist. 2 (wring sb's hand) grasp, grip, press, pump, shake, squeeze. 3 (wring a confession from sb) exact, extract, force, wrest

wrinkle n crease, crinkle, crow's foot, fold, line, pucker

wrinkle v crease, crinkle, crumple, fold, pucker, ruck up, rumple; *opp* smooth

writ n court order, decree, injunction, instruction, order, summons

write v 1 (put in writing) jot down, note down, put down, put in writing, record, scrawl, scribble, sign. 2 (create) compile, compose, create, dash off, draft, draw up, pen, produce, put together. 3 (correspond) communicate, correspond, drop sb a line, write sb a letter. **4 write off** cancel, discount, dismiss, disregard, forget about, wipe out

writer n author, biographer, columnist, compiler, contributor, correspondent, creator, diarist, dramatist, editor, essayist, ghostwriter, hack, journalist, novelist, playwright, poet, scribbler, scriptwriter, wordsmith

writhe v flail, snake, squirm, thrash about, twist, worm, wriggle

writing n 1 article, book, composition, document, essay, letter, piece, publication, work. 2 calligraphy, hand, handwriting, inscription, lettering, letters, print, scribble, script, text

wrong adj 1 (incorrect) false, inaccurate, incorrect, mistaken, untrue; *opp* correct, right, true. 2 against the law, bad,

criminal, dishonest, evil, ill-advised,
illegal, illicit, ill-judged, immoral,
improper, inappropriate, misguided,
unacceptable, unethical, unfair,
unlawful, unsuitable, wicked; **opp** good,
legal, right. **3** (there's sth wrong with
this) amiss, awry, defective, faulty,
funny, out of order, strange

wrong n abuse, atrocity, bad deed,
crime, error, evil, immorality, iniquity,
injustice, mistake, offense, outrage, sin,
unfairness, wickedness, wrong-doing;
opp right

wrongful adj criminal, dishonorable,
illegal, improper, incorrect, unethical,
unfair, unjust, unjustified, unlawful,
unwarranted, wrong

wry adj caustic, cynical, derisive, ironic,
mocking, quizzical, sarcastic, sardonic,
twisted

yard *n* **1** area, back yard, compound, court, courtyard, enclosure, farmyard, garden, quadrangle. **2** dockyard, factory, steelyard, works, workshop

yardstick *n* benchmark, criterion, gauge, guide, measure, standard

yarn *n* **1** anecdote, story, tale, tall story. **2** fiber, silk, strand, thread, wool

yawning *adj* cavernous, deep, gaping, huge, massive, vast, wide

yearly *adj*, *adv* annual, annually, each year, every year, once a year, per annum, per year

yearn *v* covet, crave, desire, eat your heart out *inf*, hanker after, hunger for, long for, pine for, want

yell *n* bellow, cry, howl, roar, scream, screech, shout, whoop, yelp, yowl

yell *v* bawl, bellow, cry, howl, roar, scream, screech, shout, whoop, yelp, yowl

yield *n* crop, earnings, harvest, income, proceeds, profit, return, revenue

yield *v* **1** bear, bring in, earn, generate, pay, produce, provide, return. **2** accede, acquiesce, admit defeat, capitulate, comply, give in, give up, give way, relinquish, submit, surrender, throw in the towel *inf*; *opp* fight on, resist, stick to your guns

young *adj* adolescent, baby, fledgling, growing, immature, infant, junior, juvenile, newborn, new, teenage, youthful

youth *n* **1** adolescence, childhood, formative years, younger days. **2** (a young person) adolescent, teenager, young man, young person, young woman. **3** (young people) children, kids *inf*, the young, young adults, the younger generation, young people

youthful *adj* childish, fresh, sprightly, well-preserved, young at heart, young-looking, young; *opp* old